Computer Bible Games With Java™

A NetBeans IDE 11 Swing Programming Tutorial

11th Edition

By Philip Conrod & Lou Tylee

BIBLEBYTE BOOKS
PO Box 701
Maple Valley, WA 98038
http://www.biblebytebooks.com

Published by:
BibleByte Books (a Publishing Division of Kidware Software, LLC)
PO Box 701
Maple Valley, Washington 98038
1.425.413.1185
www.biblebytebooks.com

Printed in the United States of America

ISBN-13: 978-1-951077-04-4 (Printed Edition)
ISBN-13: 978-1-951077-05-1 (Electronic Edition)

Illustrations: Kevin Brockschmidt
Copy Editor: Stephanie Rogers & Jessica Conrod
Compositor: Michael Rogers

About The Authors

Philip Conrod has authored, co-authored and edited over two dozen computer programming books over the past thirty years. Philip holds a bachelor's degree in Computer Information Systems and a Master's certificate in the Essentials of Business Development from Regis University. Philip has served in various Information Technology leadership roles in companies like Sundstrand Aerospace, Safeco Insurance, FamilyLife, Kenworth Truck Company, and PACCAR. Philip last served as the Chief Information Officer (CIO) for Darigold for over a decade before returning to teaching and writing full-time. Today, Philip serves as the President & Publisher of Kidware Software LLC which is based in Maple Valley, Washington.

Lou Tylee holds BS and MS degrees in Mechanical Engineering and a PhD in Electrical Engineering. Lou has been programming computers since 1969 when he took his first Fortran course in college. He has written software to control suspensions for high speed ground vehicles, monitor nuclear power plants, lower noise levels in commercial jetliners, compute takeoff speeds for jetliners, locate and identify air and ground traffic and to let kids count bunnies, learn how to spell and do math problems. He has written several on-line texts teaching Visual Basic, Visual C# and Java to thousands of people. He taught computer programming courses for over 15 years at the University of Washington and currently teaches math and engineering courses at the Oregon Institute of Technology. Lou also works as a research engineer at a major Seattle aerospace firm. He is the proud father of five children, has six grandchildren and is married to an amazing woman. Lou and his family live in Seattle, Washington.

Acknowledgements

First, I want to thank my best friend Jesus Christ for granting me the wisdom, courage and resources to publish this book. My life would be nothing without you! I also want to thank my three wonderful daughters - Stephanie, Jessica and Chloe, who helped with various aspects of the book publishing process including software testing, book editing, creative design and many other more tedious tasks like finding all the typos. I could not have accomplished this without all your hard work, love and support.

Last but definitely not least, I want to thank my multi-talented co-author, Lou Tylee, for doing all the real hard work necessary to develop, test, debug, and keep current all the 'family-friendly' applications found in this book. Lou has tirelessly poured his heart and soul into so many previous versions of this tutorial and there are so many beginners who have benefited from his work over the years. Lou is by far one of the best application developers and tutorial writers I have ever worked with. Thanks Lou for collaborating with me on this book project.

Table of Contents

1. Introduction

2. Bible Safecracker Project

3. Bible Tic Tac Toe Project

4. Bible Match Game Project

5. Noah's Ark Project

6. Elijah and the Ravens Project

7. Daniel and the Lions Project

Course Description:

COMPUTER BIBLE GAMES WITH JAVA teaches Java GUI programming concepts while providing detailed step-by-step instructions for building many fun games. The tutorial is appropriate for both kids and adults. The games built are non-violent and teach logical thinking skills.

COMPUTER BIBLE GAMES WITH JAVA explains (in simple, easy-to-follow terms) how to build a Java game project. Students learn about project design, the Java Swing controls, many elements of the Java language, and how to distribute finished projects. Game skills learned include handling multiple players, scoring, graphics, animation, and sounds. The game projects built include (in increasing difficulty level):

- **Bible Safecracker** – Decipher a secret combination to find an ancient Bible..
- **Bible Tic Tac Toe** – The classic game with a Bible Trivia Twist!
- **Bible Match Game** – Find matching pairs of hidden Bible Characters!
- **Noah's Ark** – Race the Turtles to Noah's Ark before the Great Flood
- **Elijah and the Ravens** – Move Elijah to catch the falling bread as he is fed by the Ravens
- **Daniel and the Lions** – Shoot Prayers at the Lions to protect Daniel in the Lion's Den

The product includes almost 550 pages of self-study notes, all Java source code and all needed graphics and sound files.

Course Prerequisites

To grasp the concepts presented in **COMPUTER BIBLE GAMES WITH JAVA**, you should have experience with Java programming. You should also be very familiar with the Java Swing control library. We offer a programming tutorial, **LEARN JAVA GUI APPLICATIONS**, that would help you gain this needed exposure on our Kidware Software website:

https://www.kidwaresoftware.com/learn-java-gui-applications-by-philip-conrod-and-lou-tylee-a-computer-programming-tutorial/.

You also need to have the current Java Development Kit (**JDK**) and the current version of **NetBeans**, the Integrated Development Environment (IDE) we use with this course. Complete download and installation instructions for the JDK and NetBeans are found in the Appendix (**Installing Java and NetBeans**) included with these notes.

System Requirements

You will need the following software to complete the exercises in this book:

- Microsoft Windows Vista, 7, 8 Operating System <OR> MAC OS X 10
- Oracle Java Standard Edition JDK11
- NetBeans 11

Installing and Using the Downloadable Solution Files

If you purchased this directly from our website you received an email with a special and individualized internet download link where you could download the compressed Program Solution Files. If you purchased this book through a 3rd Party Book Store like Amazon.com, the solutions files for this tutorial are included in a compressed ZIP file that is available for download directly from our website at:

http://www.kidwaresoftware.com/cbgjava11-registration.htm

Complete the online web form at this webpage above with your name, shipping address, email address, the exact title of this book, date of purchase, online or physical store name, and your order confirmation number from that store. We also ask you to include the last 4 digits of your credit card so we can match it to the credit card that was used to purchase this tutorial. After we receive all this information we will email you a download link for the Source Code Solution Files associated with this book.

Warning: If you purchased this book "used" or "second hand" you are not licensed or entitled to download the Program Solution Files. However, you can purchase the Digital Download Version of this book at a highly discounted price which allows you access to the digital source code solutions files required for completing this tutorial.

Using Computer Bible Games With Java

The course notes and code for **COMPUTER BIBLE GAMES WITH JAVA** are included in one or more ZIP file(s). Use your favorite 'unzipping' application to write all files to your computer. The course is included in the folder entitled **CBGJava**. There's a chance when you copy the files to your computer, they will be written as '**Read-Only**.' To correct this (in **Windows Explorer** or **My Computer**), right-click the **CBGJava** folder and remove the check next to **Read only**. Make sure to choose the option to apply this change to all sub-folders and files. The **CBGJava Projects** folder includes all projects developed during the course. Work through the notes and projects at your leisure.

How To Take the Course:

Computer Bible Games with Java is a self-paced course. The suggested approach is to do one class a week for seven weeks. Each week's class should require about 3 to 6 hours of your time to grasp the concepts completely. Prior to doing a particular week's work, open the class notes file for that week and print it out. Then, work through the notes at your own pace. Try to do each example as they are encountered in the notes. Work through the projects in Classes 2 through 7. If you need any help, all completed projects are included in the **CBGJava Projects** folder.

Foreword

For over 20 years I have known Philip Conrod as a best friend, fellow Christian, and my personal IT guy for a variety of computer issues that have come my way. Philip's technological expertise mixed with his spiritual gifts of knowledge and teaching have given him not only a unique set of skills for working in the Information Technology field for over 30 years but also for serving Jesus in the church. He has saved his home church thousands of dollars in needed upgrades, understanding networks intricacies and teaching staff members needed computer skills.

The "other side" of Philip's gifts lie in his amazing ability to teach. Simply put, he makes the "hard concepts" easy to understand! Whether it's doctrinal, devotional or day to day living from the Bible, student after student have grown tremendously from Philip's teaching at New Community Church. Recently I was leading a group of young adults and asked "Which mentor has influenced you the most?" Not surprisingly, Philip Conrod's name quickly rose to the top! He has, for years been a favorite Sunday school teacher for many students in our church, including my own son. Of course the highlight of each year is when a crowded house of teenagers and college graduates, of "Mr. Phil", play hours of computer games intertwined with Christian fellowship in his home every year for over 15 years. It is this very combination that makes Philip the perfect author for the *Computer Bible Games* series of programming books. Making the Bible fun, intriguing and filled with learning enables all of us to grow in our biblical knowledge. Sit back and be prepared to be challenged, captivated and without knowing it, grow in your knowledge and understanding of the Bible!

Ken B. Michell
Sr. Pastor
New Community Church
Maple Valley, Washington USA

www.newcommunitychurch.us

1

Introduction

Preview

In this first chapter, we will do an overview of how to build a Java project with a graphical user interface (GUI). You'll get a description of what is needed to complete this course, review the steps of building a Java GUI project and delve into use of an Integrated Development environment (IDE).

Introducing Computer Bible Games With Java

In this class, we will use Java to build many fun game projects with graphic user interfaces (GUI). The games are non-violent and teach logical thinking skills. They are appropriate for kids of all ages (even adults). The projects you will build are (in increasing complexity):

- **Bible Safecracker** – Decipher a secret combination to find an ancient Bible..
- **Bible Tic Tac Toe** – The classic game with a Bible Trivia Twist!
- **Bible Match Game** – Find matching pairs of hidden Bible Characters!
- **Noah's Ark** – Race the Turtles to Noah's Ark before the Great Flood
- **Elijah and the Ravens** – Move Elijah to catch the falling bread as he is fed by the Ravens
- **Daniel and the Lions** – Shoot Prayers at the Lions to protect Daniel in the Lion's Den

These projects will teach many of the skills needed to be a successful game programmer. You will learn about timing, multi-player games, scoring, simulation techniques and animation.

Each project will be addressed in a single chapter. Complete step-by-step instructions covering every project detail will be provided. Before beginning the projects, however, we will review course requirements, Java project structure and our approach to building a Java GUI project.

Requirements for Computer Bible Games With Java

To complete the games in this course, you should have a basic understanding of the Java language and its syntax, understand the structure of a Java application, how to write and use Java methods and how to compile, debug and run a Java GUI application. You should be familiar with the Java Swing control library. We briefly review each of these topics in the course, but it is a cursory review. If you haven't built Java GUI Swing projects before, we highly recommend you purchase our Java tutorial **Learn Java GUI Applications**. Please see our sister Kidware Software website for more details and ordering information for the pre-requisite **Learn Java GUI Applications** tutorial.

Regarding software, you need two things: (1) the Java Development Kit (JDK) and (2) a development environment. The JDK is a free download from the Java website. Nearly all programmers develop their Java programs using something called an **Integrated Development Environment** (IDE). There are many IDE's available for Java development purposes, some very elaborate, some very simple. In these notes, we use a free IDE called **NetBeans**. If you are comfortable with another IDE, by all means, use it. Complete download and installation instructions are provided in the Appendix (**Installing Java and NetBeans**) included with these notes.

Testing the Installation

We'll use **NetBeans** to load a Java project and to run a project. This will give us some assurance we have everything installed correctly. This will let us begin our study of the Java programming language.

Once installed, to start **NetBeans**, double-click the icon on your desktop. The NetBeans program should start. Several windows will appear on the screen.

Upon starting (after clearing the **Start Page**), my screen shows:

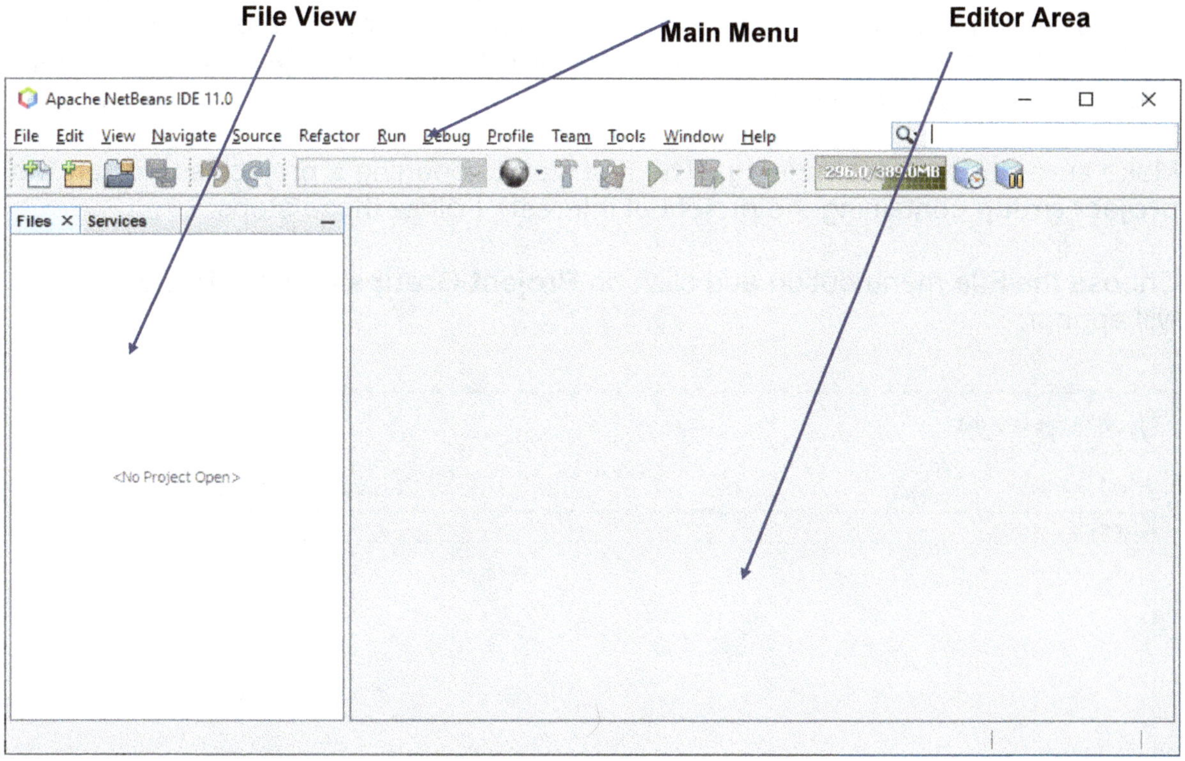

This screen displays the NetBeans **Integrated Development Environment** (**IDE**). We're going to use it to test our Java installation and see if we can get a program up and running. Note the location of the **file view** area, **editor** area and the **main menu**. The file view tells you what Java programs are available, the editor area is used to view the actual code and the main menu is used to control file access and file editing functions. It is also used to run the program.

What we want to do right now is **open a project**. Computer programs (applications) written using Java are referred to as **projects**. Projects include all the information in **files** we need for our computer program. Java projects are in **project groups**. Included with these notes are many Java projects you can open and use. Let's open one now.

Make sure **NetBeans** is running. The first step to opening a project is to **open the project group** containing the project of interest. Follow these steps:

Choose the **File** menu option and click on **Project Groups** option. This window will appear:

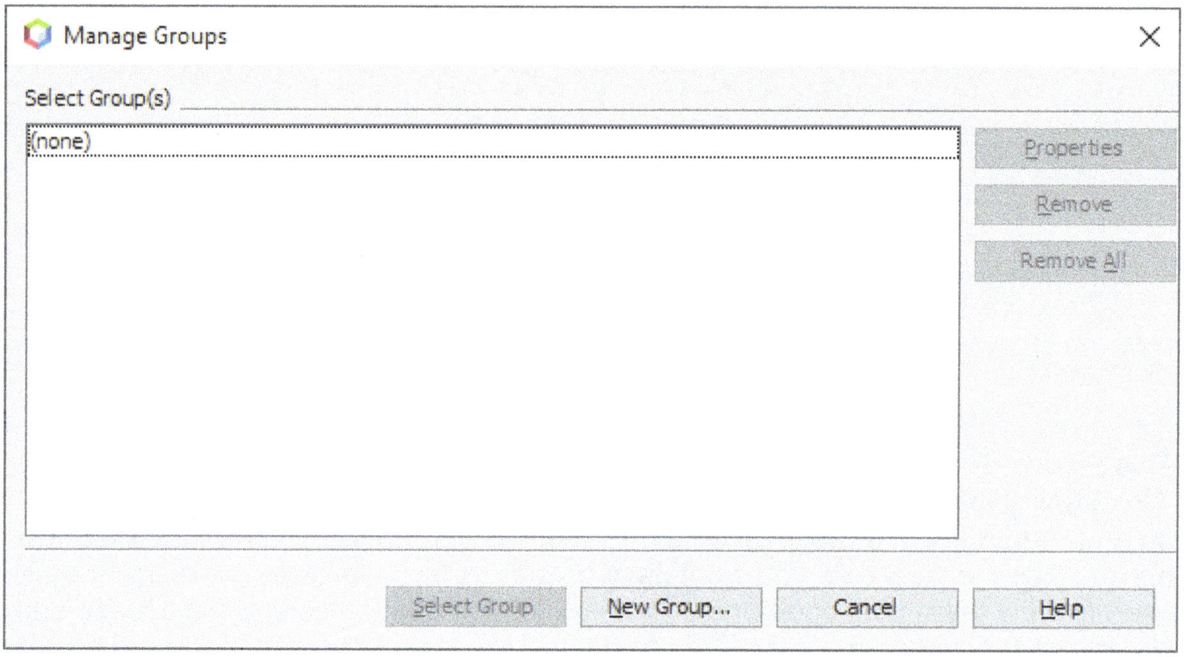

All projects in these notes are saved in a folder named **\CBGJava\CBGJava Projects**. Click **New Group**, select **Folder of Projects**, **Browse** to that folder as shown. Click **Create Group**.

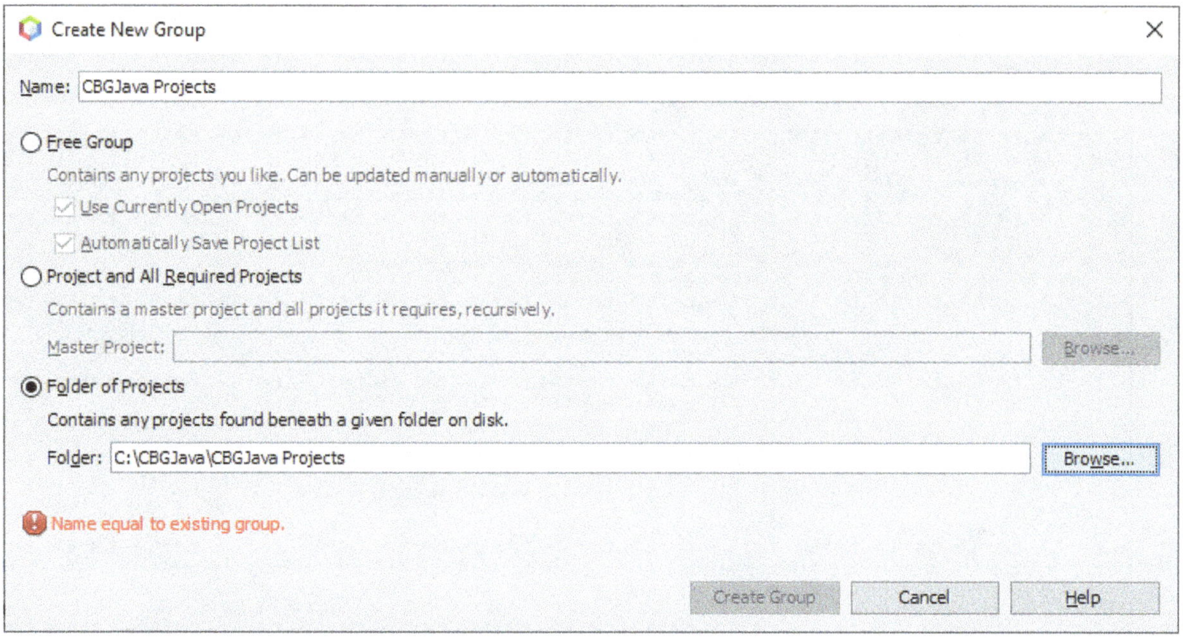

There will be many projects listed in the file view area in NetBeans. Find the project named **Welcome**. Right-click that project name and expand the Welcome project node by clicking the plus sign. Open **Source Packages**, then **welcome**. Note there is one file named **Welcome.java**. If the file contents do not appear in the editor view area, double-click that file to open it.

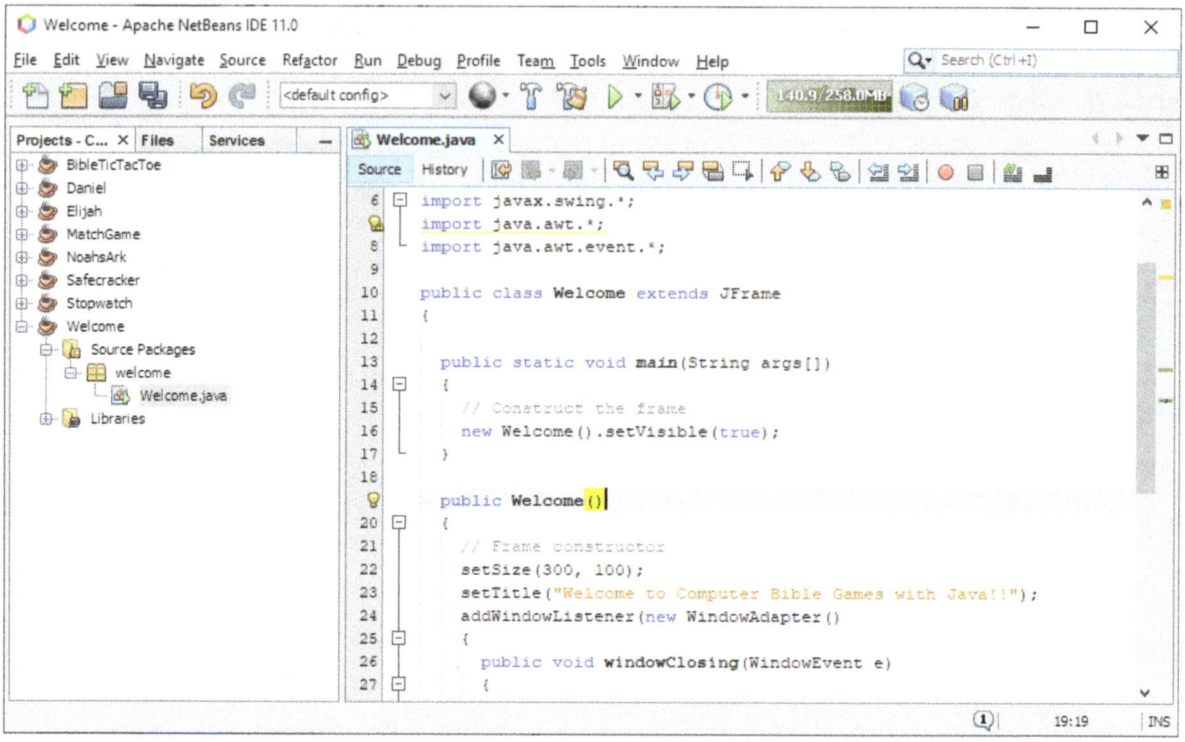

To run this project, choose **Run** from the menu and select **Run Project** (or alternately press <**F6**> on your keyboard or click the green **Run** arrow on the toolbar). An **Output** window should open and you should see the following Welcome message:

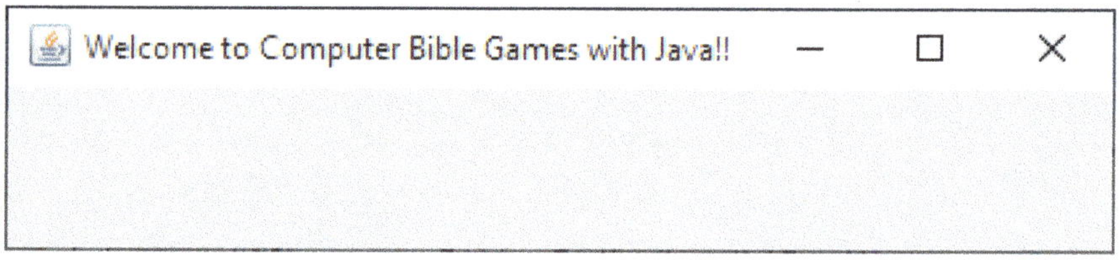

If you've gotten this far, everything has been installed correctly. If you don't see the Welcome message, something has not been installed correctly. You should probably go back and review all the steps involved with installing Java and NetBeans and make sure all steps were followed properly.

To stop this project, you click the boxed **X** in the upper right corner of the window. To stop NetBeans (don't do this right now, though):

- Select **File** in the main menu.
- Select **Exit** (at the end of the File menu).

NetBeans will close all open windows and you will be returned to the Windows desktop. Like with stopping a project, an alternate way to stop NetBeans is to click on the close button in the upper right hand corner of the main window.

Getting Help With a Java Program

As you build Java programs, there will be times when you get stuck. You will not know how to do a certain task using Java or you will receive error messages while compiling or running your program that you do not understand. What do you do in these cases? There are several options for getting help.

A highly recommended help method is to ask someone else if they know how to help you. Other Java programmers love to share their skills with people just learning the language. A second option is to look at one of the many Java books out there (you are reading one of them

The **Java** website has a wealth of information that could possibly help. The problem with the website is that there is so much information, it can be overwhelming. There are tutorials, example, forums, ... The Java **API** (application programming interface) documentation (on-line at the Sun website) is a great place to get help if you can wade through the difficult format. The Java website does offer search facilities. I often type in a few keywords and find topics that help in my pursuit of answers.

There are also hundreds of other Java websites out in WWW-land. Many websites offer forums where you can ask other Java programmers questions and get quick answers. A good way to find them is to use a search utility like **Google** or **Yahoo**. Again, type in a few keywords and many times you'll find the answer you are looking for.

As you progress as a Java programmer, you will develop your own methods of solving problems you encounter. One day, you'll be the person other programmers come to for their answers.

Structure of a Java Program

Java, like any language (computer or spoken), has a terminology all its own. Let's look at the structure of a Java program and learn some of this new terminology. A Java program (or project) is made up of a number of files. These files are called **classes**. Each of these files has Java code that performs some specific task(s). Each class file is saved with the file extension **.java**. The filename used to save a class must match the class name. One class in each project will contain something called the **main method**. Whenever you run a Java program, your computer will search for the **main** method to get things started. Hence, to run a program, you refer directly to the class containing this **main** method.

Let's see how this relates to **Welcome** project**.** This particular project has a single file named **Welcome.java**. Notice, as required, the name **Welcome** matches the class name seen in the code (public class **Welcome**). If no code is seen, simply double-click on the filename **Welcome.java**. If the project had other classes, they would be listed under the **Welcome** project folder. Notice too in the code area the word **main**. This is the **main** method we need in one of the project's classes.

That's really all we need to know about the structure of a Java program. Just remember a **program** (or project, we'll use both terms) is made up of files called **classes** that contain actual Java code. One class is the **main** class where everything starts. And, one more thing to remember is that projects are in **project groups**.

NetBeans uses a very specific directory structure for saving all of the files for a particular application. When you start a new project, it is placed in a specific folder in a specific project group. That folder will be used to store all files needed by the project. We'll take another look at the NetBeans file structure when we create our first project. You can stop NetBeans now, if you'd like.

Structure of a Java GUI Application

Let's look at the structure of a Java GUI application. In these notes, we tend to use the terms application, program and project synonymously. A GUI application consists of a **frame**, with associated **controls** and **code**. Pictorially, this is:

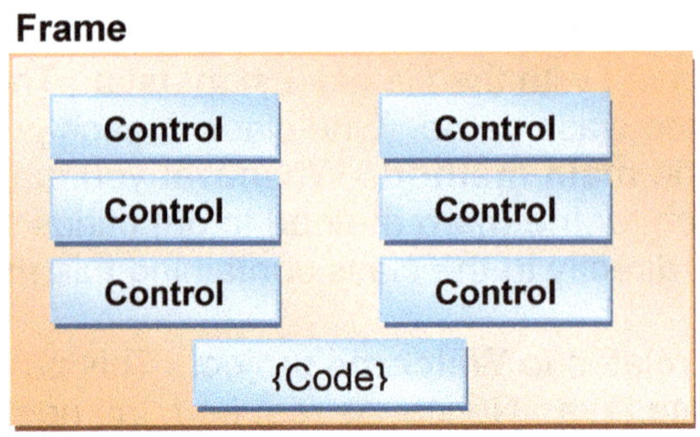

Application (Project) is made up of:

- **Frame** - window that you create for user interface (also referred to as a **form**)
- **Controls** - Graphical features positioned on frame to allow user interaction (text boxes, labels, scroll bars, buttons, etc.) (frames and controls are **objects**.) Controls are briefly discussed next.
- **Properties** - Every characteristic of a frame or control is specified by a property. Example properties include names, captions, size, color, position, and contents. Java applies default properties. You can change properties when designing the application or even when an application is executing.
- **Methods** - Built-in procedures that can be invoked to impart some action to or change or determine a property of a particular object.
- **Event Methods** - **Code** related to some object or control. This is the code that is executed when a certain event occurs. In our applications, this code will be written in the Java language (covered in detail in Chapter 2 of these notes).
- **General Methods** - **Code** not related to objects. This code must be invoked or called in the application.

The application displayed above has a single form, or frame. As we progress in this course, we will build applications with multiple forms. The code for each form will usually be stored in its own file with a **.java** extension.

We will follow three steps in building a Java GUI application:

1. Create the **frame**.
2. Create the user **interface** by placing controls on the frame.
3. **Write code** for control event methods (and perhaps write other methods).

These same steps are followed whether you are building a very simple application or one involving many controls and many lines of code. Recall, the GUI applications we build will use the Java **Swing** and **AWT** (Abstract Windows Toolkit) components.

Each of these steps require us to write Java code, and sometimes lots of code. The event-driven nature of Java applications allows you to build your application in stages and test it at each stage. You can build one method, or part of a method, at a time and try it until it works as desired. This minimizes errors and gives you, the programmer, confidence as your application takes shape.

As you progress in your programming skills, always remember to take this sequential approach to building a Java application. Build a little, test a little, modify a little and test again. You'll quickly have a completed application.

Swing Controls

The controls we use in GUI applications will be **Swing** components. These components are defined in the **javax.swing** package and all have names beginning with **J**. Here, we briefly look at several controls to give you an idea of what they are, what they look like and what they do. You will see more Swing components in several of the projects.

JFrame control:

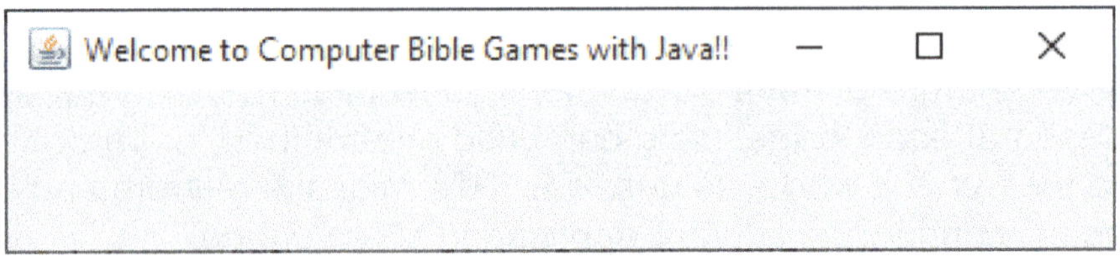

The frame control is the basic 'container' for other controls. It is the framework for a Java project. The **title** property establishes the caption information. Every application we build will start by building a **class** that **extends** the JFrame control.

JButton control:

The button control is used to start some action. The **text** property is used to establish the caption.

JLabel control:

The label control allows placement of formatted text information on a frame (**text** property).

JTextField control:

The text field control accepts a single line of typed information from the user (**text** property).

JTextArea control:

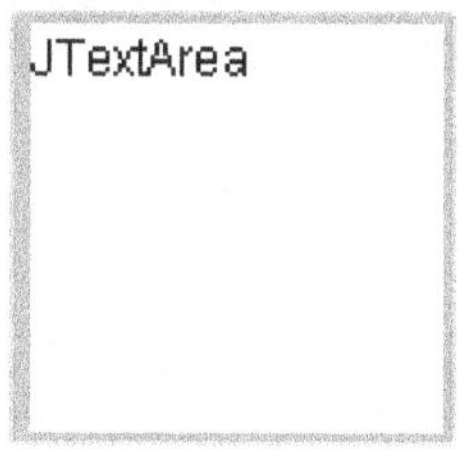

The text area control accepts multiple lines of scrollable typed information (**text** property).

JCheckBox control:

The check box control is used to provide a yes or no answer to a question.

JRadioButton control:

The radio button control is used to select from a mutually exclusive group of options. You always work with a group of radio buttons.

JComboBox control:

Combo box controls are very common in GUI applications. Users can choose an item from a drop down list (states, countries, product).

JList control:

A list control is like a combo box with the list portion always visible. Multiple selections can be made with a list control.

JScroll control:

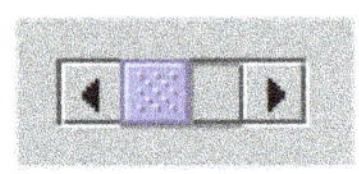

A scroll bar control is used to select from a range of values. The scroll bar is always "buddied" with another control related to the scroll bar selection.

JPanel control:

The panel control is a 'workhorse' in GUI applications – we will use many of them. It provides a convenient way of grouping related controls in a Java GUI application. And, the panel can also be used to host graphics.

Now, we'll start NetBeans and look at each step in the application development process, including using Swing controls. We will use a stopwatch application as an example.

Stopwatch - Creating a Java Project with NetBeans

We will now start building our first Java GUI application (a computer stopwatch). It might seem like a slow, long process. But, it has to be in order to cover all the necessary material. The more projects you build, the simpler this process will become. We begin by creating a new project and creating a frame. We will store all created projects in a separate project group named **Bible Games**. Create that folder now. If using Windows, you can use **Windows Explorer** or **My Computer** to that task.

If it's not already running, start **NetBeans**. The program group containing the **Welcome** project should still be there. We are going to remove this program group and create a new one. (You should only use the **CBGJava Projects** program group when you want to refer to the code included with the class notes. For all your projects, you will use your own program group).

Choose **File** from the main menu and select **Project Groups** The **Manage Groups** window appears – choose **New Group** to see

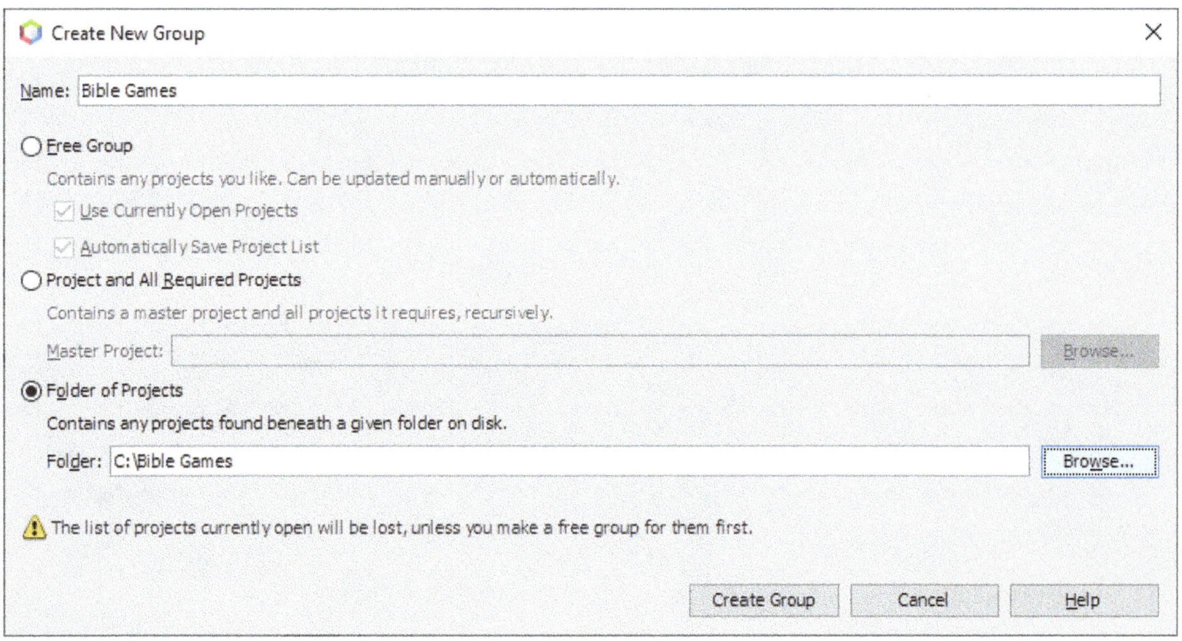

As shown, click **Folder of Projects**, then **Browse** to your **Bible Games** folder. Click **Create Group**. The project group is displayed in the file view area (it is empty).

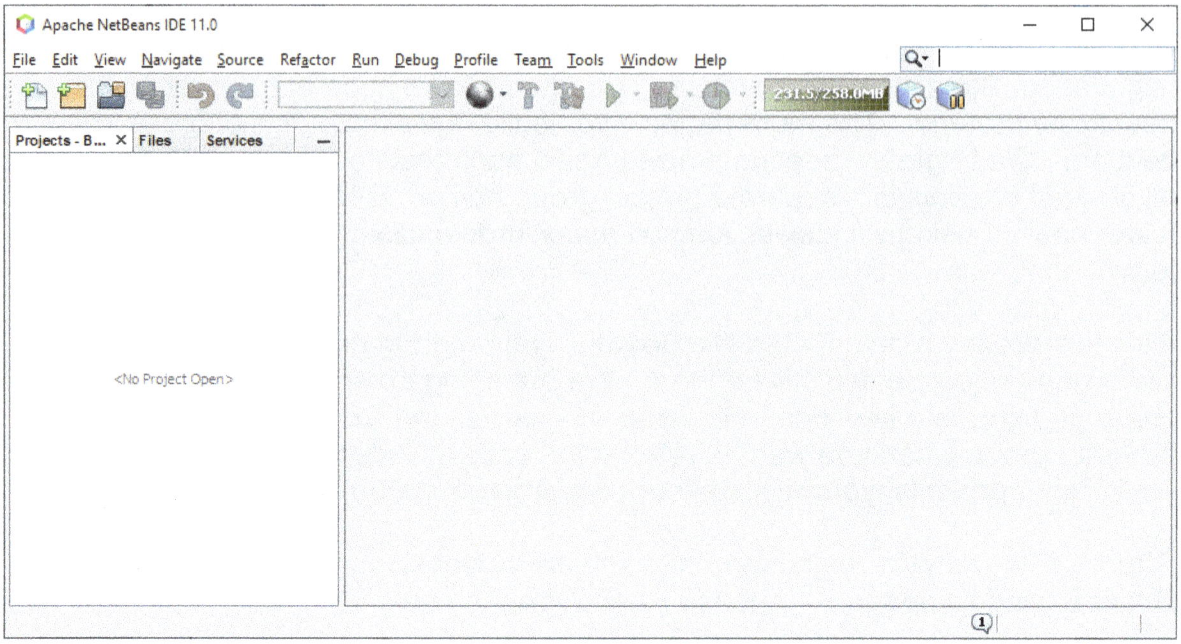

Now, we want to add a project to the project group. Pay close attention to these steps because you will repeat them every time you need to create a new Java project. Right-click the project group area in the file view and choose **New Project** to see:

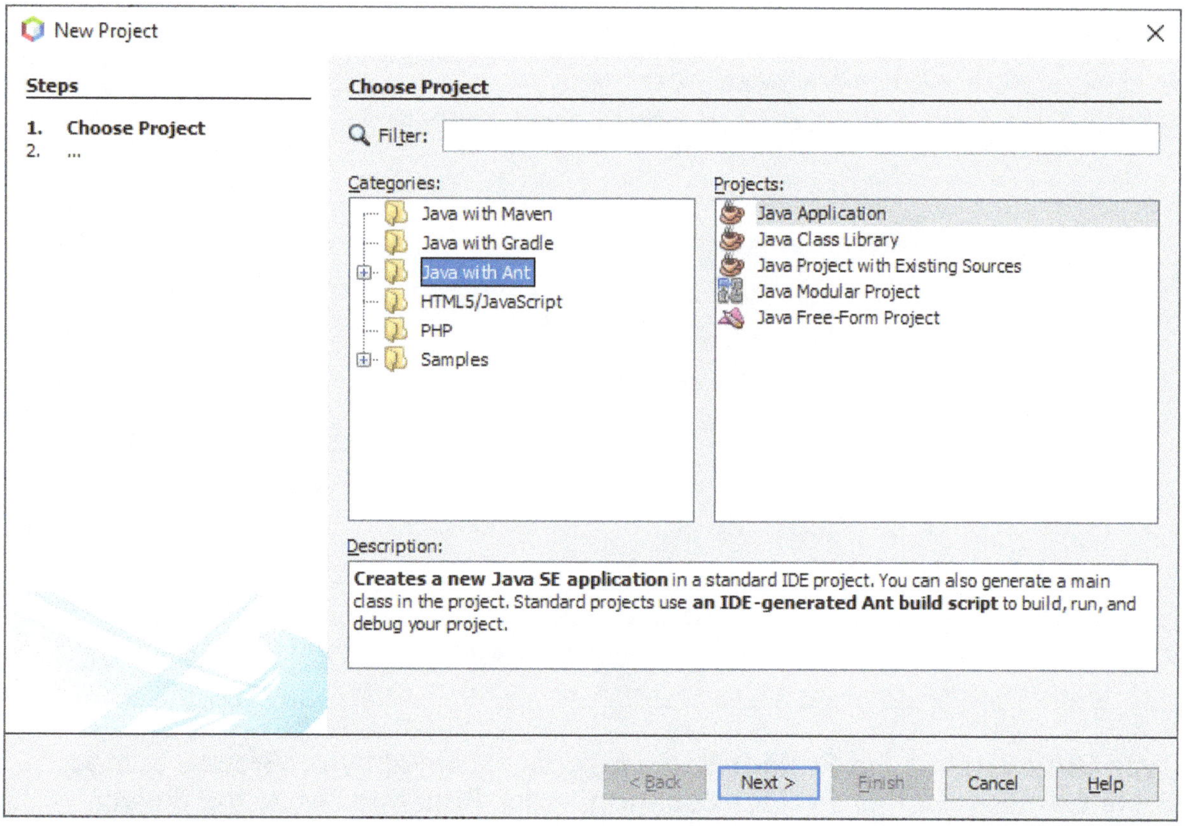

Select **Java with Ant** in **Categories** and **Java Application** in **Projects**. Click **Next**.

This window appears:

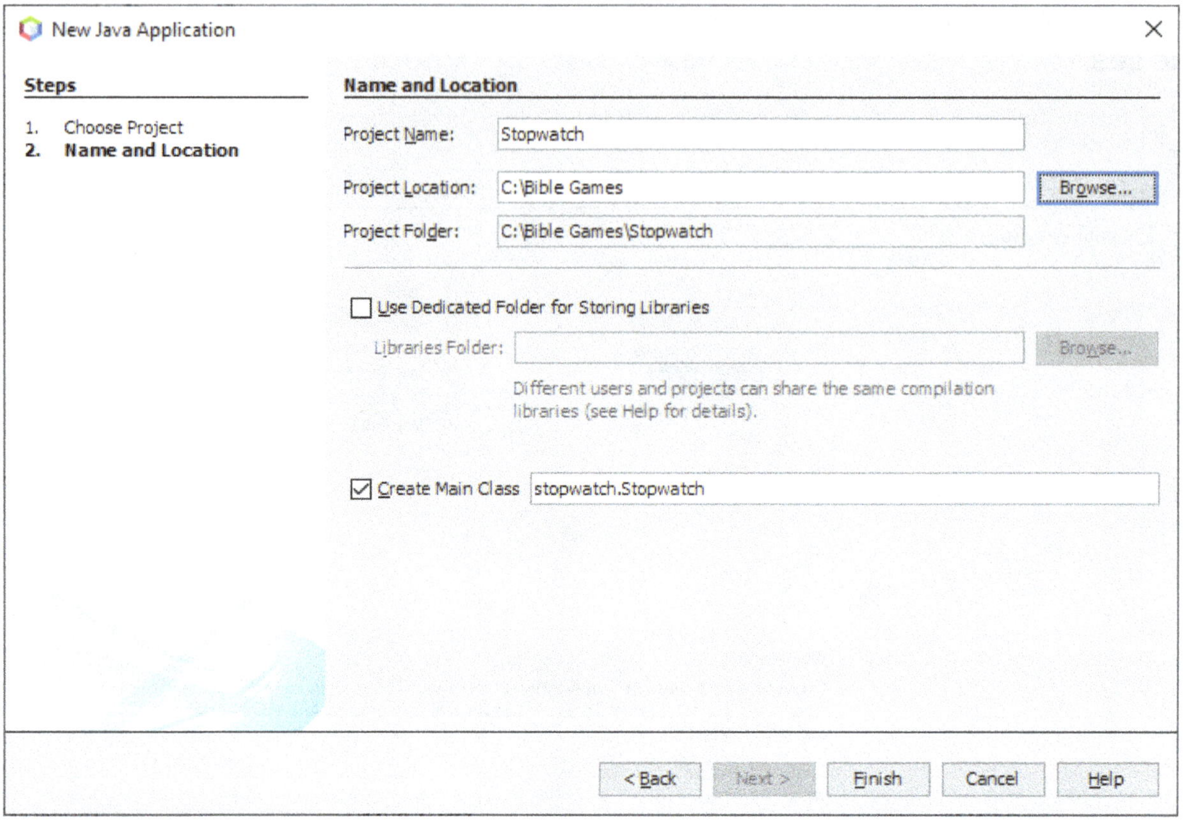

Type **Stopwatch** in the **Project Name** box (as shown above). Browse to the **Bible Games** folder for **Project Location**. Click **Finish** to create the project. Once created, click **Finish** in the resulting window.

The project group view window should now show a project (**Stopwatch**) in the project group (I've expanded all the folders):

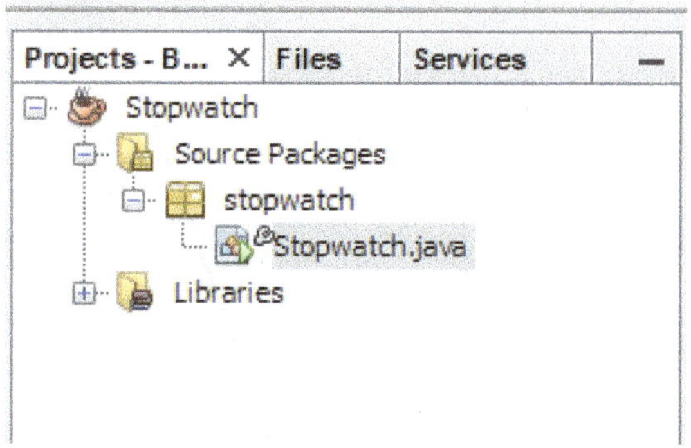

NetBeans uses a particular structure for each project you create. Under the Project main folder is a folder (**Source Packages**) with a **package** it names (in this case, **stopwatch**). In that package folder are the class files (**java** files) needed for your project. It creates a default class file (the one with your project name, **Stopwatch.java** in this case). You do not have to accept the default name (or default package name) – you can change it when creating the project, if desired. Just make sure there is a main class with the matching filename.

Double-click on the **Stopwatch.java** file to see a framework for the file in the editor view area:

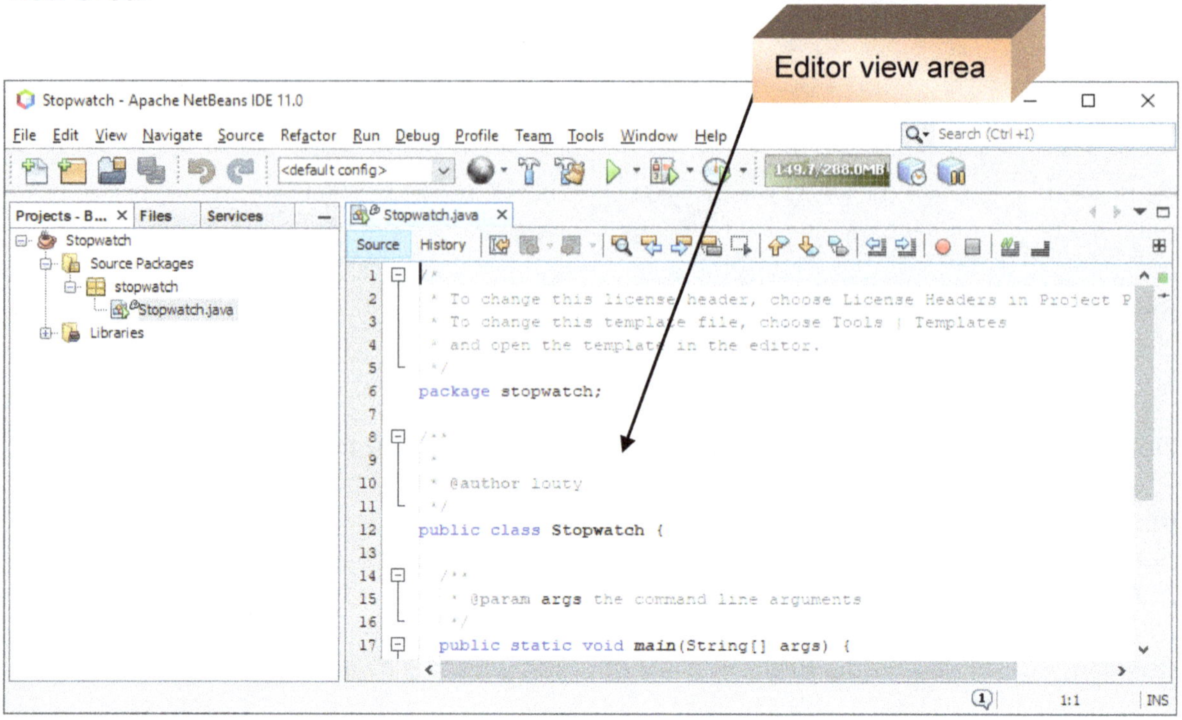

The default code created by NetBeans is:

```
/*
 * To change this license header, choose License Headers in
Project Properties.
 * To change this template file, choose Tools | Templates
 * and open the template in the editor.
 */

package stopwatch;

/**
 *
 * @author tyleel
 */
public class Stopwatch
{

  /**
   * @param args the command line arguments
   */
  public static void main(String[] args)
  {
    // TODO code application logic here
  }

}
```

We will always replace this default code with our own code (or you can modify it if you want to avoid a little typing). Delete the default code.

Recall, there are a few rules to pay attention to as you type Java code (we will go over these rules again in the next class):

- Java code requires perfection. All words must be spelled correctly.
- Java is case-sensitive, meaning upper and lower case letters are considered to be different characters. When typing code, make sure you use upper and lower case letters properly
- Java ignores any "**white space**" such as blanks. We will often use white space to make our code more readable.
- Curly **braces** are used for grouping. They mark the beginning and end of programming sections. Make sure your Java programs have an equal number of left and right braces. We call the section of code between matching braces a **block**.
- It is good coding practice to **indent** code within a block. This makes code easier to follow. NetBeans automatically indents code in blocks for you.

- Every Java statement will end with a semicolon. A **statement** is a program expression that generates some result. Note that not all Java expressions are statements (for example, the line defining the main method has no semicolon).

Stopwatch - Create a Frame

The first step in building a Java GUI application is creating a frame. At the same time we create the frame, we establish the basic framework for the entire program. The code (**Stopwatch.java**) that creates a frame within this basic framework is defined by a Java **class** of the same name:

```
/*
 * Stopwatch
 */
package stopwatch;
import javax.swing.*;
import java.awt.*;
import java.awt.event.*;
public class Stopwatch extends JFrame
{

  public static void main(String args[])
  {
    // Construct the frame
    new Stopwatch().setVisible(true);
  }

  public Stopwatch()
  {
    // Frame constructor
    setTitle("Stopwatch Application");
    setSize(300, 100);
  }
}
```

Type one line at a time, paying close attention that you type everything as shown (use the rules).

As you type, notice after you type each left brace (**{**), the NetBeans editor adds a corresponding right brace (**}**) and automatically indents the next line. This follows the rule of indenting each code block. Like the braces, when you type a left parenthesis, a matching right parenthesis is added. Also, another thing to notice is that the editor uses different colors for different things in the code. Green text represents comments. Code is in black and keywords are in blue. This coloring sometimes helps you identify mistakes you may have made in typing.

When done typing, you should see:

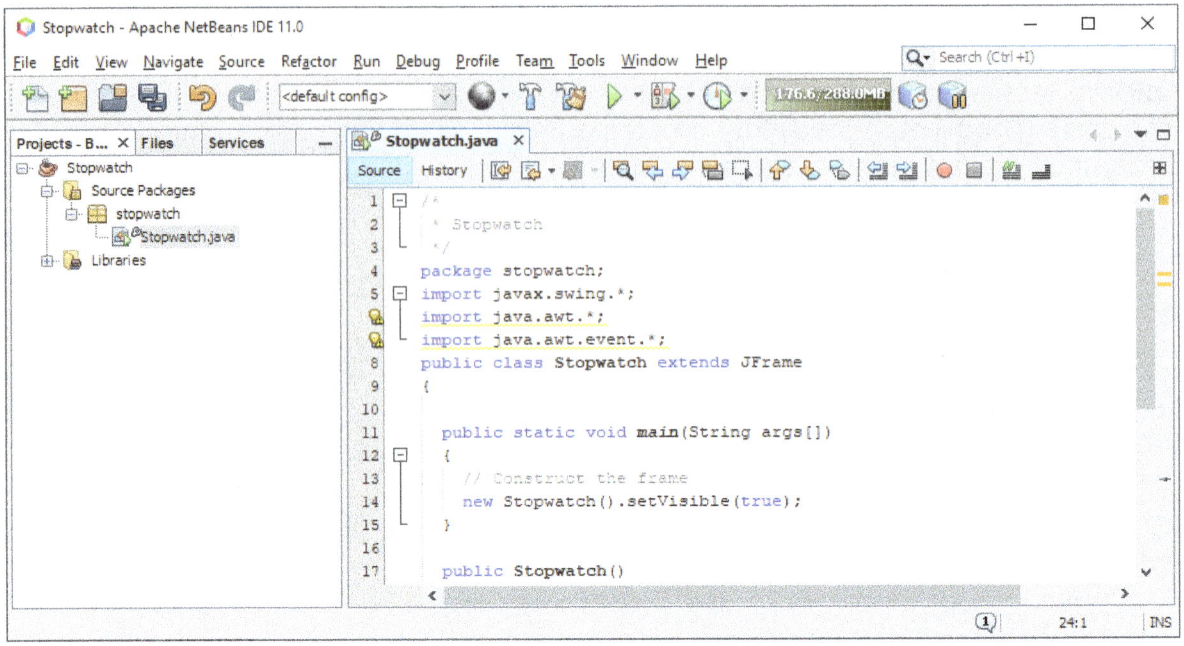

This code creates the frame by **extending** the Swing **JFrame** object, meaning it takes on all characteristics of such a frame. The code has a **constructor** for the **Stopwatch** object. You should see it executes two methods: one to set the title (**setTitle**) and one to set the size (**setSize**). The constructor is called in the **main method** to create the frame. We will use this same basic structure in <u>every</u> project built in this course. A constructor for the frame and all associated controls and control events will be built. The frame will be constructed in the main method.

Run the project (press <**F6**> or choose **Run**, then **Run Main Project** in the menu). You will see your first frame:

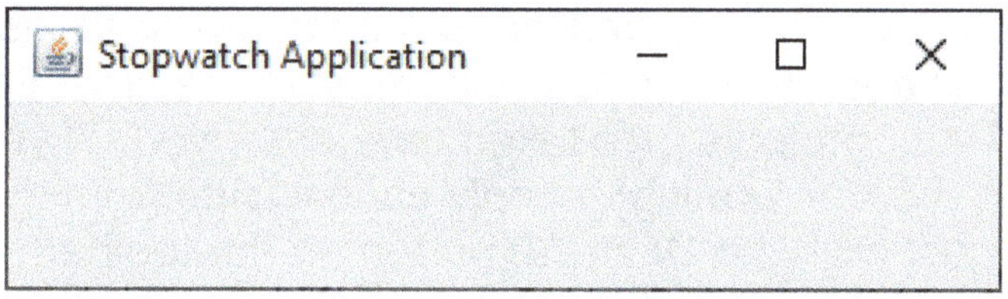

Saving Java Projects with NetBeans

Whenever you run a Java project, NetBeans automatically saves both the source files and the compiled code files for you. So, most of the time, you don't need to worry about saving your projects - it's taken care of for you. If you want to save code you are typing (before running), simply choose **File** from the main menu and click **Save All**. Or, just click the **Save All** button on the toolbar:

You do need to save the project group anytime you make a change, for example, if you add/delete files from a project or add/delete projects. This is also done using the **Save All** option. If you try to exit NetBeans and have not saved projects, NetBeans will pop up dialog boxes to inform you of such and give you an opportunity to save files before exiting.

NetBeans and Java Files

So, how does all this information about program structure, files, compiling and running fit in with NetBeans, our development environment. We have seen that Java projects are grouped in project groups. And projects are made up of different folders and files.

Using My Computer or Windows Explorer (if using Windows), go to the folder containing the **Stopwatch** project you just built. There are many folders and files. In the **src/stopwatch** folder, you will see

Stopwatch.java

This is the source code that appears in the editor view area of NetBeans. In the **build/classes/stopwatch** folder is **Stopwatch.class**. This the compiled version of Stopwatch.java (this is the file needed by the Java virtual machine). Most of the other files are used by NetBeans used to keep track of what files make up the project.

Be aware that the only true Java files here are the ones with **.java** and **.class** extensions. The other files are created and modified by our particular development environment, NetBeans. If you want to share your Java program with a friend or move your Java program to another development environment, the only files you really need to transfer are the **.java** files. These files can be used by any Java programmer or programming environment to create a running program.

Create the User Interface

Having created a frame, we now create the user interface by "placing" controls in the frame. This placement simply involves several lines of logical Java code per control desired.

An object called a **layout manager** determines how controls are arranged in a frame. Some of the layout managers and their characteristics are:

FlowLayout	Places controls in successive rows, fitting as many as possible in a given row.
BorderLayout	Places controls against any of the four frame borders.
CardLayout	Places controls on top of each other like a deck of cards.
GridLayout	Places controls within a specified rectangular grid.
GridBagLayout	Places controls with a specified very flexible rectangular grid.
BoxLayout	Arranges controls either in a row or column.
SpringLayout	Arranges controls with positions defined by sprints and struts.

In this class, we will use the **GridBagLayout**. In our opinion, it offers the nicest interface appearance. As we work through the course, you will learn more and more capabilities of this manager. Study the other layout managers if you'd like.

A frame is actually made up of several different **panes**. Controls are placed in the **content pane** of the frame. The **GridBagLayout** manager divides the content pane into a grid of rows and columns:

	Column 0	Column 1	Column 2	Column 3	Column 4	Column 5
Row 0						
Row 1						
Row 2						
Row 3						
Row 4						
Row 5						

The top row is Row 0 and row number increases as you go down the grid. The left column is Column 0 and column number increases as you move to the right in the grid.

The **GridBagConstraints** object is used for control placement and positioning within the various grid elements. Controls are placed in this grid by referring to a particular column (**gridx** location) and row (**gridy** location). Rows and columns both start at zero (0). The grid does not have to be (but can be) sized. It automatically grows as controls are added. We will see that the GridBagLayout manager is very flexible. Controls can span more than one column/row and can be spaced (using **insets**) anywhere within a grid element.

A single line of code in our frame constructor is needed to specify we are using the GridBagLayout in the frame content pane:

```
getContentPane().setLayout(new GridBagLayout());
```

To place a control in the GridBagLayout grid, we follow these steps:

- **Declare** the control.
- **Create** (construct) the control.
- Establish desired control **properties**.
- **Add** the control to the layout content pane at the desired position.

In the projects we build, all controls will be declared with **class level scope**, meaning the controls and associated properties and methods will be available to any method in the class. Hence, all controls will be declared following the left opening brace of the class, before the first method.

We will also give **meaningful names** to controls. Accepted practice is to give the control a name beginning with some description of its purpose, then concatenating the type of control at the end of the name. Such a naming convention makes reading and writing your Java code much easier. Examples of names for button, label and text field controls (the ones we use with our stopwatch example):

```
startButton
stopButton
elapsedLabel
startTextField
```

To declare a control, you type the statement:

```
ControlType controlName;
```

In the Swing library, a button control is of type **JButton**. Hence, to declare our **startButton**, we use:

```
JButton startButton;
```

To create a previously declared control, use:

```
controlName = new ControlType();
```

For our start timing button, the Java code is:

```
startButton = new JButton();
```

The process of **declaring** and **creating** a control can be combined into a single line of code. We will always do this. For our example, the control declaration would be:

```
JButton startButton = new JButton();
```

The next step is to set any desired control properties. The format for such code is:

```
controlName.setPropertyName(PropertyValue);
```

Where **setPropertyName** is a method to set a desired property. When we discuss controls in detail, we will cover many of these methods. For now, we will just give them to you. As an example, to set the text appearing on the start timing button to "**Start Timing**," you would use:

```
startButton.setText("Start Timing");
```

The next step (yes, I know there are lots of steps) is to position the control in the **GridBagLayout** grid. First, we need to declare an object of type **GridBagConstraints** to allow positioning. Assuming this object is named **gridConstraints**, the declaration is:

```
GridBagConstraints gridConstraints = new
GridBagConstraints();
```

This statement is placed near the top of the frame constructor code.

Now, we use a three-step process to place each control in the grid. Decide on an x location (**desiredColumn**) and a y location (**desiredRow**). Then, use this code for a sample control named **controlName**):

```
gridConstraints.gridx = desiredColumn;
gridConstraints.gridy = desiredRow;
getContentPane().add(controlName, gridConstraints);
```

We will place the start timing button in the upper left corner of the grid, so we use:

```
gridConstraints.gridx = 0;
gridConstraints.gridy = 0;
getContentPane().add(startButton, gridConstraints);
```

To finalize placement of controls in the frame, execute a pack method:

```
pack();
```

This "packs" the grid layout onto the frame and makes the controls visible.

In summary, decide what controls you want to place in a frame. For each control, you need:

- a **declaration** and **creation** statement (class level)
- three lines of code for **placement** (in constructor method)

Once all controls are in the frame, you must execute a **pack** method to finalize placement. We'll clear this up (hopefully) with an example.

Stopwatch – Adding Controls

Continue with the **Stopwatch** example where we created a frame. We want to build this frame:

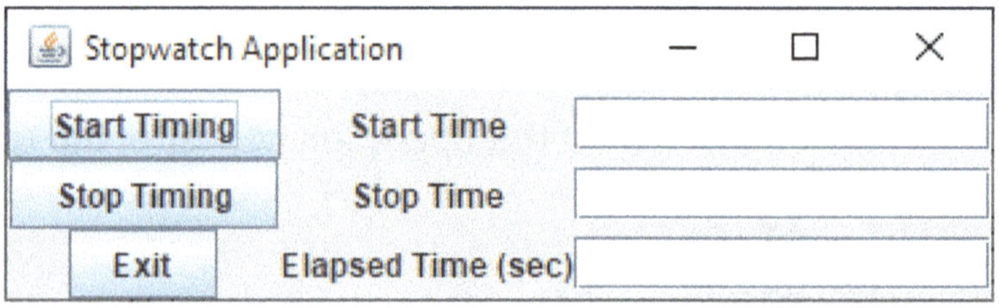

1. We will place nine controls in the frame: three buttons (**JButton** class), three labels (**JLabel** class) and three text fields (**JTextField** class). The buttons will start and stop the timing. The labels and text fields will be used to display the timing results: We will place these controls in a 3 x 3 array:

	gridx = 0	gridx = 1	gridx = 2
gridy = 0	**startButton**	**startLabel**	**startTextField**
gridy = 1	**stopButton**	**stopLabel**	**stopTextField**
gridy = 2	**exitButton**	**elapsedLabel**	**elapsedTextField**

Properties we will set in code:

startButton:

text	Start Timing
gridx	0
gridy	0

stopButton:

text	Stop Timing
gridx	0
gridy	1

exitButton:

text	Exit
gridx	0
gridy	2

startLabel:

text	Start Time
gridx	1
gridy	0

stopLabel:

text	End Time
gridx	1
gridy	1

elapsedLabel:

text	Elapsed Time (sec)
gridx	1
gridy	2

startTextField:

text	[Blank]
columns	15
gridx	2
gridy	0

stopTextField:

text	[Blank]
columns	15
gridx	2
gridy	1

elapsedTextField:

text	[Blank]
columns	15
gridx	2
gridy	2

2. First, type the code to declare the nine controls (recall these lines go after the opening left brace for the class definition):

```
JButton startButton = new JButton();
JButton stopButton = new JButton();
JButton exitButton = new JButton();
JLabel startLabel = new JLabel();
JLabel stopLabel = new JLabel();
JLabel elapsedLabel = new JLabel();;
JTextField startTextField = new JTextField();
JTextField stopTextField = new JTextField();
JTextField elapsedTextField = new JTextField();
```

3. Replace the **setSize** line in the constructor code with the line establishing the grid layout:

```
getContentPane().setLayout(new GridBagLayout());
```

4. The code to set properties of and place each of the nine controls (also goes in the constructor method):

```
GridBagConstraints gridConstraints = new
GridBagConstraints();
startButton.setText("Start Timing");
gridConstraints.gridx = 0;
gridConstraints.gridy = 0;
getContentPane().add(startButton, gridConstraints);

stopButton.setText("Stop Timing");
gridConstraints.gridx = 0;
gridConstraints.gridy = 1;
getContentPane().add(stopButton, gridConstraints);

exitButton.setText("Exit");
gridConstraints.gridx = 0;
gridConstraints.gridy = 2;
getContentPane().add(exitButton, gridConstraints);

startLabel.setText("Start Time");
gridConstraints.gridx = 1;
gridConstraints.gridy = 0;
getContentPane().add(startLabel, gridConstraints);

stopLabel.setText("Stop Time");
gridConstraints.gridx = 1;
gridConstraints.gridy = 1;
getContentPane().add(stopLabel, gridConstraints);
```

```
    elapsedLabel.setText("Elapsed Time (sec)");
    gridConstraints.gridx = 1;
    gridConstraints.gridy = 2;
    getContentPane().add(elapsedLabel, gridConstraints);

    startTextField.setText("");
    startTextField.setColumns(15);
    gridConstraints.gridx = 2;
    gridConstraints.gridy = 0;
    getContentPane().add(startTextField, gridConstraints);

    stopTextField.setText("");
    stopTextField.setColumns(15);
    gridConstraints.gridx = 2;
    gridConstraints.gridy = 1;
    getContentPane().add(stopTextField, gridConstraints);

    elapsedTextField.setText("");
    elapsedTextField.setColumns(15);
    gridConstraints.gridx = 2;
    gridConstraints.gridy = 2;
    getContentPane().add(elapsedTextField, gridConstraints);

    pack();
```

Notice how each control is located within the grid. Notice, too, how we set the number of columns for the text field controls. If we didn't do this, you wouldn't see the controls. I know there's lots of code here (and there will always be lots of code for GUI interfaces). You can choose to type the code or copy and paste from these notes into NetBeans. If you choose to type the code, notice much of the code is similar, so copy and paste operations come in very handy.

For reference, here is the complete **Stopwatch.java** code at this point (newly added code is shaded – the line setting the frame size has been deleted):

```
/*
 * Stopwatch.java
 */
package stopwatch;
import javax.swing.*;
import java.awt.*;
import java.awt.event.*;
public class Stopwatch extends JFrame
{
  // declare controls used
  JButton startButton = new JButton();
```

```
  JButton stopButton = new JButton();
  JButton exitButton = new JButton();
  JLabel startLabel = new JLabel();
  JLabel stopLabel = new JLabel();
  JLabel elapsedLabel = new JLabel();;
  JTextField startTextField = new JTextField();
  JTextField stopTextField = new JTextField();
  JTextField elapsedTextField = new JTextField();
  public static void main(String args[])
  {
    // Construct frame
    new Stopwatch().setVisible(true);
  }
  public Stopwatch()
  {
    // Frame constructor
    setTitle("Stopwatch Application");
    getContentPane().setLayout(new GridBagLayout());
    // add controls
    GridBagConstraints gridConstraints = new
GridBagConstraints();

    startButton.setText("Start Timing");
    gridConstraints.gridx = 0;
    gridConstraints.gridy = 0;
    getContentPane().add(startButton, gridConstraints);

    stopButton.setText("Stop Timing");
    gridConstraints.gridx = 0;
    gridConstraints.gridy = 1;
    getContentPane().add(stopButton, gridConstraints);

    exitButton.setText("Exit");
    gridConstraints.gridx = 0;
    gridConstraints.gridy = 2;
    getContentPane().add(exitButton, gridConstraints);

    startLabel.setText("Start Time");
    gridConstraints.gridx = 1;
    gridConstraints.gridy = 0;
    getContentPane().add(startLabel, new
GridBagConstraints());

    stopLabel.setText("Stop Time");
    gridConstraints.gridx = 1;
    gridConstraints.gridy = 1;
    getContentPane().add(stopLabel, gridConstraints);
```

```
        elapsedLabel.setText("Elapsed Time (sec)");
        gridConstraints.gridx = 1;
        gridConstraints.gridy = 2;
        getContentPane().add(elapsedLabel, gridConstraints);

        startTextField.setText("");
        startTextField.setColumns(15);
        gridConstraints.gridx = 2;
        gridConstraints.gridy = 0;
        getContentPane().add(startTextField, gridConstraints);

        stopTextField.setText("");
        stopTextField.setColumns(15);
        gridConstraints.gridx = 2;
        gridConstraints.gridy = 1;
        getContentPane().add(stopTextField, gridConstraints);

        elapsedTextField.setText("");
        elapsedTextField.setColumns(15);
        gridConstraints.gridx = 2;
        gridConstraints.gridy = 2;
        getContentPane().add(elapsedTextField, gridConstraints);

        pack();
    }
}
```

Run the project. The interface should look like this:

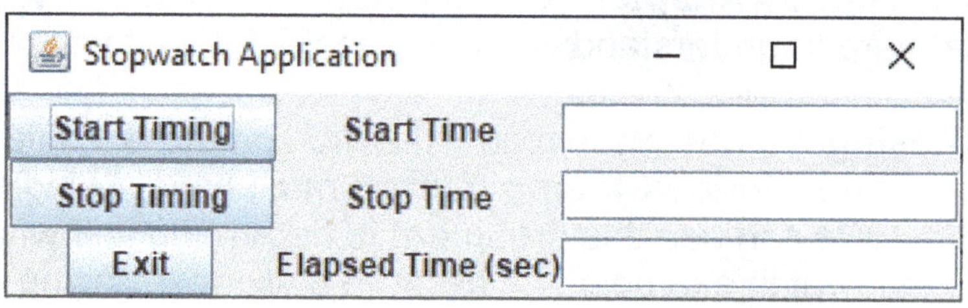

Notice how each control is located and sized in the layout of the frame. Save this project. We have no code to stop this project. To do this, select **Tools** in the NetBeans menu and choose **Stop Tool**.

Adding Event Methods

At this point, our interface has a finished look. What is missing is the code behind the control events. The next step in building a Java GUI application is to add this code. But, to add the code, we need a place to put it. We need to add event methods and their corresponding **listeners** to our application. There are two ways to add listeners, one for **AWT** objects and one for **Swing** objects. Listeners are added in the frame constructor code.

Java **event listeners** for AWT objects (primarily those for mouse and keyboard inputs) are implemented using something called **adapters** (also available from the AWT). The best way to see how to add such a listener is by example. In every project we build, we need to "listen" for the event when the user closes the window. The adapter that implements events for the frame (window) is called the **WindowAdapter** and it works with the **WindowListener**. There are certain window events that can be "listened for." In our case, we want to listen for the **windowClosing** event. The code that adds this event method to our application is:

```
addWindowListener(new WindowAdapter()
{
  public void windowClosing(WindowEvent e)
  {
        [Java code for window closing]
  }
});
```

This is actually one very long Java statement over several lines. It calls the **addWindowListener** method and, as an argument (all in parentheses), includes a **new** instance of a **WindowAdapter** event method (the **windowClosing** event). It's really not that hard to understand when you look at it, just very long!!

In the **windowClosing** method, we would write the code to execute when the window is closing. The **windowClosing** method must have a single argument (**WindowEvent e**). We can use this argument to determine just what event has occurred. In the stopwatch example, we assume a window closing event.

For Swing components, like the button, label and text field used here, event methods (**actionPerformed**) are added using the **ActionListener**. If the component is named controlName, the method is added using:

```
controlName.addActionListener(new ActionListener()
{
  public void actionPerformed(ActionEvent e)
  {
          [Java code to execute]
  }
});
```

Again, note this is just one long line of Java code. The method has a single argument (**ActionEvent e**), which tells us what particular event occurred (each control can respond to a number of events). For our stopwatch example, we will assume click events for the three button controls.

Note when we add a listener, we also need to add code for the event method. We could type the code at the same time we add the listener, but we take a different approach. When a method is added, the method code will be a single line of code invoking an "external" method where the actual code will reside. This separates the coding of method events from the code building the frame and makes for a "cleaner" code. For Swing components, we will name these external methods using a specific convention – the **control name** and **method name** will be concatenated into a new method name. Similar conventions are followed for AWT events. For our example above, the code adding such a method would be:

```
controlName.addActionListener(new ActionListener()
{
  public void actionPerformed(ActionEvent e)
  {
     controlNameActionPerformed(e);
  }
});
```

Once the method is added, the actual code is written in a method defined elsewhere in the program. The form for this method must be:

```
private void controlNameActionPerformed(ActionEvent e)
{
   [Java code to execute]
}
```

By separating the event method code from the code constructing the frame, editing, modifying and testing a Java GUI application is much easier. And, the naming convention selected makes it easier to find the event method associated with a particular control. The control event methods are usually placed after the constructor method.

Let's summarize the many steps to place a control (named **controlName** of type **controlType**) in a frame and add an event method:

- Declare and create the control (class level scope):

```
ControlType controlName = new ControlType();
```

- Position the control:

```
gridConstraints.gridx = desiredColumn;
gridConstraints.gridy = desiredRow;
getContentPane().add(controlName, gridConstraints);
```

(assumes a **gridConstraints** object has been created).

- Add the control listener:

```
controlName.addActionListener(new ActionListener()
{
  public void actionPerformed(ActionEvent e)
  {
     controlNameActionPerformed(e);
  }
});
```

- Write the control event method:

```
private void controlNameActionPerformed(ActionEvent e)
{
    [Java code to execute]
}
```

The first few times you add controls, this will seem to be a tedious process. As you develop more and more GUI applications, such additions will become second nature (and, you'll get very good at using the copy and paste features of NetBeans).

Stopwatch - Writing Code

All that's left to do is write code for the application. We write code for every event a response is needed for. In this application, there are three such events: clicking on each of the buttons.

1. Under the lines declaring the frame controls, declare three class level variables:

```
long startTime;
long stopTime;
double elapsedTime;
```

This establishes **startTime**, **endTime**, and **elapsedTime** as variables with class level scope.

2. In the frame constructor, add the **windowClosing** event method (every GUI project will need this code - place it after line establishing frame title):

```
addWindowListener(new WindowAdapter()
{
  public void windowClosing(WindowEvent e)
  {
    exitForm(e);
  }
});
```

And, add the corresponding event method code:

```
private void exitForm(WindowEvent e)
{
  System.exit(0);
}
```

This method is placed before the final right closing brace of the Stopwatch class (the normal place for methods). This one line of code tells the application to stop.

3. Let's create an **actionPerformed** event for the **startButton**. Add the listener (I place this after the code placing the control on the frame):

```
startButton.addActionListener(new ActionListener()
{
  public void actionPerformed(ActionEvent e)
  {
    startButtonActionPerformed(e);
  }
});
```

Then, add the event method after the constructor method:

```
private void startButtonActionPerformed(ActionEvent e)
{
  // click of start timing button
  startTime = System.currentTimeMillis();
  startTextField.setText(String.valueOf(startTime));
  stopTextField.setText("");
  elapsedTextField.setText("");
}
```

In this procedure, once the **Start Timing** button is clicked, we read the current time using a system function (in milliseconds, by the way) and put it in a text field using the **setText** method. We also blank out the other text fields. In the code above (and in all code in these notes), any line beginning with two slashes (//) is a comment. You decide whether you want to type these lines or not. They are not needed for proper application operation.

4. Now, add a listener for the **actionPerformed** event method for the **stopButton**:

```
stopButton.addActionListener(new ActionListener()
{
  public void actionPerformed(ActionEvent e)
  {
    stopButtonActionPerformed(e);
  }
});
```

Then, add this event method after the **startButtonActionPerformed** method:

```
private void stopButtonActionPerformed(ActionEvent e)
{
  // click of stop timing button
  stopTime = System.currentTimeMillis();
  stopTextField.setText(String.valueOf(stopTime));
  elapsedTime = (stopTime - startTime) / 1000.0;
  elapsedTextField.setText(String.valueOf(elapsedTime));
}
```

Here, when the **Stop Timing** button is clicked, we read the current time (**stopTime**), compute the elapsed time (in seconds), and put both values in their corresponding text field controls.

5. Finally, we need code in the **actionPerformed** method for the **exitButton** control. Add the listener:

```
exitButton.addActionListener(new ActionListener()
{
  public void actionPerformed(ActionEvent e)
  {
    exitButtonActionPerformed(e);
  }
});
```

Now, add the method:

```
private void exitButtonActionPerformed(ActionEvent e)
{
  System.exit(0);
}
```

This routine simply closes the frame once the **Exit** button is clicked.

For reference, the complete, final **Stopwatch.java** code is (newly added code is shaded):

```
/*
 * Stopwatch.java
*/
package stopwatch;
import javax.swing.*;
import java.awt.*;
import java.awt.event.*;

public class Stopwatch extends JFrame
{

  // declare controls used
  JButton startButton = new JButton();
  JButton stopButton = new JButton();
  JButton exitButton = new JButton();
  JLabel startLabel = new JLabel();
  JLabel stopLabel = new JLabel();
  JLabel elapsedLabel = new JLabel();;
  JTextField startTextField = new JTextField();
  JTextField stopTextField = new JTextField();
  JTextField elapsedTextField = new JTextField();

  // declare class level variables
  long startTime;
  long stopTime;
  double elapsedTime;

  public static void main(String args[])
  {
    new Stopwatch().setVisible(true);
  }

  public Stopwatch()
  {
    // frame constructor
    setTitle("Stopwatch Application");
    addWindowListener(new WindowAdapter()
    {
      public void windowClosing(WindowEvent e)
      {
        exitForm(e);
      }
    });
    getContentPane().setLayout(new GridBagLayout());
```

```
    // add controls
    GridBagConstraints gridConstraints = new
GridBagConstraints();
    startButton.setText("Start Timing");
    gridConstraints.gridx = 0;
    gridConstraints.gridy = 0;
    getContentPane().add(startButton, gridConstraints);
    startButton.addActionListener(new ActionListener()
    {
      public void actionPerformed(ActionEvent e)
      {
        startButtonActionPerformed(e);
      }
    });

    stopButton.setText("Stop Timing");
    gridConstraints.gridx = 0;
    gridConstraints.gridy = 1;
    getContentPane().add(stopButton, gridConstraints);
    stopButton.addActionListener(new ActionListener()
    {
      public void actionPerformed(ActionEvent e)
      {
        stopButtonActionPerformed(e);
       }
    });

    exitButton.setText("Exit");
    gridConstraints.gridx = 0;
    gridConstraints.gridy = 2;
    getContentPane().add(exitButton, gridConstraints);
    exitButton.addActionListener(new ActionListener()
    {
      public void actionPerformed(ActionEvent e)
      {
        exitButtonActionPerformed(e);
      }
    });

    startLabel.setText("Start Time");
    gridConstraints.gridx = 1;
    gridConstraints.gridy = 0;
    getContentPane().add(startLabel, new
GridBagConstraints());

    stopLabel.setText("Stop Time");
```

```
    gridConstraints.gridx = 1;
    gridConstraints.gridy = 1;
    getContentPane().add(stopLabel, gridConstraints);

    elapsedLabel.setText("Elapsed Time (sec)");
    gridConstraints.gridx = 1;
    gridConstraints.gridy = 2;
    getContentPane().add(elapsedLabel, gridConstraints);

    startTextField.setText("");
    startTextField.setColumns(15);
    gridConstraints.gridx = 2;
    gridConstraints.gridy = 0;
    getContentPane().add(startTextField, new
GridBagConstraints());

    stopTextField.setText("");
    stopTextField.setColumns(15);
    gridConstraints.gridx = 2;
    gridConstraints.gridy = 1;
    getContentPane().add(stopTextField, gridConstraints);

    elapsedTextField.setText("");
    elapsedTextField.setColumns(15);
    gridConstraints.gridx = 2;
    gridConstraints.gridy = 2;
    getContentPane().add(elapsedTextField, gridConstraints);
    pack();
  }

  private void startButtonActionPerformed(ActionEvent e)
  {
    // click of start timing button
    startTime = System.currentTimeMillis();
    startTextField.setText(String.valueOf(startTime));
    stopTextField.setText("");
    elapsedTextField.setText("");
  }

  private void stopButtonActionPerformed(ActionEvent e)
  {
     // click of stop timing button
    stopTime = System.currentTimeMillis();
    stopTextField.setText(String.valueOf(stopTime));
    elapsedTime = (stopTime - startTime) / 1000.0;
    elapsedTextField.setText(String.valueOf(elapsedTime));
  }
```

```
  private void exitButtonActionPerformed(ActionEvent e)
  {
    System.exit(0);
  }

  private void exitForm(WindowEvent e)
  {
    System.exit(0);
  }

}
```

Study this code to see where all the methods go.

Now, run the application (press <**F6**>). Try it out. If your application doesn't run, recheck to make sure the code is typed properly. Save your application. This is saved as **Stopwatch Project** in the **Projects** program group in **\CBGJava\CBGJava Projects** folder. Here's what I got when I tried:

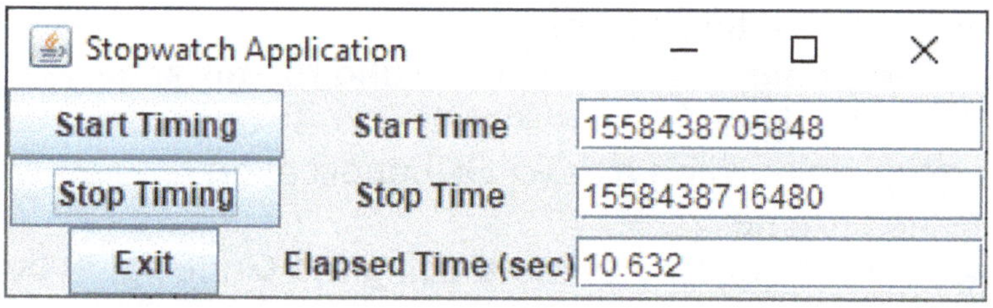

If you have the time, here are some other things you may try with the **Stopwatch**. To make these changes will require research on your part (use web sites, other books, other programmers) to find answers. This is an important skill to have – how to improve existing applications by discovering new things. The solutions to the problems and exercises at the end of this class' notes can also shed some light on these challenges:

A. Try changing the frame background color.

B. Notice you can press the 'Stop Timing' button before the 'Start Timing' button. This shouldn't be so. Change the application so you can't do this. And make it such that you can't press the 'Start Timing' until 'Stop Timing' has been pressed. Hint: Look at the button **enabled** property.

C. Can you think of how you can continuously display the 'End Time' and 'Elapsed Time'? This is a little tricky because of the event-driven nature of Java. Look at the **Timer** class (do a little Java research). By setting the **delay** property of this class to **1000**, it will generate its own events every one second. Put code similar to that in the event method for the **stopButton** in the Timer class' actionPerformed method and see what happens. Also, see the exercise at the end of the class for help on this one.

Chapter Review

After completing this chapter, you should understand:

- The prerequisites for this course
- How to use NetBeans to build, compile and run an application
- The structure of a Java GUI application
- The three steps in building a Java GUI application
- How to create a frame
- How to place a control on the frame using the GridBagLayout
- Proper control naming convention
- How to add event listeners and event methods
- How to add code to event methods

2

Bible Safecracker Project

Review and Preview

We've completed our review of building Java GUI projects using NetBeans (or any IDE you choose). We now start building some kid games. For each project built, we provide step-by-step instructions in designing and building the form's graphic interface and detailed explanations of the code behind the projects.

The first project we build is a **Bible Safecracker** that asks you to guess a secret combination of numbers using clues from the computer. This lets you break into the old abandoned safe to rescue an ancient and valuable Bible.

Bible Safecracker Project Preview

In this chapter, we will build a **Bible Safecracker** game. A bank safe is locked and can only be opened if you enter the proper combination. The combination can be 2 to 4 non-repeating digits (digits range from 1 to 9). After each guess, you are told how many digits are correct and how many are in the correct location. Based on this information, you make another guess. You continue guessing until you get the correct combination or stop the game.

The finished project is saved as **Safecracker** in the **\CBGJava\CBGJava Projects** project group. Start NetBeans (or your IDE). Open the specified project group. Make **Safecracker** the selected project. Run the project. You will see:

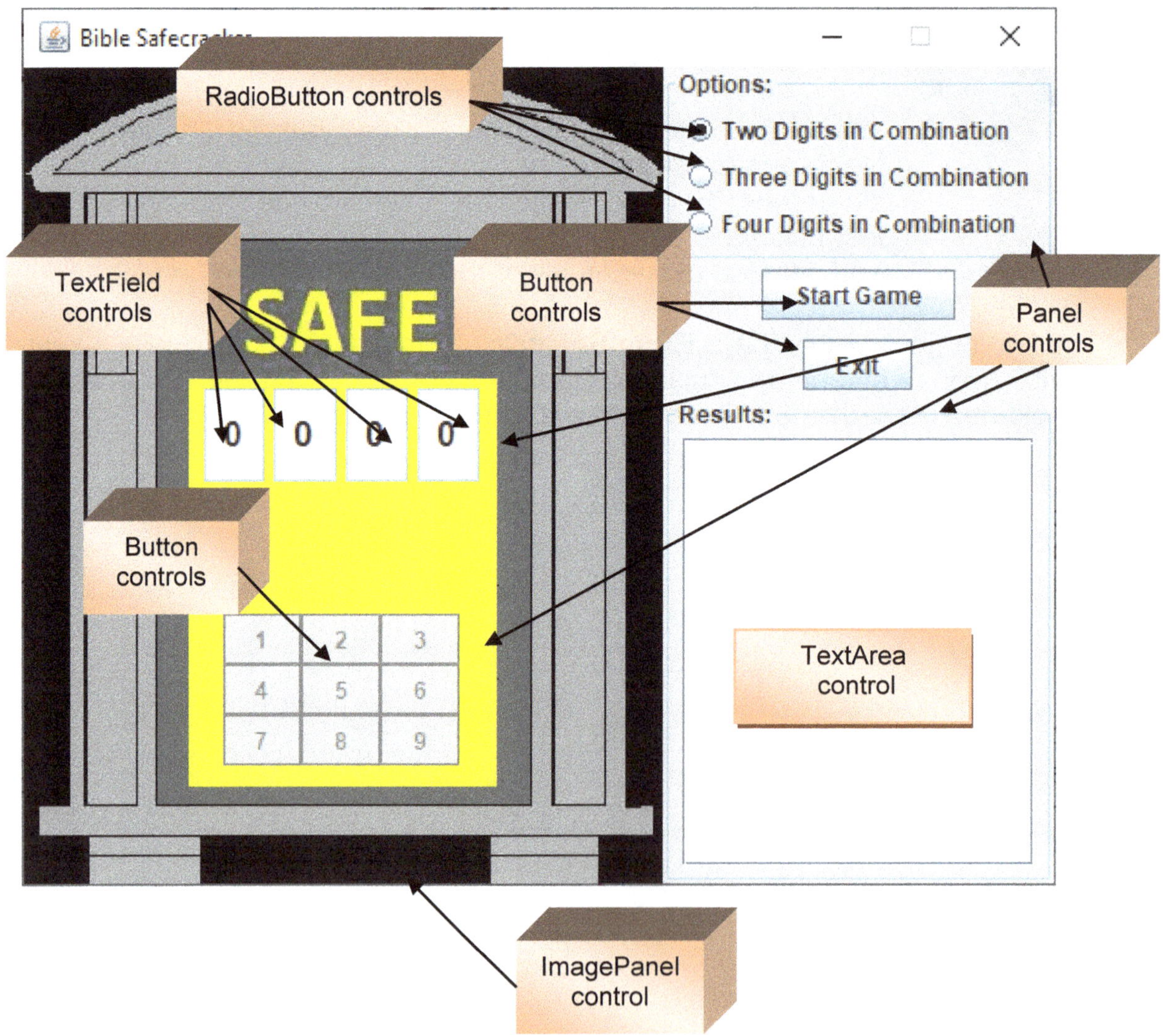

On the left is an image panel control displaying the bank safe (we will show you how to create such a control – it is a panel that hosts an image). A panel control holds four text field controls to display the entered combination and another panel contains nine button controls that form a keypad to enter the combination. On the right are two panel controls and two button controls. The first panel holds three radio buttons to select game options. The second panel holds a scrollable text area control to display the results of a guess. The two buttons are used to start and stop the game and to exit the program.

The game initially appears in its 'stopped' state, waiting for you to choose game options (how many digits in the combination and whether digits can repeat). The bank vault is disabled – no combination can be entered. I've selected 3 digits in the combination:

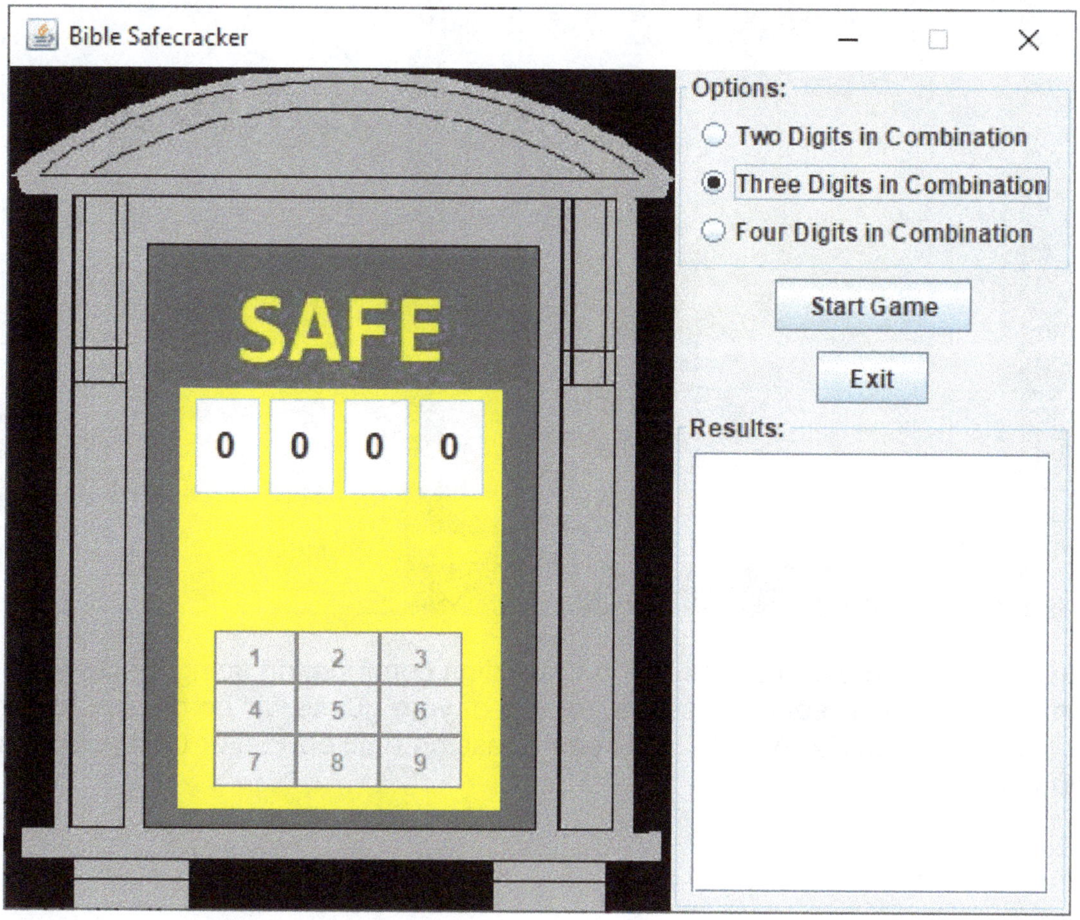

Click the **Start Game** button to start playing. Its caption will change (now reading **Stop Game**) and the **Options** panel and **Exit** button will become disabled. The panel control in the vault is now enabled showing a text field control for each digit in the combination and activating the 9 button keypad. We call this the 'playing' state:

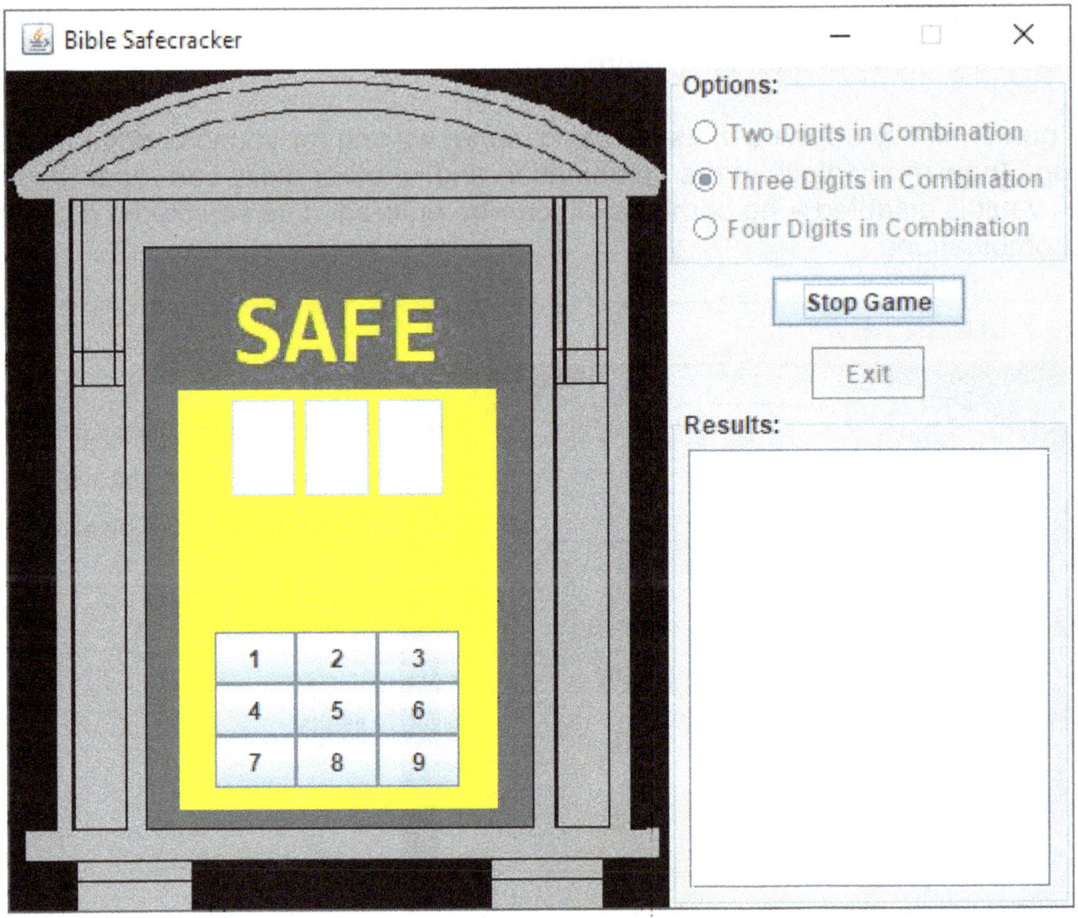

In this state, you make a guess at the three digit combination using the keypad in the bank safe. After each guess, the results of your guess will be displayed in the text box in the **Results** panel. You keep guessing until correct or until you press **Stop Game**.

Enter a guess; I entered 123:

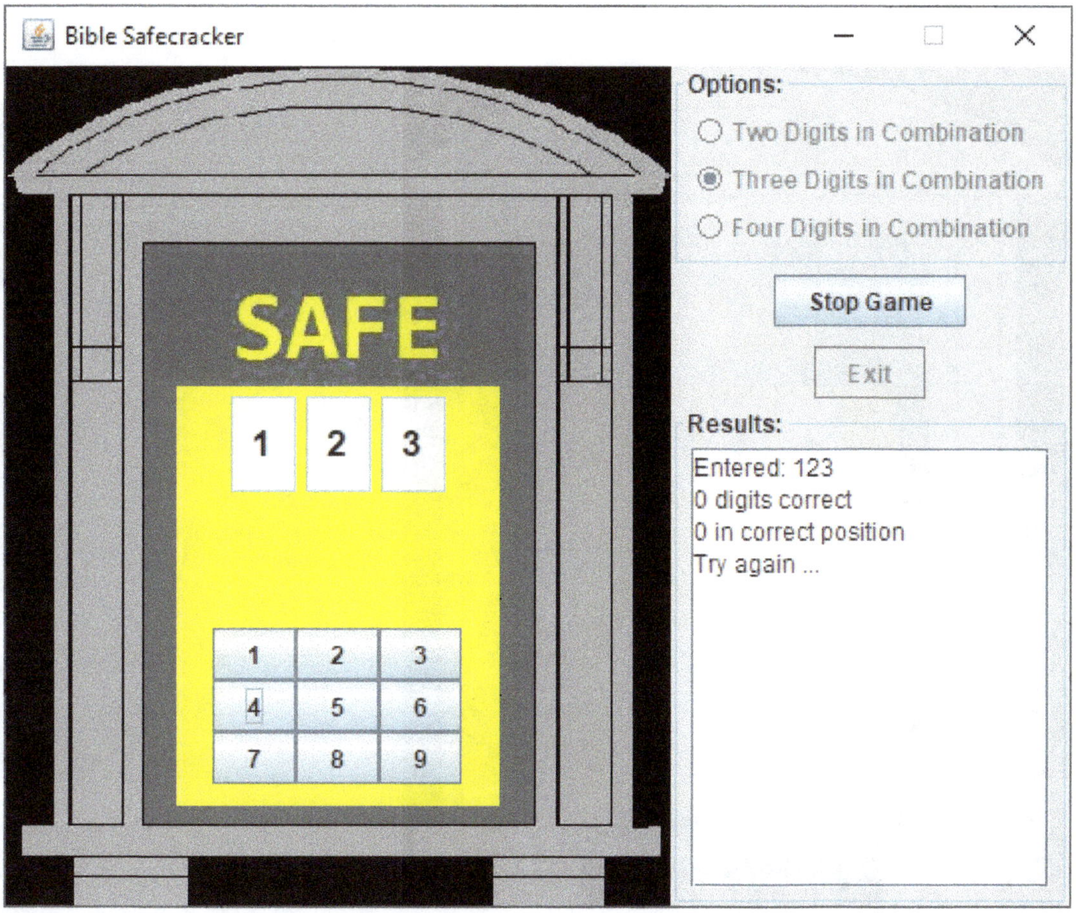

As a guess is entered, notice several things. Once a button is pressed, the corresponding digit appears in the proper text field. Also, the pressed button is disabled since the digits can't repeat. Once three buttons are pressed, the results are shown. You are told how many digits in your guess were correct and how many were in the correct position. If incorrect, you will hear an 'uh-oh' sound. Obviously, my guess was not very good!

When I try 456, I see:

Much better. Now, I know that the combination has either a 4 and a 5, a 4 and a 6, or a 5 and a 6. I also know none of the digits are in their proper position.

What if I try 745 (I assumed the 4 and 5 should stay and shifted them over)

Since only 1 digit is now correct, I know the 6 is definitely in the combination. I think you're starting to see how the game works.

I continued playing until finally, after entering 648:

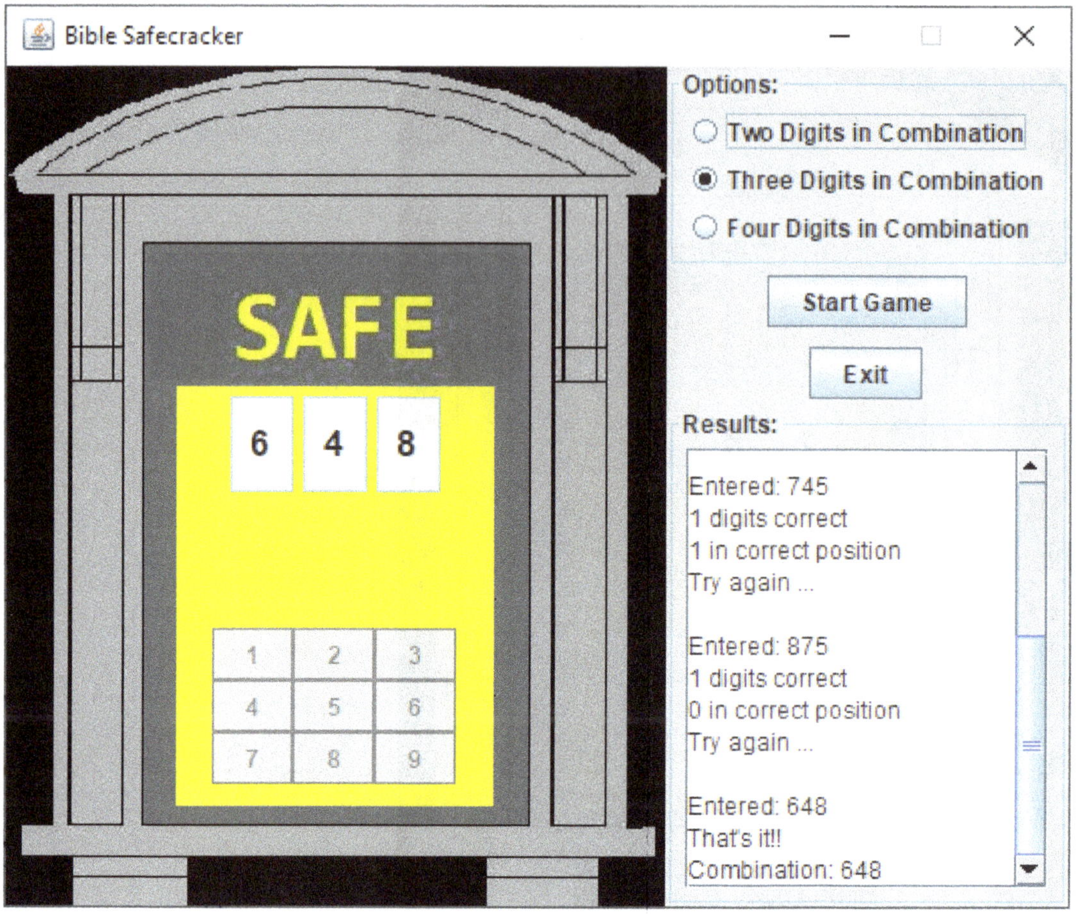

The correct combination was entered! A little celebratory sound is heard. The game returns to its stopped state to allow another game or to stop the program.

Continue playing the game to understand its operation. Click **Exit** when you're done to stop the game. Open the code file and skim over the code, if you like.

You will now build this project in stages. As you build Java projects, we always recommend taking a slow, step-by-step process. It minimizes programming errors and helps build your confidence as things come together in a complete project. This is the approach we will take on all projects in these notes.

We address **frame design**. We discuss the controls needed to build the frame, establish initial control properties and discuss how to change the state of the controls. And, we address **code design**. We discuss how to form the secret combination, how to gather user input and how to check an entered combination. We also discuss how to have several events invoke a single method. Before diving into this first project, however, we review some of the 'tricks' in using the grid bag layout manager.

Frame Design – GridBagLayout Manager

We use the **GridBagLayout** manager to set up our Java GUI projects (you can, of course, choose to use any layout manager you want). Recall, with this manager, a grid is used to place controls:

	gridx = 0	gridx = 1	gridx = 2	gridx = 3	gridx = 4
gridy = 0					
gridy = 1					
gridy = 2					
gridy = 3					
gridy = 4					
gridy = 5					

The **GridBagConstraints** object is used for control placement and positioning within the various grid elements. Controls are placed in this grid by referring to a particular column (**gridx** location) and row (**gridy** location). We have seen that the grid (and frame) automatically grows as controls are added. Column widths are set by the "widest" control in a particular column. And, row heights are set by the "tallest" control in a particular row.

There are other variables associated with **GridBagConstraints** that can be used to adjust control size and, hence, associated column, row, and frame size. A control can occupy more than one column or row. The number of columns spanned by a control is set with the **gridwidth** variable; the number of rows spanned is set with the **gridheight** variable. By default, a control fills one row and one column. If we have a GridBagConstraints object named **gridConstraints**, a control will occupy two rows and three columns, starting in the second column (gridx = 1) and fourth row (gridy = 3), with this code:

```
gridConstraints.gridx = 1;
gridConstraints.gridy = 3;
gridConstraints.gridheight = 2;
gridConstraints.gridwidth = 3;
```

In our example grid, this control would be placed like this:

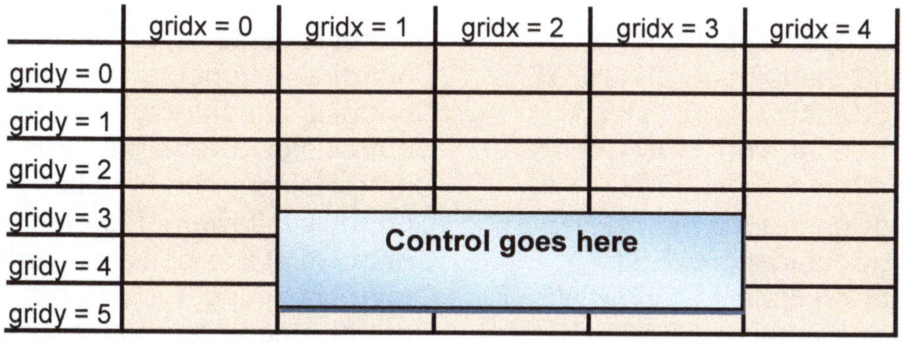

A particular control may completely fill its region or may not. If the control is smaller than its allocated region, its dimensions may be adjusted to fill the region – use the **fill** variable. There are four values:

GridBagConstraints.NONE	Control is not resized (default value)
GridBagConstraints.HORIZONTAL	Control width fills display area.
GridBagConstraints.VERTICAL	Control height fills display area.
GridBagConstraints.BOTH	Control fills entire display area.

With our example **gridConstraints** object, a control will grow to fill the region width using:

```
gridConstraints.fill = GridBagConstraints.HORIZONTAL;
```

This control would look like this in its grid region:

Smaller changes in control size can be made using the **ipadx** and **ipady** variables. These determine how much a control size is to be increased beyond its minimum size (in each direction). To add five pixels to the width and height of a control using our **gridConstraints** example:

```
gridConstraints.ipadx = 5;
gridConstraints.ipady = 5;
```

If you choose not to expand a control to fill its area, its position within its allocated area is set with the **anchor** variable. There are nine possible values:

GridBagConstraints.NORTH	Control is centered at top
GridBagConstraints.NORTHEAST	Control is in upper right corner
GridBagConstraints.EAST	Control is at right, centered vertically
GridBagConstraints.SOUTHEAST	Control is in lower right corner
GridBagConstraints.SOUTH	Control is centered at bottom
GridBagConstraints.SOUTHWEST	Control is in lower left corner
GridBagConstraints.WEST	Control is at left, centered vertically
GridBagConstraints.NORTHWEST	Control is in upper left corner
GridBagConstraints.CENTER	Control is centered horizontally and vertically

To center a control (in both directions) in its display area, use:

```
gridConstraints.anchor = GridBagConstraints.CENTER;
```

This control would look like this in its grid region:

If a control completely fills its allocated display area, a border region (free space) can be established around the control using the **Insets** object. Four values are used to define the **top**, **left**, **bottom** and **right** side margins from the side of the display area. The default is **Insets(0, 0, 0, 0)**. With our example, if we want 10 pixels of space at the top and bottom, 20 on the left and 30 on the right, we would use:

```
gridConstraints.insets = new Insets(10, 20, 10, 30);
```

This control would look something like this in its grid region:

Once the **gridConstraints** are established for a control, it is added to the frame's content pane using the add method. If the control is **myControl**, the code syntax is:

```
getContentPane().add(myControl, gridConstraints);
```

Many times, we add controls to a panel control (with its own **GridBayLayout** manager) within a frame. If the panel is named **myPanel**, the code to add **myControl** is:

```
myPanel.add(myControl, gridConstraints);
```

I think you see the flexibility available with the **GridBagLayout** manager. You are encouraged to learn these ideas and use them to "beautify" your GUI interfaces. Remember to establish all grid constraint values before adding a control to the grid.

Building an interface is an "art," not a science. You will see the process involves lots of trial and error and adjustments. And sometimes, you get results you would never expect – components may not appear as you wish or may not appear at all! The bottom line is – once all adjustments are made, your completed frame size is established. Let's look at one final task - how to center the frame in the screen.

First, to place a frame (**width** by **height** in size) at a horizontal position **left** and vertical position **top**, we use the **setBounds** method:

```
setBounds(left, top, width, height);
```

All the dimensions are **int** types and measured in pixels. To center a frame in the computer screen, we need to know find **left** and **top**.

To find the centering position, we need two things: the dimensions of the frame (use **getWidth** and **getHeight** methods) and the dimensions of the screen. The dimensions of the screen are held in the frame's '**toolkit'**. A **Dimension** object holds the information we need. To retrieve this object, use:

```
Dimension screenSize =
Toolkit.getDefaultToolkit().getScreenSize();
```

With this, **screenSize.width** holds the screen width and **screenSize.height** holds the screen height. So, the code to center the frame using **setBounds** is:

```
setBounds((int) (0.5 * (screenSize.width - getWidth())),
(int) (0.5 * (screenSize.height - getHeight())),
getWidth(), getHeight());
```

This code needs to be after the **pack** method in the code establishing the frame, so that proper frame size is used. We'll use this centering code in every application built in the remainder of this course. Any initializations for a project will be placed after this line in the frame constructor.

Bible Safecracker Frame Design

We can begin building the **Bible Safecracker** game project. Before starting, make sure you have established a project group on your computer for building Java projects. Always save your projects in this project group. Do not save them in the project group used in these notes (**\CBGJava\CBGJava Projects** folder). Leave this project group intact so you can always reference the finished projects, if needed.

Let's build the frame. Start a new project in your Java project group – name it **Safecracker**. Delete default code in file named **Safecracker.java**. Once started, we suggest you immediately save the project with the name you chose. This sets up the folder and file structure needed for your project. Build the basic frame with these properties:

Safecracker Frame:

title	Bible Safecracker
resizable	false

The code is:

```
/*
 * Safecracker.java
 */
package safecracker;
import javax.swing.*;
import java.awt.*;
import java.awt.event.*;

public class Safecracker extends JFrame
{

  public static void main(String args[])
  {
    // create frame
    new Safecracker().setVisible(true);
  }

  public Safecracker()
  {
    // frame constructor
    setTitle("Bible Safecracker");
    setResizable(false);
    addWindowListener(new WindowAdapter()
    {
      public void windowClosing(WindowEvent evt)
```

```
        {
          exitForm(evt);
        }
      });
      getContentPane().setLayout(new GridBagLayout());
      GridBagConstraints gridConstraints;

      pack();
      Dimension screenSize =
  Toolkit.getDefaultToolkit().getScreenSize();
      setBounds((int) (0.5 * (screenSize.width -
  getWidth())), (int) (0.5 * (screenSize.height -
  getHeight())), getWidth(), getHeight());
    }

    private void exitForm(WindowEvent evt)
    {
      System.exit(0);
    }
  }
```

We use similar code to start each project. It builds the frame, sets up the layout manager and includes code to exit the application. Run the code to make sure the frame (at least, what there is of it at this point) appears and is centered on the screen:

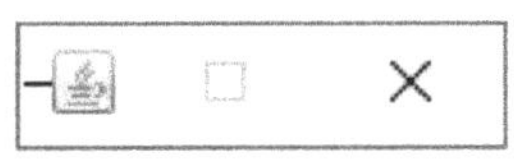

Let's populate our frame with other controls. All code for creating the frame and placing controls (except declarations) goes in the **Safecracker** constructor.

We start by putting four panel controls on the frame. The **GridBagLayout** is:

	gridx = 0	gridx = 1
gridy = 0	**safePanel**	**optionsPanel**
gridy = 1		**buttonsPanel**
gridy = 2		**resultsPanel**

We use lots of panels in building Java GUI projects. They are useful for sizing the frames and can be used to hold other controls. The **safePanel** will hold the safe graphic, the combination display and the keypad for combination entry. The **optionsPanel** will hold the radio buttons used to specify the number of digits in the combination. The **buttonsPanel** will hold the two button controls. The **resultsPanel** holds the text area displaying the results after entry of a combination. Each panel will be built individually We start with the **safePanel**.

The **safePanel** is an **ImagePanel** control, which is an extended version of the **JPanel** control. We want to use a background image (the safe) in the panel, but the JPanel control does not have an image property. We can get around this by using the object-oriented nature of Java by extending the JPanel control with a new **img** property. The code that does this is (found on the Internet by the way):

```
class ImagePanel extends JPanel
{
  private Image img;
  public ImagePanel(Image img)
  {
   this.img = img;
  }
  public void paintComponent(Graphics g)
  {
    g.drawImage(img, 0, 0, null);
  }
}
```

Add this code after the class describing the **Safecracker** project.

Let's construct the **safePanel** control (with graphic) and put it in the frame. Use these properties:

safePanel (ImagePanel):

img	safe.jpg (included in the **\CBGJava\CBGJava Projects\Safecracker** folder)
size	330, 420

Make sure to copy the **safe.jpg** graphic file into the folder you use to build your project. The panel size matches the size of the graphic.

Declare and create the panel (goes after the class definition):

```
ImagePanel safePanel = new ImagePanel(new
ImageIcon("safe.jpg").getImage());
```

The code to set the properties and place the panel in the frame (goes in the **Safecracker** constructor after the layout manager is defined):

```
safePanel.setPreferredSize(new Dimension(330, 420));
safePanel.setLayout(new GridBagLayout());
gridConstraints = new GridBagConstraints();
gridConstraints.gridx = 0;
gridConstraints.gridy = 0;
gridConstraints.gridheight = 3;
getContentPane().add(safePanel, gridConstraints);
```

As a reminder of where particular code segments go, here is the complete code at this point (additions are shaded):

```
/*
 * Safecracker.java
 */

import javax.swing.*;
import java.awt.*;
import java.awt.event.*;

public class Safecracker extends JFrame
{
  ImagePanel safePanel = new ImagePanel(new
ImageIcon("safe.jpg").getImage());
  public static void main(String args[])
  {
    // create frame
    new Safecracker().setVisible(true);
  }
```

```
  public Safecracker()
  {
    // frame constructor
    setTitle("Bible Safecracker");
    setResizable(false);
    addWindowListener(new WindowAdapter()
    {
      public void windowClosing(WindowEvent evt)
      {
        exitForm(evt);
      }
    });
    getContentPane().setLayout(new GridBagLayout());
    GridBagConstraints gridConstraints;

    safePanel.setPreferredSize(new Dimension(330, 420));
    safePanel.setLayout(new GridBagLayout());
    gridConstraints = new GridBagConstraints();
    gridConstraints.gridx = 0;
    gridConstraints.gridy = 0;
    gridConstraints.gridheight = 3;
    getContentPane().add(safePanel, gridConstraints);

    pack();
    Dimension screenSize =
Toolkit.getDefaultToolkit().getScreenSize();
    setBounds((int) (0.5 * (screenSize.width -
getWidth())), (int) (0.5 * (screenSize.height -
getHeight())), getWidth(), getHeight());
  }

  private void exitForm(WindowEvent evt)
  {
    System.exit(0);
  }
}

class ImagePanel extends JPanel
{
  private Image img;
  public ImagePanel(Image img)
  {
   this.img = img;
  }
  public void paintComponent(Graphics g)
  {
```

```
      g.drawImage(img, 0, 0, null);
    }
  }
```

Run. The safe graphic should appear:

The **safePanel** will hold two other panel (JPanel) controls. The **GridBagLayout** for safePanel is:

	gridx = 0
gridy = 0	**comboPanel**
gridy = 1	**keyPanel**

comboPanel holds the controls used to display the combination, while **keyPanel** holds the buttons used to enter the combination.

The panel properties:

comboPanel:

size	160, 110
background	Yellow
gridx	0
gridy	0
insets	110, 0, 0, 0

keyPanel:

size	160, 100
background	Yellow
gridx	0
gridy	1

The sizing and position properties were obtained via trial and error.

These new panels are declared using:

```
JPanel comboPanel = new JPanel();
JPanel keyPanel = new JPanel();
```

The panels are placed in the **safePanel** using:

```
comboPanel.setPreferredSize(new Dimension(160, 110));
safePanel.setLayout(new GridBagLayout());
comboPanel.setBackground(Color.YELLOW);
gridConstraints = new GridBagConstraints();
gridConstraints.gridx = 0;
gridConstraints.gridy = 0;
gridConstraints.insets = new Insets(110, 0, 0, 0);
safePanel.add(comboPanel, gridConstraints);
```

```
keyPanel.setPreferredSize(new Dimension(160, 100));
keyPanel.setLayout(new GridBagLayout());
keyPanel.setBackground(Color.YELLOW);
gridConstraints = new GridBagConstraints();
gridConstraints.gridx = 0;
gridConstraints.gridy = 1;
safePanel.add(keyPanel, gridConstraints);
```

Add this code in the proper locations. Run to see:

The blank yellow panels appear on the safe graphic.

The **comboPanel** will hold four text field controls used to display the combination. The **GridBagLayout** for comboPanel is:

	gridx = 0	gridx = 1	gridx = 2	gridx = 3
gridy = 0	comboTextField[0]	comboTextField[1]	comboTextField[2]	comboTextField[3]

The text field properties:

comboTextField[i]:

size	32, 48
editable	false
background	White
text	0
horizontalAlignment	Center
font	Arial, Bold, 18
gridx	i
gridy	0

These text fields are declared using:

```
JTextField[] comboTextField = new JTextField[4];
```

The text fields are placed in the **comboPanel** using (place this code after the code positioning the comboPanel):

```
for (int i = 0; i < 4; i++)
{
  comboTextField[i] = new JTextField();
  comboTextField[i].setPreferredSize(new Dimension(32,
48));
  comboTextField[i].setEditable(false);
  comboTextField[i].setBackground(Color.WHITE);
  comboTextField[i].setText("0");

comboTextField[i].setHorizontalAlignment(SwingConstants.CE
NTER);
  comboTextField[i].setFont(new Font("Arial", Font.BOLD,
18));
  gridConstraints = new GridBagConstraints();
  gridConstraints.gridx = i;
  gridConstraints.gridy = 0;
  comboPanel.add(comboTextField[i], gridConstraints);
}
```

Add this code in the proper locations. Run to see:

We're making progress! The combination display is visible.

The **keyPanel** will hold nine button controls used to enter the combination. The **GridBagLayout** for keyPanel is:

	gridx = 0	gridx = 1	gridx = 2
gridy = 0	**keyButton[0]**	**keyButton[1]**	**keyButton[2]**
gridy = 1	**keyButton[3]**	**keyButton[4]**	**keyButton[5]**
gridy = 2	**keyButton[6]**	**keyButton[7]**	**keyButton[8]**

The text field properties:

keyButton[0]:
text 1
gridx 0
gridy 0

keyButton[1]:
text 2
gridx 1
gridy 0

keyButton[2]:
text 3
gridx 2
gridy 0

keyButton[3]:
text 4
gridx 0
gridy 1

keyButton[4]:
text 5
gridx 1
gridy 1

keyButton[5]:
text 6
gridx 2
gridy 1

keyButton[6]:

text	7
gridx	0
gridy	2

keyButton[7]:

text	8
gridx	1
gridy	2

keyButton[8]:

text	9
gridx	2
gridy	2

These buttons are declared using:

```
JButton[] keyButton = new JButton[9];
```

The buttons are placed in the **keyPanel** using (place this code after the code positioning the keyPanel):

```
for (int i = 0; i < 9; i++)
{
  keyButton[i] = new JButton();
  keyButton[i].setText(String.valueOf(i + 1));
  gridConstraints = new GridBagConstraints();
  gridConstraints.gridx = i % 3;
  gridConstraints.gridy = i / 3;
  keyPanel.add(keyButton[i], gridConstraints);
  keyButton[i].addActionListener(new ActionListener()
  {
    public void actionPerformed(ActionEvent e)
    {
      keyButtonActionPerformed(e);
    }
  });
}
```

Note how the loop index (**i**) is used to set properties.

This code also adds listeners for each button. The method called when a button is clicked is **keyButtonActionPerformed**. Add this empty method with the other methods:

```
private void keyButtonActionPerformed(ActionEvent e)
{
}
```

Add code in the proper locations. Run to see:

The keys appear. The **safePanel** control is complete. Let's move to the other three panels on the frame.

The **optionsPanel** will hold three radio button controls used to select the number of digits in the combination. The **GridBagLayout** for optionsPanel is:

	gridx = 0
gridy = 0	**twoDigitsRadioButton**
gridy =1	**threeDigitsRadioButton**
gridy = 2	**fourDigitsRadioButton**

The panel and radio button properties:

optionsPanel:

size	200, 100
title	Options:
gridx	1 (on frame)
gridy	0 (on frame)

twoDigitsRadioButton:

text	Two Digits in Combination
buttonGroup	digitsButtonGroup
selected	true
gridx	0 (on optionsPanel)
gridy	0 (on optionsPanel)
anchor	WEST

threeDigitsRadioButton:

text	Three Digits in Combination
buttonGroup	digitsButtonGroup
gridx	0 (on optionsPanel)
gridy	1 (on optionsPanel)
anchor	WEST

fourDigitsRadioButton:

text	Four Digits in Combination
gridx	0 (on optionsPanel)
gridy	2 (on optionsPanel)
anchor	WEST

These controls are declared using:

```
JPanel optionsPanel = new JPanel();
ButtonGroup digitsButtonGroup = new ButtonGroup();
JRadioButton twoDigitsRadioButton = new JRadioButton();
JRadioButton threeDigitsRadioButton = new JRadioButton();
JRadioButton fourDigitsRadioButton = new JRadioButton();
```

The radio buttons are placed in the **optionsPanel** (which is placed in the frame) using:

```
optionsPanel.setPreferredSize(new Dimension(200, 100));
optionsPanel.setBorder(BorderFactory.createTitledBorder("O
ptions:"));
optionsPanel.setLayout(new GridBagLayout());
gridConstraints = new GridBagConstraints();
gridConstraints.gridx = 1;
gridConstraints.gridy = 0;
getContentPane().add(optionsPanel, gridConstraints);

twoDigitsRadioButton.setText("Two Digits in Combination");
twoDigitsRadioButton.setSelected(true);
digitsButtonGroup.add(twoDigitsRadioButton);
gridConstraints = new GridBagConstraints();
gridConstraints.gridx = 0;
gridConstraints.gridy = 0;
gridConstraints.anchor = GridBagConstraints.WEST;
optionsPanel.add(twoDigitsRadioButton, gridConstraints);

threeDigitsRadioButton.setText("Three Digits in
Combination");
digitsButtonGroup.add(threeDigitsRadioButton);
gridConstraints = new GridBagConstraints();
gridConstraints.gridx = 0;
gridConstraints.gridy = 1;
gridConstraints.anchor = GridBagConstraints.WEST;
optionsPanel.add(threeDigitsRadioButton, gridConstraints);

fourDigitsRadioButton.setText("Four Digits in
Combination");
digitsButtonGroup.add(fourDigitsRadioButton);
gridConstraints = new GridBagConstraints();
gridConstraints.gridx = 0;
gridConstraints.gridy = 2;
gridConstraints.anchor = GridBagConstraints.WEST;
optionsPanel.add(fourDigitsRadioButton, gridConstraints);
```

Add this code in the proper locations. Run to see:

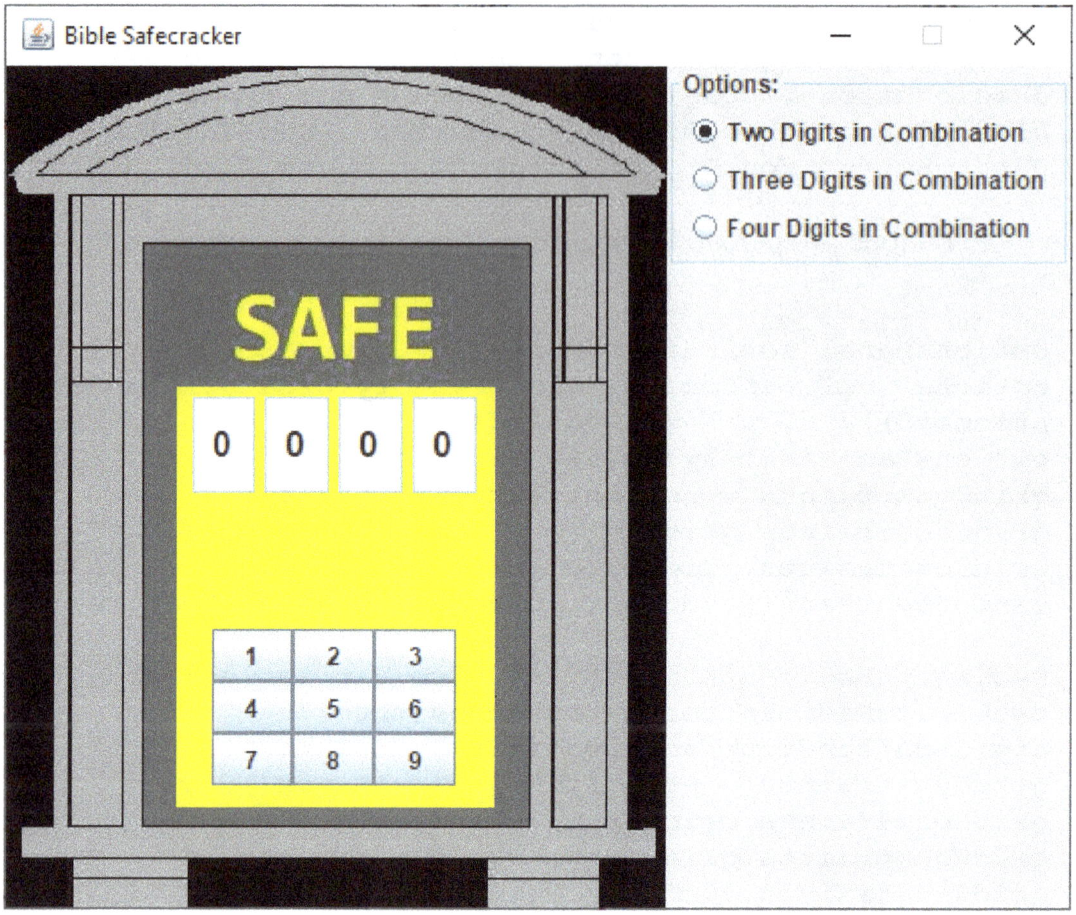

The options panel is displayed.

The **buttonsPanel** will hold two buttons used to control game play. The **GridBagLayout** for buttonsPanel is:

	gridx = 0
gridy = 0	**startStopButton**
gridy =1	**exitButton**

The panel and button properties:

buttonsPanel:

size	200, 70
gridx	1 (on frame)
gridy	1 (on frame)

startStopButton:

text	Start Game
gridx	0 (on buttonsPanel)
gridy	0 (on buttonsPanel)

exitButton:

text	Exit
gridx	0 (on buttonsPanel)
gridy	1 (on buttonsPanel)

These controls are declared using:

```
JPanel buttonsPanel = new JPanel();
JButton startStopButton = new JButton();
JButton exitButton = new JButton();
```

The buttons are placed in the **buttonsPanel** (which is placed in the frame) using:

```
buttonsPanel.setPreferredSize(new Dimension(200, 70));
buttonsPanel.setLayout(new GridBagLayout());
gridConstraints = new GridBagConstraints();
gridConstraints.gridx = 1;
gridConstraints.gridy = 1;
getContentPane().add(buttonsPanel, gridConstraints);

startStopButton.setText("Start Game");
gridConstraints = new GridBagConstraints();
gridConstraints.gridx = 0;
gridConstraints.gridy = 0;
buttonsPanel.add(startStopButton, gridConstraints);
startStopButton.addActionListener(new ActionListener()
{
```

```
    public void actionPerformed(ActionEvent e)
    {
      startStopButtonActionPerformed(e);
    }
  });

  exitButton.setText("Exit");
  gridConstraints = new GridBagConstraints();
  gridConstraints.gridx = 0;
  gridConstraints.gridy = 1;
  gridConstraints.insets = new Insets(10, 0, 0, 0);
  buttonsPanel.add(exitButton, gridConstraints);
  exitButton.addActionListener(new ActionListener()
  {
    public void actionPerformed(ActionEvent e)
    {
      exitButtonActionPerformed(e);
    }
  });
```

This code also adds listeners for each button. Add these empty methods with the other methods:

```
private void startStopButtonActionPerformed(ActionEvent e)
{
}

private void exitButtonActionPerformed(ActionEvent e)
{
}
```

Add this code in the proper locations. Run to see:

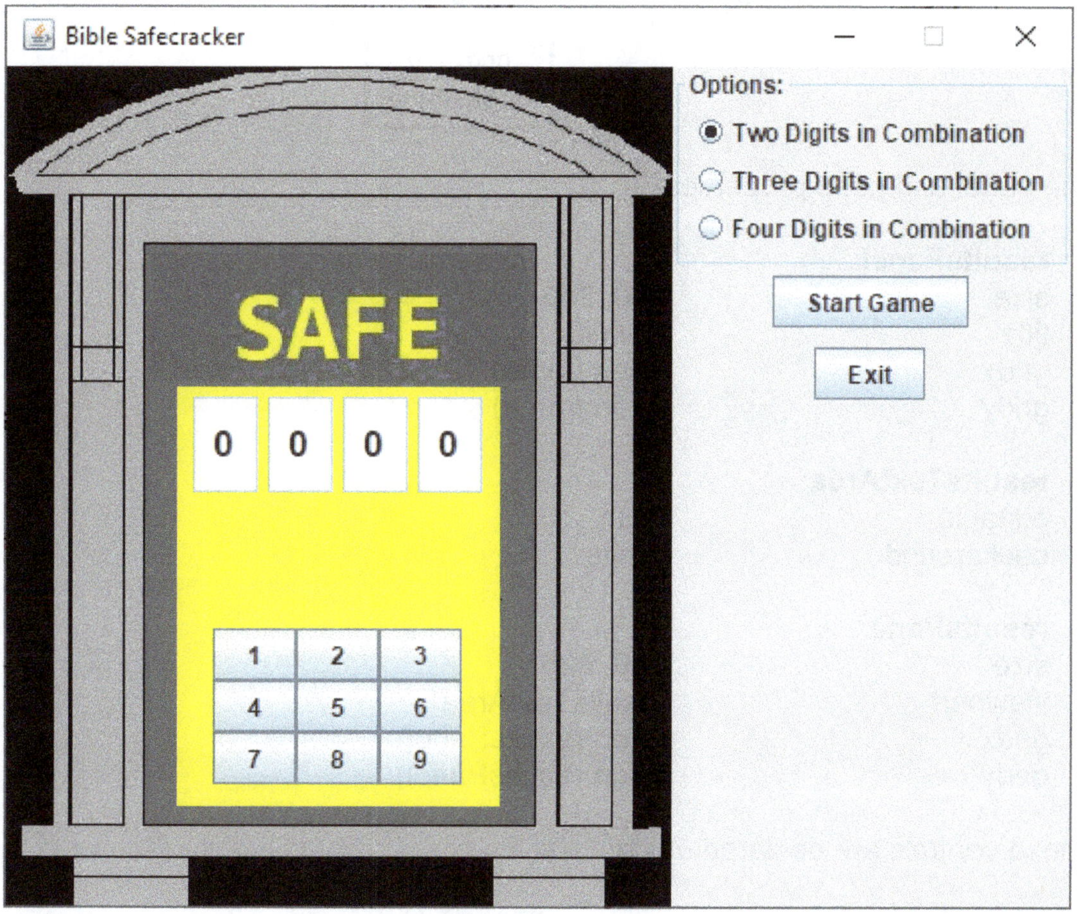

The button controls are displayed. One more panel and we're done with the frame design.

The **resultsPanel** will hold a scroll pane (which has a text area) used to display results of a combination guess. The **GridBagLayout** for resultsPanel is:

	gridx = 0
gridy = 0	**resultsPanel**

The panel and pane properties:

resultsPanel:

size	200, 250
title	Results:
gridx	1 (on frame)
gridy	2 (on frame)

resultsTextArea:

editable	false
background	White

resultsPane:

size	180, 220
viewport	resultsTextArea
gridx	0 (on resultsPanel)
gridy	0 (on resultsPanel)

These controls are declared using:

```
JPanel resultsPanel = new JPanel();
JScrollPane resultsPane = new JScrollPane();
JTextArea resultsTextArea = new JTextArea();
```

The buttons are placed in the **resultsPanel** (which is placed in the frame) using:

```
resultsPanel.setPreferredSize(new Dimension(200, 250));
resultsPanel.setBorder(BorderFactory.createTitledBorder("R
esults:"));
resultsPanel.setLayout(new GridBagLayout());
gridConstraints = new GridBagConstraints();
gridConstraints.gridx = 1;
gridConstraints.gridy = 2;
getContentPane().add(resultsPanel, gridConstraints);

resultsTextArea.setEditable(false);
resultsTextArea.setBackground(Color.WHITE);
resultsPane.setPreferredSize(new Dimension(180, 220));
resultsPane.setViewportView(resultsTextArea);
gridConstraints = new GridBagConstraints();
```

```
gridConstraints.gridx = 0;
gridConstraints.gridy = 0;
resultsPanel.add(resultsPane, gridConstraints);
```

Add this code in the proper locations. Run to see:

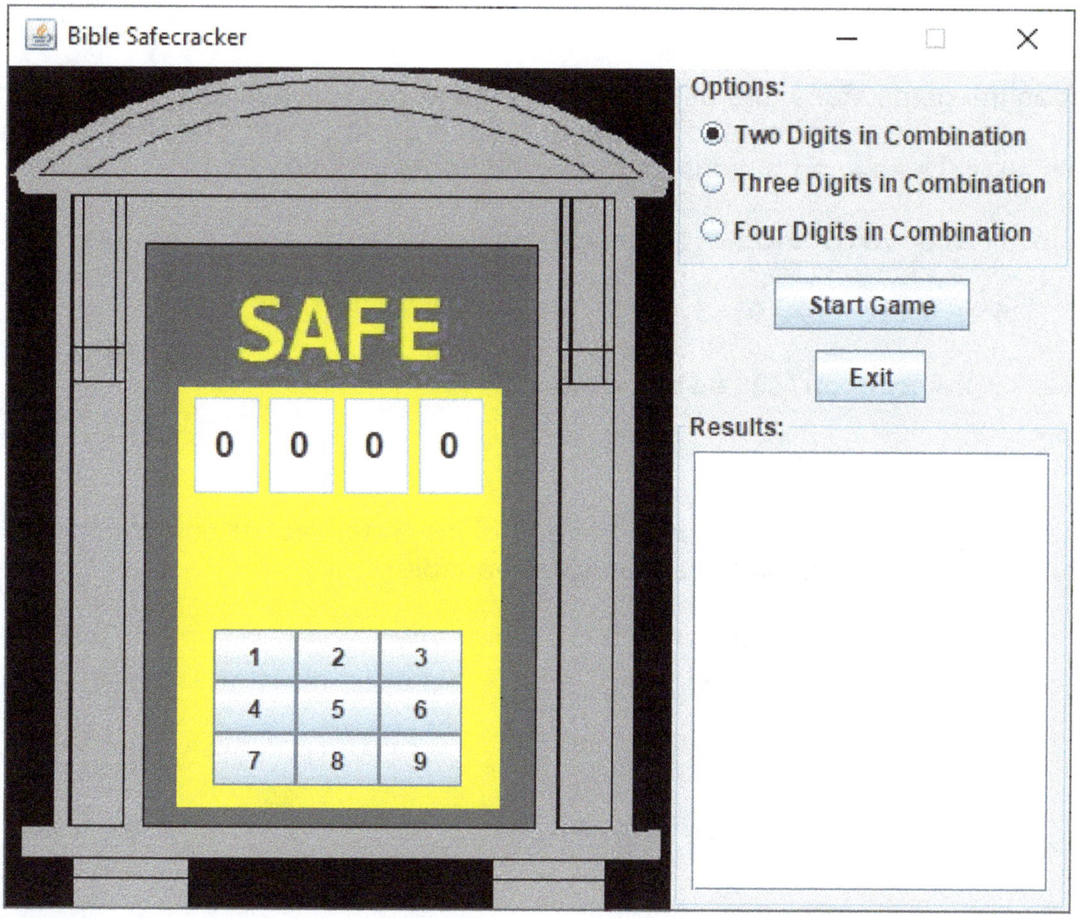

This completes the frame design. You should be able to identify all the controls in the game.

We will begin writing code for the game. We will write the code in several steps. As a first step, we will write the code that starts the game and establishes its 'stopped' state. Then, we look at how to go to 'playing' state following clicking of the **Start Game** button. During the code development process, recognize you may modify a particular method several times before arriving at the finished product.

Code Design – Initializing Stopped State

Any time we start a project, there are certain initializations that must take place. Let's look at the initializations needed in the **Safecracker** game. All initialization code is placed in the frame constructor after all the controls have been added to the frame.

When the game starts, the user should not be able to click the keys in the bank until options are selected and the game is started. Add this general method which sets all of the key pad buttons to a selected boolean state (**a**):

```
private void setKeyButtons(boolean a)
{
  for (int i = 0; i < 9; i++)
  {
    keyButton[i].setEnabled(a);
  }
}
```

Then, add this one line of code at the end of the **Safecracker** constructor code (following the line setting the **screenSize** variable):

```
setKeyButtons(false);
```

Run the project to make sure the frame is properly initialized. Do this and you'll see in the 'stopped' state (using default properties), the **Bible Safecracker** game looks like this:

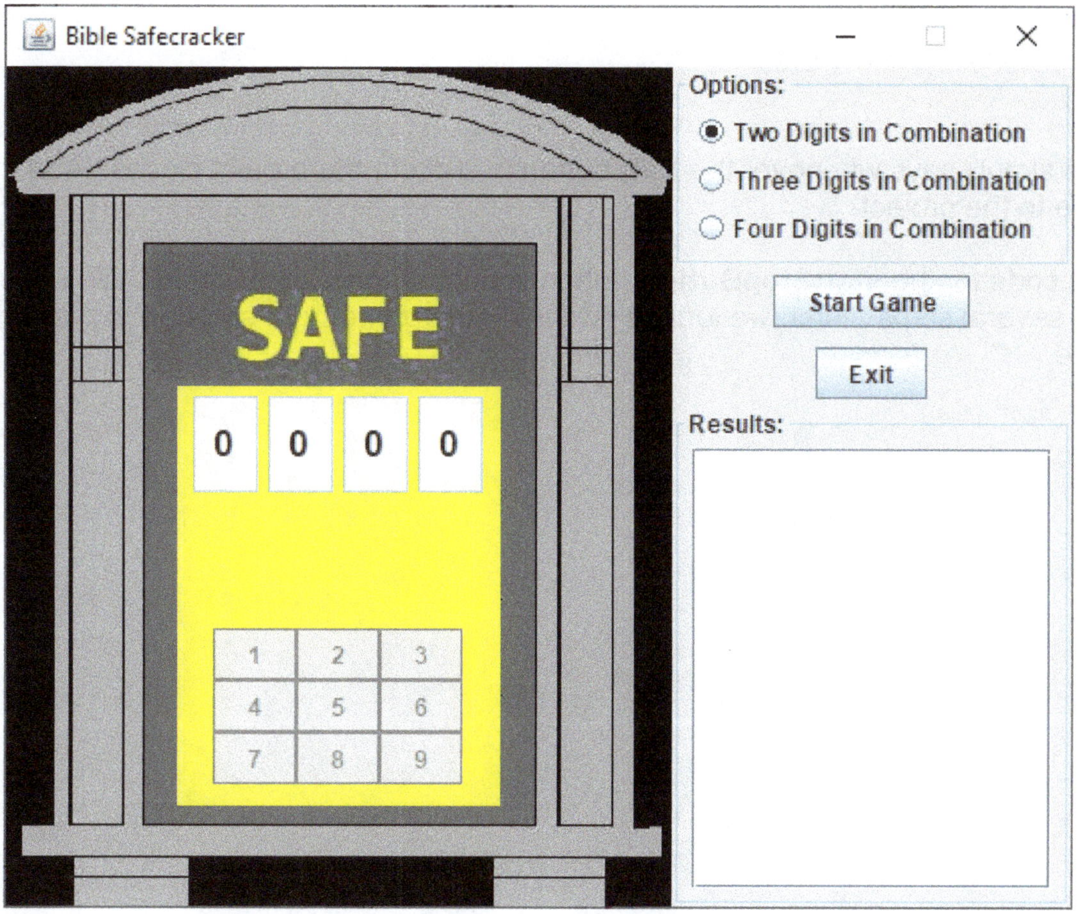

Note the keypad buttons are 'grayed-out' as desired. Try clicking one; you can't. We have two choices at this point – either choose some options and click **startStopButton** (the button with **Start Game**) or click **exitButton** (the button with **Exit**).

The code for exiting is simple. The **exitButtonActionListener** method (currently empty) is:

```
private void exitButtonActionPerformed(ActionEvent e)
{
  System.exit(0);
}
```

This simply says whenever the **Exit** button is clicked, the project closes. Add this code to the project.

The code for the **startStopButton** button is much more complicated. We will build it in several steps. First, we look at switching the game from stopped to playing state.

Code Design – Stopped to Playing State

When the user clicks the **Start Game** button in 'stopped' state, several things must happen to switch the **Bible Safecracker** game to 'playing' state:

- Change the **text** property of **startStopButton** to **Stop Game**.
- Disable the radio buttons (don't allow selection of options while playing).
- Disable **exitButton**.
- Enable the keypad buttons (allow entering a combination)
- Blank out **resultsTextArea** (delete previous results).
- Display proper number of text field controls to show combination.
- Determine secret combination.
- Allow user to input combination.
- Check to see if input combination matches secret combination – provide results.

Right now, we will implement each of these steps except those establishing the secret combination and accepting and checking user input. Those steps will be addressed separately.

Add this line to the class level declarations to define a variable for the number of digits in the combination:

```
int numberDigits;
```

The code for the **startStopButtonActionPerformed** method that implements all but the last three steps in the above method is:

```
private void startStopButtonActionPerformed(ActionEvent e)
{
  startStopButton.setText("Stop Game");
  twoDigitsRadioButton.setEnabled(false);
  threeDigitsRadioButton.setEnabled(false);
  fourDigitsRadioButton.setEnabled(false);
  exitButton.setEnabled(false);
  setKeyButtons(true);
  resultsTextArea.setText("");
  // determine number of digits and set up labels
  if (twoDigitsRadioButton.isSelected())
  {
    numberDigits = 2;
  }
  else if (threeDigitsRadioButton.isSelected())
  {
    numberDigits = 3;
  }
  else
  {
    numberDigits = 4;
  }
  for (int i = 0; i < numberDigits; i++)
  {
    comboTextField[i].setVisible(true);
    comboTextField[i].setText("");
  }
  if (numberDigits != 4)
  {
    for (int i = numberDigits; i < 4; i++)
    {
      comboTextField[i].setVisible(false);
    }
  }
}
```

Notice how the text field control array (**comboTextField**) is used to display the needed controls for the displayed combination.

Save and run the project. Click **Start Game** and the game should switch to 'playing' state (assumes 2 digits in combination):

Make sure the number of text field controls displayed in the bank area match the option selected. Notice the **Stop Game** button does nothing at the moment. Let's fix that. Stop the project.

Code Design – Playing to Stopped State

When the user clicks the **Stop Game** button in 'playing' state, several things must happen to switch the **Bible Safecracker** game to 'stopped' state:

- Change the **text** property of **startStopButton** to **Start Game**.
- Enable radio buttons.
- Enable **exitButton**.
- Disable keypad buttons.

The button now marked **Stop Game** is the **startStopButton** button. We have already added some code to its **actionPerformed** method. It is common practice to have one button control have multiple purposes - we just need to have some way to distinguish which "mode" the button is in when it is clicked. In this project, we use the text property of the button. If the text property is **Start Game**, we switch to 'playing' mode. If the text property is **Stop Game**, we switch to 'stopped' mode. The code that does this is (modifications to the current **actionPerformed** method code are shaded):

```
private void startStopButtonActionPerformed(ActionEvent e)
{
  if (startStopButton.getText().equals("Start Game"))
  {
    startStopButton.setText("Stop Game");
    twoDigitsRadioButton.setEnabled(false);
    threeDigitsRadioButton.setEnabled(false);
    fourDigitsRadioButton.setEnabled(false);
    exitButton.setEnabled(false);
    setKeyButtons(true);
    resultsTextArea.setText("");
    // determine number of digits and set up labels
    if (twoDigitsRadioButton.isSelected())
    {
      numberDigits = 2;
    }
    else if (threeDigitsRadioButton.isSelected())
    {
      numberDigits = 3;
    }
    else
    {
      numberDigits = 4;
    }
    for (int i = 0; i < numberDigits; i++)
    {
      comboTextField[i].setVisible(true);
```

```
        comboTextField[i].setText("");
      }
      if (numberDigits != 4)
      {
        for (int i = numberDigits; i < 4; i++)
        {
          comboTextField[i].setVisible(false);
        }
      }
    }
    else
    {
      startStopButton.setText("Start Game");
      twoDigitsRadioButton.setEnabled(true);
      threeDigitsRadioButton.setEnabled(true);
      fourDigitsRadioButton.setEnabled(true);
      exitButton.setEnabled(true);
      setKeyButtons(false);
    }
  }
```

Save and run the project. You should be able to now move from 'stopped' to 'playing' state and back. Make sure you can display 2, 3 or 4 digits in the combination. Try the **Exit** button. We can now look at the three missing steps in the program: generating a secret combination and accepting and checking user input.

Code Design – Generating Secret Combination

A critical step in the **Bible Safecracker** project is to generate the secret combination the game player is trying to guess. Using the options selected, we know the combination can be from 2 to 4 digits. We have also specified none of the digits can repeat.

Since repeated digits are not allowed, for each digit in the combination, we generate a random number from 1 to 9, but only add it to the combination if it has not been used before. The code snippet that accomplishes this for our game is:

```
// determine combination
secretCombo = "";
int j;
boolean uniqueDigit;
for (int i = 0; i < numberDigits; i++)
{
  // select unique digit
  do
  {
    j = myRandom.nextInt(9) + 1;
    uniqueDigit = true;
    if (i != 0)
    {
      for (int k = 0; k < i; k++)
      {
        if
(String.valueOf(secretCombo.charAt(k)).equals(String.value
Of(j)))
          uniqueDigit = false;
      }
    }
  }
  while (!uniqueDigit);
  secretCombo += String.valueOf(j);
}
```

We'll step you through this code to see what's going on. A string variable (**secretCombo**) is used to store the combination. It is initially blank. One digit at a time (a total of **numberDigits**) is added to **secretCombo** using string concatenation.

A random digit **j** (from 1 to 9) is generated. We then look at the current digits in the code to see if this newly generated digit is unique. If so, it is added to **secretCombo**. If not unique, a new random digit is generated. All of this logic is implemented in a **do** loop. Study how we examine the individual digits in **secretCombo** using the **charAt** method. The returned values are **char** type, so we need to convert to **String** before comparing. Let's try this new code.

Since we are using random numbers, include this **import** statement near the top of the code listing (with the other import statements):

```
import java.util.Random;
```

Add these class level variable declarations to define the secret combination and establish the random number object:

```
String secretCombo;
Random myRandom = new Random();
```

Add the given snippet to the **startStopButtonActionPerformed** method as shown in the shaded code below:

```
private void startStopButtonActionPerformed(ActionEvent e)
{
  if (startStopButton.getText().equals("Start Game"))
  {
    startStopButton.setText("Stop Game");
    twoDigitsRadioButton.setEnabled(false);
    threeDigitsRadioButton.setEnabled(false);
    fourDigitsRadioButton.setEnabled(false);
    exitButton.setEnabled(false);
    setKeyButtons(true);
    resultsTextArea.setText("");
    // determine number of digits and set up labels
    if (twoDigitsRadioButton.isSelected())
    {
      numberDigits = 2;
    }
    else if (threeDigitsRadioButton.isSelected())
    {
      numberDigits = 3;
    }
    else
    {
      numberDigits = 4;
    }
    for (int i = 0; i < numberDigits; i++)
    {
      comboTextField[i].setVisible(true);
      comboTextField[i].setText("");
    }
    if (numberDigits != 4)
    {
      for (int i = numberDigits; i < 4; i++)
      {
        comboTextField[i].setVisible(false);
      }
    }
    // determine combination
    secretCombo = "";
    int j;
    boolean uniqueDigit;
    for (int i = 0; i < numberDigits; i++)
    {
      // select unique digit
      do
```

```
        {
          j = myRandom.nextInt(9) + 1;
          uniqueDigit = true;
          if (i != 0)
          {
            for (int k = 0; k < i; k++)
            {
              if
(String.valueOf(secretCombo.charAt(k)).equals(String.value
Of(j)))
                uniqueDigit = false;
            }
          }
        }
        while (!uniqueDigit);
        secretCombo += String.valueOf(j);
      }
    }
    else
    {
      startStopButton.setText("Start Game");
      twoDigitsRadioButton.setEnabled(true);
      threeDigitsRadioButton.setEnabled(true);
      fourDigitsRadioButton.setEnabled(true);
      exitButton.setEnabled(true);
      setKeyButtons(false);
    }
  }
```

We can now generate a secret combination, but have no way of seeing what it is. Let's change that. Many times while developing a project, you want to check results before the project is complete. This means adding temporary code just for debugging purposes. Place this line after the closing bracket in the code generating the combination:

```
System.out.println(secretCombo);
```

This will write the generated combination in the **Output** window of the the IDE allowing you to see if the combination meets the requirements (proper number of digits and proper repeating/non-repeating of digits).

Save and run the project. Click **Start Game**. Open the **output** window of your IDE and look at the generated combination. Make sure it meets the selected options requirement. Click **Stop Game**. Repeat this process for various combinations to make sure the combination is being generated correctly. When done, delete the debug line from the code. We're now ready to accept the player's guess at the secret combination using the 9 keypad buttons.

Code Design – Accepting Player Input

Once the secret combination has been generated, the next step is to allow the user to enter his or her guess at the combination. This is done using the 9 number buttons on the panel control in the bank graphic. The steps followed are:

- Click a button to enter a digit.
- If this is the first number in the combination, clear out any previous guess in label controls.
- Determine which button was clicked.
- Disable the clicked button since repeating digits are not allowed.
- Add the number on the clicked button to the user's input combination.
- Display the number in the proper label control.
- If all digits have been entered, enable the number buttons and compare the user's input to the actual combination, else repeat these steps.

The code to perform these steps will be placed in the method named **keyButtonActionPerformed** (currently empty). This method is set to handle a click event for all 9 buttons used for input (**keyButton** array).

Add these class level variables to store the combination entered by the user and the number of digits entered:

```
int digitsEntered;
String enteredCombo;
```

Initialize the value of these two new variables using the shaded code in **startStopButtonActionPerformed**:

```
private void startStopButtonActionPerformed(ActionEvent e)
{
  if (startStopButton.getText().equals("Start Game"))
  {
    startStopButton.setText("Stop Game");
    twoDigitsRadioButton.setEnabled(false);
    threeDigitsRadioButton.setEnabled(false);
    fourDigitsRadioButton.setEnabled(false);
    exitButton.setEnabled(false);
    setKeyButtons(true);
    resultsTextArea.setText("");
    // determine number of digits and set up labels
    if (twoDigitsRadioButton.isSelected())
    {
      numberDigits = 2;
    }
    else if (threeDigitsRadioButton.isSelected())
    {
      numberDigits = 3;
    }
    else
    {
      numberDigits = 4;
    }
    for (int i = 0; i < numberDigits; i++)
    {
      comboTextField[i].setVisible(true);
      comboTextField[i].setText("");
    }
    if (numberDigits != 4)
    {
      for (int i = numberDigits; i < 4; i++)
      {
        comboTextField[i].setVisible(false);
      }
    }
    // determine combination
    secretCombo = "";
    int j;
    boolean uniqueDigit;
    for (int i = 0; i < numberDigits; i++)
    {
      // select unique digit
      do
```

```
        {
          j = myRandom.nextInt(9) + 1;
          uniqueDigit = true;
          if (i != 0)
          {
            for (int k = 0; k < i; k++)
            {
              if
(String.valueOf(secretCombo.charAt(k)).equals(String.value
Of(j)))
                uniqueDigit = false;
            }
          }
        }
        while (!uniqueDigit);
        secretCombo += String.valueOf(j);
      }
      enteredCombo = "";
      digitsEntered = 0;
    }
    else
    {
      startStopButton.setText("Start Game");
      twoDigitsRadioButton.setEnabled(true);
      threeDigitsRadioButton.setEnabled(true);
      fourDigitsRadioButton.setEnabled(true);
      exitButton.setEnabled(true);
      setKeyButtons(false);
    }
  }
```

Add this code to the **keyButtonActionPerformed** method.. This implements the needed steps to check the user's input:

```
private void keyButtonActionPerformed(ActionEvent e)
{
  String n;
  // determine which button was clicked
  // ActionCommand is text on button
  n = e.getActionCommand();
  // disable button since digits can't repeat
  keyButton[Integer.valueOf(n).intValue() -
1].setEnabled(false);
  // if first button in combo, clear out label boxes
  if (digitsEntered == 0)
  {
    comboTextField[0].setText("");
    comboTextField[1].setText("");
    comboTextField[2].setText("");
    comboTextField[3].setText("");
  }
  // add button to code
  enteredCombo += n;
  digitsEntered++;
  comboTextField[digitsEntered - 1].setText(n);
  // if all digits entered, check combo
  if (digitsEntered == numberDigits)
  {
    // reset combo buttons
    for (int i = 0; i < 9; i++)
        keyButton[i].setEnabled(true);
    // check combination
    System.out.println(enteredCombo);
  }
}
```

Notice the **getActionCommand** method returns the text property of the clicked button. This is the corresponding digit (the variable **n**). We have used a **println** statement to print the complete entered combination in the IDE **Output** window. Logic to check this combination is next.

Save and run the project. Make sure the entered combination looks correct (has the proper number of digits, in the correct order and following repeatability rules). Make sure the keypad buttons are re-enabled after entering a combination. Let's complete the game by comparing the player's input to the actual combination and displaying the results.

Code Design – Checking Player Input

We now have the capability to generate a secret combination and obtain the player's guess at that combination. We need the code that compares the two string variables and displays the results. If it's a match, great! If not, we tell the player how many digits are correct and how many are in the correct position. This is some of the trickier code.

Once the user has complete their input, we follow these steps:

- Display the user's guess (**enteredCombo**) in **resultsTextArea**.
- If user's guess (**enteredCombo**) equals the actual combination (**secretCombo**), return the game to stopped state and let the user know they guessed the combination.
- If incorrect guess, determine number of correct digits and number in correct positions. Display this information in **resultsTextArea**.
- Clear user's guess to allow another try.

All of the code to perform these steps is placed in the **keyButtonActionPerformed** method.

Place the shaded code in the **keyButtonActionPerformed** method to implement these steps (we deleted the **println** statement):

```
private void keyButtonActionPerformed(ActionEvent e)
{
  String n;
  // determine which button was clicked
  // ActionCommand is text on button
  n = e.getActionCommand();
  // disable button since digits can't repeat
  keyButton[Integer.valueOf(n).intValue() -
1].setEnabled(false);
  // if first button in combo, clear out label boxes
  if (digitsEntered == 0)
  {
    comboTextField[0].setText("");
    comboTextField[1].setText("");
    comboTextField[2].setText("");
    comboTextField[3].setText("");
  }
  // add button to code
  enteredCombo += n;
  digitsEntered++;
  comboTextField[digitsEntered - 1].setText(n);
  // if all digits entered, check combo
```

```
  if (digitsEntered == numberDigits)
  {
    // reset combo buttons
    for (int i = 0; i < 9; i++)
        keyButton[i].setEnabled(true);
    // check combination
    resultsTextArea.append("Entered: " + enteredCombo +
"\n");
    if (enteredCombo.equals(secretCombo))
      startStopButton.doClick();
    else
    {
      numberRight = 0;
      for (int i = 0; i < numberDigits; i++)
      {
        n = String.valueOf(enteredCombo.charAt(i));
        for (int j = 0; j < numberDigits; j++)
          if
(n.equals(String.valueOf(secretCombo.charAt(j))))
            numberRight++;
      }
      // how many in correct position
      positionRight = 0;
      for (int i = 0; i < numberDigits; i++)
        if (secretCombo.charAt(i) ==
enteredCombo.charAt(i))
          positionRight++;
      resultsTextArea.append(String.valueOf(numberRight) +
" digits correct" + "\n");
      resultsTextArea.append(String.valueOf(positionRight)
+ " in correct position" + "\n");
      resultsTextArea.append("Try again ..." + "\n\n");
      // clear combo to try again
      enteredCombo = "";
      digitsEntered = 0;
    }
  }
}
```

You should be able to follow the above code. It first counts the number of correct digits in the user's input. The code to see if digits are in correct position just compares each digit in **enteredCombo** and **secretCombo**. All the results are displayed in the **resultsTextArea** text box using the **append** method.

If the correct combination is entered, we want to return to 'stopped' state. An easy way to do this (and the way we did) is simply programmatically click on the **Stop Game** button using the **doClick** method. Using this approach, though, we need to add some code to the **startStopButtonActionPerformed** method. The new code is used to distinguish between stopping the game before guessing the combination and stopping because the combination has been guessed. Make the shaded changes to the **startStopButtonActionPerformed** method:

```
private void startStopButtonActionPerformed(ActionEvent e)
{
  if (startStopButton.getText().equals("Start Game"))
  {
    startStopButton.setText("Stop Game");
    twoDigitsRadioButton.setEnabled(false);
    threeDigitsRadioButton.setEnabled(false);
    fourDigitsRadioButton.setEnabled(false);
    exitButton.setEnabled(false);
    setKeyButtons(true);
    resultsTextArea.setText("");
    // determine number of digits and set up labels
    if (twoDigitsRadioButton.isSelected())
    {
      numberDigits = 2;
    }
    else if (threeDigitsRadioButton.isSelected())
    {
      numberDigits = 3;
    }
    else
    {
      numberDigits = 4;
    }
    for (int i = 0; i < numberDigits; i++)
    {
      comboTextField[i].setVisible(true);
      comboTextField[i].setText("");
    }
    if (numberDigits != 4)
    {
      for (int i = numberDigits; i < 4; i++)
      {
        comboTextField[i].setVisible(false);
      }
    }
    // determine combination
    secretCombo = "";
    int j;
```

```
    boolean uniqueDigit;
    for (int i = 0; i < numberDigits; i++)
    {
      // select unique digit
      do
      {
        j = myRandom.nextInt(9) + 1;
        uniqueDigit = true;
        if (i != 0)
        {
          for (int k = 0; k < i; k++)
          {
            if
(String.valueOf(secretCombo.charAt(k)).equals(String.value
Of(j)))
              uniqueDigit = false;
          }
        }
      }
      while (!uniqueDigit);
      secretCombo += String.valueOf(j);
    }
    enteredCombo = "";
    digitsEntered = 0;
  }
  else
  {
    if (enteredCombo.equals(secretCombo))
      resultsTextArea.append("That's it!!" + "\n");
    else
      resultsTextArea.append("Game Stopped" + "\n");
    resultsTextArea.append("Combination: " + secretCombo);
    startStopButton.setText("Start Game");
    twoDigitsRadioButton.setEnabled(true);
    threeDigitsRadioButton.setEnabled(true);
    fourDigitsRadioButton.setEnabled(true);
    exitButton.setEnabled(true);
    setKeyButtons(false);
  }
}
```

Save and run the project. The game is now fully functional. Try playing it a few times to make sure things are working okay. It still needs just one more thing.

Sounds in Java

You may have never used sounds in your projects. Or you may have used the the one sound available with Java, a simple beep generated using:

```
Toolkit.getDefaultToolkit().beep();
```

This unexciting sound plays through the computer's built-in speaker, if there is one. Multimedia presentations and games feature elaborate sounds that take advantage of stereo sound cards. To play such sounds in Java involves just a bit of trickery.

We look at playing two particular types of sounds: **AU** files (a common Sun audio format) and **WAV** files. Most sounds you hear played in Windows applications are saved as WAV files. These are the files formed when you record using one of the many sound recorder programs available.

The Java sound capabilities are part of the **java.applet.*** package. This package is used to implement Java applications on the Internet. But we can still use these capabilities in our GUI applications. It just requires a little work. There are two steps involved in playing sound files: (1) load the sound as an audio clip and (2) play the sound.

A sound file is loaded using the **newAudioClip** method. If we name the sound **mySound**, the sound is loaded using:

```
mySound = Applet.newAudioClip(mySoundURL);
```

where **mySoundURL** is the "address" of the sound file. You may note that URL is an Internet address (universal resource locator) – this is because the sound utilities are part of the applet package. Does this mean our sounds must be stored on the Internet somewhere? No. By forming a special URL as the argument, we can load sound files from our project folder, just like we have loaded graphics files.

A URL for use in the **newAudioClip** method is formed using the Java **URL** method (in the **java.net.URL** package). If the sound file is **mySoundFile** (**String** type), the URL is formed with:

```
mySoundURL = new URL("file:" + mySoundFile);
```

The addition of the "**file:**" string tells Java the sound is loaded from a file rather than the Internet. This assumes the sound file is located in the project folder. If it is in another folder, you need to "prepend" the file name with the appropriate directory information.

We need to consider one last thing. The URL can only be formed within a **try/catch** loop to catch potential exceptions. Hence, the complete code segment to load a sound (**mySound**) from a file (**mySoundFile**) is:

```
try
{
  mySound = Applet.newAudioClip(new URL("file:" +
mySoundFile));
}
catch (Exception ex)
{
   [Error message]
}
```

Such code to create sounds is usually placed in at the end of your application's constructor with all sounds declared as class level variables.

Once we have created a sound clip, there are three methods used to play or stop the corresponding sound. To play **mySound** one time, use the **play** method:

```
mySound.play();
```

To play the sound in a continuous loop, use the **loop** method:

```
mySound.loop();
```

To stop the sound from playing, use the **stop** method:

```
mySound.stop();
```

It's that easy.

It is normal practice to include any sound files an application uses in the project folder. This makes them easily accessible. As such, when distributing your application to other users, you must remember to include the sound files in the package.

Code Design – Adding Sounds

The text feedback of the **Bible Safecracker** game is a bit boring. Let's snazz it up a bit by adding sounds. In the **\CBGJava\CBGJava Projects\Safecracker** folder are two wav files that can be used for sound. The file **uhoh.wav** is an 'uh-oh' sound we'll use for incorrect guesses. The **tada.wav** file is a celebratory sound we'll use for correct guesses. These files will be loaded when the project starts. Copy the two sound files to your project's folder.

Add these **import** statements:

```
import java.net.URL;
import java.applet.*;
```

Add these class level declarations to represent the two sounds:

```
AudioClip wrongSound;
AudioClip correctSound;
```

Add these lines at the end of the **Safecracker** constructor (following the line that initializes the keypad status) to establish the sound objects:

```
try
{
  wrongSound = Applet.newAudioClip(new URL("file:" +
"uhoh.wav"));
  correctSound = Applet.newAudioClip(new URL("file:" +
"tada.wav"));
}
catch (Exception ex)
{
  System.out.println("Error loading sound files");
}
```

This code assumes the sound files are in your project's folder.

Lastly, play the two sounds at the appropriate (shaded) locations in the **keyButtonActionPerformed** method:

```
private void keyButtonActionPerformed(ActionEvent e)
{
  String n;
  // determine which button was clicked
  // ActionCommand is text on button
  n = e.getActionCommand();
  // disable button since digits can't repeat
  keyButton[Integer.valueOf(n).intValue() -
1].setEnabled(false);
  // if first button in combo, clear out label boxes
  if (digitsEntered == 0)
  {
    comboTextField[0].setText("");
    comboTextField[1].setText("");
    comboTextField[2].setText("");
    comboTextField[3].setText("");
  }
  // add button to code
  enteredCombo += n;
  digitsEntered++;
  comboTextField[digitsEntered - 1].setText(n);
  // if all digits entered, check combo
  if (digitsEntered == numberDigits)
  {
    // reset combo buttons
    for (int i = 0; i < 9; i++)
        keyButton[i].setEnabled(true);
    // check combination
    resultsTextArea.append("Entered: " + enteredCombo +
"\n");
    if (enteredCombo.equals(secretCombo))
    {
      correctSound.play();
      startStopButton.doClick();
    }
    else
    {
      wrongSound.play();
      numberRight = 0;
      for (int i = 0; i < numberDigits; i++)
      {
        n = String.valueOf(enteredCombo.charAt(i));
        for (int j = 0; j < numberDigits; j++)
```

```
          if
(n.equals(String.valueOf(secretCombo.charAt(j))))
            numberRight++;
      }
      // how many in correct position
      positionRight = 0;
      for (int i = 0; i < numberDigits; i++)
        if (secretCombo.charAt(i) ==
enteredCombo.charAt(i))
          positionRight++;
      resultsTextArea.append(String.valueOf(numberRight) +
" digits correct" + "\n");
      resultsTextArea.append(String.valueOf(positionRight)
+ " in correct position" + "\n");
      resultsTextArea.append("Try again ..." + "\n\n");
      // clear combo to try again
      enteredCombo = "";
      digitsEntered = 0;
    }
  }
}
```

Save and run the project. You should now have a complete, running version of the **Bible Safecracker** game (the complete code listing is given at the end of the chapter). Have fun playing it! See if you can come up with some kind of winning strategy. Here's a game I played using 3 non-repeating digits. First, I tried 123 (obviously not a good guess) and heard 'uh-oh':

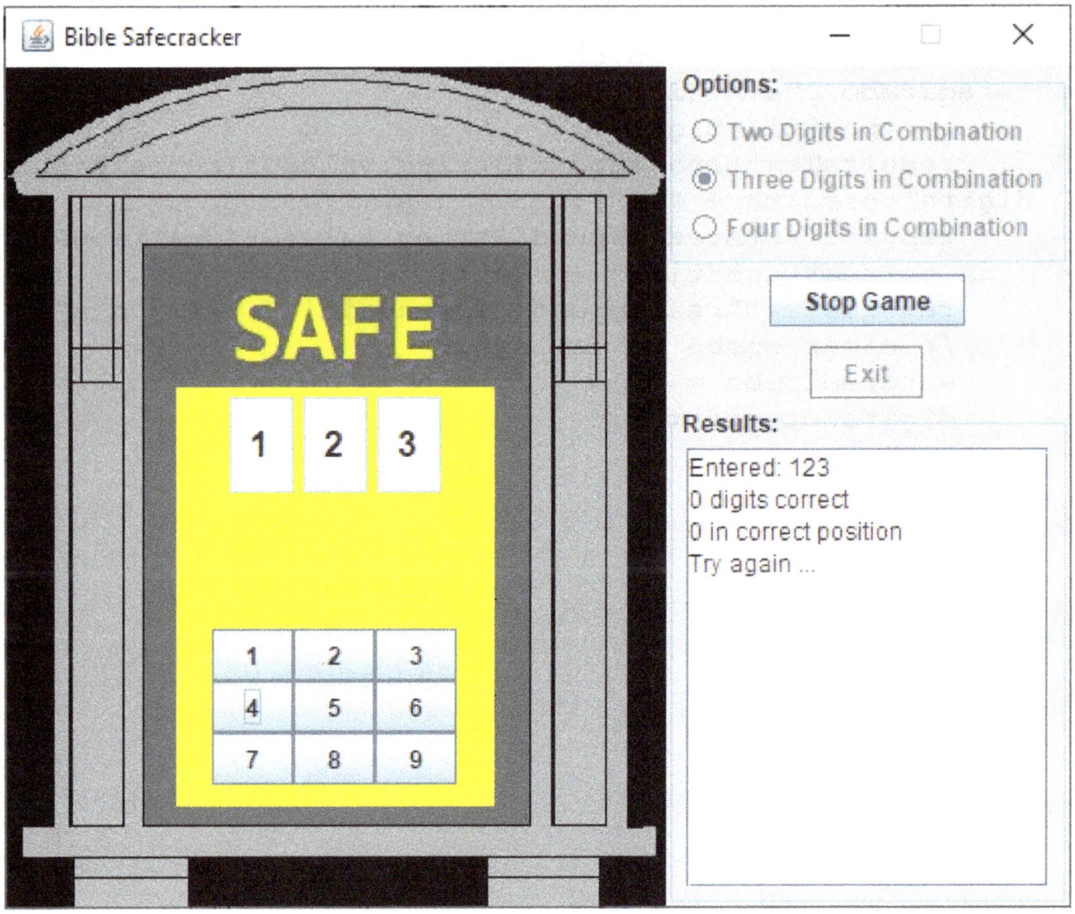

Next try was 456:

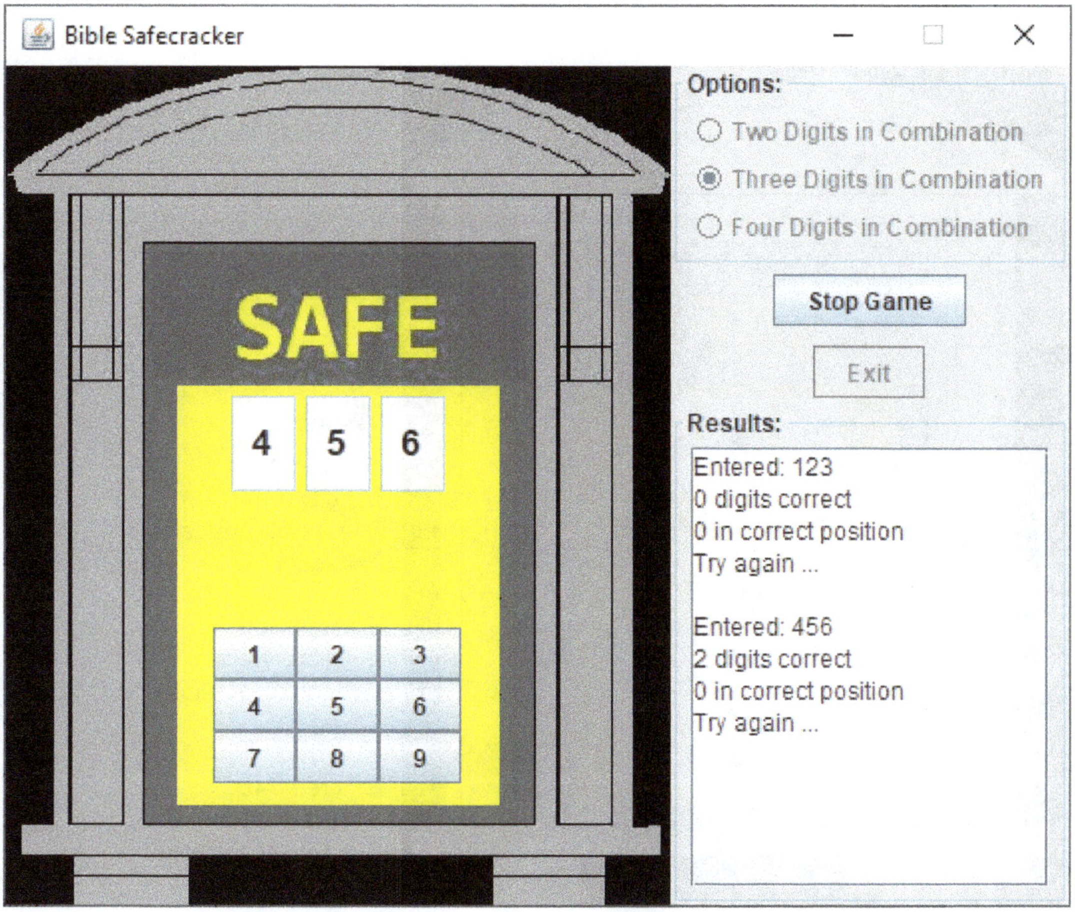

Much better – two digits are correct. I have some valuable information.

Next, I tried 745, digressing a bit:

After one more guess, I entered 648:

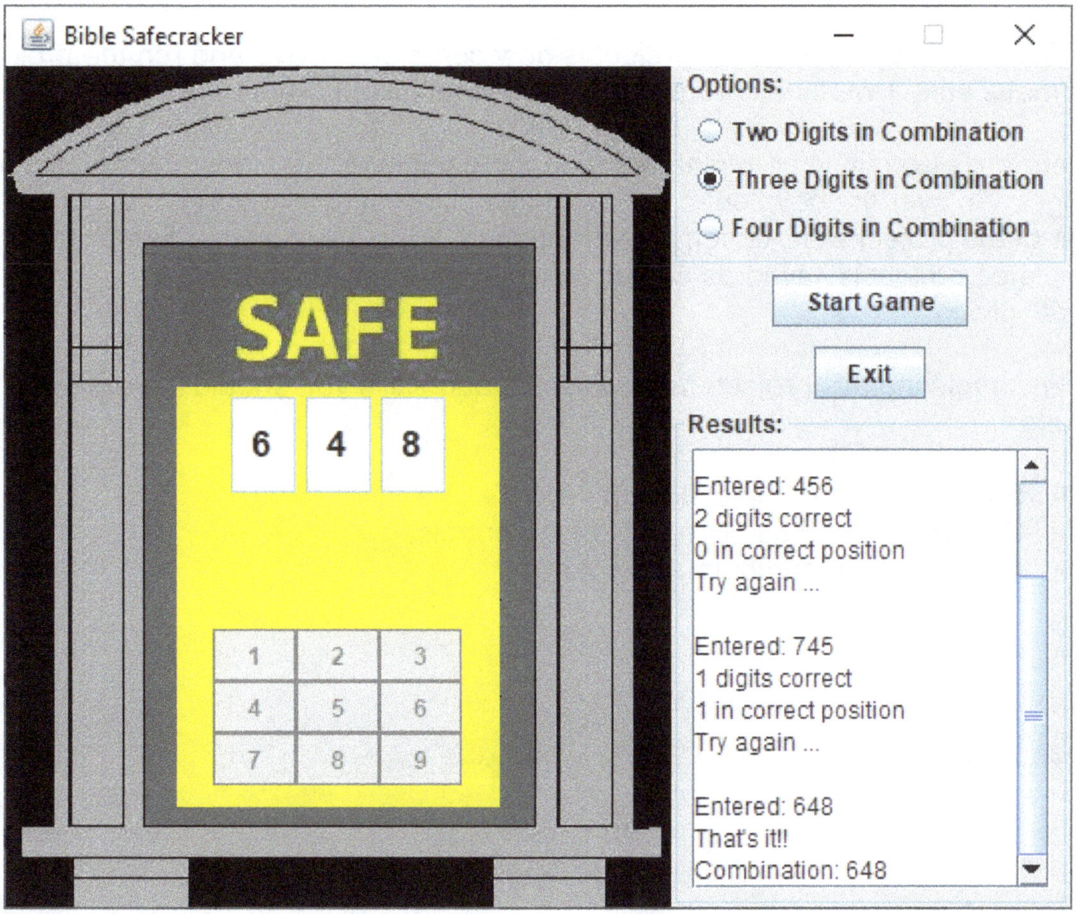

The correct combination was entered! A little celebratory sound was heard and the game returned to its stopped state.

Bible Safecracker Project Review

The **Bible Safecracker** game project is now complete. Save and run the project and make sure it works as promised. Check that all options work correctly.

If there are errors in your implementation, go back over the steps of form and code design. Go over the developed code – make sure you understand how different parts of the project were coded. As mentioned in the beginning of this chapter, the completed project is saved as **Safecracker** in the **\CBGJava\CBGJava Projects** project group.

While completing this project, new concepts and skills you should have gained include:

- Proper steps in project design.
- Capabilities and use of many Java controls.
- Using random numbers and sounds.

Bible Safecracker Project Enhancements

There are always things you can do to improve a project. At the end of each chapter, we will give you some ideas for the current project. For the **Bible Safecracker** game, some possibilities are:

- Add an option so the digits in the combination can repeat (perhaps use a check box control). You will need to modify the code that generates and checks the combination. You will also have to make sure the keypad buttons are not disabled after clicking. Do you see how such an option makes the game easier to play?
- To make the game simpler for smaller children, you might like to have combinations that use fewer than the 9 digits on the keypad. For example, a three digit code that only uses the numbers from 1 to 3 would be much easier to guess. You would need logic to decide which keys to keep on the keypad.
- After each guess, you might like to provide a hint on how to proceed.
- After a correct combination, maybe have more dramatic results. Perhaps, have the bank graphic disappear and a pile of treasure appear.

Bible Safecracker Project Java Code Listing

```
/*
 * Safecracker.java
 */
package safecracker;
import javax.swing.*;
import java.awt.*;
import java.awt.event.*;
import java.util.Random;
import java.net.URL;
import java.applet.*;

public class Safecracker extends JFrame
{
  ImagePanel safePanel = new ImagePanel(new
ImageIcon("safe.jpg").getImage());
  JPanel comboPanel = new JPanel();
  JPanel keyPanel = new JPanel();
  JPanel optionsPanel = new JPanel();
  JPanel buttonsPanel = new JPanel();
  JPanel resultsPanel = new JPanel();

  JTextField[] comboTextField = new JTextField[4];
  JButton[] keyButton = new JButton[9];
  ButtonGroup digitsButtonGroup = new ButtonGroup();
  JRadioButton twoDigitsRadioButton = new JRadioButton();
  JRadioButton threeDigitsRadioButton = new JRadioButton();
  JRadioButton fourDigitsRadioButton = new JRadioButton();
  JButton startStopButton = new JButton();
  JButton exitButton = new JButton();
  JScrollPane resultsPane = new JScrollPane();
  JTextArea resultsTextArea = new JTextArea();

  int numberDigits;
  String secretCombo;
  Random myRandom = new Random();
  int digitsEntered;
  String enteredCombo;

  AudioClip wrongSound;
  AudioClip correctSound;

  public static void main(String args[])
```

```
  {
    // create frame
    new Safecracker().setVisible(true);
  }

  public Safecracker()
  {
    // frame constructor
    setTitle("Bible Safecracker");
    setResizable(false);
    addWindowListener(new WindowAdapter()
    {
      public void windowClosing(WindowEvent evt)
      {
        exitForm(evt);
      }
    });
    getContentPane().setLayout(new GridBagLayout());
    GridBagConstraints gridConstraints;

    safePanel.setPreferredSize(new Dimension(330, 420));
    safePanel.setLayout(new GridBagLayout());
    gridConstraints = new GridBagConstraints();
    gridConstraints.gridx = 0;
    gridConstraints.gridy = 0;
    gridConstraints.gridheight = 3;
    getContentPane().add(safePanel, gridConstraints);

    comboPanel.setPreferredSize(new Dimension(160, 110));
    safePanel.setLayout(new GridBagLayout());
    comboPanel.setBackground(Color.YELLOW);
    gridConstraints = new GridBagConstraints();
    gridConstraints.gridx = 0;
    gridConstraints.gridy = 0;
    gridConstraints.insets = new Insets(110, 0, 0, 0);
    safePanel.add(comboPanel, gridConstraints);

    for (int i = 0; i < 4; i++)
    {
      comboTextField[i] = new JTextField();
      comboTextField[i].setPreferredSize(new Dimension(32,
48));
      comboTextField[i].setEditable(false);
      comboTextField[i].setBackground(Color.WHITE);
      comboTextField[i].setText("0");
```

```
comboTextField[i].setHorizontalAlignment(SwingConstants.CENT
ER);
      comboTextField[i].setFont(new Font("Arial", Font.BOLD,
18));
      gridConstraints = new GridBagConstraints();
      gridConstraints.gridx = i;
      gridConstraints.gridy = 0;
      comboPanel.add(comboTextField[i], gridConstraints);
    }

    keyPanel.setPreferredSize(new Dimension(160, 100));
    keyPanel.setLayout(new GridBagLayout());
    keyPanel.setBackground(Color.YELLOW);
    gridConstraints = new GridBagConstraints();
    gridConstraints.gridx = 0;
    gridConstraints.gridy = 1;
    safePanel.add(keyPanel, gridConstraints);

    for (int i = 0; i < 9; i++)
    {
      keyButton[i] = new JButton();
      keyButton[i].setText(String.valueOf(i + 1));
      gridConstraints = new GridBagConstraints();
      gridConstraints.gridx = i % 3;
      gridConstraints.gridy = i / 3;
      keyPanel.add(keyButton[i], gridConstraints);
      keyButton[i].addActionListener(new ActionListener()
      {
        public void actionPerformed(ActionEvent e)
        {
          keyButtonActionPerformed(e);
        }
      });
    }

    optionsPanel.setPreferredSize(new Dimension(200, 100));

optionsPanel.setBorder(BorderFactory.createTitledBorder("Opt
ions:"));
    optionsPanel.setLayout(new GridBagLayout());
    gridConstraints = new GridBagConstraints();
    gridConstraints.gridx = 1;
    gridConstraints.gridy = 0;
    getContentPane().add(optionsPanel, gridConstraints);
```

```
    twoDigitsRadioButton.setText("Two Digits in
Combination");
    twoDigitsRadioButton.setSelected(true);
    digitsButtonGroup.add(twoDigitsRadioButton);
    gridConstraints = new GridBagConstraints();
    gridConstraints.gridx = 0;
    gridConstraints.gridy = 0;
    gridConstraints.anchor = GridBagConstraints.WEST;
    optionsPanel.add(twoDigitsRadioButton, gridConstraints);

    threeDigitsRadioButton.setText("Three Digits in
Combination");
    digitsButtonGroup.add(threeDigitsRadioButton);
    gridConstraints = new GridBagConstraints();
    gridConstraints.gridx = 0;
    gridConstraints.gridy = 1;
    gridConstraints.anchor = GridBagConstraints.WEST;
    optionsPanel.add(threeDigitsRadioButton,
gridConstraints);

    fourDigitsRadioButton.setText("Four Digits in
Combination");
    digitsButtonGroup.add(fourDigitsRadioButton);
    gridConstraints = new GridBagConstraints();
    gridConstraints.gridx = 0;
    gridConstraints.gridy = 2;
    gridConstraints.anchor = GridBagConstraints.WEST;
    optionsPanel.add(fourDigitsRadioButton,
gridConstraints);

    buttonsPanel.setPreferredSize(new Dimension(200, 70));
    buttonsPanel.setLayout(new GridBagLayout());
    gridConstraints = new GridBagConstraints();
    gridConstraints.gridx = 1;
    gridConstraints.gridy = 1;
    getContentPane().add(buttonsPanel, gridConstraints);

    startStopButton.setText("Start Game");
    gridConstraints = new GridBagConstraints();
    gridConstraints.gridx = 0;
    gridConstraints.gridy = 0;
    buttonsPanel.add(startStopButton, gridConstraints);
    startStopButton.addActionListener(new ActionListener()
    {
      public void actionPerformed(ActionEvent e)
      {
        startStopButtonActionPerformed(e);
```

```
      }
    });

    exitButton.setText("Exit");
    gridConstraints = new GridBagConstraints();
    gridConstraints.gridx = 0;
    gridConstraints.gridy = 1;
    gridConstraints.insets = new Insets(10, 0, 0, 0);
    buttonsPanel.add(exitButton, gridConstraints);
    exitButton.addActionListener(new ActionListener()
    {
      public void actionPerformed(ActionEvent e)
      {
        exitButtonActionPerformed(e);
      }
    });

    resultsPanel.setPreferredSize(new Dimension(200, 250));

resultsPanel.setBorder(BorderFactory.createTitledBorder("Res
ults:"));
    resultsPanel.setLayout(new GridBagLayout());
    gridConstraints = new GridBagConstraints();
    gridConstraints.gridx = 1;
    gridConstraints.gridy = 2;
    getContentPane().add(resultsPanel, gridConstraints);

    resultsTextArea.setEditable(false);
    resultsTextArea.setBackground(Color.WHITE);
    resultsPane.setPreferredSize(new Dimension(180, 220));
    resultsPane.setViewportView(resultsTextArea);
    gridConstraints = new GridBagConstraints();
    gridConstraints.gridx = 0;
    gridConstraints.gridy = 0;
    resultsPanel.add(resultsPane, gridConstraints);

    pack();
    Dimension screenSize =
Toolkit.getDefaultToolkit().getScreenSize();
    setBounds((int) (0.5 * (screenSize.width - getWidth())),
(int) (0.5 * (screenSize.height - getHeight())), getWidth(),
getHeight());

    setKeyButtons(false);
    try
    {
```

```
      wrongSound = Applet.newAudioClip(new URL("file:" +
"uhoh.wav"));
      correctSound = Applet.newAudioClip(new URL("file:" +
"tada.wav"));
    }
    catch (Exception ex)
    {
      System.out.println("Error loading sound files");
    }
  }

  private void keyButtonActionPerformed(ActionEvent e)
  {
    String n;
    int numberRight, positionRight;
    // determine which button was clicked
    // ActionCommand is text on button
    n = e.getActionCommand();
    // disable button since digits can't repeat
    keyButton[Integer.valueOf(n).intValue() -
1].setEnabled(false);
    // if first button in combo, clear out label boxes
    if (digitsEntered == 0)
    {
      comboTextField[0].setText("");
      comboTextField[1].setText("");
      comboTextField[2].setText("");
      comboTextField[3].setText("");
    }
    // add button to code
    enteredCombo += n;
    digitsEntered++;
    comboTextField[digitsEntered - 1].setText(n);
    // if all digits entered, check combo
    if (digitsEntered == numberDigits)
    {
      // reset combo buttons
      setKeyButtons(true);
      // check combination
      resultsTextArea.append("Entered: " + enteredCombo +
"\n");
      if (enteredCombo.equals(secretCombo))
      {
        correctSound.play();
        startStopButton.doClick();
      }
      else
```

```
      {
        wrongSound.play();
        numberRight = 0;
        for (int i = 0; i < numberDigits; i++)
        {
          n = String.valueOf(enteredCombo.charAt(i));
          for (int j = 0; j < numberDigits; j++)
            if
(n.equals(String.valueOf(secretCombo.charAt(j))))
              numberRight++;
        }
        // how many in correct position
        positionRight = 0;
        for (int i = 0; i < numberDigits; i++)
          if (secretCombo.charAt(i) ==
enteredCombo.charAt(i))
            positionRight++;
        resultsTextArea.append(String.valueOf(numberRight) +
" digits correct" + "\n");
        resultsTextArea.append(String.valueOf(positionRight)
+ " in correct position" + "\n");
        resultsTextArea.append("Try again ..." + "\n\n");
        // clear combo to try again
        enteredCombo = "";
        digitsEntered = 0;
      }
    }
  }

  private void startStopButtonActionPerformed(ActionEvent e)
  {
    if (startStopButton.getText().equals("Start Game"))
    {
      startStopButton.setText("Stop Game");
      twoDigitsRadioButton.setEnabled(false);
      threeDigitsRadioButton.setEnabled(false);
      fourDigitsRadioButton.setEnabled(false);
      exitButton.setEnabled(false);
      setKeyButtons(true);
      resultsTextArea.setText("");
      // determine number of digits and set up labels
      if (twoDigitsRadioButton.isSelected())
      {
        numberDigits = 2;
      }
      else if (threeDigitsRadioButton.isSelected())
      {
```

```
          numberDigits = 3;
        }
        else
        {
          numberDigits = 4;
        }
        for (int i = 0; i < numberDigits; i++)
        {
          comboTextField[i].setVisible(true);
          comboTextField[i].setText("");
        }
        if (numberDigits != 4)
        {
          for (int i = numberDigits; i < 4; i++)
          {
            comboTextField[i].setVisible(false);
          }
        }
        // determine combination
        secretCombo = "";
        int j;
        boolean uniqueDigit;
        for (int i = 0; i < numberDigits; i++)
        {
          // select unique digit
          do
          {
            j = myRandom.nextInt(9) + 1;
            uniqueDigit = true;
            if (i != 0)
            {
              for (int k = 0; k < i; k++)
              {
                if
(String.valueOf(secretCombo.charAt(k)).equals(String.valueOf
(j)))
                  uniqueDigit = false;
              }
            }
          }
          while (!uniqueDigit);
          secretCombo += String.valueOf(j);
        }
        enteredCombo = "";
        digitsEntered = 0;
      }
      else
```

```
    {
      if (enteredCombo.equals(secretCombo))
        resultsTextArea.append("That's it!!" + "\n");
      else
        resultsTextArea.append("Game Stopped" + "\n");
      resultsTextArea.append("Combination: " + secretCombo);
      startStopButton.setText("Start Game");
      twoDigitsRadioButton.setEnabled(true);
      threeDigitsRadioButton.setEnabled(true);
      fourDigitsRadioButton.setEnabled(true);
      exitButton.setEnabled(true);
      setKeyButtons(false);
    }
  }

  private void exitButtonActionPerformed(ActionEvent e)
  {
    System.exit(0);
  }

  private void setKeyButtons(boolean a)
  {
    for (int i = 0; i < 9; i++)
    {
      keyButton[i].setEnabled(a);
    }
  }

  private void exitForm(WindowEvent evt)
  {
    System.exit(0);
  }
}

class ImagePanel extends JPanel
{
  private Image img;
  public ImagePanel(Image img)
  {
   this.img = img;
  }
  public void paintComponent(Graphics g)
  {
    g.drawImage(img, 0, 0, null);
  }
}
```

3

Bible Tic Tac Toe Project

Review and Preview

The next project we build is the classic **Tic Tac Toe** game, where you try to line up 3 X's or 3 O's in a 3 by 3 grid. We'll develop a two player version and one where you can play against the computer. Then we will add Bible Trivia questions to answer before you can make a move in the Single Player version.

Tic Tac Toe Project Preview

In this chapter, we will build a **Tic Tac Toe** game. This is purportedly the first game ever programmed on a computer and one of the first ever programmed by Bill Gates when he was a teenager at Lakeside School in Seattle. The object of the game is line up 3 X markers or 3 O markers in a 3 by 3 grid. The markers can run horizontally, vertically or diagonally. Turns alternate between players. The version we build here allows two players to compete against each other or to have a single player compete against a pretty smart computer.

The finished project is saved as **TicTacToe** in the **\CBGJava\CBGJava Projects** project group. Start NetBeans (or your IDE). Open the specified project group. Make **TicTacToe** the selected project. Run the project. You will see:

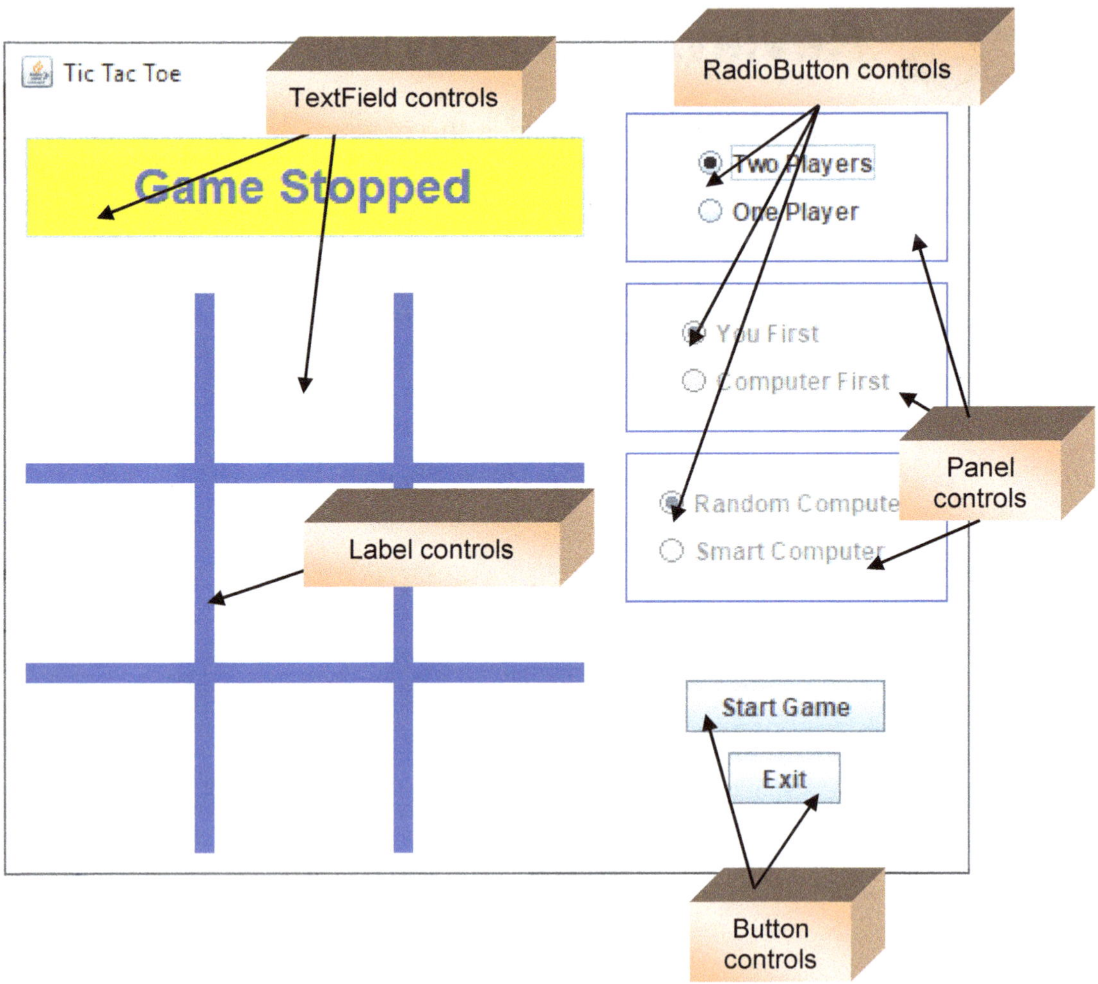

On the left is the grid for playing **Tic Tac Toe**. A text field is used to tell you whose turn it is. Text fields are also used to mark X's and O's in the grid. Skinny label controls are used to form the dark blue grid. On the right are three panel controls and two button controls. Each panel holds two radio button controls used to establish game options. The two button controls are used to start and stop the game and to exit the program.

The game appears in its 'stopped' state, the grid is cleared and waiting for you to choose game options (one or two players and, if one player, who goes first and how smart you want the computer to be). The grid is disabled – no marks can be made (by clicking the grid). I've selected a one player game, where I go first (giving me X's) and a smart computer:

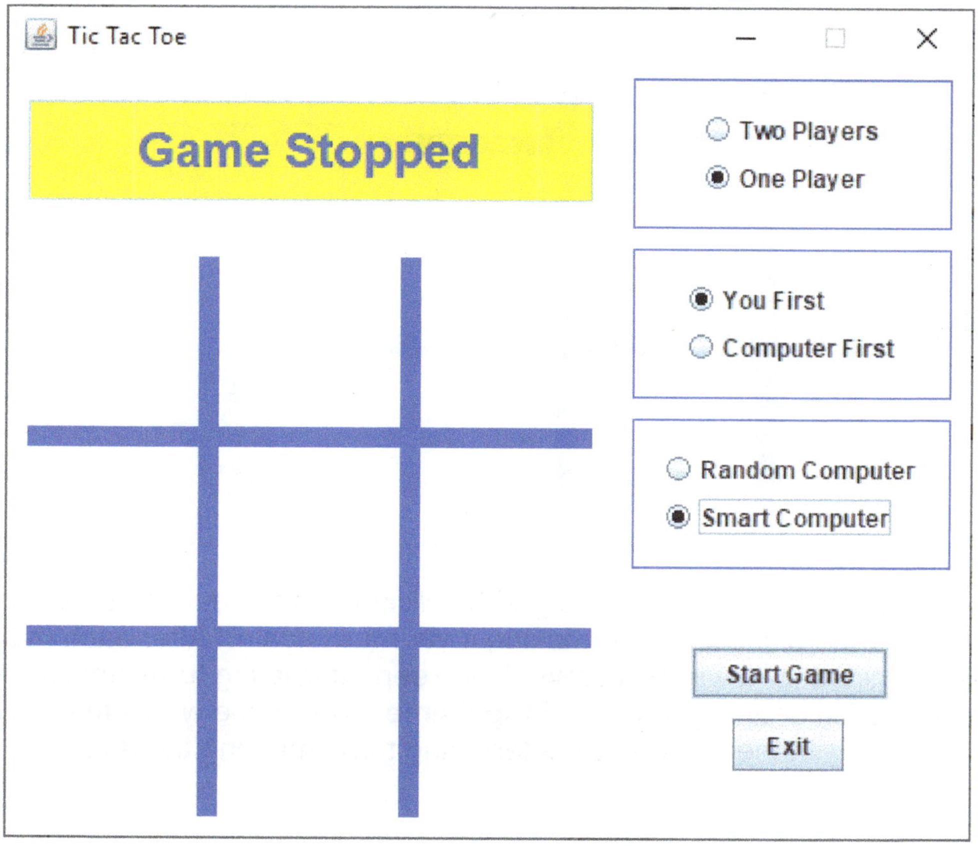

Click the **Start Game** button to start playing. Its caption will change (now reading **Stop Game**) and the options group boxes and **Exit** button will become disabled. The label at the top of the grid says **X's Turn**. X always goes first in this game (whether it's you, the human player, or the computer).

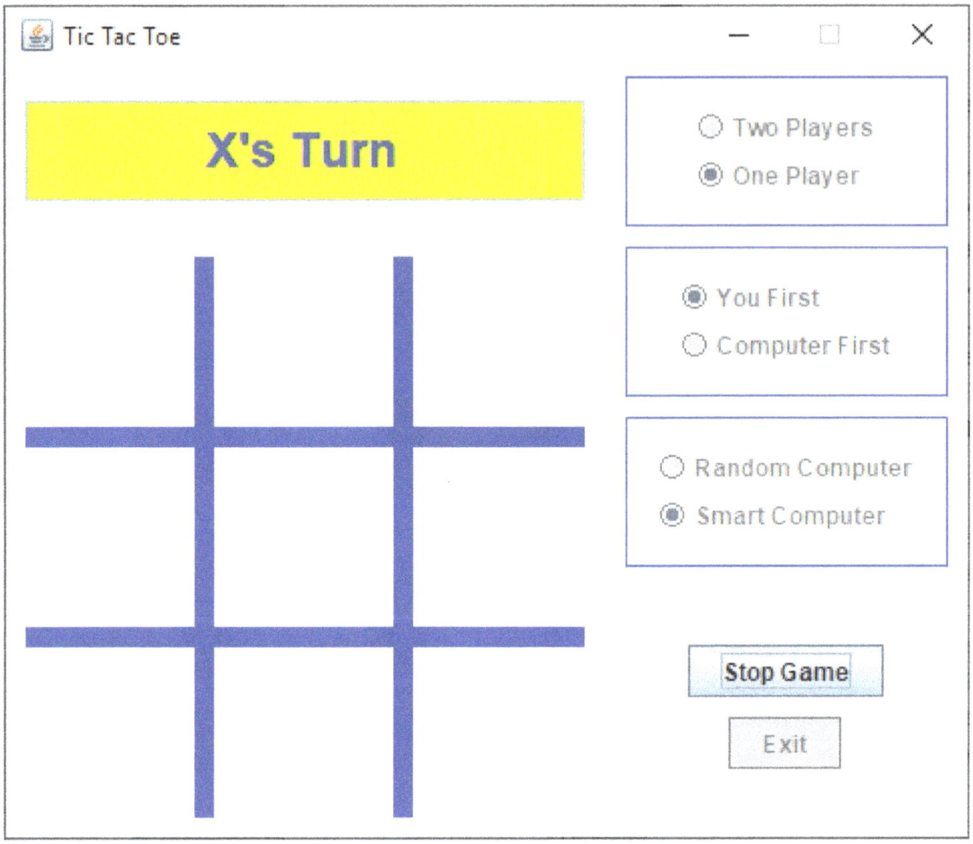

In this state, you make a mark in the grid by clicking on the desired square. The computer will then place its mark, making it your turn again. After each mark, the board is examined for a win or a draw. You keep alternating turns until there is a win, the grid is full or until you press **Stop Game**. The game works the same way for two players, with the two players alternating turns marking the grid.

Enter a mark; I chose the center square and the computer immediately placed its mark (an O) in the upper left corner:

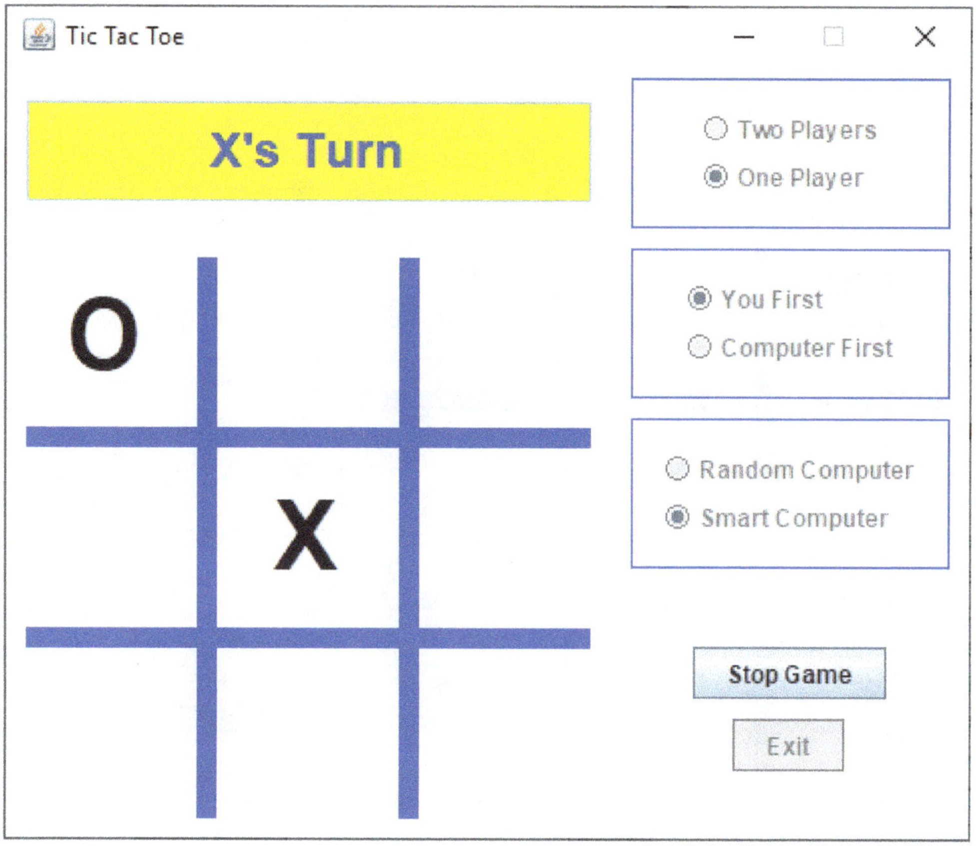

I try the lower left corner and the computer blocks me from winning:

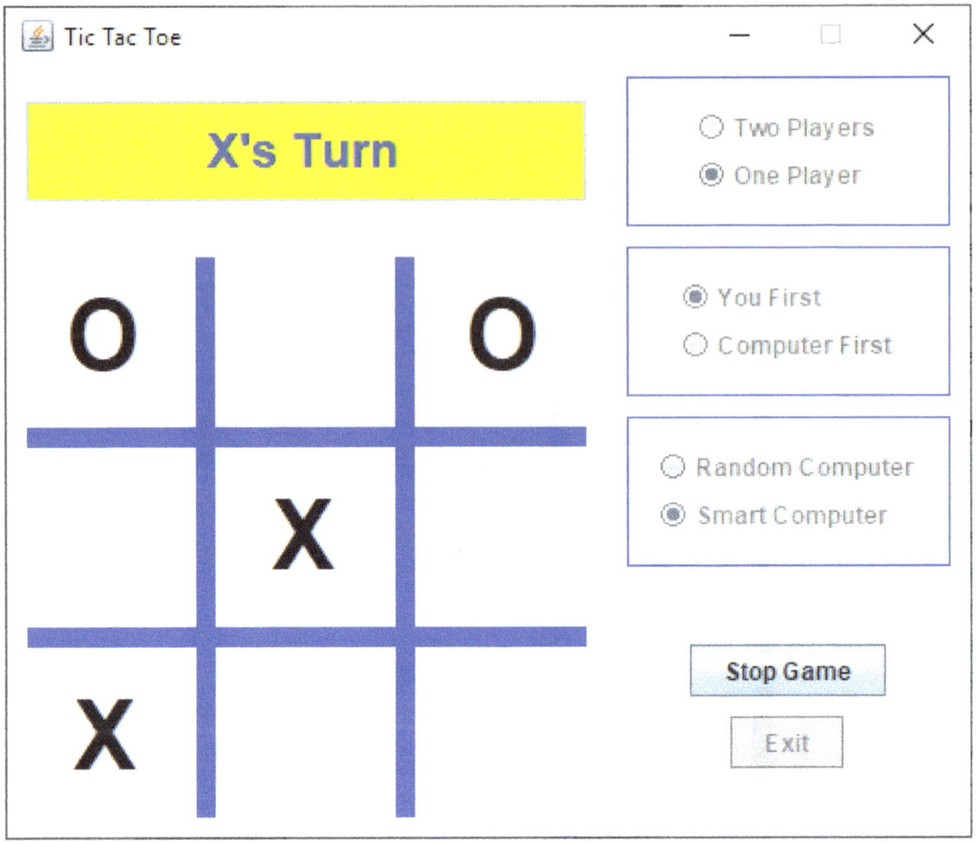

I block the computer's possible win by putting an X in the middle box of the top row. Then, the computer blocks me with a move to the middle of the bottom row:

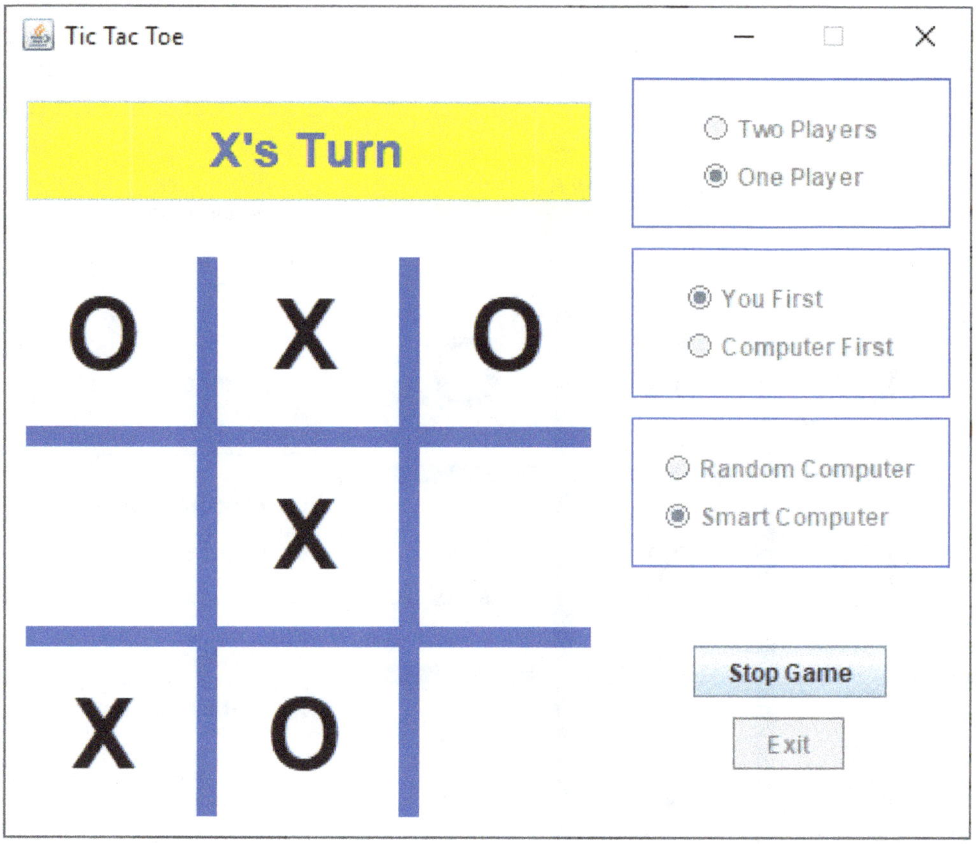

Looks like no one is going to win here.

I continued playing (moving to the right of the middle row and, following the computer's block, a move to the right of the bottom row) until finally we ended in a draw:

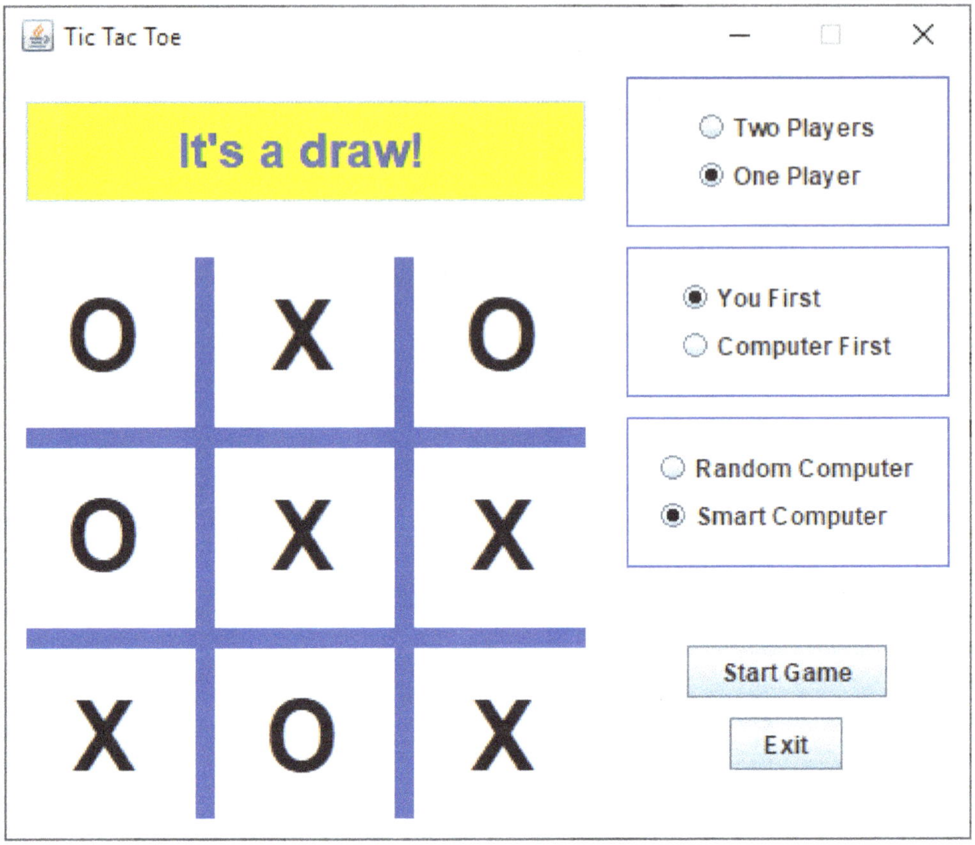

Looks like the computer is pretty smart! We'll see how this intelligence is programmed later. Notice the game returns to its stopped state to allow another game or to stop the program.

Continue playing the game to understand its operation. Try using the **Random Computer** option (the computer just makes random moves making it easier to beat). Click **Exit** when you're done to stop the game. Open the code file and look over the code, if you like.

You will now build this project in stages. As you build Java projects, we always recommend taking a slow, step-by-step process. It minimizes programming errors and helps build your confidence as things come together in a complete project.

We address **frame design**. We discuss the controls needed to build the frame, establish initial control properties and discuss how to change the state of the controls. And, we address **code design**. We discuss how to mark the grid, handle multiple players, check for a win and decide how to make computer-generated moves.

Tic Tac Toe Frame Design

We begin building the **Tic Tac Toe** game project. Let's build the frame. Start a new project in your Java Project group – name it **TicTacToe**. Delete default code in file named **TicTacToe.java**. Once started, we suggest you immediately save the project with a name you choose. This sets up the folder and file structure needed for your project.

Build the basic frame with these properties:

TicTacToe Frame:

title	Tic Tac Toe
background	White
resizable	false

The code is:

```
/*
 * TicTacToe.java
 */
package tictactoe;
import javax.swing.*;
import java.awt.*;
import java.awt.event.*;

public class TicTacToe extends JFrame
{
  public static void main(String args[])
  {
    // create frame
    new TicTacToe().setVisible(true);
  }

  public TicTacToe()
  {
    // frame constructor
    setTitle("Tic Tac Toe");
    getContentPane().setBackground(Color.WHITE);
    setResizable(false);
    addWindowListener(new WindowAdapter()
    {
      public void windowClosing(WindowEvent evt)
      {
        exitForm(evt);
      }
    });
```

```
      getContentPane().setLayout(new GridBagLayout());
      GridBagConstraints gridConstraints;

      pack();
      Dimension screenSize =
  Toolkit.getDefaultToolkit().getScreenSize();
      setBounds((int) (0.5 * (screenSize.width -
  getWidth())), (int) (0.5 * (screenSize.height -
  getHeight())), getWidth(), getHeight());
    }

    private void exitForm(WindowEvent evt)
    {
      System.exit(0);
    }
  }
```

This code builds the frame, sets up the layout manager and includes code to exit the application. Run the code to make sure the frame (at least, what there is of it at this point) appears and is centered on the screen:

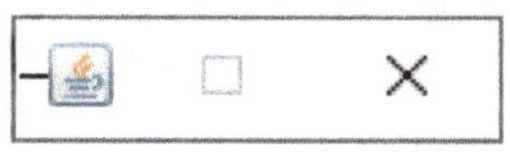

Let's populate our frame with other controls. All code for creating the frame and placing controls (except declarations) goes in the **TicTacToe** constructor.

We start by putting a text field control and five panel controls on the frame. The **GridBagLayout** is:

	gridx = 0	gridx = 1
gridy = 0	**messageTextField**	**playersPanel**
gridy = 1	**gamePanel**	**firstPanel**
gridy = 2		**computerPanel**
gridy = 3		**buttonsPanel**

The **messageTextField** control is used for messaging. The **gamePanel** will be used to display the marks (X and O) and to form the grid. The **playersPanel** will hold radio buttons selecting the number of players. The **firstPanel** will host radio buttons deciding who goes first in a one player game. The **computerPanel** holds radio buttons that decide how smart the computer is. And the **buttonsPanel** will hold the two button controls. We will build each panel separately. Let's begin with the first column (which includes gamePanel) in the grid layout .

Add the **messageTextField** and **gamePanel** controls to the frame with these properties:

messageTextField:	
size	280, 50
editable	false
background	Yellow
foreground	Blue
text	X's Move
horizontalAlignment	Center
font	Arial, Bold, Size 24
gridx	0
gridy	0
insets	10, 10, 10, 10

gamePanel:	
size	280, 280
background	White
gridx	0
gridy	1
insets	10, 10, 10, 10

These controls are declared using:

```
JTextField messageTextField = new JTextField();
JPanel gamePanel = new JPanel();
```

The controls are placed in the frame using this code:

```
messageTextField = new JTextField();
messageTextField.setPreferredSize(new Dimension(280, 50));
messageTextField.setEditable(false);
messageTextField.setBackground(Color.YELLOW);
messageTextField.setForeground(Color.BLUE);
messageTextField.setText("X's Move");
messageTextField.setHorizontalAlignment(SwingConstants.CEN
TER);
messageTextField.setFont(new Font("Arial", Font.BOLD,
24));
gridConstraints = new GridBagConstraints();
gridConstraints.gridx = 0;
gridConstraints.gridy = 0;
gridConstraints.insets = new Insets(10, 10, 10, 10);
getContentPane().add(messageTextField, gridConstraints);
```

```
gamePanel.setPreferredSize(new Dimension(280, 280));
gamePanel.setBackground(Color.WHITE);
gamePanel.setLayout(new GridBagLayout());
gridConstraints = new GridBagConstraints();
gridConstraints.gridx = 0;
gridConstraints.gridy = 1;
gridConstraints.gridheight = 3;
gridConstraints.insets = new Insets(10, 10, 10, 10);
getContentPane().add(gamePanel, gridConstraints);
```

Add this code in the proper locations. Run to see:

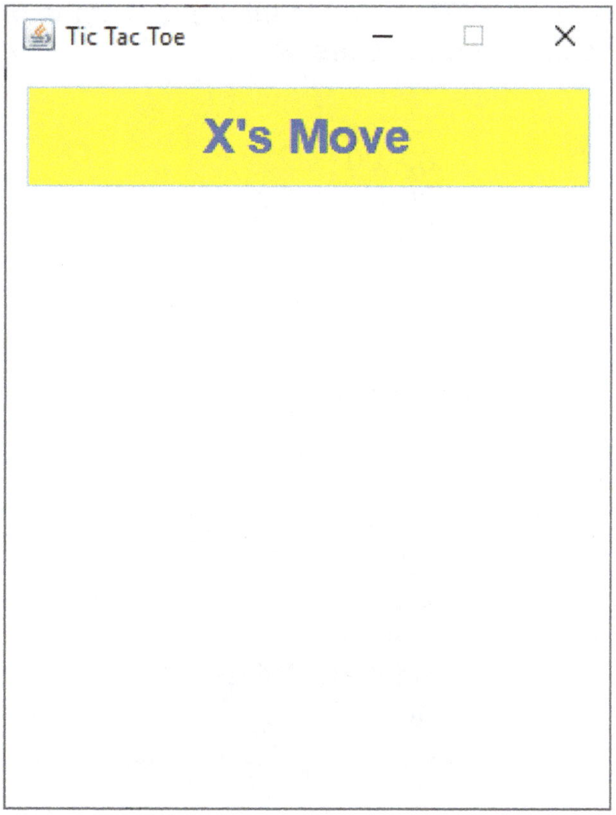

The text field and empty game panel are shown. Let's build the game panel next.

The **gamePanel** control will hold nine text field controls (to display the marks) and four skinny label controls to form a grid. The **GridBagLayout** is:

	gridx = 0	gridx = 1	gridx = 2	gridx = 3	gridx = 4
gridy = 0	**boxTextField[0]**	**gridLabel[2]**	**boxTextField[1]**	**gridLabel[3]**	**boxTextField[2]**
gridy = 1			**gridLabel[0]**		
gridy = 2	**boxTextField[3]**		**boxTextField[4]**		**boxTextField[5]**
gridy = 3			**gridLabel[1]**		
gridy = 4	**boxTextField[6]**		**boxTextField[7]**		**boxTextField[8]**

gridLabel[2] and **gridLabel[3]** extend to the bottom of the grid (we can't show that on this table. The control properties are:

boxTextField[0]:

size	80, 80
editable	false
background	White
horizontalAlignment	Center
font	Arial, Bold, Size 48
border	null
gridx	0
gridy	0

boxTextField[1]:

size	80, 80
editable	false
background	White
horizontalAlignment	Center
font	Arial, Bold, Size 48
border	null
gridx	2
gridy	0

boxTextField[2]:

size	80, 80
editable	false
background	White
horizontalAlignment	Center
font	Arial, Bold, Size 48
border	null
gridx	4
gridy	0

boxTextField[3]:

size	80, 80
editable	false
background	White
horizontalAlignment	Center
font	Arial, Bold, Size 48
border	null
gridx	2
gridy	0

boxTextField[4]:

size	80, 80
editable	false
background	White
horizontalAlignment	Center
font	Arial, Bold, Size 48
border	null
gridx	2
gridy	2

boxTextField[5]:

size	80, 80
editable	false
background	White
horizontalAlignment	Center
font	Arial, Bold, Size 48
border	null
gridx	4
gridy	2

boxTextField[6]:

size	80, 80
editable	false
background	White
horizontalAlignment	Center
font	Arial, Bold, Size 48
border	null
gridx	0
gridy	4

boxTextField[7]:

size	80, 80
editable	false
background	White
horizontalAlignment	Center
font	Arial, Bold, Size 48
border	null
gridx	2
gridy	4

boxTextField[8]:

size	80, 80
editable	false
background	White
horizontalAlignment	Center
font	Arial, Bold, Size 48
border	null
gridx	4
gridy	4

gridLabel[0]:

size	280, 10
opaque	true
background	Blue
gridx	0
gridy	1
gridwidth	5
insets	5, 0, 5, 0

gridLabel[1]:

size	280, 10
opaque	true
background	Blue
gridx	0
gridy	3
gridwidth	5
insets	5, 0, 5, 0

gridLabel[2]:

size	10, 280
opaque	true
background	Blue
gridx	1
gridy	0
gridheight	5
insets	0, 5, 0, 5

gridLabel[3]:

size	10, 280
opaque	true
background	Blue
gridx	3
gridy	0
gridheight	5
insets	0, 5, 0, 5

Declare the controls using:

```
JTextField[] boxTextField = new JTextField[9];
JLabel[] gridLabel = new JLabel[4];
```

Add the controls to the **gamePanel** using:

```
for (int i = 0; i < 9; i++)
{
  boxTextField[i] = new JTextField();
  boxTextField[i].setPreferredSize(new Dimension(80, 80));
  boxTextField[i].setEditable(false);
  boxTextField[i].setBackground(Color.WHITE);

boxTextField[i].setHorizontalAlignment(SwingConstants.CENT
ER);
  boxTextField[i].setFont(new Font("Arial", Font.BOLD,
48));
  boxTextField[i].setBorder(null);
  gridConstraints = new GridBagConstraints();
  gridConstraints.gridx = 2 * (i % 3);
  gridConstraints.gridy = 2 * (i / 3);
  gamePanel.add(boxTextField[i], gridConstraints);
  boxTextField[i].addMouseListener(new MouseAdapter()
  {
public void mousePressed(MouseEvent e)
{
  boxTextFieldMousePressed(e);
}
```

```
    });
  }

  gridLabel[0] = new JLabel();
  gridLabel[0].setPreferredSize(new Dimension(280, 10));
  gridLabel[0].setOpaque(true);
  gridLabel[0].setBackground(Color.BLUE);
  gridConstraints = new GridBagConstraints();
  gridConstraints.gridx = 0;
  gridConstraints.gridy = 1;
  gridConstraints.gridwidth = 5;
  gridConstraints.insets = new Insets(5, 0, 5, 0);
  gamePanel.add(gridLabel[0], gridConstraints);

  gridLabel[1] = new JLabel();
  gridLabel[1].setPreferredSize(new Dimension(280, 10));
  gridLabel[1].setOpaque(true);
  gridLabel[1].setBackground(Color.BLUE);
  gridConstraints = new GridBagConstraints();
  gridConstraints.gridx = 0;
  gridConstraints.gridy = 3;
  gridConstraints.gridwidth = 5;
  gridConstraints.insets = new Insets(5, 0, 5, 0);
  gamePanel.add(gridLabel[1], gridConstraints);

  gridLabel[2] = new JLabel();
  gridLabel[2].setPreferredSize(new Dimension(10, 280));
  gridLabel[2].setOpaque(true);
  gridLabel[2].setBackground(Color.BLUE);
  gridConstraints = new GridBagConstraints();
  gridConstraints.gridx = 1;
  gridConstraints.gridy = 0;
  gridConstraints.gridheight = 5;
  gridConstraints.insets = new Insets(0, 5, 0, 5);
  gamePanel.add(gridLabel[2], gridConstraints);

  gridLabel[3] = new JLabel();
  gridLabel[3].setPreferredSize(new Dimension(10, 280));
  gridLabel[3].setOpaque(true);
  gridLabel[3].setBackground(Color.BLUE);
  gridConstraints = new GridBagConstraints();
  gridConstraints.gridx = 3;
  gridConstraints.gridy = 0;
  gridConstraints.gridheight = 5;
  gridConstraints.insets = new Insets(0, 5, 0, 5);
  gamePanel.add(gridLabel[3], gridConstraints);
```

Notice how the loop index (**i**) is used to set the text field positioning.

This code also adds mouse listeners for each text field. The method called when a text field is clicked with the mouse **boxTextFieldMousePressed**. Add this empty method with the other methods:

```
private void boxTextFieldMousePressed(MouseEvent e)
{
}
```

Add code in the proper locations. Run to see the empty grid:

Let's add the remaining panels.

The **playersPanel** will hold two radio button controls used to select the number of players in the game. The **GridBagLayout** for optionsPanel is:

	gridx = 0
gridy = 0	**twoPlayersRadioButton**
gridy =1	**onePlayerRadioButton**

The panel and radio button properties:

playersPanel:

size	160, 75
border	Line, Blue
gridx	1 (on frame)
gridy	0 (on frame)
insets	5, 10, 5, 10

twoPlayersRadioButton:

text	Two Players
background	White
buttonGroup	playersButtonGroup
selected	true
gridx	0 (on playersPanel)
gridy	0 (on playersPanel)
anchor	WEST

onePlayerRadioButton:

text	One Player
background	White
buttonGroup	playersButtonGroup
gridx	0 (on optionsPanel)
gridy	1 (on optionsPanel)
anchor	WEST

These controls are declared using:

```
JPanel playersPanel = new JPanel();
ButtonGroup playersButtonGroup = new ButtonGroup();
JRadioButton twoPlayersRadioButton = new JRadioButton();
JRadioButton onePlayerRadioButton = new JRadioButton();
```

The radio buttons are placed in the **playersPanel** (which is placed in the frame) using:

```
playersPanel.setPreferredSize(new Dimension(160, 75));
playersPanel.setBackground(Color.WHITE);
playersPanel.setBorder(BorderFactory.createLineBorder(Colo
r.BLUE));
playersPanel.setLayout(new GridBagLayout());
gridConstraints = new GridBagConstraints();
gridConstraints.gridx = 1;
gridConstraints.gridy = 0;
gridConstraints.insets = new Insets(5, 10, 5, 10);
getContentPane().add(playersPanel, gridConstraints);

twoPlayersRadioButton.setText("Two Players");
twoPlayersRadioButton.setBackground(Color.WHITE);
twoPlayersRadioButton.setSelected(true);
playersButtonGroup.add(twoPlayersRadioButton);
gridConstraints = new GridBagConstraints();
gridConstraints.gridx = 0;
gridConstraints.gridy = 0;
gridConstraints.anchor = GridBagConstraints.WEST;
playersPanel.add(twoPlayersRadioButton, gridConstraints);
twoPlayersRadioButton.addActionListener(new
ActionListener()
{
  public void actionPerformed(ActionEvent e)
  {
    twoPlayersRadioButtonActionPerformed(e);
  }
});

onePlayerRadioButton.setText("One Player");
onePlayerRadioButton.setBackground(Color.WHITE);
playersButtonGroup.add(onePlayerRadioButton);
gridConstraints = new GridBagConstraints();
gridConstraints.gridx = 0;
gridConstraints.gridy = 1;
gridConstraints.anchor = GridBagConstraints.WEST;
playersPanel.add(onePlayerRadioButton, gridConstraints);
```

```
onePlayerRadioButton.addActionListener(new
ActionListener()
{
  public void actionPerformed(ActionEvent e)
  {
    onePlayerRadioButtonActionPerformed(e);
  }
});
```

We added listeners for the two radio buttons. Add these empty methods to handle button selections:

```
private void
twoPlayersRadioButtonActionPerformed(ActionEvent e)
{
}

private void
onePlayerRadioButtonActionPerformed(ActionEvent e)
{
}
```

Add this code in the proper locations. Run to see:

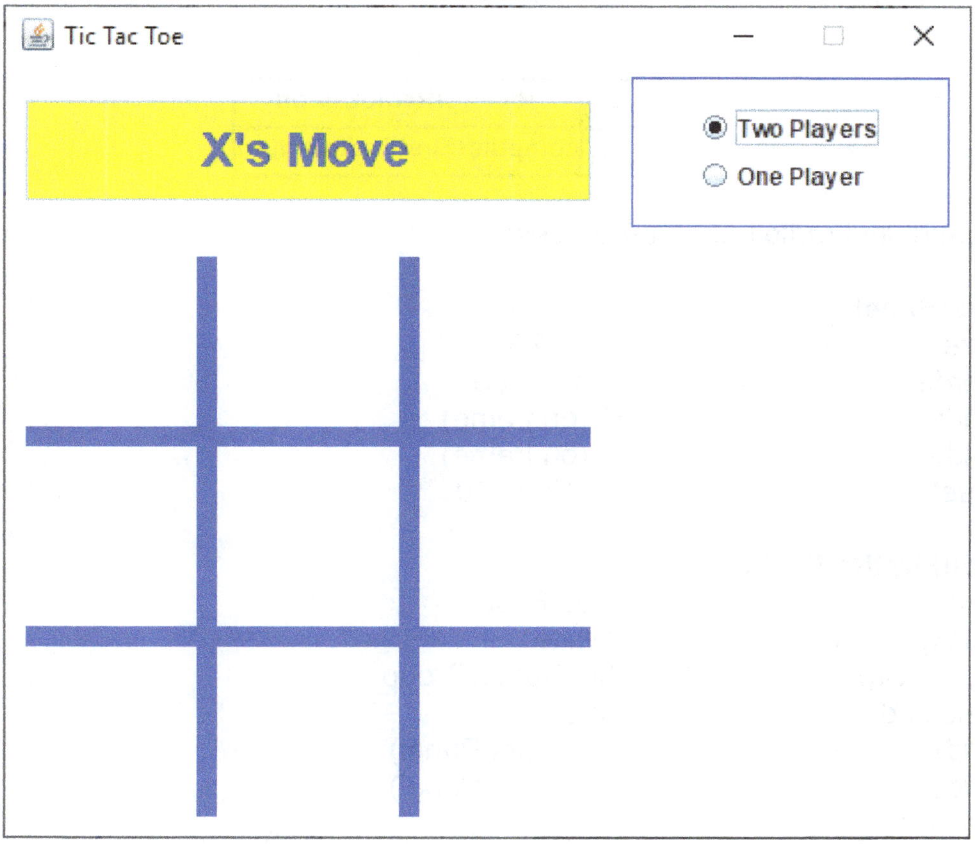

The players panel is displayed.

The **firstPanel** will hold two radio button controls used to determine who goes first in a one player game. The **GridBagLayout** for firstPanel is:

	gridx = 0
gridy = 0	**youFirstRadioButton**
gridy =1	**computerFirstRadioButton**

The panel and radio button properties:

firstPanel:

size	160, 75
border	Line, Blue
gridx	1 (on frame)
gridy	1 (on frame)
insets	5, 10, 5, 10

youFirstRadioButton:

text	You First
background	White
buttonGroup	firstButtonGroup
selected	true
gridx	0 (on firstPanel)
gridy	0 (on firstPanel)
anchor	WEST

computerFirstRadioButton:

text	Computer First
background	White
buttonGroup	firstButtonGroup
gridx	0 (on firstPanel)
gridy	1 (on firstPanel)
anchor	WEST

These controls are declared using:

```
JPanel firstPanel = new JPanel();
ButtonGroup firstButtonGroup = new ButtonGroup();
JRadioButton youFirstRadioButton = new JRadioButton();
JRadioButton computerFirstRadioButton = new
JRadioButton();
```

The radio buttons are placed in the **firstPanel** (which is placed in the frame) using:

```
firstPanel.setPreferredSize(new Dimension(160, 75));
firstPanel.setBackground(Color.WHITE);
firstPanel.setBorder(BorderFactory.createLineBorder(Color.
BLUE));
firstPanel.setLayout(new GridBagLayout());
gridConstraints = new GridBagConstraints();
gridConstraints.gridx = 1;
gridConstraints.gridy = 1;
gridConstraints.insets = new Insets(5, 10, 5, 10);
getContentPane().add(firstPanel, gridConstraints);

youFirstRadioButton.setText("You First");
youFirstRadioButton.setBackground(Color.WHITE);
youFirstRadioButton.setSelected(true);
firstButtonGroup.add(youFirstRadioButton);
gridConstraints = new GridBagConstraints();
gridConstraints.gridx = 0;
gridConstraints.gridy = 0;
gridConstraints.anchor = GridBagConstraints.WEST;
firstPanel.add(youFirstRadioButton, gridConstraints);

computerFirstRadioButton.setText("Computer First");
computerFirstRadioButton.setBackground(Color.WHITE);
firstButtonGroup.add(computerFirstRadioButton);
gridConstraints = new GridBagConstraints();
gridConstraints.gridx = 0;
gridConstraints.gridy = 1;
gridConstraints.anchor = GridBagConstraints.WEST;
firstPanel.add(computerFirstRadioButton, gridConstraints);
```

Add this code in the proper locations. Run to see:

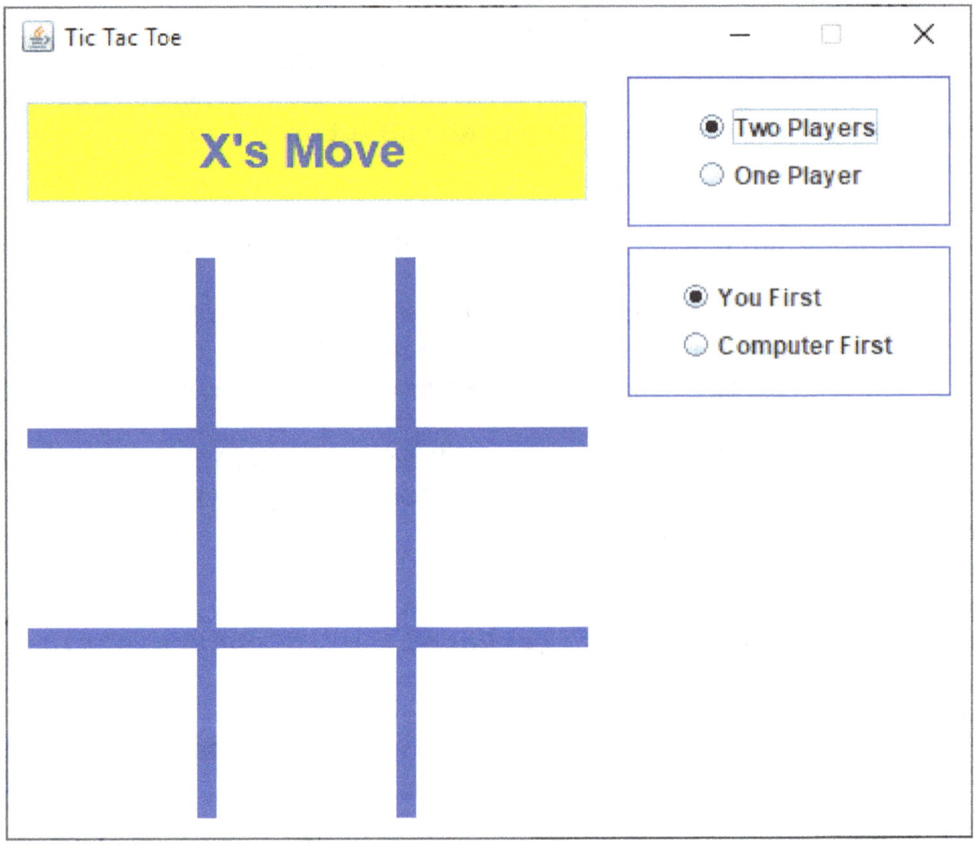

The first panel is displayed.

The **computerPanel** will hold two radio button controls used to how smart the computer is in a one player game. The **GridBagLayout** for computerPanel is:

	gridx = 0
gridy = 0	**randomRadioButton**
gridy =1	**smartRadioButton**

The panel and radio button properties:

computerPanel:

size	160, 75
border	Line, Blue
gridx	1 (on frame)
gridy	2 (on frame)
insets	5, 10, 5, 10

randomRadioButton:

text	Random Computer
background	White
buttonGroup	computerButtonGroup
selected	true
gridx	0 (on computerPanel)
gridy	0 (on computerPanel)
anchor	WEST

smartRadioButton:

text	Smart Computer
background	White
buttonGroup	computerButtonGroup
gridx	0 (on computerPanel)
gridy	1 (on computerPanel)
anchor	WEST

These controls are declared using:

```
JPanel computerPanel = new JPanel();
ButtonGroup computerButtonGroup = new ButtonGroup();
JRadioButton randomRadioButton = new JRadioButton();
JRadioButton smartRadioButton = new JRadioButton();
```

The radio buttons are placed in the **computerPanel** (which is placed in the frame) using:

```
computerPanel.setPreferredSize(new Dimension(160, 75));
computerPanel.setBackground(Color.WHITE);
computerPanel.setBorder(BorderFactory.createLineBorder(Col
or.BLUE));
computerPanel.setLayout(new GridBagLayout());
gridConstraints = new GridBagConstraints();
gridConstraints.gridx = 1;
gridConstraints.gridy = 2;
gridConstraints.insets = new Insets(5, 10, 5, 10);
getContentPane().add(computerPanel, gridConstraints);

randomRadioButton.setText("Random Computer");
randomRadioButton.setBackground(Color.WHITE);
randomRadioButton.setSelected(true);
computerButtonGroup.add(randomRadioButton);
gridConstraints = new GridBagConstraints();
gridConstraints.gridx = 0;
gridConstraints.gridy = 0;
gridConstraints.anchor = GridBagConstraints.WEST;
computerPanel.add(randomRadioButton, gridConstraints);

smartRadioButton.setText("Smart Computer");
smartRadioButton.setBackground(Color.WHITE);
computerButtonGroup.add(smartRadioButton);
gridConstraints = new GridBagConstraints();
gridConstraints.gridx = 0;
gridConstraints.gridy = 1;
gridConstraints.anchor = GridBagConstraints.WEST;
computerPanel.add(smartRadioButton, gridConstraints);
```

Add this code in the proper locations. Run to see:

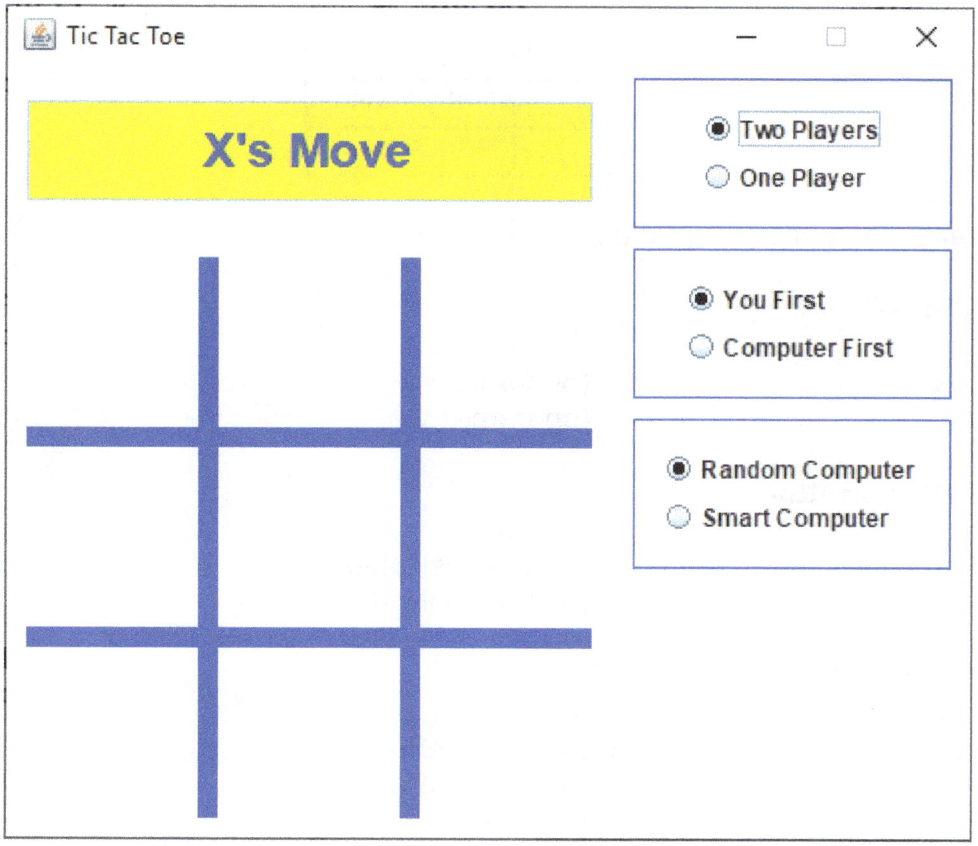

The computer panel is displayed.

The **buttonsPanel** will hold two buttons used to control game play. The **GridBagLayout** for buttonsPanel is:

	gridx = 0
gridy = 0	**startStopButton**
gridy =1	**exitButton**

The panel and button properties:

buttonsPanel:	
size	160, 70
gridx	1 (on frame)
gridy	3 (on frame)

startStopButton:	
text	Start Game
gridx	0 (on buttonsPanel)
gridy	0 (on buttonsPanel)

exitButton:	
text	Exit
gridx	0 (on buttonsPanel)
gridy	1 (on buttonsPanel)
insets	10, 0, 0, 0

These controls are declared using:

```
JPanel buttonsPanel = new JPanel();
JButton startStopButton = new JButton();
JButton exitButton = new JButton();
```

The buttons are placed in the **buttonsPanel** (which is placed in the frame) using:

```
buttonsPanel.setPreferredSize(new Dimension(160, 70));
buttonsPanel.setBackground(Color.WHITE);
buttonsPanel.setLayout(new GridBagLayout());
gridConstraints = new GridBagConstraints();
gridConstraints.gridx = 1;
gridConstraints.gridy = 3;
getContentPane().add(buttonsPanel, gridConstraints);

startStopButton.setText("Start Game");
gridConstraints = new GridBagConstraints();
gridConstraints.gridx = 0;
gridConstraints.gridy = 0;
buttonsPanel.add(startStopButton, gridConstraints);
```

```
startStopButton.addActionListener(new ActionListener()
{
  public void actionPerformed(ActionEvent e)
  {
    startStopButtonActionPerformed(e);
  }
});

exitButton.setText("Exit");
gridConstraints = new GridBagConstraints();
gridConstraints.gridx = 0;
gridConstraints.gridy = 1;
gridConstraints.insets = new Insets(10, 0, 0, 0);
buttonsPanel.add(exitButton, gridConstraints);
exitButton.addActionListener(new ActionListener()
{
  public void actionPerformed(ActionEvent e)
  {
    exitButtonActionPerformed(e);
  }
});
```

This code also adds listeners for each button. Add these empty methods with the other methods:

```
private void startStopButtonActionPerformed(ActionEvent e)
{
}

private void exitButtonActionPerformed(ActionEvent e)
{
}
```

Add this code in the proper locations. Run to see:

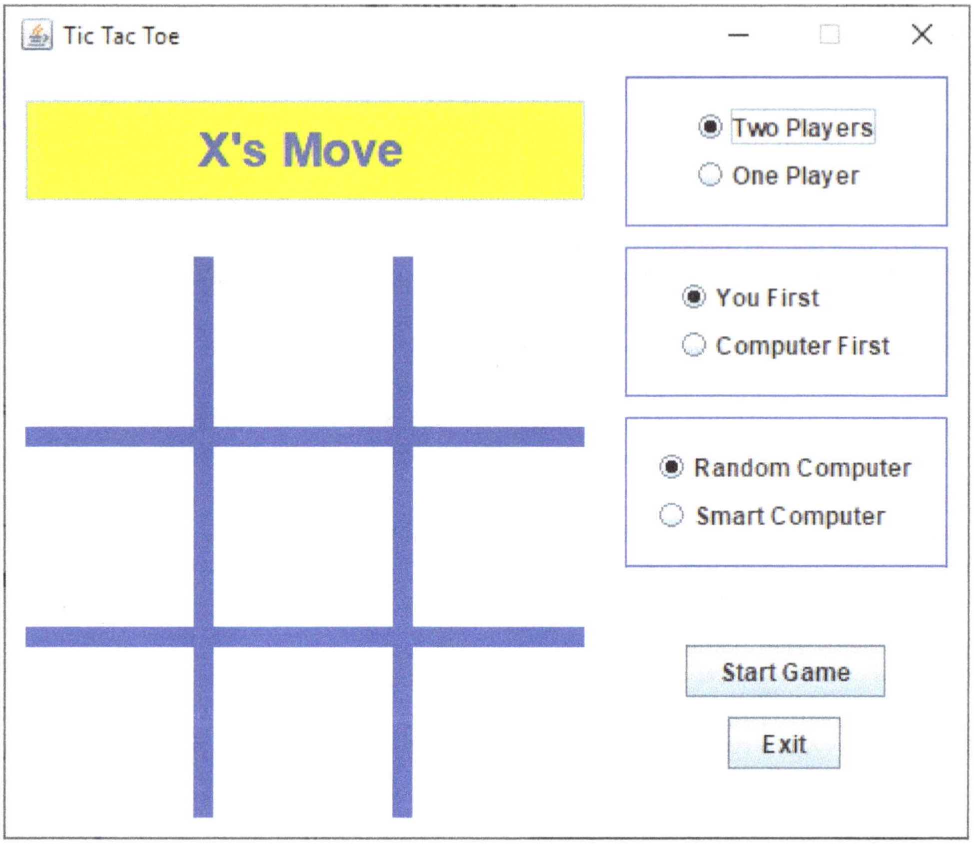

This completes the frame design. You should be able to identify all the controls in the game.

We will begin writing code for the game. We will write the code in several steps. As a first step, we will write the code that starts the game and establishes its 'stopped' state. Then, we look at how to go to 'playing' state following clicking of the **Start Game** button. During the code development process, recognize you may modify a particular method several times before arriving at the finished product.

Code Design – Initializing Stopped State

Any time we start a project, there are certain initializations that must take place. Let's look at the initializations needed in the **Tic Tac Toe** game. All initializations are done at the end of the frame's constructor method.

We want to set a message in the **messageTextField** control. And, we want the game to initially be in **Two Players** mode so we disable the radio buttons in the **firstPanel** and **computerPanel** (these are options associated with a one player game). Add this code to the end of the **TicTacToe** constructor (following the line establishing **screenSize**):

```
messageTextField.setText("Game Stopped");
youFirstRadioButton.setEnabled(false);
computerFirstRadioButton.setEnabled(false);
randomRadioButton.setEnabled(false);
smartRadioButton.setEnabled(false);
```

Run the project to make sure the frame is properly initialized. Do this and you'll see in the 'stopped' state (using default properties), the **Tic Tac Toe** game looks like this:

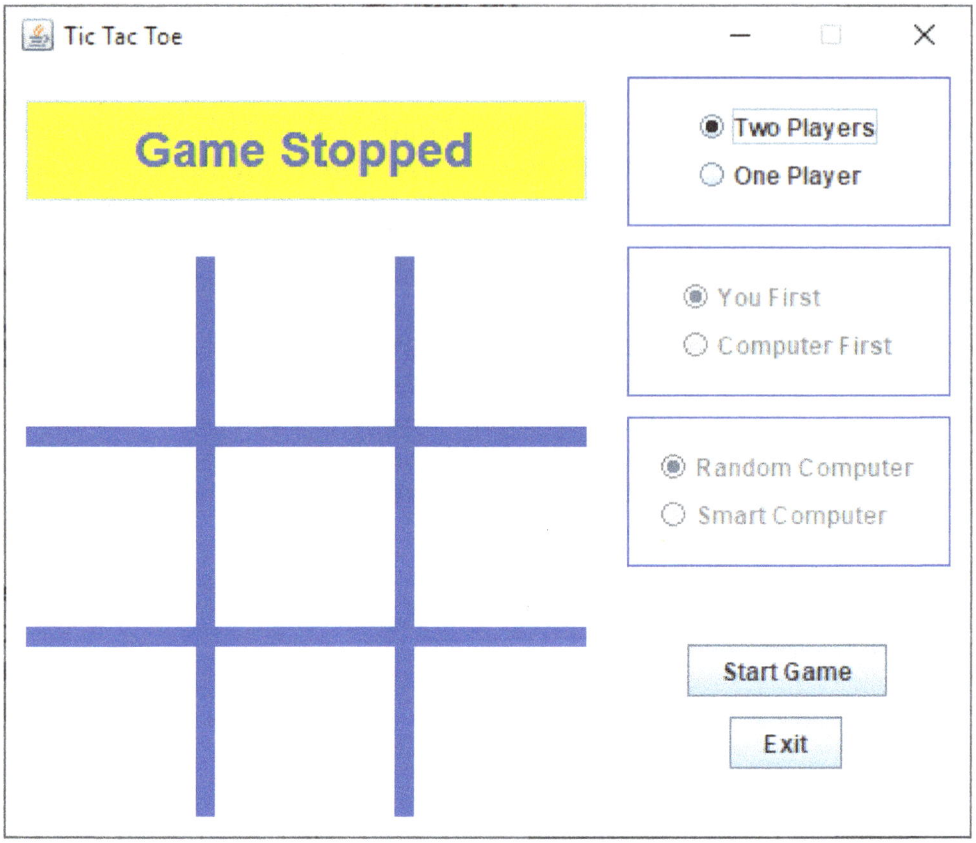

As desired, the game initializes in **Two Players** mode (you can't choose who goes first or how smart the computer is). We have two choices at this point: click **startStopButton** (the button with **Start Game**) or click **exitButton** (the button with **Exit**). We could also change to **One Player** mode – we will address this option in some detail later.

The code for exiting is simple. The **exitButtonActionPerformed** event:

```
private void exitButtonActionPerformed(ActionEvent e)
{
  System.exit(0);
}
```

This simply says whenever the **Exit** button is clicked, the project closes. Add this code to the code window.

The code for the **startStopButton** button is much more complicated. We will build it in several steps. First, we look at switching the game from stopped to playing state.

Code Design –Stopped to Playing State

When the user clicks the **Start Game** button in the 'stopped' state, several things must happen to switch the **Tic Tac Toe** game to 'playing' state:

- Change the **text** property of **startStopButton** to **Stop Game**.
- Disable all radio buttons (don't allow selection of options while playing).
- Disable **exitButton**.
- Establish this as X's turn (since X always goes first).
- Blank out text field controls displaying marks.
- Allow player to input a mark on the grid.

We establish three variables in the class level declarations to help keep track of where we are in the game:

```
boolean xTurn;
boolean canClick = false;
int numberClicks;
```

If **xTurn** is **true**, it is X's turn, otherwise it is O's turn. **canClick** is used to determine if it's okay to click on the text field controls. It is **true** when playing, **false** (the initial value) when stopped. **numberClicks** keeps track of how many of the grid labels have been clicked on (9 maximum).

The code for the **startStopButtonActionPerformed** method that implements the steps in the above method and initializes the new variables is:

```
private void startStopButtonActionPerformed(ActionEvent e)
{
  startStopButton.setText("Stop Game");
  twoPlayersRadioButton.setEnabled(false);
  onePlayerRadioButton.setEnabled(false);
  youFirstRadioButton.setEnabled(false);
  computerFirstRadioButton.setEnabled(false);
  randomRadioButton.setEnabled(false);
  smartRadioButton.setEnabled(false);
  exitButton.setEnabled(false);
  xTurn = true;
  messageTextField.setText("X's Turn");
  // reset boxes
  for (int i = 0; i < 9; i++)
    boxTextField[i].setText("");
  canClick = true;
  numberClicks = 0;
}
```

Can you see how the needed steps are implemented in code?

Save and run the project. Click **Start Game** and the game should switch to two player 'playing' state:

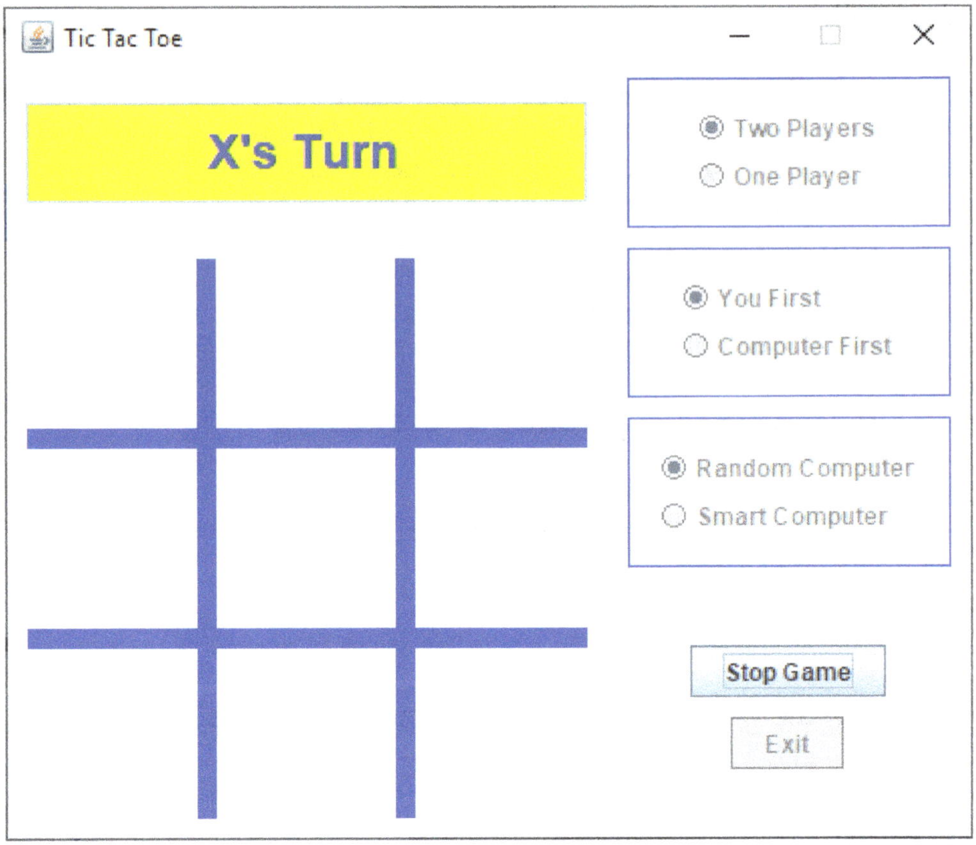

The game is waiting for the first player to click one of the grid locations (we'll write code for that soon). Notice the **Stop Game** button does nothing at the moment. Let's fix that. Stop the project.

Code Design –Playing to Stopped State

When the user clicks the **Stop Game** button in the two player 'playing' state, several things must happen to switch the **Tic Tac Toe** game to 'stopped' state:

- Change the **text** property of **startStopButton** to **Start Game**.
- Display **Game Stopped** message.
- Enable radio buttons in players panel.
- Enable radio buttons in first panel and computer panel, if one player game.
- Enable **exitButton**.
- Set **canClick** to **false.**

We use logic similar to what we did for the **Safecracker** game – modifying the code for **startStopButton**. The code that does these steps is (modifications to the current **startStopButtonActionPerformed** method code are shaded):

```
private void startStopButtonActionPerformed(ActionEvent e)
{
  if (startStopButton.getText().equals("Start Game"))
  {
    startStopButton.setText("Stop Game");
    twoPlayersRadioButton.setEnabled(false);
    onePlayerRadioButton.setEnabled(false);
    youFirstRadioButton.setEnabled(false);
    computerFirstRadioButton.setEnabled(false);
    randomRadioButton.setEnabled(false);
    smartRadioButton.setEnabled(false);
    exitButton.setEnabled(false);
    xTurn = true;
    messageTextField.setText("X's Turn");
    // reset boxes
    for (int i = 0; i < 9; i++)
      boxTextField[i].setText("");
    canClick = true;
    numberClicks = 0;
  }
  else
  {
    startStopButton.setText("Start Game");
    messageTextField.setText("Game Stopped");
    twoPlayersRadioButton.setEnabled(true);
    onePlayerRadioButton.setEnabled(true);
    if (onePlayerRadioButton.isSelected())
    {
      youFirstRadioButton.setEnabled(true);
      computerFirstRadioButton.setEnabled(true);
```

```
            randomRadioButton.setEnabled(true);
            smartRadioButton.setEnabled(true);
          }
          exitButton.setEnabled(true);
          canClick = false;
        }
      }
```

Save and run the project. You should be able to now move from ‘stopped’ to ‘playing’ state and back. When stopped, make sure the proper radio buttons appear for the one and two player options. Let’s write the code for the two player game, first looking at how to mark the grid.

Code Design –Marking Grid

In the **Tic Tac Toe** two player game, when a player clicks a box in the grid, we want the proper mark (X or O) to appear. After each mark, we then need to see if anyone won. If there is no win, and there are still empty locations, we switch to the next player.

So, when a grid box is clicked, we follow these steps:

- Make sure there is not a mark there already.
- Increment **numberClicks**.
- Place proper mark in corresponding text box control (**X** if **xTurn** is **true**, otherwise **O**).
- Switch to next player (not needed if there is a win or draw).
- Check for win. If there is a win, declare the winner and stop the game.
- Check if **numberClicks = 9** (board is full with no win). If so, declare the game a draw and stop.

Anticipating that a human can choose a box or the computer can choose a box (in one player game), we first write a general method that implements the above steps (not checking for a win yet, though). Add this general method (**markClickedBox**) which has an argument the index of the selected box:

```
private void markClickedBox(int i)
{
  String whoWon = "";
  // if already clicked then exit
  if (!boxTextField[i].getText().equals(""))
    return;
  numberClicks++;
  if (xTurn)
  {
    boxTextField[i].setText("X");
    xTurn = false;
    messageTextField.setText("O's Turn");
  }
  else
  {
    boxTextField[i].setText("O");
    xTurn = true;
    messageTextField.setText("X's Turn");
  }
  // check for win - will establish a value for WhoWon
  if (!whoWon.equals(""))
  {
    messageTextField.setText(whoWon + " wins!");
```

```
        startStopButton.doClick();
        return;
      }
      else if (numberClicks == 9)
      {
        // draw
        messageTextField.setText("It's a draw!");
        startStopButton.doClick();
        return;
      }
    }
```

Let's look at this code. The argument **i** is the index of the text field control (**boxTextField**) that was selected. If there is already a mark there (not blank), the method is exited. If blank, the proper mark is placed in **boxTextField[i]**. After this, we check for a win (right now just in a comment line – we'll fix that soon). If the variable **whoWon** is not blank (will be established by the check win logic), we declare the winner. Otherwise, we exit allowing other elements of the grid to be selected until the grid is full, declaring a draw.

Let's use this new method to allow selection of boxes using the mouse. The code to do this goes in the **boxTextFieldMousePressed** method (currently empty). This method is invoked whenever any of the nine text field controls are clicked by the mouse. The tricky part is – how to determine which of the nine controls was clicked. An Internet search yielded the necessary logic. The mouse press method has a **MouseEvent** argument, **e**. The following method uses this argument and returns a **Point** object (**p**) that has the coordinates of the upper left corner of the clicked component (relative to the panel hosting the component):

```
Point p = e.getComponent().getLocation();
```

So, for our case, **p.x** and **p.y** represent the upper left corner of the clicked text field (relative to the **gamePanel** which hosts the text fields). The corresponding coordinates for the text fields can be obtained using **getX** and **getY** methods.

We can use these methods to determine which box is clicked by the mouse and, in turn, place a mark in the clicked box (using the **markClickedBox** method) Add this code to the **boxTextAreaMousePressed** method:

```
private void boxTextFieldMousePressed(MouseEvent e)
{
  if (canClick)
  {
    int i;
    // get upper left corner of clicked box
    Point p = e.getComponent().getLocation();
    // determine index based on p
    for (i = 0; i < 9; i++)
    {
      if (p.x == boxTextField[i].getX() && p.y ==
boxTextField[i].getY())
        break;
    }
    markClickedBox(i);
  }
}
```

Make sure you see how this works.

Save and run the project. You should be able to click on each of the grid locations, placing X's and O's there in alternate turns. Once you have filled all the grid locations, the game will be returned to stopped state. Wins will not be recognized. Here's what I got when I tried it:

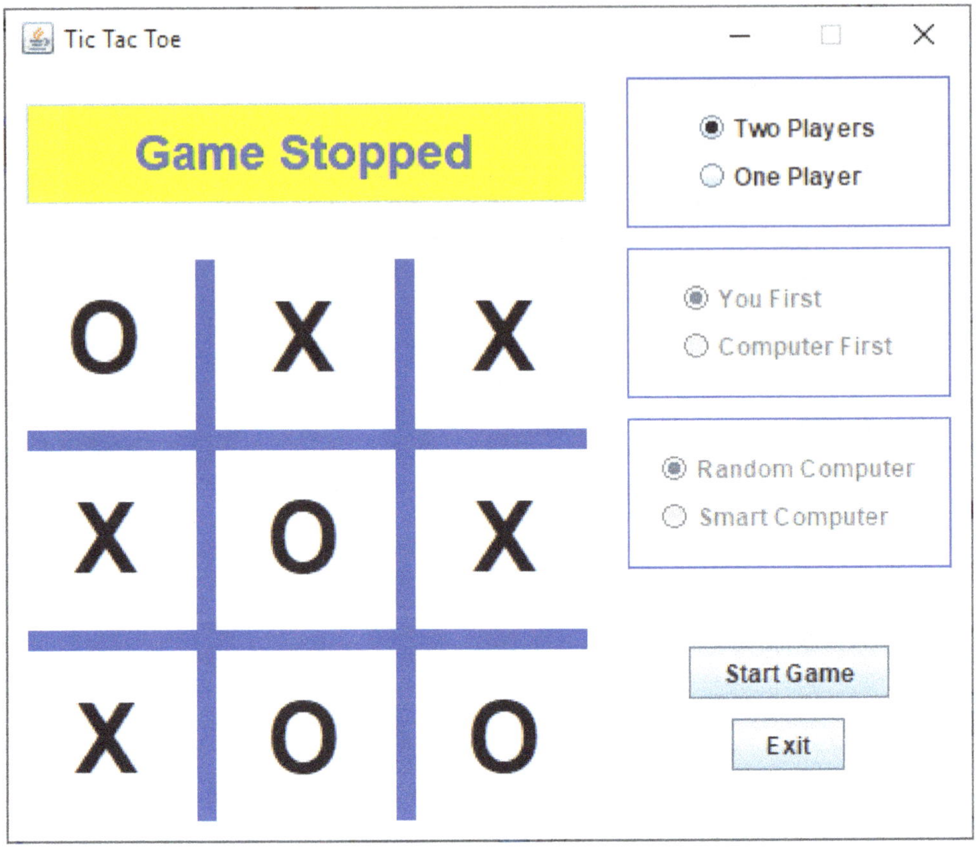

As expected, the computer completely missed the fact that O (Player 2) got a **Tic Tac Toe**!! Let's fix that. We will use a method to return a value for the **whoWon** variable used in the code.

Code Design – Checking For Win

We will build a general method (named **checkForWin**) that examines the playing grid and determines if there is a winner. If so, the win will be identified and the method will return a string variable holding the marker (**X** or **O**) for the winner or a blank if there is no winner. Let's establish a strategy for doing this.

There are eight possible ways to win (3 horizontal, 3 vertical, 2 diagonal). Recall the indices of the **boxTextField** array used in the playing grid are laid out in this manner:

0	1	2
3	4	5
6	7	8

If we declare a string array named **possibleWins**, its 8 elements would be:

```
possibleWins[0] = "012"
possibleWins[1] = "345"
possibleWins[2] = "678"
possibleWins[3] = "036"
possibleWins[4] = "147"
possibleWins[5] = "258"
possibleWins[6] = "048"
possibleWins[7] = "246"
```

So our win logic would be to go through each possible win and see if the corresponding elements of **boxTextField** all contain the same mark (**X** or **O**, but not blank). If so, a winner is declared.

Add this class level declaration to the code window:

```
String[] possibleWins = new String[8];
```

Add this code at the end of the **TicTacToe** constructor to establish values for the array:

```
// possible wins
possibleWins[0] = "012";
possibleWins[1] = "345";
possibleWins[2] = "678";
possibleWins[3] = "036";
possibleWins[4] = "147";
possibleWins[5] = "258";
possibleWins[6] = "048";
possibleWins[7] = "246";
```

Add the general method **checkForWin** to your project:

```
private String checkForWin()
{
  String winner = "";
  int[] boxNumber = new int[3];
  String[] mark = new String[3];
  // check all possible for wins
  for (int i = 0; i < 8; i++)
  {
    for (int j = 0; j < 3; j++)
    {
      boxNumber[j] =
Integer.valueOf(String.valueOf(possibleWins[i].charAt(j)))
.intValue();
      mark[j] = boxTextField[boxNumber[j]].getText();
    }
    if (mark[0].equals(mark[1]) && mark[0].equals(mark[2])
&& mark[1].equals(mark[2]) && !mark[0].equals(""))
    {
      // we have a winner
      winner = mark[0];
      for (int j = 0; j < 3; j++)

boxTextField[boxNumber[j]].setBackground(Color.RED);
    }
  }
  return (winner);
}
```

This code goes through all the possible wins. If all the marks in a particular horizontal, vertical or diagonal row match, the background color of that row is changed to red and the corresponding winner returned. Study the code to see how it works. The **boxNumber** array holds the indices of the **boxTextField** array for each possible win.

We can now modify the **markClickedbox** method to check for wins, but we need one other modification. Notice when a win or draw is declared, we stop the game by performing a click on **startStopButton**. We need some way to distinguish between this method of stopping the game and just having a player click the stop button (which stops the game before a win or draw is declared). Add this variable to the class level declarations:

```
boolean gameOver;
```

If **gameOver** is **true**, there has been a win or draw. If **false**, the **Stop Game** button was clicked before the game ended.

Make the shaded changes to the **startStopButtonActionPerformed** method:

```
private void startStopButtonActionPerformed(ActionEvent e)
{
  if (startStopButton.getText().equals("Start Game"))
  {
    startStopButton.setText("Stop Game");
    twoPlayersRadioButton.setEnabled(false);
    onePlayerRadioButton.setEnabled(false);
    youFirstRadioButton.setEnabled(false);
    computerFirstRadioButton.setEnabled(false);
    randomRadioButton.setEnabled(false);
    smartRadioButton.setEnabled(false);
    exitButton.setEnabled(false);
    xTurn = true;
    messageTextField.setText("X's Turn");
    // reset boxes
    for (int i = 0; i < 9; i++)
    {
      boxTextField[i].setText("");
      boxTextField[i].setBackground(Color.WHITE);
    }
    canClick = true;
    numberClicks = 0;
    gameOver = false;
  }
  else
  {
    startStopButton.setText("Start Game");
    if (!gameOver)
      messageTextField.setText("Game Stopped");
    twoPlayersRadioButton.setEnabled(true);
    onePlayerRadioButton.setEnabled(true);
    if (onePlayerRadioButton.isSelected())
    {
      youFirstRadioButton.setEnabled(true);
      computerFirstRadioButton.setEnabled(true);
      randomRadioButton.setEnabled(true);
      smartRadioButton.setEnabled(true);
    }
    exitButton.setEnabled(true);
    canClick = false;
  }
}
```

These changes do several things. The text field controls' **background** is restored to **White**, in case a win was displayed. The **gameOver** variable is set to **false** when starting a new game. And, the **Game Stopped** message is not displayed if **gameOver** is **true** (meaning a winner or draw is declared).

Now, modify (changes are shaded) the **markClickedBox** method to incorporate the **checkForWin** method and the new **gameOver** variable:

```
private void markClickedBox(int i)
{
  String whoWon = "";
  // if already clicked then exit
  if (!boxTextField[i].getText().equals(""))
    return;
  numberClicks++;
  if (xTurn)
  {
    boxTextField[i].setText("X");
    xTurn = false;
    messageTextField.setText("O's Turn");
  }
  else
  {
    boxTextField[i].setText("O");
    xTurn = true;
    messageTextField.setText("X's Turn");
  }
  // check for win - will establish a value for WhoWon
  whoWon = checkForWin();
  if (!whoWon.equals(""))
  {
    messageTextField.setText(whoWon + " wins!");
    gameOver = true;
    startStopButton.doClick();
    return;
  }
  else if (numberClicks == 9)
  {
    // draw
    messageTextField.setText("It's a draw!");
    gameOver = true;
    startStopButton.doClick();
    return;
  }
}
```

Save and run the project. You and a friend should be able to compete with wins and draws properly determined. Here is a replay of the game I tried before (notice the win by O is now declared):

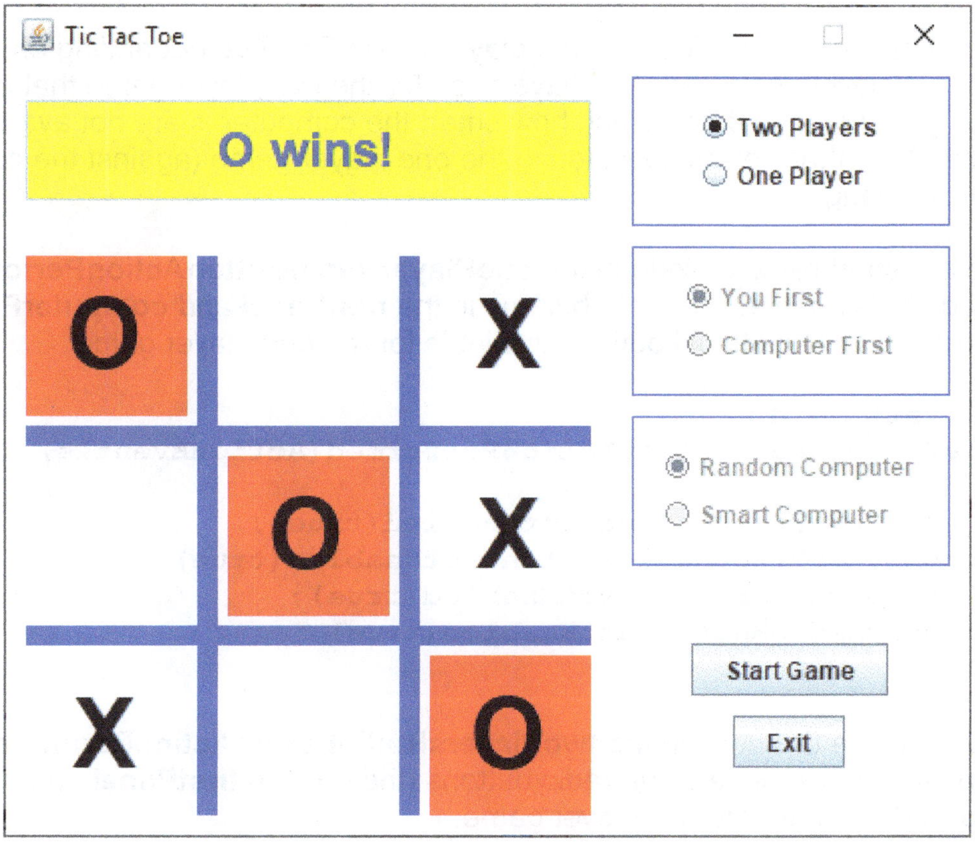

The two player game is now complete. Let's start looking at how to implement a one player game versus a computer opponent. We'll start easy, just having the computer make random moves (no brains!). This will help us establish the logic of switching players when the computer is one of them.

Code Design – Number of Players Selection

Different options are available to the player of **Tic Tac Toe** depending on the number of players selected. We have seen for the two player game that the choice of who goes first and determining how smart the computer is are not available as options. Now that we are considering the one player game (against the computer), this must change.

Place this short piece of code in the **onePlayerRadioButtonActionPerformed** method. This enables the radio buttons in the **firstPanel** and **computerPanel** controls to allow additional options available for the one player game:

```
private void
onePlayerRadioButtonActionPerformed(ActionEvent e)
{
  youFirstRadioButton.setEnabled(true);
  computerFirstRadioButton.setEnabled(true);
  randomRadioButton.setEnabled(true);
  smartRadioButton.setEnabled(true);
}
```

Likewise, place this code in the **twoPlayersRadioButtonActionPerformed** method to disable these same radio buttons (the ones in **firstPanel** and **computerPanel**) for the two player game:

```
private void
twoPlayersRadioButtonActionPerformed(ActionEvent e)
{
  youFirstRadioButton.setEnabled(false);
  computerFirstRadioButton.setEnabled(false);
  randomRadioButton.setEnabled(false);
  smartRadioButton.setEnabled(false);
}
```

Save and run the project to make sure the player choices work as desired.

Code Design – Random Computer Moves

A big part of allowing the computer to play against a human (you, the player) is to decide what “thought processes” to give the computer. We’re allowing two choices: a **random computer** and a **smart computer**. We’ll start by coding up the random computer. This will get all the logic of implementing computer moves along with human moves working properly. Then, we’ll move on to a smart computer, developing a formidable opponent.

All of the logic behind a computer move will be implemented in a general method named **computerTurn**. For random moves, it will simply choose (at random) one of the empty boxes in the grid and place a marker in that box (X if computer goes first, O if human goes first).

Add this import statement to allow use of random numbers:

```
import java.util.Random;
```

And, add a random object to the class level declarations area of the code window:

```
Random myRandom = new Random();
```

Place this general method **computerTurn** in your project:

```
private void computerTurn()
{
  int selectedBox;
  int i, n;
  if (randomRadioButton.isSelected())
  {
    // random logic
    // put mark in Nth available square
    n = myRandom.nextInt(9 - numberClicks) + 1;
    i = 0;
    for (selectedBox = 0; selectedBox < 9; selectedBox++)
    {
      if (boxTextField[selectedBox].getText().equals(""))
        i++;
      if (i == n)
        break;
    }
    // put mark in SelectedBox
    markClickedBox(selectedBox);
  }
  else
```

```
    {
      // smart computer
    }
  }
```

The logic behind the code in **computerTurn** is straightforward. At any time, we have **9 - numberClicks** empty boxes in the grid. The code selects a random number from **1** to **9 – numberClicks** and counts ahead that number of empty boxes to identify the box to mark. To mark the identified box, **boxTextField[selectedBox]**, we simulate a click on that box by calling the **markClickedBox** method with **selectedBox** as the argument. The program will know whether to place an X or O in the box based on previously implemented logic.

Now, let's implement the **computerTurn** method to allow the computer to play. We need to modify two methods. First, when we start a game, if the computer moves first, we need to invoke **computerTurn**. Make the shaded changes to the **startStopButtonActionPerformed** method:

```
private void startStopButtonActionPerformed(ActionEvent e)
{
  if (startStopButton.getText().equals("Start Game"))
  {
    startStopButton.setText("Stop Game");
    twoPlayersRadioButton.setEnabled(false);
    onePlayerRadioButton.setEnabled(false);
    youFirstRadioButton.setEnabled(false);
    computerFirstRadioButton.setEnabled(false);
    randomRadioButton.setEnabled(false);
    smartRadioButton.setEnabled(false);
    exitButton.setEnabled(false);
    xTurn = true;
    messageTextField.setText("X's Turn");
    // reset boxes
    for (int i = 0; i < 9; i++)
    {
      boxTextField[i].setText("");
      boxTextField[i].setBackground(Color.WHITE);
    }
    canClick = true;
    numberClicks = 0;
    gameOver = false;
    if (computerFirstRadioButton.isSelected())
      computerTurn();
  }
  else
  {
```

```
      startStopButton.setText("Start Game");
      if (!gameOver)
        messageTextField.setText("Game Stopped");
      twoPlayersRadioButton.setEnabled(true);
      onePlayerRadioButton.setEnabled(true);
      if (onePlayerRadioButton.isSelected())
      {
        youFirstRadioButton.setEnabled(true);
        computerFirstRadioButton.setEnabled(true);
        randomRadioButton.setEnabled(true);
        smartRadioButton.setEnabled(true);
      }
      exitButton.setEnabled(true);
      canClick = false;
    }
  }
```

And, after a mark is placed by the human player, the computer needs to take a turn. This logic is in the **markClickedBox** method. The needed changes are shaded:

```
  private void markClickedBox(int i)
  {
    String whoWon = "";
    // if already clicked then exit
    if (!boxTextField[i].getText().equals(""))
      return;
    numberClicks++;
    if (xTurn)
    {
      boxTextField[i].setText("X");
      xTurn = false;
      messageTextField.setText("O's Turn");
    }
    else
    {
      boxTextField[i].setText("O");
      xTurn = true;
      messageTextField.setText("X's Turn");
    }
    // check for win - will establish a value for WhoWon
    whoWon = checkForWin();
    if (!whoWon.equals(""))
    {
      messageTextField.setText(whoWon + " wins!");
      gameOver = true;
      startStopButton.doClick();
```

```
      return;
    }
    else if (numberClicks == 9)
    {
      // draw
      messageTextField.setText("It's a draw!");
      gameOver = true;
      startStopButton.doClick();
      return;
    }
    if (onePlayerRadioButton.isSelected())
      if ((xTurn && computerFirstRadioButton.isSelected())
|| (!xTurn && youFirstRadioButton.isSelected()))
        computerTurn();
}
```

With the added code, the computer takes a turn when it goes first and it's X's turn or takes a turn when the human goes first and it's O's turn.

Save and run the game. Choose the one player option and make sure **Random Computer** is selected. Try playing a few games (you go first, computer going first). Make sure things work properly, you should see the computer is pretty easy to beat! Here's a game I won when I went first:

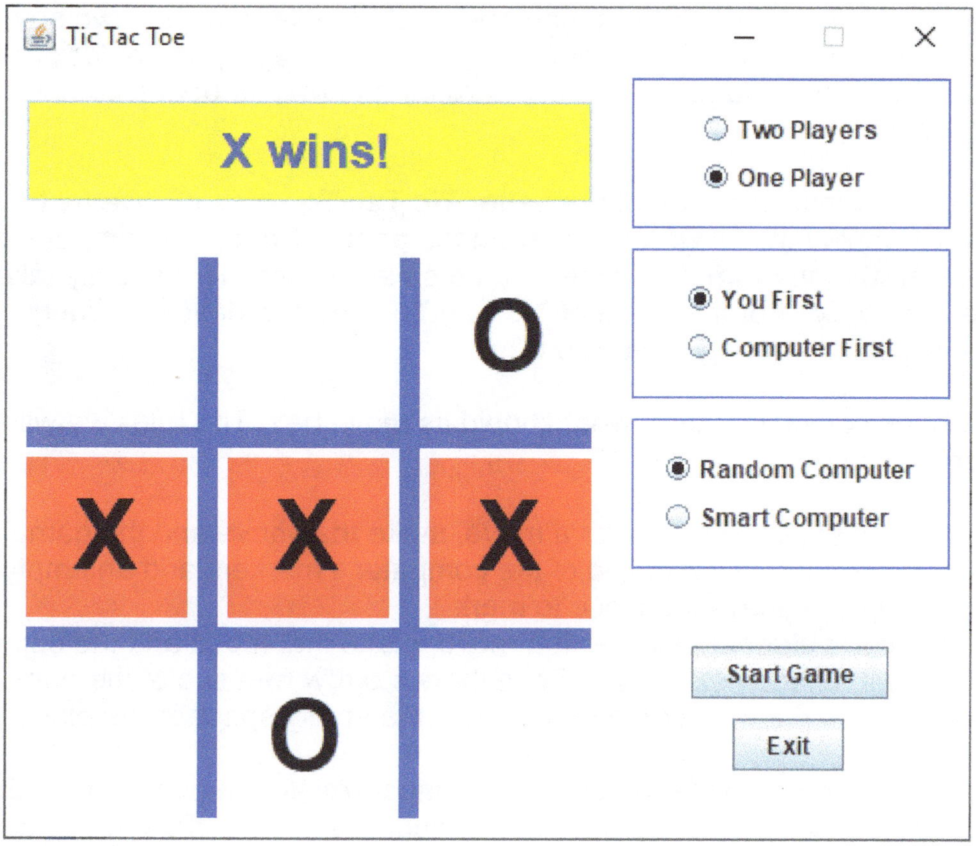

Code Design – Smart Computer Moves

We've come to one of the more fun and more challenging parts of this game project. How can we make our computer a smarter opponent? In any game where a computer is playing against a human, we must be able to write down some rules that give the computer the appearance of intelligence. Many computer opponents are unbeatable. For example, it is very hard for a human to beat a computer at the game of chess.

So how do we make our computer a better **Tic Tac Toe** player? We try to imbed choices we would make if we were playing the game. So for the computer to be a smart player, the programmer needs to be a smart player. This usually takes practice and study. For the game of **Tic Tac Toe**, we can develop a fairly simple, yet very intelligent strategy. Let's do it.

When it is the computer's turn, what should its move be? The rules we will use are (in order of choice):

1. If the computer can win with a move, make that move and the game is over. So, if there's a row with two of the computer's markers and an empty space, the empty space is the place to mark!
2. If the computer can block with a move, make that move and the opponent can't win on the next move. So, if there's a row with two of the human player's markers and an empty space, the empty space is the place to mark!
3. If there is no possible win or possible block, make a move in this order: center square, one of the four corner squares, or one of the four side squares.

I think you see this logic makes sense. You may wonder about Step 3 – why we choose that particular order. Recall there are 8 possible ways to win in **Tic Tac Toe** (3 horizontal, 3 vertical, 2 diagonal). The center square is needed in 4 of these, any one corner is involved in 3 possibilities, while any side is involved in just 2 wins. Hence, the order of choices is made on basic probabilities. Let's implement this logic in code.

Here is the modified **computerTurn** method that implements this 'smart' logic. The changes are shaded:

```
private void computerTurn()
{
  int selectedBox;
  int i, n;
  int j, k;
  String computerMark, playerMark, markToFind;
  int[] boxNumber = new int[3];
  String[] mark = new String[3];
  int emptyBox;
  int[] bestMoves = { 4, 0, 2, 6, 8, 1, 3, 5, 7 };
  if (randomRadioButton.isSelected())
  {
    // random logic
    // put mark in Nth available square
    n = myRandom.nextInt(9 - numberClicks) + 1;
    i = 0;
    for (selectedBox = 0; selectedBox < 9; selectedBox++)
    {
      if (boxTextField[selectedBox].getText().equals(""))
        i++;
      if (i == n)
        break;
    }
    // put mark in SelectedBox
    markClickedBox(selectedBox);
  }
  else
  {
    // smart computer
    // determine who has what mark
    if (computerFirstRadioButton.isSelected())
    {
      computerMark = "X";
      playerMark = "O";
    }
    else
    {
      computerMark = "O";
      playerMark = "X";
    }
    // Step 1 (K = 1) - check for win - see if two boxes
hold computer mark and one is empty
    // Step 2 (K = 2) - check for block - see if two boxes
hold player mark and one is empty
```

```
    for (k = 1; k <= 2; k++)
    {
      if (k == 1)
        markToFind = computerMark;
      else
        markToFind = playerMark;
      for (i = 0; i < 8; i++)
      {
        n = 0;
        emptyBox = 0;
        for (j = 0; j < 3; j++)
        {
          boxNumber[j] =
Integer.valueOf(String.valueOf(possibleWins[i].charAt(j)))
.intValue();
          mark[j] = boxTextField[boxNumber[j]].getText();
          if (mark[j].equals(markToFind))
            n++;
          else if (mark[j].equals(""))
            emptyBox = boxNumber[j];
        }
        if (n == 2 && emptyBox != 0)
        {
          // mark empty box to win (K = 1) or block (K =
2)
          markClickedBox(emptyBox);
          return;
        }
      }
    }
    // Step 3 - find next best move
    for (i = 0; i < 9; i++)
    {
      if (boxTextField[bestMoves[i]].getText().equals(""))
      {
        markClickedBox(bestMoves[i]);
        return;
      }
    }
  }
}
```

In the ‘smart’ logic, we first find out whether the computer has X or O. Steps 1 and 2 of the computer logic are done in a for loop with k as index. In that loop, we go through all the possible wins looking for a row with 2 identical marks and an empty box. For k=1, we look for the computer’s mark and an empty box – giving the computer a win on the next move. For k=2, we look for the human’s mark and an empty box – giving the computer a block on the next move. If neither Step 1 or Step 2 is successful, we move to Step 3. The next best moves are listed in desired order in the array **bestMoves**. In Step 3, we go through this array, finding the first empty box available and move there.

Save and run the project. The game is now fully functional. Try playing it against the computer. You should find it can’t be beat. The best you can do against the computer is a draw. Before leaving, let’s add a couple of sounds.

Code Design – Adding Sounds

We know sounds make games a bit more fun. Let's add a couple to the Tick Tac Toe game. In the **\CBGJava\CBGJava Projects\TicTacToe** folder are two wav files that can be used for sound. The file **beep.wav** is a sound we'll use for games that end a draw. The **tada.wav** file is a celebratory sound we'll use for wins by either player. These files will be loaded when the project starts. Copy the two sound files to your project's folder.

Add these import statements:

```
import java.net.URL;
import java.applet.*;
```

And, add these class level declarations to represent the two sounds:

```
AudioClip drawSound;
AudioClip winSound;
```

Add these lines at the end of the **TicTacToe** constructor code to establish the sound objects:

```
try
{
  drawSound = Applet.newAudioClip(new URL("file:" +
"beep.wav"));
  winSound = Applet.newAudioClip(new URL("file:" +
"tada.wav"));
}
catch (Exception ex)
{
  System.out.println("Error loading sound files");
}
```

Make sure you copy the two sound files to your project folder.

Lastly, play the two sounds at the appropriate (shaded) locations in the **markClickedBox** method:

```
private void markClickedBox(int i)
{
  String whoWon = "";
  // if already clicked then exit
  if (!boxTextField[i].getText().equals(""))
    return;
  numberClicks++;
  if (xTurn)
  {
    boxTextField[i].setText("X");
    xTurn = false;
    messageTextField.setText("O's Turn");
  }
  else
  {
    boxTextField[i].setText("O");
    xTurn = true;
    messageTextField.setText("X's Turn");
  }
  // check for win - will establish a value for WhoWon
  whoWon = checkForWin();
  if (!whoWon.equals(""))
  {
    winSound.play();
    messageTextField.setText(whoWon + " wins!");
    gameOver = true;
    startStopButton.doClick();
    return;
  }
  else if (numberClicks == 9)
  {
    // draw
    drawSound.play();
    messageTextField.setText("It's a draw!");
    gameOver = true;
    startStopButton.doClick();
    return;
  }
  if (onePlayerRadioButton.isSelected())
    if ((xTurn && computerFirstRadioButton.isSelected())
|| (!xTurn && youFirstRadioButton.isSelected()))
      computerTurn();
}
```

Save and run the project. You should now have a complete, running version of the **Tic Tac Toe** game (the complete code listing is given at the end of the chapter). Have fun playing it! Again, you will see the computer can't be beat. Here's a game I played against a 'smart' computer where I went first, taking the middle square:

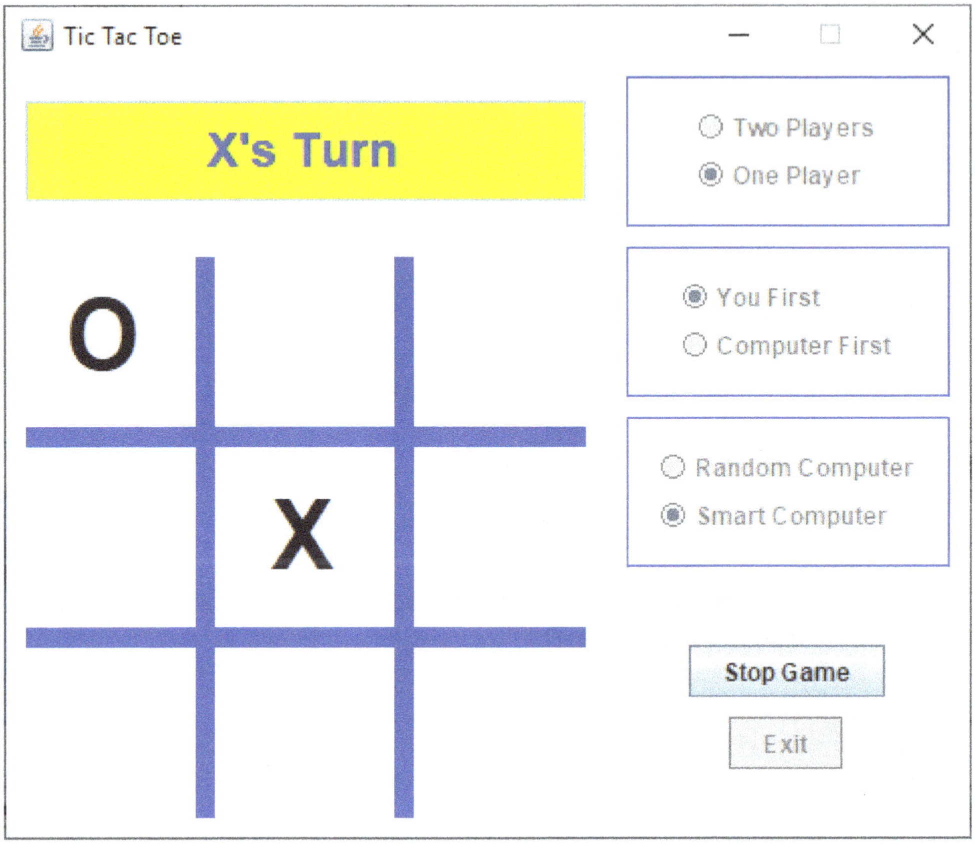

Notice, based on the logic we implemented, since the computer couldn't win or block, it took its next best move, the first available corner square.

My next move was the lower left corner:

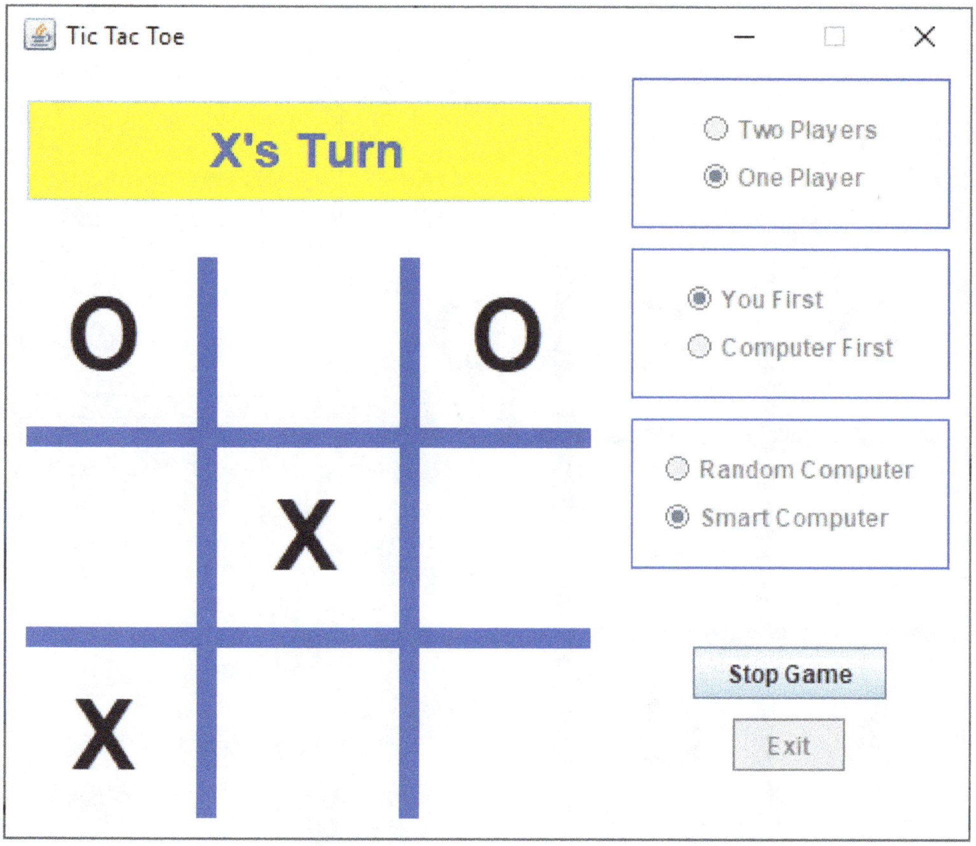

The computer logic implemented block my next move.

My next move was to block the computer, who in turn blocked me:

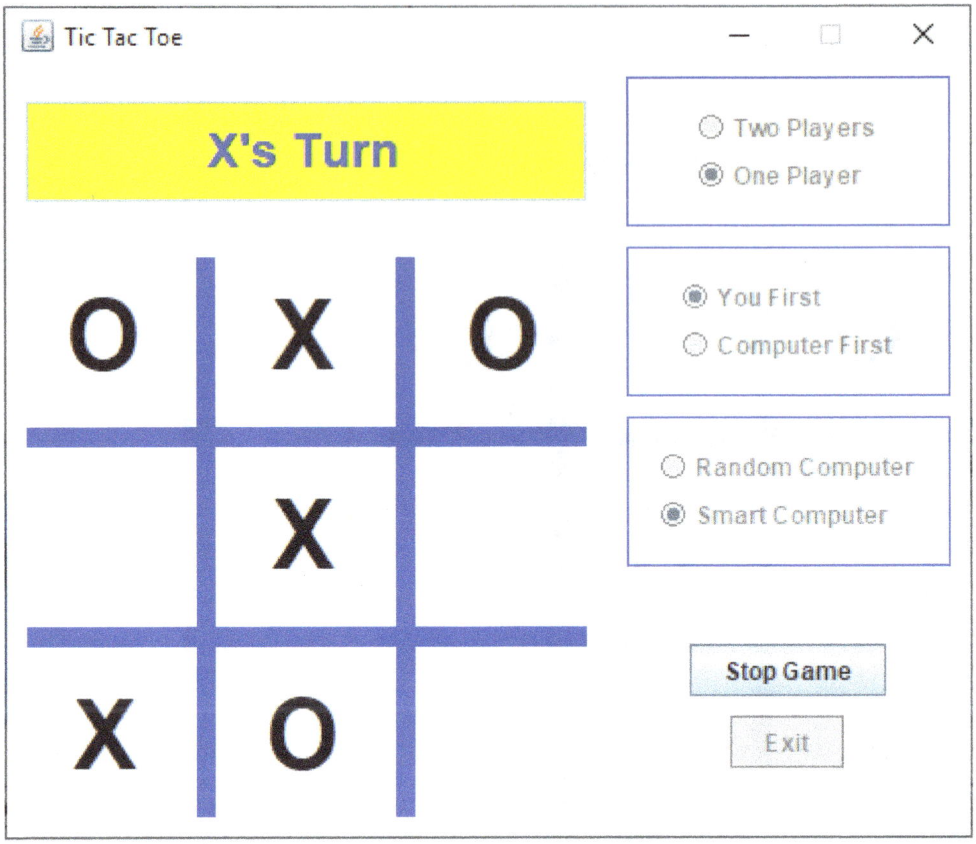

I continued playing (moving to the right of the middle row and, following the computer's block, a move to the right of the bottom row) until finally we ended in a draw:

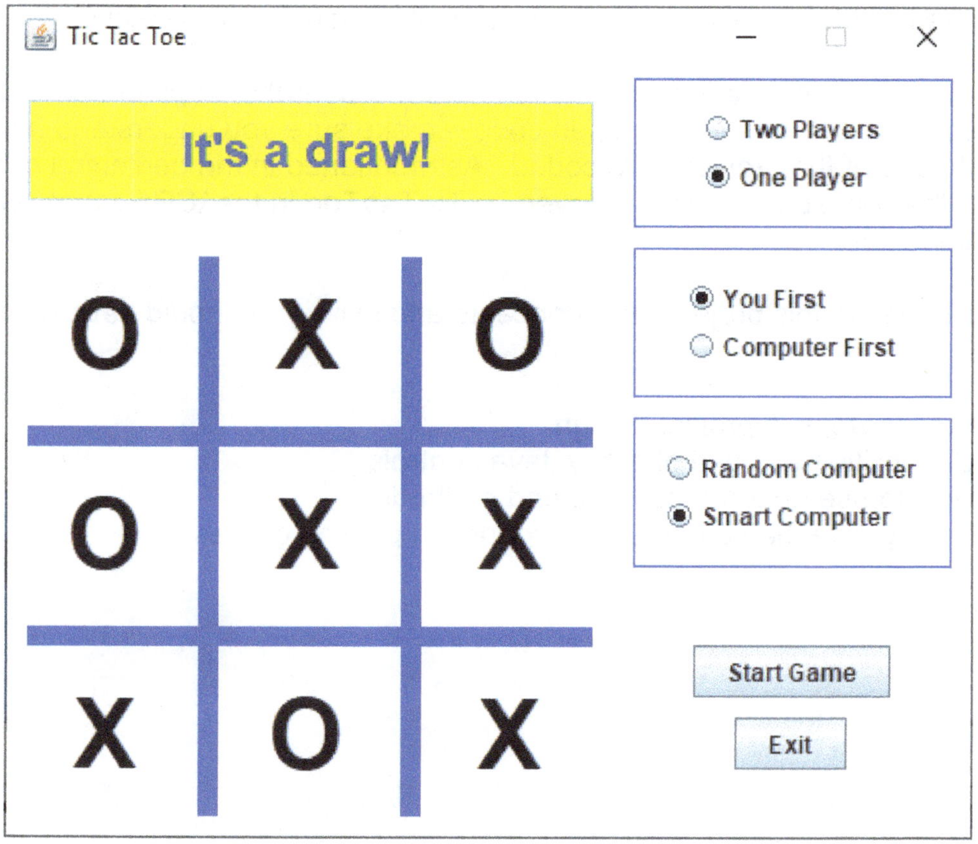

I heard the little beep and the computer's ready to play again.

Tic Tac Toe Project Review

The **Tic Tac Toe** game project is now complete. Save and run the project and make sure it works as promised. Check that all options work correctly.

If there are errors in your implementation, go back over the steps of frame and code design. Go over the developed code – make sure you understand how different parts of the project were coded. As mentioned in the beginning of this chapter, the completed project is saved as **TicTacToe** in the **\CBGJava\CBGJava Projects** folder.

While completing this project, new concepts and skills you should have gained include:

- Proper steps in project design.
- Capabilities and use of many Java controls.
- How to use general methods and methods.
- How to give the computer intelligence in playing games.

Tic Tac Toe Project Enhancements

There are several ways to improve the **Tic Tac Toe** game. Some possibilities are:

- Use label controls instead of text field controls in the grid. With such a change, you could use something other than X's and O's to mark the squares. Try using small digital photos (jpeg files).
- Add better messaging with a computer opponent. As implemented, the computer quickly makes its move. Perhaps, add a delay (see the Timer object) and perhaps some color changes in the grid so the computer has time to tell you where its move will be.
- In the current computer logic (Step 3), the computer always picks corners or sides in the same order. To make things a bit more unpredictable, add logic so the computer makes corner or side moves randomly based on the number of corner or side boxes that are empty.
- The computer in this game is pretty smart, but can be made smarter. Between Steps 2 and 3 in the current computer logic, we could add another step where the computer would be more aggressive. In this new step, have the computer search for horizontal, vertical or diagonal rows with one of its markers and two empty squares. By choosing one of the empty squares, the computer forces your next move. Even better is to find a place where with an additional mark, the computer sets up two wins, making it impossible for you to block him.
- For little kids, maybe the computer is a bit too smart. The random computer is an option, but goes to the other extreme of maybe not being smart enough. A change would be to add levels of intelligence – having the computer use its 'smart' logic sometimes and its 'random' logic sometimes. To do this, you could generate a random number from 1 to 100 and based on some threshold, determine whether to make a smart move or random move. By varying the threshold, you can make the computer extremely smart or not so smart. We implement such logic in the next game project, **Match Game**.

Tic Tac Toe Project Java Code Listing

```
/*
 * TicTacToe.java
 */
package tictactoe;
import javax.swing.*;
import java.awt.*;
import java.awt.event.*;
import java.util.Random;
import java.net.URL;
import java.applet.*;

public class TicTacToe extends JFrame
{
  JTextField messageTextField = new JTextField();
  JPanel gamePanel = new JPanel();
  JTextField[] boxTextField = new JTextField[9];
  JLabel[] gridLabel = new JLabel[4];
  JPanel playersPanel = new JPanel();
  ButtonGroup playersButtonGroup = new ButtonGroup();
  JRadioButton twoPlayersRadioButton = new JRadioButton();
  JRadioButton onePlayerRadioButton = new JRadioButton();
  JPanel firstPanel = new JPanel();
  ButtonGroup firstButtonGroup = new ButtonGroup();
  JRadioButton youFirstRadioButton = new JRadioButton();
  JRadioButton computerFirstRadioButton = new
JRadioButton();
  JPanel computerPanel = new JPanel();
  ButtonGroup computerButtonGroup = new ButtonGroup();
  JRadioButton randomRadioButton = new JRadioButton();
  JRadioButton smartRadioButton = new JRadioButton();
  JPanel buttonsPanel = new JPanel();
  JButton startStopButton = new JButton();
  JButton exitButton = new JButton();

  boolean xTurn;
  boolean canClick = false;
  int numberClicks;
  String[] possibleWins = new String[8];
  boolean gameOver;
  Random myRandom = new Random();

  AudioClip drawSound;
  AudioClip winSound;
```

```
  public static void main(String args[])
  {
    // create frame
    new TicTacToe().setVisible(true);
  }

  public TicTacToe()
  {
    // frame constructor
    setTitle("Tic Tac Toe");
    getContentPane().setBackground(Color.WHITE);
    setResizable(false);
    addWindowListener(new WindowAdapter()
    {
      public void windowClosing(WindowEvent evt)
      {
        exitForm(evt);
      }
    });
    getContentPane().setLayout(new GridBagLayout());

    messageTextField = new JTextField();
    messageTextField.setPreferredSize(new Dimension(280,
50));
    messageTextField.setEditable(false);
    messageTextField.setBackground(Color.YELLOW);
    messageTextField.setForeground(Color.BLUE);
    messageTextField.setText("X's Move");

messageTextField.setHorizontalAlignment(SwingConstants.CENTE
R);
    messageTextField.setFont(new Font("Arial", Font.BOLD,
24));
    GridBagConstraints gridConstraints = new
GridBagConstraints();
    gridConstraints.gridx = 0;
    gridConstraints.gridy = 0;
    gridConstraints.insets = new Insets(10, 10, 10, 10);
    getContentPane().add(messageTextField, gridConstraints);

    gamePanel.setPreferredSize(new Dimension(280, 280));
    gamePanel.setBackground(Color.WHITE);
    gamePanel.setLayout(new GridBagLayout());
    gridConstraints = new GridBagConstraints();
    gridConstraints.gridx = 0;
    gridConstraints.gridy = 1;
    gridConstraints.gridheight = 3;
```

```
    gridConstraints.insets = new Insets(10, 10, 10, 10);
    getContentPane().add(gamePanel, gridConstraints);

    for (int i = 0; i < 9; i++)
    {
      boxTextField[i] = new JTextField();
      boxTextField[i].setPreferredSize(new Dimension(80,
80));
      boxTextField[i].setEditable(false);
      boxTextField[i].setBackground(Color.WHITE);

boxTextField[i].setHorizontalAlignment(SwingConstants.CENTER
);
      boxTextField[i].setFont(new Font("Arial", Font.BOLD,
48));
      boxTextField[i].setBorder(null);
      gridConstraints = new GridBagConstraints();
      gridConstraints.gridx = 2 * (i % 3);
      gridConstraints.gridy = 2 * (i / 3);
      gamePanel.add(boxTextField[i], gridConstraints);
      boxTextField[i].addMouseListener(new MouseAdapter()
      {
        public void mousePressed(MouseEvent e)
        {
          boxTextFieldMousePressed(e);
        }
      });
    }

    gridLabel[0] = new JLabel();
    gridLabel[0].setPreferredSize(new Dimension(280, 10));
    gridLabel[0].setOpaque(true);
    gridLabel[0].setBackground(Color.BLUE);
    gridConstraints = new GridBagConstraints();
    gridConstraints.gridx = 0;
    gridConstraints.gridy = 1;
    gridConstraints.gridwidth = 5;
    gridConstraints.insets = new Insets(5, 0, 5, 0);
    gamePanel.add(gridLabel[0], gridConstraints);

    gridLabel[1] = new JLabel();
    gridLabel[1].setPreferredSize(new Dimension(280, 10));
    gridLabel[1].setOpaque(true);
    gridLabel[1].setBackground(Color.BLUE);
    gridConstraints = new GridBagConstraints();
    gridConstraints.gridx = 0;
    gridConstraints.gridy = 3;
```

```
    gridConstraints.gridwidth = 5;
    gridConstraints.insets = new Insets(5, 0, 5, 0);
    gamePanel.add(gridLabel[1], gridConstraints);

    gridLabel[2] = new JLabel();
    gridLabel[2].setPreferredSize(new Dimension(10, 280));
    gridLabel[2].setOpaque(true);
    gridLabel[2].setBackground(Color.BLUE);
    gridConstraints = new GridBagConstraints();
    gridConstraints.gridx = 1;
    gridConstraints.gridy = 0;
    gridConstraints.gridheight = 5;
    gridConstraints.insets = new Insets(0, 5, 0, 5);
    gamePanel.add(gridLabel[2], gridConstraints);

    gridLabel[3] = new JLabel();
    gridLabel[3].setPreferredSize(new Dimension(10, 280));
    gridLabel[3].setOpaque(true);
    gridLabel[3].setBackground(Color.BLUE);
    gridConstraints = new GridBagConstraints();
    gridConstraints.gridx = 3;
    gridConstraints.gridy = 0;
    gridConstraints.gridheight = 5;
    gridConstraints.insets = new Insets(0, 5, 0, 5);
    gamePanel.add(gridLabel[3], gridConstraints);

    playersPanel.setPreferredSize(new Dimension(160, 75));
    playersPanel.setBackground(Color.WHITE);

playersPanel.setBorder(BorderFactory.createLineBorder(Color.
BLUE));
    playersPanel.setLayout(new GridBagLayout());
    gridConstraints = new GridBagConstraints();
    gridConstraints.gridx = 1;
    gridConstraints.gridy = 0;
    gridConstraints.insets = new Insets(5, 10, 5, 10);
    getContentPane().add(playersPanel, gridConstraints);

    twoPlayersRadioButton.setText("Two Players");
    twoPlayersRadioButton.setBackground(Color.WHITE);
    twoPlayersRadioButton.setSelected(true);
    playersButtonGroup.add(twoPlayersRadioButton);
    gridConstraints = new GridBagConstraints();
    gridConstraints.gridx = 0;
    gridConstraints.gridy = 0;
    gridConstraints.anchor = GridBagConstraints.WEST;
```

```
    playersPanel.add(twoPlayersRadioButton,
gridConstraints);
    twoPlayersRadioButton.addActionListener(new
ActionListener()
    {
      public void actionPerformed(ActionEvent e)
      {
        twoPlayersRadioButtonActionPerformed(e);
      }
    });

    onePlayerRadioButton.setText("One Player");
    onePlayerRadioButton.setBackground(Color.WHITE);
    playersButtonGroup.add(onePlayerRadioButton);
    gridConstraints = new GridBagConstraints();
    gridConstraints.gridx = 0;
    gridConstraints.gridy = 1;
    gridConstraints.anchor = GridBagConstraints.WEST;
    playersPanel.add(onePlayerRadioButton, gridConstraints);
    onePlayerRadioButton.addActionListener(new
ActionListener()
    {
      public void actionPerformed(ActionEvent e)
      {
        onePlayerRadioButtonActionPerformed(e);
      }
    });

    firstPanel.setPreferredSize(new Dimension(160, 75));
    firstPanel.setBackground(Color.WHITE);

firstPanel.setBorder(BorderFactory.createLineBorder(Color.BL
UE));
    firstPanel.setLayout(new GridBagLayout());
    gridConstraints = new GridBagConstraints();
    gridConstraints.gridx = 1;
    gridConstraints.gridy = 1;
    gridConstraints.insets = new Insets(5, 10, 5, 10);
    getContentPane().add(firstPanel, gridConstraints);

    youFirstRadioButton.setText("You First");
    youFirstRadioButton.setBackground(Color.WHITE);
    youFirstRadioButton.setSelected(true);
    firstButtonGroup.add(youFirstRadioButton);
    gridConstraints = new GridBagConstraints();
    gridConstraints.gridx = 0;
    gridConstraints.gridy = 0;
```

```
    gridConstraints.anchor = GridBagConstraints.WEST;
    firstPanel.add(youFirstRadioButton, gridConstraints);

    computerFirstRadioButton.setText("Computer First");
    computerFirstRadioButton.setBackground(Color.WHITE);
    firstButtonGroup.add(computerFirstRadioButton);
    gridConstraints = new GridBagConstraints();
    gridConstraints.gridx = 0;
    gridConstraints.gridy = 1;
    gridConstraints.anchor = GridBagConstraints.WEST;
    firstPanel.add(computerFirstRadioButton,
gridConstraints);

    computerPanel.setPreferredSize(new Dimension(160, 75));
    computerPanel.setBackground(Color.WHITE);

computerPanel.setBorder(BorderFactory.createLineBorder(Color
.BLUE));
    computerPanel.setLayout(new GridBagLayout());
    gridConstraints = new GridBagConstraints();
    gridConstraints.gridx = 1;
    gridConstraints.gridy = 2;
    gridConstraints.insets = new Insets(5, 10, 5, 10);
    getContentPane().add(computerPanel, gridConstraints);

    randomRadioButton.setText("Random Computer");
    randomRadioButton.setBackground(Color.WHITE);
    randomRadioButton.setSelected(true);
    computerButtonGroup.add(randomRadioButton);
    gridConstraints = new GridBagConstraints();
    gridConstraints.gridx = 0;
    gridConstraints.gridy = 0;
    gridConstraints.anchor = GridBagConstraints.WEST;
    computerPanel.add(randomRadioButton, gridConstraints);

    smartRadioButton.setText("Smart Computer");
    smartRadioButton.setBackground(Color.WHITE);
    computerButtonGroup.add(smartRadioButton);
    gridConstraints = new GridBagConstraints();
    gridConstraints.gridx = 0;
    gridConstraints.gridy = 1;
    gridConstraints.anchor = GridBagConstraints.WEST;
    computerPanel.add(smartRadioButton, gridConstraints);

    buttonsPanel.setPreferredSize(new Dimension(160, 70));
    buttonsPanel.setBackground(Color.WHITE);
    buttonsPanel.setLayout(new GridBagLayout());
```

```
    gridConstraints = new GridBagConstraints();
    gridConstraints.gridx = 1;
    gridConstraints.gridy = 3;
    getContentPane().add(buttonsPanel, gridConstraints);

    startStopButton.setText("Start Game");
    gridConstraints = new GridBagConstraints();
    gridConstraints.gridx = 0;
    gridConstraints.gridy = 0;
    buttonsPanel.add(startStopButton, gridConstraints);
    startStopButton.addActionListener(new ActionListener()
    {
      public void actionPerformed(ActionEvent e)
      {
        startStopButtonActionPerformed(e);
      }
    });

    exitButton.setText("Exit");
    gridConstraints = new GridBagConstraints();
    gridConstraints.gridx = 0;
    gridConstraints.gridy = 1;
    gridConstraints.insets = new Insets(10, 0, 0, 0);
    buttonsPanel.add(exitButton, gridConstraints);
    exitButton.addActionListener(new ActionListener()
    {
      public void actionPerformed(ActionEvent e)
      {
        exitButtonActionPerformed(e);
      }
    });

    pack();
    Dimension screenSize =
Toolkit.getDefaultToolkit().getScreenSize();
    setBounds((int) (0.5 * (screenSize.width - getWidth())),
(int) (0.5 * (screenSize.height - getHeight())), getWidth(),
getHeight());

    messageTextField.setText("Game Stopped");
    youFirstRadioButton.setEnabled(false);
    computerFirstRadioButton.setEnabled(false);
    randomRadioButton.setEnabled(false);
    smartRadioButton.setEnabled(false);
    // possible wins
    possibleWins[0] = "012";
    possibleWins[1] = "345";
```

```
    possibleWins[2] = "678";
    possibleWins[3] = "036";
    possibleWins[4] = "147";
    possibleWins[5] = "258";
    possibleWins[6] = "048";
    possibleWins[7] = "246";
    try
    {
      drawSound = Applet.newAudioClip(new URL("file:" +
"beep.wav"));
      winSound = Applet.newAudioClip(new URL("file:" +
"tada.wav"));
    }
    catch (Exception ex)
    {
      System.out.println("Error loading sound files");
    }
  }

  private void exitForm(WindowEvent evt)
  {
    System.exit(0);
  }

  private void boxTextFieldMousePressed(MouseEvent e)
  {
    if (canClick)
    {
      int i;
      // get upper left corner of clicked box
      Point p = e.getComponent().getLocation();
      // determine index based on p
      for (i = 0; i < 9; i++)
      {
        if (p.x == boxTextField[i].getX() && p.y ==
boxTextField[i].getY())
          break;
      }
      markClickedBox(i);
    }
  }

  private void
twoPlayersRadioButtonActionPerformed(ActionEvent e)
  {
    youFirstRadioButton.setEnabled(false);
    computerFirstRadioButton.setEnabled(false);
```

```
    randomRadioButton.setEnabled(false);
    smartRadioButton.setEnabled(false);
   }

  private void
onePlayerRadioButtonActionPerformed(ActionEvent e)
  {
    youFirstRadioButton.setEnabled(true);
    computerFirstRadioButton.setEnabled(true);
    randomRadioButton.setEnabled(true);
    smartRadioButton.setEnabled(true);
  }

  private void startStopButtonActionPerformed(ActionEvent e)
  {
    if (startStopButton.getText().equals("Start Game"))
    {
      startStopButton.setText("Stop Game");
      twoPlayersRadioButton.setEnabled(false);
      onePlayerRadioButton.setEnabled(false);
      youFirstRadioButton.setEnabled(false);
      computerFirstRadioButton.setEnabled(false);
      randomRadioButton.setEnabled(false);
      smartRadioButton.setEnabled(false);
      exitButton.setEnabled(false);
      xTurn = true;
      messageTextField.setText("X's Turn");
      // reset boxes
      for (int i = 0; i < 9; i++)
      {
        boxTextField[i].setText("");
        boxTextField[i].setBackground(Color.WHITE);
      }
      canClick = true;
      numberClicks = 0;
      gameOver = false;
      if (computerFirstRadioButton.isSelected())
        computerTurn();
    }
    else
    {
      startStopButton.setText("Start Game");
      if (!gameOver)
        messageTextField.setText("Game Stopped");
      twoPlayersRadioButton.setEnabled(true);
      onePlayerRadioButton.setEnabled(true);
      if (onePlayerRadioButton.isSelected())
```

```
      {
        youFirstRadioButton.setEnabled(true);
        computerFirstRadioButton.setEnabled(true);
        randomRadioButton.setEnabled(true);
        smartRadioButton.setEnabled(true);
      }
      exitButton.setEnabled(true);
      canClick = false;
    }
  }

  private void exitButtonActionPerformed(ActionEvent e)
  {
    System.exit(0);
  }

  private void markClickedBox(int i)
  {
    String whoWon = "";
    // if already clicked then exit
    if (!boxTextField[i].getText().equals(""))
      return;
    numberClicks++;
    if (xTurn)
    {
      boxTextField[i].setText("X");
      xTurn = false;
      messageTextField.setText("O's Turn");
    }
    else
    {
      boxTextField[i].setText("O");
      xTurn = true;
      messageTextField.setText("X's Turn");
    }
    // check for win - will establish a value for WhoWon
    whoWon = checkForWin();
    if (!whoWon.equals(""))
    {
      winSound.play();
      messageTextField.setText(whoWon + " wins!");
      gameOver = true;
      startStopButton.doClick();
      return;
    }
    else if (numberClicks == 9)
    {
```

```
      // draw
      drawSound.play();
      messageTextField.setText("It's a draw!");
      gameOver = true;
      startStopButton.doClick();
      return;
    }
    if (onePlayerRadioButton.isSelected())
      if ((xTurn && computerFirstRadioButton.isSelected())
|| (!xTurn && youFirstRadioButton.isSelected()))
        computerTurn();
  }

  private String checkForWin()
  {
    String winner = "";
    int[] boxNumber = new int[3];
    String[] mark = new String[3];
    // check all possible for wins
    for (int i = 0; i < 8; i++)
    {
      for (int j = 0; j < 3; j++)
      {
        boxNumber[j] =
Integer.valueOf(String.valueOf(possibleWins[i].charAt(j))).i
ntValue();
        mark[j] = boxTextField[boxNumber[j]].getText();
      }
      if (mark[0].equals(mark[1]) && mark[0].equals(mark[2])
&& mark[1].equals(mark[2]) && !mark[0].equals(""))
      {
        // we have a winner
        winner = mark[0];
        for (int j = 0; j < 3; j++)

boxTextField[boxNumber[j]].setBackground(Color.RED);
      }
    }
    return (winner);
  }

  private void computerTurn()
  {
    int selectedBox;
    int i, n;
    int j, k;
    String computerMark, playerMark, markToFind;
```

```
    int[] boxNumber = new int[3];
    String[] mark = new String[3];
    int emptyBox;
    int[] bestMoves = { 4, 0, 2, 6, 8, 1, 3, 5, 7 };

    if (randomRadioButton.isSelected())
    {
      // random logic
      // put mark in Nth available square
      n = myRandom.nextInt(9 - numberClicks) + 1;
      i = 0;
      for (selectedBox = 0; selectedBox < 9; selectedBox++)
      {
        if (boxTextField[selectedBox].getText().equals(""))
          i++;
        if (i == n)
          break;
      }
      // put mark in SelectedBox
      markClickedBox(selectedBox);
    }
    else
    {
      // smart computer
            // determine who has what mark
      if (computerFirstRadioButton.isSelected())
      {
        computerMark = "X";
        playerMark = "O";
      }
      else
      {
        computerMark = "O";
        playerMark = "X";
      }
      // Step 1 (K = 1) - check for win - see if two boxes
hold computer mark and one is empty
      // Step 2 (K = 2) - check for block - see if two boxes
hold player mark and one is empty
      for (k = 1; k <= 2; k++)
      {
        if (k == 1)
          markToFind = computerMark;
        else
          markToFind = playerMark;
        for (i = 0; i < 8; i++)
        {
```

```
          n = 0;
          emptyBox = 0;
          for (j = 0; j < 3; j++)
          {
            boxNumber[j] =
Integer.valueOf(String.valueOf(possibleWins[i].charAt(j))).i
ntValue();
            mark[j] = boxTextField[boxNumber[j]].getText();
            if (mark[j].equals(markToFind))
              n++;
            else if (mark[j].equals(""))
              emptyBox = boxNumber[j];
          }
          if (n == 2 && emptyBox != 0)
          {
            // mark empty box to win (K = 1) or block (K =
2)
            markClickedBox(emptyBox);
            return;
          }
        }
      }
      // Step 3 - find next best move
      for (i = 0; i < 9; i++)
      {
        if (boxTextField[bestMoves[i]].getText().equals(""))
        {
          markClickedBox(bestMoves[i]);
          return;
        }
      }
    }
  }

}
```

Bible Tic Tac Toe
Trivia Game Enhancement

A fun adaptation to the one player version of this game is to require the player to correctly answer a question before making a choice on the **Tic Tac Toe** grid. In the adaptation here, the player answers questions about the Bible. Other questions can be used, if desired.

We take you through the steps to make the program modifications. The finished program is saved as **BibleTicTacToe** in the **\CBGJava\CBGJava Projects** folder.

Enlarge Frame, Add New Controls

We need to add a few new controls – a non-editable text area (**questionTextArea**) to display the question, a text field control (**answerTestField**) for the user to type an answer, and a button to click to check the answer (**checkButton**

The new controls will be placed under the **Tic Tac Toe** grid. The modified frame **GridBagLayout** is:

	gridx = 0	gridx = 1
gridy = 0	**messageTextField**	**playersPanel**
gridy = 1	**gamePanel**	**firstPanel**
gridy = 2		**computerPanel**
gridy = 3		**buttonsPanel**
gridy = 4	**questionTextArea**	
gridy = 5	**answerTextField**	**checkButton**

Add the new controls to the frame with these properties:

questionTextArea:

size	450, 40
editable	false
font	Arial, Plain, Size 14
lineWrap	true
wrapWordStyle	true
gridx	0
gridy	4
gridwidth	2

answerTextField:

size	280, 25
font	Arial, Plain, Size 14
gridx	0
gridy	5
insets	0, 0, 10, 0

checkButton:

text	Check Answer
gridx	1
gridy	5
insets	10, 10, 10, 10

These controls are declared using:

```
JTextArea questionTextArea = new JTextArea();
JTextField answerTextField = new JTextField();
JButton checkButton = new JButton();
```

The controls are placed in the frame using this code:

```
questionTextArea = new JTextArea();
questionTextArea.setPreferredSize(new Dimension(450, 40));
questionTextArea.setFont(new Font("Arial", Font.PLAIN,
14));
questionTextArea.setLineWrap(true);
questionTextArea.setWrapStyleWord(true);
questionTextArea.setEditable(false);
gridConstraints = new GridBagConstraints();
gridConstraints.gridx = 0;
gridConstraints.gridy = 4;
gridConstraints.gridwidth = 2;
getContentPane().add(questionTextArea, gridConstraints);

answerTextField = new JTextField();
answerTextField.setPreferredSize(new Dimension(280, 25));
answerTextField.setFont(new Font("Arial", Font.PLAIN,
14));
gridConstraints = new GridBagConstraints();
gridConstraints.gridx = 0;
gridConstraints.gridy = 5;
gridConstraints.insets = new Insets(0, 0, 10, 0);
getContentPane().add(answerTextField, gridConstraints);

checkButton.setText("Check Answer");
gridConstraints = new GridBagConstraints();
gridConstraints.gridx = 1;
gridConstraints.gridy = 5;
gridConstraints.insets = new Insets(0, 0, 10, 0);
getContentPane().add(checkButton, gridConstraints);
checkButton.addActionListener(new ActionListener()
{
  public void actionPerformed(ActionEvent e)
  {
checkButtonActionPerformed(e);
  }
});
```

This code also adds a listeners for the button. Add this empty method with the other methods:

```
private void checkButtonActionPerformed(ActionEvent e)
{
}
```

Save and **Run** the program. You will see the modified frame:

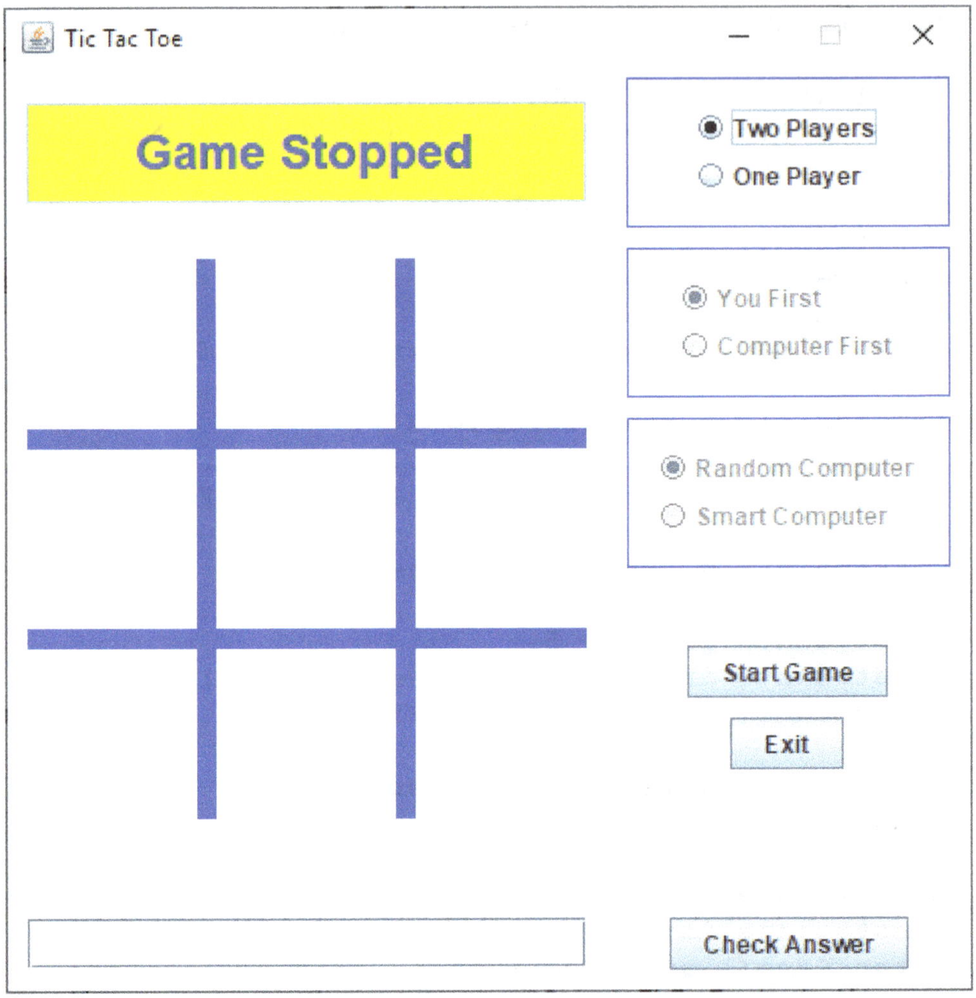

No question is seen since that control (**questionTextArea**) is blank.

We don't want the question/answer controls and **Check Answer** button to initially appear, so add these lines (to hide the controls) at the end of the frame constructor (must be after the `pack()` line of code):

```
questionTextArea.setVisible(false);
answerTextField.setVisible(false);
checkButton.setVisible(false);
```

Save and **Run** the program again to make sure the controls don't appear.

Add Questions and Answers

The questions and answers used in the modified game are stored in arrays (**qChoice** for the questions, **aChoice** for the answers). We use a variable **numberQuestions** that represents the number of question and answer pairs. As mentioned, we use Bible questions here – 73 of them. You can use your own questions by putting the needed information in the two arrays and adjusting **numberQuestions**. And, the program assumes that answers (and questions) are in all upper case letters.

Add the needed variable declarations:

```
int numberQuestions = 73;
String[] qChoice = new String[numberQuestions];
String[] aChoice = new String[numberQuestions];
```

Add this code to the end of the frame constructor method; you probably want to copy and paste these lines into your code, rather than type them:

```
numberQuestions = 73;
qChoice[0] = "WHAT INSTRUMENT WILL BE HEARD AT JESUS' 2ND
COMING?";
aChoice[0] = "TRUMPET";
qChoice[1] = "WHO DID JESUS SAY SO LOVED THE WORLD THAT HE
GAVE IS ONLY SON?";
aChoice[1] = "GOD";
qChoice[2] = "WHAT NAME DID THE ANGEL TELL MARY TO GIVE TO
HER SON?";
aChoice[2] = "JESUS";
qChoice[3] = "WHO DID GOD INSTRUCT TO BUILD AN ARK BEFORE
THE FLOOD?";
aChoice[3] = "NOAH";
qChoice[4] = "WHAT PERSON DID GOD ASK TO OFFER HIS ONLY
SON AS A SACRIFICE?";
aChoice[4] = "ABRAHAM";
qChoice[5] = "WHO DREAMED THAT ANGELS WERE CLIMBING UP AND
DOWN A LADDER?";
aChoice[5] = "JACOB";
qChoice[6] = "WHICH OF THE TWELVE ISRAELITE BROTHERS WAS
SOLD INTO SLAVERY?";
aChoice[6] = "JOSEPH";
qChoice[7] = "WHAT JUDGE WON A BATTLE WITH ONLY 300
UNARMED MEN?";
aChoice[7] = "GIDEON";
qChoice[8] = "WHAT PROPHET WAS DEDICATED TO THE LORD AT
BIRTH BY HIS MOTHER HANNAH?";
```

```
aChoice[8] = "SAMUEL";
qChoice[9] = "WHAT KINGWAS 'A MAN AFTER GOD'S OWN
HEART?'";
aChoice[9] = "DAVID";
qChoice[10] = "WHAT PROPHET WENT TO DAVID WHEN HE
SINNED?";
aChoice[10] = "NATHAN";
qChoice[11] = "WHAT PROPHET RECEIVED THE MANTLE FROM
ELIJAH?";
aChoice[11] = "ELISHA";
qChoice[12] = "WHAT BROTHER OF MOSES BECAME A PRIEST?";
aChoice[12] = "AARON";
qChoice[13] = "WHAT GOOD KING RULED AFTER HIS EVIL FATHER
AHAZ?";
aChoice[13] = "HEZEKIAH";
qChoice[14] = "WHAT FAMOUS NAME DID GOD GIVE TO JACOB?";
aChoice[14] = "ISRAEL";
qChoice[15] = "WHICH OF SAUL'S SONS DID DAVID LOVE AS A
BROTHER?";
aChoice[15] = "JONATHAN";
qChoice[16] = "WHICH OF ADAM AND EVE'S SONS SLEW HIS
BROTHER?";
aChoice[16] = "CAIN";
qChoice[17] = "WHICH OF ADAM AND EVE'S SONS SACRIFICED A
SHEEP TO GOD?";
aChoice[17] = "ABEL";
qChoice[18] = "THROUGH WHICH OF ABRAHAM'S SONS WAS GOD'S
COVENANT PROMISED?";
aChoice[18] = "ISAAC";
qChoice[19] = "WHAT WOMAN CAME ON A CAMEL TO MARRY
ISAAC?";
aChoice[19] = "REBEKAH";
qChoice[20] = "WHAT WOMAN GAVE BIRTH TO ISAAC IN HER OLD
AGE?";
aChoice[20] = "SARAH";
qChoice[21] = "WHAT WOMAN BECAME THE EARTHLY MOTHER OF THE
SAVIOUR?";
aChoice[21] = "MARY";
qChoice[22] = "WHO WAS THE MOTHER OF JOHN THE BAPTIST?";
aChoice[22] = "ELISABETH";
qChoice[23] = "WHICH WOMAN COMPLAINED THAT HER SISTER
WASN'T HELPING?";
aChoice[23] = "MARTHA";
qChoice[24] = "WHICH OF JESUS' APOSTLES BETRAYED HIM WITH
A KISS?";
aChoice[24] = "JUDAS";
```

```
qChoice[25] = "WHAT APOSTLE GAVE HIS WITNESS TO KING
AGRIPPA?";
aChoice[25] = "PAUL";
qChoice[26] = "WHO ACCOMPANIED PAUL ON HIS 2ND MISSIONARY
TRIP?";
aChoice[26] = "SILAS";
qChoice[27] = "WHAT KING WAS RULING PALESTINE WHEN JESUS
WAS BORN?";
aChoice[27] = "HEROD";
qChoice[28] = "WHO CAME TO JESUS BY NIGHT TO ASK HIM
QUESTIONS?";
aChoice[28] = "NICODEMUS";
qChoice[29] = "WHO ASKED JESUS TO SHOW THEM THE FATHER?";
aChoice[29] = "PHILIP";
qChoice[30] = "WHAT IS THE NAME OF THE ARCHANGEL?";
aChoice[30] = "MICHAEL";
qChoice[31] = "WHAT WAS PETER'S NAME BEFORE JESUS CHANGED
IT?";
aChoice[31] = "SIMON";
qChoice[32] = "WHO WASHED HIS HANDS JUST BEFORE JESUS WAS
CRUCIFIED?";
aChoice[32] = "PILATE";
qChoice[33] = "WHO WAS THE ROMAN EMPEROR AT THE TIME OF
JESUS' DEATH?";
aChoice[33] = "CAESAR";
qChoice[34] = "WHO WAS ALMOST PURSUADED TO BECOME A
CHRISTIAN?";
aChoice[34] = "AGRIPPA";
qChoice[35] = "WHO WAS TRAINED BY AQUILLA AND PRICILLA?";
aChoice[35] = "APPOLOS";
qChoice[36] = "WHO WENT WITH PAUL ON HIS 1ST MISSIONARY
TRIP?";
aChoice[36] = "BARNABAS";
qChoice[37] = "WHO WAS GIVEN A REVELATION ON THE ISLE OF
PATMOS?";
aChoice[37] = "JOHN";
qChoice[38] = "WHERE DID MARY AND MARTHA AND LAZARUS
LIVE?";
aChoice[38] = "BETHANY";
qChoice[39] = "IN WHAT TOWN WAS THE STABLE WHERE JESUS WAS
BORN?";
aChoice[39] = "BETHLEHEM";
qChoice[40] = "ON WHAT ROAD DID JESUS APPEAR TO TWO
DISCIPLES?";
aChoice[40] = "EMMAUS";
qChoice[41] = "WHOSE WALLS DID JOSHUA MARCH AROUND FOR 7
DAYS?";
```

```
aChoice[41] = "JERICHO";
qChoice[42] = "ON WHAT ROAD DID THE SAMARITAN FIND AN
INJURED MAN?";
aChoice[42] = "JERICHO";
qChoice[43] = "WHERE DID LOT LIVE BEFORE THE CITY WAS
DESTROYED?";
aChoice[43] = "SODOM";
qChoice[44] = "IN WHAT COUNTRY DID JESUS MEET A WOMAN BY A
WELL?";
aChoice[44] = "SAMARIA";
qChoice[45] = "JESUS LIVED AS A YOUNG BOY IN WHAT
VILLAGE?";
aChoice[45] = "NAZARETH";
qChoice[46] = "WHERE DID PETER LIVE WHILE HE WAS A
FISHERMAN?";
aChoice[46] = "CAPERNAUM";
qChoice[47] = "JOHN ADDRESSED HIS 7TH LETTER TO WHAT
CITY?";
aChoice[47] = "LAODICEA";
qChoice[48] = "WHERE DID PAUL LIVE BEFORE BECOMING AN
APOSTLE?";
aChoice[48] = "TARSUS";
qChoice[49] = "WHAT WAS THE NAME OF THE VERY FIRST
GARDEN?";
aChoice[49] = "EDEN";
qChoice[50] = "IN WHAT COUNTRY WAS DANIEL IN A LIONS'
DEN?";
aChoice[50] = "BABYLONIA";
qChoice[51] = "PHAROAH WAS THE RULER OF WHAT COUNTRY?";
aChoice[51] = "EGYPT";
qChoice[52] = "WHAT CITY DID GOD TELL JONAH TO GO TO?";
aChoice[52] = "NINEVEH";
qChoice[53] = "ON WHAT MOUNTAIN DID NOAH'S ARK COME TO
REST?";
aChoice[53] = "ARARAT";
qChoice[54] = "WHAT COUNTRY IS FAMOUS FOR ITS CEDAR
TREES?";
aChoice[54] = "LEBANON";
qChoice[55] = "WHAT LOCATION IS CALLED 'THE PLACE OF THE
SKULL?'";
aChoice[55] = "GOLGOTHA";
qChoice[56] = "WHAT GREEK WORD MEANS THE SAME AS
'MESSIAH?'";
aChoice[56] = "CHRIST";
qChoice[57] = "WHAT WERE JESUS' FOLLOWERS CALLED IN
ANTIOCH?";
aChoice[57] = "CHRISTIANS";
```

```
qChoice[58] = "WHAT DID JESUS SAY HE WOULD BUILD ON A
ROCK?";
aChoice[58] = "CHURCH";
qChoice[59] = "WHAT WAS WRITTEN ON TWO TABLES OF STONE?";
aChoice[59] = "COMMANDMENTS";
qChoice[60] = "WHAT WAS THE AGREEMENT GOD MADE WITH MAN
CALLED?";
aChoice[60] = "COVENANT";
qChoice[61] = "WHAT WILL GOD DO WHEN YOU CONFESS YOUR
SINS?";
aChoice[61] = "FORGIVE";
qChoice[62] = "WHAT IS A NON-JEWISH PERSON CALLED?";
aChoice[62] = "GENTILE";
qChoice[63] = "WHAT IS TO BE PREACHED TO ALL THE WORLD?";
aChoice[63] = "GOSPEL";
qChoice[64] = "WHAT RETURNS TO GOD UPON A PERSON'S
DEATH?";
aChoice[64] = "SPIRIT";
qChoice[65] = "WHAT IS THE SEVENTH DAY OF THE WEEK
CALLED?";
aChoice[65] = "SABBATH";
qChoice[66] = "WHAT IS THE FIRST FRUIT OF THE SPIRIT?";
aChoice[66] = "LOVE";
qChoice[67] = "WHAT WAS A PERSON WHO TOLD THE FUTURE?";
aChoice[67] = "PROPHET";
qChoice[68] = "WHERE WAS GOD WORSHIPPED IN THE
WILDERNESS?";
aChoice[68] = "TABERNACLE";
qChoice[69] = "WHERE DID JESUS CAST OUT THE MONEY
CHANGERS?";
aChoice[69] = "TEMPLE";
qChoice[70] = "WHERE DID JESUS STAND UP AND READ FROM
ISAIAH?";
aChoice[70] = "SYNAGOGUE";
qChoice[71] = "WHAT DID JESUS ILLUSTRATE WITH A MUSTARD
SEED?";
aChoice[71] = "FAITH";
qChoice[72] = "WHAT INSTRUMENT DID DAVID PLAY FOR KING
SAUL?";
aChoice[72] = "HARP";
```

Save and **Run** the program to make sure there are no errors. No question (or answer) will appear. We fix that next.

Display Question

Questions should appear during the one player game when it's not the computer's turn. The first place this could happen is when the game starts.

When the game starts, if it is a one player game, we need to display the controls that display the question (and allow checking the answer). In addition, if the player goes first, we need to display a question. If it is a two player game, we need to hide the question/answer controls.

Make the shaded changes to the **startStopButtonActionPerformed** method to incorporate these steps:

```
private void startStopButtonActionPerformed(ActionEvent e)
{
  if (startStopButton.getText().equals("Start Game"))
  {
    startStopButton.setText("Stop Game");
    twoPlayersRadioButton.setEnabled(false);
    onePlayerRadioButton.setEnabled(false);
    youFirstRadioButton.setEnabled(false);
    computerFirstRadioButton.setEnabled(false);
    randomRadioButton.setEnabled(false);
    smartRadioButton.setEnabled(false);
    exitButton.setEnabled(false);
    xTurn = true;
    messageTextField.setText("X's Turn");
    // reset boxes
    for (int i = 0; i < 9; i++)
    {
      boxTextField[i].setText("");
      boxTextField[i].setBackground(Color.WHITE);
    }
    canClick = true;
    numberClicks = 0;
    gameOver = false;
    if (onePlayerRadioButton.isSelected())
    {
      // clear question/answer
      questionTextArea.setText("");
      answerTextField.setText("");
      questionTextArea.setVisible(true);
      answerTextField.setVisible(true);
      checkButton.setVisible(true);
      if (computerFirstRadioButton.isSelected())
        computerTurn();
```

```
        else
          askQuestion();
      }
      else
      {
        questionTextArea.setVisible(false);
        answerTextField.setVisible(false);
        checkButton.setVisible(false);
      }
    }
    else
    {
      startStopButton.setText("Start Game");
      if (!gameOver)
        messageTextField.setText("Game Stopped");
      twoPlayersRadioButton.setEnabled(true);
      onePlayerRadioButton.setEnabled(true);
      if (onePlayerRadioButton.isSelected())
      {
        youFirstRadioButton.setEnabled(true);
        computerFirstRadioButton.setEnabled(true);
        randomRadioButton.setEnabled(true);
        smartRadioButton.setEnabled(true);
      }
      exitButton.setEnabled(true);
      canClick = false;
    }
  }
```

In a one player game, the controls are displayed (after clearing them). If the player goes first, a question is displayed using the **askQuestion** method. In the two player game, the new controls are hidden.

Add the **askQuestion** method to the program:

```
private void askQuestion()
{
  // pick question at random
  tries = 0;
  correctAnswer = false;
  questionIndex = myRandom.nextInt(numberQuestions);
  questionTextArea.setText(qChoice[questionIndex]);
  answerTextField.setText("");
}
```

A variable **tries** keeps track of how many guesses at the answer have been made and a variable **correctAnswer** tells us if the entered answer is correct (initially **false**). A random question (**questionIndex**) is selected and the corresponding question displayed. You need to add the corresponding declarations:

```
int tries;
boolean correctAnswer;
int questionIndex;
```

Save and **Run** the program. Choose a one player game, where you go first. Click **Start Game** and a random question will appear:

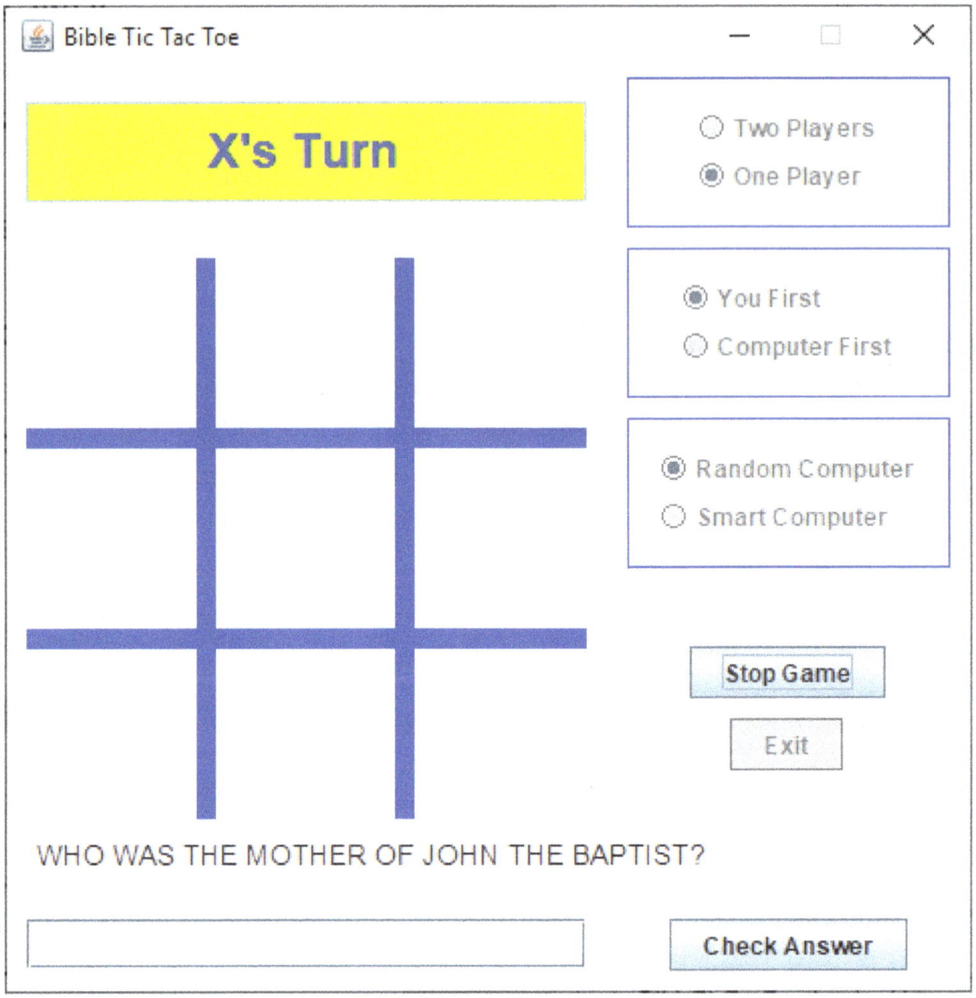

We have no logic to check an answer yet. All we can do is click **Stop Game**. When we do this, we want any displayed question/answer to disappear. Make the shaded changes to the **startStopButtonActionPerformed** method:

```
private void startStopButtonActionPerformed(ActionEvent e)
{
  if (startStopButton.getText().equals("Start Game"))
  {
    startStopButton.setText("Stop Game");
    twoPlayersRadioButton.setEnabled(false);
    onePlayerRadioButton.setEnabled(false);
    youFirstRadioButton.setEnabled(false);
    computerFirstRadioButton.setEnabled(false);
    randomRadioButton.setEnabled(false);
    smartRadioButton.setEnabled(false);
    exitButton.setEnabled(false);
    xTurn = true;
    messageTextField.setText("X's Turn");
    // reset boxes
    for (int i = 0; i < 9; i++)
    {
      boxTextField[i].setText("");
      boxTextField[i].setBackground(Color.WHITE);
    }
    canClick = true;
    numberClicks = 0;
    gameOver = false;
    if (onePlayerRadioButton.isSelected())
    {
      // clear question/answer
      questionTextArea.setText("");
      answerTextField.setText("");
      questionTextArea.setVisible(true);
      answerTextField.setVisible(true);
      checkButton.setVisible(true);
      if (computerFirstRadioButton.isSelected())
        computerTurn();
      else
        askQuestion();
    }
    else
    {
      questionTextArea.setVisible(false);
      answerTextField.setVisible(false);
      checkButton.setVisible(false);
    }
  }
```

```
    else
    {
      startStopButton.setText("Start Game");
      if (!gameOver)
        messageTextField.setText("Game Stopped");
      twoPlayersRadioButton.setEnabled(true);
      onePlayerRadioButton.setEnabled(true);
      if (onePlayerRadioButton.isSelected())
      {
        youFirstRadioButton.setEnabled(true);
        computerFirstRadioButton.setEnabled(true);
        randomRadioButton.setEnabled(true);
        smartRadioButton.setEnabled(true);
      }
      exitButton.setEnabled(true);
      canClick = false;
      // clear question/answer
      questionTextArea.setText("");
      answerTextField.setText("");
    }
  }
```

Save and **Run** the program. Make sure the new stop code works as advertised.

We're nearly ready to allow typing answers to the questions and checking if they are right. Before doing this, we need to recognize there is one other place in the code where we need to display a question – after the computer takes a turn. This is a very simple two line addition (shaded code) to the **markClickedBox** method:

```
  private void markClickedBox(int i)
  {
    String whoWon = "";
    // if already clicked then exit
    if (!boxTextField[i].getText().equals(""))
      return;
    numberClicks++;
    if (xTurn)
    {
      boxTextField[i].setText("X");
      xTurn = false;
      messageTextField.setText("O's Turn");
    }
    else
    {
      boxTextField[i].setText("O");
      xTurn = true;
      messageTextField.setText("X's Turn");
```

```
    }
    // check for win - will establish a value for WhoWon
    whoWon = checkForWin();
    if (!whoWon.equals(""))
    {
      winSound.play();
      messageTextField.setText(whoWon + " wins!");
      gameOver = true;
      startStopButton.doClick();
      return;
    }
    else if (numberClicks == 9)
    {
      // draw
      drawSound.play();
      messageTextField.setText("It's a draw!");
      gameOver = true;
      startStopButton.doClick();
      return;
    }
    if (onePlayerRadioButton.isSelected())
      if ((xTurn && computerFirstRadioButton.isSelected())
|| (!xTurn && youFirstRadioButton.isSelected()))
        computerTurn();
      else
        askQuestion();
}
```

When play switches to the player in a one player game, another random question is displayed using the **askQuestion** method.

Answer Question

Once a question is displayed, a correct answer to the question must be typed before the player is allowed to make a **Tic Tac Toe** selection in the grid. To make this task a bit easier, with each incorrect guess, the computer will give the player a hint to the answer by providing one of the letters.

The player types an answer and clicks the **Check Answer** button. When this occurs, we follow these steps:

- Increment **tries** variable by one.
- Convert user input (**yourAnswer**) to all upper case.
- Compare **yourAnswer** to correct answer.
- If **yourAnswer** is correct, set **correctAnswer** to **true** and inform the player to click the grid.
- If **yourAnswer** is incorrect, show the player the first **tries** letters in the correct answer.

Notice how we use the **tries** variable to decide how many letters to show the player as a hint.

The code behind this logic is placed in the **checkButtonActionPerformed** method. Add this code to the currently empty method:

```
private void checkButtonActionPerformed(ActionEvent e)
{
  String yourAnswer;
  //check for correct answer
  tries++;
  if (tries > aChoice[questionIndex].length())
    tries = aChoice[questionIndex].length();
  yourAnswer = answerTextField.getText().toUpperCase();
  if (yourAnswer.equals(aChoice[questionIndex]))
  {
    answerTextField.setText(yourAnswer + " - CORRECT.
CLICK GRID.");
    correctAnswer = true;
  }
  else

answerTextField.setText(aChoice[questionIndex].substring(0
, tries));
}
```

We make sure **tries** never exceeds the length of the correct answer.

One last change and we're done. While the player is answering a question, we want to make sure the grid cannot be clicked. Make the shaded changes to the **boxTextFieldMousePressed** method:

```
private void boxTextFieldMousePressed(MouseEvent e)
{
  if (canClick)
  {
    // if one player game, cannot click if correct answer
has not been entered
    if (onePlayerRadioButton.isSelected() && correctAnswer
== false)
       return;
    int i;
    // get upper left corner of clicked box
    Point p = e.getComponent().getLocation();
    // determine index based on p
    for (i = 0; i < 9; i++)
    {
      if (p.x == boxTextField[i].getX() && p.y ==
boxTextField[i].getY())
         break;
    }
    markClickedBox(i);
  }
}
```

With the added lines, the grid cannot be clicked in a one player game until the question has been correctly answered (**correctAnswer** is **true**).

Play the Game

The **Bible Tic Tac Toe** game is complete. Again, it plays just like the one player version of the **Tic Tac Toe** game with the only difference being the player needs to answer a question before clicking the grid. Notice the player will always get a turn because eventually (after checking the answer numerous times), the player will be given the correct answer. Let's try it.

Save and **Run** the program. Choose the one player option with you going first – I chose a **Smart** computer. Click **Start Game**. My window shows (you will probably see a different question):

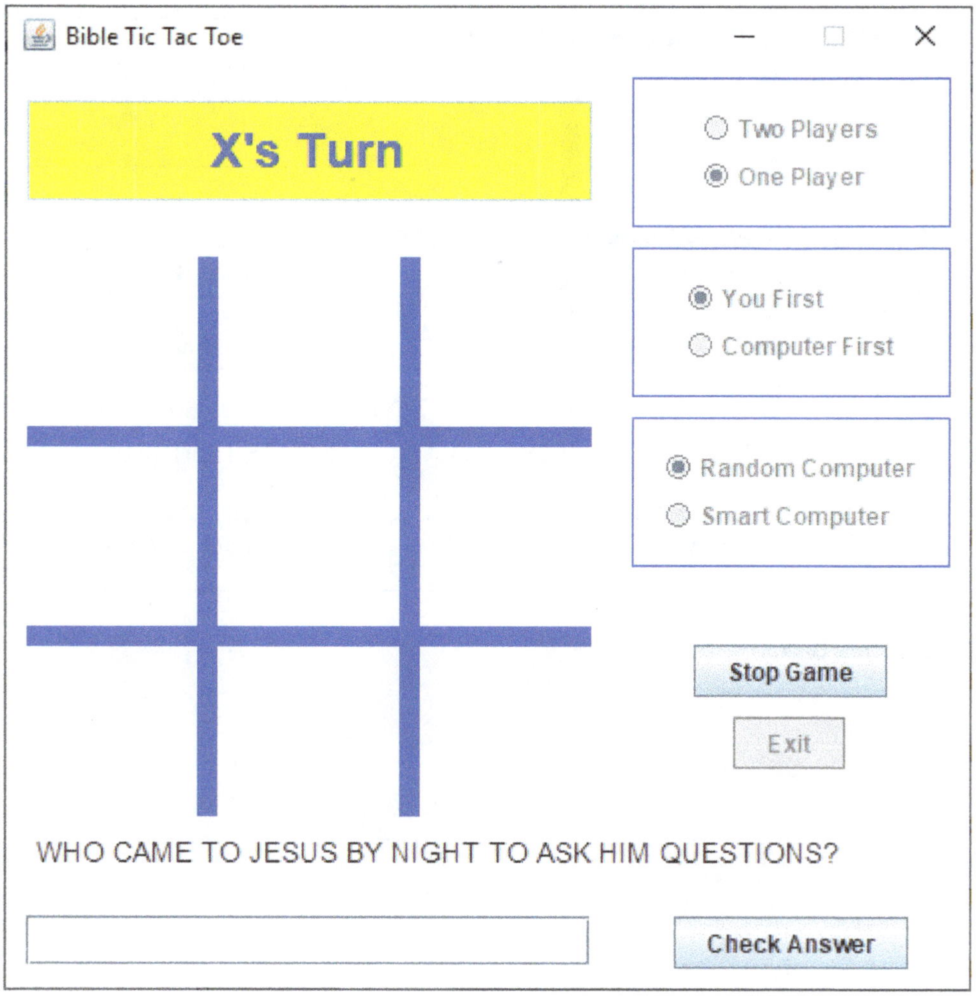

I know the answer. I type **NICODEMUS** and click **Check Answer** to see:

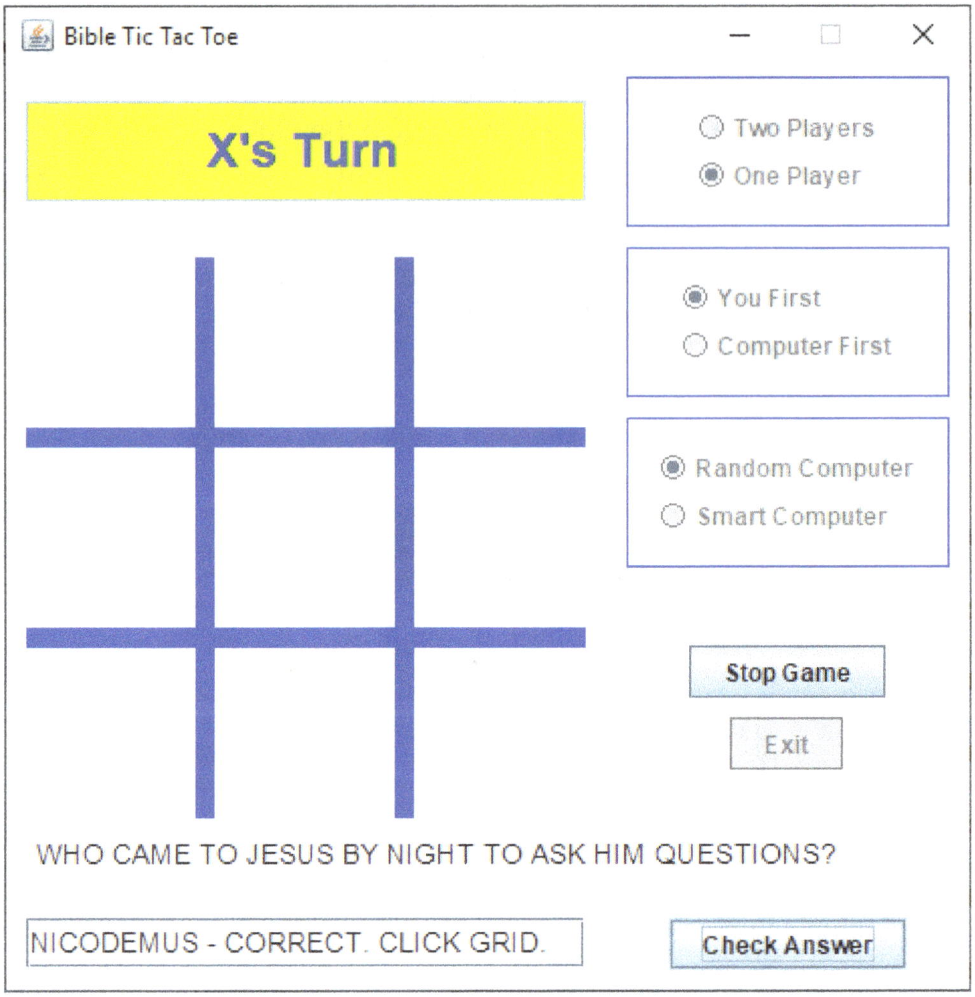

I click the middle box.

An X appears. The computer takes a turn (upper right corner) and I have another question to answer:

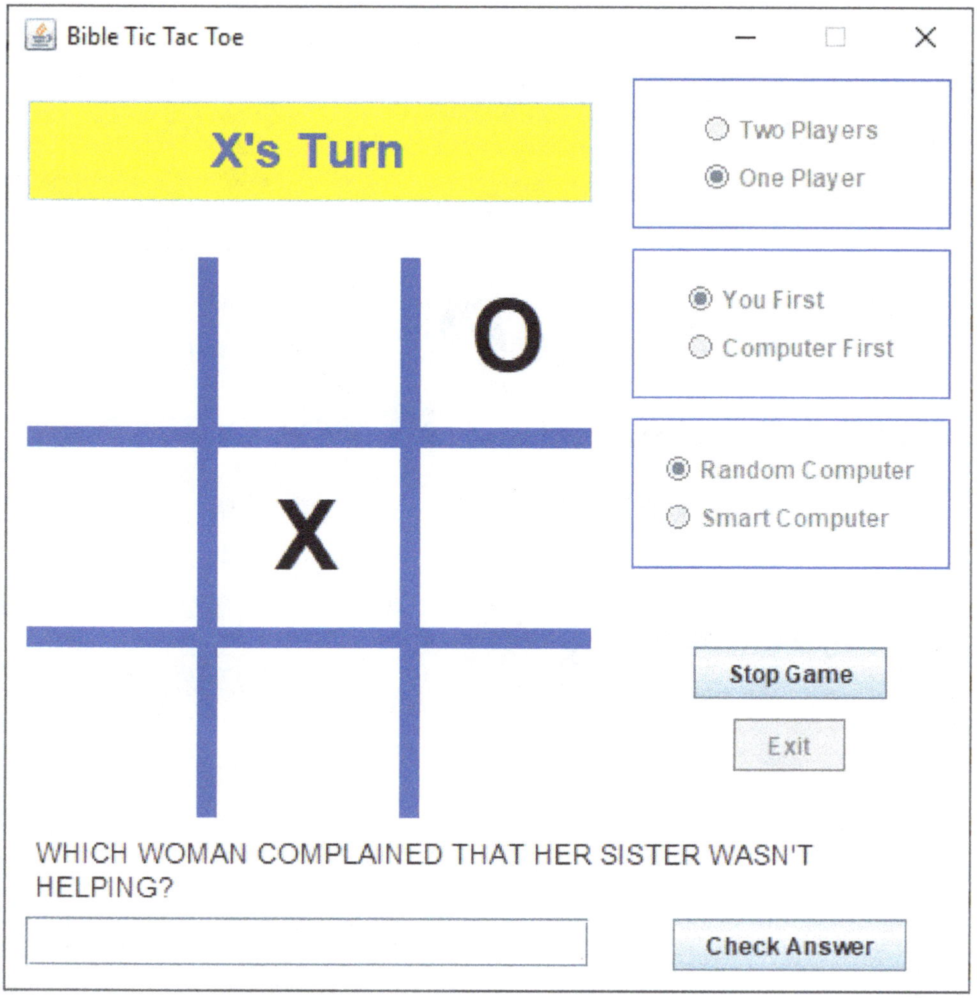

I don't know the answer.

I click **Check Answer** three times to get a clue that makes sense (the first three letters):

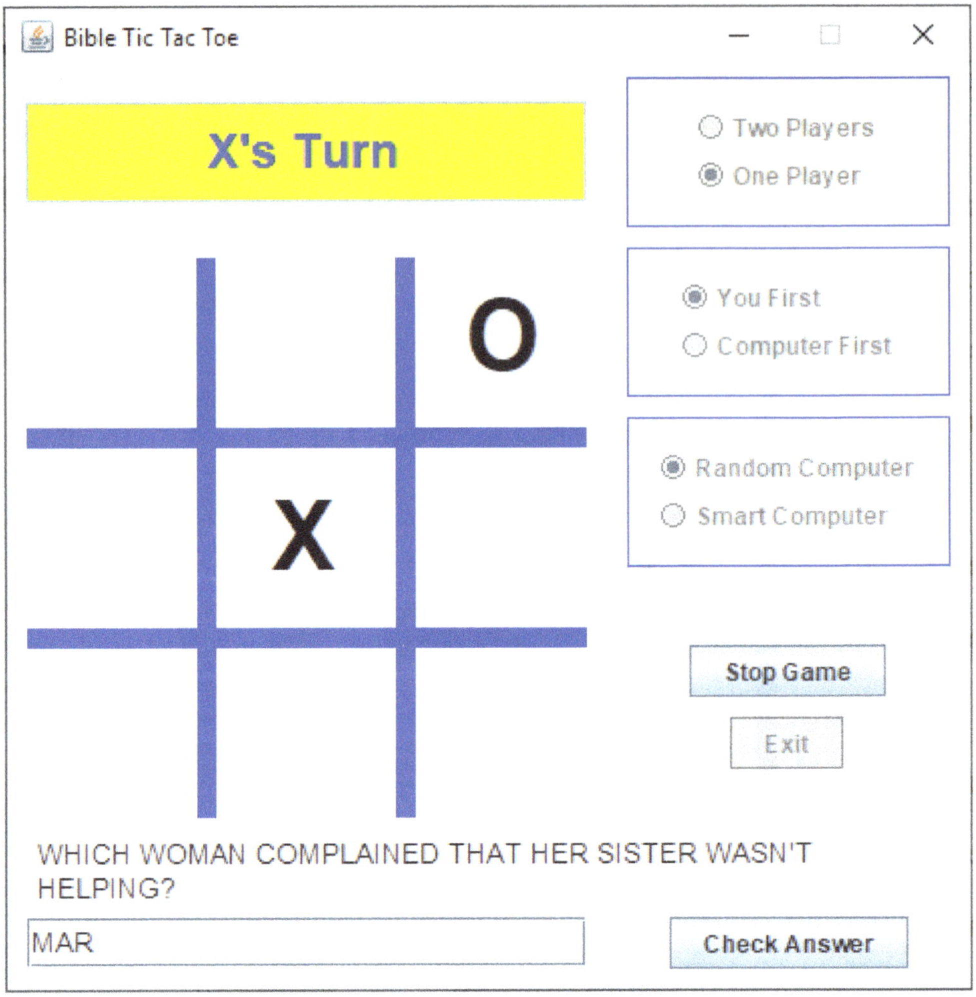

This helps. I think the answer is **MARTHA**.

I was right! I click the upper left corner of the grid. The computer takes another turn (lower right corner) and I have another question to answer:

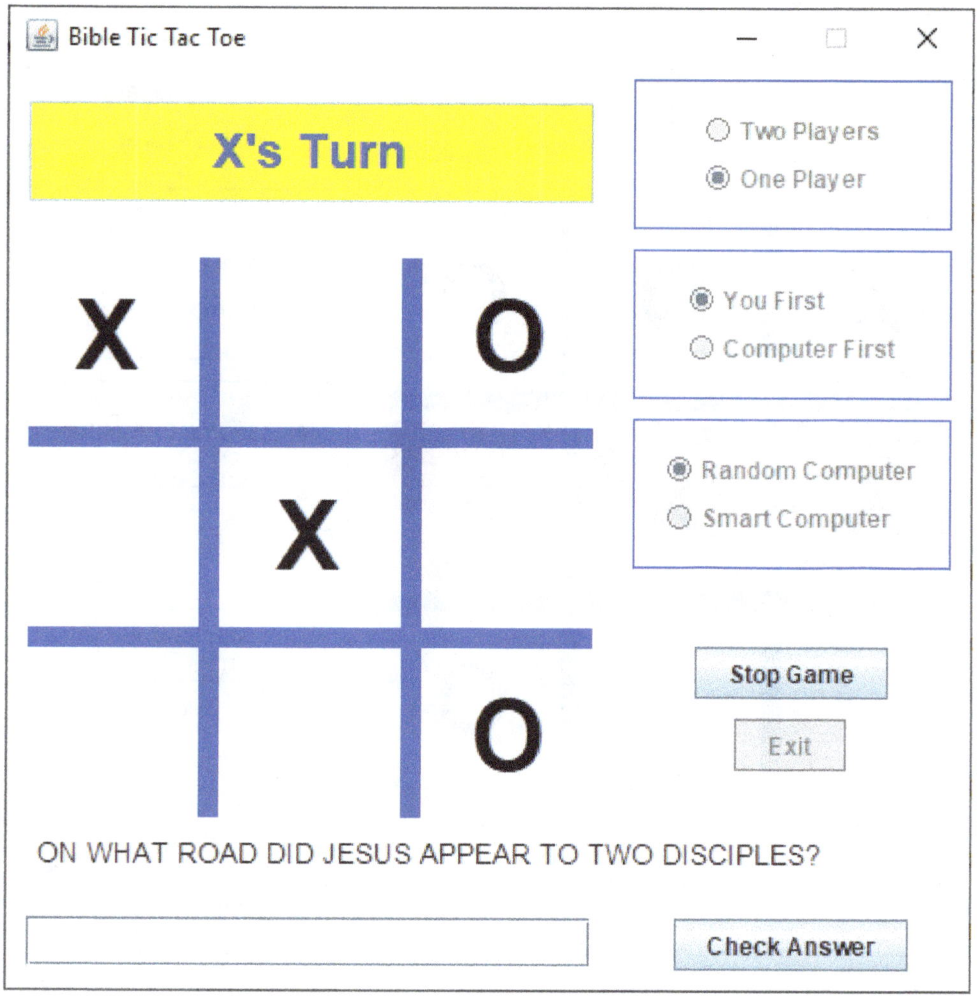

I continued playing until I won:

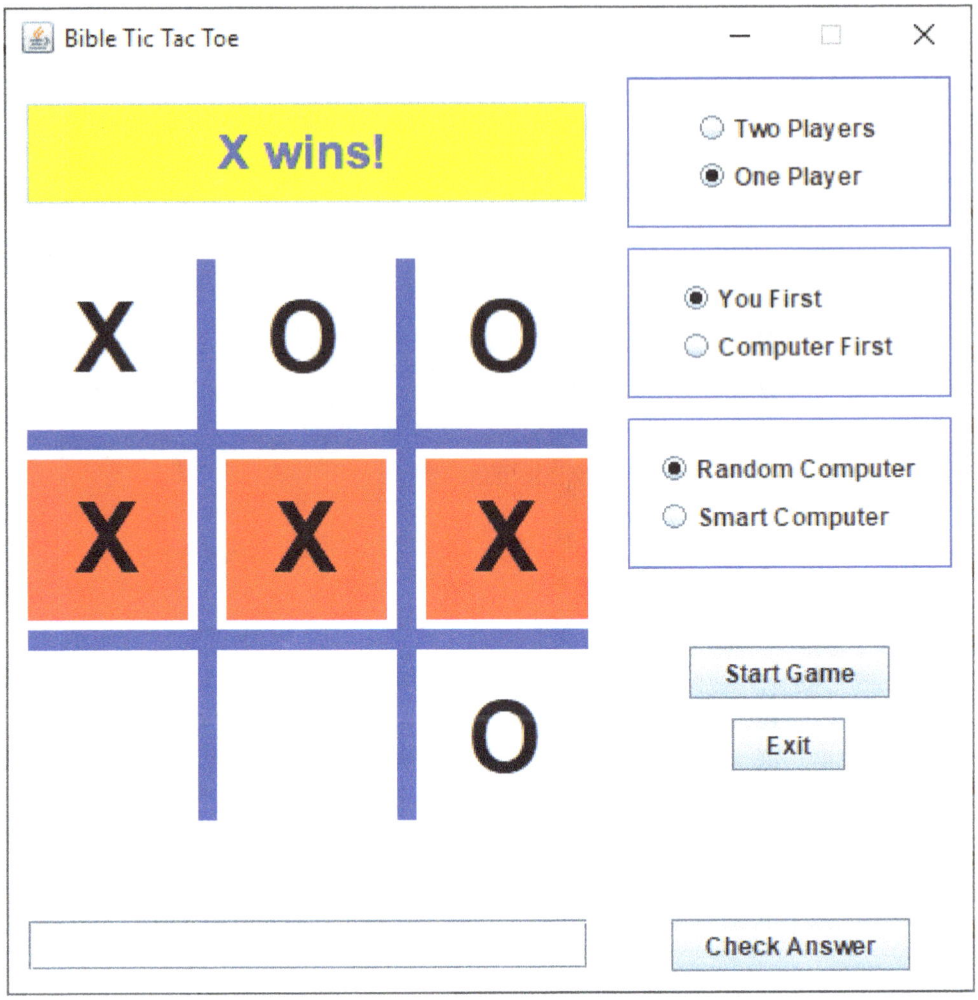

One Last Change

We said the game was complete, but not quite. To give a more pleasant appearance, let's add some biblical graphics at the bottom of the form.

There are seven graphics included in the **\CBGJava\CBGJava Projects\Bible TicTacToe** folder:

Daniel.jpg

Elijah.jpg

Noah.jpg

Prodigal.jpg

Shepherd.jpg

Woman.jpg

Bible.jpg

We will draw these along the bottom of the frame.

Declare a panel control (**displayPanel**) to host these graphics:

```
GraphicsPanel displayPanel = new GraphicsPanel();
```

This uses a **GraphicsPanel** class to allow drawing of the images. Add this object to your code after the **TicTacToe** class:

```
class GraphicsPanel extends JPanel
{
  public GraphicsPanel()
  {
  }
  public void paintComponent(Graphics g)
  {
    Graphics2D g2D = (Graphics2D) g;
    super.paintComponent(g2D);
    Image myImage = new
ImageIcon("Prodigal.jpg").getImage();
    g2D.drawImage(myImage, 0, 0, 70, 100, this);
    myImage = new ImageIcon("Woman.jpg").getImage();
    g2D.drawImage(myImage, 70, 0, 70, 100, this);
    myImage = new ImageIcon("Daniel.jpg").getImage();
    g2D.drawImage(myImage, 140, 0, 70, 100, this);
    myImage = new ImageIcon("Bible.jpg").getImage();
    g2D.drawImage(myImage, 210, 0, 70, 100, this);
    myImage = new ImageIcon("Noah.jpg").getImage();
    g2D.drawImage(myImage, 280, 0, 70, 100, this);
    myImage = new ImageIcon("Shepherd.jpg").getImage();
    g2D.drawImage(myImage, 350, 0, 70, 100, this);
    myImage = new ImageIcon("Elijah.jpg").getImage();
    g2D.drawImage(myImage, 420, 0, 70, 100, this);

    g2D.dispose();
  }
}
```

By using this **GraphicsPanel** class, the images are persistent (or always on) the frame.

Now, add the panel at the bottom of the frame using this code in the frame constructor:

```
displayPanel.setPreferredSize(new Dimension(490, 100));
displayPanel.setBackground(Color.WHITE);
gridConstraints = new GridBagConstraints();
gridConstraints.gridx = 0;
gridConstraints.gridy = 6;
gridConstraints.gridwidth = 2;
gridConstraints.insets = new Insets(0, 0, 10, 0);
getContentPane().add(displayPanel, gridConstraints);
```

Lastly, draw the graphics on the panel using this line of code (put it in the frame constructor after the **pack()** statement; I put this right before the code defining the questions):

```
displayPanel.repaint();
```

Save and **Run** the program to see the graphics:

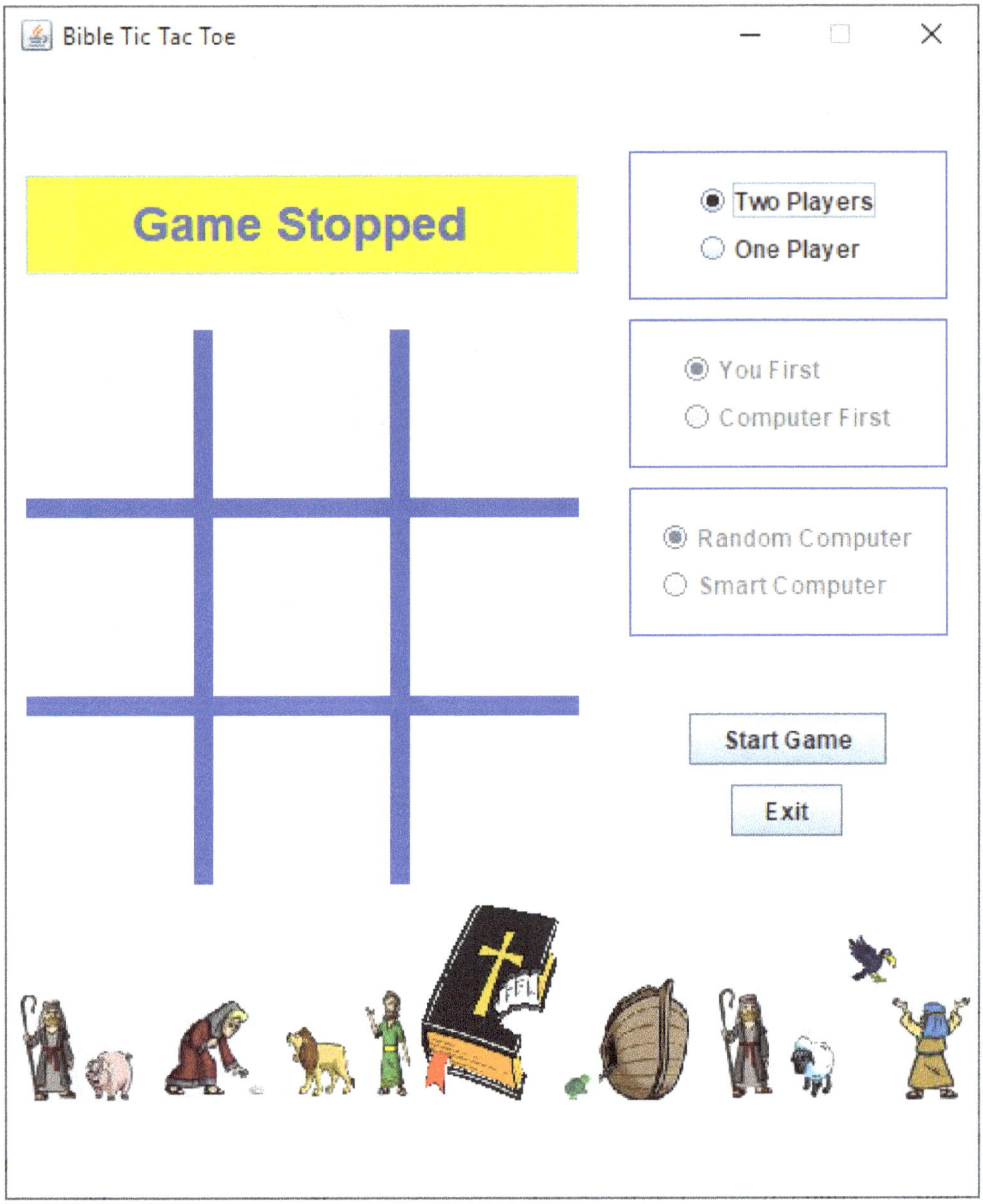

Now, we're really done – enjoy the game!

Bible Tic Tac Toe Project Review

The **Bible Tic Tac Toe** game project is now complete. Save and run the project and make sure it works as promised. Check that all options work correctly.

If there are errors in your implementation, go back over the steps of frame and code design. Go over the developed code – make sure you understand how different parts of the project were coded. As mentioned in the beginning of this chapter, the completed project is saved as **BibleTicTacToe** in the **\CBGJava\CBGJava Projects** folder.

While completing this project, new concepts and skills you should have gained include:

- Proper steps in project design.
- Capabilities and use of many Java controls.
- How to use general methods and methods.
- How to give the computer intelligence in playing games.

4

Bible Match Game Project

Review and Preview

The next project we build is a **Bible Match Game**. This is a one or two player game - play against a friend, the computer, or play alone. Ten pairs of pictures are hidden on a playing board. The object of the game is to find matching pairs by remembering picture locations. We'll see how to generate an array of random integers and how to use the timer object for delays.

Bible Match Game Project Preview

In this chapter, we will build a **Bible Match Game**. Ten pairs of pictures are hidden on a playing board. The object is to find matching pairs. Turns alternate between players – an extra turn is earned with each match. The version we build here allows two players to compete against each other or to have a single player play a solitaire version or compete against the computer.

The finished project is saved as **MatchGame** in the **\CBGJava\CBGJava Projects** project group. Start NetBeans (or your IDE). Open the specified project group. Make **MatchGame** the selected project. Run the project. You will see:

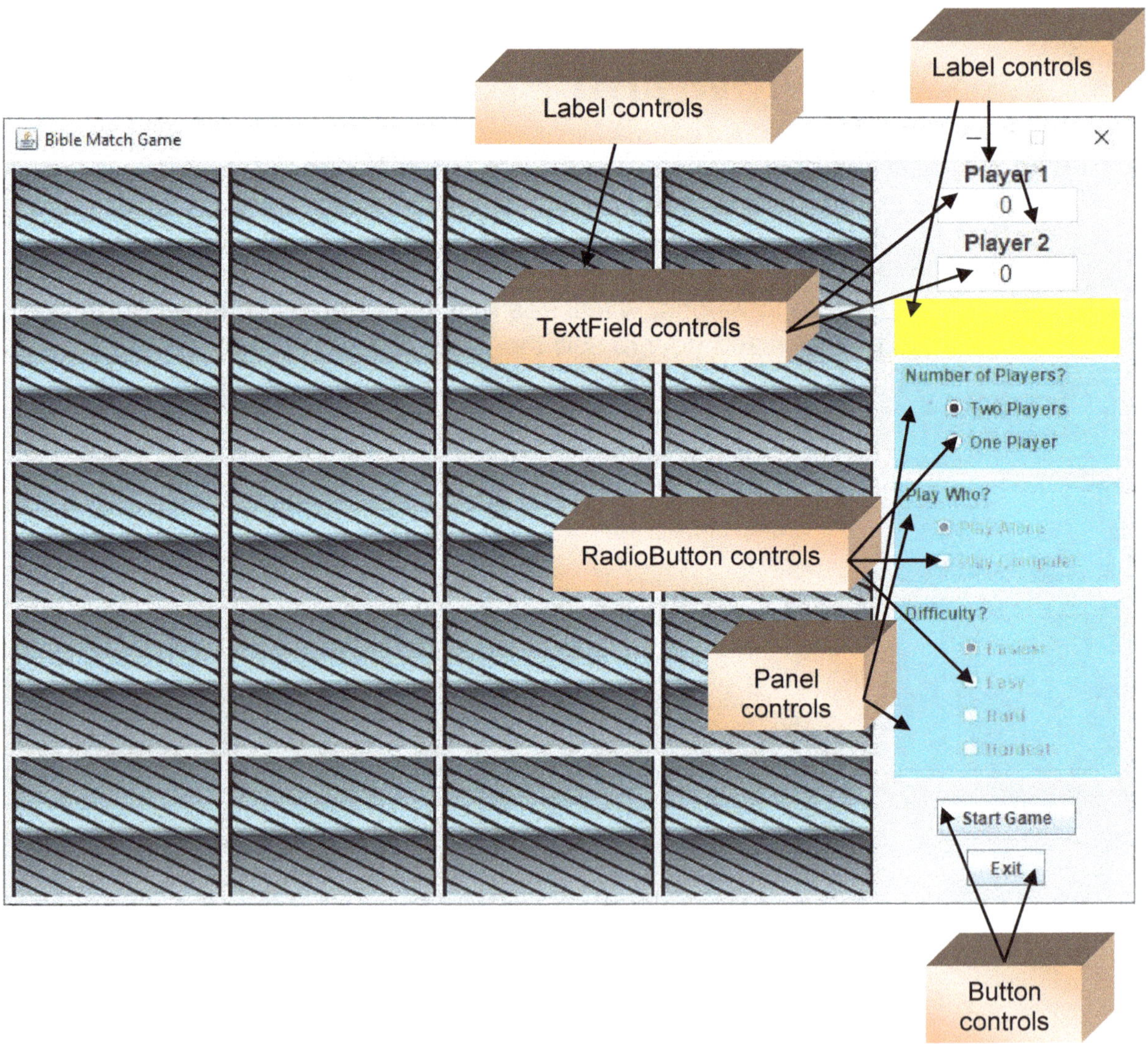

On the left is the picture display area for **Bible Match Game**. Each picture is displayed in a label control. On the right are label and text field controls used to display scoring. There are also three panel controls and two button controls. Each panel holds radio button controls used to establish game options. The two button controls are used to start and stop the game and to exit the program.

The game appears in its 'stopped' state, the label controls holding pictures are covered and waiting for you to choose game options. You can choose one or two players. If one player, you can choose to play alone or against the computer. If playing the computer, you can choose how smart you want the computer to be (**Difficulty**). As options are selected, the labels used for scoring change their headings to match the selections. I've selected a one player game, against the computer with a **Hard** difficulty:

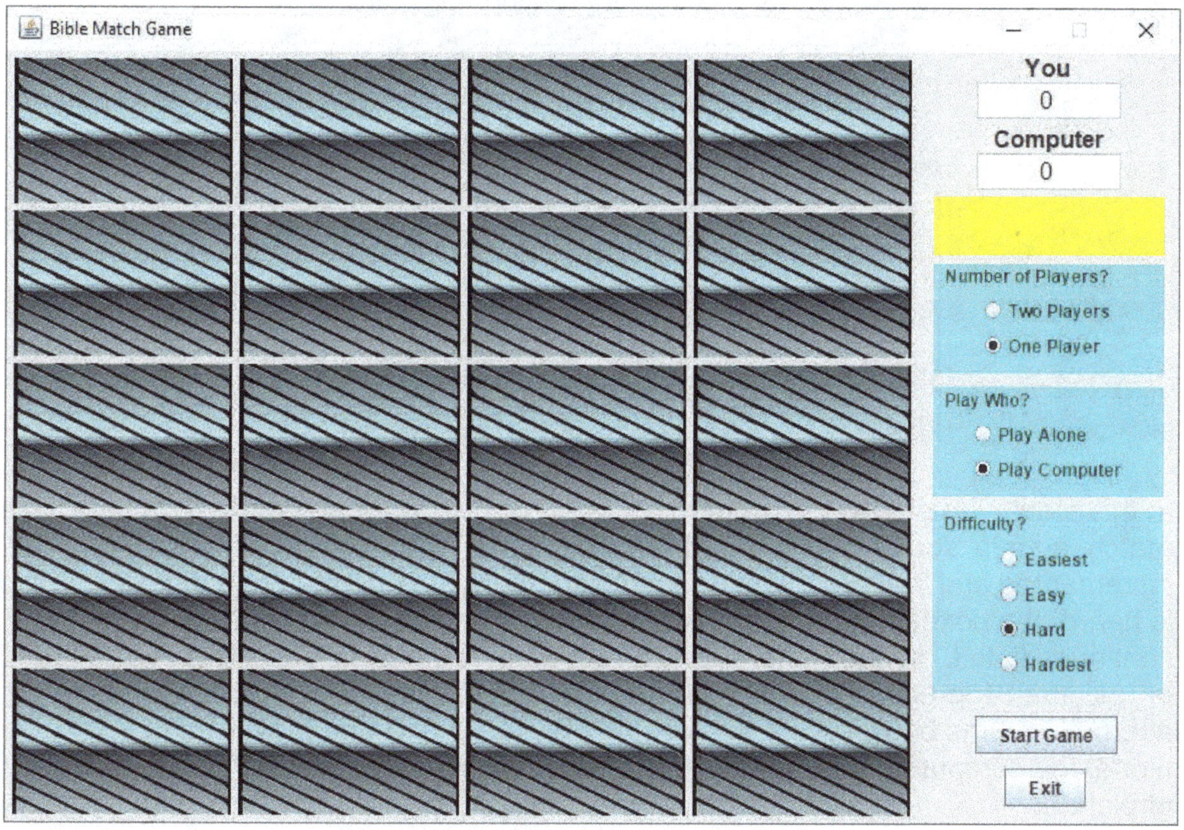

Click the **Start Game** button to start playing. Its caption will change (now reading **Stop Game**) and the options group boxes and **Exit** button will become disabled. The message area says **Pick a Box**. When playing the computer, you go first.

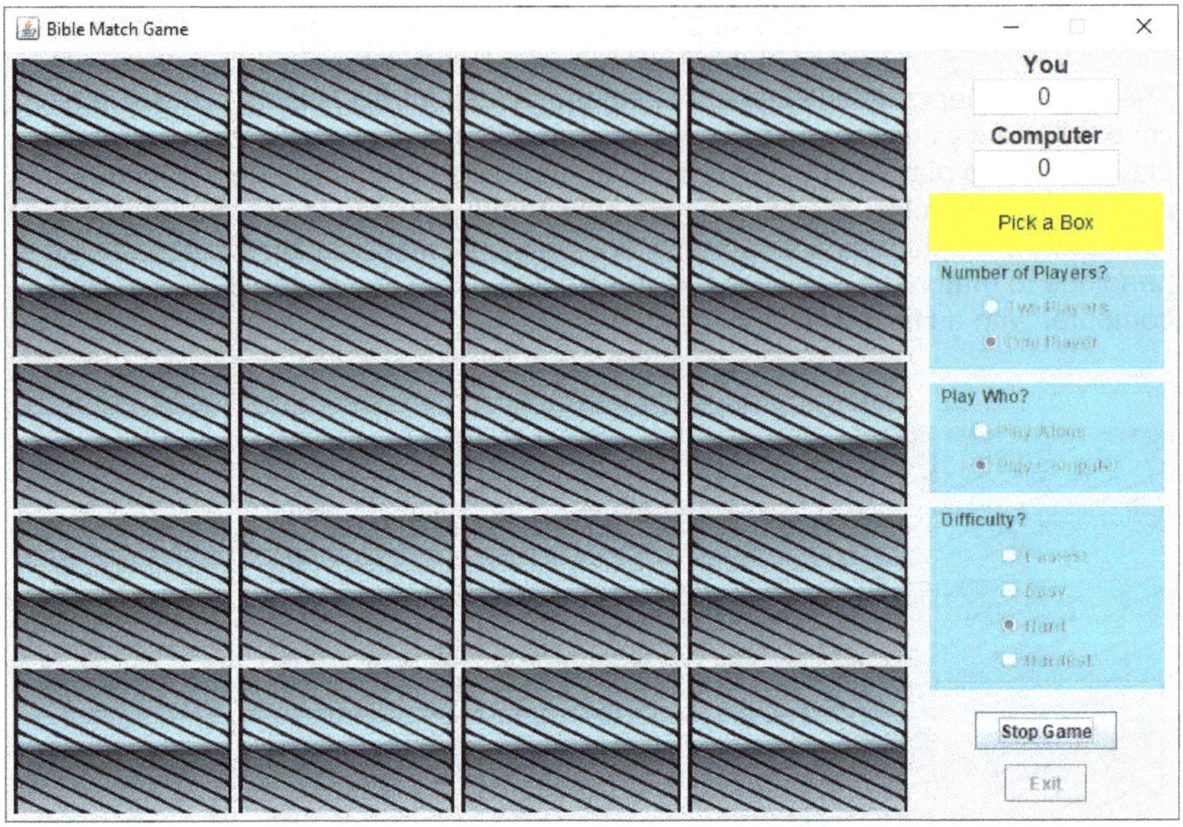

In this state, you pick two boxes to see what pictures are behind them. If there is a match, a ‘tada’ sound will be heard, the boxes are removed, your score incremented and you are given another turn. If there is no match, a different sound is heard, the boxes are recovered and it becomes the computer’s turn. Play continues in this manner (alternating turns) until all the matching pictures are found or until the **Stop Game** button is clicked. Play is similar for a two player game, alternating turns between the two people playing. For a one player game, playing alone, the computer keeps track of how many tries it takes you to find all 10 pairs of pictures.

I selected the first two boxes and see:

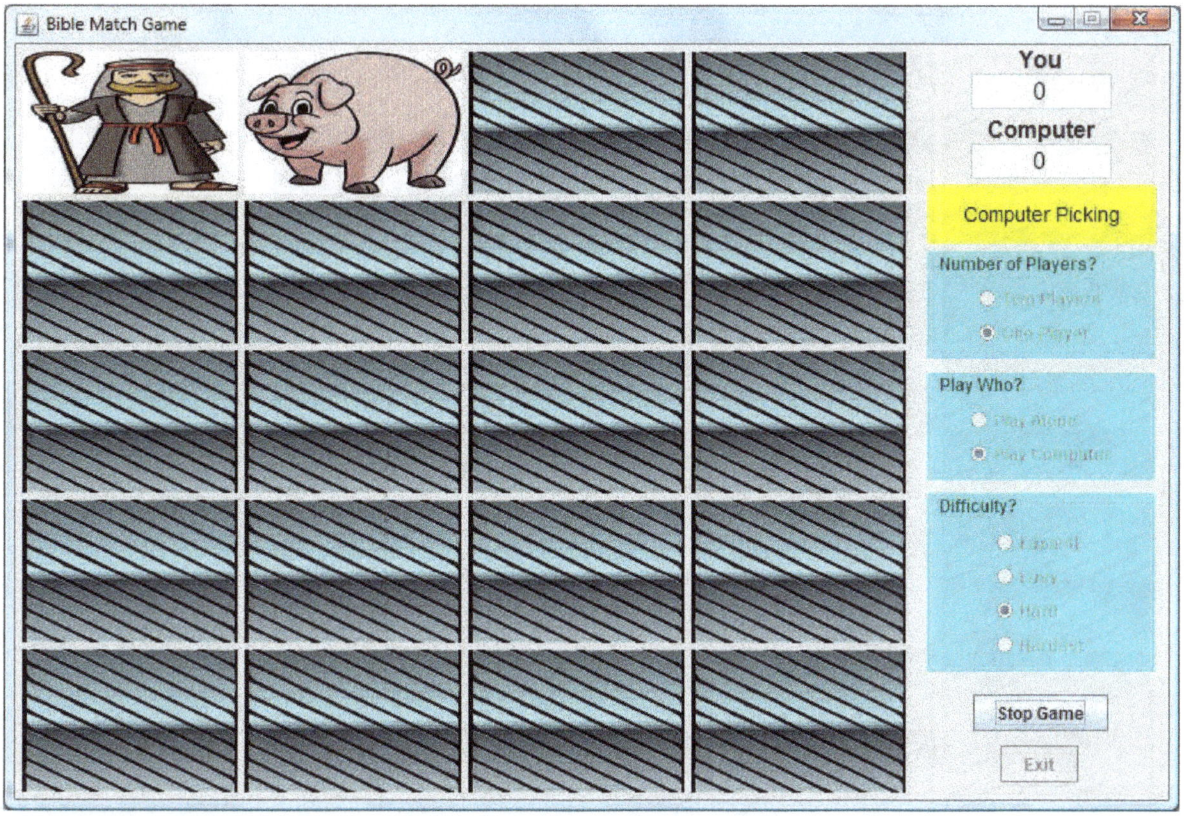

It's a shepherd and a pig. I hear a 'boing' sound and the board returns to it's covered state. You will most likely see different pictures when you run the game because we are using random numbers.

It then becomes the computer's turn. It's choices are:

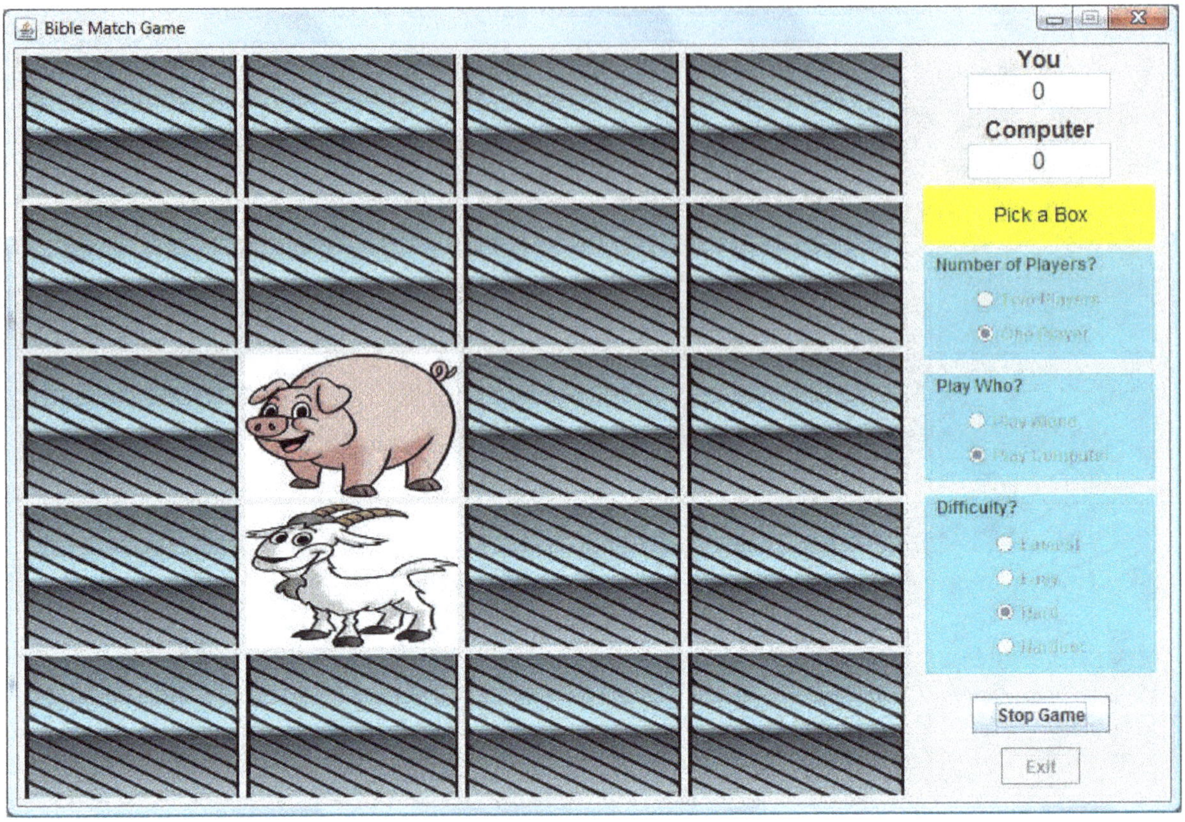

Not a match … but we've seen that pig before. I think you know the next move.

Picking the second box in the top row and the second box in the third row, I get a match. The pictures are removed, my score is incremented and it's my turn again:

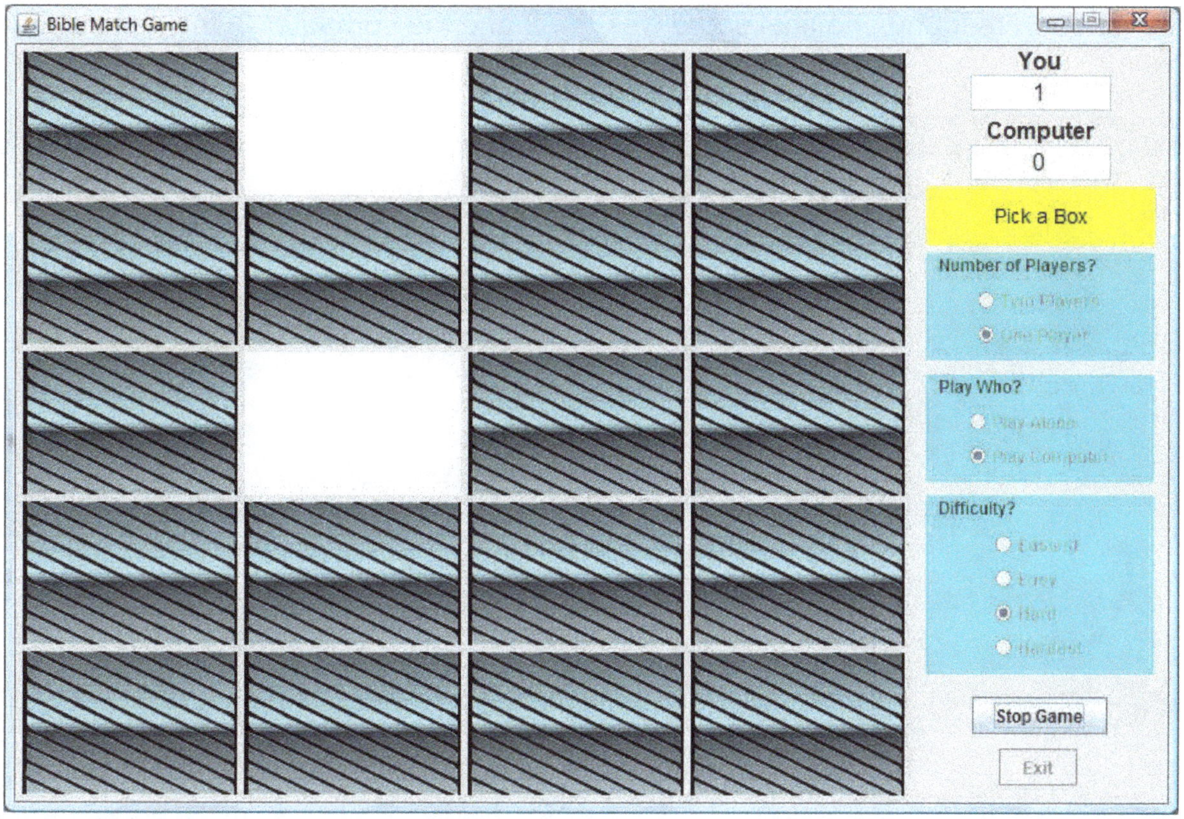

The game continues in this same manner, alternating turns between you and the computer. When there is a match, you or the computer get an additional turn. I continued playing this game against a pretty smart computer. Once all the matches were found, the final score was me 2 and the computer 8, the computer won!

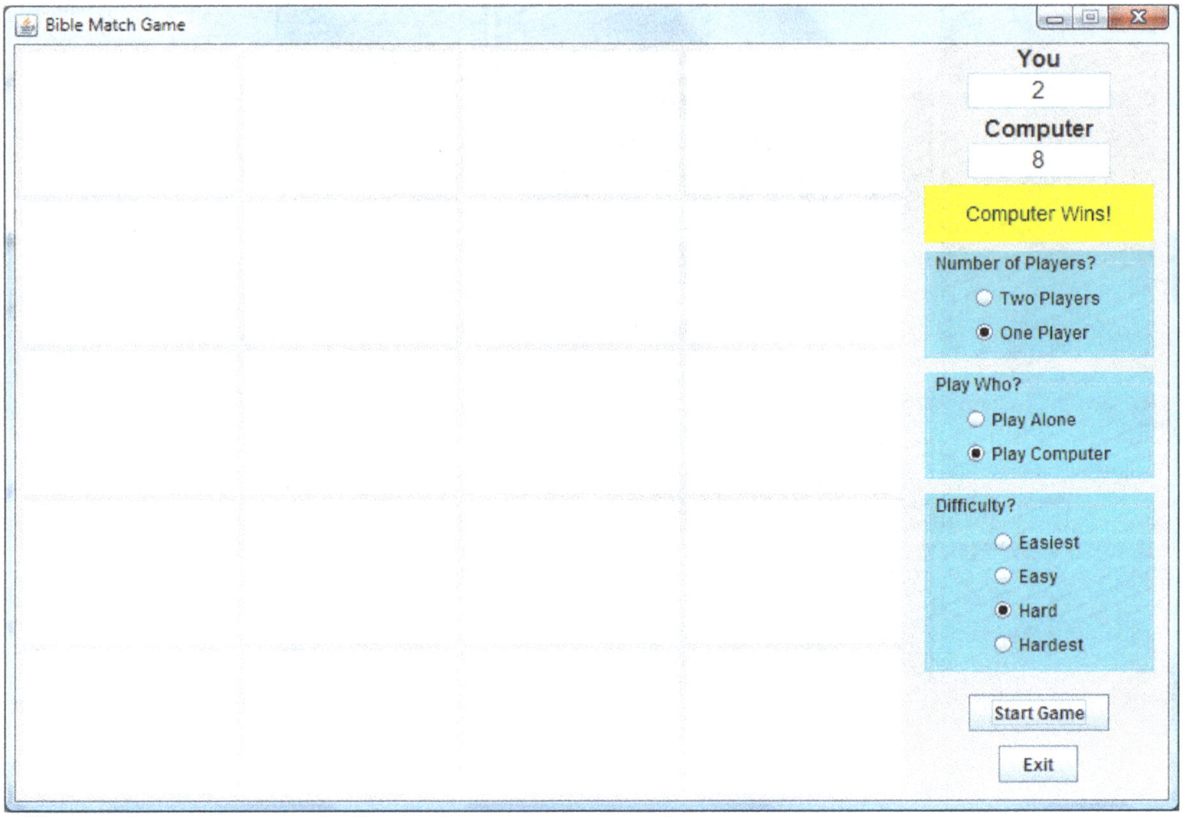

Notice the game returns to its stopped state to allow another game or to stop the program by clicking **Exit**.

Continue playing the game to understand its operation. Try using the two player game and the one player game where you **Play Alone**. Or, in the one player game against the computer, try different levels of difficulty. You will find at the **Hardest** level, the computer is nearly impossible to beat. Click **Exit** when you're done to stop the game. Open the code file and look over the code, if you like.

You will now build this project in stages. As you build Java projects, we always recommend taking a slow, step-by-step process. It minimizes programming errors and helps build your confidence as things come together in a complete project.

We address **frame design**. We discuss the controls needed to build the frame, establish initial control properties (including using your own pictures in the game) and discuss how to change the state of the controls. And, we address **code design**. We discuss how to display the pairs of pictures, check for a match, handle multiple players, and decide how to make computer-generated moves. We also discuss how to "scramble" the pictures and the use of timer objects for delays.

Bible Match Game Frame Design

We begin building the **Bible Match Game** project. Let's build the frame. Start a new project in your Java Project group – name it **MatchGame**. Delete default code in file named **MatchGame.java**. Once started, we suggest you immediately save the project with a name you choose. This sets up the folder and file structure needed for your project.

Build the basic frame with these properties:

MatchGame Frame:

title	Bible Match Game
resizable	false

The code is:

```
/*
 * MatchGame.java
 */
package matchgame;
import javax.swing.*;
import java.awt.*;
import java.awt.event.*;

public class MatchGame extends JFrame
{

  public static void main(String args[])
  {
    // create frame
    new MatchGame().setVisible(true);
  }

  public MatchGame()
  {
    // frame constructor
    setTitle("Bible Match Game");
    setResizable(false);
    addWindowListener(new WindowAdapter()
    {
      public void windowClosing(WindowEvent evt)
      {
        exitForm(evt);
      }
    });
    getContentPane().setLayout(new GridBagLayout());
```

```
        GridBagConstraints gridConstraints;

        pack();
        Dimension screenSize =
    Toolkit.getDefaultToolkit().getScreenSize();
        setBounds((int) (0.5 * (screenSize.width -
    getWidth())), (int) (0.5 * (screenSize.height -
    getHeight())), getWidth(), getHeight());
      }

      private void exitForm(WindowEvent evt)
      {
        System.exit(0);
      }
    }
```

This code builds the frame, sets up the layout manager and includes code to exit the application. Run the code to make sure the frame (at least, what there is of it at this point) appears and is centered on the screen:

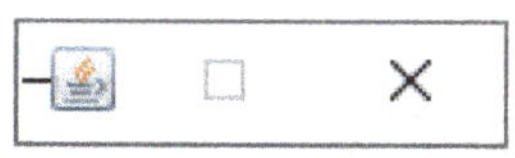

Let's populate our frame with other controls. All code for creating the frame and placing controls (except declarations) goes in the **MatchGame** constructor.

We start by putting six panel controls on the frame. The **GridBagLayout** is:

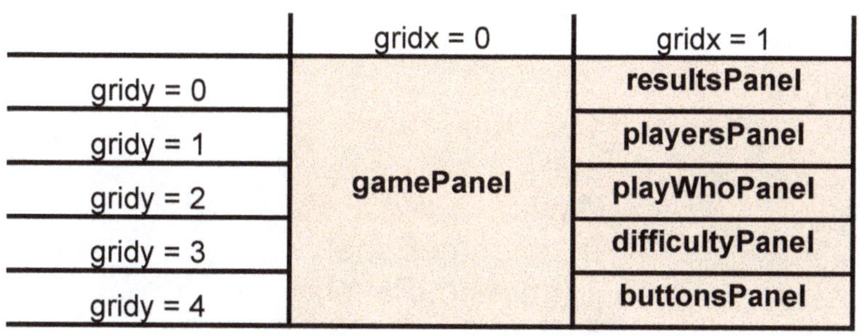

The **gamePanel** will be used to display the pictures in label controls. The **resultsPanel** will hold scoring and message controls. The **playersPanel** will hold radio buttons selecting the number of players. The **playWhoPanel** will host radio buttons deciding (in a one player game) if you play solitaire or against the computer. The **difficultyPanel** holds radio buttons that decide how smart the computer is. And the **buttonsPanel** will hold the two button controls. We will build each panel separately. Let's begin with the gamePanel.

The **gamePanel** will hold twenty label controls (in a 5 rows by 4 columns grid) used to display the hidden pictures. The **GridBagLayout** for gamePanel is:

	gridx = 0	gridx = 1	gridx = 2	gridx = 3
gridy = 0	pictureLabel[0]	pictureLabel[1]]	pictureLabel[2]	pictureLabel[3]
gridy = 1	pictureLabel[4]	pictureLabel[5]	pictureLabel[6]	pictureLabel[7]
gridy = 2	pictureLabel[8]	pictureLabel[9]	pictureLabel[10]	pictureLabel[11]
gridy = 3	pictureLabel[12]	pictureLabel[13]	pictureLabel[14]	pictureLabel[15]
gridy = 4	pictureLabel[16]	pictureLabel[17]	pictureLabel[18]	pictureLabel[19]

Add the **gamePanel** to the frame and **pictureLabel** controls to the panel with these properties:

gamePanel:

size	625, 530
gridx	0 (on frame)
gridy	0 (on frame)
gridheight	5

pictureLabel[0]:

size	150, 100
opaque	true
background	White
gridx	0 (on gamePanel)
gridy	0 (on gamePanel)
insets	5, 5, 0, 0

pictureLabel[1]:

size	150, 100
opaque	true
background	White
gridx	0 (on gamePanel)
gridy	1 (on gamePanel)
insets	5, 5, 0, 0

pictureLabel[2]:

size	150, 100
opaque	true
background	White
gridx	0 (on gamePanel)
gridy	2 (on gamePanel)
insets	5, 5, 0, 0

pictureLabel[3]:

size	150, 100

opaque	true
background	White
gridx	0 (on gamePanel)
gridy	3 (on gamePanel)
insets	5, 5, 0, 5

pictureLabel[4]:

size	150, 100
opaque	true
background	White
gridx	1 (on gamePanel)
gridy	0 (on gamePanel)
insets	5, 5, 0, 0

pictureLabel[5]:

size	150, 100
opaque	true
background	White
gridx	1 (on gamePanel)
gridy	1 (on gamePanel)
insets	5, 5, 0, 0

pictureLabel[6]:

size	150, 100
opaque	true
background	White
gridx	1 (on gamePanel)
gridy	2 (on gamePanel)
insets	5, 5, 0, 0

pictureLabel[7]:

size	150, 100
opaque	true
background	White
gridx	1 (on gamePanel)
gridy	3 (on gamePanel)
insets	5, 5, 0, 5

pictureLabel[8]:

size	150, 100
opaque	true
background	White
gridx	2 (on gamePanel)
gridy	0 (on gamePanel)
insets	5, 5, 0, 0

pictureLabel[9]:

size	150, 100
opaque	true
background	White
gridx	2 (on gamePanel)
gridy	1 (on gamePanel)
insets	5, 5, 0, 0

pictureLabel[10]:

size	150, 100
opaque	true
background	White
gridx	2 (on gamePanel)
gridy	2 (on gamePanel)
insets	5, 5, 0, 0

pictureLabel[11]:

size	150, 100
opaque	true
background	White
gridx	2 (on gamePanel)
gridy	3 (on gamePanel)
insets	5, 5, 0, 5

pictureLabel[12]:

size	150, 100
opaque	true
background	White
gridx	3 (on gamePanel)
gridy	0 (on gamePanel)
insets	5, 5, 0, 0

pictureLabel[13]:

size	150, 100
opaque	true
background	White
gridx	3 (on gamePanel)
gridy	1 (on gamePanel)
insets	5, 5, 0, 0

pictureLabel[14]:

size	150, 100
opaque	true
background	White
gridx	3 (on gamePanel)
gridy	2 (on gamePanel)
insets	5, 5, 0, 0

pictureLabel[15]:

size	150, 100
opaque	true
background	White
gridx	3 (on gamePanel)
gridy	3 (on gamePanel)
insets	5, 5, 0, 5

pictureLabel[16]:

size	150, 100
opaque	true
background	White
gridx	4 (on gamePanel)
gridy	0 (on gamePanel)
insets	5, 5, 5, 0

pictureLabel[17]:

size	150, 100
opaque	true
background	White
gridx	4 (on gamePanel)
gridy	1 (on gamePanel)
insets	5, 5, 5, 0

pictureLabel[18]:

size	150, 100
opaque	true
background	White
gridx	4 (on gamePanel)
gridy	2 (on gamePanel)
insets	5, 5, 5, 0

pictureLabel[19]:

size	150, 100
opaque	true
background	White
gridx	4 (on gamePanel)
gridy	3 (on gamePanel)
insets	5, 5, 5, 5

The gamePanel size and label control insets were selected to insure 5 pixel spacing of all labels from other labels and from the edges of the panel.

These controls are declared using:

```
JPanel gamePanel = new JPanel();
JLabel[] pictureLabel = new JLabel[20];
```

The controls are placed in the frame using this code:

```
gamePanel.setPreferredSize(new Dimension(625, 530));
gamePanel.setLayout(new GridBagLayout());
gridConstraints = new GridBagConstraints();
gridConstraints.gridx = 0;
gridConstraints.gridy = 0;
gridConstraints.gridheight = 5;
getContentPane().add(gamePanel, gridConstraints);
```

```
for (int i = 0; i < 20; i++)
{
  pictureLabel[i] = new JLabel();
  pictureLabel[i].setPreferredSize(new Dimension(150,
100));
  pictureLabel[i].setOpaque(true);
  pictureLabel[i].setBackground(Color.WHITE);
  gridConstraints = new GridBagConstraints();
  gridConstraints.gridx = i % 4;
  gridConstraints.gridy = i / 4;
  gridConstraints.insets = new Insets(5, 5, 0, 0);
  if (gridConstraints.gridx == 3)
    gridConstraints.insets = new Insets(5, 5, 0, 5);
  if (gridConstraints.gridy == 4)
    gridConstraints.insets = new Insets(5, 5, 5, 0);
  if (gridConstraints.gridx == 3 && gridConstraints.gridy
== 4)
    gridConstraints.insets = new Insets(5, 5, 5, 5);
  gamePanel.add(pictureLabel[i], gridConstraints);
  pictureLabel[i].addMouseListener(new MouseAdapter()
  {
    public void mousePressed(MouseEvent e)
    {
      pictureLabelMousePressed(e);
    }
  });
}
```

Note how the loop index (**i**) is used to set proper label control properties (gridx, gridy). This code also adds mouse listeners for each label. The method called when a label is clicked with the mouse **pictureLabelMousePressed**. Add this empty method with the other methods:

```
private void pictureLabelMousePressed(MouseEvent e)
{
}
```

Add code in the proper locations. Run to see:

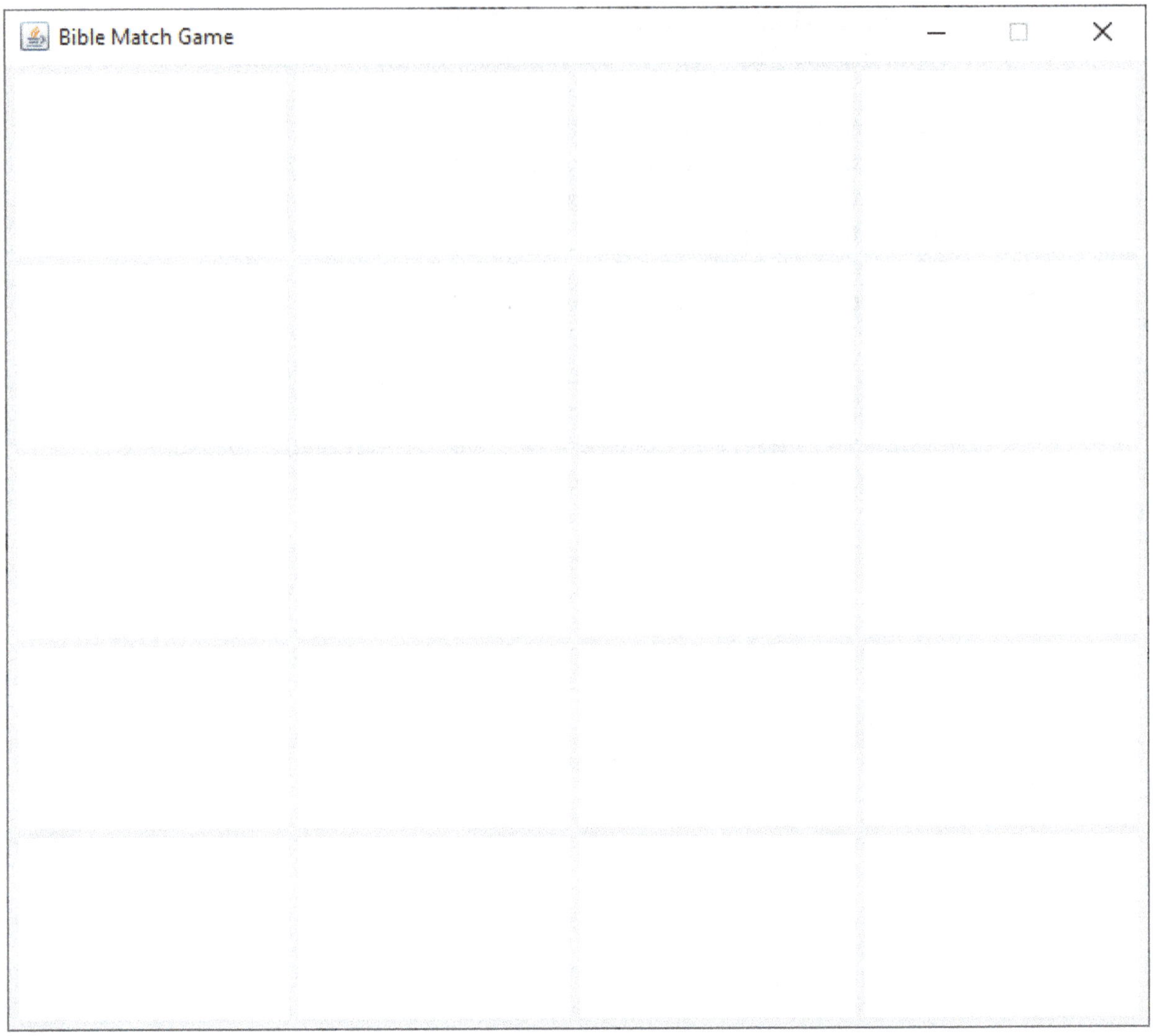

The empty label controls appear in the grid. The **gamePanel** control is complete. Let's move to the remaining panels on the frame.

The **resultsPanel** holds three label controls and two text fields to display scores and messages. The **GridBagLayout** for resultsPanel is:

	gridx = 0
gridy = 0	**player1Label**
gridy = 1	**scoreTextField[0]**
gridy = 2	**Player2Label**
gridy = 3	**scoreTextField[1]**
gridy = 4	**messageLabel**

The control properties are:

resultsPanel:

size	160, 140
gridx	1 (on frame)
gridy	0 (on frame)

player1Label:

text	Player 1
font	Arial, Bold, Size 16
gridx	0 (on resultsPanel)
gridy	0 (on resultsPanel)

scoreTextField[0]:

size	100, 25
text	0
editable	false
background	White
horizontalAlignment	CENTER
font	Arial, Plain, Size 16
gridx	0 (on resultsPanel)
gridy	1 (on results Panel)

player2Label:

text	Player 2
font	Arial, Bold, Size 16
gridx	0 (on resultsPanel)
gridy	2 (on resultsPanel)

scoreTextField[1]:

size	100, 25
text	0
editable	false
background	White
horizontalAlignment	CENTER
font	Arial, Plain, Size 16
gridx	0 (on resultsPanel)
gridy	3 (on results Panel)

messageLabel:

size	160, 40
opaque	true
background	Yellow
horizontalAlignment	CENTER
text	[blank]
font	Arial, Plain, Size 14
gridx	0 (on resultsPanel)
gridy	4 (on resultsPanel)
insets	5, 0, 0, 0

Declare the controls using:

```
JPanel resultsPanel = new JPanel();
JLabel player1Label = new JLabel();
JLabel player2Label = new JLabel();
JTextField[] scoreTextField = new JTextField[2];
JLabel messageLabel = new JLabel();
```

Add the controls to the **resultsPanel** (which is placed in the frame) using:

```
resultsPanel.setPreferredSize(new Dimension(160, 140));
resultsPanel.setLayout(new GridBagLayout());
gridConstraints = new GridBagConstraints();
gridConstraints.gridx = 1;
gridConstraints.gridy = 0;
getContentPane().add(resultsPanel, gridConstraints);

player1Label.setText("Player 1");
player1Label.setFont(new Font("Arial", Font.BOLD, 16));
gridConstraints = new GridBagConstraints();
gridConstraints.gridx = 0;
gridConstraints.gridy = 0;
resultsPanel.add(player1Label, gridConstraints);

scoreTextField[0] = new JTextField();
scoreTextField[0].setPreferredSize(new Dimension(100,
25));
scoreTextField[0].setText("0");
scoreTextField[0].setEditable(false);
scoreTextField[0].setBackground(Color.WHITE);
scoreTextField[0].setHorizontalAlignment(SwingConstants.CE
NTER);
scoreTextField[0].setFont(new Font("Arial", Font.PLAIN,
16));
gridConstraints = new GridBagConstraints();
gridConstraints.gridx = 0;
gridConstraints.gridy = 1;
resultsPanel.add(scoreTextField[0], gridConstraints);

player2Label.setText("Player 2");
player2Label.setFont(new Font("Arial", Font.BOLD, 16));
gridConstraints = new GridBagConstraints();
gridConstraints.gridx = 0;
gridConstraints.gridy = 2;
gridConstraints.insets = new Insets(5, 0, 0, 0);
resultsPanel.add(player2Label, gridConstraints);

scoreTextField[1] = new JTextField();
scoreTextField[1].setPreferredSize(new Dimension(100,
25));
scoreTextField[1].setText("0");
scoreTextField[1].setEditable(false);
scoreTextField[1].setBackground(Color.WHITE);
scoreTextField[1].setHorizontalAlignment(SwingConstants.CE
NTER);
```

```
scoreTextField[1].setFont(new Font("Arial", Font.PLAIN,
16));
gridConstraints = new GridBagConstraints();
gridConstraints.gridx = 0;
gridConstraints.gridy = 3;
resultsPanel.add(scoreTextField[1], gridConstraints);

messageLabel.setPreferredSize(new Dimension(160, 40));
messageLabel.setOpaque(true);
messageLabel.setBackground(Color.YELLOW);
messageLabel.setHorizontalAlignment(SwingConstants.CENTER)
;
messageLabel.setText("");
messageLabel.setFont(new Font("Arial", Font.PLAIN, 14));
gridConstraints = new GridBagConstraints();
gridConstraints.gridx = 0;
gridConstraints.gridy = 4;
gridConstraints.insets = new Insets(5, 0, 0, 0);
resultsPanel.add(messageLabel, gridConstraints);
```

Add this code in the proper locations. Run to see:

The new controls appear.

The **playersPanel** will hold two radio button controls used to select the number of players in the game. The **GridBagLayout** for optionsPanel is:

	gridx = 0
gridy = 0	**twoPlayersRadioButton**
gridy =1	**onePlayerRadioButton**

The panel and radio button properties:

playersPanel:

size	160, 75
background	Cyan
title	Number of Players?
gridx	1 (on frame)
gridy	1 (on frame)
insets	5, 10, 5, 10

twoPlayersRadioButton:

text	Two Players
background	Cyan
buttonGroup	playersButtonGroup
selected	true
gridx	0 (on playersPanel)
gridy	0 (on playersPanel)
anchor	WEST

onePlayerRadioButton:

text	One Player
background	Cyan
buttonGroup	playersButtonGroup
gridx	0 (on optionsPanel)
gridy	1 (on optionsPanel)
anchor	WEST

These controls are declared using:

```
JPanel playersPanel = new JPanel();
ButtonGroup playersButtonGroup = new ButtonGroup();
JRadioButton twoPlayersRadioButton = new JRadioButton();
JRadioButton onePlayerRadioButton = new JRadioButton();
```

The radio buttons are placed in the **playersPanel** (which is placed in the frame) using:

```
playersPanel.setPreferredSize(new Dimension(160, 75));
playersPanel.setBackground(Color.CYAN);
playersPanel.setBorder(BorderFactory.createTitledBorder("N
umber of Players?"));
playersPanel.setLayout(new GridBagLayout());
gridConstraints = new GridBagConstraints();
gridConstraints.gridx = 1;
gridConstraints.gridy = 1;
gridConstraints.insets = new Insets(5, 10, 5, 10);
getContentPane().add(playersPanel, gridConstraints);

twoPlayersRadioButton.setText("Two Players");
twoPlayersRadioButton.setBackground(Color.CYAN);
twoPlayersRadioButton.setSelected(true);
playersButtonGroup.add(twoPlayersRadioButton);
gridConstraints = new GridBagConstraints();
gridConstraints.gridx = 0;
gridConstraints.gridy = 0;
gridConstraints.anchor = GridBagConstraints.WEST;
playersPanel.add(twoPlayersRadioButton, gridConstraints);
twoPlayersRadioButton.addActionListener(new
ActionListener()
{
  public void actionPerformed(ActionEvent e)
  {
    twoPlayersRadioButtonActionPerformed(e);
  }
});

onePlayerRadioButton.setText("One Player");
onePlayerRadioButton.setBackground(Color.CYAN);
playersButtonGroup.add(onePlayerRadioButton);
gridConstraints = new GridBagConstraints();
gridConstraints.gridx = 0;
gridConstraints.gridy = 1;
gridConstraints.anchor = GridBagConstraints.WEST;
playersPanel.add(onePlayerRadioButton, gridConstraints);
```

```
onePlayerRadioButton.addActionListener(new
ActionListener()
{
  public void actionPerformed(ActionEvent e)
  {
    onePlayerRadioButtonActionPerformed(e);
  }
});
```

We added listeners for the two radio buttons. Add these empty methods to handle button selections:

```
private void
twoPlayersRadioButtonActionPerformed(ActionEvent e)
{
}

private void
onePlayerRadioButtonActionPerformed(ActionEvent e)
{
}
```

Add this code in the proper locations. Run to see:

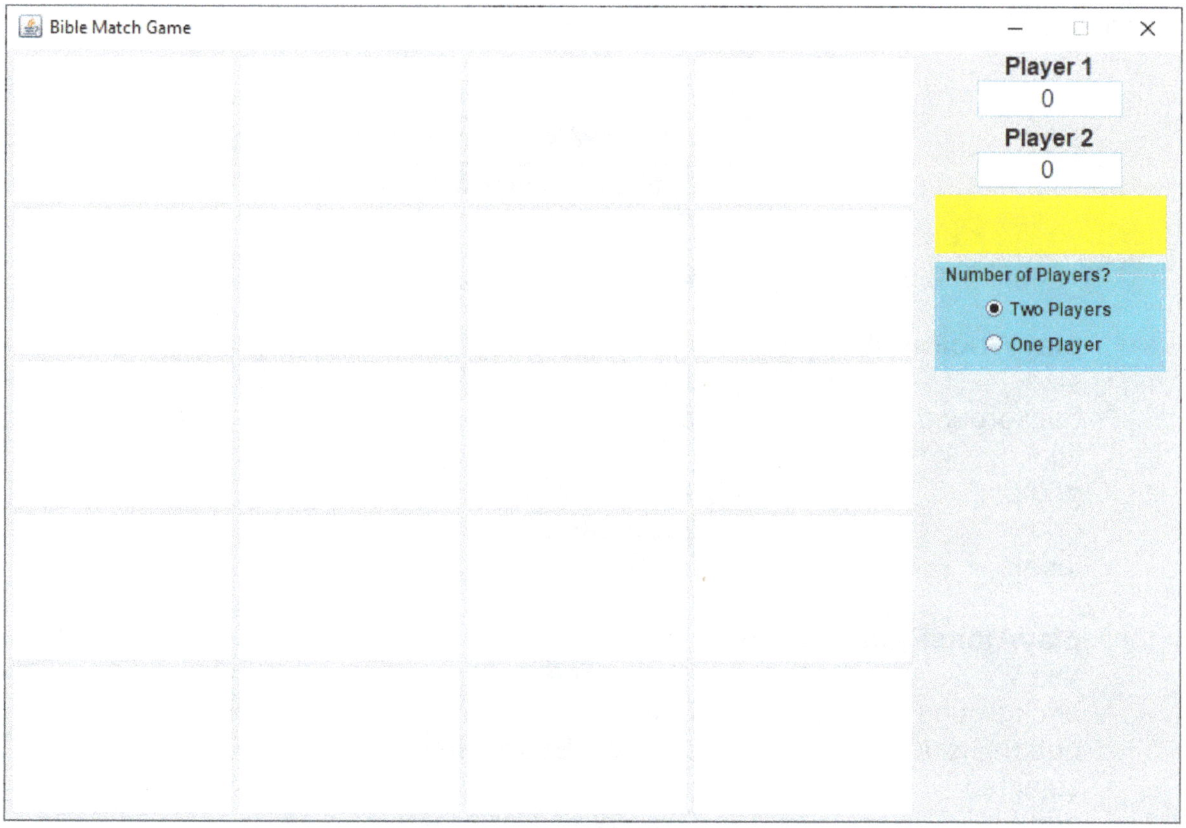

The players panel is displayed.

The **playWhoPanel** will hold two radio button controls used to determine (in a one player game) if you play alone or play against the computer. The **GridBagLayout** for playWhoPanel is:

	gridx = 0
gridy = 0	**playAloneRadioButton**
gridy =1	**playComputerRadioButton**

The panel and radio button properties:

playWhoPanel:

size	160, 75
background	Cyan
title	Play Who?
gridx	1 (on frame)
gridy	2 (on frame)
insets	5, 10, 5, 10

playAloneRadioButton:

text	Play Alone
background	Cyan
buttonGroup	playWhoButtonGroup
selected	true
gridx	0 (on playWhoPanel)
gridy	0 (on playWhoPanel)
anchor	WEST

playComputerRadioButton:

text	Play Computer
background	Cyan
buttonGroup	playWhoButtonGroup
gridx	0 (on playWhoPanel)
gridy	1 (on playWhoPanel)
anchor	WEST

These controls are declared using:

```
JPanel playWhoPanel = new JPanel();
ButtonGroup playWhoButtonGroup = new ButtonGroup();
JRadioButton playAloneRadioButton = new JRadioButton();
JRadioButton playComputerRadioButton = new JRadioButton();
```

The radio buttons are placed in the **playWhoPanel** (which is placed in the frame) using:

```
playWhoPanel.setPreferredSize(new Dimension(160, 75));
playWhoPanel.setBackground(Color.CYAN);
playWhoPanel.setBorder(BorderFactory.createTitledBorder("P
lay Who?"));
playWhoPanel.setLayout(new GridBagLayout());
gridConstraints = new GridBagConstraints();
gridConstraints.gridx = 1;
gridConstraints.gridy = 2;
gridConstraints.insets = new Insets(5, 10, 5, 10);
getContentPane().add(playWhoPanel, gridConstraints);

playAloneRadioButton.setText("Play Alone");
playAloneRadioButton.setBackground(Color.CYAN);
playAloneRadioButton.setSelected(true);
playWhoButtonGroup.add(playAloneRadioButton);
gridConstraints = new GridBagConstraints();
gridConstraints.gridx = 0;
gridConstraints.gridy = 0;
gridConstraints.anchor = GridBagConstraints.WEST;
playWhoPanel.add(playAloneRadioButton, gridConstraints);
playAloneRadioButton.addActionListener(new
ActionListener()
{
  public void actionPerformed(ActionEvent e)
  {
    playAloneRadioButtonActionPerformed(e);
  }
});

playComputerRadioButton.setText("Play Computer");
playComputerRadioButton.setBackground(Color.CYAN);
playWhoButtonGroup.add(playComputerRadioButton);
gridConstraints = new GridBagConstraints();
gridConstraints.gridx = 0;
gridConstraints.gridy = 1;
gridConstraints.anchor = GridBagConstraints.WEST;
```

```
playWhoPanel.add(playComputerRadioButton,
gridConstraints);
playComputerRadioButton.addActionListener(new
ActionListener()
{
  public void actionPerformed(ActionEvent e)
  {
    playComputerRadioButtonActionPerformed(e);
  }
});
```

We added listeners for the two radio buttons. Add these empty methods to handle button selections:

```
private void
playAloneRadioButtonActionPerformed(ActionEvent e)
{
}

private void
playComputerRadioButtonActionPerformed(ActionEvent e)
{
}
```

Add this code in the proper locations. Run to see:

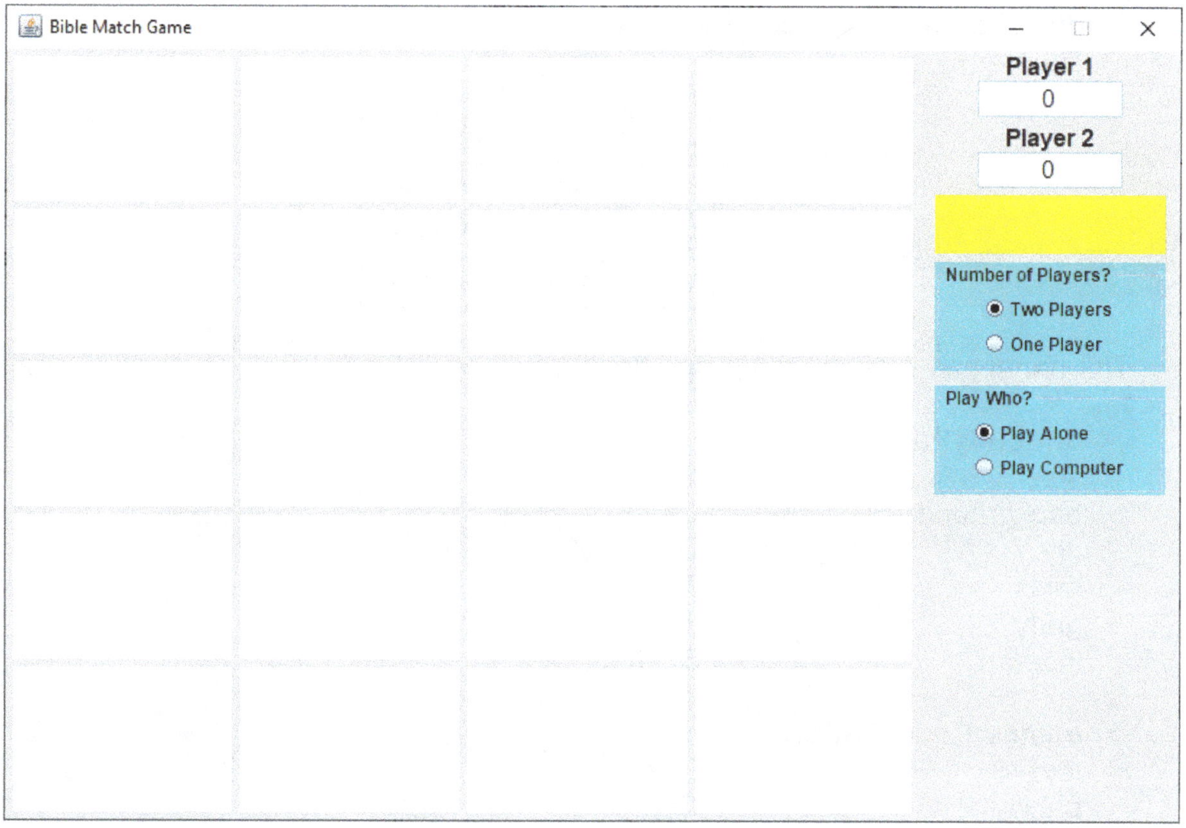

The play who panel is displayed.

The **difficultyPanel** will hold four radio button controls used to determine (in a one player game against the computer) how smart the computer is. The **GridBagLayout** for difficultyPanel is:

	gridx = 0
gridy = 0	**easiestRadioButton**
gridy =1	**easyRadioButton**
gridy = 2	**hardRadioButton**
gridy = 3	**hardestRadioButton**

The panel and radio button properties:

difficultyPanel:

size	160, 125
background	Cyan
title	Difficulty?
gridx	1 (on frame)
gridy	3 (on frame)
insets	5, 10, 5, 10

easiestRadioButton:

text	Easiest
background	Cyan
buttonGroup	difficultyButtonGroup
selected	true
gridx	0 (on difficultyPanel)
gridy	0 (on difficultyWhoPanel)
anchor	WEST

easyRadioButton:

text	Easy
background	Cyan
buttonGroup	difficultyButtonGroup
gridx	0 (on difficultyPanel)
gridy	1 (on difficultyWhoPanel)
anchor	WEST

hardRadioButton:

text	Hard
background	Cyan
buttonGroup	difficultyButtonGroup
gridx	0 (on difficultyPanel)
gridy	2 (on difficultyWhoPanel)
anchor	WEST

hardestRadioButton:

text	Hardest
background	Cyan
buttonGroup	difficultyButtonGroup
gridx	0 (on difficultyPanel)
gridy	3 (on difficultyWhoPanel)
anchor	WEST

These controls are declared using:

```
JPanel difficultyPanel = new JPanel();
ButtonGroup difficultyButtonGroup = new ButtonGroup();
JRadioButton easiestRadioButton = new JRadioButton();
JRadioButton easyRadioButton = new JRadioButton();
JRadioButton hardRadioButton = new JRadioButton();
JRadioButton hardestRadioButton = new JRadioButton();
```

The radio buttons are placed in the **difficultyPanel** (which is placed in the frame) using:

```
difficultyPanel.setPreferredSize(new Dimension(160, 125));
difficultyPanel.setBackground(Color.CYAN);
difficultyPanel.setBorder(BorderFactory.createTitledBorder
("Difficulty?"));
difficultyPanel.setLayout(new GridBagLayout());
gridConstraints = new GridBagConstraints();
gridConstraints.gridx = 1;
gridConstraints.gridy = 3;
gridConstraints.insets = new Insets(5, 10, 5, 10);
getContentPane().add(difficultyPanel, gridConstraints);

easiestRadioButton.setText("Easiest");
easiestRadioButton.setBackground(Color.CYAN);
easiestRadioButton.setSelected(true);
difficultyButtonGroup.add(easiestRadioButton);
gridConstraints = new GridBagConstraints();
gridConstraints.gridx = 0;
gridConstraints.gridy = 0;
gridConstraints.anchor = GridBagConstraints.WEST;
difficultyPanel.add(easiestRadioButton, gridConstraints);
easiestRadioButton.addActionListener(new ActionListener()
{
  public void actionPerformed(ActionEvent e)
  {
    easiestRadioButtonActionPerformed(e);
  }
});
```

```
easyRadioButton.setText("Easy");
easyRadioButton.setBackground(Color.CYAN);
easyRadioButton.setSelected(true);
difficultyButtonGroup.add(easyRadioButton);
gridConstraints = new GridBagConstraints();
gridConstraints.gridx = 0;
gridConstraints.gridy = 1;
gridConstraints.anchor = GridBagConstraints.WEST;
difficultyPanel.add(easyRadioButton, gridConstraints);
easyRadioButton.addActionListener(new ActionListener()
{
  public void actionPerformed(ActionEvent e)
  {
    easyRadioButtonActionPerformed(e);
  }
});

hardRadioButton.setText("Hard");
hardRadioButton.setBackground(Color.CYAN);
hardRadioButton.setSelected(true);
difficultyButtonGroup.add(hardRadioButton);
gridConstraints = new GridBagConstraints();
gridConstraints.gridx = 0;
gridConstraints.gridy = 2;
gridConstraints.anchor = GridBagConstraints.WEST;
difficultyPanel.add(hardRadioButton, gridConstraints);
hardRadioButton.addActionListener(new ActionListener()
{
  public void actionPerformed(ActionEvent e)
  {
    hardRadioButtonActionPerformed(e);
  }
});

hardestRadioButton.setText("Hardest");
hardestRadioButton.setBackground(Color.CYAN);
hardestRadioButton.setSelected(true);
difficultyButtonGroup.add(hardestRadioButton);
gridConstraints = new GridBagConstraints();
gridConstraints.gridx = 0;
gridConstraints.gridy = 3;
gridConstraints.anchor = GridBagConstraints.WEST;
difficultyPanel.add(hardestRadioButton, gridConstraints);
hardestRadioButton.addActionListener(new ActionListener()
{
  public void actionPerformed(ActionEvent e)
```

```
    {
      hardestRadioButtonActionPerformed(e);
    }
  });
```

We added listeners for the four radio buttons. Add these empty methods to handle button selections:

```
private void easiestRadioButtonActionPerformed(ActionEvent
e)
{
}

private void easyRadioButtonActionPerformed(ActionEvent e)
{
}

private void hardRadioButtonActionPerformed(ActionEvent e)
{
}

private void hardestRadioButtonActionPerformed(ActionEvent
e)
{
}
```

Add this code in the proper locations. Run to see:

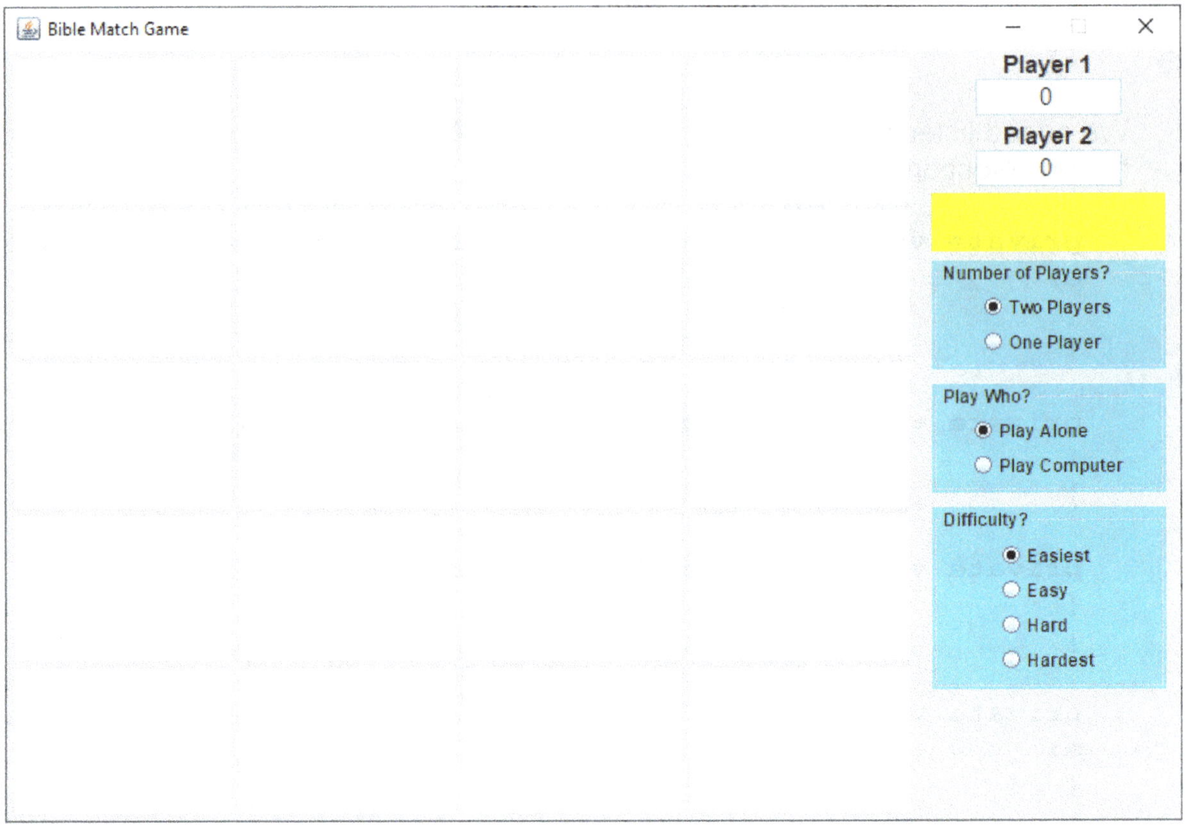

The difficulty panel is displayed.

The **buttonsPanel** will hold two buttons used to control game play. The **GridBagLayout** for buttonsPanel is:

	gridx = 0
gridy = 0	**startStopButton**
gridy =1	**exitButton**

The panel and button properties:

buttonsPanel:	
size	160, 70
gridx	1 (on frame)
gridy	4 (on frame)
startStopButton:	
text	Start Game
gridx	0 (on buttonsPanel)
gridy	0 (on buttonsPanel)
exitButton:	
text	Exit
gridx	0 (on buttonsPanel)
gridy	1 (on buttonsPanel)
insets	10, 0, 0, 0

These controls are declared using:

```
JPanel buttonsPanel = new JPanel();
JButton startStopButton = new JButton();
JButton exitButton = new JButton();
```

The buttons are placed in the **buttonsPanel** (which is placed in the frame) using:

```
buttonsPanel.setPreferredSize(new Dimension(160, 70));
buttonsPanel.setLayout(new GridBagLayout());
gridConstraints = new GridBagConstraints();
gridConstraints.gridx = 1;
gridConstraints.gridy = 4;
getContentPane().add(buttonsPanel, gridConstraints);

startStopButton.setText("Start Game");
gridConstraints = new GridBagConstraints();
gridConstraints.gridx = 0;
gridConstraints.gridy = 0;
buttonsPanel.add(startStopButton, gridConstraints);
startStopButton.addActionListener(new ActionListener()
```

```
{
  public void actionPerformed(ActionEvent e)
  {
    startStopButtonActionPerformed(e);
  }
});

exitButton.setText("Exit");
gridConstraints = new GridBagConstraints();
gridConstraints.gridx = 0;
gridConstraints.gridy = 1;
gridConstraints.insets = new Insets(10, 0, 0, 0);
buttonsPanel.add(exitButton, gridConstraints);
exitButton.addActionListener(new ActionListener()
{
  public void actionPerformed(ActionEvent e)
  {
    exitButtonActionPerformed(e);
  }
});
```

This code also adds listeners for each button. Add these empty methods with the other methods:

```
private void startStopButtonActionPerformed(ActionEvent e)
{
}

private void exitButtonActionPerformed(ActionEvent e)
{
}
```

Add this code in the proper locations. Run to see:

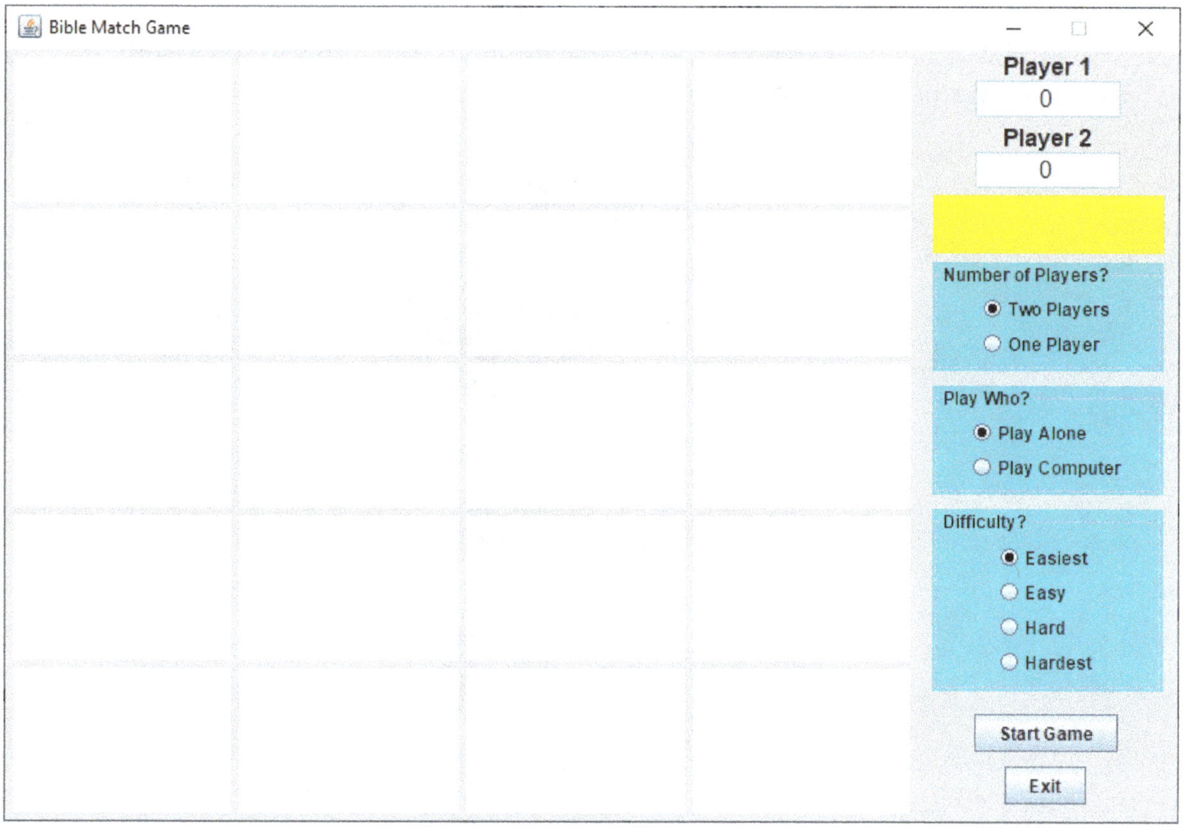

This completes the frame design. You should be able to identify all the controls in the game. Before looking at the code, let's see how to select the pictures used in the game.

Picture Selection

The ten bible pictures used in the game are included in the **\CBGJava\CBGJava Projects\MatchGame** folder:

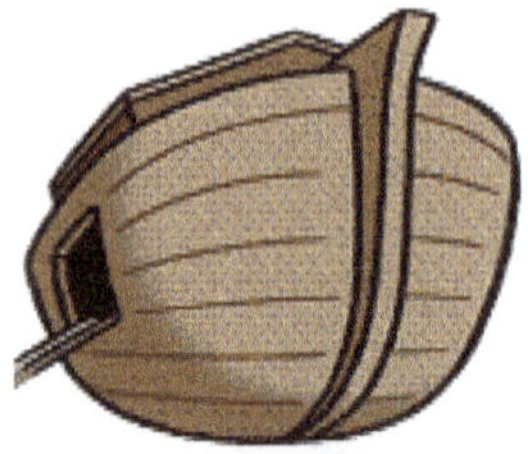

ark.gif

daniel.gif

elijah.gif

goat.gif

lion.gif

pig.gif

raven.gif

sheep.gif

shepherd.gif

woman.gif

Copy each of these files to your project's folder.

One additional image you need is the one used to cover a label box before it is uncovered. Also located in the **\CBGJava\CBGJava Projects\MatchGame** folder is a file named **cover.jpg** that has this picture:

Copy this file to your project folder.

We will now begin writing code for the game. After writing code for the first two projects, **Safecracker** and **Tic Tac Toe**, you should know there are certain standard steps needed to get a working project. Since you should be familiar with these steps by now, in discussing the code for **Bible Match Game**, we will combine some steps to speed up the coding process.

We will write the code in several steps. As a first step, we will write the code that initializes the game. Then, we look at going from 'stopped' state to 'playing' state and back. During the code development process, recognize you may modify a particular method several times before arriving at the finished product.

Code Design – Initializing Stopped State

Any time we start a project, there are certain initializations that must take place. Let's look at the initializations needed in the **Bible Match Game**. All initializations are done at the end of the frame's constructor method.

We will use an **ImageIcon** array (**picture**) to hold the 10 pictures that are used in the game and an additional ImageIcon (**cover**) to hold the cover image. Add declarations for these variables in the class level declarations area:

```
ImageIcon[] picture = new ImageIcon[10];
ImageIcon cover = new ImageIcon();
```

Another initialization is to set the game in **Two Players** mode. As such, we will disable the radio buttons in the **playWhoPanel** and **difficultyPanel**. We will be enabling and disabling radio buttons many times in this game, so let's add three methods that facilitate this process. Add these three methods to your code. One is used to set the enabled property of the radio buttons in the **playersPanel**, one for the **playWhoPanel** and one for the **difficultyPanel** (in each method the boolean argument **a** specifies the desired state, true or false):

```
private void setPlayersButtons(boolean a)
{
  onePlayerRadioButton.setEnabled(a);
  twoPlayersRadioButton.setEnabled(a);
}

private void setPlayWhoButtons(boolean a)
{
  playAloneRadioButton.setEnabled(a);
  playComputerRadioButton.setEnabled(a);
}

 private void setDifficultyButtons(boolean a)
  {
  easiestRadioButton.setEnabled(a);
  easyRadioButton.setEnabled(a);
  hardRadioButton.setEnabled(a);
  hardestRadioButton.setEnabled(a);
}
```

Add this code at the end of the **MatchGame** constructor code:

```
picture[0] = new ImageIcon("clara.jpg");
picture[1] = new ImageIcon("toby.jpg");
picture[2] = new ImageIcon("Blue hills.jpg");
picture[3] = new ImageIcon("Sunset.jpg");
picture[4] = new ImageIcon("Water lilies.jpg");
picture[5] = new ImageIcon("Winter.jpg");
picture[6] = new ImageIcon("spaceneedle.jpg");
picture[7] = new ImageIcon("market.jpg");
picture[8] = new ImageIcon("safeco.jpg");
picture[9] = new ImageIcon("qwest.jpg");
cover = new ImageIcon("cover.jpg");
for (int i = 0; i < 20; i++)
  pictureLabel[i].setIcon(cover);
setPlayWhoButtons(false);
setDifficultyButtons(false);
```

In the above code, if you are using your own pictures, change the graphics file names as appropriate (again, make sure the files are in your project folder or they will not load).

Run the project to make sure the game is properly initialized. Do this and you'll see in the 'stopped' state (using default properties), the **Bible Match Game** looks like this:

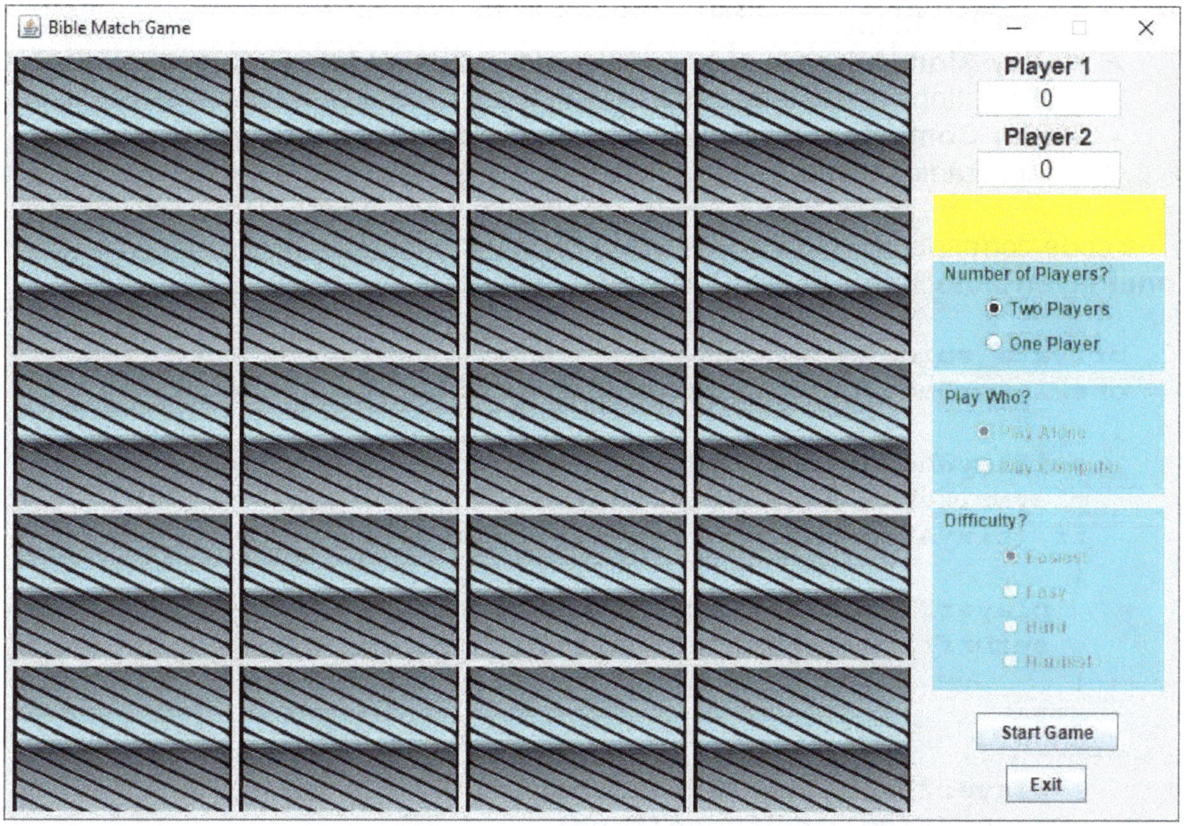

As desired, the game initializes in **Two Players** mode. The label controls are all 'covered.' We have three choices at this point: change to **One Player** mode, click **startStopButton** (the button with **Start Game**) or click **exitButton** (the button with **Exit**).

If we click on the **One Player** button, different options are available and the labels displaying the scoring information must change. The following must happen:

- Enable the radio buttons in play who panel.
- Set **player1Label text** to **You**.
- If **Play Alone** option is selected, set **player2Label text** to **Guesses**, disable radio buttons in difficulty panel.
- If **Play Computer** option is selected, set **player2Label text** to **Computer**, enable radio buttons in difficulty panel.

The code corresponding to these steps is placed in the **onePlayerRadioButtonActionPerformed** method:

```
private void
onePlayerRadioButtonActionPerformed(ActionEvent e)
{
  setPlayWhoButtons(true);
  player1Label.setText("You");
  if (playAloneRadioButton.isSelected())
  {
    player2Label.setText("Guesses");
    setDifficultyButtons(false);
  }
  else
  {
    player2Label.setText("Computer");
    setDifficultyButtons(true);
  }
}
```

In one player mode, we can select **Play Alone** or **Play Computer**. If a user clicks **Play Alone**, we need to make sure the radio buttons in the difficulty panel are disabled and that the **text** property of **player2Label** reads **Guesses**. Use this code in the **playAloneRadioButtonActionPerformed** method:

```
private void
playAloneRadioButtonActionPerformed(ActionEvent e)
{
  setDifficultyButtons(false);
  player2Label.setText("Guesses");
}
```

Conversely, if a user clicks **Play Computer**, we need to make sure the difficulty radio buttons are enabled and that the **text** property of **player2Label** reads **Computer**. Use this code in the **playComputerRadioButtonActionPerformed** method:

```
private void
playComputerRadioButtonActionPerformed(ActionEvent e)
{
  setDifficultyButtons(true);
  player2Label.setText("Computer");
}
```

Lastly, we need code for the **twoPlayersRadioButtonActionPerformed** method to return to two player mode. When this button is clicked, we disable the radio buttons in the play who panel and the difficulty radio buttons and return the label headers to their default values:

```
private void
twoPlayersRadioButtonActionPerformed(ActionEvent e)
{
  setPlayWhoButtons(false);
  setDifficultyButtons(false);
  player1Label.setText("Player 1");
  player2Label.setText("Player 2");
}
```

What about code for clicking on either of the two button controls (**Start Game** or **Exit**)? The code for exiting is simple. The **exitButtonActionPerformed** method:

```
private void exitButtonActionPerformed(ActionEvent e)
{
  System.exit(0);
}
```

This simply says whenever the **Exit** button is clicked, the project closes. Add this code.

The code for the **startStopButton** is much more complicated. We will build it in several steps. First, we look at changing the form from 'stopped' to 'playing' and back to 'stopped' state. Before doing this, let's make sure our new initialization code is working. Save and run the project. It will be in two player mode. Click **One Player**; you should see:

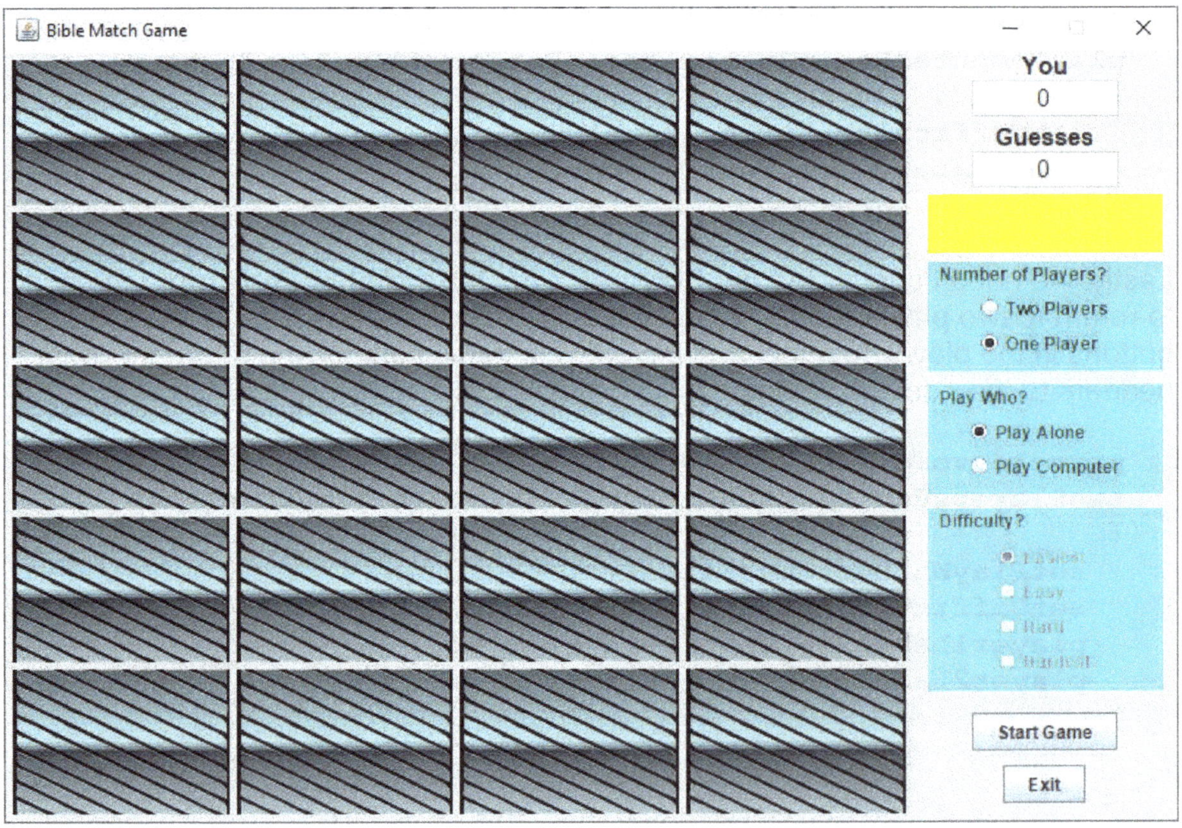

Notice the label controls change. The **Play Who** panel is enabled and the **Difficulty** panel is disabled.

Now, click **Play Computer** and the label controls again change and the **Difficulty** panel is enabled:

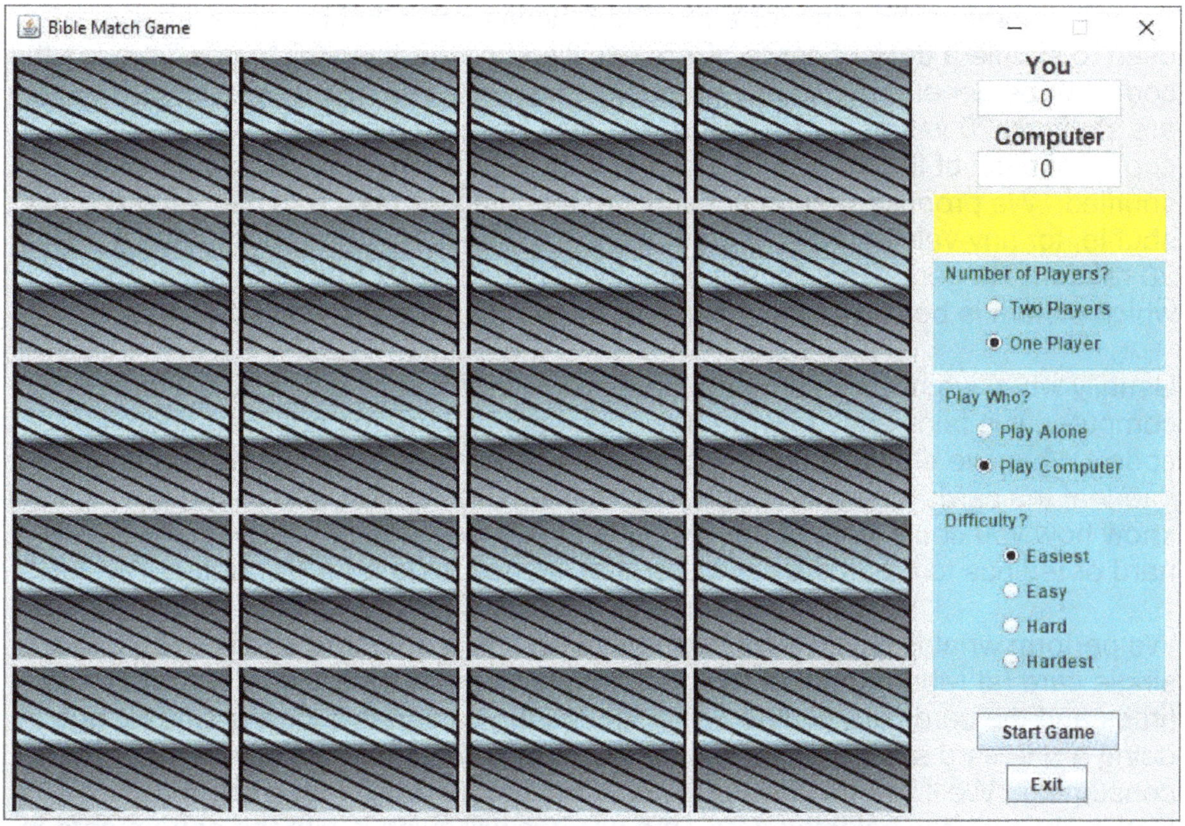

Finally, make sure when you click **Two Players**, the form returns to two player mode.

We're nearly ready to begin looking at the code behind the **Start Game** button. A key step in starting this game is to 'hide' two copies of each picture behind the 20 label controls. There are 10 pictures, represented in the array **picture**, with indices from 0 to 9. We want to randomly place two copies of each index in another array (with 20 elements). The elements of this second array tell us which picture is behind which picture box control. We need some way to shuffle integer indices around. This is actually a very common game task which can be used for shuffling cards, selecting multiple choice answers, or here to hide pictures. We will build a general method to perform this task.

Code Design – Integer Shuffling

We will be presenting code for a **shuffle** process, so called because it can be used to shuffle a deck of cards. Here, we'll just be shuffling 20 "cards," though the code can be generalized to any number of "cards." You might be asking, why we are shuffling 20 values, not 10, since we only have 10 pictures? We need two copies of each of the 10 picture indices, hence there are 20 total items being shuffled. We propose randomly shuffling the integers from 0 to 19. After the shuffle, for any value greater than 9, we will subtract 10. This will give us a list of 20 random integers. This list will have two of each index from 0 to 9, telling us which picture is behind which picture box control. Let's see how to do this.

Usually when we need a computer version of something we can do without a computer, it is fairly easy to write down the steps taken and duplicate them in code. When we shuffle a deck of cards, we separate the deck in two parts, then interleaf the cards as we fan each part, making that familiar shuffling noise. I don't know how you could write code to do this. We'll take another approach which is hard or tedious to do off the computer, but is easy to do on a computer.

We perform what is called a "one card shuffle." In a one card shuffle, you pull a single card (at random) out of the deck and lay it aside on a pile. Repeat this 52 times and the cards are shuffled. Try it! I think you see this idea is simple, but doing a one card shuffle with a real deck of cards would be awfully time-consuming. We'll use the idea of a one card shuffle here, with a slight twist. Rather than lay the selected card on a pile, we will swap it with the bottom card in the stack of cards remaining to be shuffled. This takes the selected card out of the deck and replaces it with the remaining bottom card. The result is the same as if we lay it aside.

Here's how the shuffle works with n numbers:

- Start with a list of n consecutive integers.
- Randomly pick one item from the list. Swap that item with the last item. You now have one fewer items in the list to be sorted (called the remaining list), or n is now n - 1.
- Randomly pick one item from the remaining list. Swap it with the item on the bottom of the remaining list. Again, your remaining list now has one fewer items.
- Repeatedly remove one item from the remaining list and swap it with the item on the bottom of the remaining list until you have run out of items. When done, the list will have been replaced with the original list in random order.

The code to do a one card shuffle, or sort n integers, is placed in a general method named **nRandomIntegers**. The single argument is **n** the number of integers to sort. The method returns an array containing the randomly sorted integers. The returned array is zero-based, returning random integers from 0 to n - 1, not 1 to n. If you need integers from 1 to n, just simply add 1 to each value in the returned array! The code is:

```
private int[] nRandomIntegers(int n)
{
  /*
  *  Returns n randomly sorted integers 0 -> n - 1
  */
  int[] nIntegers = new int[n];
  int temp, s;
  Random sortRandom = new Random();
  //  initialize array from 0 to n - 1
  for (int i = 0; i < n; i++)
  {
    nIntegers[i] = i;
  }
  //  i is number of items remaining in list
  for (int i = n; i >= 1; i--)
  {
    s = sortRandom.nextInt(i);
    temp = nIntegers[s];
    nIntegers[s] = nIntegers[i - 1];
    nIntegers[i - 1] = temp;
  }
  return(nIntegers);
}
```

You should be able to see each step of the shuffle method. This method is general (sorting n integers) and can be used in other projects requiring random lists of integers.

Add the **nRandomIntegers** method to your **Bible Match Game** project. Also, since we are using random numbers, we need this import statement:

```
import java.util.Random;
```

The shuffle method will be used to hide the 10 pictures behind the 20 picture box controls. In the project, we will use a class level array **pictureIndex** (dimensioned to 20) to hold the randomly sorted integers (the shuffled picture indices). Add this class level declaration to your project:

```
int[] pictureIndex = new int[20];
```

The snippet of code that does a shuffle (and adjusts the values greater than 10) is:

```
pictureIndex = nRandomIntegers(20);
for (int i = 0; i < 20; i++)
  if (pictureIndex[i] > 9)
    pictureIndex[i] -= 10;
```

Let's look at an example of how this works. If I run this snippet of code through a little example, the 20 elements of **pictureIndex** returned from one particular call to **nRandomIntegers** are (arranged like our picture boxes):

14	11	15	1
17	2	10	0
5	18	7	8
16	12	19	13
6	4	3	9

You should see all the integers from 0 to 19. Now, subtracting 10 from each value greater than 9 yields:

4	1	5	1
7	2	0	0
5	8	7	8
6	2	9	3
6	4	3	9

As desired, we now have random pairs of the integers from 0 to 9. Matching pairs of integers represent matching pairs of pictures in **Bible Match Game**.

How do we know what picture is behind what picture box control? Say we have a label control, represented by element **i** of the array **pictureLabel[i]**. To determine the picture, examine **pictureIndex[i]**; call this value **j**. The picture in this label is then **picture[j]**, element **j** of the array holding the 10 pictures being used. To set the **IconImage** property, the proper line of code is:

```
pictureLabel[i].setIcon(picture[pictureIndex[i]]);
```

We can now use the shuffling method to start building the code behind the **startStopButton** control.

Code Design – Stopped to Playing to Stopped State

In the **Safecracker** and **Tic Tac Toe** projects, the button to start and stop the game was the same control. That is also the case here. We will look at the code behind this control (**startStopButton**) to both start and stop the game.

When the user clicks the **Start Game** button in the 'stopped' state, several things must happen to switch **Bible Match Game** to 'playing' state:

- Change the **text** property of **startStopButton** to **Stop Game**.
- Initialize scores and corresponding label controls to zero.
- Initialize number of pictures remaining (20).
- Shuffle pictures using **nRandomIntegers** method.
- Initialize label controls for displaying pictures.
- Disable radio buttons in all panel controls (don't allow selection of options while playing).
- Disable **exitButton**.
- Establish this as Player 1's turn.
- Set message to player.
- Allow player to click on label controls.

Conversely, when the user clicks the **Stop Game** button in 'playing' state, several things must happen to switch **Bible Match Game** to 'stopped' state:

- Change the **text** property of **startStopButton** to **Start Game**.
- Enable radio buttons in players panel.
- Enable radio buttons in play who panel, if one player game.
- Enable radio buttons in difficulty panel, if one player game and playing computer.
- Enable **exitButton**.
- Stop allowing clicking on label controls.
- If game is not over, display **Game Stopped** message.

First, let's look at the code to start the game. We establish several variables in the class level declarations to help keep track of where we are in the game:

```
int picturesRemaining;
int[] score = new int[2];
boolean[] pictureFound = new boolean[20];
int playerNumber, choiceNumber;
int[] choice = new int[2];
boolean canClick = false;
boolean gameOver;
```

picturesRemaining tells us how many pictures are still hidden, while the **score** array holds the two players scores (number of matched pictures found). The **pictureFound** array tells us whether a picture behind the corresponding picture box control has been uncovered (so it can't be clicked twice). **playerNumber** tells us whose turn it is and **choiceNumber** tells whether it is the player's first choice on the playing board or second choice. The **choice** array holds the indices of the two picture boxes selected. **canClick** is used to determine if it's okay to click on the picture box controls. It is **true** when playing, **false** (the initial value) when stopped. Finally, **gameOver** is used to tell us whether the game is actually over (**true** if all pictures uncovered) or the **Stop Game** button was clicked before completing a game (**false**).

The code for the **startStopButtonActionPerformed** method that implements the steps for clicking on **Start Game** and initializes the new variables is:

```
private void startStopButtonActionPerformed(ActionEvent e)
{
  if (startStopButton.getText().equals("Start Game"))
  {
    startStopButton.setText("Stop Game");
    score[0] = 0;
    score[1] = 0;
    scoreTextField[0].setText("0");
    scoreTextField[1].setText("0");
    picturesRemaining = 20;
    pictureIndex = nRandomIntegers(20);
    for (int i = 0; i < 20; i++)
    {
      if (pictureIndex[i] > 9)
        pictureIndex[i] -= 10;
      pictureFound[i] = false;
      pictureLabel[i].setIcon(cover);
    }
    playerNumber = 1;
    choiceNumber = 1;
    if (twoPlayersRadioButton.isSelected())
```

```
        messageLabel.setText("Player 1, Pick a Box");
      else
        messageLabel.setText("Pick a Box");
      setNumberPlayersButtons(false);
      setPlayWhoButtons(false);
      setDifficultyButtons(false);
      exitButton.setEnabled(false);
      canClick = true;
      gameOver = false;
    }
    else
    {
      // stop game
    }
  }
```

The steps follow should be clear. Note especially where the "shuffling" routine was used to form the **pictureIndex** array.

Save and run the project. Click on **Start Game** and you should see:

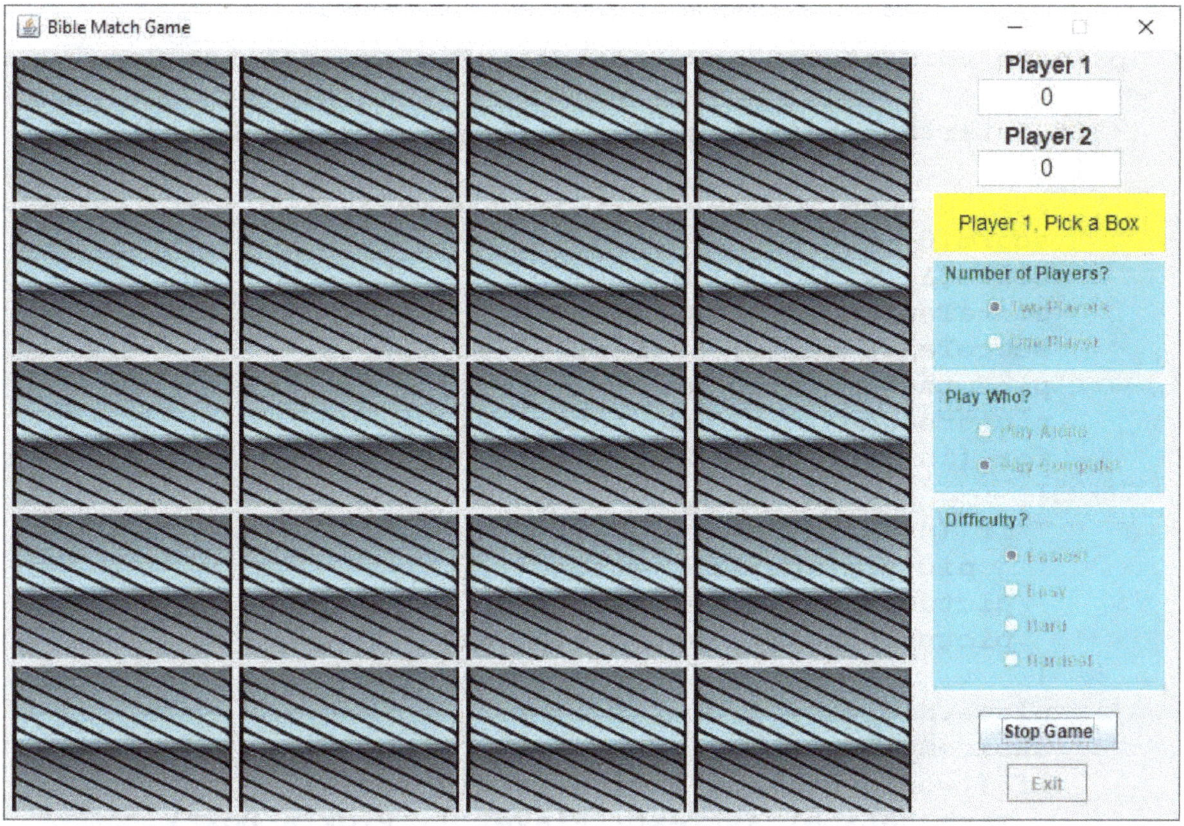

The only noticeable change is the two player message in the label control (**Player 1, Pick a Box**). Stop the project (you can't click **Stop Game** yet) and try the other options if you'd like.

The code for the **btnStartStop Click** event that implements the steps for clicking on **Stop Game** is (additions are shaded):

```
private void startStopButtonActionPerformed(ActionEvent e)
{
  if (startStopButton.getText().equals("Start Game"))
  {
    startStopButton.setText("Stop Game");
    score[0] = 0;
    score[1] = 0;
    scoreTextField[0].setText("0");
    scoreTextField[1].setText("0");
    picturesRemaining = 20;
    pictureIndex = nRandomIntegers(20);
    for (int i = 0; i < 20; i++)
    {
      if (pictureIndex[i] > 9)
        pictureIndex[i] -= 10;
      pictureFound[i] = false;
      pictureLabel[i].setIcon(cover);
    }
    playerNumber = 1;
    choiceNumber = 1;
    if (twoPlayersRadioButton.isSelected())
      messageLabel.setText("Player 1, Pick a Box");
    else
      messageLabel.setText("Pick a Box");
    setNumberPlayersButtons(false);
    setPlayWhoButtons(false);
    setDifficultyButtons(false);
    exitButton.setEnabled(false);
    canClick = true;
    gameOver = false;
  }
  else
  {
    // stop game
    startStopButton.setText("Start Game");
    setNumberPlayersButtons(true);
    if (onePlayerRadioButton.isSelected())
    {
      setPlayWhoButtons(true);
      if (playComputerRadioButton.isSelected())
        setDifficultyButtons(true);
    }
    exitButton.setEnabled(true);
    canClick = false;
```

```
      if (!gameOver)
        messageLabel.setText("Game Stopped");
    }
  }
```

Notice how we determine which panels holding radio buttons should be disabled/enabled and how we decide if the **Game Stopped** message is used. Other messages will appear (developed in later code) if a game is played to completion (**gameOver** is **True**).

Save and run the project. You should be able to now move from 'stopped' to 'playing' state and back. Make sure the panels are in the proper state for the one and two player options. Let's write the code for the two player game, first looking at how to display a picture following a click on a label control.

Code Design –Displaying Pictures

In the **Bible Match Game** two player game, when a player clicks a label on the game panel, we want the proper picture to appear. After clicking a second label, another picture is displayed and we see if there is a match. If there is a match, the pictures are removed and the player is given another turn. If there is no match, the pictures are hidden again and we switch to the next player.

So, when a label is clicked, we follow these steps:

- Make sure the box has not already been clicked.
- Display picture.
- If first choice, allow second choice and display that picture. Compare the two pictures.
- If pictures match:
  - Play matching sound.
  - Remove labels with pictures from frame
  - Increment proper player score by 1.
  - Decrement **picturesRemaining** by 2.
  - If **picturesRemaining = 0**, set **gameOver** to **true**, determine winner, play game over sound and stop game.
  - If **picturesRemaining != 0**, give player another turn.
- If pictures do not match:
  - Play no match sound.
  - Replace pictures with ‘cover’ graphic.
  - Swap players.

We’ll code all of these steps in a bit. But first, notice we refer to playing sounds. In previous games, we added sounds at the very end. We know all games use sounds so, from now on, they will be added when needed in projects. We use three sounds in this game. In the **\CBGJava\CBGJava Projects\Match Game** folder are three wav files that can be used for sound. The **tada.wav** file is a sound we’ll use when two pictures match. The **boing.wav** file is used when there is no match. And, the **wow.wav** sound is used when a game is over. Copy the three sound files to your project’s folder.

Add these import statements:

```
import java.net.URL;
import java.applet.*;
```

And, add these class level declarations to represent the two sounds:

```
AudioClip matchSound;
AudioClip noMatchSound;
AudioClip gameOverSound;
```

Add ths code to the end of the **MatchGame** constructor code:

```
try
{
  matchSound = Applet.newAudioClip(new URL("file:" +
"tada.wav"));
  noMatchSound = Applet.newAudioClip(new URL("file:" +
"boing.wav"));
  gameOverSound = Applet.newAudioClip(new URL("file:" +
"wow.wav"));
}
catch (Exception ex)
{
  System.out.println("Error loading sound files");
}
```

Now the coding of displaying a picture in a selected label. Like in the **Tic Tac Toe** project, we anticipate that a human can choose a label or the computer can choose a label (in one player game versus the computer), we first write a general method that implements the above steps (not checking for a win yet, though). Add this class level variable (to indicate the selected label):

```
int labelSelected;
```

Add this general method (**showSelectedLabel**) which uses **labelSelected** to display the corresponding picture:

```
private void showSelectedLabel()
{

pictureLabel[labelSelected].setIcon(picture[pictureIndex[l
abelSelected]]);
  pictureFound[labelSelected] = true;
  if (choiceNumber == 1)
  {
    choice[0] = labelSelected;
    choiceNumber = 2;
    if (twoPlayersRadioButton.isSelected())
    {
      messageLabel.setText("Player " +
String.valueOf(playerNumber) + ", Pick Another");
      canClick = true;
    }
    else
    {
      // one player logic
    }
  }
  else
  {
    choice[1] = labelSelected;
    choiceNumber = 1;
    if (pictureIndex[choice[0]] ==
pictureIndex[choice[1]])
    {
      // a match
      matchSound.play();
      pictureLabel[choice[0]].setIcon(null);
      pictureLabel[choice[1]].setIcon(null);
      score[playerNumber - 1]++;
      scoreTextField[playerNumber -
1].setText(String.valueOf(score[playerNumber - 1]));
      picturesRemaining -= 2;
```

```
        if (picturesRemaining == 0)
        {
          gameOver = true;
          gameOverSound.play();
          if (twoPlayersRadioButton.isSelected())
          {
            if (score[0] > score[1])
              messageLabel.setText("Player 1 Wins!");
            else if (score[1] > score[0])
              messageLabel.setText("Player 2 Wins!");
            else
              messageLabel.setText("It's a Tie!");
          }
          else
          {
            // one player logic
          }
          startStopButton.doClick();
          return;
        }
        // another turn
        if (twoPlayersRadioButton.isSelected())
        {
          messageLabel.setText("Player " +
String.valueOf(playerNumber) + ", Pick Again");
          canClick = true;
        }
        else
        {
          // one player logic
        }
      }
      else
      {
        //no match
        noMatchSound.play();
        pictureFound[choice[0]] = false;
        pictureFound[choice[1]] = false;
        pictureLabel[choice[0]].setIcon(cover);
        pictureLabel[choice[1]].setIcon(cover);
        // swap players
        if (twoPlayersRadioButton.isSelected())
        {
          if (playerNumber == 1)
            playerNumber = 2;
          else
            playerNumber = 1;
```

```
            messageLabel.setText("Player " +
String.valueOf(playerNumber) + ", Pick a Box");
            canClick = true;
          }
          else
          {
            // one player logic
          }
        }
      }
    }
```

I know this is a lot of code to throw at you at once, but it's simply a straightforward implementation of the listed steps (except for determining the value of **labelSelected**; we'll look at that next). Now that you're becoming a great game programmer, you should be able to follow the logic. It's similar to that used in the **Tic Tac Toe** game. The picture behind the selected label (**picture[pictureIndex[labelSelected]]**) is displayed. If this is the first choice (**choiceNumber = 1**), we tell the player to pick again (using **messageLabel**).

Following display of the second choice, we look to see if the two selections match. The selected boxes are stored in the **choice** array. If there is a match, the pictures are removed, a sound is played and we check to see if all the pictures have been selected. If pictures remain, the same player is given another turn. Similarly, for no match, a sound is heard, the pictures are recovered and players are swapped.

All of this code is for a two player game. Notice, however, we have left "hooks" (represented by comment statements) for later modifications for a one player game.

Let's use this method to allow selection of labels using the mouse. The code to do this goes in the **pictureLabelMousePressed** method (currently empty). To determine which label is clicked, we use the same logic developed in the **Tic Tac Toe** game, checking the upper left corner of the clicked label. Add this code to the **pictureLabelMousePressed** method:

```
private void pictureLabelMousePressed(MouseEvent e)
{
  // determine which label was clicked
  // get upper left corner of clicked label
  Point p = e.getComponent().getLocation();
  // determine index based on p
  for (labelSelected = 0; labelSelected < 20;
labelSelected++)
  {
    if (p.x == pictureLabel[labelSelected].getX() && p.y
== pictureLabel[labelSelected].getY())
      break;
  }
  if (!canClick || pictureFound[labelSelected])
    return;
  // show image behind selected label box
  canClick = false;
  showSelectedLabel();
}
```

Clicking any of the twenty label controls used to display pictures will invoke this method. The first part of the code determines the index of the element of label control array that was clicked (the variable **labelSelected**). If the box has already been clicked (or **canClick** is **false**), the method is exited. Otherwise, we show the picture behind the label using the **showSelectedLabel** method.

Save and run the project. Try playing the two player game with a friend or by yourself. You will notice a problem. When you click on the first label, the picture displays fine. When you click the second label, though, nothing is seen. You'll hear a sound indicating a match or no match, but you won't see the second picture. The code executes so quickly the display of the pictures cannot keep up! We need to slow things down a bit be inserting a delay. To do this, we use the Java **timer** object. Since this may not be a familiar topic, we'll do a quick review.

Timer Object

A **timer object** generates an event every **delay** milliseconds. The code in the timer's corresponding **actionPerformed** method is executed with each such event. Other control events can be detected while the timer object processes events in the background. This multi-tasking allows more than one thing to be happening in your application.

Timer **Properties**:

delay	Number of milliseconds (there are 1000 milliseconds in one second) between each invocation of the timer object's **actionPerformed** method.
running	Boolean value indicating if timer is running.

Timer **Methods**:

start	Used to start timer object.
stop	Used to stop timer.
isRunning	Method that returns boolean value indicating whether timer is running (generating events).

Timer **Events**:

actionPerformed	Event method invoked every **delay** milliseconds while timer object's **running** property is **true**.

To use a timer object, you first declare it using the standard syntax. For a timer named **myTimer**, the code is:

```
Timer myTimer;
```

The constructor for the timer object specifies the **delay** and adds the event (**actionPerformed**) method, using an **ActionListener**, in a single step. The syntax is:

```
myTimer = new Timer(delay, new ActionListener()
{
  public void actionPerformed(ActionEvent e)
  {
    myTimerActionPerformed(e);
  }
});
```

And, the corresponding event code would be placed in a **myTimerActionPerformed** method:

```
private void myTimerActionPerformed(ActionEvent e)
{
   [method code]
}
```

To use the **timer** object, we add it to our application the same as any object. You write code in the timer object's **actionPerformed** method. This is the code you want to repeat every **delay** milliseconds

You 'turn on' a timer in code using the **start** method:

```
myTimer.start();
```

and it is turned off using the **stop** method:

```
myTimer.stop();
```

To check if the timer is on, use the **isRunning** method:

```
myTimer.isRunning();
```

If this method returns a boolean true, the timer is on.

Applications can (and many times do) have multiple timer objects. You need separate timer objects (and event methods) if you have events that occur with different regularity (different **delay** values). Timer objects are used for two primary purposes. First, as we do here, you can use a timer object to implement some 'wait time' established by the **delay** property. In this case, you simply start the timer and when the delay is reached, have the **actionPerformed** event turn its corresponding timer off. Second, you use timer objects to periodically repeat some code segment. This is very useful for graphics animation. We will do this in the remaining three projects in these notes.

Typical use of **timer** object:

- Declare timer, assigning an identifiable **name**. For **myTimer**, the statement is:

```
Timer myTimer;
```

- Establish a **delay** value. Create the timer using specified constructor, adding the **actionPerformed** method. Write the method code.
- At some point in your application, start the timer. Also, have capability to turn the timer off, when desired.

Code Design – Adding Delays

In the **Bible Match Game**, we want to implement a delay of some duration following the code that displays a selected label. We chose to delay for 0.5 seconds (500 milliseconds). You can choose another value if you want.

To implement this delay, first declare a timer object:

```
Timer displayTimer;
```

Add it to the project (creating the event method, **displayTimerActionPerformed**) with this code:

```
displayTimer = new Timer(500, new ActionListener()
{
  public void actionPerformed(ActionEvent e)
  {
    displayTimerActionPerformed(e);
  }
});
```

Add the empty method:

```
private void displayTimerActionPerformed(ActionEvent e)
{
}
```

The way this will work is: following display of a picture, we start the timer object (**delayTimer**). This will implement a wait of **delay** milliseconds (500 milliseconds in this case) until the code in the **displayTimerActionPerformed** method is executed. The code in that method will be the code that currently follows the picture display line (the shaded code below, in **showSelectedLabel** method):

```
private void showSelectedLabel()
{

pictureLabel[labelSelected].setIcon(picture[pictureIndex[l
abelSelected]]);
  pictureFound[labelSelected] = true;
   if (choiceNumber == 1)
  {
    choice[0] = labelSelected;
    choiceNumber = 2;
    if (twoPlayersRadioButton.isSelected())
    {
      messageLabel.setText("Player " +
String.valueOf(playerNumber) + ", Pick Another");
      canClick = true;
    }
    else
    {
      // one player logic
    }
  }
  else
  {
    choice[1] = labelSelected;
    choiceNumber = 1;
    if (pictureIndex[choice[0]] ==
pictureIndex[choice[1]])
    {
      // a match
      matchSound.play();
      pictureLabel[choice[0]].setIcon(null);
      pictureLabel[choice[1]].setIcon(null);
      score[playerNumber - 1]++;
      scoreTextField[playerNumber -
1].setText(String.valueOf(score[playerNumber - 1]));
      picturesRemaining -= 2;
      if (picturesRemaining == 0)
      {
        gameOver = true;
        gameOverSound.play();
        if (twoPlayersRadioButton.isSelected())
```

```
        {
          if (score[0] > score[1])
            messageLabel.setText("Player 1 Wins!");
          else if (score[1] > score[0])
            messageLabel.setText("Player 2 Wins!");
          else
            messageLabel.setText("It's a Tie!");
        }
        else
        {
          // one player logic
        }
        startStopButton.doClick();
        return;
      }
      // another turn
      if (twoPlayersRadioButton.isSelected())
      {
        messageLabel.setText("Player " +
String.valueOf(playerNumber) + ", Pick Again");
        canClick = true;
      }
      else
      {
        // one player logic
      }
    }
    else
    {
      //no match
      noMatchSound.play();
      pictureFound[choice[0]] = false;
      pictureFound[choice[1]] = false;
      pictureLabel[choice[0]].setIcon(cover);
      pictureLabel[choice[1]].setIcon(cover);
      // swap players
      if (twoPlayersRadioButton.isSelected())
      {
        if (playerNumber == 1)
          playerNumber = 2;
        else
          playerNumber = 1;
        messageLabel.setText("Player " +
String.valueOf(playerNumber) + ", Pick a Box");
        canClick = true;
      }
      else
```

```
        {
          // one player logic
        }
      }
    }
  }
```

Before this code is executed, we stop the timer to insure the code is only processed one time.

So first replace all the above shaded code (make sure you save the deleted code) with a single line of code that turns on the timer (new line is shaded):

```
private void showSelectedLabel()
{

pictureLabel[labelSelected].setIcon(picture[pictureIndex[l
abelSelected]]);
  pictureFound[labelSelected] = true;
  displayTimer.start();
}
```

Now, put the code you just deleted from the **showSelectedLabel** method in the **delayTimerActionPerformed** method, adding the line to turn off the timer at the beginning (shaded):

```
private void displayTimerActionPerformed(ActionEvent e)
{
  displayTimer.stop();
  if (choiceNumber == 1)
  {
    choice[0] = labelSelected;
    choiceNumber = 2;
    if (twoPlayersRadioButton.isSelected())
    {
      messageLabel.setText("Player " +
String.valueOf(playerNumber) + ", Pick Another");
      canClick = true;
    }
    else
    {
      // one player logic
    }
  }
  else
  {
    choice[1] = labelSelected;
```

```
    choiceNumber = 1;
    if (pictureIndex[choice[0]] ==
pictureIndex[choice[1]])
    {
      // a match
      matchSound.play();
      pictureLabel[choice[0]].setIcon(null);
      pictureLabel[choice[1]].setIcon(null);
      score[playerNumber - 1]++;
      scoreTextField[playerNumber -
1].setText(String.valueOf(score[playerNumber - 1]));
      picturesRemaining -= 2;
      if (picturesRemaining == 0)
      {
        gameOver = true;
        gameOverSound.play();
        if (twoPlayersRadioButton.isSelected())
        {
          if (score[0] > score[1])
            messageLabel.setText("Player 1 Wins!");
          else if (score[1] > score[0])
            messageLabel.setText("Player 2 Wins!");
          else
            messageLabel.setText("It's a Tie!");
        }
        else
        {
          // one player logic
        }
        startStopButton.doClick();
        return;
      }
      // another turn
      if (twoPlayersRadioButton.isSelected())
      {
        messageLabel.setText("Player " +
String.valueOf(playerNumber) + ", Pick Again");
        canClick = true;
      }
      else
      {
        // one player logic
      }
    }
    else
    {
      //no match
```

```
        noMatchSound.play();
        pictureFound[choice[0]] = false;
        pictureFound[choice[1]] = false;
        pictureLabel[choice[0]].setIcon(cover);
        pictureLabel[choice[1]].setIcon(cover);
        // swap players
        if (twoPlayersRadioButton.isSelected())
        {
          if (playerNumber == 1)
            playerNumber = 2;
          else
            playerNumber = 1;
          messageLabel.setText("Player " +
String.valueOf(playerNumber) + ", Pick a Box");
          canClick = true;
        }
        else
        {
          // one player logic
        }
      }
    }
  }
```

Make sure you see how this all works – it's actually kind of simple. The picture displays, the timer starts, 0.5 seconds elapses, giving time for the picture to display, the timer is turned off and the code in the timer method (**delayTimerActionPerformed**) executes.

Save and run the project. You and a friend should now be able to play a two player version of **Bible Match Game** with the pictures appearing correctly. When a match is found, you will hear a 'tada' sound and the pictures will disappear. When no match is found, you will hear a 'boing' sound and the pictures will be recovered. When done, you'll hear a crowd saying "wow". Give it a try. I played a two player game by myself. Here's the form after three matches have been found (2 by **Player 1**, 1 by **Player 2**) and one box has been uncovered:

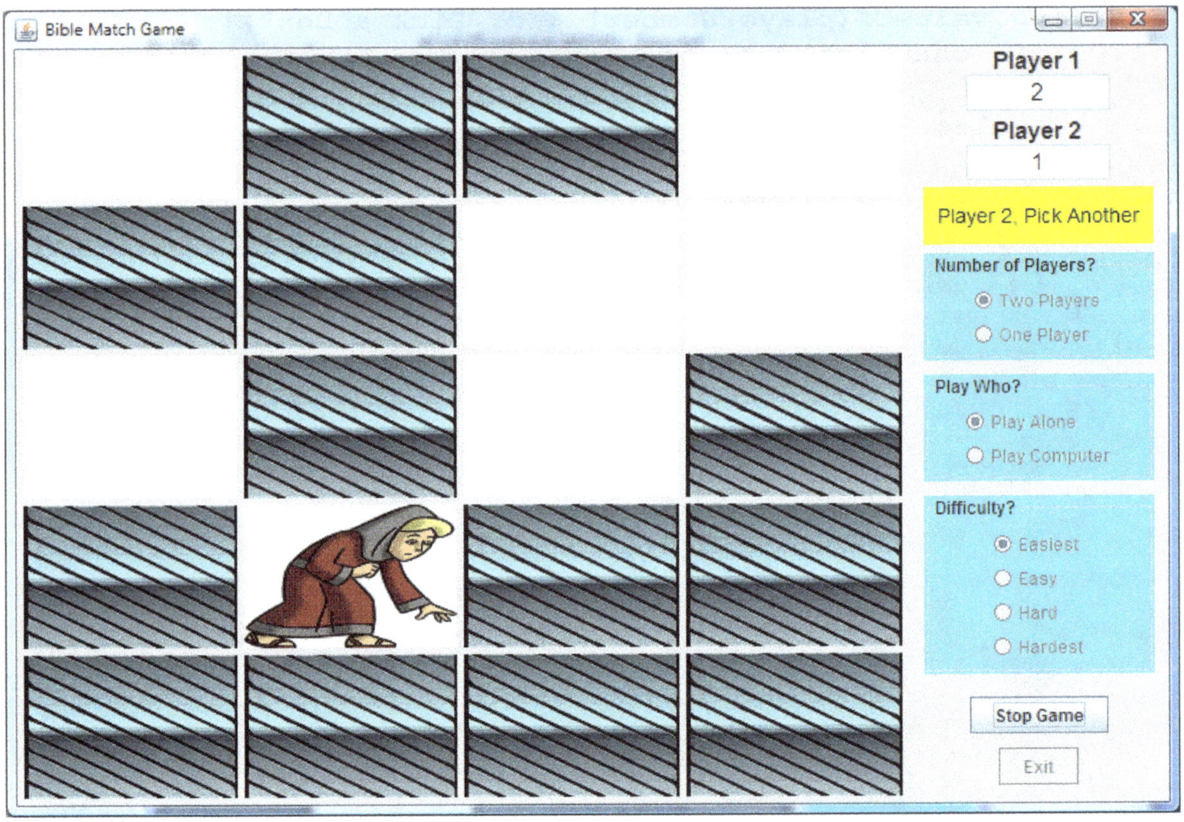

Playing the game to completion, the form looks like this, where we could now select other options and play again:

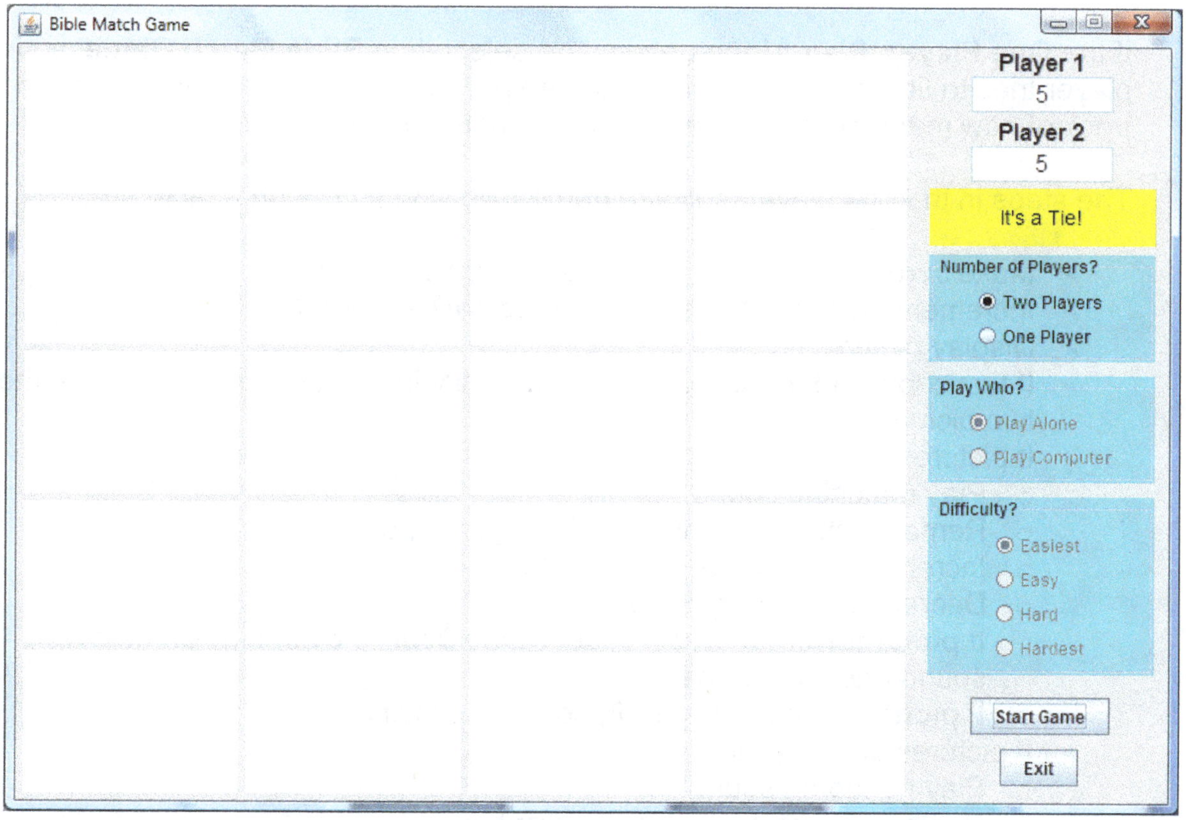

It's a tie! Actually, I was Player 1 and Player 2. In such a case, when you don't have a playing partner, it's fun to play alone or play the computer. Let's code up those options now.

Code Design - One Player, Solitaire Game

If the **One Player**, **Play Alone** options are selected in **Bible Match Game**, a single player tries to find matching pictures on the playing form. The computer keeps track of how many guesses it takes until all matches have been found.

The steps in the one player, solitaire game following a click on a label are:

- Make sure the label has not already been selected.
- Increment number of guesses (use **scoreTextField[1]**)
- Display picture.
- If first choice, allow second choice and display that picture. Compare the two pictures.
- If pictures match:
  - Play matching sound.
  - Remove labels with pictures from game panel.
  - Increment number of matches by 1.
  - Decrement **picturesRemaining** by 2.
  - If **picturesRemaining = 0**, set **gameOver** to **true**, play game over sound and stop game.
  - If **picturesRemaining != 0**, continue playing.
- If pictures do not match:
  - Play no match sound.
  - Replace pictures with 'cover' graphic.
  - Continue playing.

To implement these steps, we first make the shaded modifications to the **showSelectedMethod** method:

```
private void showSelectedLabel()
{
  // one player/solitaire game
  if (onePlayerRadioButton.isSelected() &&
playAloneRadioButton.isSelected())
  {
    score[1]++;
    scoreTextField[1].setText(String.valueOf(score[1]));
  }

pictureLabel[labelSelected].setIcon(picture[pictureIndex[l
abelSelected]]);
  pictureFound[labelSelected] = true;
  displayTimer.start();
}
```

And we make additional modifications (shaded code) to the **displayTimerActionPerformedMethod**:

```
private void displayTimerActionPerformed(ActionEvent e)
{
  displayTimer.stop();
  if (choiceNumber == 1)
  {
    choice[0] = labelSelected;
    choiceNumber = 2;
    if (twoPlayersRadioButton.isSelected())
    {
      messageLabel.setText("Player " +
String.valueOf(playerNumber) + ", Pick Another");
      canClick = true;
    }
    else
    {
    // one player logic
      if (playerNumber == 1)
      {
        messageLabel.setText("Pick Another Box");
        canClick = true;
      }
      else
      {
        // play computer logic
      }
    }
  }
  else
  {
    choice[1] = labelSelected;
    choiceNumber = 1;
    if (pictureIndex[choice[0]] ==
pictureIndex[choice[1]])
    {
      // a match
      matchSound.play();
      pictureLabel[choice[0]].setIcon(null);
      pictureLabel[choice[1]].setIcon(null);
      score[playerNumber - 1]++;
      scoreTextField[playerNumber -
1].setText(String.valueOf(score[playerNumber - 1]));
      picturesRemaining -= 2;
      if (picturesRemaining == 0)
      {
```

```
        gameOver = true;
        gameOverSound.play();
        if (twoPlayersRadioButton.isSelected())
        {
          if (score[0] > score[1])
            messageLabel.setText("Player 1 Wins!");
          else if (score[1] > score[0])
            messageLabel.setText("Player 2 Wins!");
          else
            messageLabel.setText("It's a Tie!");
        }
        else
        {
          // one player logic
          if (playAloneRadioButton.isSelected())
            messageLabel.setText("All Matches Found!");
          else
          {
            // play computer logic
          }
        }
        startStopButton.doClick();
        return;
      }
      // another turn
      if (twoPlayersRadioButton.isSelected())
      {
        messageLabel.setText("Player " +
String.valueOf(playerNumber) + ", Pick Again");
        canClick = true;
      }
      else
      {
        // one player logic
        if (playerNumber == 1)
        {
          messageLabel.setText("Pick a Box");
          canClick = true;
        }
        else
        {
          // play computer logic
        }
      }
    }
    else
    {
```

```
        //no match
        noMatchSound.play();
        pictureFound[choice[0]] = false;
        pictureFound[choice[1]] = false;
        pictureLabel[choice[0]].setIcon(cover);
        pictureLabel[choice[1]].setIcon(cover);
        // swap players
        if (twoPlayersRadioButton.isSelected())
        {
          if (playerNumber == 1)
            playerNumber = 2;
          else
            playerNumber = 1;
          messageLabel.setText("Player " +
String.valueOf(playerNumber) + ", Pick a Box");
          canClick = true;
        }
        else
        {
          // one player logic
          if (playerNumber == 1)
          {
            messageLabel.setText("Pick a Box");
            canClick = true;
          }
          else
          {
            // play computer logic
          }
        }
      }
    }
}
```

Again, note we have left "hooks" (comment statements) for one player game versus the computer (**play computer logic**).

Save and run the game. Click **One Player** and make sure **Play Alone** is selected. Click **Start Game.** Here's the first box I uncovered:

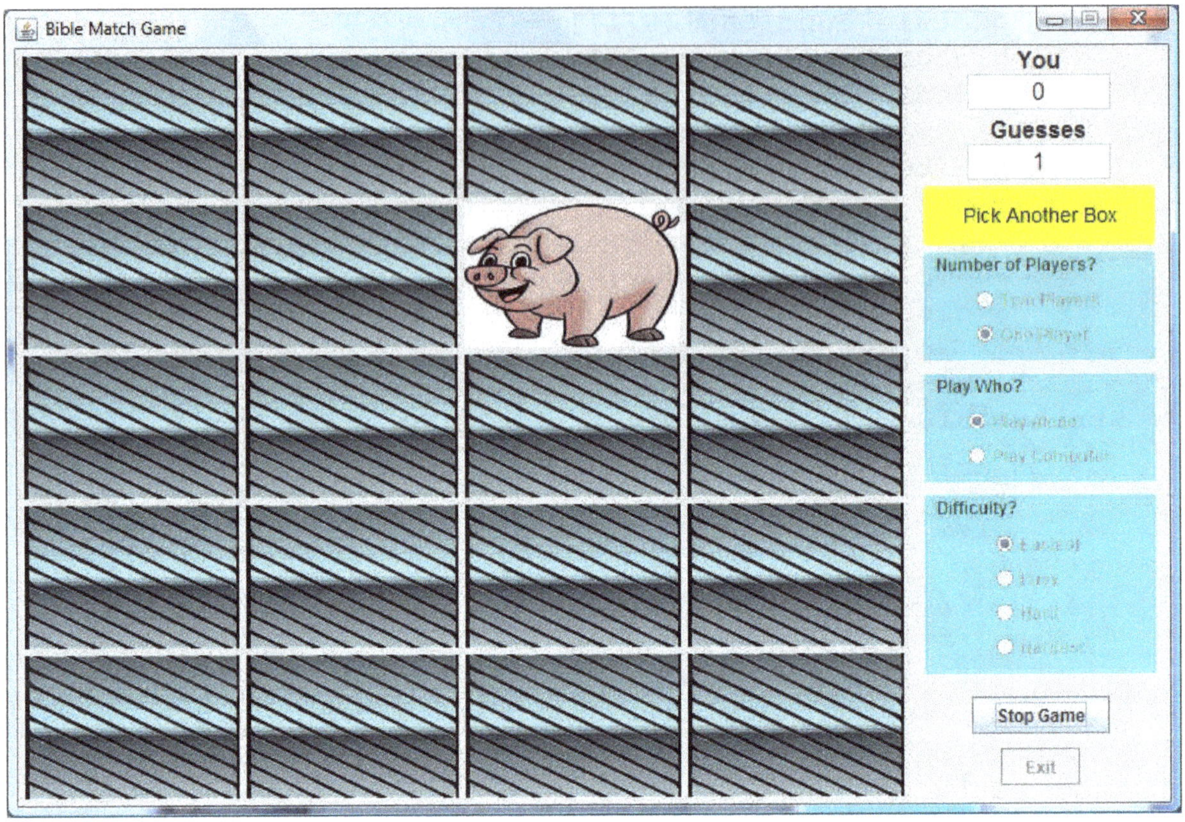

I uncovered another, but no match.

From here on, you just keep uncovering pictures. The computer keeps track of how many guesses (pictures uncovered) it took you to find all the matches. Here's the form once I finished (I did pretty well – it took me 62 guesses):

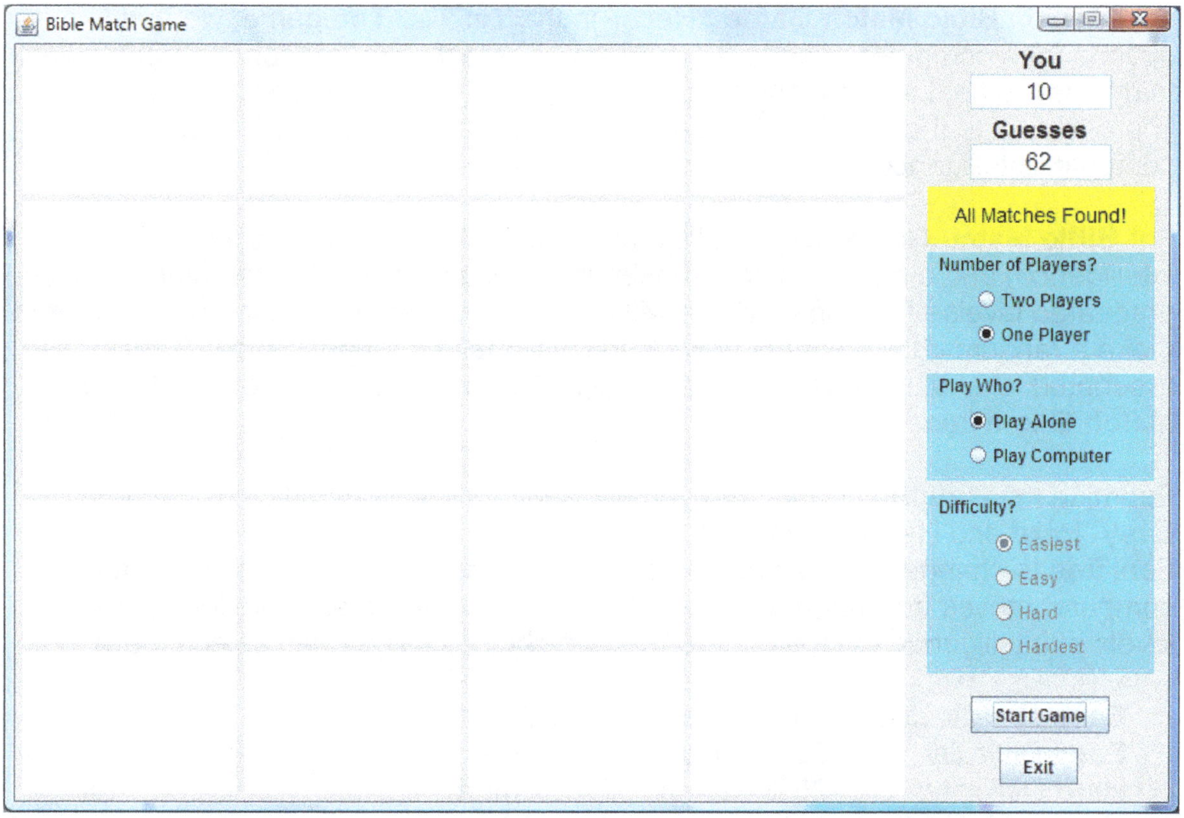

Now, let's see how to change the game to play against the computer.

Code Design – Computer Moves

It's time to give some intelligence to the computer, trying to make it a reasonable opponent in **Bible Match Game**. Recall in the **Tic Tac Toe** game, we had two options for a computer opponent: **random** or **smart**. The random opponent was fairly easy to beat and the smart opponent was impossible to beat. As an improvement to the **Tic Tac Toe** game, we suggested graduated levels of computer intelligence. We will take that approach here.

For **Bible Match Game**, we will still develop logic for a **random** choice (minimum intelligence) and a **smart** choice (maximum intelligence) by the computer. To give graduated levels of intelligence, we will decide how often we want the computer to make a random choice versus how often it will make a smart choice. That graduated level of intelligence is selected in the **Difficulty** panel on the **Bible Match Game** frame.

Examine the **Difficulty** panel and you will see four levels of difficulty: **Easiest**, **Easy**, **Hard** and **Hardest**. We will set some rules for intelligence at each level. Feel free to change these if you'd like. These rules establish what percentage of computer moves are random and what percentage are smart. Obviously lower levels of intelligence will have more random choices. The rules selected are:

Easiest Difficulty:	75% Random, 25% Smart
Easy Difficulty:	50% Random, 50% Smart
Hard Difficulty:	25% Random, 75% Smart
Hardest Difficulty:	10% Random, 90% Smart

So even at the highest level of difficulty, we allow that the computer can make a mistake.

Let's build a framework for implementing a computer opponent, then develop the code for a random or a smart move. Add these class level declarations:

```
Random myRandom = new Random();
boolean smartComputer;
int difficulty = 1;
```

We will use a random number (using the **myRandom** object) to determine whether a random (**smartComputer** is **false**) or smart (**smartComputer** is **true**) move is to be made, based on the value of **difficulty** (initialized at 1, the **Easy** level). The resulting label to be uncovered will be represented by **labelSelected**.

Code the **ActionPerformed** methods for the four radio buttons used to set **difficulty**:

```
private void easiestRadioButtonActionPerformed(ActionEvent
e)
{
  difficulty = 1;
}

private void easyRadioButtonActionPerformed(ActionEvent e)
{
  difficulty = 2;
}

private void hardRadioButtonActionPerformed(ActionEvent e)
{
  difficulty = 3;
}

private void hardestRadioButtonActionPerformed(ActionEvent
e)
{
  difficulty = 4;
}
```

Code two empty methods (**randomChoice** and **smartChoice**) that return the selected box for the random and smart computer options:

```
private int randomChoice()
{
  return(0);
}

private int smartChoice()
{
  return(0);
}
```

We'll add some code to these soon.

Add a general method (**computerTurn**) that generates the computer's selection based on the selected difficulty and corresponding rules for move generation:

```
private void computerTurn()
{
  int threshold = 0;
  if (choiceNumber == 1)
  {
    switch (difficulty)
    {
      case 1:
        threshold = 25;
        break;
      case 2:
        threshold = 50;
        break;
      case 3:
        threshold = 75;
        break;
      case 4:
        threshold = 90;
        break;
    }
    if (myRandom.nextInt(100) < threshold)
      smartComputer = true;
    else
      smartComputer = false;
  }
  if (smartComputer)
    labelSelected = smartChoice();
  else
    labelSelected = randomChoice();
```

```
    showSelectedLabel();
  }
```

In this code, if it's the first choice (**choiceNumber = 1**), we decide whether we have a smart computer for both computer selections. This is done by establishing a **threshold** (from 0 to 100) based on difficulty. The higher the threshold, the smarter the computer. We then generate a random number from 0 to 99. If this number is less than the threshold, we use a smart computer (**smartComputer** is **true**). In such a case, the **labelSelected** will be found using the **smartChoice** method (which has no code yet). If **smartComputer** is **false**, we obtain **labelSelected** from the **randomChoice** method (also empty). Once, we know **labelSelected**, we display the corresponding picture by calling the **showSelectedLabel** method.

And, we need to modify the **displayTimerActionPerformed** method to allow a computer opponent (recall the "hooks" are marked by comment statements). In a game against the computer, the computer is Player 2 – you always get to go first. These shaded modifications simply call **computerTurn** at the proper time and swap players when appropriate:

```
  private void displayTimerActionPerformed(ActionEvent e)
  {
    displayTimer.stop();
    if (choiceNumber == 1)
    {
      choice[0] = labelSelected;
      choiceNumber = 2;
      if (twoPlayersRadioButton.isSelected())
      {
        messageLabel.setText("Player " +
  String.valueOf(playerNumber) + ", Pick Another");
        canClick = true;
      }
      else
      {
      // one player logic
        if (playerNumber == 1)
        {
          messageLabel.setText("Pick Another Box");
          canClick = true;
        }
        else
        {
          // play computer logic
          messageLabel.setText("Picking Another");
          computerTurn();
          return;
```

```
        }
      }
    }
    else
    {
      choice[1] = labelSelected;
      choiceNumber = 1;
      if (pictureIndex[choice[0]] ==
pictureIndex[choice[1]])
      {
        // a match
        matchSound.play();
        pictureLabel[choice[0]].setIcon(null);
        pictureLabel[choice[1]].setIcon(null);
        score[playerNumber - 1]++;
        scoreTextField[playerNumber -
1].setText(String.valueOf(score[playerNumber - 1]));
        picturesRemaining -= 2;
        if (picturesRemaining == 0)
        {
          gameOver = true;
          gameOverSound.play();
          if (twoPlayersRadioButton.isSelected())
          {
            if (score[0] > score[1])
              messageLabel.setText("Player 1 Wins!");
            else if (score[1] > score[0])
              messageLabel.setText("Player 2 Wins!");
            else
              messageLabel.setText("It's a Tie!");
          }
          else
          {
            // one player logic
            if (playAloneRadioButton.isSelected())
              messageLabel.setText("All Matches Found!");
            else
            {
              // play computer logic
              if (score[0] > score[1])
                messageLabel.setText("You Win!");
              else if (score[1] > score[0])
                messageLabel.setText("Computer Wins!");
              else
                messageLabel.setText("It's a Tie!");
            }
          }
```

```
          startStopButton.doClick();
          return;
        }
        // another turn
        if (twoPlayersRadioButton.isSelected())
        {
          messageLabel.setText("Player " +
String.valueOf(playerNumber) + ", Pick Again");
          canClick = true;
        }
        else
        {
          // one player logic
          if (playerNumber == 1)
          {
            messageLabel.setText("Pick a Box");
            canClick = true;
          }
          else
          {
            // play computer logic
            messageLabel.setText("Picking Again");
            computerTurn();
            return;
          }
        }
      }
      else
      {
        //no match
        noMatchSound.play();
        pictureFound[choice[0]] = false;
        pictureFound[choice[1]] = false;
        pictureLabel[choice[0]].setIcon(cover);
        pictureLabel[choice[1]].setIcon(cover);
        // swap players
        if (twoPlayersRadioButton.isSelected())
        {
          if (playerNumber == 1)
            playerNumber = 2;
          else
            playerNumber = 1;
          messageLabel.setText("Player " +
String.valueOf(playerNumber) + ", Pick a Box");
          canClick = true;
        }
        else
```

```
          {
            // one player logic
            if (playComputerRadioButton.isSelected())
            {
              if (playerNumber == 1)
                playerNumber = 2;
              else
                playerNumber = 1;
            }
            if (playerNumber == 1)
            {
              messageLabel.setText("Pick a Box");
              canClick = true;
            }
            else
            {
              // play computer logic
              messageLabel.setText("Computer Picking");
              choiceNumber = 1;
              computerTurn();
              return;
            }
          }
        }
      }
    }
```

The framework is in place. If you trying running the game, the **Two Player** and **One Player**, **Play Alone** options will still work. Playing against the computer will not work because we need code for the **randomChoice** and **smartChoice** methods. We'll do **randomChoice** first.

Code Design – Random Computer

For random moves, the computer will simply choose (at random) one of the available labels on the game panel. This code is very similar to the random move code for the **Tic Tac Toe** game.

Replace the single line currently in the **randomChoice** method with the shaded code:

```
private int randomChoice()
{
  int count, n, rc;
  if (choiceNumber == 1)
    n = myRandom.nextInt(picturesRemaining) + 1;
  else
    n = myRandom.nextInt(picturesRemaining - 1) + 1;
  count = 0;
  for (rc = 0; rc < 20; rc++)
  {
    if (!pictureFound[rc])
      count++;
    if (count == n)
      break;
  }
  return(rc);
}
```

The logic behind this code is straightforward. We either have **picturesRemaining** unselected labels (if it's the first choice) or **picturesRemaining – 1** unselected labels (if it's the second choice). The code selects a random number within this range and counts ahead that number of unselected labels to identify the index of the label to choose (returned as **rc**).

We can test our random logic, but there's one problem. If (in **computerTurn**) we select a smart computer, there is no code in the corresponding method (**smartMove**). To make things work, replace the current line in the **smartMove** method with the shaded line:

```
private int smartChoice()
{
  return(RandomChoice());
}
```

We're simply making the smart computer be random (temporarily) to allow testing of the computer move logic.

Save and run the **Bible Match Game** project. Select the **One Player**, **Play Computer** options. **Difficulty** doesn't matter since all code is random at the moment. Click **Start Game**. You go first, trying to find matching pictures. Once it's the computer's turn, notice two things. First, the pictures are uncovered (in pairs) randomly, very seldom do they match. Second, the pictures appear and disappear very quickly.

We can slow things down using another **timer** object (named **delayTimer**) to add some delay (we'll choose one second). Declare this timer:

```
Timer delayTimer;
```

and add it to the frame with a 1000 millisecond delay (one second):

```
delayTimer = new Timer(1000, new ActionListener()
{
  public void actionPerformed(ActionEvent e)
  {
    delayTimerActionPerformed(e);
  }
});
```

Rather than immediately display the pictures in the **computerTurn** method, we will start the **timer** object. We move the line of code that displays the picture into the **delayTimerActionPerformed** method. With a 1000 millisecond **delay** property, the pictures will remain on the form for 1 second. You may adjust this amount of delay if you like. So, the **delayTimerActionPerformed** event method is:

```
private void delayTimerActionPerformed(ActionEvent e)
{
  delayTimer.stop();
  showSelectedLabel();
}
```

Here we turn off the timer to stop the delay and display the picture with the line of code moved from the **computerTurn** method.

Replace the last line in the **computerTurn** method (the call to the **showSelectedLabel** method) with the single shaded line that starts the timer object:

```
private void computerTurn()
{
  int threshold = 0;
  if (choiceNumber == 1)
  {
    switch (difficulty)
    {
      case 1:
        threshold = 25;
        break;
      case 2:
        threshold = 50;
        break;
      case 3:
        threshold = 75;
        break;
      case 4:
        threshold = 90;
        break;
    }
    if (myRandom.nextInt(100) < threshold)
      smartComputer = true;
    else
      smartComputer = false;
  }
  if (smartComputer)
    labelSelected = smartChoice();
  else
    labelSelected = randomChoice();
  delayTimer.start();
}
```

Save and run the game again. Select **One Player** and **Play Computer**. Again, **Difficulty** does not matter. Click **Start Game**. You can now play against a random computer that has been slowed down a bit. You'll see the computer is not that smart, making it pretty easy for you to win. We'll fix that next by coding up a far more intelligent and formidable computer opponent. Here's a game I played (the computer did find two matches – the last two!):

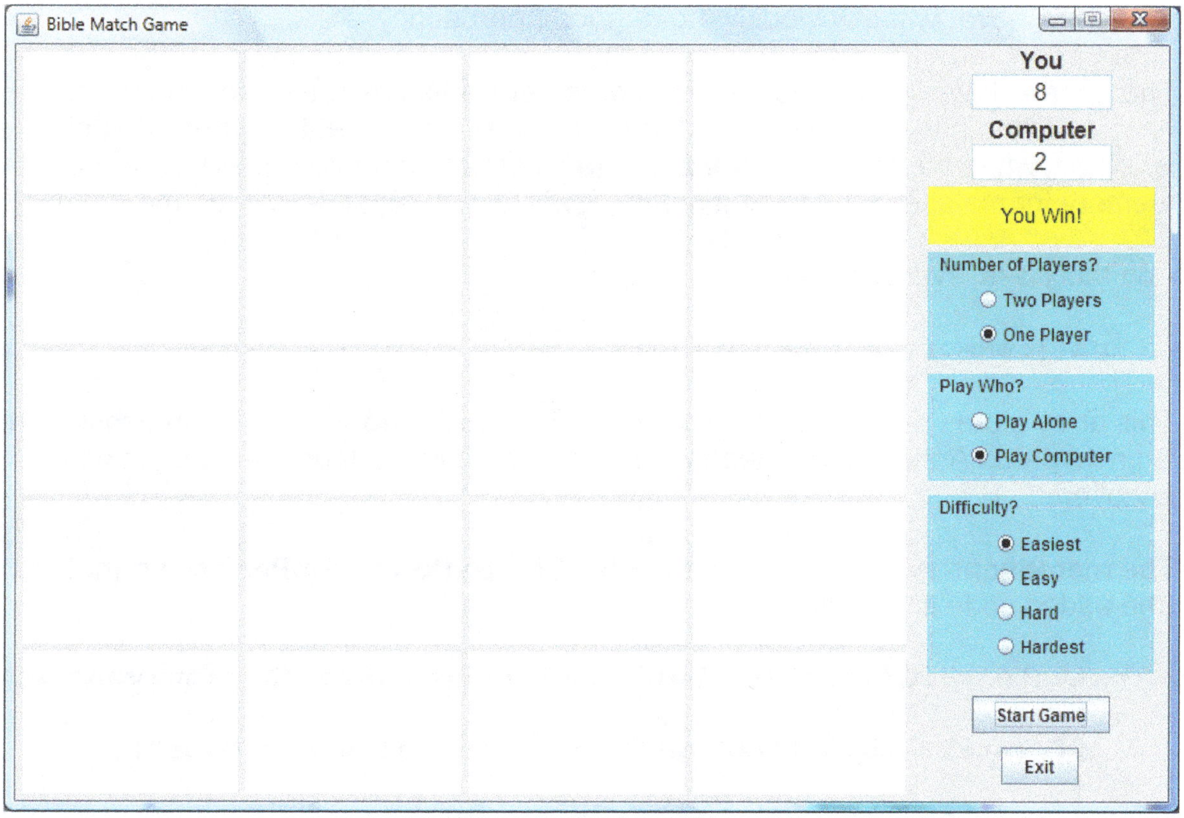

Code Design – Smart Computer

So how can we make the computer a better **Bible Match Game** opponent? Well, we could cheat! Since the computer generated the random numbers to hide the pictures behind the labels, the computer knows where everything is. Once it's the computer's turn, it could just go through that list and find all the matching pairs. You could never win. Obviously, not a good approach.

The approach we'll take is to give the computer perfect memory. In other words, once a picture has been uncovered, the computer will remember where that picture is. Then, when the computer has a turn (as a smart computer), it will search its memory for matches. If it finds a match, it will take it. First, let's code the memory.

Add this class level declaration:

```
int[] memory = new int[20];
```

This array stores the indices of pictures behind the 20 label objects as each picture is uncovered. A zero value means the picture behind the label has not yet been uncovered.

The **memory** array is initialized in the **startStopButtonActionPerformed** method (the added code is shaded):

```
private void startStopButtonActionPerformed(ActionEvent e)
{
  if (startStopButton.getText().equals("Start Game"))
  {
    startStopButton.setText("Stop Game");
    score[0] = 0;
    score[1] = 0;
    scoreTextField[0].setText("0");
    scoreTextField[1].setText("0");
    picturesRemaining = 20;
    pictureIndex = nRandomIntegers(20);
    for (int i = 0; i < 20; i++)
    {
      if (pictureIndex[i] > 9)
        pictureIndex[i] -= 10;
      pictureFound[i] = false;
      pictureLabel[i].setIcon(cover);
      memory[i] = 0;
    }
    playerNumber = 1;
    choiceNumber = 1;
    if (twoPlayersRadioButton.isSelected())
```

```
        messageLabel.setText("Player 1, Pick a Box");
      else
        messageLabel.setText("Pick a Box");
      setNumberPlayersButtons(false);
      setPlayWhoButtons(false);
      setDifficultyButtons(false);
      exitButton.setEnabled(false);
      canClick = true;
      gameOver = false;
    }
    else
    {
      // stop game
      startStopButton.setText("Start Game");
      setNumberPlayersButtons(true);
      if (onePlayerRadioButton.isSelected())
      {
        setPlayWhoButtons(true);
        if (playComputerRadioButton.isSelected())
          setDifficultyButtons(true);
      }
      exitButton.setEnabled(true);
      canClick = false;
      if (!gameOver)
        messageLabel.setText("Game Stopped");
    }
}
```

The values in the **memory** array are established in the **displayTimerActionPerformed** method. The needed changes are shaded:

```
private void displayTimerActionPerformed(ActionEvent e)
{
  displayTimer.stop();
  if (choiceNumber == 1)
  {
    choice[0] = labelSelected;
    choiceNumber = 2;
    memory[labelSelected] = pictureIndex[labelSelected];
    if (twoPlayersRadioButton.isSelected())
    {
      messageLabel.setText("Player " +
String.valueOf(playerNumber) + ", Pick Another");
      canClick = true;
    }
    else
    {
    // one player logic
      if (playerNumber == 1)
      {
        messageLabel.setText("Pick Another Box");
        canClick = true;
      }
      else
      {
        // play computer logic
        messageLabel.setText("Picking Another");
        computerTurn();
        return;
      }
    }
  }
  else
  {
    choice[1] = labelSelected;
    choiceNumber = 1;
    memory[labelSelected] = pictureIndex[labelSelected];
    if (pictureIndex[choice[0]] ==
pictureIndex[choice[1]])
    {
      // a match
      matchSound.play();
      pictureLabel[choice[0]].setIcon(null);
      pictureLabel[choice[1]].setIcon(null);
```

```
      // clear memory so boxes are not checked again for
match
       memory[choice[0]] = 0;
       memory[choice[1]] = 0;
       score[playerNumber - 1]++;
       scoreTextField[playerNumber -
1].setText(String.valueOf(score[playerNumber - 1]));
       picturesRemaining -= 2;
       if (picturesRemaining == 0)
       {
         gameOver = true;
         gameOverSound.play();
         if (twoPlayersRadioButton.isSelected())
         {
           if (score[0] > score[1])
             messageLabel.setText("Player 1 Wins!");
           else if (score[1] > score[0])
             messageLabel.setText("Player 2 Wins!");
           else
             messageLabel.setText("It's a Tie!");
         }
         else
         {
           // one player logic
           if (playAloneRadioButton.isSelected())
             messageLabel.setText("All Matches Found!");
           else
           {
             // play computer logic
             if (score[0] > score[1])
               messageLabel.setText("You Win!");
             else if (score[1] > score[0])
               messageLabel.setText("Computer Wins!");
             else
               messageLabel.setText("It's a Tie!");
           }
         }
         startStopButton.doClick();
         return;
       }
       // another turn
       if (twoPlayersRadioButton.isSelected())
       {
         messageLabel.setText("Player " +
String.valueOf(playerNumber) + ", Pick Again");
         canClick = true;
       }
```

```
        else
        {
          // one player logic
          if (playerNumber == 1)
          {
            messageLabel.setText("Pick a Box");
            canClick = true;
          }
          else
          {
            // play computer logic
            messageLabel.setText("Picking Again");
            computerTurn();
            return;
          }
        }
      }
      else
      {
        //no match
        noMatchSound.play();
        pictureFound[choice[0]] = false;
        pictureFound[choice[1]] = false;
        pictureLabel[choice[0]].setIcon(cover);
        pictureLabel[choice[1]].setIcon(cover);
        // swap players
        if (twoPlayersRadioButton.isSelected())
        {
          if (playerNumber == 1)
            playerNumber = 2;
          else
            playerNumber = 1;
          messageLabel.setText("Player " +
String.valueOf(playerNumber) + ", Pick a Box");
          canClick = true;
        }
        else
        {
          // one player logic
          if (playComputerRadioButton.isSelected())
          {
            if (playerNumber == 1)
              playerNumber = 2;
            else
              playerNumber = 1;
          }
          if (playerNumber == 1)
```

```
          {
            messageLabel.setText("Pick a Box");
            canClick = true;
          }
          else
          {
            // play computer logic
            messageLabel.setText("Computer Picking");
            choiceNumber = 1;
            computerTurn();
            return;
          }
        }
      }
    }
}
```

Now, how do we use the **memory** array to make a smart move? The rules we will use for the computer's two choices are:

Choice 1:
1. Check **memory** array for a match.
2. If a match is found, select the first matching label control.
3. If no match is found, select a random label.

Choice 2:
1. If a match was found with Choice 1, select the second matching label.
2. If no match was found with Choice 1, check again for a match (the random choice in Choice 1 may match a picture stored in memory).
3. If a match is found, select the matching label.
4. If no match is found, select a random label.

Let's implement this logic in code.

First, add the general method **checkForMatch**. This method returns two integers in an array. If these both of these integers are non-zero, it tells the computer which two picture boxes have matching pictures:

```
private int[] checkForMatch()
{
  int[] matches = new int[2];
  matches[0] = 0;
  matches[1] = 0;
  for (int i = 0; i < 20; i++)
  {
    for (int j = 0; j < 20; j++)
    {
      if (memory[i] != 0 && memory[i] == memory[j] && i !=
j)
      {
        matches[0] = i;
        matches[1] = j;
      }
    }
  }
  return(matches);
}
```

This method does a simple comparison of all labels looking for matching non-zero values in the **memory** array.

Add a class level declaration for an integer array (**matchFound**) that will be used to store the matching picture boxes:

```
int[] matchFound = new int[2];
```

Now, remove the current **return** statement from the **SmartChoice** method (the one returning a random choice). Replace that method with this code which implements the smart computer steps outlined above:

```
private int smartChoice()
{
  int sc;
  if (choiceNumber == 1)
  {
    matchFound = checkForMatch();
    if (matchFound[0] != 0 && matchFound[1] != 0)
      sc = matchFound[0];
    else
      sc = randomChoice();
  }
  else
  {
    if (matchFound[0] != 0 && matchFound[1] != 0)
      sc = matchFound[1];
    else
    {
      matchFound = checkForMatch();
      if (matchFound[0] != 0 && matchFound[1] != 0)
      {
        if (matchFound[0] != choice[0])
          sc = matchFound[0];
        else
          sc = matchFound[1];
      }
      else
        sc = randomChoice();
    }
  }
  return (sc);
}
```

Save and run the project. The game is now fully functional (the complete code listing is given at the end of the chapter). Try playing it against the computer with the **Hardest** difficulty. You should find it is very hard to beat. Continue playing seeing how the various levels of difficulty do indeed adjust the computer's intelligence. Here's a game I played with **Hard** difficulty. I selected the first two boxes and see:

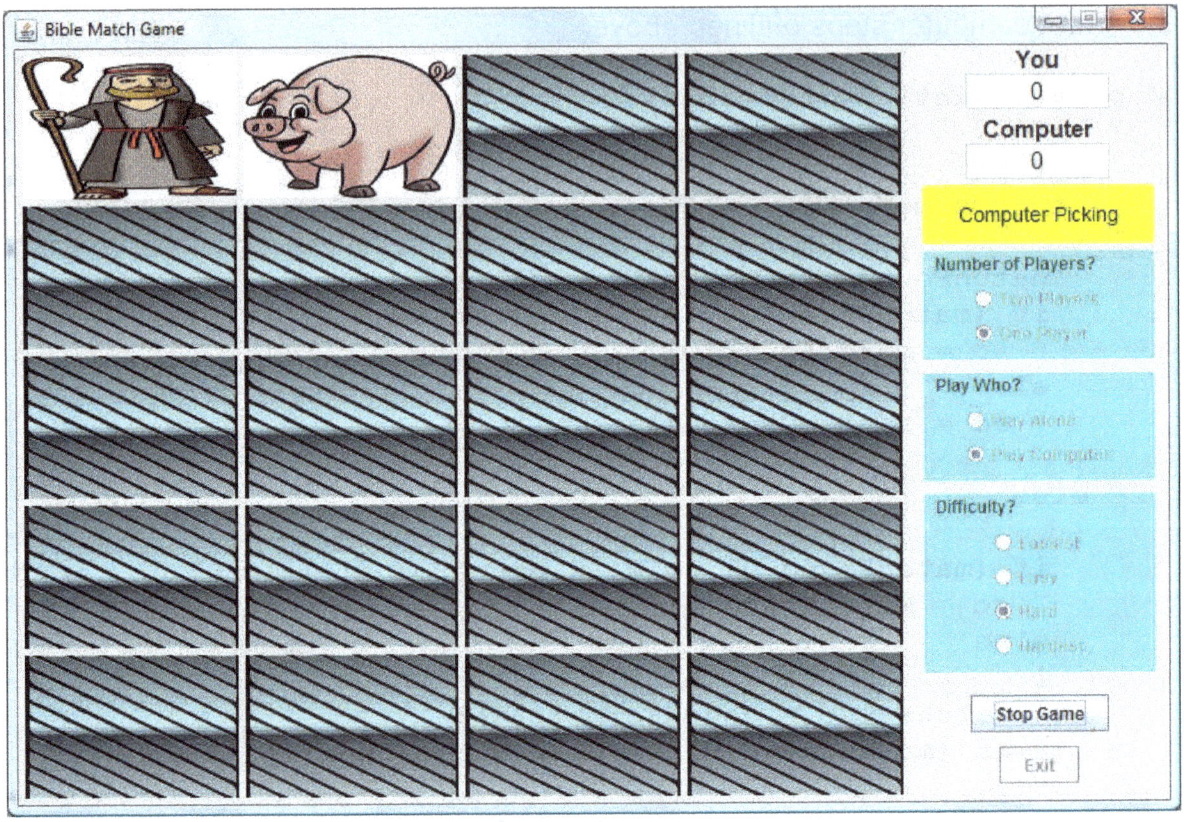

It's a shepherd and a pig; nice pictures, but not a match.

It then becomes the computer's turn. It's choices are:

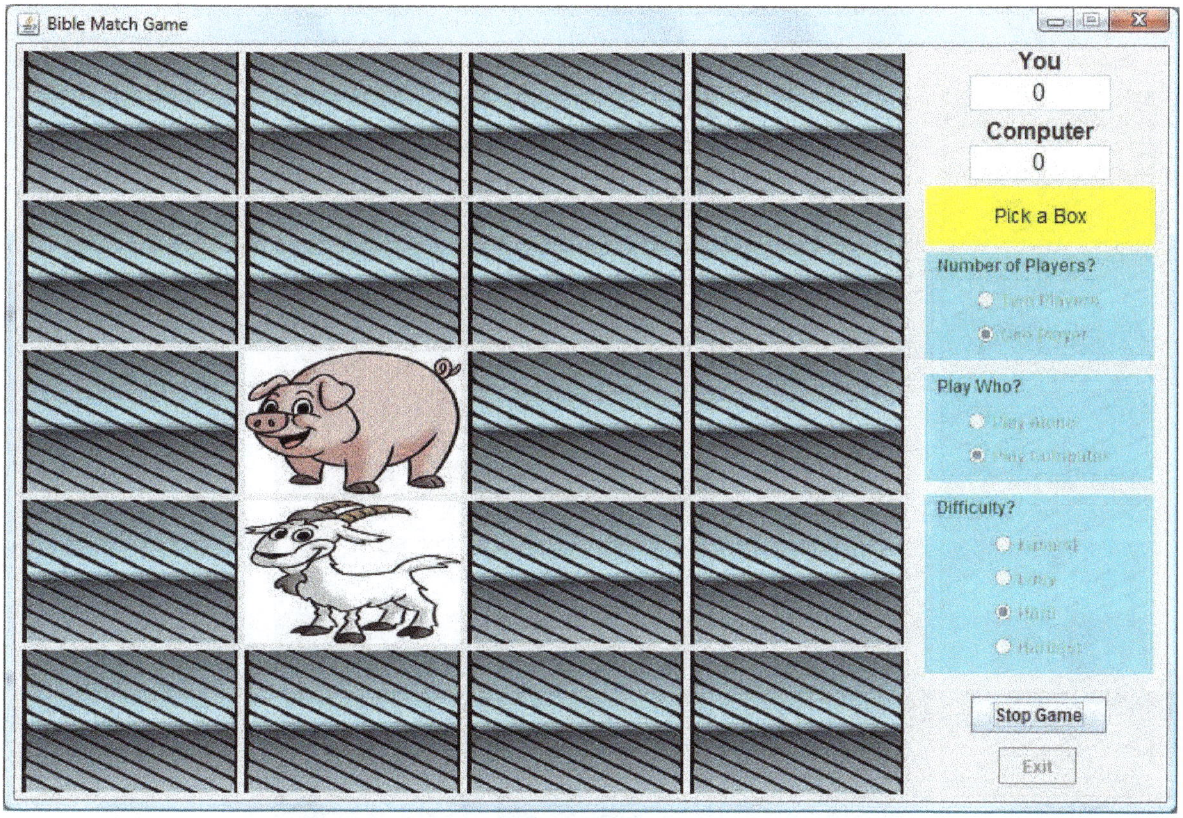

Not a match … but we've seen that pig before.

Picking the second box in the top row and the second box in the third row, I get a match. The pictures are removed, my score is incremented and it's my turn again:

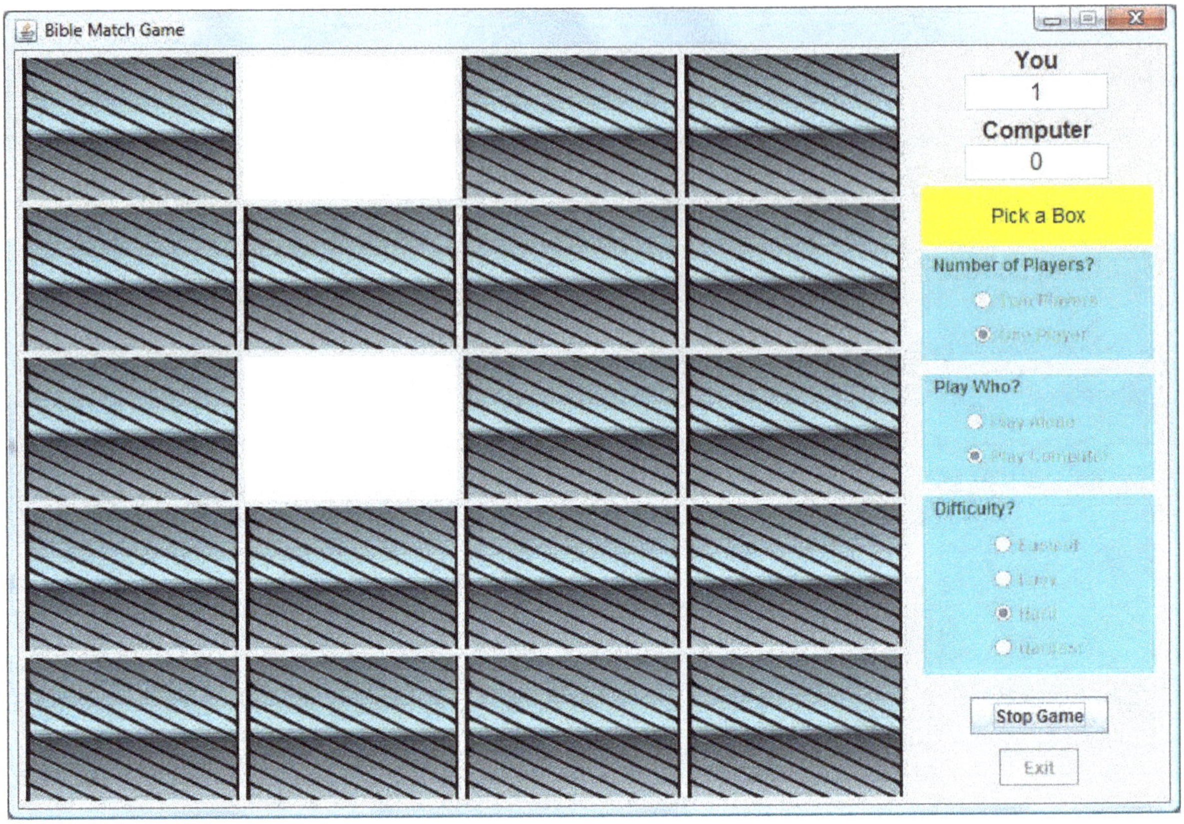

Once all the matches were found, the final score was me 2 and the computer 8, I lost!

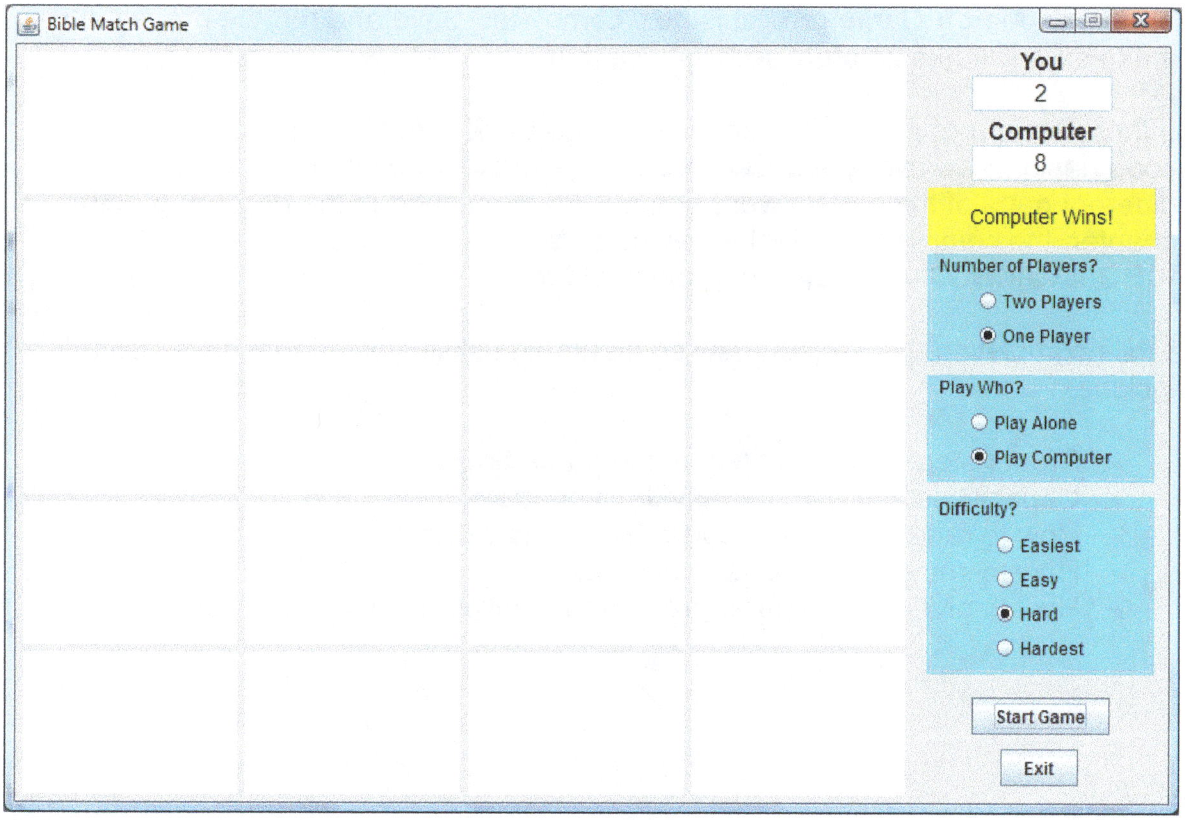

Bible Match Game Project Review

The **Bible Match Game** project is now complete. Save and run the project and make sure it works as promised. Check that all options work correctly.

If there are errors in your implementation, go back over the steps of frame and code design. Go over the developed code – make sure you understand how different parts of the project were coded. As mentioned in the beginning of this chapter, the completed project is saved as **MatchGame** in the **\CBGJava\CBGJava Projects** project folder.

While completing this project, new concepts and skills you should have gained include:

- Proper steps in game design and game flow.
- Capabilities and use of many Java controls.
- How to randomly sort integers (shuffle numbers).
- How to implement delays in games.
- How to give the computer graduated intelligence in playing games.

Bible Match Game Project Enhancements

There are several ways to improve the **Bible Match Game** project. Some possibilities are:

- As written, the human player can click on labels while the computer is making a move. Implement logic to disallow this.
- Make the number of labels displaying pictures adjustable for an added difficulty adjustment (fewer boxes for little kids).
- Add additional levels of difficulty by having finer adjustments on the threshold between random and smart computer moves.
- As written, a player could theoretically find all ten pairs without giving the other player a chance. Perhaps, rewrite the game so a player only gets one extra turn after a match.
- The computer in this game is pretty smart, but it can be smarter. How you ask? If the computer uncovers a picture that has no match, its next choice could be a picture that's already been uncovered. This would not give the computer any more information about hidden pictures, but it also does not give you, the opponent, any needed information either.

Bible Match Game Project Java Code Listing

```
/*
 * MatchGame.java
 */
package matchgame;
import javax.swing.*;
import java.awt.*;
import java.awt.event.*;
import java.util.Random;
import java.net.URL;
import java.applet.*;


public class MatchGame extends JFrame
{

  JPanel gamePanel = new JPanel();
  JLabel[] pictureLabel = new JLabel[20];
  JPanel resultsPanel = new JPanel();
  JLabel player1Label = new JLabel();
  JLabel player2Label = new JLabel();
  JTextField[] scoreTextField = new JTextField[2];
  JLabel messageLabel = new JLabel();
  JPanel playersPanel = new JPanel();
  ButtonGroup playersButtonGroup = new ButtonGroup();
  JRadioButton twoPlayersRadioButton = new JRadioButton();
  JRadioButton onePlayerRadioButton = new JRadioButton();
  JPanel playWhoPanel = new JPanel();
  ButtonGroup playWhoButtonGroup = new ButtonGroup();
  JRadioButton playAloneRadioButton = new JRadioButton();
  JRadioButton playComputerRadioButton = new JRadioButton();
  JPanel difficultyPanel = new JPanel();
  ButtonGroup difficultyButtonGroup = new ButtonGroup();
  JRadioButton easiestRadioButton = new JRadioButton();
  JRadioButton easyRadioButton = new JRadioButton();
  JRadioButton hardRadioButton = new JRadioButton();
  JRadioButton hardestRadioButton = new JRadioButton();
  JPanel buttonsPanel = new JPanel();
  JButton startStopButton = new JButton();
  JButton exitButton = new JButton();

  ImageIcon[] picture = new ImageIcon[10];
  ImageIcon cover = new ImageIcon();
```

```
int[] pictureIndex = new int[20];
int picturesRemaining;
int[] score = new int[2];
boolean[] pictureFound = new boolean[20];
int playerNumber, choiceNumber;
int[] choice = new int[2];
boolean canClick = false;
boolean gameOver;
int labelSelected;
Random myRandom = new Random();
boolean smartComputer;
int difficulty = 1;
int[] memory = new int[20];
int[] matchFound = new int[2];


AudioClip matchSound;
AudioClip noMatchSound;
AudioClip gameOverSound;

Timer displayTimer;
Timer delayTimer;

public static void main(String args[])
{
  // create frame
  new MatchGame().setVisible(true);
}

public MatchGame()
{
  // frame constructor
  setTitle("Bible Match Game");
  setResizable(false);
  addWindowListener(new WindowAdapter()
  {
    public void windowClosing(WindowEvent evt)
    {
      exitForm(evt);
    }
  });
  getContentPane().setLayout(new GridBagLayout());
  GridBagConstraints gridConstraints;

  gamePanel.setPreferredSize(new Dimension(625, 530));
  gamePanel.setLayout(new GridBagLayout());
  gridConstraints = new GridBagConstraints();
```

```
    gridConstraints.gridx = 0;
    gridConstraints.gridy = 0;
    gridConstraints.gridheight = 5;
    getContentPane().add(gamePanel, gridConstraints);

    for (int i = 0; i < 20; i++)
    {
      pictureLabel[i] = new JLabel();
      pictureLabel[i].setPreferredSize(new Dimension(150,
100));
      pictureLabel[i].setOpaque(true);
      pictureLabel[i].setBackground(Color.WHITE);
      gridConstraints = new GridBagConstraints();
      gridConstraints.gridx = i % 4;
      gridConstraints.gridy = i / 4;
      gridConstraints.insets = new Insets(5, 5, 0, 0);
      if (gridConstraints.gridx == 3)
        gridConstraints.insets = new Insets(5, 5, 0, 5);
      if (gridConstraints.gridy == 4)
        gridConstraints.insets = new Insets(5, 5, 5, 0);
      if (gridConstraints.gridx == 3 &&
gridConstraints.gridy == 4)
        gridConstraints.insets = new Insets(5, 5, 5, 5);
      gamePanel.add(pictureLabel[i], gridConstraints);
      pictureLabel[i].addMouseListener(new MouseAdapter()
      {
        public void mousePressed(MouseEvent e)
        {
          pictureLabelMousePressed(e);
        }
      });
    }

    resultsPanel.setPreferredSize(new Dimension(160, 140));
    resultsPanel.setLayout(new GridBagLayout());
    gridConstraints = new GridBagConstraints();
    gridConstraints.gridx = 1;
    gridConstraints.gridy = 0;
    getContentPane().add(resultsPanel, gridConstraints);

    player1Label.setText("Player 1");
    player1Label.setFont(new Font("Arial", Font.BOLD, 16));
    gridConstraints = new GridBagConstraints();
    gridConstraints.gridx = 0;
    gridConstraints.gridy = 0;
    resultsPanel.add(player1Label, gridConstraints);
```

```
    scoreTextField[0] = new JTextField();
    scoreTextField[0].setPreferredSize(new Dimension(100,
25));
    scoreTextField[0].setText("0");
    scoreTextField[0].setEditable(false);
    scoreTextField[0].setBackground(Color.WHITE);

scoreTextField[0].setHorizontalAlignment(SwingConstants.CENT
ER);
    scoreTextField[0].setFont(new Font("Arial", Font.PLAIN,
16));
    gridConstraints = new GridBagConstraints();
    gridConstraints.gridx = 0;
    gridConstraints.gridy = 1;
    resultsPanel.add(scoreTextField[0], gridConstraints);

    player2Label.setText("Player 2");
    player2Label.setFont(new Font("Arial", Font.BOLD, 16));
    gridConstraints = new GridBagConstraints();
    gridConstraints.gridx = 0;
    gridConstraints.gridy = 2;
    gridConstraints.insets = new Insets(5, 0, 0, 0);
    resultsPanel.add(player2Label, gridConstraints);

    scoreTextField[1] = new JTextField();
    scoreTextField[1].setPreferredSize(new Dimension(100,
25));
    scoreTextField[1].setText("0");
    scoreTextField[1].setEditable(false);
    scoreTextField[1].setBackground(Color.WHITE);

scoreTextField[1].setHorizontalAlignment(SwingConstants.CENT
ER);
    scoreTextField[1].setFont(new Font("Arial", Font.PLAIN,
16));
    gridConstraints = new GridBagConstraints();
    gridConstraints.gridx = 0;
    gridConstraints.gridy = 3;
    resultsPanel.add(scoreTextField[1], gridConstraints);

    messageLabel.setPreferredSize(new Dimension(160, 40));
    messageLabel.setOpaque(true);
    messageLabel.setBackground(Color.YELLOW);

messageLabel.setHorizontalAlignment(SwingConstants.CENTER);
    messageLabel.setText("");
    messageLabel.setFont(new Font("Arial", Font.PLAIN, 14));
```

```
    gridConstraints = new GridBagConstraints();
    gridConstraints.gridx = 0;
    gridConstraints.gridy = 4;
    gridConstraints.insets = new Insets(5, 0, 0, 0);
    resultsPanel.add(messageLabel, gridConstraints);

    playersPanel.setPreferredSize(new Dimension(160, 75));
    playersPanel.setBackground(Color.CYAN);

playersPanel.setBorder(BorderFactory.createTitledBorder("Num
ber of Players?"));
    playersPanel.setLayout(new GridBagLayout());
    gridConstraints = new GridBagConstraints();
    gridConstraints.gridx = 1;
    gridConstraints.gridy = 1;
    gridConstraints.insets = new Insets(5, 10, 5, 10);
    getContentPane().add(playersPanel, gridConstraints);

    twoPlayersRadioButton.setText("Two Players");
    twoPlayersRadioButton.setBackground(Color.CYAN);
    twoPlayersRadioButton.setSelected(true);
    playersButtonGroup.add(twoPlayersRadioButton);
    gridConstraints = new GridBagConstraints();
    gridConstraints.gridx = 0;
    gridConstraints.gridy = 0;
    gridConstraints.anchor = GridBagConstraints.WEST;
    playersPanel.add(twoPlayersRadioButton,
gridConstraints);
    twoPlayersRadioButton.addActionListener(new
ActionListener()
    {
      public void actionPerformed(ActionEvent e)
      {
        twoPlayersRadioButtonActionPerformed(e);
      }
    });

    onePlayerRadioButton.setText("One Player");
    onePlayerRadioButton.setBackground(Color.CYAN);
    playersButtonGroup.add(onePlayerRadioButton);
    gridConstraints = new GridBagConstraints();
    gridConstraints.gridx = 0;
    gridConstraints.gridy = 1;
    gridConstraints.anchor = GridBagConstraints.WEST;
    playersPanel.add(onePlayerRadioButton, gridConstraints);
    onePlayerRadioButton.addActionListener(new
ActionListener()
```

```
    {
      public void actionPerformed(ActionEvent e)
      {
        onePlayerRadioButtonActionPerformed(e);
      }
    });

    playWhoPanel.setPreferredSize(new Dimension(160, 75));
    playWhoPanel.setBackground(Color.CYAN);

playWhoPanel.setBorder(BorderFactory.createTitledBorder("Pla
y Who?"));
    playWhoPanel.setLayout(new GridBagLayout());
    gridConstraints = new GridBagConstraints();
    gridConstraints.gridx = 1;
    gridConstraints.gridy = 2;
    gridConstraints.insets = new Insets(5, 10, 5, 10);
    getContentPane().add(playWhoPanel, gridConstraints);

    playAloneRadioButton.setText("Play Alone");
    playAloneRadioButton.setBackground(Color.CYAN);
    playAloneRadioButton.setSelected(true);
    playWhoButtonGroup.add(playAloneRadioButton);
    gridConstraints = new GridBagConstraints();
    gridConstraints.gridx = 0;
    gridConstraints.gridy = 0;
    gridConstraints.anchor = GridBagConstraints.WEST;
    playWhoPanel.add(playAloneRadioButton, gridConstraints);
    playAloneRadioButton.addActionListener(new
ActionListener()
    {
      public void actionPerformed(ActionEvent e)
      {
        playAloneRadioButtonActionPerformed(e);
      }
    });

    playComputerRadioButton.setText("Play Computer");
    playComputerRadioButton.setBackground(Color.CYAN);
    playWhoButtonGroup.add(playComputerRadioButton);
    gridConstraints = new GridBagConstraints();
    gridConstraints.gridx = 0;
    gridConstraints.gridy = 1;
    gridConstraints.anchor = GridBagConstraints.WEST;
    playWhoPanel.add(playComputerRadioButton,
gridConstraints);
```

```
    playComputerRadioButton.addActionListener(new
ActionListener()
    {
      public void actionPerformed(ActionEvent e)
      {
        playComputerRadioButtonActionPerformed(e);
      }
    });

    difficultyPanel.setPreferredSize(new Dimension(160,
125));
    difficultyPanel.setBackground(Color.CYAN);

difficultyPanel.setBorder(BorderFactory.createTitledBorder("
Difficulty?"));
    difficultyPanel.setLayout(new GridBagLayout());
    gridConstraints = new GridBagConstraints();
    gridConstraints.gridx = 1;
    gridConstraints.gridy = 3;
    gridConstraints.insets = new Insets(5, 10, 5, 10);
    getContentPane().add(difficultyPanel, gridConstraints);

    easiestRadioButton.setText("Easiest");
    easiestRadioButton.setBackground(Color.CYAN);
    easiestRadioButton.setSelected(true);
    difficultyButtonGroup.add(easiestRadioButton);
    gridConstraints = new GridBagConstraints();
    gridConstraints.gridx = 0;
    gridConstraints.gridy = 0;
    gridConstraints.anchor = GridBagConstraints.WEST;
    difficultyPanel.add(easiestRadioButton,
gridConstraints);
    easiestRadioButton.addActionListener(new
ActionListener()
    {
      public void actionPerformed(ActionEvent e)
      {
        easiestRadioButtonActionPerformed(e);
      }
    });

    easyRadioButton.setText("Easy");
    easyRadioButton.setBackground(Color.CYAN);
    easyRadioButton.setSelected(true);
    difficultyButtonGroup.add(easyRadioButton);
    gridConstraints = new GridBagConstraints();
    gridConstraints.gridx = 0;
```

```
    gridConstraints.gridy = 1;
    gridConstraints.anchor = GridBagConstraints.WEST;
    difficultyPanel.add(easyRadioButton, gridConstraints);
    easyRadioButton.addActionListener(new ActionListener()
    {
      public void actionPerformed(ActionEvent e)
      {
        easyRadioButtonActionPerformed(e);
      }
    });

    hardRadioButton.setText("Hard");
    hardRadioButton.setBackground(Color.CYAN);
    hardRadioButton.setSelected(true);
    difficultyButtonGroup.add(hardRadioButton);
    gridConstraints = new GridBagConstraints();
    gridConstraints.gridx = 0;
    gridConstraints.gridy = 2;
    gridConstraints.anchor = GridBagConstraints.WEST;
    difficultyPanel.add(hardRadioButton, gridConstraints);
    hardRadioButton.addActionListener(new ActionListener()
    {
      public void actionPerformed(ActionEvent e)
      {
        hardRadioButtonActionPerformed(e);
      }
    });

    hardestRadioButton.setText("Hardest");
    hardestRadioButton.setBackground(Color.CYAN);
    hardestRadioButton.setSelected(true);
    difficultyButtonGroup.add(hardestRadioButton);
    gridConstraints = new GridBagConstraints();
    gridConstraints.gridx = 0;
    gridConstraints.gridy = 3;
    gridConstraints.anchor = GridBagConstraints.WEST;
    difficultyPanel.add(hardestRadioButton,
gridConstraints);
    hardestRadioButton.addActionListener(new
ActionListener()
    {
      public void actionPerformed(ActionEvent e)
      {
        hardestRadioButtonActionPerformed(e);
      }
    });
```

```
buttonsPanel.setPreferredSize(new Dimension(160, 70));
buttonsPanel.setLayout(new GridBagLayout());
gridConstraints = new GridBagConstraints();
gridConstraints.gridx = 1;
gridConstraints.gridy = 4;
getContentPane().add(buttonsPanel, gridConstraints);

startStopButton.setText("Start Game");
gridConstraints = new GridBagConstraints();
gridConstraints.gridx = 0;
gridConstraints.gridy = 0;
buttonsPanel.add(startStopButton, gridConstraints);
startStopButton.addActionListener(new ActionListener()
{
  public void actionPerformed(ActionEvent e)
  {
    startStopButtonActionPerformed(e);
  }
});

exitButton.setText("Exit");
gridConstraints = new GridBagConstraints();
gridConstraints.gridx = 0;
gridConstraints.gridy = 1;
gridConstraints.insets = new Insets(10, 0, 0, 0);
buttonsPanel.add(exitButton, gridConstraints);
exitButton.addActionListener(new ActionListener()
{
  public void actionPerformed(ActionEvent e)
  {
    exitButtonActionPerformed(e);
  }
});

displayTimer = new Timer(500, new ActionListener()
{
  public void actionPerformed(ActionEvent e)
  {
    displayTimerActionPerformed(e);
  }
});

delayTimer = new Timer(1000, new ActionListener()
{
  public void actionPerformed(ActionEvent e)
  {
    delayTimerActionPerformed(e);
```

```
      }
    });

    pack();
    Dimension screenSize =
Toolkit.getDefaultToolkit().getScreenSize();
    setBounds((int) (0.5 * (screenSize.width - getWidth())),
(int) (0.5 * (screenSize.height - getHeight())),

getWidth(), getHeight());

    picture[0] = new ImageIcon("ark.gif");
    picture[1] = new ImageIcon("daniel.gif");
    picture[2] = new ImageIcon("elijah.gif");
    picture[3] = new ImageIcon("goat.gif");
    picture[4] = new ImageIcon("lion.gif");
    picture[5] = new ImageIcon("pig.gif");
    picture[6] = new ImageIcon("raven.gif");
    picture[7] = new ImageIcon("sheep.gif");
    picture[8] = new ImageIcon("shepherd.gif");
    picture[9] = new ImageIcon("woman.gif");
    cover = new ImageIcon("cover.jpg");
    for (int i = 0; i < 20; i++)
      pictureLabel[i].setIcon(cover);

    setPlayWhoButtons(false);
    setDifficultyButtons(false);
    try
    {
      matchSound = Applet.newAudioClip(new URL("file:" +
"tada.wav"));
      noMatchSound = Applet.newAudioClip(new URL("file:" +
"boing.wav"));
      gameOverSound = Applet.newAudioClip(new URL("file:" +
"wow.wav"));
    }
    catch (Exception ex)
    {
      System.out.println("Error loading sound files");
    }
  }

  private void exitForm(WindowEvent evt)
  {
    System.exit(0);
  }
```

```
  private void pictureLabelMousePressed(MouseEvent e)
  {
    // determine which label was clicked
    // get upper left corner of clicked label
    Point p = e.getComponent().getLocation();
    // determine index based on p
    for (labelSelected = 0; labelSelected < 20;
labelSelected++)
    {
      if (p.x == pictureLabel[labelSelected].getX() && p.y
== pictureLabel[labelSelected].getY())
        break;
    }
    if (!canClick || pictureFound[labelSelected])
      return;
    // show image behind selected label box
    canClick = false;
    showSelectedLabel();
  }

  private void
twoPlayersRadioButtonActionPerformed(ActionEvent e)
  {
    setPlayWhoButtons(false);
    setDifficultyButtons(false);
    player1Label.setText("Player 1");
    player2Label.setText("Player 2");
  }

  private void
onePlayerRadioButtonActionPerformed(ActionEvent e)
  {
    setPlayWhoButtons(true);
    player1Label.setText("You");
    if (playAloneRadioButton.isSelected())
    {
      player2Label.setText("Guesses");
      setDifficultyButtons(false);
    }
    else
    {
      player2Label.setText("Computer");
      setDifficultyButtons(true);
    }
 }
```

```
  private void
playAloneRadioButtonActionPerformed(ActionEvent e)
  {
    setDifficultyButtons(false);
    player2Label.setText("Guesses");
  }

  private void
playComputerRadioButtonActionPerformed(ActionEvent e)
  {
    setDifficultyButtons(true);
    player2Label.setText("Computer");
  }

  private void easiestRadioButtonActionPerformed(ActionEvent
e)
  {
    difficulty = 1;
  }

  private void easyRadioButtonActionPerformed(ActionEvent e)
  {
    difficulty = 2;
  }

  private void hardRadioButtonActionPerformed(ActionEvent e)
  {
    difficulty = 3;
  }

  private void hardestRadioButtonActionPerformed(ActionEvent
e)
  {
    difficulty = 4;
  }

  private void startStopButtonActionPerformed(ActionEvent e)
  {
    if (startStopButton.getText().equals("Start Game"))
    {
      startStopButton.setText("Stop Game");
      score[0] = 0;
      score[1] = 0;
      scoreTextField[0].setText("0");
      scoreTextField[1].setText("0");
      picturesRemaining = 20;
      pictureIndex = nRandomIntegers(20);
```

```
      for (int i = 0; i < 20; i++)
      {
        if (pictureIndex[i] > 9)
          pictureIndex[i] -= 10;
        pictureFound[i] = false;
        pictureLabel[i].setIcon(cover);
        memory[i] = 0;
      }
      playerNumber = 1;
      choiceNumber = 1;
      if (twoPlayersRadioButton.isSelected())
        messageLabel.setText("Player 1, Pick a Box");
      else
        messageLabel.setText("Pick a Box");
      setNumberPlayersButtons(false);
      setPlayWhoButtons(false);
      setDifficultyButtons(false);
      exitButton.setEnabled(false);
      canClick = true;
      gameOver = false;
    }
    else
    {
      // stop game
      startStopButton.setText("Start Game");
      setNumberPlayersButtons(true);
      if (onePlayerRadioButton.isSelected())
      {
        setPlayWhoButtons(true);
        if (playComputerRadioButton.isSelected())
          setDifficultyButtons(true);
      }
      exitButton.setEnabled(true);
      canClick = false;
      if (!gameOver)
        messageLabel.setText("Game Stopped");
    }
  }

  private void exitButtonActionPerformed(ActionEvent e)
  {
   System.exit(0);
  }

  private void setNumberPlayersButtons(boolean a)
  {
    onePlayerRadioButton.setEnabled(a);
```

```
      twoPlayersRadioButton.setEnabled(a);
    }

    private void setPlayWhoButtons(boolean a)
    {
      playAloneRadioButton.setEnabled(a);
      playComputerRadioButton.setEnabled(a);
    }

    private void setDifficultyButtons(boolean a)
    {
      easiestRadioButton.setEnabled(a);
      easyRadioButton.setEnabled(a);
      hardRadioButton.setEnabled(a);
      hardestRadioButton.setEnabled(a);
    }

    private int[] nRandomIntegers(int n)
    {
      /*
      *  Returns n randomly sorted integers 0 -> n - 1
      */
      int[] nIntegers = new int[n];
      int temp, s;
      Random sortRandom = new Random();
      //  initialize array from 0 to n - 1
      for (int i = 0; i < n; i++)
      {
        nIntegers[i] = i;
      }
      //  i is number of items remaining in list
      for (int i = n; i >= 1; i--)
      {
        s = sortRandom.nextInt(i);
        temp = nIntegers[s];
        nIntegers[s] = nIntegers[i - 1];
        nIntegers[i - 1] = temp;
      }
      return(nIntegers);
    }

    private void showSelectedLabel()
    {
      // one player/solitaire game
      if (onePlayerRadioButton.isSelected() &&
playAloneRadioButton.isSelected())
      {
```

```
      score[1]++;
      scoreTextField[1].setText(String.valueOf(score[1]));
    }

pictureLabel[labelSelected].setIcon(picture[pictureIndex[lab
elSelected]]);
    pictureFound[labelSelected] = true;
    displayTimer.start();
  }

  private void displayTimerActionPerformed(ActionEvent e)
  {
    displayTimer.stop();
    if (choiceNumber == 1)
    {
      choice[0] = labelSelected;
      choiceNumber = 2;
      memory[labelSelected] = pictureIndex[labelSelected];
      if (twoPlayersRadioButton.isSelected())
      {
        messageLabel.setText("Player " +
String.valueOf(playerNumber) + ", Pick Another");
        canClick = true;
      }
      else
      {
      // one player logic
        if (playerNumber == 1)
        {
          messageLabel.setText("Pick Another Box");
          canClick = true;
        }
        else
        {
          // play computer logic
          messageLabel.setText("Picking Another");
          computerTurn();
          return;
        }
      }
    }
    else
    {
      choice[1] = labelSelected;
      choiceNumber = 1;
      memory[labelSelected] = pictureIndex[labelSelected];
```

```
      if (pictureIndex[choice[0]] ==
pictureIndex[choice[1]])
      {
        // a match
        matchSound.play();
        pictureLabel[choice[0]].setIcon(null);
        pictureLabel[choice[1]].setIcon(null);
       // clear memory so boxes are not checked again for
match
        memory[choice[0]] = 0;
        memory[choice[1]] = 0;
        score[playerNumber - 1]++;
        scoreTextField[playerNumber -
1].setText(String.valueOf(score[playerNumber - 1]));
        picturesRemaining -= 2;
        if (picturesRemaining == 0)
        {
          gameOver = true;
          gameOverSound.play();
          if (twoPlayersRadioButton.isSelected())
          {
            if (score[0] > score[1])
              messageLabel.setText("Player 1 Wins!");
            else if (score[1] > score[0])
              messageLabel.setText("Player 2 Wins!");
            else
              messageLabel.setText("It's a Tie!");
          }
          else
          {
            // one player logic
            if (playAloneRadioButton.isSelected())
              messageLabel.setText("All Matches Found!");
            else
            {
              // play computer logic
              if (score[0] > score[1])
                messageLabel.setText("You Win!");
              else if (score[1] > score[0])
                messageLabel.setText("Computer Wins!");
              else
                messageLabel.setText("It's a Tie!");
            }
          }
          startStopButton.doClick();
          return;
        }
```

```
        // another turn
        if (twoPlayersRadioButton.isSelected())
        {
          messageLabel.setText("Player " +
String.valueOf(playerNumber) + ", Pick Again");
          canClick = true;
        }
        else
        {
          // one player logic
          if (playerNumber == 1)
          {
            messageLabel.setText("Pick a Box");
            canClick = true;
          }
          else
          {
            // play computer logic
            messageLabel.setText("Picking Again");
            computerTurn();
            return;
          }
        }
      }
      else
      {
        //no match
        noMatchSound.play();
        pictureFound[choice[0]] = false;
        pictureFound[choice[1]] = false;
          pictureLabel[choice[0]].setIcon(cover);
        pictureLabel[choice[1]].setIcon(cover);
        // swap players
        if (twoPlayersRadioButton.isSelected())
        {
          if (playerNumber == 1)
            playerNumber = 2;
          else
            playerNumber = 1;
          messageLabel.setText("Player " +
String.valueOf(playerNumber) + ", Pick a Box");
          canClick = true;
        }
        else
        {
          // one player logic
          if (playComputerRadioButton.isSelected())
```

```
        {
          if (playerNumber == 1)
            playerNumber = 2;
          else
            playerNumber = 1;
        }
        if (playerNumber == 1)
        {
          messageLabel.setText("Pick a Box");
          canClick = true;
        }
        else
        {
          // play computer logic
          messageLabel.setText("Computer Picking");
          choiceNumber = 1;
          computerTurn();
          return;
        }
      }
    }
  }
}

private int randomChoice()
{
  int count, n, rc;
  if (choiceNumber == 1)
    n = myRandom.nextInt(picturesRemaining) + 1;
  else
    n = myRandom.nextInt(picturesRemaining - 1) + 1;
  count = 0;
  for (rc = 0; rc < 20; rc++)
  {
    if (!pictureFound[rc])
      count++;
    if (count == n)
      break;
  }
  return(rc);
}

private int smartChoice()
{
  int sc;
  if (choiceNumber == 1)
  {
```

```
      matchFound = checkForMatch();
      if (matchFound[0] != 0 && matchFound[1] != 0)
        sc = matchFound[0];
      else
        sc = randomChoice();
    }
    else
    {
      if (matchFound[0] != 0 && matchFound[1] != 0)
        sc = matchFound[1];
      else
      {
        matchFound = checkForMatch();
        if (matchFound[0] != 0 && matchFound[1] != 0)
        {
          if (matchFound[0] != choice[0])
            sc = matchFound[0];
          else
            sc = matchFound[1];
        }
        else
          sc = randomChoice();
      }
    }
    return (sc);
  }

  private void computerTurn()
  {
    int threshold = 0;
    if (choiceNumber == 1)
    {
      switch (difficulty)
      {
        case 1:
          threshold = 25;
          break;
        case 2:
          threshold = 50;
          break;
        case 3:
          threshold = 75;
          break;
        case 4:
          threshold = 90;
          break;
      }
```

```
      if (myRandom.nextInt(100) < threshold)
        smartComputer = true;
      else
        smartComputer = false;
    }
    if (smartComputer)
      labelSelected = smartChoice();
    else
      labelSelected = randomChoice();
    delayTimer.start();
  }

  private void delayTimerActionPerformed(ActionEvent e)
  {
    delayTimer.stop();
    showSelectedLabel();
  }

  private int[] checkForMatch()
  {
    int[] matches = new int[2];
    matches[0] = 0;
    matches[1] = 0;
    for (int i = 0; i < 20; i++)
    {
      for (int j = 0; j < 20; j++)
      {
        if (memory[i] != 0 && memory[i] == memory[j] && i !=
j)
        {
          matches[0] = i;
          matches[1] = j;
        }
      }
    }
    return(matches);
  }

}
```

5

Noah's Ark Project

Preview

In Genesis, Noah was commanded by God to take two of every kind of animal into the ark. In this chapter, we build a game where turtles race to get on Noah's Ark. You pick two turtles (out of ten maximum) and see if your turtles are the winners. The purpose of this Bible story is to remember that God has promised never to flood the earth again. God displays a beautiful rainbow in the sky to remind us of His promises to us.

Noah's Ark Project Preview

In this chapter, we will build the **Noah's Ark** game. It's a simple game. Up to 10 turtles line up to race to the ark. You select two turtles you want to win the race. Clicking a '**Start**' button gets the race going. The turtles then move across the screen toward the finish line.

The finished project is saved as **NoahsArk** in the **\CBGJava\CBGJava Projects** project group. Start NetBeans (or your IDE). Open the specified project group. Make **NoahsArk** the selected project. Run the project. You will see:

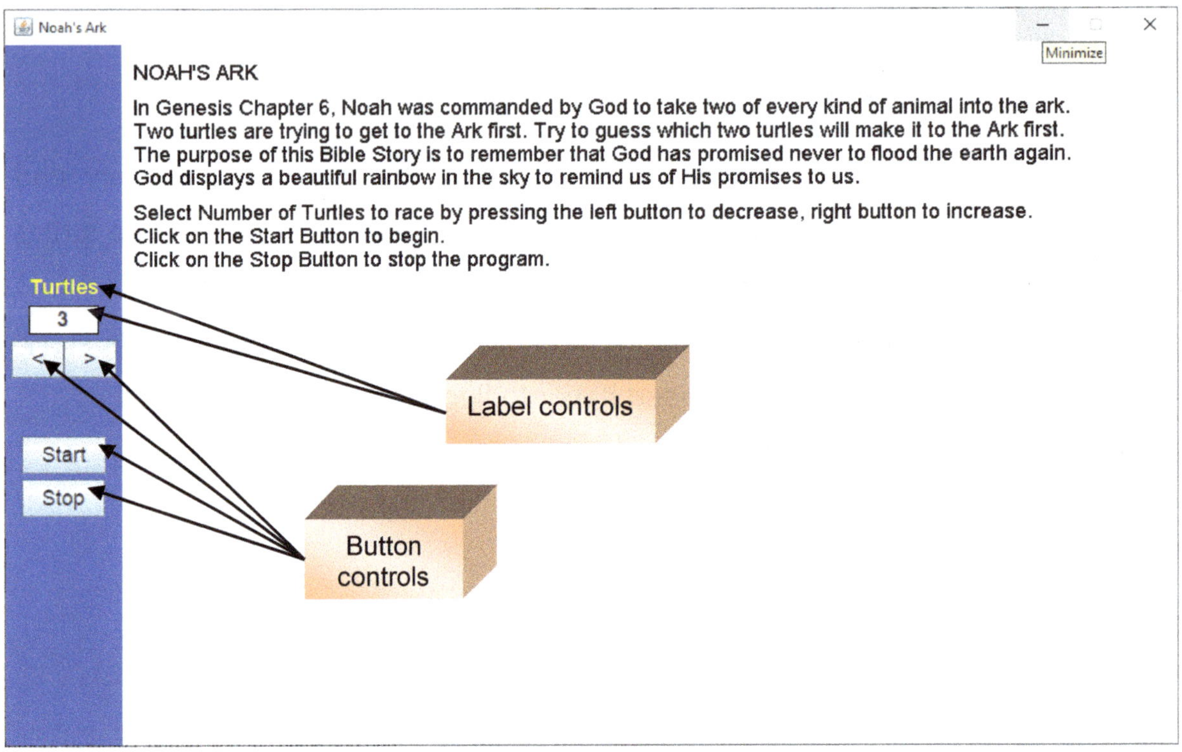

Labels are used to display the number of turtles in the race. Four button controls are included: two to change the number of turtles, one to start the game and one to stop. A game description and program instructions are given. At this point, you can click the **Start** button to start the game, click arrow buttons to change the number of turtles racing or click **Stop** to stop the program.

Change the number of turtles if you want (I picked five) by clicking the little arrows under **Number of Turtles**. Click the **Start** button to start playing. The program instructions disappear. Five turtles are poised, ready to race. This is the game's 'stopped' state:

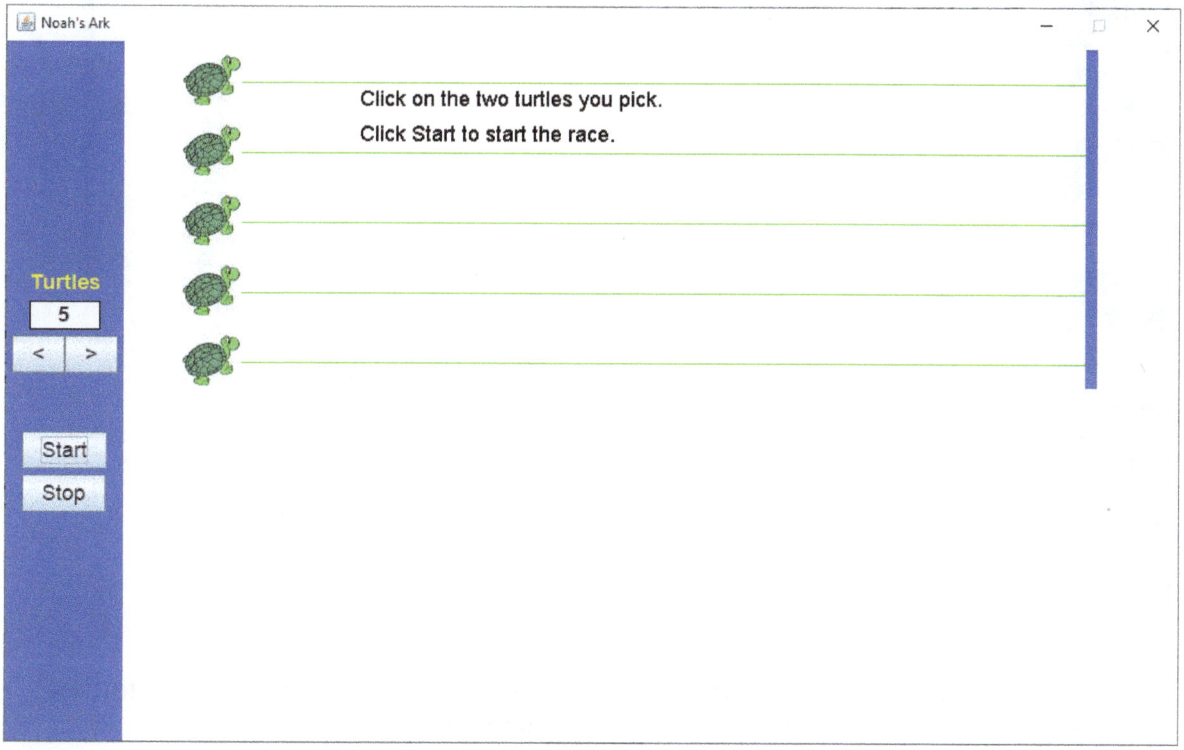

In this state, you pick two turtles you want to win the race. To do this, simple click on your selected turtle with the mouse – a red X will appear next to the selected turtle. Once two turtles are selected, you can start the race by clicking **Start**. If you select two turtles and want to change your mind, click on a selected turtle and the red X will disappear allowing you to pick another.

Choose two turtles. I picked the top one and the bottom one:

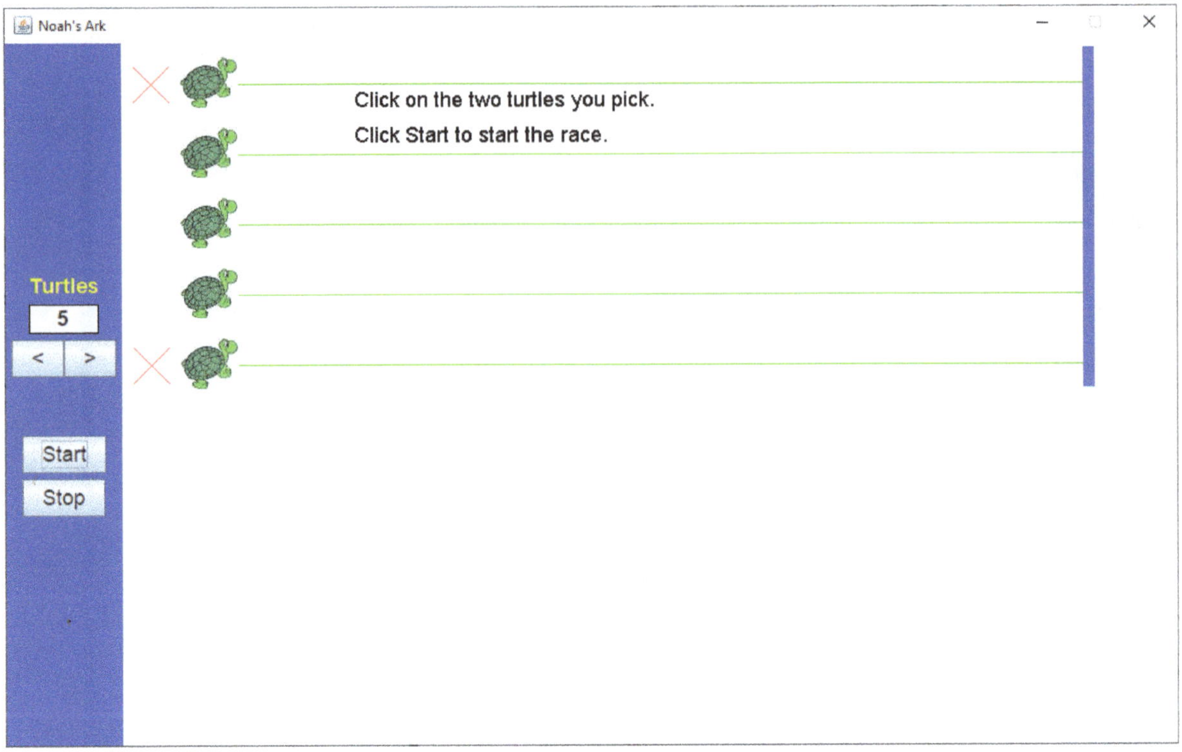

I then click **Start**. The race is on. The program is in 'moving' state. The turtles move across the screen until two cross the finish line.

Here's the results:

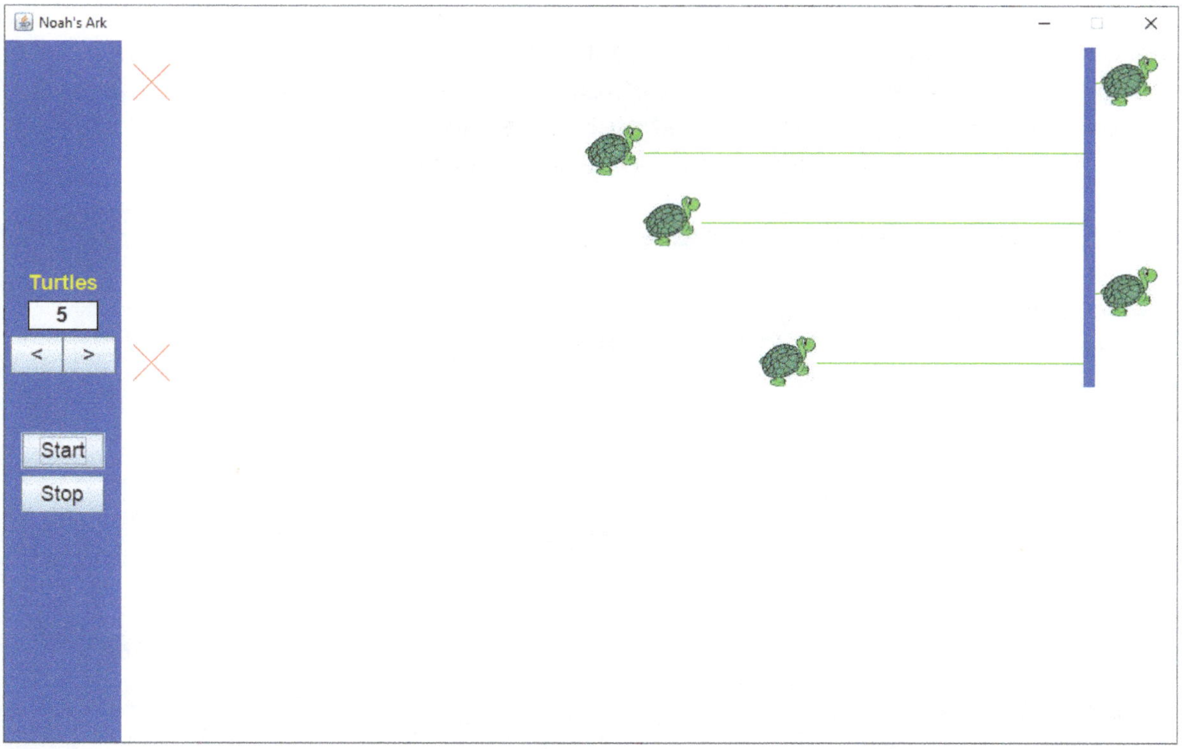

One of my turtles won! At this point, if you want, you can change the number of turtles. You can also click **Start** to race again or click **Stop** to stop the program. Continue playing the game to understand its operation.

You will now build this program in stages. As you build Java programs, we always recommend taking a slow, step-by-step process. It minimizes programming errors and helps build your confidence as things come together in a complete program. We address **frame design**, discussing sizing of panels and control placement. And, we address **code design**. We discuss how to use the buttons, how to display the racing turtles, and how to move the turtles.

Noah's Ark Frame Design

We begin building the **Noah's Ark** project. Start a new project in your Java project group – name it **NoahsArk**. Delete default code in file named **NoahsArk.java**. Once started, we suggest you immediately save the project with a name you choose. This sets up the folder and file structure needed for your project.

Build the basic frame with these properties:

Noah Frame:

title	Noah's Ark
resizable	false

The code is:

```
/*
 * NoahsArk.java
 */
package noahsark;
import javax.swing.*;
import java.awt.*;
import java.awt.event.*;
import java.awt.geom.*;

public class NoahsArk extends JFrame
{

  public static void main(String args[])
  {
    // create frame
    new NoahsArk().setVisible(true);
  }

  public NoahsArk()
  {
    // frame constructor
    setTitle("Noah's Ark");
    setResizable(false);
    addWindowListener(new WindowAdapter()
    {
      public void windowClosing(WindowEvent evt)
      {
        exitForm(evt);
      }
    });
    getContentPane().setLayout(new GridBagLayout());
```

```
      GridBagConstraints gridConstraints;

      pack();
      Dimension screenSize =
  Toolkit.getDefaultToolkit().getScreenSize();
      setBounds((int) (0.5 * (screenSize.width -
  getWidth())), (int) (0.5 * (screenSize.height -
  getHeight())), getWidth(), getHeight());
    }

    private void exitForm(WindowEvent evt)
    {
      System.exit(0);
    }
  }
```

This code builds the frame, sets up the layout manager and includes code to exit the application. Run the code to make sure the frame (at least, what there is of it at this point) appears and is centered on the screen:

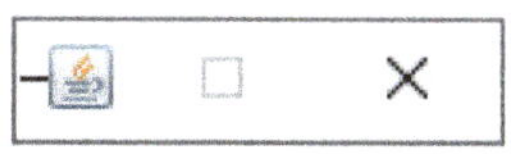

Let's populate our frame with other controls. All code for creating the frame and placing controls (except declarations) goes in the **NoahsArk** constructor.

The frame uses two panel controls. **controlPanel** holds the labels and buttons for game control, while **gamePanel** displays the racing turtles. The **GridBagLayout** is:

	gridx = 0	gridx = 1
gridy = 0	**controlPanel**	**gamePanel**

Since **gamePanel** hosts graphics elements (images, lines), it will be a 'graphics panel.' Each such panel (example below is named **GraphicsPanel**) will be a separate class with a **paintComponent** method where any graphics are drawn:

```
class GraphicsPanel extends JPanel
{
  public void paintComponent(Graphics g)
  {
    Graphics2D g2D = (Graphics2D) g;
    super.paintComponent(g2D);

    g2D.dispose();  }
}
```

Recall we introduced such panels in other projects.

The properties for each panel are:

controlPanel:	
size	100, 600
background	Blue
gridx	0
gridy	0

gamePanel:	
size	900, 600
background	White
gridx	1
gridy	0

Declare each panel using:

```
JPanel controlPanel = new JPanel();
GraphicsPanel gamePanel = new GraphicsPanel();
```

Add the panels to the frame using this code:

```
controlPanel.setPreferredSize(new Dimension(100, 600));
controlPanel.setBackground(Color.BLUE);
controlPanel.setLayout(new GridBagLayout());
gridConstraints = new GridBagConstraints();
gridConstraints.gridx = 0;
gridConstraints.gridy = 0;
getContentPane().add(controlPanel, gridConstraints);

gamePanel.setPreferredSize(new Dimension(900, 600));
gamePanel.setBackground(Color.WHITE);
gridConstraints = new GridBagConstraints();
gridConstraints.gridx = 1;
gridConstraints.gridy = 0;
getContentPane().add(gamePanel, gridConstraints);
```

After the **Noah** main class, add this 'graphics' panel framework:

```
class GraphicsPanel extends JPanel
{
  public GraphicsPanel()
  {
  }
  public void paintComponent(Graphics g)
  {
    Graphics2D g2D = (Graphics2D) g;
    super.paintComponent(g2D);

    g2D.dispose();
  }
}
```

All graphic elements will be drawn in the **paintComponent** methods of these classes.

Save, run. You will see the empty panel controls on the frame. This is the finished frame size.

We need to add some elements to the **controlPanel**.

The **controlPanel** holds controls used to display status of the **Noah's Ark** game and control its operation. The **GridBagLayout** is:

	gridx = 0	gridx = 1
gridy = 0	**turtleLabel**	
gridy = 1	**turtleTextField**	
gridy = 2	**decreaseButton**	**increaseButton**
gridy = 3	**startButton**	
gridy = 4	**stopButton**	

The label and text field controls display the number of turtles. Buttons are used to change the number of turtles and start and stop the game.

Control properties are:

turtleLabel:

text	Turtles
foreground	Yellow
font	Arial, Bold, Size 18
gridx	0
gridy	0
gridwidth	2

turtleTextField:

size	60, 25
border	Black line
text	0
editable	false
background	White
horizontalAlignment	CENTER
font	Arial, Bold, Size 18
gridx	0
gridy	1
gridwidth	2
insets	5, 0, 0, 0

decreaseButton:

text	<
font	Arial, Plain, Size 18
gridx	0
gridy	2
insets	5, 0, 0, 0

increaseButton:

text	>
font	Arial, Plain, Size 18
gridx	1
gridy	2
insets	5, 0, 0, 0

startButton:

text	Start
font	Arial, Plain, Size 18
gridx	0
gridy	3
gridwidth	2
insets	50, 0, 0, 0

stopButton:

text	Stop
font	Arial, Plain, Size 18
gridx	0
gridy	4
gridwidth	2
insets	5, 0, 0, 0

Use these declarations for the control panel elements:

```
JLabel turtleLabel = new JLabel();
JTextField turtleTextField = new JTextField();
JButton decreaseButton = new JButton();
JButton increaseButton = new JButton();
JButton startButton = new JButton();
JButton stopButton = new JButton();
```

And, this code adds the controls:

```
turtleLabel.setText("Turtles");
turtleLabel.setForeground(Color.YELLOW);
turtleLabel.setFont(new Font("Arial", Font.BOLD, 18));
gridConstraints = new GridBagConstraints();
gridConstraints.gridx = 0;
gridConstraints.gridy = 0;
gridConstraints.gridwidth = 2;
controlPanel.add(turtleLabel, gridConstraints);
```

```
turtleTextField.setPreferredSize(new Dimension(60, 25));
turtleTextField.setBorder(BorderFactory.createLineBorder(C
olor.BLACK));
turtleTextField.setText("0");
turtleTextField.setEditable(false);
turtleTextField.setBackground(Color.WHITE);
turtleTextField.setHorizontalAlignment(SwingConstants.CENT
ER);
turtleTextField.setFont(new Font("Arial", Font.BOLD, 18));
gridConstraints = new GridBagConstraints();
gridConstraints.gridx = 0;
gridConstraints.gridy = 1;
gridConstraints.gridwidth = 2;
gridConstraints.insets = new Insets(5, 0, 0, 0);
controlPanel.add(turtleTextField, gridConstraints);

decreaseButton.setText("<");
decreaseButton.setFont(new Font("Arial", Font.PLAIN, 18));
gridConstraints = new GridBagConstraints();
gridConstraints.gridx = 0;
gridConstraints.gridy = 2;
gridConstraints.insets = new Insets(5, 0, 0, 0);
controlPanel.add(decreaseButton, gridConstraints);
decreaseButton.addActionListener(new ActionListener()
{
  public void actionPerformed(ActionEvent e)
  {
    decreaseButtonActionPerformed(e);
  }
});
```

```
increaseButton.setText(">");
increaseButton.setFont(new Font("Arial", Font.PLAIN, 18));
gridConstraints = new GridBagConstraints();
gridConstraints.gridx = 1;
gridConstraints.gridy = 2;
gridConstraints.insets = new Insets(5, 0, 0, 0);
controlPanel.add(increaseButton, gridConstraints);
increaseButton.addActionListener(new ActionListener()
{
  public void actionPerformed(ActionEvent e)
  {
    increaseButtonActionPerformed(e);
  }
});

startButton.setText("Start");
startButton.setFont(new Font("Arial", Font.PLAIN, 18));
gridConstraints = new GridBagConstraints();
gridConstraints.gridx = 0;
gridConstraints.gridy = 3;
gridConstraints.gridwidth = 2;
gridConstraints.insets = new Insets(50, 0, 0, 0);
controlPanel.add(startButton, gridConstraints);
startButton.addActionListener(new ActionListener()
{
  public void actionPerformed(ActionEvent e)
  {
    startButtonActionPerformed(e);
  }
});

stopButton.setText("Stop");
stopButton.setFont(new Font("Arial", Font.PLAIN, 18));
gridConstraints = new GridBagConstraints();
gridConstraints.gridx = 0;
gridConstraints.gridy = 4;
gridConstraints.gridwidth = 2;
gridConstraints.insets = new Insets(5, 0, 0, 0);
controlPanel.add(stopButton, gridConstraints);
stopButton.addActionListener(new ActionListener()
{
  public void actionPerformed(ActionEvent e)
  {
    stopButtonActionPerformed(e);
  }
});
```

And, add these four empty methods:

```
private void decreaseButtonActionPerformed(ActionEvent e)
{
}

private void increaseButtonActionPerformed(ActionEvent e)
{
}

private void startButtonActionPerformed(ActionEvent e)
{
}

private void stopButtonActionPerformed(ActionEvent e)
{
}
```

Run the project so see:

The controls are there. The frame design is complete.

We now begin writing code for the **Noah's Ark** game. We will write the code in several steps. As a first step, we will write the code that starts the game and establishes its 'initial' state. Then, we look at how to go to 'stopped' state following clicking of the **Start** button from initial state. Lastly, we write code to race the turtles once **Start** is clicked again. During the code development process, recognize you may modify a particular procedure several times before arriving at the finished product.

Code Design – Initial State (Instructions)

Any time we start a program, there are certain initializations that must take place. Let's look at the initializations needed in the **Noah's Ark** game. When the program first begins, we want to display the game instructions (when **firstTime** is true). We also initialize the number of turtles (**numberOfTurtles**) and the game status (**gameStatus**). These initializations are in the **Noah** frame constructor.

We declare three variables (**firstTime**, **numberOfTurtles**, and **gameStatus**). Do this in the class level declarations area:

```
static boolean firstTime = true;
static int numberOfTurtles;
static String gameStatus;
```

The variables are declared **static** because they will be needed in the **gamePanel paintComponent** method.

Add this code at the end of the frame constructor:

```
numberOfTurtles = 3;
gameStatus = "Initial";
turtleTextField.setText(String.valueOf(numberOfTurtles));
```

As mentioned, we set **numberOfTurtles** to **3** and the **gameStatus** to "**Initial**".

In this initial state, with **firstTime = true**, we want to display the game instructions. The code to do this is placed in the graphics panel **paintComponent** method. Add the shaded code:

```
public void paintComponent(Graphics g)
{
  Graphics2D g2D = (Graphics2D) g;
  super.paintComponent(g2D);

  if (NoahsArk.firstTime)
  {
    // draw instructions
    g2D.setFont(new Font("Arial", Font.PLAIN, 18));
    g2D.setPaint(Color.BLACK);
    g2D.drawString("NOAH'S ARK", 10, 30);
    g2D.drawString("In Genesis Chapter 6, Noah was
commanded by God to take two of every kind of animal into
the ark.", 10, 60);
    g2D.drawString("Two turtles are trying to get to the
Ark first. Try to guess which two turtles will make it to
the Ark first.", 10, 80);
    g2D.drawString("The purpose of this Bible Story is to
remember that God has promised never to flood the earth
again.", 10, 100);
    g2D.drawString("God displays a beautiful rainbow in
the sky to remind us of His promises to us.", 10, 120);
    g2D.drawString("Select Number of Turtles to race by
pressing the left button to decrease, right button to
increase.", 10, 150);
    g2D.drawString("Click on the Start Button to begin.",
10, 170);
    g2D.drawString("Click on the Stop Button to stop the
program.", 10, 190);
  }

  g2D.dispose();
}
```

The instructions are 'drawn' in the **gamePanel** using the **drawString** method. The positions of each line of text were found using trial and error.

Save and **Run** the program to see:

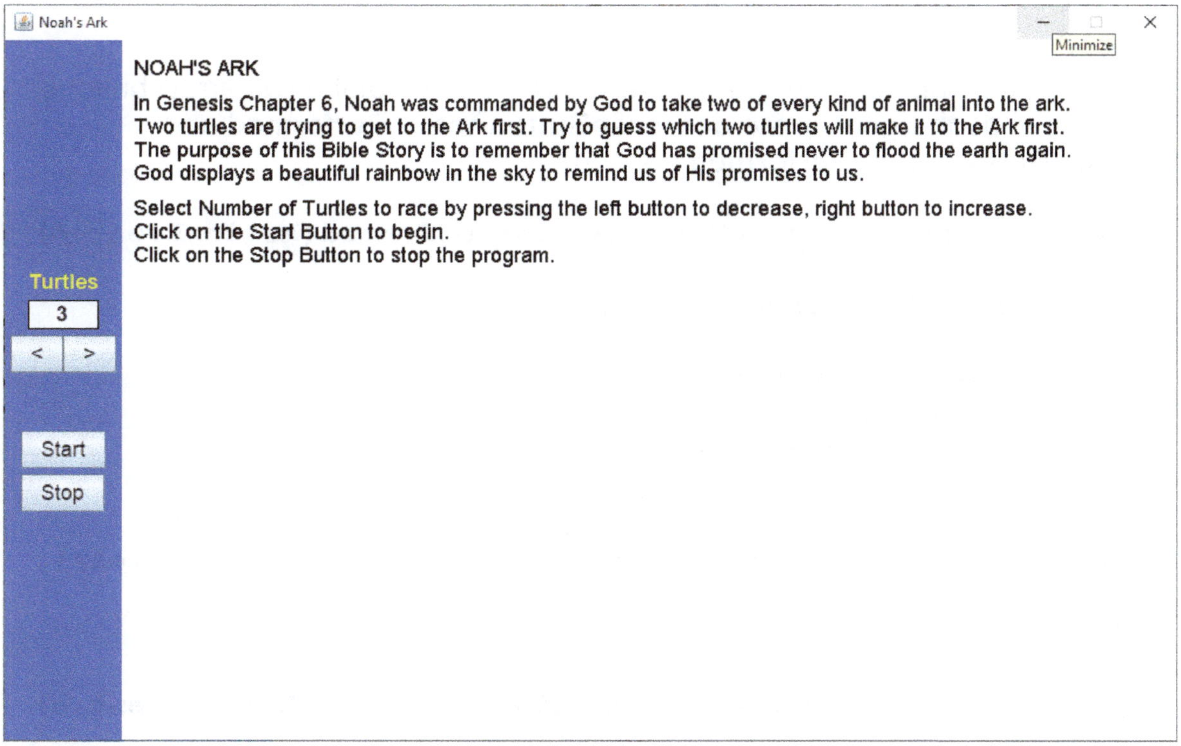

Code Design – Select Number of Turtles

To change the number of turtles, a user clicks on either of the two arrow buttons. The code to do this goes in the **decreaseButtonActionPerformed** and in**creaseButtonActionPerformed** methods:

```
private void decreaseButtonActionPerformed(ActionEvent e)
{
  if (gameStatus.equals("Initial"))
  {
    // decrease number of turtles
    numberOfTurtles--;
    if (numberOfTurtles < 3)
      numberOfTurtles = 3;

turtleTextField.setText(String.valueOf(numberOfTurtles));
  }
}

private void increaseButtonActionPerformed(ActionEvent e)
{
  if (gameStatus.equals("Initial"))
  {
    // increase number of turtles
    numberOfTurtles++;
    if (numberOfTurtles > 10)
      numberOfTurtles = 10;

turtleTextField.setText(String.valueOf(numberOfTurtles));
  }
}
```

The code is straightforward. The number of turtles can only be changed when the game is in "**Initial**" state. If the **<** button is clicked, we decrease the number of turtles by one (minimum of 3). If the **>** button is clicked, we increase the number of turtles (maximum of 10). The new value for the number of turtles is then displayed.

Save and **Run** the program. Make sure the arrow buttons work – make sure the number of turtles is always between 3 and 10. Here's my run where I changed the number of turtles to five:

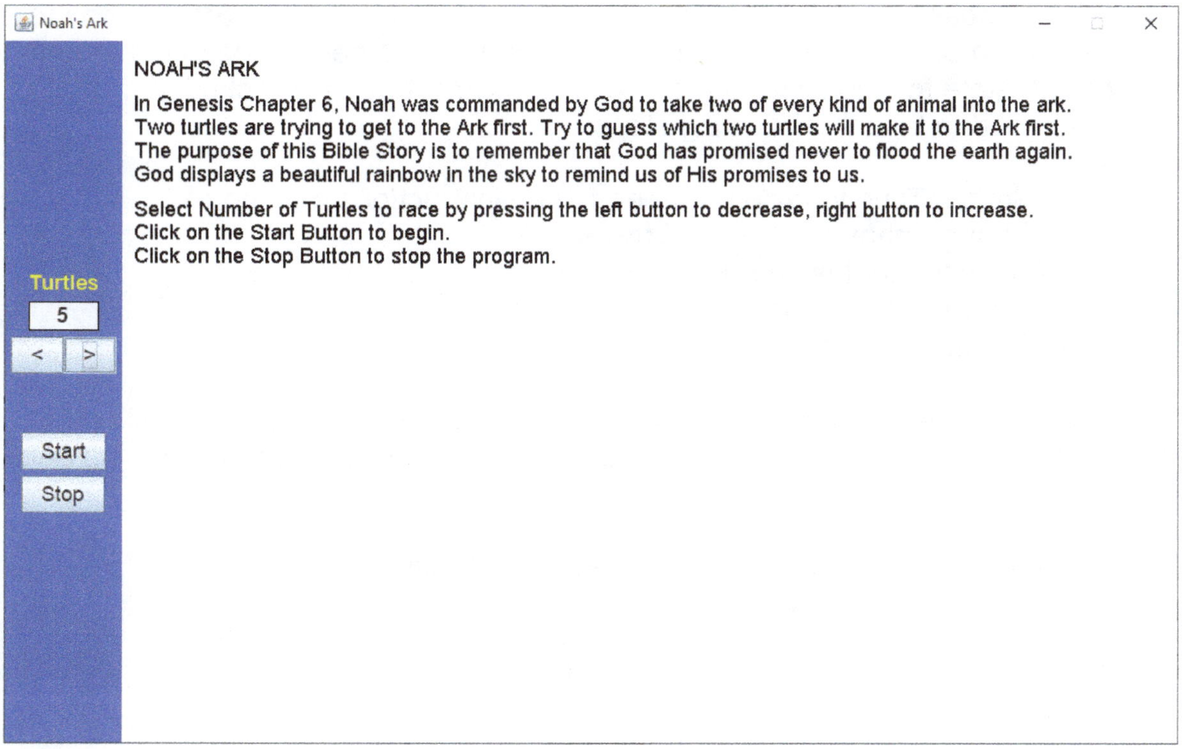

Code Design – Initial to Stopped State

Once the number of turtles is finalized, the next step is to click the **Start** button to allow selection of the turtles you want to win. Hence, we need code to move from the "**Initial**" state to "**Stopped**" state. When the **Start** button is clicked in "**Initial**" state, we need to take the following steps:

- Set firstTime to false (no need to see instructions any more)
- Change **gameStatus** to "**Stopped**"
- Draw the turtles and "lane lines" for each
- Draw the finish line
- Display instructions for the user

To draw the turtles, we divide the race region into 10 equal size areas (set up for the maximum number of turtles). We then just move down the screen adding each turtle.

The image file **turtle.jpg** is used to represent the turtle:

The turtle is 50 pixels wide and 45 pixels high. This file is included in the **\CBGJava\CBGJava Projects\NoahsArk** folder. Copy it to your project folder.

Now, add this code to **startButtonActionPerformed** method::

```
private void startButtonActionPerformed(ActionEvent e)
{
  firstTime = false;
  if (gameStatus.equals("Initial"))
  {
    //clicked start
    gameStatus = "Stopped";
    turtlesSelected = 0;
    for (int i = 0; i < numberOfTurtles; i++)
    {
       turtlePicked[i] = 0;
       turtlePosition[i] = 50;
    }
    gamePanel.repaint();
  }
}
```

This code sets up some variables so the turtles can be drawn. Once established, a **repaint** of the **gamePanel** will do the drawing.

Four new variables are introduced. **turtlesSelected** (the number of turtles picked by the user) is initialized at zero. The array **turtlePicked** is used to keep track of which turtles are selected by the user. **turtlePosition** is an array that keeps track of where each turtle is. The turtle image variable is **turtle**. Add these lines in the class level declarations area:

```
static int turtlesSelected;
static int[] turtlePicked = new int[10];
static int[] turtlePosition = new int[10];
static Image turtle = new
ImageIcon("turtle.jpg").getImage();
```

As mentioned, once all these variables are established, the **repaint** of the **gamePanel** does the actual drawing. Add the shaded code to the **gamePanel paintComponent** method:

```
public void paintComponent(Graphics g)
{
  Graphics2D g2D = (Graphics2D) g;
  super.paintComponent(g2D);

  if (NoahsArk.firstTime)
  {
    // draw instructions
    g2D.setFont(new Font("Arial", Font.PLAIN, 18));
    g2D.setPaint(Color.BLACK);
    g2D.drawString("NOAH'S ARK", 10, 30);
    g2D.drawString("In Genesis Chapter 6, Noah was
commanded by God to take two of every kind of animal into
the ark.", 10, 60);
    g2D.drawString("Two turtles are trying to get to the
Ark first. Try to guess which two turtles will make it to
the Ark first.", 10, 80);
    g2D.drawString("The purpose of this Bible Story is to
remember that God has promised never to flood the earth
again.", 10, 100);
    g2D.drawString("God displays a beautiful rainbow in
the sky to remind us of His promises to us.", 10, 120);
    g2D.drawString("Select Number of Turtles to race by
pressing the left button to decrease, right button to
increase.", 10, 150);
    g2D.drawString("Click on the Start Button to begin.",
10, 170);
    g2D.drawString("Click on the Stop Button to stop the
program.", 10, 190);
  }
  else
  {
    Line2D.Double myLine;
    //draw turtles
    for (int i = 0; i < NoahsArk.numberOfTurtles; i++)
    {
      g2D.setPaint(Color.GREEN);
      myLine = new
Line2D.Double(NoahsArk.turtlePosition[i], i * 60 + 35,
820, i * 60 + 35);
      g2D.draw(myLine);
      g2D.drawImage(NoahsArk.turtle,
NoahsArk.turtlePosition[i], i * 60 + 10, 50, 45, this);
```

```
      }
      // draw finish line
      g2D.setPaint(Color.BLUE);
      Rectangle2D.Double myRectangle = new
Rectangle2D.Double(820, 5, 10, NoahsArk.numberOfTurtles *
60 - 10);
      g2D.fill(myRectangle);
      if (NoahsArk.gameStatus.equals("Stopped"))
      {
        g2D.setFont(new Font("Arial", Font.PLAIN, 18));
        g2D.setPaint(Color.BLACK);
        g2D.drawString("Click on the two turtles you pick.",
200, 55);
        g2D.drawString("Click Start to start the race.",
200, 85);
      }
    }

    g2D.dispose();
  }
```

You should see how the different graphic methods draw the turtles, the finish line and connecting green lines. If the game is in "**Stopped**" state, instructions are provided.

Save and **Run** the program. Choose a number of turtles (I picked 5). Click **Start** and you should see:

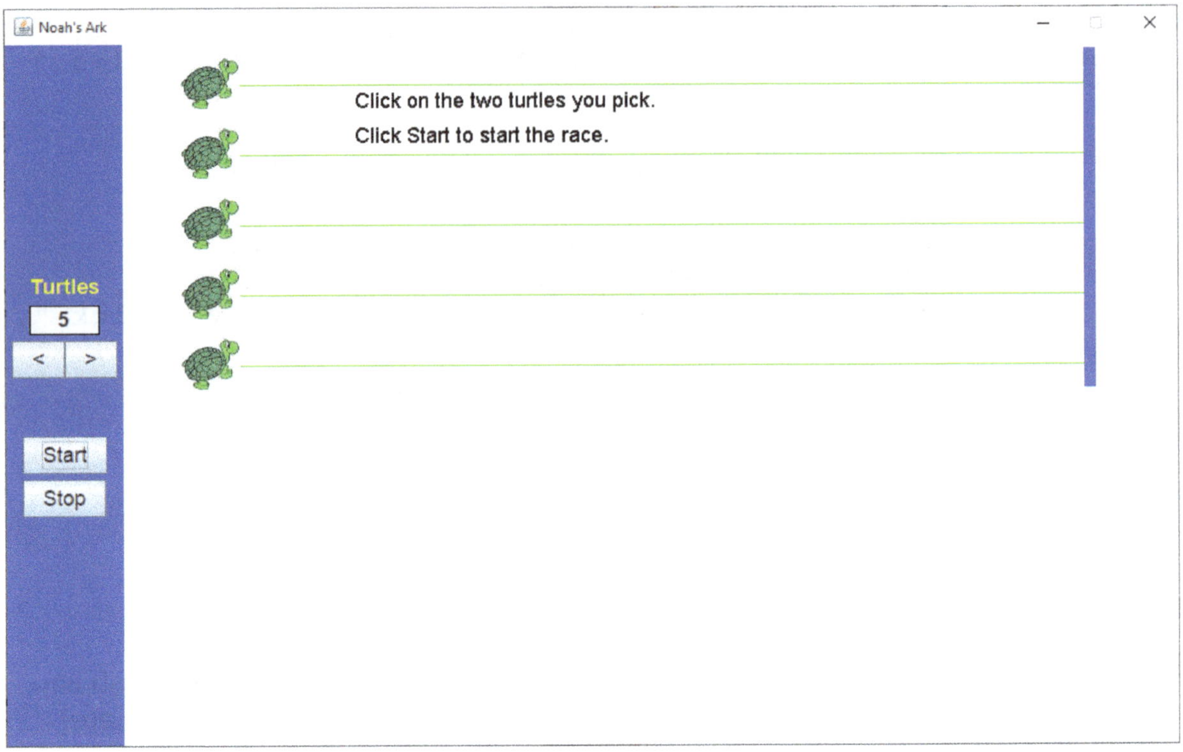

The next step is to select two turtles you want in the race. We do that selection code soon. But first, let's take care of one last thing you can do while in "**Initial**" state – stop the program.

Code Design – Stop the Program

One last thing you can do while the game is in "**Initial**" state is to click on the **Stop** button. This will stop the game. The code here is simple. Add the few lines in the **stopButtonActionPerformed** method:

```
private void stopButtonActionPerformed(ActionEvent e)
{
  if (gameStatus.equals("Initial"))
    // clicked stop
    System.exit(0);
}
```

As desired, if the **Stop** button is clicked, the program ends.

Save and **Run** the program. Make sure the **Stop** button works.

Code Design – Selecting Turtles

Once the game is in "**Stopped**" state, the user picks the two turtles they want in the **Noah's Ark** race. To detect clicks on a turtle, we need to know their initial location and size. From the code placing the turtles on **gamePanel**, you should see that for turtle i (where **i** goes from **0** to **numberOfTurtles - 1**):

located at (50, i * 60 +10), width 50, height 45

The array **turtlePicked** is used to tell us which turtles have been selected. A red **X** will appear next to a selected turtle. Once two turtles are selected (**turtlesSelected = 2**), you can start the race by clicking **Start**. If you select two turtles and want to change your mind, click on a selected turtle and the red **X** will disappear allowing you to pick another.

When a turtle i is clicked, the following steps are taken:

- If turtle has been selected selected previously, decrement **turtlesSelected**, set **turtlePicked[i]** to **0**. Remove red **X** next to turtle.
- If turtle has not been selected and **turtlesSelected** is less than 2, increment **turtlesSelected**, set **turtlePicked[i]** to **1**. Draw red **X** next to turtle.

We do the steps in this order to make sure we don't click on a turtle that has already been selected.

We need to detect mouse clicks on **gamePanel**. Add this code in the frame constructor after the code adding **gamePanel** to the frame:

```
gamePanel.addMouseListener(new MouseAdapter()
{
  public void mousePressed(MouseEvent e)
  {
    gamePanelMousePressed(e);
  }
});
```

And, the code for turtle selection is placed in the **gamePanelMousePressed** method:

```
private void gamePanelMousePressed(MouseEvent e)
{
  int turtleClicked;
  if (gameStatus == "Stopped")
  {
    // want to pick two and only two turtles
    //which turtle clicked
    turtleClicked = (int) ((e.getY() - 10) / 60);
    //if clicked before, remove from list
    if (turtlePicked[turtleClicked] == 1)
    {
      turtlesSelected--;
      turtlePicked[turtleClicked] = 0;
    }
    else if (turtlesSelected < 2)
    {
      //add to list if two have not been selected yet
      turtlesSelected++;
      turtlePicked[turtleClicked] = 1;
    }
  }
  gamePanel.repaint();
}
```

You should see how the clicks on the turtles are handled.

The code above decides which turtles are selected. The marking X's are drawn in the panel's **paintComponent** method. Add the shaded code that goes through the **turtlePicked** array to see which turtles to mark:

```
public void paintComponent(Graphics g)
{
  Graphics2D g2D = (Graphics2D) g;
  super.paintComponent(g2D);

  if (NoahsArk.firstTime)
  {
    // draw instructions
    g2D.setFont(new Font("Arial", Font.PLAIN, 18));
    g2D.setPaint(Color.BLACK);
    g2D.drawString("NOAH'S ARK", 10, 30);
    g2D.drawString("In Genesis Chapter 6, Noah was
commanded by God to take two of every kind of animal into
the ark.", 10, 60);
```

```
    g2D.drawString("Two turtles are trying to get to the
Ark first. Try to guess which two turtles will make it to
the Ark first.", 10, 80);
    g2D.drawString("The purpose of this Bible Story is to
remember that God has promised never to flood the earth
again.", 10, 100);
    g2D.drawString("God displays a beautiful rainbow in
the sky to remind us of His promises to us.", 10, 120);
    g2D.drawString("Select Number of Turtles to race by
pressing the left button to decrease, right button to
increase.", 10, 150);
    g2D.drawString("Click on the Start Button to begin.",
10, 170);
    g2D.drawString("Click on the Stop Button to stop the
program.", 10, 190);
  }
  else
  {
    Line2D.Double myLine;
    //draw turtles
    for (int i = 0; i < NoahsArk.numberOfTurtles; i++)
    {
      g2D.setPaint(Color.GREEN);
      myLine = new
Line2D.Double(NoahsArk.turtlePosition[i], i * 60 + 35,
820, i * 60 + 35);
      g2D.draw(myLine);
      g2D.drawImage(NoahsArk.turtle,
NoahsArk.turtlePosition[i], i * 60 + 10, 50, 45, this);
      // mark selected turtles
      if (NoahsArk.turtlePicked[i] == 1)
      {
        g2D.setPaint(Color.RED);
        myLine = new Line2D.Double(10, i * 60 + 20, 40, i
* 60 + 50);
        g2D.draw(myLine);
        myLine = new Line2D.Double(10, i * 60 + 50, 40, i
* 60 + 20);
        g2D.draw(myLine);
      }
    }
    // draw finish line
    g2D.setPaint(Color.BLUE);
    Rectangle2D.Double myRectangle = new
Rectangle2D.Double(820, 5, 10, NoahsArk.numberOfTurtles *
60 - 10);
    g2D.fill(myRectangle);
```

```
      if (NoahsArk.gameStatus.equals("Stopped"))
      {
        g2D.setFont(new Font("Arial", Font.PLAIN, 18));
        g2D.setPaint(Color.BLACK);
        g2D.drawString("Click on the two turtles you pick.",
  200, 55);
        g2D.drawString("Click Start to start the race.",
  200, 85);
      }
    }

    g2D.dispose();
  }
```

Save and **Run** the program. Choose a number of turtles (I picked 5). Click **Start**. Then, select two turtles for your race. I picked the first and last turtle:

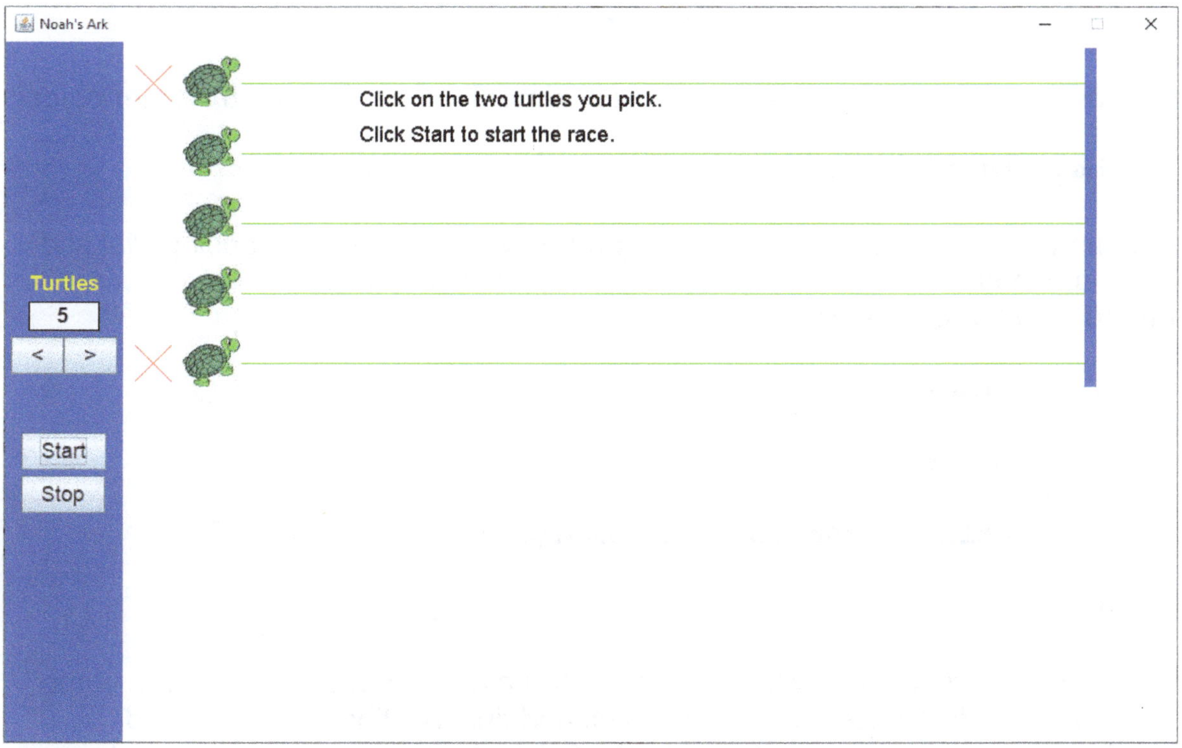

Make sure you can 'unselect' a turtle. Now, let's race!

Code Design - Stopped to Moving State

Once turtles are selected, we click the **Start** button to get the race started, moving to "**Moving**" state. So, when the **Start** button is clicked in "**Stopped**" state, we take these steps:

- Change **gameStatus** to "**Moving**".
- Clear instructions.
- For each turtle, pick a random final position before the finish line.
- Pick two winners at random. Assign these winners final positions after the finish line.
- Move the turtles to their final positions.
- Change **gameStatus** to "**Initial**" to allow another race.

What we do is pick two of the displayed turtles to be winners. These turtles finish across the line – all others finish before the line.

To move the turtles, we use a timer object (**timerTurtle**). Declare the timer object:

```
Timer turtleTimer;
```

Add the timer object to the project using a **delay** of 100 msec (set using trial and error) and add a listener (in the frame constructor code) for the **turtleTimerActionPerformed** method:

```
turtleTimer = new Timer(100, new ActionListener()
{
  public void actionPerformed(ActionEvent e)
  {
    turtleTimerActionPerformed(e);
  }
});
```

Once the timer is started, with each generated event, we move each turtle some fraction of the difference between its initial and final postion. This method provides a smooth animation from start to finish. With the turtles, we want to move each from its starting position to final position in 5000 milliseconds (5 seconds). Since **delay** is 100 milliseconds, we move each turtle 1/50th of its moved distance with each timer event. You can change these values if you want.

The code that starts the turtles moving is shaded in the **start** procedure:

```
private void startButtonActionPerformed(ActionEvent e)
{
  firstTime = false;
  if (gameStatus.equals("Initial"))
  {
    //clicked start
    gameStatus = "Stopped";
    turtlesSelected = 0;
    for (int i = 0; i < numberOfTurtles; i++)
    {
       turtlePicked[i] = 0;
       turtlePosition[i] = 50;
    }
    gamePanel.repaint();
  }
  else if (gameStatus == "Stopped" && turtlesSelected ==
2)
  {
    //clicked start after picking two turtles
    gameStatus = "Moving";
    //set start position/get final positions
    numberMoves = 0;
    for (int i = 0; i < numberOfTurtles; i++)
    {
      turtlePosition[i] = 50;
      finalPosition[i] = 400 + myRandom.nextInt(360);
    }
    // pick two winners
    winner[0] = 0;
    winner[1] = 0;
    while (winner[0] == winner[1])
    {
      winner[0] = myRandom.nextInt(numberOfTurtles);
      winner[1] = myRandom.nextInt(numberOfTurtles);
    }
    finalPosition[winner[0]] = 850;
    finalPosition[winner[1]] = 850;
    turtleTimer.start();
  }
}
```

Notice how the final positions and winners are determined. Several new variables are introduced and are declared in the class level declarations area:

```
int numberMoves;
int[] finalPosition = new int[10];
int[] winner = new int[2];
Random myRandom = new Random();
```

numberMoves is how many times the timer method has been called. **finalPosition** is the array of final positions. The **winner** array holds the two winners. **myRandom** is used to generate random locations. The random number generator requires this import statement:

```
import java.util.Random;
```

Motion begins by starting **turtleTimer**. The code that moves the turtles is placed in the **timTurtle Tick** event procedure:

```
private void turtleTimerActionPerformed(ActionEvent e)
{
  //increment number of moves and positions
  numberMoves++;
  for (int i = 0; i < numberOfTurtles; i++)
    turtlePosition[i] += (finalPosition[i] - 50) / 50;
  gamePanel.repaint();
  if (numberMoves == 49)
  {
    turtleTimer.stop();
    gameStatus = "Initial";
  }
}
```

After each movement,the **gamePanel** is repainted. Once the turtles reach the finish line, you can play again by choosing a new number of turtles (if you want) and click **Start**. Or, you can click **Stop** to end the program.

One last time, **Save** and **Run** the program. Choose a number of turtles (again, I picked 5). Click **Start**, choose two turtles (I chose the top and bottom ones). Click **Start** –and the turtles start the race. Here's the middle of my race:

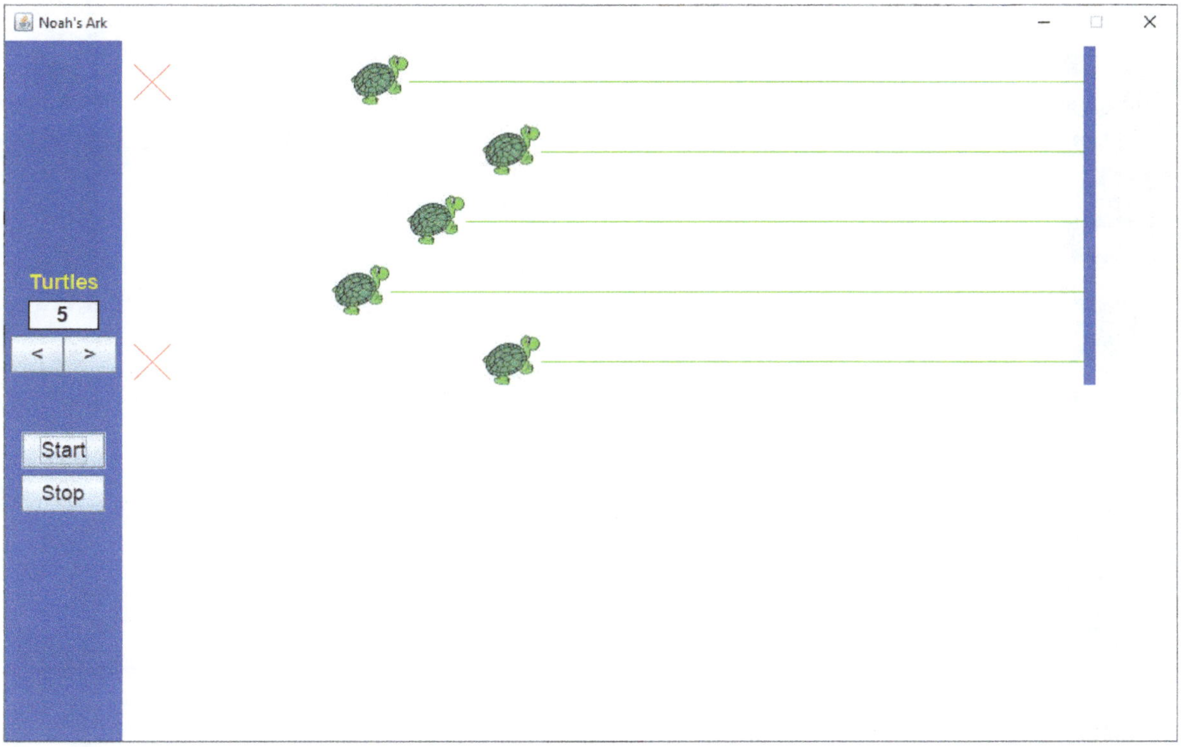

And the finish:

Our work is done. Enjoy the game!

Noah's Ark Project Review

The **Noah's Ark** program is now complete. **Save** and **Run** the program and make sure it works as promised. Check that all options work correctly.

If there are errors in your implementation, go back over the steps of form and code design. Go over the developed code – make sure you understand how different parts of the program were coded. As mentioned in the beginning of this chapter, the finished project is saved as **NoahsArk** in the **\CBGJava\CBGJava Projects** folder.

Noah's Ark Project Java Code Listing

```
/*
 * NoahsArk.java
 */

package noahsark;
import javax.swing.*;
import java.awt.*;
import java.awt.event.*;
import java.awt.geom.*;
import java.util.Random;

public class NoahsArk extends JFrame
{
  JPanel controlPanel = new JPanel();
  GraphicsPanel gamePanel = new GraphicsPanel();
  JLabel turtleLabel = new JLabel();
  JTextField turtleTextField = new JTextField();
  JButton decreaseButton = new JButton();
  JButton increaseButton = new JButton();
  JButton startButton = new JButton();
  JButton stopButton = new JButton();
  Timer turtleTimer;


  static boolean firstTime = true;
  static int numberOfTurtles;
  static String gameStatus;
  static int turtlesSelected;
  static int[] turtlePicked = new int[10];
  static int[] turtlePosition = new int[10];
  static Image turtle = new
ImageIcon("turtle.jpg").getImage();

  int numberMoves;
  int[] finalPosition = new int[10];
  int[] winner = new int[2];
  Random myRandom = new Random();


  public static void main(String args[])
  {
    // create frame
    new NoahsArk().setVisible(true);
```

```
  }

  public NoahsArk()
  {
    // frame constructor
    setTitle("Noah's Ark");
    setResizable(false);
    addWindowListener(new WindowAdapter()
    {
      public void windowClosing(WindowEvent evt)
      {
        exitForm(evt);
      }
    });
    getContentPane().setLayout(new GridBagLayout());
    GridBagConstraints gridConstraints;

    controlPanel.setPreferredSize(new Dimension(100, 600));
    controlPanel.setBackground(Color.BLUE);
    controlPanel.setLayout(new GridBagLayout());
    gridConstraints = new GridBagConstraints();
    gridConstraints.gridx = 0;
    gridConstraints.gridy = 0;
    getContentPane().add(controlPanel, gridConstraints);

    turtleLabel.setText("Turtles");
    turtleLabel.setForeground(Color.YELLOW);
    turtleLabel.setFont(new Font("Arial", Font.BOLD, 18));
    gridConstraints = new GridBagConstraints();
    gridConstraints.gridx = 0;
    gridConstraints.gridy = 0;
    gridConstraints.gridwidth = 2;
    controlPanel.add(turtleLabel, gridConstraints);

    turtleTextField.setPreferredSize(new Dimension(60, 25));

turtleTextField.setBorder(BorderFactory.createLineBorder(Colo
r.BLACK));
    turtleTextField.setText("0");
    turtleTextField.setEditable(false);
    turtleTextField.setBackground(Color.WHITE);

turtleTextField.setHorizontalAlignment(SwingConstants.CENTER)
;
    turtleTextField.setFont(new Font("Arial", Font.BOLD,
18));
    gridConstraints = new GridBagConstraints();
```

```
    gridConstraints.gridx = 0;
    gridConstraints.gridy = 1;
    gridConstraints.gridwidth = 2;
    gridConstraints.insets = new Insets(5, 0, 0, 0);
    controlPanel.add(turtleTextField, gridConstraints);

    decreaseButton.setText("<");
    decreaseButton.setFont(new Font("Arial", Font.PLAIN,
18));
    gridConstraints = new GridBagConstraints();
    gridConstraints.gridx = 0;
    gridConstraints.gridy = 2;
    gridConstraints.insets = new Insets(5, 0, 0, 0);
    controlPanel.add(decreaseButton, gridConstraints);
    decreaseButton.addActionListener(new ActionListener()
    {
      public void actionPerformed(ActionEvent e)
      {
        decreaseButtonActionPerformed(e);
      }
    });

    increaseButton.setText(">");
    increaseButton.setFont(new Font("Arial", Font.PLAIN,
18));
    gridConstraints = new GridBagConstraints();
    gridConstraints.gridx = 1;
    gridConstraints.gridy = 2;
    gridConstraints.insets = new Insets(5, 0, 0, 0);
    controlPanel.add(increaseButton, gridConstraints);
    increaseButton.addActionListener(new ActionListener()
    {
      public void actionPerformed(ActionEvent e)
      {
        increaseButtonActionPerformed(e);
      }
    });

    startButton.setText("Start");
    startButton.setFont(new Font("Arial", Font.PLAIN, 18));
    gridConstraints = new GridBagConstraints();
    gridConstraints.gridx = 0;
    gridConstraints.gridy = 3;
    gridConstraints.gridwidth = 2;
    gridConstraints.insets = new Insets(50, 0, 0, 0);
    controlPanel.add(startButton, gridConstraints);
    startButton.addActionListener(new ActionListener()
```

```
{
  public void actionPerformed(ActionEvent e)
  {
    startButtonActionPerformed(e);
  }
});

stopButton.setText("Stop");
stopButton.setFont(new Font("Arial", Font.PLAIN, 18));
gridConstraints = new GridBagConstraints();
gridConstraints.gridx = 0;
gridConstraints.gridy = 4;
gridConstraints.gridwidth = 2;
gridConstraints.insets = new Insets(5, 0, 0, 0);
controlPanel.add(stopButton, gridConstraints);
stopButton.addActionListener(new ActionListener()
{
  public void actionPerformed(ActionEvent e)
  {
    stopButtonActionPerformed(e);
  }
});


gamePanel.setPreferredSize(new Dimension(900, 600));
gamePanel.setBackground(Color.WHITE);
gridConstraints = new GridBagConstraints();
gridConstraints.gridx = 1;
gridConstraints.gridy = 0;
getContentPane().add(gamePanel, gridConstraints);
gamePanel.addMouseListener(new MouseAdapter()
{
  public void mousePressed(MouseEvent e)
  {
    gamePanelMousePressed(e);
  }
});

turtleTimer = new Timer(100, new ActionListener()
{
  public void actionPerformed(ActionEvent e)
  {
    turtleTimerActionPerformed(e);
  }
});
```

```
    pack();
    Dimension screenSize =
Toolkit.getDefaultToolkit().getScreenSize();
    setBounds((int) (0.5 * (screenSize.width - getWidth())),
(int) (0.5 * (screenSize.height - getHeight())), getWidth(),
getHeight());

    numberOfTurtles = 3;
    gameStatus = "Initial";
    turtleTextField.setText(String.valueOf(numberOfTurtles));
 }

  private void decreaseButtonActionPerformed(ActionEvent e)
  {
    if (gameStatus.equals("Initial"))
    {
      // decrease number of turtles
      numberOfTurtles--;
      if (numberOfTurtles < 3)
        numberOfTurtles = 3;

turtleTextField.setText(String.valueOf(numberOfTurtles));
    }
  }

  private void increaseButtonActionPerformed(ActionEvent e)
  {
    if (gameStatus.equals("Initial"))
    {
      // increase number of turtles
      numberOfTurtles++;
      if (numberOfTurtles > 10)
        numberOfTurtles = 10;

turtleTextField.setText(String.valueOf(numberOfTurtles));
    }
  }

  private void startButtonActionPerformed(ActionEvent e)
  {
    firstTime = false;
    if (gameStatus.equals("Initial"))
    {
      //clicked start
      gameStatus = "Stopped";
      turtlesSelected = 0;
      for (int i = 0; i < numberOfTurtles; i++)
```

```
    {
      turtlePicked[i] = 0;
      turtlePosition[i] = 50;
    }
    gamePanel.repaint();
  }
  else if (gameStatus == "Stopped" && turtlesSelected == 2)
  {
    //clicked start after picking two turtles
    gameStatus = "Moving";
    //set start position/get final positions
    numberMoves = 0;
    for (int i = 0; i < numberOfTurtles; i++)
    {
      turtlePosition[i] = 50;
      finalPosition[i] = 400 + myRandom.nextInt(360);
    }
    // pick two winners
    winner[0] = 0;
    winner[1] = 0;
    while (winner[0] == winner[1])
    {
      winner[0] = myRandom.nextInt(numberOfTurtles);
      winner[1] = myRandom.nextInt(numberOfTurtles);
    }
    finalPosition[winner[0]] = 850;
    finalPosition[winner[1]] = 850;
    turtleTimer.start();
  }
}

private void stopButtonActionPerformed(ActionEvent e)
{
  if (gameStatus.equals("Initial"))
    // clicked stop
    System.exit(0);
}

private void gamePanelMousePressed(MouseEvent e)
{
  int turtleClicked;
  if (gameStatus == "Stopped")
  {
    // want to pick two and only two turtles
    //which turtle clicked
    turtleClicked = (int) ((e.getY() - 10) / 60);
    //if clicked before, remove from list
```

```
      if (turtlePicked[turtleClicked] == 1)
      {
        turtlesSelected--;
        turtlePicked[turtleClicked] = 0;
      }
      else if (turtlesSelected < 2)
      {
        //add to list if two have not been selected yet
        turtlesSelected++;
        turtlePicked[turtleClicked] = 1;
      }
    }
    gamePanel.repaint();
  }

  private void turtleTimerActionPerformed(ActionEvent e)
  {
    //increment number of moves and positions
    numberMoves++;
    for (int i = 0; i < numberOfTurtles; i++)
      turtlePosition[i] += (finalPosition[i] - 50) / 50;
    gamePanel.repaint();
    if (numberMoves == 49)
    {
      turtleTimer.stop();
      gameStatus = "Initial";
    }
  }


  private void exitForm(WindowEvent evt)
  {
    System.exit(0);
  }
}

class GraphicsPanel extends JPanel
{
  public GraphicsPanel()
  {
  }
  public void paintComponent(Graphics g)
  {
    Graphics2D g2D = (Graphics2D) g;
    super.paintComponent(g2D);

   if (NoahsArk.firstTime)
```

```
    {
      // draw instructions
      g2D.setFont(new Font("Arial", Font.PLAIN, 18));
      g2D.setPaint(Color.BLACK);
      g2D.drawString("NOAH'S ARK", 10, 30);
      g2D.drawString("In Genesis Chapter 6, Noah was
commanded by God to take two of every kind of animal into the
ark.", 10, 60);
      g2D.drawString("Two turtles are trying to get to the
Ark first. Try to guess which two turtles will make it to the
Ark first.", 10, 80);
      g2D.drawString("The purpose of this Bible Story is to
remember that God has promised never to flood the earth
again.", 10, 100);
      g2D.drawString("God displays a beautiful rainbow in the
sky to remind us of His promises to us.", 10, 120);
      g2D.drawString("Select Number of Turtles to race by
pressing the left button to decrease, right button to
increase.", 10, 150);
      g2D.drawString("Click on the Start Button to begin.",
10, 170);
      g2D.drawString("Click on the Stop Button to stop the
program.", 10, 190);
    }
        else
    {
      Line2D.Double myLine;
      //draw turtles
      for (int i = 0; i < NoahsArk.numberOfTurtles; i++)
      {
         g2D.setPaint(Color.GREEN);
        myLine = new
Line2D.Double(NoahsArk.turtlePosition[i], i * 60 + 35, 820, i
* 60 + 35);
        g2D.draw(myLine);
        g2D.drawImage(NoahsArk.turtle,
NoahsArk.turtlePosition[i], i * 60 + 10, 50, 45, this);
        // mark selected turtles
        if (NoahsArk.turtlePicked[i] == 1)
        {
          g2D.setPaint(Color.RED);
          myLine = new Line2D.Double(10, i * 60 + 20, 40, i *
60 + 50);
          g2D.draw(myLine);
          myLine = new Line2D.Double(10, i * 60 + 50, 40, i *
60 + 20);
          g2D.draw(myLine);
```

```
        }
      }
       // draw finish line
      g2D.setPaint(Color.BLUE);
      Rectangle2D.Double myRectangle = new
Rectangle2D.Double(820, 5, 10, NoahsArk.numberOfTurtles * 60
- 10);
      g2D.fill(myRectangle);
      if (NoahsArk.gameStatus.equals("Stopped"))
      {
        g2D.setFont(new Font("Arial", Font.PLAIN, 18));
        g2D.setPaint(Color.BLACK);
        g2D.drawString("Click on the two turtles you pick.",
200, 55);
        g2D.drawString("Click Start to start the race.", 200,
85);
      }
    }

    g2D.dispose();
  }
}
```

6

Elijah and the Ravens

Preview

In I Kings, God sends ravens to drop bread for Elijah while he hides from King Ahab. In this game, you try to catch as many falling loaves of bread as possible to feed Elijah. God always provides for our needs."

Elijah and the Ravens Program Preview

In this chapter, we will build the **Elijah and the Ravens** game. Flying ravens drop loaves of bread from the sky. You position Elijah under the falling loaves to catch them for food.

The finished project is saved as **Elijah** in the **\CBGJava\CBGJava Projects** project group. Start NetBeans (or your IDE). Open the specified project group. Make **Elijah** the selected project. Run the project. You will see:

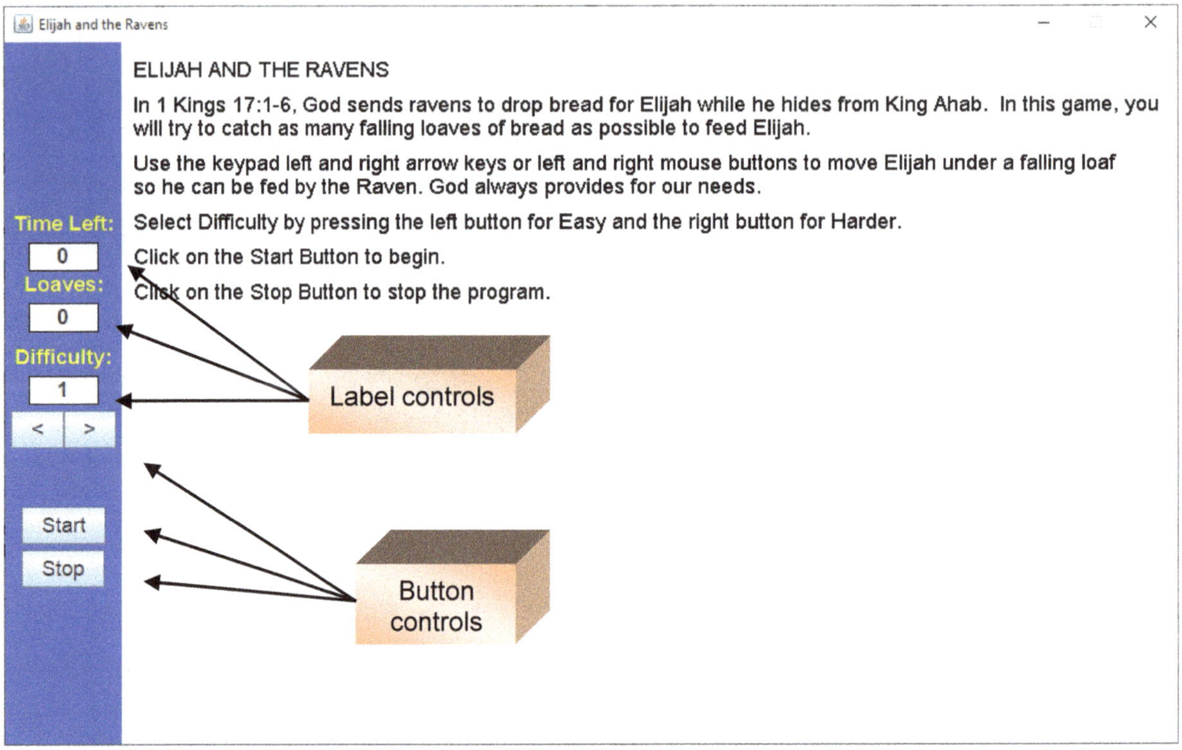

Labels are used for instructions and to display game information (time remaining, loaves caught, difficulty). Two buttons are used to change the difficulty, one to start the game and one to stop.

The game appears in its 'initial' state. A game description and program instructions are given. At this point, you can click the **Start** button to start the game, click arrow buttons to change the game difficulty or click **Stop** to stop the program. Change the difficulty if you want (I picked 3) by clicking the little arrows under **Difficulty**. Click the **Start** button to start playing. The program instructions disappear. A raven appears at the top of the screen holding a loaf of bread. Elijah is at the bottom of the screen. The loaf of bread will start falling. This is the game's 'playing' state:

You move Elijah under the falling loaf to catch it. You can move Elijah using the keypad arrow keys (**NumLock** must be on) or by holding down the left or right mouse button. When the loaf reaches Elijah, you score a point (under **Loaves**). If the loaf passes without catching it, you score nothing. Either way, another raven appears dropping another loaf.

Here's a screen where Elijah is about to catch a loaf of bread:

The game continues for 60 seconds. The remaining time is shown under **Time Left**. You are given your final score at this point. Here's mine:

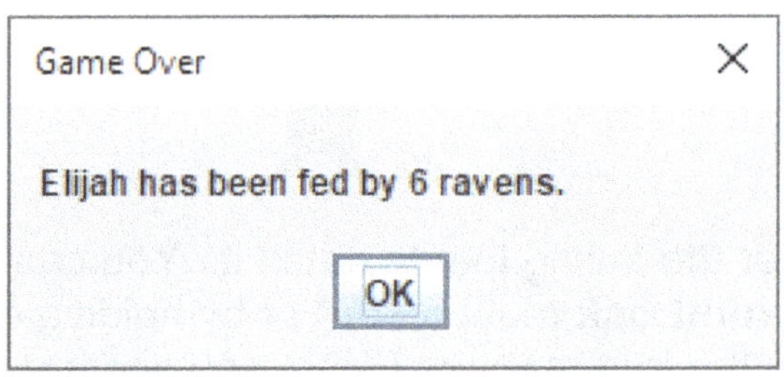

Next, if you want, you can change the difficulty – higher difficulties give you faster dropping bread. You can also click **Start** to race again or click **Stop** to stop the program. Continue playing the game to understand its operation.

You will now build this program in stages. As you build Java programs, we always recommend taking a slow, step-by-step process. It minimizes programming errors and helps build your confidence as things come together in a complete program. We address **frame design**. And, we address **code design**. We discuss how to use the buttons, how to display the raven, the bread and Elijah, and how to move the different graphic images and detect whether a loaf of bread has been caught.

Elijah and the Ravens Frame Design

We begin building the **Elijah** project. Start a new project in your Java project group – name it **Elijah**. Delete default code in **Elijah.java**. Once started, we suggest you immediately save the project with a name you choose. This sets up the folder and file structure needed for your project.

Build the basic frame with these properties:

Elijah Frame:

title	Elijah and the Ravens
resizable	false

The code is:

```
/*
 * Elijah.java
 */
package elijah;
import javax.swing.*;
import java.awt.*;
import java.awt.event.*;
import java.awt.geom.*;
import java.util.Random;

public class Elijah extends JFrame
{
  public static void main(String args[])
  {
    // create frame
    new Elijah().setVisible(true);
  }

  public Elijah()
  {
    // frame constructor
    setTitle("Elijah and the Ravens");
    setResizable(false);
    addWindowListener(new WindowAdapter()
    {
      public void windowClosing(WindowEvent evt)
      {
        exitForm(evt);
      }
    });
    getContentPane().setLayout(new GridBagLayout());
```

```
      GridBagConstraints gridConstraints;

      pack();
      Dimension screenSize =
Toolkit.getDefaultToolkit().getScreenSize();
      setBounds((int) (0.5 * (screenSize.width -
getWidth())), (int) (0.5 * (screenSize.height -
getHeight())), getWidth(), getHeight());
    }
   private void exitForm(WindowEvent evt)
   {
      System.exit(0);
   }
}
```

This code builds the frame, imports the needed packages, sets up the layout manager and includes code to exit the application. Run the code to make sure the frame (at least, what there is of it at this point) appears and is centered on the screen:

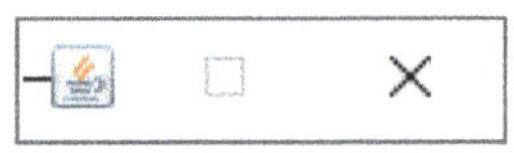

Let's populate our frame with other controls. All code for creating the frame and placing controls (except declarations) goes in the **Elijah** constructor.

The frame uses two panel controls. **controlPanel** holds the labels and buttons for game control, while **gamePanel** displays the game grid. The **GridBagLayout** is:

	gridx = 0	gridx = 1
gridy = 0	**controlPanel**	**gamePanel**

Since **gamePanel** hosts graphics elements (images, lines), it will be a 'graphics panel.' Each such panel (example below is named **GraphicsPanel**) will be a separate class with a **paintComponent** method where any graphics are drawn:

```
class GraphicsPanel extends JPanel
{
  public void paintComponent(Graphics g)
  {
    Graphics2D g2D = (Graphics2D) g;
    super.paintComponent(g2D);

    g2D.dispose();  }
}
```

Recall we introduced such panels in other projects.

The properties for each panel are:

controlPanel:	
size	100, 600
background	Blue
gridx	0
gridy	0

gamePanel:	
size	900, 600
background	White
gridx	1
gridy	0

Declare each panel using:

```
JPanel controlPanel = new JPanel();
GraphicsPanel gamePanel = new GraphicsPanel();
```

Add the panels to the frame using this code:

```
// control panel
controlPanel.setPreferredSize(new Dimension(100, 600));
controlPanel.setBackground(Color.BLUE);
controlPanel.setLayout(new GridBagLayout());
gridConstraints = new GridBagConstraints();
gridConstraints.gridx = 0;
gridConstraints.gridy = 0;
getContentPane().add(controlPanel, gridConstraints);

// game panel
gamePanel.setPreferredSize(new Dimension(900, 600));
gamePanel.setBackground(Color.WHITE);
gridConstraints = new GridBagConstraints();
gridConstraints.gridx = 1;
gridConstraints.gridy = 0;
getContentPane().add(gamePanel, gridConstraints);
```

After the **Elijah** main class, add this ‘graphics’ panel framework:

```
class GraphicsPanel extends JPanel
{
  public GraphicsPanel()
  {
  }
  public void paintComponent(Graphics g)
  {
    Graphics2D g2D = (Graphics2D) g;
    super.paintComponent(g2D);

    g2D.dispose();
  }
}
```

All graphic elements will be drawn in the **paintComponent** methods of these classes.

Save, run. You will see the empty panel controls on the frame. This is the finished frame size.

We need to add elements to the **controlPanel**.

The **controlPanel** holds controls used to display status of the **Elijah** game and control part of its operation. The **GridBagLayout** is:

	gridx = 0	gridx = 1
gridy = 0	**timeLabel**	
gridy = 1	**timeTextField**	
gridy = 2	**scoreLabel**	
gridy = 3	**scoreTextField**	
gridy = 4	**difficultyLabel**	
gridy = 5	**difficultyTextField**	
gridy = 6	**decreaseButton**	**increaseButton**
gridy = 7	**startButton**	
gridy = 8	**stopButton**	

The label and text field controls display the time remaining, the loaves caught and the difficulty. Buttons are used to change the difficulty and start and stop the game.

Control properties are:

timeLabel:

text	Time Left:
foreground	Yellow
font	Arial, Bold, Size 18
gridx	0
gridy	0
gridwidth	2
insets	10, 0, 0, 0

timeTextField:

size	60, 25
border	Black line
text	0
editable	false
background	White
horizontalAlignment	CENTER
font	Arial, Bold, Size 18
gridx	0
gridy	1
gridwidth	2
insets	5, 0, 0, 0

scoreLabel:

text	Loaves:
foreground	Yellow
font	Arial, Bold, Size 18
gridx	0
gridy	2
gridwidth	2

scoreTextField:

size	60, 25
border	Black line
text	0
editable	false
background	White
horizontalAlignment	CENTER
font	Arial, Bold, Size 18
gridx	0
gridy	3
gridwidth	2
insets	5, 0, 0, 0

difficultyLabel:

text	Difficulty:
foreground	Yellow
font	Arial, Bold, Size 18
gridx	0
gridy	4
gridwidth	2
insets	10, 0, 0, 0

difficultyTextField:

size	60, 25
border	Black line
text	1
editable	false
background	White
horizontalAlignment	CENTER
font	Arial, Bold, Size 18
gridx	0
gridy	5
gridwidth	2
insets	5, 0, 0, 0

decreaseButton:

text	<
font	Arial, Plain, Size 18
gridx	0
gridy	6
insets	5, 0, 0, 0

increaseButton:

text	>
font	Arial, Plain, Size 18
gridx	1
gridy	6
insets	5, 0, 0, 0

startButton:

text	Start
font	Arial, Plain, Size 18
gridx	0
gridy	7
gridwidth	2
insets	50, 0, 0, 0

stopButton:

text	Stop
font	Arial, Plain, Size 18
gridx	0
gridy	8
gridwidth	2
insets	5, 0, 0, 0

Use these declarations for the control panel elements:

```
JLabel timeLabel = new JLabel();
JTextField timeTextField = new JTextField();
JLabel scoreLabel = new JLabel();
JTextField scoreTextField = new JTextField();
JLabel difficultyLabel = new JLabel();
JTextField difficultyTextField = new JTextField();
JButton decreaseButton = new JButton();
JButton increaseButton = new JButton();
JButton startButton = new JButton();
JButton stopButton = new JButton();
```

And, this code adds the controls:

```
timeLabel.setText("Time Left:");
timeLabel.setForeground(Color.YELLOW);
timeLabel.setFont(new Font("Arial", Font.BOLD, 18));
gridConstraints = new GridBagConstraints();
gridConstraints.gridx = 0;
gridConstraints.gridy = 0;
gridConstraints.gridwidth = 2;
gridConstraints.insets = new Insets(10, 0, 0, 0);
controlPanel.add(timeLabel, gridConstraints);

timeTextField.setPreferredSize(new Dimension(60, 25));
timeTextField.setBorder(BorderFactory.createLineBorder(Col
or.BLACK));
timeTextField.setText("0");
timeTextField.setEditable(false);
timeTextField.setBackground(Color.WHITE);
timeTextField.setHorizontalAlignment(SwingConstants.CENTER
);
timeTextField.setFont(new Font("Arial", Font.BOLD, 18));
gridConstraints = new GridBagConstraints();
gridConstraints.gridx = 0;
gridConstraints.gridy = 1;
gridConstraints.gridwidth = 2;
gridConstraints.insets = new Insets(5, 0, 0, 0);
controlPanel.add(timeTextField, gridConstraints);

scoreLabel.setText("Loaves:");
scoreLabel.setForeground(Color.YELLOW);
scoreLabel.setFont(new Font("Arial", Font.BOLD, 18));
gridConstraints = new GridBagConstraints();
gridConstraints.gridx = 0;
gridConstraints.gridy = 2;
gridConstraints.gridwidth = 2;
controlPanel.add(scoreLabel, gridConstraints);
```

```
scoreTextField.setPreferredSize(new Dimension(60, 25));
scoreTextField.setBorder(BorderFactory.createLineBorder
(Color.BLACK));
scoreTextField.setText("0");
scoreTextField.setEditable(false);
scoreTextField.setBackground(Color.WHITE);
scoreTextField.setHorizontalAlignment(SwingConstants.CENTE
R);
scoreTextField.setFont(new Font("Arial", Font.BOLD, 18));
gridConstraints = new GridBagConstraints();
gridConstraints.gridx = 0;
gridConstraints.gridy = 3;
gridConstraints.gridwidth = 2;
gridConstraints.insets = new Insets(5, 0, 0, 0);
controlPanel.add(scoreTextField, gridConstraints);

difficultyLabel.setText("Difficulty:");
difficultyLabel.setForeground(Color.YELLOW);
difficultyLabel.setFont(new Font("Arial", Font.BOLD, 18));
gridConstraints = new GridBagConstraints();
gridConstraints.gridx = 0;
gridConstraints.gridy = 4;
gridConstraints.gridwidth = 2;
gridConstraints.insets = new Insets(10, 0, 0, 0);
controlPanel.add(difficultyLabel, gridConstraints);

difficultyTextField.setPreferredSize(new Dimension(60,
25));
difficultyTextField.setBorder(BorderFactory.createLineBord
er(Color.BLACK));
difficultyTextField.setText("1");
difficultyTextField.setEditable(false);
difficultyTextField.setBackground(Color.WHITE);
difficultyTextField.setHorizontalAlignment(SwingConstants.
CENTER);
difficultyTextField.setFont(new Font("Arial", Font.BOLD,
18));
gridConstraints = new GridBagConstraints();
gridConstraints.gridx = 0;
gridConstraints.gridy = 5;
gridConstraints.gridwidth = 2;
gridConstraints.insets = new Insets(5, 0, 0, 0);
controlPanel.add(difficultyTextField, gridConstraints);
```

```
decreaseButton.setText("<");
decreaseButton.setFont(new Font("Arial", Font.PLAIN, 18));
gridConstraints = new GridBagConstraints();
gridConstraints.gridx = 0;
gridConstraints.gridy = 6;
gridConstraints.insets = new Insets(5, 0, 0, 0);
controlPanel.add(decreaseButton, gridConstraints);
decreaseButton.addActionListener(new ActionListener()
{
  public void actionPerformed(ActionEvent e)
  {
    decreaseButtonActionPerformed(e);
  }
});

increaseButton.setText(">");
increaseButton.setFont(new Font("Arial", Font.PLAIN, 18));
gridConstraints = new GridBagConstraints();
gridConstraints.gridx = 1;
gridConstraints.gridy = 6;
gridConstraints.insets = new Insets(5, 0, 0, 0);
controlPanel.add(increaseButton, gridConstraints);
increaseButton.addActionListener(new ActionListener()
{
  public void actionPerformed(ActionEvent e)
  {
    increaseButtonActionPerformed(e);
  }
});

startButton.setText("Start");
startButton.setFont(new Font("Arial", Font.PLAIN, 18));
gridConstraints = new GridBagConstraints();
gridConstraints.gridx = 0;
gridConstraints.gridy = 7;
gridConstraints.gridwidth = 2;
gridConstraints.insets = new Insets(50, 0, 0, 0);
controlPanel.add(startButton, gridConstraints);
startButton.addActionListener(new ActionListener()
{
  public void actionPerformed(ActionEvent e)
  {
    startButtonActionPerformed(e);
  }
});
```

```
stopButton.setText("Stop");
stopButton.setFont(new Font("Arial", Font.PLAIN, 18));
gridConstraints = new GridBagConstraints();
gridConstraints.gridx = 0;
gridConstraints.gridy = 8;
gridConstraints.gridwidth = 2;
gridConstraints.insets = new Insets(5, 0, 0, 0);
controlPanel.add(stopButton, gridConstraints);
stopButton.addActionListener(new ActionListener()
{
  public void actionPerformed(ActionEvent e)
  {
    stopButtonActionPerformed(e);
  }
});
```

And, add these four empty methods:

```
private void decreaseButtonActionPerformed(ActionEvent e)
{
}

private void increaseButtonActionPerformed(ActionEvent e)
{
}

private void startButtonActionPerformed(ActionEvent e)
{
}

private void stopButtonActionPerformed(ActionEvent e)
{
}
```

Run the project to see:

The labels, text fields and buttons for the control panel are in place. The frame design. Nothing needs to be added (for now) to the game panel.

We now begin writing code for the **Elijah and the Ravens** game. We will write the code in several steps. As a first step, we will write the code that starts the program and establishes its 'initial' state. Then, we look at how to go to 'playing' state (positioning the graphics elements) following clicking of the **Start** button. We then write code to move the bread down the screen, move Elijah (using mouse clicks or keyboard presses), and check for caught loaves of bread. During the code development process, recognize you may modify a particular method several times before arriving at the finished product.

Code Design – Initial State (Instructions)

Any time we start a program, there are certain initializations that must take place. Let's look at the initializations needed in the **Elijah and the Ravens** game. When the program first begins, we want to display the game instructions (when **firstTime** is true). We also initialize the difficulty (**difficulty**) and the game status (**gameStatus**). These initializations are in **Elijah** frame constructor.

We declare three variables (**firstTime**, **difficulty** and, **gameStatus**). Do this in the class level declarations area:

```
static boolean firstTime = true;
int difficulty;
static String gameStatus;
```

firstTime and **gameStatus** are declared **static** because they will be needed in the **gamePanel paintComponent** method.

Add this code at the end of the frame constructor:

```
difficulty = 1;
gameStatus = "Initial";
difficultyTextField.setText(String.valueOf(difficulty));
```

As mentioned, we initialize **difficulty** to **1** and the **gameStatus** to "**Initial**".

In this initial state, with **firstTime = true**, we want to display the game instructions. The code to do this is placed in the graphics panel **paintComponent** method. Add the shaded code:

```
public void paintComponent(Graphics g)
{
  Graphics2D g2D = (Graphics2D) g;
  super.paintComponent(g2D);
  if (Elijah.firstTime)
  {
    // draw instructions
    g2D.setFont(new Font("Arial", Font.PLAIN, 18));
    g2D.setPaint(Color.BLACK);
    g2D.drawString("ELIJAH AND THE RAVENS", 10, 30);
    g2D.drawString("In 1 Kings 17:1-6, God sends ravens to
drop bread for Elijah while he hides from King Ahab.  In
this game, you ", 10, 60);
    g2D.drawString("will try to catch as many falling
loaves of bread as possible to feed Elijah.", 10, 80);
    g2D.drawString("Use the keypad left and right arrow
keys or left and right mouse buttons to move Elijah under
a falling loaf", 10, 110);
    g2D.drawString("so he can be fed by the Raven. God
always provides for our needs.", 10, 130);
    g2D.drawString("Select Difficulty by pressing the left
button for Easy and the right button for Harder.", 10,
160);
    g2D.drawString("Click on the Start Button to begin.",
10, 190);
    g2D.drawString("Click on the Stop Button to stop the
program.", 10, 220);
  }
  g2D.dispose();
}
```

Save and **Run** the program to see:

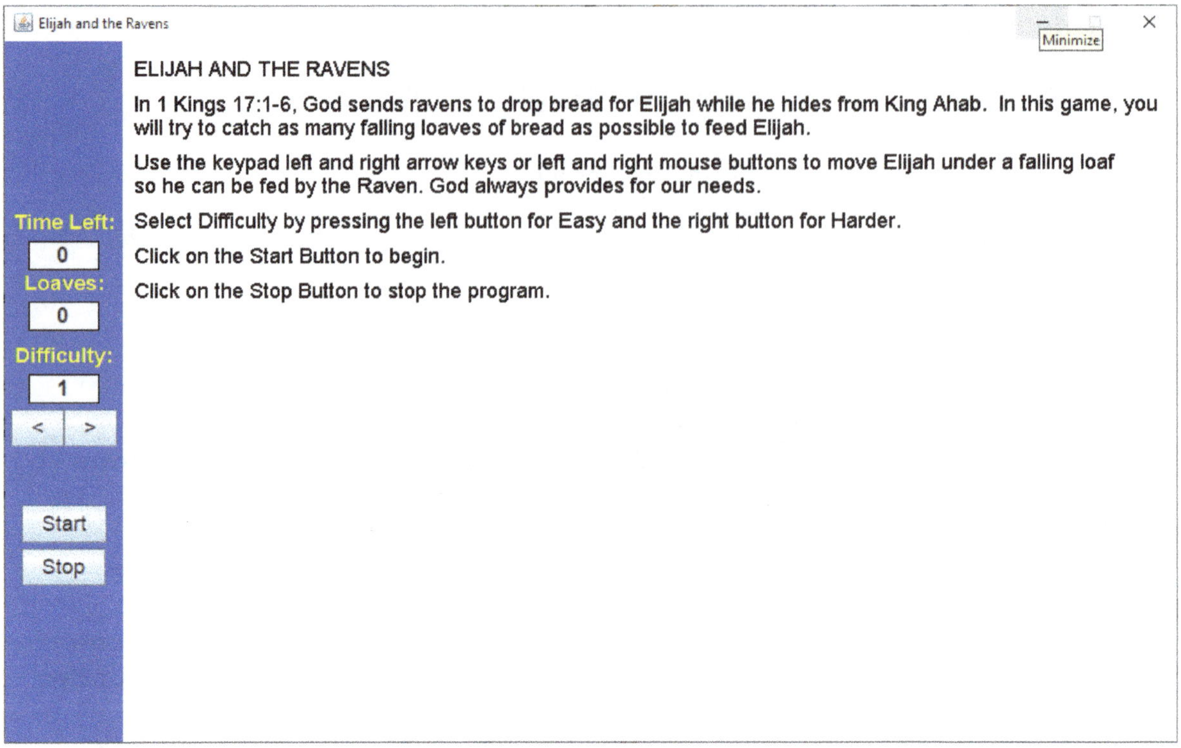

Code Design – Select Difficulty

The **difficulty** variable is used to determine how fast the bread falls (the higher the difficulty, the faster it falls). To change the difficulty, a user clicks on either of the two arrow buttons. The code to do this goes in the **decreaseButtonActionPerformed** and **increaseButtonActionPerformed** methods:

```
private void decreaseButtonActionPerformed(ActionEvent e)
{
  if (gameStatus.equals("Initial"))
  {
    // decrease difficulty
    difficulty--;
    if (difficulty < 1)
      difficulty = 1;

difficultyTextField.setText(String.valueOf(difficulty));
  }
 }

private void increaseButtonActionPerformed(ActionEvent e)
{
  if (gameStatus.equals("Initial"))
  {
    // increase difficulty
    difficulty++;
    if (difficulty > 10)
      difficulty = 10;
  difficultyTextField.setText(String.valueOf(difficulty));
  }
}
```

The code is straightforward. The difficulty can only be changed when the game is in "**Initial**" state. If the **<** button is clicked, we decrease the difficulty by one (minimum of 1). If the **>** button is clicked, we increase the difficulty (maximum of 10). The new value for the difficulty is then displayed in **difficultyTextField**.

Save and **Run** the program. Make sure the arrow buttons work – make sure the difficulty is always between 1 and 10. Here's my run where I changed the difficulty to three:

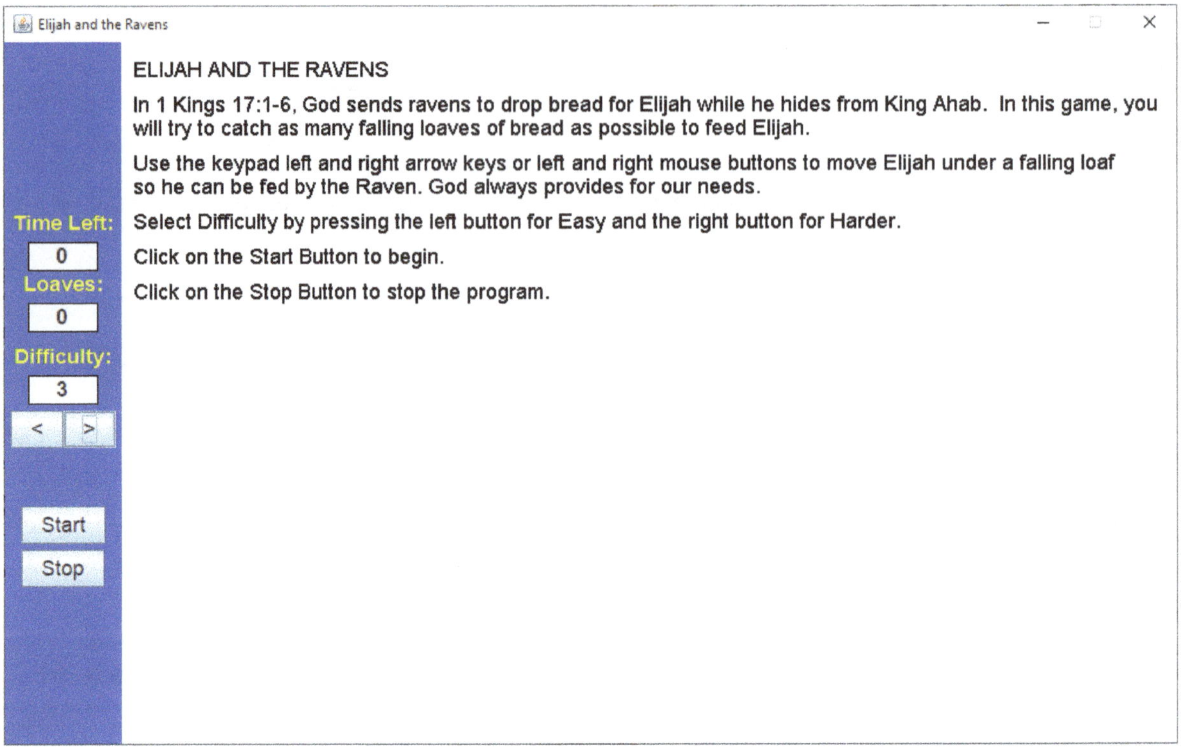

Code Design – Position Elijah

Once the difficulty is set, the next step is to click the **Start** button to allow the game to begin. Hence, we need code to move from the "**Initial**" state to what we'll call "**Playing**" state. When the **Start** button is clicked in "**Initial**" state, we need to take the following steps:

- Change **gameStatus** to "**Playing**"
- Clear the screen.
- Initialize score and time left.
- Place Elijah at bottom of screen
- Randomly place Raven and bread at top of screen
- Start dropping bread

There is a lot to do here, so we will take it in steps. First, we'll initialize variables and position Elijah at the bottom of the screen.

Two variables are used in game control. **timeLeft** is an integer value telling us how much time is left in the game (in milliseconds). We choose to let a game last 60 seconds. **score** tells us how many loaves of bread have been caught by Elijah. Add these general variable declarations:

```
int timeLeft;
int score;
```

The image file **Elijah.gif** and is used for Elijah (image variable **elijah**):

Elijah.gif

This file is included in the **\CBGJava\CBGJava Projects\Elijah** folder. Copy it to your project folder.

In the code, we determine both the width (**elijahW**) and height of this graphic (**elijahH**). Elijah is positioned at the bottom of the screen, near the middle. The variables **elijahX** and **elijahY** tell us where Elijah is. **elijahDeltaX** is used to tell us how much to move Elijah with each button click or mouse press. All of these variables will be helpful when checking to see if Elijah catches or misses falling bread. Add these new variable declarations:

```
static int elijahW, elijahH, elijahX, elijahY;
int elijahDeltaX;
static Image elijah = new
ImageIcon("Elijah.gif").getImage();
```

As usual, variables needed by the game panel are prefaced as **static**.

Add this code to the **startButtonActionPerformed** method:

```
private void startButtonActionPerformed(ActionEvent e)
{
  // clicked start
  firstTime = false;
  gameStatus = "Playing";
  //time/score
  timeLeft = 60 * 1000; // milliseconds remaining
  score = 0;
  DisplayTimeScore();
  //Elijah
  elijahW = elijah.getWidth(this);
  elijahH = elijah.getHeight(this);
  elijahDeltaX = 5;
  elijahX = 375;
  elijahY = gamePanel.getHeight() - elijahH;
  gamePanel.repaint();
}
```

You should be able to identify each step in this new code. We clear the area and set variables. We establish the variables for Elijah and position him at the bottom (in the **gamePanel repaint**).

Add the shaded lines to the **paintComponent** method to draw Elijah:

```
public void paintComponent(Graphics g)
{
  Graphics2D g2D = (Graphics2D) g;
  super.paintComponent(g2D);
  if (Elijah.firstTime)
  {
    // draw instructions
    g2D.setFont(new Font("Arial", Font.PLAIN, 18));
    g2D.setPaint(Color.BLACK);
    g2D.drawString("ELIJAH AND THE RAVENS", 10, 30);
    g2D.drawString("In 1 Kings 17:1-6, God sends ravens to
drop bread for Elijah while he hides from King Ahab.  In
this game, you ", 10, 60);
    g2D.drawString("will try to catch as many falling
loaves of bread as possible to feed Elijah.", 10, 80);
    g2D.drawString("Use the keypad left and right arrow
keys or left and right mouse buttons to move Elijah under
a falling loaf", 10, 110);
    g2D.drawString("so he can be fed by the Raven. God
always provides for our needs.", 10, 130);
```

```
    g2D.drawString("Select Difficulty by pressing the left
button for Easy and the right button for Harder.", 10,
160);
    g2D.drawString("Click on the Start Button to begin.",
10, 190);
    g2D.drawString("Click on the Stop Button to stop the
program.", 10, 220);
  }
  else if (Elijah.gameStatus.equals("Playing"))
  {
    // position Elijah
    g2D.drawImage(Elijah.elijah, Elijah.elijahX,
Elijah.elijahY, this);
  }
  g2D.dispose();
}
```

In **startButtonActionPerformed**, notice this line of code:

```
DisplayTimeScore();
```

This line calls a method that updates the displayed value for **timeLeft** and **score**. Add this method at the end of your program:

```
private void DisplayTimeScore()
{
  timeTextField.setText(String.valueOf((int) (timeLeft /
1000)));
  scoreTextField.setText(String.valueOf(score));
}
```

Here, we set the appropriate values in **timeTextField** and **scoreTextField**. Note how we convert milliseconds to seconds.

Save and **Run** the program. Choose a difficulty (I picked 3). Click **Start** and you should see:

Notice the displayed values for **Time Left** and **Loaves**. Notice Elijah down there waiting for bread to fall. Let's get a raven and loaf of bread on the screen.

Code Design – Position Raven and Bread

The last initialization step is to randomly place the raven (image variable **raven**) and bread (image variable **bread**) at the top of the screen. The image files **Raven.gif** and **Bread.gif** are used:

Raven.gif

Bread.gif

These files are included in the **\CBGJava\CBGJava Projects\Elijah** folder. Copy them to your project folder.

We determine the width and height of the raven (**ravenW** and **ravenH**) and the width and height for the bread (**breadW** and **breadH**). These help in determining if Elijah catches a loaf of bread. Add these general declarations:

```
static int ravenW, ravenH, ravenX;
static int breadW, breadH, breadX, breadY;
Random myRandom = new Random();
static Image raven = new
ImageIcon("Raven.gif").getImage();
static Image bread = new
ImageIcon("Bread.gif").getImage();
```

ravenX is the x position of the raven (the y position is zero – the top of the screen). The bread is a (**breadX**, **breadY**). **myRandom** is needed for random number generation.

Add the shaded code to the **startButtonActionPerformed** method:

```
private void startButtonActionPerformed(ActionEvent e)
{
  // clicked start
  firstTime = false;
  gameStatus = "Playing";
  //time/score
  timeLeft = 60 * 1000; // milliseconds remaining
  score = 0;
  DisplayTimeScore();
  //Elijah
  elijahW = elijah.getWidth(this);
  elijahH = elijah.getHeight(this);
  elijahDeltaX = 5;
  elijahX = 375;
  elijahY = gamePanel.getHeight() - elijahH;
  //Raven
  ravenW = raven.getWidth(this);
  ravenH = raven.getHeight(this);
  //Bread
  breadW = bread.getWidth(this);
  breadH = bread.getHeight(this);
  PositionRavenAndBread();
  gamePanel.repaint();
}
```

The above code uses a separate method (**PositionRavenAndBread**) to randomly place the raven and bread on the screen. Add this method to your program:

```
private void PositionRavenAndBread()
{
  ravenX = myRandom.nextInt(gamePanel.getWidth() -
ravenW);
  breadX = (int) (ravenX + 0.5 * (ravenW - breadW));
  breadY = ravenH - 20;
}
```

Notice how the random horizontal position is selected. The coordinates **breadX** and **breadY** let us know where a falling loaf of bread is at all times.

Add the shaded lines to the **paintComponent** method to draw the raven and the bread:

```
public void paintComponent(Graphics g)
{
  Graphics2D g2D = (Graphics2D) g;
  super.paintComponent(g2D);
  if (Elijah.firstTime)
  {
    // draw instructions
    g2D.setFont(new Font("Arial", Font.PLAIN, 18));
    g2D.setPaint(Color.BLACK);
    g2D.drawString("ELIJAH AND THE RAVENS", 10, 30);
    g2D.drawString("In 1 Kings 17:1-6, God sends ravens to
drop bread for Elijah while he hides from King Ahab.  In
this game, you ", 10, 60);
    g2D.drawString("will try to catch as many falling
loaves of bread as possible to feed Elijah.", 10, 80);
    g2D.drawString("Use the keypad left and right arrow
keys or left and right mouse buttons to move Elijah under
a falling loaf", 10, 110);
    g2D.drawString("so he can be fed by the Raven. God
always provides for our needs.", 10, 130);
    g2D.drawString("Select Difficulty by pressing the left
button for Easy and the right button for Harder.", 10,
160);
    g2D.drawString("Click on the Start Button to begin.",
10, 190);
    g2D.drawString("Click on the Stop Button to stop the
program.", 10, 220);
  }
  else if (Elijah.gameStatus.equals("Playing"))
  {
    // position Elijah
    g2D.drawImage(Elijah.elijah, Elijah.elijahX,
Elijah.elijahY, this);
    // position raven and bread
    g2D.drawImage(Elijah.raven, Elijah.ravenX, 0, this);
    g2D.drawImage(Elijah.bread, Elijah.breadX,
Elijah.breadY, this);
  }
  g2D.dispose();
}
```

Save and **Run** the program. Set the **Difficulty** (I used 3). Click **Start**. The complete initialized game is now seen:

We still need to code to get the bread to drop and to move Elijah along the bottom of the screen. We write code to do these steps soon. But first, let's take care of one last thing you can do while in "**Initial**" state – stop the program.

Code Design – Stop the Program

One last thing you can do while the game is in "**Initial**" state is to click on the **Stop** button. This will stop the program. The code here is simple. Add these lines to the **stopButtonActionPerformed** method:

```
private void stopButtonActionPerformed(ActionEvent e)
{
  if (gameStatus.equals("Initial"))
    // clicked stop
    System.exit(0);
}
```

As desired, if the **Stop** button is clicked, the program ends.

Save and **Run** the program. Make sure the **Stop** button works. This completes the code for moving from "**Initial**" game status to "**Playing**" status. Now, let's look at code to move Elijah along the bottom of the screen.

Code Design – Dropping Bread

Once the game begins, the loaf of bread will drop. You move Elijah along the bottom of the screen to try and catch the dropping bread. Here we do the code that drops the bread. A variable **breadSpeed** will determine how fast the bread drops down the screen. Add this general declaration:

```
int breadSpeed;
```

We assign **BreadSpeed** based on the value of **Difficulty**:

```
breadSpeed = 0.5 * difficulty + 3;
```

Note, the higher the difficulty, the faster the speed. You can change this if you like.

A timer object (**gameTimer**) is used to control bread motion. Declare the timer object:

```
Timer gameTimer;
```

Add the timer object to the project using a **delay** of 50 msec (set using trial and error) and add a listener (in the frame constructor code) for the **gameTimerActionPerformed** method:

```
gameTimer = new Timer(50, new ActionListener()
{
  public void actionPerformed(ActionEvent e)
  {
    gameTimerActionPerformed(e);
  }
});
```

Add the shaded lines to the **startButtonActionPerformed** method to turn on the timer and set the value for **breadSpeed**:

```
private void startButtonActionPerformed(ActionEvent e)
{
  // clicked start
  firstTime = false;
  gameStatus = "Playing";
  //time/score
  timeLeft = 60 * 1000; // milliseconds remaining
  score = 0;
  DisplayTimeScore();
  //Elijah
  elijahW = elijah.getWidth(this);
  elijahH = elijah.getHeight(this);
  elijahDeltaX = 5;
  elijahX = 375;
  elijahY = gamePanel.getHeight() - elijahH;
  //Raven
  ravenW = raven.getWidth(this);
  ravenH = raven.getHeight(this);
  //Bread
  breadW = bread.getWidth(this);
  breadH = bread.getHeight(this);
  PositionRavenAndBread();
  gamePanel.repaint();
  //start timer
  breadSpeed = (int)(0.5 * difficulty + 3); // base on
difficulty
  gameTimer.start();
}
```

The bread position is updated in the **gameTimerActionPerformed** method. Use this code:

```
private void gameTimerActionPerformed(ActionEvent e)
{
  // move bread
  breadY = breadY + breadSpeed;
  gamePanel.repaint();
}
```

With each timer event, the bread vertical position changes and the game panel is repainted.

Save and **Run** the program. Click **Start**. The bread is falling:

But it just keeps on falling! We need to add two more pieces of code – one to move Elijah under the bread and one to determine whether Elijah has caught the bread.

Code Design – Moving Elijah

The object of the game is to move Elijah under falling bread so he can catch the loaves for food. Elijah can be moved using two different methods. First, he can be moved by using the left and right arrow buttons on the numeric keypad (this will not work with the cursor control keys). With each key press, we change **elijahX** by **elijahDeltaX** (defined a while ago) in the appropriate direction. We use a new variable **keyPressed** to keep track of which key is being held. Add the general declaration (initializing **keyPressed** to "**None"**):

```
String keyPressed = "None";
```

We detect key presses (and key releases) using the game panel's **KeyPressed** and **KeyReleased** methods. Add this code in the frame constructor after the code that adds **gamePanel** to the frame:

```
gamePanel.addKeyListener(new KeyAdapter()
{
  public void keyPressed(KeyEvent e)
  {
    moveKeyPressed(e);
  }
});
  gamePanel.addKeyListener(new KeyAdapter()
{
  public void keyReleased(KeyEvent e)
  {
    moveKeyReleased(e);
  }
});
```

With this, when a key is pressed, the method **moveKeyPressed** is called. When a key is released, the method **moveKeyReleased** is called.

To detect these key presses, we must make sure **gamePanel** always has focus during game play. To do this, we add this line at the end of the startButtonActionPerformed method:

```
gamePanel.requestFocus();
```

This insures once a game starts, the panel has focus.

Now, add this code to the **moveKeyPressed** and **moveKeyReleased** methods:

```
private void moveKeyPressed(KeyEvent e)
{
  int k = e.getKeyCode();
  if (k == e.VK_NUMPAD4)
    keyPressed = "Left";
  else if (k == e.VK_NUMPAD6)
    keyPressed = "Right";
}

private void moveKeyReleased(KeyEvent e)
{
  keyPressed = "None";
}
```

The first method tells us which key is being pressed (**keyPressed**). It is used in the **gameTimerActionPerformed** method to update the position of Elijah. When the second method is called, **keyPressed** is set back to "**None**".

Add the shaded code to the **gameTimerActionPerformed** method:

```
private void gameTimerActionPerformed(ActionEvent e)
{
  // move bread
  breadY = breadY + breadSpeed;
  // move elijah
  if (keyPressed.equals("Left"))
  {
    elijahX -= elijahDeltaX;
    if (elijahX < 0)
      elijahX = 0;
  }
  else if (keyPressed.equals("Right"))
  {
    elijahX += elijahDeltaX;
    if (elijahX > gamePanel.getWidth() - elijahW)
      elijahX =gamePanel.getWidth() - elijahW;
  }
  gamePanel.repaint();
}
```

If the left key is pressed, Elijah's position is decremented by **elijahDeltaX** – if the right key is pressed, the position is incremented by **elijahDeltaX**.

Save and **Run** the program. Click **Start**. Try moving Elijah using the left and right arrow keys on the numeric keypad (make sure **NumLock** is on):

Here I've moved him far to the left.

When we started this section, we said there were two ways to move Elijah. Let's write code for the second method – using the left and mouse button keys. It's a fairly easy change – the code is nearly identical to that used for key presses. Define a variable to keep track of the pressed button (**buttonPressed**):

```
String buttonPressed = "None";
```

We detect mouse presses (and mouse releases) using the game panel's **MousePressed** and **MouseReleased** methods. Add this code in the frame constructor after the code that adds **gamePanel** to the frame:

```
gamePanel.addMouseListener(new MouseAdapter()
{
  public void mousePressed(MouseEvent e)
  {
    moveMousePressed(e);
  }
});
gamePanel.addMouseListener(new MouseAdapter()
{
  public void mouseReleased(MouseEvent e)
  {
    moveMouseReleased(e);
  }
});
```

With this, when a mouse button is pressed, the method **moveMousePressed** is called. When a mouse button is released, the method **moveKeyReleased** is called.

Add this code to the **moveMousePressed** and **moveMouseReleased** methods:

```
private void moveMousePressed(MouseEvent e)
{
  // check for left or right mouse button.y to move Elijah
  if (e.getButton() == MouseEvent.BUTTON1)
    buttonPressed = "Left";
  else if (e.getButton() == MouseEvent.BUTTON3)
    buttonPressed = "Right";
}
```

```
private void moveMouseReleased(MouseEvent e)
{
  buttonPressed = "None";
}
```

With these, when the mouse is over the game panel, the left and right mouse buttons replicate the action of clicking on the left and right arrow keys on the keypad.

Add the shaded change to the **gameTimerActionPerformed** method:

```
private void gameTimerActionPerformed(ActionEvent e)
{
  // move bread
  breadY = breadY + breadSpeed;
  // move elijah
  if (keyPressed.equals("Left") ||
buttonPressed.equals("Left"))
  {
    elijahX -= elijahDeltaX;
    if (elijahX < 0)
      elijahX = 0;
  }
  else if (keyPressed.equals("Right") ||
buttonPressed.equals("Right"))
  {
    elijahX += elijahDeltaX;
    if (elijahX > gamePanel.getWidth() - elijahW)
      elijahX =gamePanel.getWidth() - elijahW;
  }
  gamePanel.repaint();
}
```

In this code, if the left mouse button is being held down, Elijah moves to the left. Similarly, if the right mouse button is being held down, Elijah moves to the right. In the changes, we just use the code we used for the arrow keys.

Save and **Run** the program. Make sure you can move Elijah with both the keypad arrow keys and by using the mouse buttons. Recall the mouse must be over the panel for the mouse buttons to work properly.

Code Design – Catching Bread

When the bread approaches the bottom of the screen, we need to see if Elijah catches it. The code to do this check is in the **gameTimerActionPerformed** method. We need to do two things:

- Check to see if the bread has been caught. If so, make the bread disappear, increment score and make raven and bread reappear at a random location at the top of the screen.
- Check to see if bread has reached the same vertical position of Elijah without being caught. If so, start a new raven and bread.

How do we know if Elijah catches the bread? We want to see if the Elijah graphic collides with the bread graphic. The check cannot be made until the bread passes the top of Elijah. This happens when:

```
BreadY + BreadH > ElijahY
```

We will use a boolean variable (**passed**) to see if this is true. Once this condition is met, we can see that Elijah collides with bread (or catches it) when:

```
ElijahX + ElijahW > BreadX && ElijahX < BreadX + BreadW
```

This says that the right side of Elijah must be "farther right" than the left side of the bread and the left side of Elijah must be "farther left" than the right side of the bread. Another boolean variable (**collision**) is used to check this condition.

Declare the two new variables:

```
boolean passed;
boolean collision;
```

Add the shaded code to the **gameTimerActionPerformed** method:

```
private void gameTimerActionPerformed(ActionEvent e)
{
  // move bread
  breadY = breadY + breadSpeed;
  // move elijah
  if (keyPressed.equals("Left") ||
buttonPressed.equals("Left"))
  {
    elijahX -= elijahDeltaX;
    if (elijahX < 0)
      elijahX = 0;
  }
  else if (keyPressed.equals("Right") ||
buttonPressed.equals("Right"))
  {
    elijahX += elijahDeltaX;
    if (elijahX > gamePanel.getWidth() - elijahW)
      elijahX =gamePanel.getWidth() - elijahW;
  }
  // check for bread collision or passed elijah
  passed = false;
  collision = false;
  if (breadY + breadH > elijahY)
  {
    passed = true;
    if (elijahX + elijahW > breadX && elijahX < breadX +
breadW)
      collision = true;
  }
  if (passed)
  {
    if (collision)
      score++;
    PositionRavenAndBread();
  }
  DisplayTimeScore();
  gamePanel.repaint();
}
```

You should see how the listed steps are implemented. In particular, note how a new raven is positioned once **passed** is **true** (and how the score is incremented if **collision** is also **true**.

Save and **Run** the program. Change **Difficulty** if you want (I used 3). Click **Start**. Now when you move Elijah under a falling loaf, the score will increment and another raven will appear. If Elijah misses a loaf, the score will not increment and another raven will appear. Here's my screen after catching five loaves and waiting on another:

Code Design – Stop the Game

We're almost done. With the current code, you can play the game as long as you like – notice the displayed **Time Left** is always 60. We need to implement the logic that ends the game after 60 seconds (and updates the time display). To do this, add the shaded code to the **gameTimerActionPerformed** method:

```
private void gameTimerActionPerformed(ActionEvent e)
{
  // move bread
  breadY = breadY + breadSpeed;
  // move elijah
  if (keyPressed.equals("Left") ||
buttonPressed.equals("Left"))
  {
    elijahX -= elijahDeltaX;
    if (elijahX < 0)
      elijahX = 0;
  }
  else if (keyPressed.equals("Right") ||
buttonPressed.equals("Right"))
  {
    elijahX += elijahDeltaX;
    if (elijahX > gamePanel.getWidth() - elijahW)
      elijahX =gamePanel.getWidth() - elijahW;
  }
  // check for bread collision or passed elijah
  passed = false;
  collision = false;
  if (breadY + breadH > elijahY)
  {
    passed = true;
    if (elijahX + elijahW > breadX && elijahX < breadX +
breadW)
      collision = true;
  }
  if (passed)
  {
    if (collision)
      score++;
    PositionRavenAndBread();
  }
  // update time
  timeLeft -= gameTimer.getDelay();
  DisplayTimeScore();
  if (timeLeft == 0)
```

```
    {
      gameTimer.stop();
      JOptionPane.showConfirmDialog(null, "Elijah has been
fed by " + score + " ravens.", "Game Over",
JOptionPane.DEFAULT_OPTION, JOptionPane.PLAIN_MESSAGE);
      gameStatus = "Initial";
    }
    gamePanel.repaint();
  }
```

In this new code, with each **Tick** event, the **timeLeft** is decremented by **delay**. Once **timeLeft** is zero, the timer is turned off and the results displayed.

Save and **Run** the program. Click **Start**. The time will count down. Here's my game in the middle:

And here's my final result:

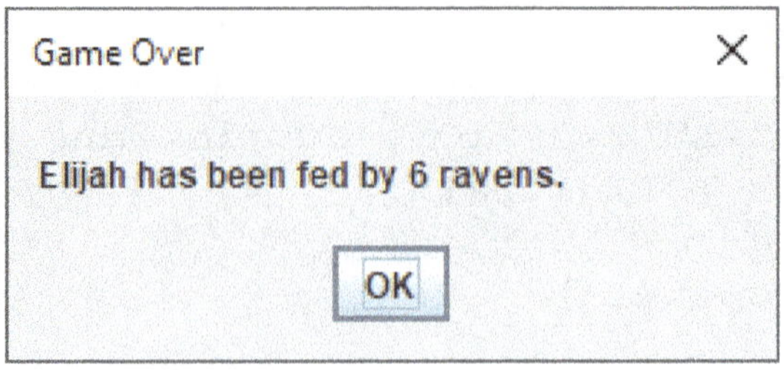

I did okay.

Just one last change. You may want to stop a game before 60 seconds goes by. To do this, you can click the **Stop** button while the game is in "**Playing**" status. The code here is simple. Add the few shaded lines at the end of the **stopButtonActionPerformed** method:

```
private void stopButtonActionPerformed(ActionEvent e)
{
  if (gameStatus.equals("Initial"))
    // clicked stop
    System.exit(0);
  else
  {
    //clicked stop while playing
    gameStatus = "Initial";
      JOptionPane.showConfirmDialog(null, "You stopped the
game.", "Game Over", JOptionPane.DEFAULT_OPTION,
JOptionPane.PLAIN_MESSAGE);
    gamePanel.repaint();
  }
}
```

Here, when stopped is pressed the game screen is cleared and a message displayed.

Save and **Run** the program. Click **Start**, then click **Stop**. You should see this message:

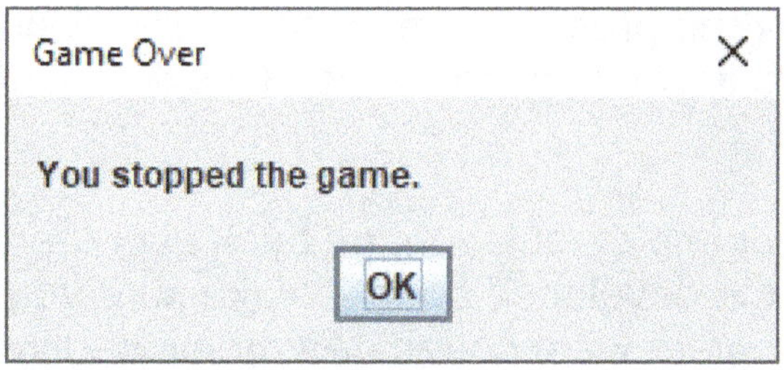

The game is now complete.

Elijah and the Ravens Program Review

The **Elijah and the Ravens** program is now complete. **Save** and **Run** the program and make sure it works as promised. Check that all options work correctly.

If there are errors in your implementation, go back over the steps of window and code design. Go over the developed code – make sure you understand how different parts of the program were coded. As mentioned in the beginning of this chapter, the completed program is saved as **Elijah** in the **\CBGJava\CBGJava Projects** folder.

Elijah and the Lions Project Java Code Listing

```
/*
 * Elijah.java
 */

package elijah;
import javax.swing.*;
import java.awt.*;
import java.awt.event.*;
import java.awt.geom.*;
import java.util.Random;

public class Elijah extends JFrame
{
JPanel controlPanel = new JPanel();
GraphicsPanel gamePanel = new GraphicsPanel();
JLabel timeLabel = new JLabel();
JTextField timeTextField = new JTextField();
JLabel scoreLabel = new JLabel();
JTextField scoreTextField = new JTextField();
JLabel difficultyLabel = new JLabel();
JTextField difficultyTextField = new JTextField();
JButton decreaseButton = new JButton();
JButton increaseButton = new JButton();
JButton startButton = new JButton();
JButton stopButton = new JButton();
Timer gameTimer;

static boolean firstTime = true;
int difficulty;
static String gameStatus;
int timeLeft;
int score;
static int elijahW, elijahH, elijahX, elijahY;
int elijahDeltaX;
static Image elijah = new
ImageIcon("Elijah.gif").getImage();
static int ravenW, ravenH, ravenX;
static int breadW, breadH, breadX, breadY;
Random myRandom = new Random();
static Image raven = new ImageIcon("Raven.gif").getImage();
static Image bread = new ImageIcon("Bread.gif").getImage();
int breadSpeed;
```

```
  String keyPressed = "None";
String buttonPressed = "None";
boolean passed;
boolean collision;

  public static void main(String args[])
  {
    // create frame
    new Elijah().setVisible(true);
  }

  public Elijah()
  {
    // frame constructor
    setTitle("Elijah and the Ravens");
    setResizable(false);
    addWindowListener(new WindowAdapter()
    {
      public void windowClosing(WindowEvent evt)
      {
        exitForm(evt);
      }
    });
    getContentPane().setLayout(new GridBagLayout());
    GridBagConstraints gridConstraints;

// control panel
controlPanel.setPreferredSize(new Dimension(100, 600));
controlPanel.setBackground(Color.BLUE);
controlPanel.setLayout(new GridBagLayout());
gridConstraints = new GridBagConstraints();
gridConstraints.gridx = 0;
gridConstraints.gridy = 0;
getContentPane().add(controlPanel, gridConstraints);

  timeLabel.setText("Time Left:");
timeLabel.setForeground(Color.YELLOW);
timeLabel.setFont(new Font("Arial", Font.BOLD, 18));
gridConstraints = new GridBagConstraints();
gridConstraints.gridx = 0;
gridConstraints.gridy = 0;
gridConstraints.gridwidth = 2;
gridConstraints.insets = new Insets(10, 0, 0, 0);
controlPanel.add(timeLabel, gridConstraints);

timeTextField.setPreferredSize(new Dimension(60, 25));
```

```
timeTextField.setBorder(BorderFactory.createLineBorder(Color
.BLACK));
timeTextField.setText("0");
timeTextField.setEditable(false);
timeTextField.setBackground(Color.WHITE);
timeTextField.setHorizontalAlignment(SwingConstants.CENTER);
timeTextField.setFont(new Font("Arial", Font.BOLD, 18));
gridConstraints = new GridBagConstraints();
gridConstraints.gridx = 0;
gridConstraints.gridy = 1;
gridConstraints.gridwidth = 2;
gridConstraints.insets = new Insets(5, 0, 0, 0);
controlPanel.add(timeTextField, gridConstraints);

  scoreLabel.setText("Loaves:");
scoreLabel.setForeground(Color.YELLOW);
scoreLabel.setFont(new Font("Arial", Font.BOLD, 18));
gridConstraints = new GridBagConstraints();
gridConstraints.gridx = 0;
gridConstraints.gridy = 2;
gridConstraints.gridwidth = 2;
controlPanel.add(scoreLabel, gridConstraints);

scoreTextField.setPreferredSize(new Dimension(60, 25));
scoreTextField.setBorder(BorderFactory.createLineBorder(Colo
r.BLACK));
scoreTextField.setText("0");
scoreTextField.setEditable(false);
scoreTextField.setBackground(Color.WHITE);
scoreTextField.setHorizontalAlignment(SwingConstants.CENTER)
;
scoreTextField.setFont(new Font("Arial", Font.BOLD, 18));
gridConstraints = new GridBagConstraints();
gridConstraints.gridx = 0;
gridConstraints.gridy = 3;
gridConstraints.gridwidth = 2;
gridConstraints.insets = new Insets(5, 0, 0, 0);
controlPanel.add(scoreTextField, gridConstraints);

  difficultyLabel.setText("Difficulty:");
difficultyLabel.setForeground(Color.YELLOW);
difficultyLabel.setFont(new Font("Arial", Font.BOLD, 18));
gridConstraints = new GridBagConstraints();
gridConstraints.gridx = 0;
gridConstraints.gridy = 4;
gridConstraints.gridwidth = 2;
gridConstraints.insets = new Insets(10, 0, 0, 0);
```

```
controlPanel.add(difficultyLabel, gridConstraints);

difficultyTextField.setPreferredSize(new Dimension(60, 25));
difficultyTextField.setBorder(BorderFactory.createLineBorder
(Color.BLACK));
difficultyTextField.setText("1");
difficultyTextField.setEditable(false);
difficultyTextField.setBackground(Color.WHITE);
difficultyTextField.setHorizontalAlignment(SwingConstants.CE
NTER);
difficultyTextField.setFont(new Font("Arial", Font.BOLD,
18));
gridConstraints = new GridBagConstraints();
gridConstraints.gridx = 0;
gridConstraints.gridy = 5;
gridConstraints.gridwidth = 2;
gridConstraints.insets = new Insets(5, 0, 0, 0);
controlPanel.add(difficultyTextField, gridConstraints);

decreaseButton.setText("<");
decreaseButton.setFont(new Font("Arial", Font.PLAIN, 18));
gridConstraints = new GridBagConstraints();
gridConstraints.gridx = 0;
gridConstraints.gridy = 6;
gridConstraints.insets = new Insets(5, 0, 0, 0);
controlPanel.add(decreaseButton, gridConstraints);
decreaseButton.addActionListener(new ActionListener()
{
  public void actionPerformed(ActionEvent e)
  {
    decreaseButtonActionPerformed(e);
  }
});

increaseButton.setText(">");
increaseButton.setFont(new Font("Arial", Font.PLAIN, 18));
gridConstraints = new GridBagConstraints();
gridConstraints.gridx = 1;
gridConstraints.gridy = 6;
gridConstraints.insets = new Insets(5, 0, 0, 0);
controlPanel.add(increaseButton, gridConstraints);
increaseButton.addActionListener(new ActionListener()
{
  public void actionPerformed(ActionEvent e)
  {
    increaseButtonActionPerformed(e);
  }
```

```
});

startButton.setText("Start");
startButton.setFont(new Font("Arial", Font.PLAIN, 18));
gridConstraints = new GridBagConstraints();
gridConstraints.gridx = 0;
gridConstraints.gridy = 7;
gridConstraints.gridwidth = 2;
gridConstraints.insets = new Insets(50, 0, 0, 0);
controlPanel.add(startButton, gridConstraints);
startButton.addActionListener(new ActionListener()
{
  public void actionPerformed(ActionEvent e)
  {
    startButtonActionPerformed(e);
  }
});

stopButton.setText("Stop");
stopButton.setFont(new Font("Arial", Font.PLAIN, 18));
gridConstraints = new GridBagConstraints();
gridConstraints.gridx = 0;
gridConstraints.gridy = 8;
gridConstraints.gridwidth = 2;
gridConstraints.insets = new Insets(5, 0, 0, 0);
controlPanel.add(stopButton, gridConstraints);
stopButton.addActionListener(new ActionListener()
{
  public void actionPerformed(ActionEvent e)
  {
    stopButtonActionPerformed(e);
  }
});

// game panel
gamePanel.setPreferredSize(new Dimension(900, 600));
gamePanel.setBackground(Color.WHITE);
gridConstraints = new GridBagConstraints();
gridConstraints.gridx = 1;
gridConstraints.gridy = 0;
getContentPane().add(gamePanel, gridConstraints);
  gamePanel.addKeyListener(new KeyAdapter()
{
  public void keyPressed(KeyEvent e)
  {
    moveKeyPressed(e);
  }
```

```
});
  gamePanel.addKeyListener(new KeyAdapter()
{
  public void keyReleased(KeyEvent e)
  {
    moveKeyReleased(e);
  }
});
gamePanel.addMouseListener(new MouseAdapter()
{
  public void mousePressed(MouseEvent e)
  {
    moveMousePressed(e);
  }
});
gamePanel.addMouseListener(new MouseAdapter()
{
  public void mouseReleased(MouseEvent e)
  {
    moveMouseReleased(e);
  }
});

gameTimer = new Timer(50, new ActionListener()
{
  public void actionPerformed(ActionEvent e)
  {
    gameTimerActionPerformed(e);
  }
});

    pack();
    Dimension screenSize =
Toolkit.getDefaultToolkit().getScreenSize();
    setBounds((int) (0.5 * (screenSize.width - getWidth())),
(int) (0.5 * (screenSize.height - getHeight())), getWidth(),
getHeight());
  difficulty = 1;
  gameStatus = "Initial";
  difficultyTextField.setText(String.valueOf(difficulty));
 }

  private void decreaseButtonActionPerformed(ActionEvent e)
  {
  if (gameStatus.equals("Initial"))
  {
    // decrease difficulty
```

```
    difficulty--;
    if (difficulty < 1)
      difficulty = 1;
  difficultyTextField.setText(String.valueOf(difficulty));
  }
  }

  private void increaseButtonActionPerformed(ActionEvent e)
  {
  if (gameStatus.equals("Initial"))
  {
    // increase difficulty
    difficulty++;
    if (difficulty > 10)
      difficulty = 10;
  difficultyTextField.setText(String.valueOf(difficulty));
  }
  }

private void startButtonActionPerformed(ActionEvent e)
{
  // clicked start
  firstTime = false;
  gameStatus = "Playing";
  //time/score
  timeLeft = 60 * 1000; // milliseconds remaining
  score = 0;
  DisplayTimeScore();
  //Elijah
  elijahW = elijah.getWidth(this);
  elijahH = elijah.getHeight(this);
  elijahDeltaX = 5;
  elijahX = 375;
  elijahY = gamePanel.getHeight() - elijahH;
    //Raven
  ravenW = raven.getWidth(this);
  ravenH = raven.getHeight(this);
  //Bread
  breadW = bread.getWidth(this);
  breadH = bread.getHeight(this);
  PositionRavenAndBread();
  gamePanel.repaint();
  //start timer
  breadSpeed = (int)(0.5 * difficulty + 3); // base on
difficulty
  gameTimer.start();
  gamePanel.requestFocus();
```

```
}

private void gameTimerActionPerformed(ActionEvent e)
{
  // move bread
  breadY = breadY + breadSpeed;
  // move elijah
  if (keyPressed.equals("Left") ||
buttonPressed.equals("Left"))
  {
    elijahX -= elijahDeltaX;
    if (elijahX < 0)
      elijahX = 0;
  }
  else if (keyPressed.equals("Right") ||
buttonPressed.equals("Right"))
  {
    elijahX += elijahDeltaX;
    if (elijahX > gamePanel.getWidth() - elijahW)
      elijahX =gamePanel.getWidth() - elijahW;
  }
  // check for bread collision or passed elijah
  passed = false;
  collision = false;
  if (breadY + breadH > elijahY)
  {
    passed = true;
    if (elijahX + elijahW > breadX && elijahX < breadX +
breadW)
      collision = true;
  }
  if (passed)
  {
    if (collision)
      score++;
    PositionRavenAndBread();
  }
  // update time
  timeLeft -= gameTimer.getDelay();
  DisplayTimeScore();
  if (timeLeft == 0)
  {
    gameTimer.stop();
    JOptionPane.showConfirmDialog(null, "Elijah has been fed
by " + score + " ravens.", "Game Over",
JOptionPane.DEFAULT_OPTION, JOptionPane.PLAIN_MESSAGE);
    gameStatus = "Initial";
```

```
    }
    gamePanel.repaint();
}

    private void DisplayTimeScore()
{
    timeTextField.setText(String.valueOf((int) (timeLeft /
1000)));
    scoreTextField.setText(String.valueOf(score));
}

private void PositionRavenAndBread()
{
    ravenX = myRandom.nextInt(gamePanel.getWidth() - ravenW);
    breadX = (int) (ravenX + 0.5 * (ravenW - breadW));
    breadY = ravenH - 20;
}

private void stopButtonActionPerformed(ActionEvent e)
{
    if (gameStatus.equals("Initial"))
      // clicked stop
      System.exit(0);
    else
    {
      //clicked stop while playing
      gameStatus = "Initial";
        JOptionPane.showConfirmDialog(null, "You stopped the
game.", "Game Over", JOptionPane.DEFAULT_OPTION,
JOptionPane.PLAIN_MESSAGE);
       gamePanel.repaint();
    }
}

    private void moveKeyPressed(KeyEvent e)
{
    int k = e.getKeyCode();
if (k == e.VK_NUMPAD4)
keyPressed = "Left";
    else if (k == e.VK_NUMPAD6)
    keyPressed = "Right";
}

    private void moveKeyReleased(KeyEvent e)
{
keyPressed = "None";
}
```

```
private void moveMousePressed(MouseEvent e)
{
  // check for left or right mouse button.y to move Elijah
  if (e.getButton() == MouseEvent.BUTTON1)
    buttonPressed = "Left";
  else if (e.getButton() == MouseEvent.BUTTON3)
    buttonPressed = "Right";
}

private void moveMouseReleased(MouseEvent e)
{
buttonPressed = "None";
}

  private void exitForm(WindowEvent evt)
  {
    System.exit(0);
  }
}

class GraphicsPanel extends JPanel
{
  public GraphicsPanel()
  {
  }

  public void paintComponent(Graphics g)
  {
    Graphics2D g2D = (Graphics2D) g;
    super.paintComponent(g2D);
  if (Elijah.firstTime)
  {
    // draw instructions
    g2D.setFont(new Font("Arial", Font.PLAIN, 18));
    g2D.setPaint(Color.BLACK);
    g2D.drawString("ELIJAH AND THE RAVENS", 10, 30);
    g2D.drawString("In 1 Kings 17:1-6, God sends ravens to
drop bread for Elijah while he hides from King Ahab.  In
this game, you ", 10, 60);
    g2D.drawString("will try to catch as many falling loaves
of bread as possible to feed Elijah.", 10, 80);
    g2D.drawString("Use the keypad left and right arrow keys
or left and right mouse buttons to move Elijah under a
falling loaf", 10, 110);
    g2D.drawString("so he can be fed by the Raven. God
always provides for our needs.", 10, 130);
```

```
    g2D.drawString("Select Difficulty by pressing the left
button for Easy and the right button for Harder.", 10, 160);
    g2D.drawString("Click on the Start Button to begin.",
10, 190);
    g2D.drawString("Click on the Stop Button to stop the
program.", 10, 220);
  }
  else if (Elijah.gameStatus.equals("Playing"))
  {
  // position Elijah
  g2D.drawImage(Elijah.elijah, Elijah.elijahX,
Elijah.elijahY, this);
  // position raven and bread
  g2D.drawImage(Elijah.raven, Elijah.ravenX, 0, this);
  g2D.drawImage(Elijah.bread, Elijah.breadX, Elijah.breadY,
this);
  }
    g2D.dispose();
  }
}
```

7

Daniel and the Lions Project

Preview

In Daniel, King Darius is tricked into putting Daniel into the lion's den. Daniel prays for God's protection and god sends His Angel to shut the lion's mouth. In this chapter, you build a computer game based on this story. Daniel is surrounded by lion's in a grid. As he moves, they move closer to him. He shoots prayers at the lions to dispatch them.

Daniel and the Lions Project Preview

In this chapter, we will build the **Daniel and the Lions** game. Daniel is placed in a grid with a number of lions (and four rocks). The idea is for Daniel to dispatch (eliminate) each lion by shooting a prayer at it. The game is over when Daniel has dispatched all the lions or the moving lions reach Daniel first.

The finished project is saved as **Daniel** in the **\CBGJava\CBGJava Projects** project group. Start NetBeans (or your IDE). Open the specified project group. Make **Daniel** the selected project. Run the project. You will see:

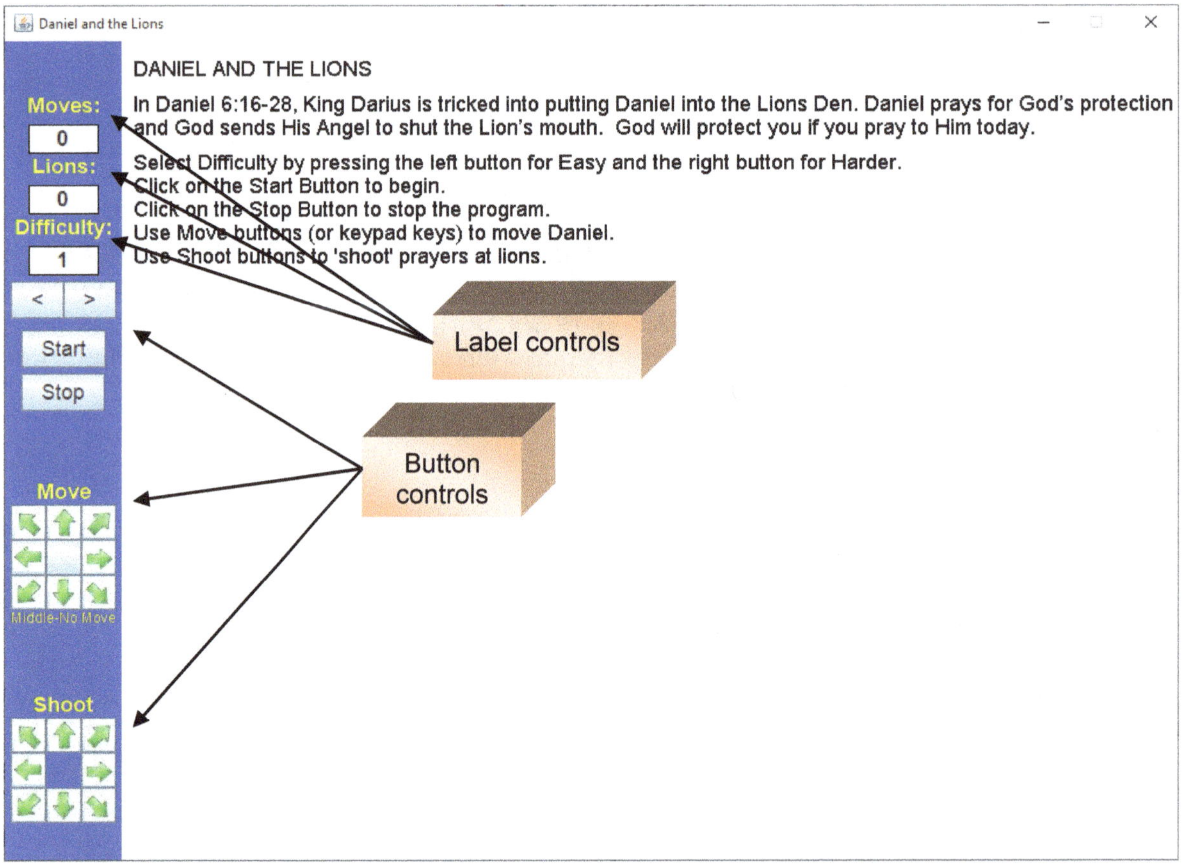

Labels are used for instructions and to display game information (number of moves, number of lions, difficulty). There are many button controls. Two are used to change the difficulty, one to start the game and one to stop. Nine button controls (with arrows) are used to move Daniel, while eight buttons (with arrows) are used to shoot prayers at lions.

The game appears in its 'initial' state. A game description and program instructions are given. At this point, you can click the **Start** button to start the game, click arrow buttons to change the game **Difficulty** or click **Stop** to stop the program. Change the **Difficulty** if you want. The higher the difficulty, the more lions that Daniel must dispatch. I set the value to **3** by clicking the little arrows under **Difficulty**. Click the **Start** button to start playing. The program instructions disappear. Daniel and the lions appear in the game grid This is the game's '**DanielMove'** state:

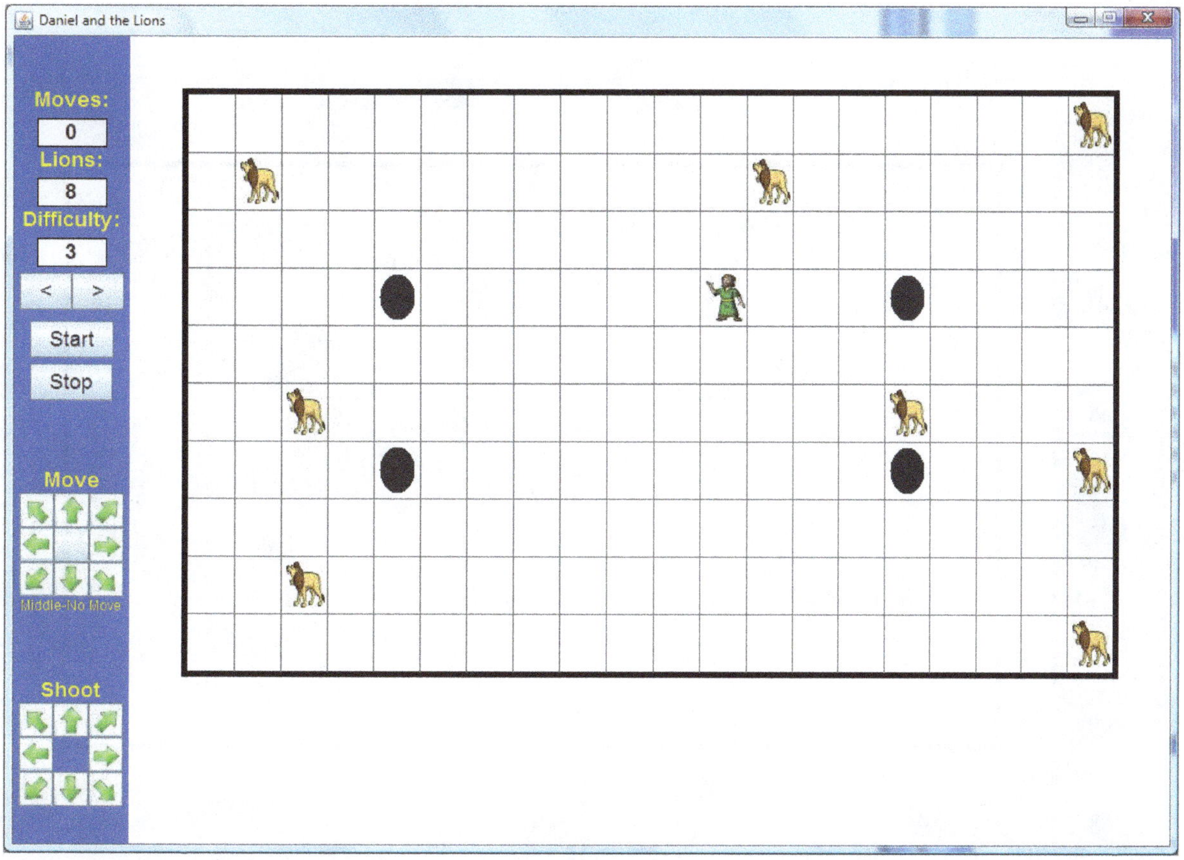

You can see Daniel near the middle of the grid. A number of lions are in the grid along with four rocks (gray ovals). In the upper left corner you are shown how many **Moves** you have taken and how many **Lions** remain. You have two choices. You can move Daniel by clicking one of the arrows under **Move** (or alternately use corresponding key on the numeric keypad). Or, you can shoot a prayer at a lion by clicking one of the green arrows under **Shoot**.

If you move Daniel, he will move one square in the chosen direction (or click the middle to have him remain where he is). Following his move, all the lions will move closer to Daniel, so be careful. Note lions cannot move through the rocks. If you shoot a prayer, it will travel in the selected direction. If it intercepts a lion, that lion is dispatched (taken out of the grid). A prayer will not move through a rock. The goal of the game is to dispatch all the lions before one reaches Daniel.

In our example, notice there are no lions in the direct path of a 'prayer shot' so we can only move Daniel. We try to stay away from lions so I click the down **Move** button:

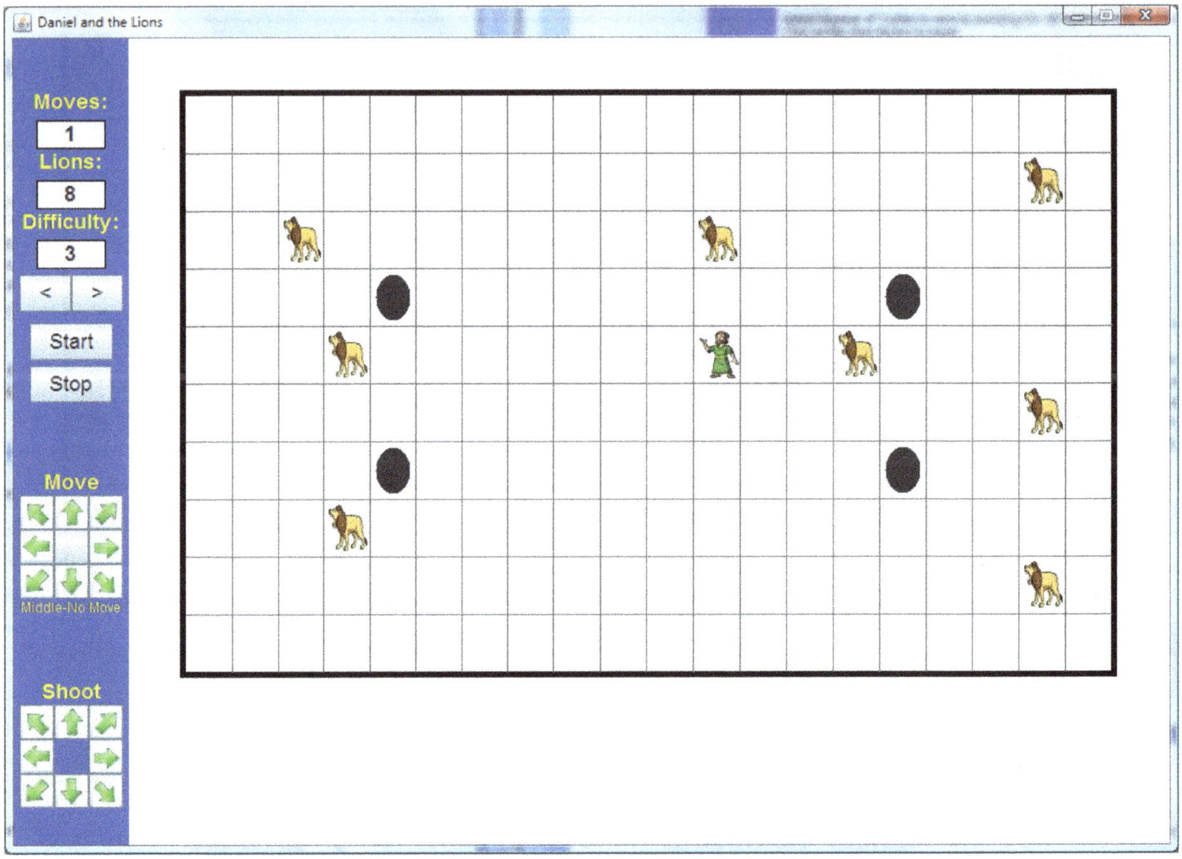

Notice how the lions have all moved closer to Daniel. There are many in shot range. The one above Daniel is closest, so I click the up **Shoot** arrow.

Here's the result of my shot. One lion is dispatched, but the others continue to close in on Daniel:

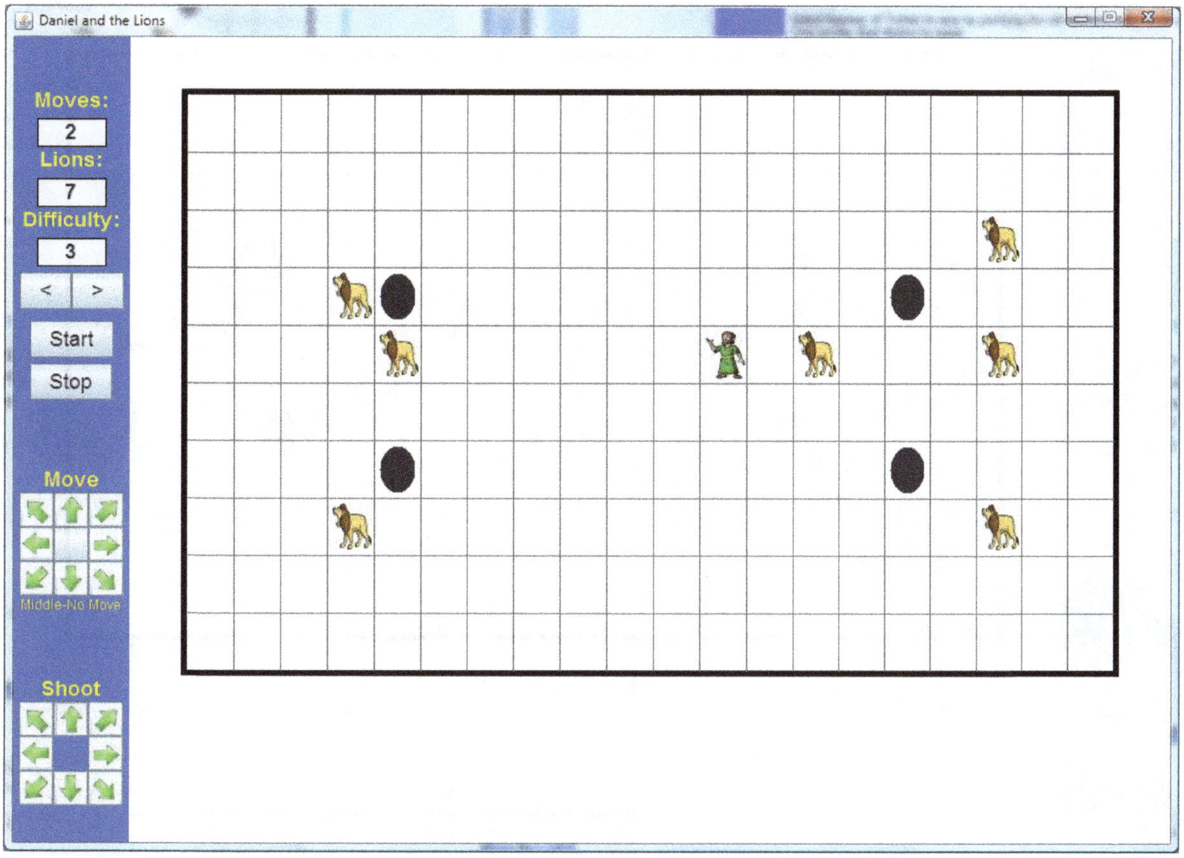

Now I need to shoot the one to the right (it's closest).

After that shot, I see:

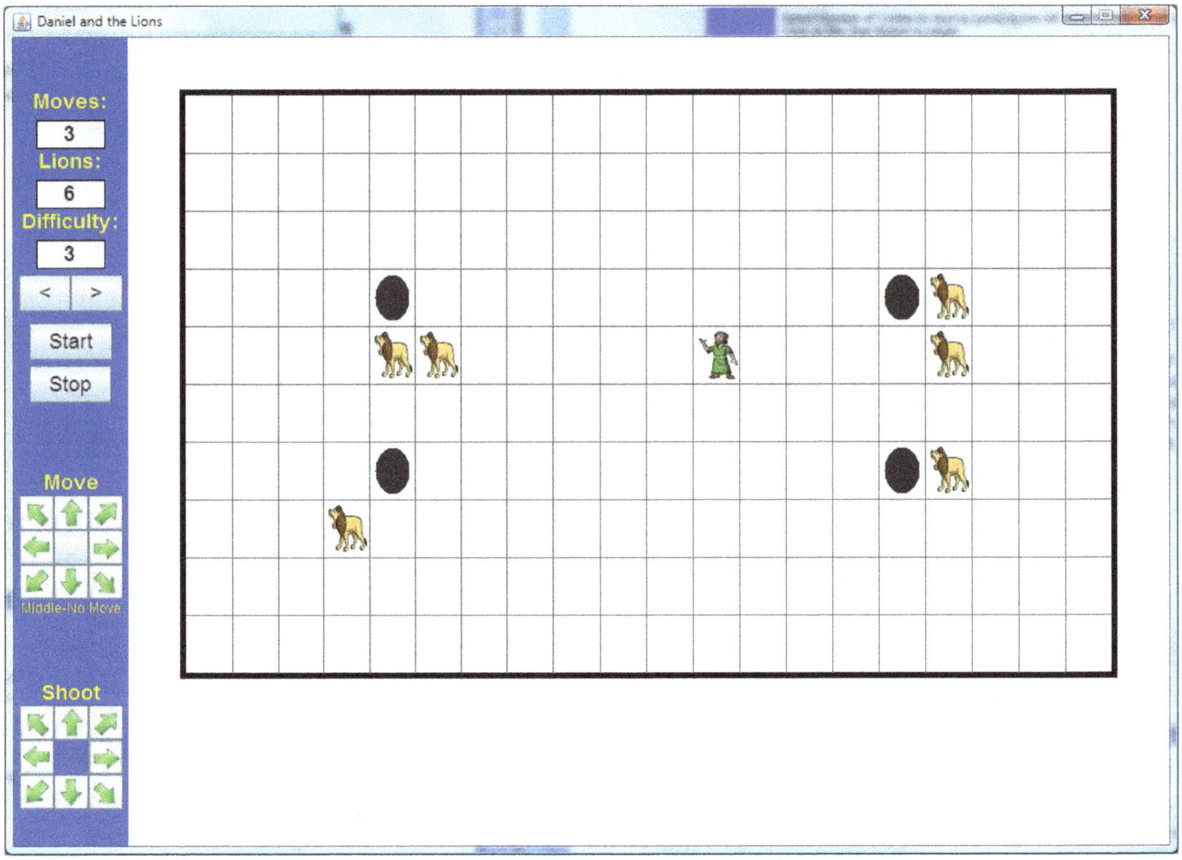

A shot to the right, then two to the left eliminates three more lions. At that point, other lions move into range.

After several shots in to the left and right, I see:

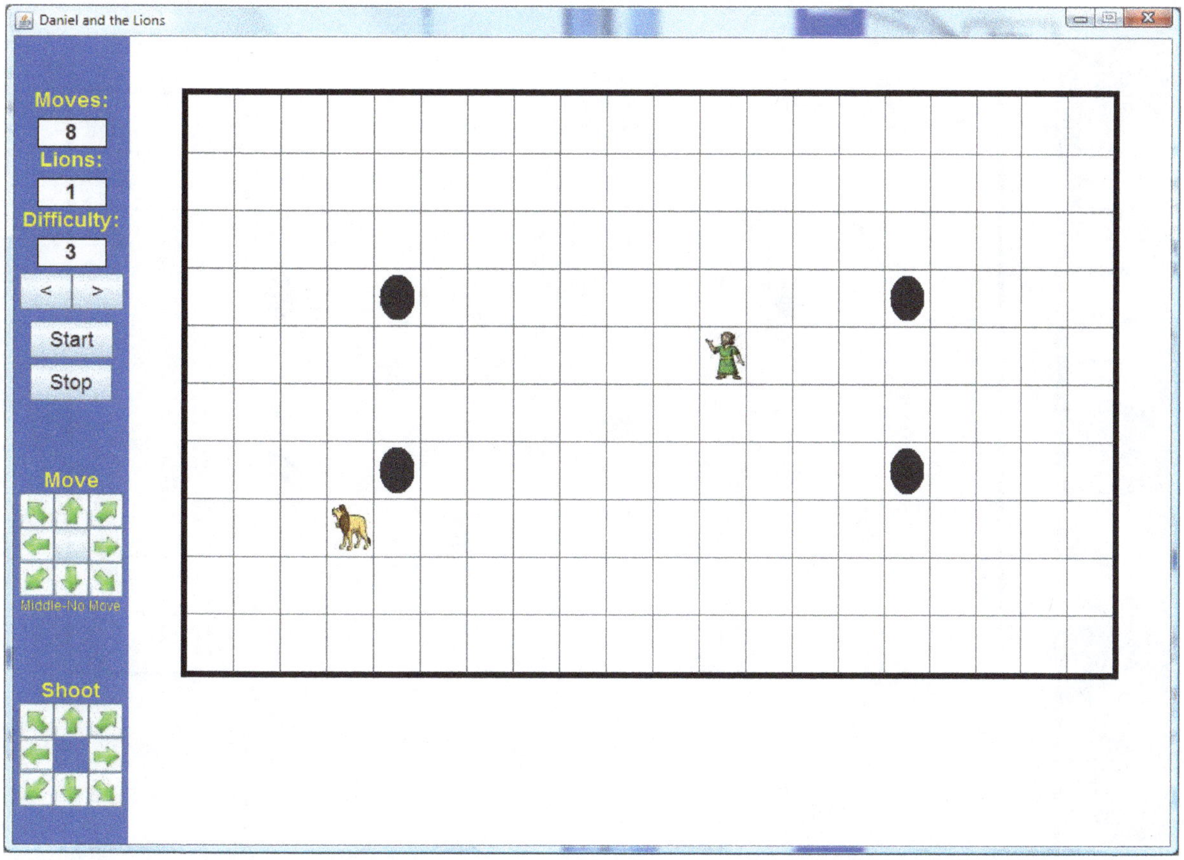

The last lion is behind a rock and can't see Daniel. And, Daniel can't shoot a prayer either. His only option is to move until the lion is in prayer shot range.

Three moves down and we have:

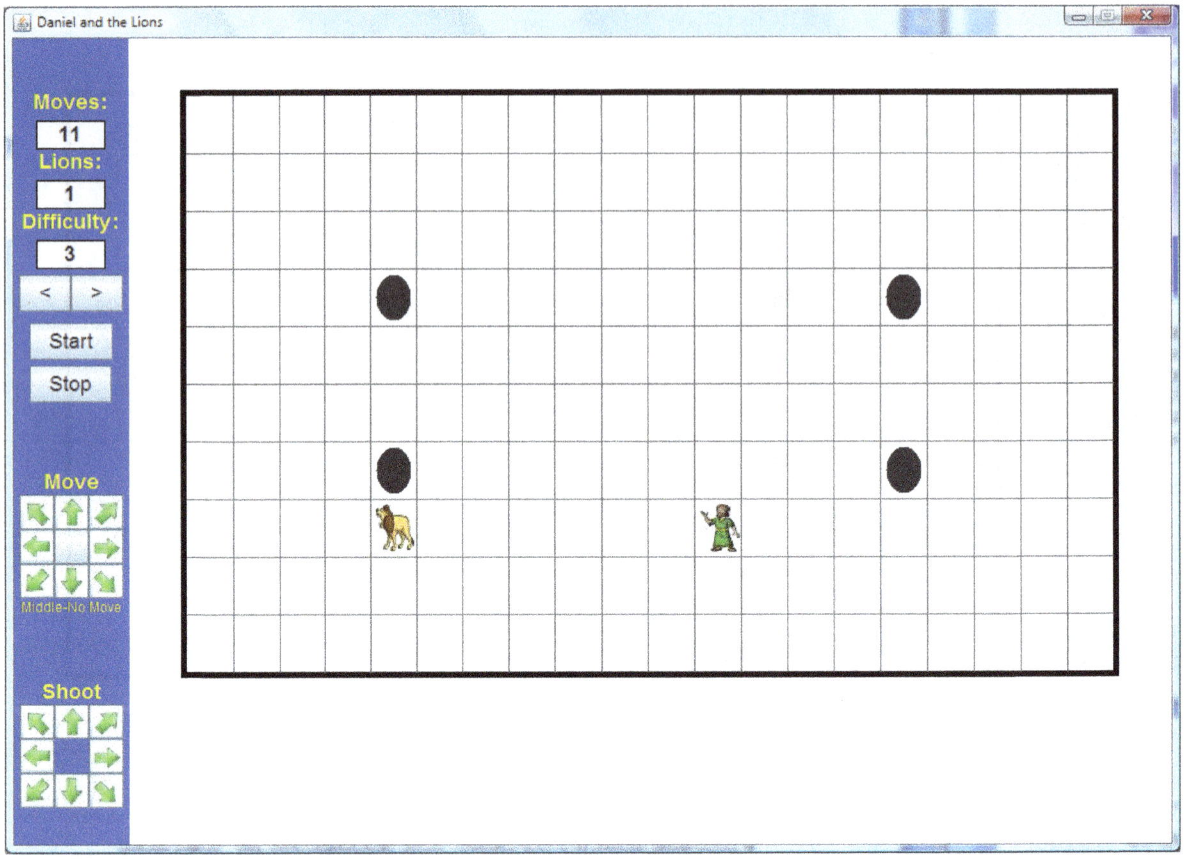

The lion can now be dispatched with a shot to the left.

You should see how the game is played. When a lion is in range, take a shot. If a lion gets stuck behind a rock, you need to move Daniel until the lion moves in range. I continued this game and dispatched all 8 lions in just 12 moves. At this point, I got this message:

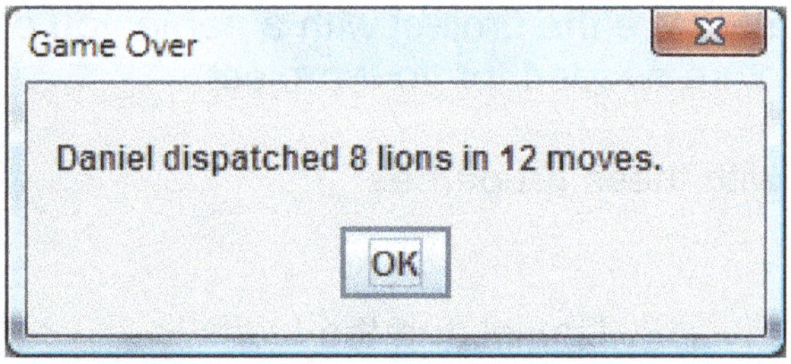

If you aren't successful in dispatching all the lions, you will see this message:

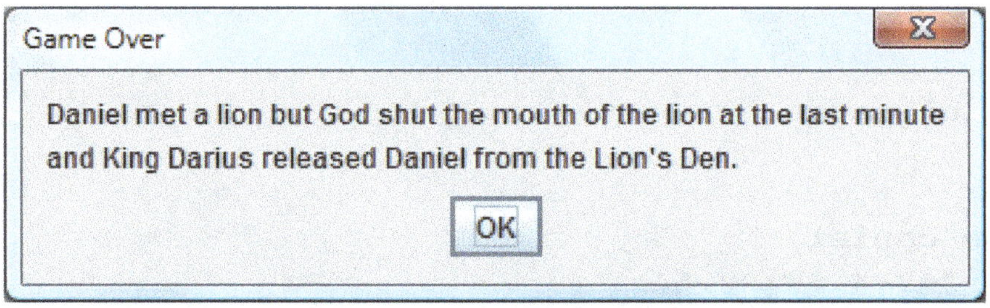

When a game is over, you can change the **Difficulty**. You can also click **Start** to play again or click **Stop** to stop the program. Continue playing the game to understand its operation.

You will now build this project in stages. As you build Java programs, we always recommend taking a slow, step-by-step process. It minimizes programming errors and helps build your confidence as things come together in a complete program. We address **frame design**. And, we address **code design**. We discuss how to use the buttons, how to draw the grid, how to display Daniel, the lions and the rocks, and how to move Daniel and the lions.

Daniel and the Lions Frame Design

We begin building the **Daniel** project. Start a new project in your Java project group – name it **Daniel**. Delete default code in **Daniel.java**. Once started, we suggest you immediately save the project with a name you choose. This sets up the folder and file structure needed for your project.

Build the basic frame with these properties:

Daniel Frame:

title	Daniel and the Lions
resizable	false

The code is:

```
/*
 * Daniel.java
 */

package daniel;
import javax.swing.*;
import java.awt.*;
import java.awt.event.*;
import java.awt.geom.*;
import java.util.Random;

public class Daniel extends JFrame
{
  public static void main(String args[])
  {
    // create frame
    new Daniel().setVisible(true);
  }

  public Daniel()
  {
    // frame constructor
    setTitle("Daniel and the Lions");
    setResizable(false);
    addWindowListener(new WindowAdapter()
    {
      public void windowClosing(WindowEvent evt)
      {
        exitForm(evt);
      }
    });
```

```
    getContentPane().setLayout(new GridBagLayout());
    GridBagConstraints gridConstraints;

    pack();
    Dimension screenSize =
Toolkit.getDefaultToolkit().getScreenSize();
    setBounds((int) (0.5 * (screenSize.width -
getWidth())), (int) (0.5 * (screenSize.height -
getHeight())), getWidth(), getHeight());
 }

  private void exitForm(WindowEvent evt)
  {
    System.exit(0);
  }
}
```

This code builds the frame, imports the needed packages, sets up the layout manager and includes code to exit the application. Run the code to make sure the frame (at least, what there is of it at this point) appears and is centered on the screen:

Let's populate our frame with other controls. All code for creating the frame and placing controls (except declarations) goes in the **Daniel** constructor.

The frame uses several panel controls. **controlPanel** holds the labels and buttons for game control, movePanel holds the buttons to move Daniel, shootPanel holds the buttons to shoot prayers, while **gamePanel** displays the game grid. The **GridBagLayout** is:

	gridx = 0	gridx = 1
gridy = 0	**controlPanel**	**gamePanel**
gridy = 1	**movePanel**	
gridy = 2	**shootPanel**	

Since **gamePanel** hosts graphics elements (images, lines), it will be a 'graphics panel.' Each such panel (example below is named **GraphicsPanel**) will be a separate class with a **paintComponent** method where any graphics are drawn:

```
class GraphicsPanel extends JPanel
{
  public void paintComponent(Graphics g)
  {
    Graphics2D g2D = (Graphics2D) g;
    super.paintComponent(g2D);

    g2D.dispose();   }
}
```

Recall we introduced such panels in other projects.

The properties for each panel are:

controlPanel:

size	100, 350
background	Blue
gridx	0
gridy	0

movePanel:

size	100, 175
background	Blue
gridx	0
gridy	1

shootPanel:

size	100, 175
background	Blue
gridx	0
gridy	2

gamePanel:

size	900, 700
background	White
gridx	1
gridy	0
gridheight	3

Declare each panel using:

```
JPanel controlPanel = new JPanel();
JPanel movePanel = new JPanel();
JPanel shootPanel = new JPanel();
GraphicsPanel gamePanel = new GraphicsPanel();
```

Add the panels to the frame using this code:

```
// control panel
controlPanel.setPreferredSize(new Dimension(100, 350));
controlPanel.setBackground(Color.BLUE);
controlPanel.setLayout(new GridBagLayout());
gridConstraints = new GridBagConstraints();
gridConstraints.gridx = 0;
gridConstraints.gridy = 0;
getContentPane().add(controlPanel, gridConstraints);

// move panel
movePanel.setPreferredSize(new Dimension(100, 175));
movePanel.setBackground(Color.BLUE);
movePanel.setLayout(new GridBagLayout());
gridConstraints = new GridBagConstraints();
gridConstraints.gridx = 0;
gridConstraints.gridy = 1;
getContentPane().add(movePanel, gridConstraints);

// shoot panel
shootPanel.setPreferredSize(new Dimension(100, 175));
shootPanel.setBackground(Color.BLUE);
shootPanel.setLayout(new GridBagLayout());
gridConstraints = new GridBagConstraints();
gridConstraints.gridx = 0;
gridConstraints.gridy = 2;
getContentPane().add(shootPanel, gridConstraints);

// game panel
gamePanel.setPreferredSize(new Dimension(900, 700));
gamePanel.setBackground(Color.WHITE);
gridConstraints = new GridBagConstraints();
gridConstraints.gridx = 1;
gridConstraints.gridy = 0;
gridConstraints.gridheight = 3;
getContentPane().add(gamePanel, gridConstraints);
```

After the **Daniel** main class, add this 'graphics' panel framework:

```
class GraphicsPanel extends JPanel
{
  public GraphicsPanel()
  {
  }
  public void paintComponent(Graphics g)
  {
    Graphics2D g2D = (Graphics2D) g;
    super.paintComponent(g2D);

    g2D.dispose();
  }
}
```

All graphic elements will be drawn in the **paintComponent** methods of these classes.

Save, run. You will see the empty panel controls on the frame. This is the finished frame size.

We need to add elements to the three blue panels. First, we do the **controlPanel**.

The **controlPanel** holds controls used to display status of the **Daniel** game and control part of its operation. The **GridBagLayout** is:

	gridx = 0	gridx = 1
gridy = 0	**movesLabel**	
gridy = 1	**movesTextField**	
gridy = 2	**lionsLabel**	
gridy = 3	**lionsTextField**	
gridy = 4	**difficultyLabel**	
gridy = 5	**difficultyTextField**	
gridy = 6	**decreaseButton**	**increaseButton**
gridy = 7	**startButton**	
gridy = 8	**stopButton**	

The label and text field controls display the number of moves, the lions left and the difficulty. Buttons are used to change the number of turtles and start and stop the game.

Control properties are:

movesLabel:

text	Moves:
foreground	Yellow
font	Arial, Bold, Size 18
gridx	0
gridy	0
gridwidth	2
insets	10, 0, 0, 0

movesTextField:

size	60, 25
border	Black line
text	0
editable	false
background	White
horizontalAlignment	CENTER
font	Arial, Bold, Size 18
gridx	0
gridy	1
gridwidth	2
insets	5, 0, 0, 0

lionsLabel:

text	Lions:
foreground	Yellow
font	Arial, Bold, Size 18
gridx	0
gridy	2
gridwidth	2

lionsTextField:

size	60, 25
border	Black line
text	0
editable	false
background	White
horizontalAlignment	CENTER
font	Arial, Bold, Size 18
gridx	0
gridy	3
gridwidth	2
insets	5, 0, 0, 0

difficultyLabel:

text	Difficulty:
foreground	Yellow
font	Arial, Bold, Size 18
gridx	0
gridy	4
gridwidth	2

difficultyTextField:

size	60, 25
border	Black line
text	1
editable	false
background	White
horizontalAlignment	CENTER
font	Arial, Bold, Size 18
gridx	0
gridy	5
gridwidth	2
insets	5, 0, 0, 0

decreaseButton:

text	<
font	Arial, Plain, Size 18
gridx	0
gridy	6
insets	5, 0, 0, 0

increaseButton:

text	>
font	Arial, Plain, Size 18
gridx	1
gridy	6
insets	5, 0, 0, 0

startButton:

text	Start
font	Arial, Plain, Size 18
gridx	0
gridy	7
gridwidth	2
insets	10, 0, 0, 0

stopButton:

text	Stop
font	Arial, Plain, Size 18
gridx	0
gridy	8
gridwidth	2
insets	5, 0, 0, 0

Use these declarations for the control panel elements:

```
JLabel movesLabel = new JLabel();
JTextField movesTextField = new JTextField();
JLabel lionsLabel = new JLabel();
JTextField lionsTextField = new JTextField();
JLabel difficultyLabel = new JLabel();
JTextField difficultyTextField = new JTextField();
JButton decreaseButton = new JButton();
JButton increaseButton = new JButton();
JButton startButton = new JButton();
JButton stopButton = new JButton();
```

And, this code adds the controls:

```
movesLabel.setText("Moves:");
movesLabel.setForeground(Color.YELLOW);
movesLabel.setFont(new Font("Arial", Font.BOLD, 18));
gridConstraints = new GridBagConstraints();
gridConstraints.gridx = 0;
gridConstraints.gridy = 0;
gridConstraints.gridwidth = 2;
gridConstraints.insets = new Insets(10, 0, 0, 0);
controlPanel.add(movesLabel, gridConstraints);

movesTextField.setPreferredSize(new Dimension(60, 25));
movesTextField.setBorder(BorderFactory.createLineBorder(Co
lor.BLACK));
movesTextField.setText("0");
movesTextField.setEditable(false);
movesTextField.setBackground(Color.WHITE);
movesTextField.setHorizontalAlignment(SwingConstants.CENTE
R);
movesTextField.setFont(new Font("Arial", Font.BOLD, 18));
gridConstraints = new GridBagConstraints();
gridConstraints.gridx = 0;
gridConstraints.gridy = 1;
gridConstraints.gridwidth = 2;
gridConstraints.insets = new Insets(5, 0, 0, 0);
controlPanel.add(movesTextField, gridConstraints);

  lionsLabel.setText("Lions:");
lionsLabel.setForeground(Color.YELLOW);
lionsLabel.setFont(new Font("Arial", Font.BOLD, 18));
gridConstraints = new GridBagConstraints();
gridConstraints.gridx = 0;
gridConstraints.gridy = 2;
gridConstraints.gridwidth = 2;
controlPanel.add(lionsLabel, gridConstraints);
```

```
lionsTextField.setPreferredSize(new Dimension(60, 25));
lionsTextField.setBorder(BorderFactory.createLineBorder(Co
lor.BLACK));
lionsTextField.setText("0");
lionsTextField.setEditable(false);
lionsTextField.setBackground(Color.WHITE);
lionsTextField.setHorizontalAlignment(SwingConstants.CENTE
R);
lionsTextField.setFont(new Font("Arial", Font.BOLD, 18));
gridConstraints = new GridBagConstraints();
gridConstraints.gridx = 0;
gridConstraints.gridy = 3;
gridConstraints.gridwidth = 2;
gridConstraints.insets = new Insets(5, 0, 0, 0);
controlPanel.add(lionsTextField, gridConstraints);

  difficultyLabel.setText("Difficulty:");
difficultyLabel.setForeground(Color.YELLOW);
difficultyLabel.setFont(new Font("Arial", Font.BOLD, 18));
gridConstraints = new GridBagConstraints();
gridConstraints.gridx = 0;
gridConstraints.gridy = 4;
gridConstraints.gridwidth = 2;
controlPanel.add(difficultyLabel, gridConstraints);

difficultyTextField.setPreferredSize(new Dimension(60,
25));
difficultyTextField.setBorder(BorderFactory.createLineBord
er(Color.BLACK));
difficultyTextField.setText("1");
difficultyTextField.setEditable(false);
difficultyTextField.setBackground(Color.WHITE);
difficultyTextField.setHorizontalAlignment(SwingConstants.
CENTER);
difficultyTextField.setFont(new Font("Arial", Font.BOLD,
18));
gridConstraints = new GridBagConstraints();
gridConstraints.gridx = 0;
gridConstraints.gridy = 5;
gridConstraints.gridwidth = 2;
gridConstraints.insets = new Insets(5, 0, 0, 0);
controlPanel.add(difficultyTextField, gridConstraints);
```

```
decreaseButton.setText("<");
decreaseButton.setFont(new Font("Arial", Font.PLAIN, 18));
gridConstraints = new GridBagConstraints();
gridConstraints.gridx = 0;
gridConstraints.gridy = 6;
gridConstraints.insets = new Insets(5, 0, 0, 0);
controlPanel.add(decreaseButton, gridConstraints);
decreaseButton.addActionListener(new ActionListener()
{
  public void actionPerformed(ActionEvent e)
  {
    decreaseButtonActionPerformed(e);
  }
});

increaseButton.setText(">");
increaseButton.setFont(new Font("Arial", Font.PLAIN, 18));
gridConstraints = new GridBagConstraints();
gridConstraints.gridx = 1;
gridConstraints.gridy = 6;
gridConstraints.insets = new Insets(5, 0, 0, 0);
controlPanel.add(increaseButton, gridConstraints);
increaseButton.addActionListener(new ActionListener()
{
  public void actionPerformed(ActionEvent e)
  {
    increaseButtonActionPerformed(e);
  }
});

startButton.setText("Start");
startButton.setFont(new Font("Arial", Font.PLAIN, 18));
gridConstraints = new GridBagConstraints();
gridConstraints.gridx = 0;
gridConstraints.gridy = 7;
gridConstraints.gridwidth = 2;
gridConstraints.insets = new Insets(10, 0, 0, 0);
controlPanel.add(startButton, gridConstraints);
startButton.addActionListener(new ActionListener()
{
  public void actionPerformed(ActionEvent e)
  {
    startButtonActionPerformed(e);
  }
});
```

```
stopButton.setText("Stop");
stopButton.setFont(new Font("Arial", Font.PLAIN, 18));
gridConstraints = new GridBagConstraints();
gridConstraints.gridx = 0;
gridConstraints.gridy = 8;
gridConstraints.gridwidth = 2;
gridConstraints.insets = new Insets(5, 0, 0, 0);
controlPanel.add(stopButton, gridConstraints);
stopButton.addActionListener(new ActionListener()
{
  public void actionPerformed(ActionEvent e)
  {
    stopButtonActionPerformed(e);
  }
});
```

And, add these four empty methods:

```
private void decreaseButtonActionPerformed(ActionEvent e)
{
}

private void increaseButtonActionPerformed(ActionEvent e)
{
}

private void startButtonActionPerformed(ActionEvent e)
{
}

private void stopButtonActionPerformed(ActionEvent e)
{
}
```

Run the project so see:

The labels, text fields and buttons for the control panel are in place. Next, let's add the labels and buttons to **movePanel**.

The **movePanel** holds the buttons used to move Daniel around the grid. It also holds a couple of labels. The **GridBagLayout** is:

	gridx = 0	gridx = 1	gridx = 2
gridy = 0	**moveLabel**		
gridy = 1	**moveUpLeftButton**	**moveUpButton**	**moveUpRightButton**
gridy = 2	**moveLeftButton**	**noMoveButton**	**moveRightButton**
gridy = 3	**moveDownLeftButton**	**moveDownButton**	**moveDownRightButton**
gridy = 4	**noMoveLabel**		

There are nine buttons! We will add each button individually. It's lots of code, so use your copy and paste skills. All the arrow graphics are in the **\CBGJava\CBGJava Projects\Daniel** folder.

Control properties are:

moveLabel:

text	Move
foreground	Yellow
font	Arial, Bold, Size 18
gridx	0
gridy	0
gridwidth	3

moveUpLeftButton:

icon	UpLeft.jpg
size	30, 30
gridx	0
gridy	1

moveUpButton:

icon	Up.jpg
size	30, 30
gridx	1
gridy	1

moveUpRightButton:

icon	UpRight.jpg
size	30, 30
gridx	2
gridy	1

moveLeftButton:

icon	UpLeft.jpg
size	30, 30
gridx	0
gridy	2

noMoveButton:

size	30, 30
gridx	1
gridy	2

moveRightButton:

icon	Right.jpg
size	30, 30
gridx	2
gridy	2

moveDownLeftButton:

icon	DownLeft.jpg
size	30, 30
gridx	0
gridy	3

moveDownButton:

icon	Down.jpg
size	30, 30
gridx	1
gridy	3

moveDownRightButton:

icon	DownRight.jpg
size	30, 30
gridx	2
gridy	3

noMoveLabel:

text	Middle-No Move
foreground	Yellow
font	Arial, Plain, Size 12
gridx	0
gridy	4
gridwidth	3

Use these declarations for the move panel elements:

```
JLabel moveLabel = new JLabel();
JLabel noMoveLabel = new JLabel();
JButton moveUpLeftButton = new JButton();
JButton moveUpButton = new JButton();
JButton moveUpRightButton = new JButton();
JButton moveLeftButton = new JButton();
JButton noMoveButton = new JButton();
JButton moveRightButton = new JButton();
JButton moveDownLeftButton = new JButton();
JButton moveDownButton = new JButton();
JButton moveDownRightButton = new JButton();
```

And, this code (yes, there's lots of it) adds the controls:

```
moveLabel.setText("Move");
moveLabel.setForeground(Color.YELLOW);
moveLabel.setFont(new Font("Arial", Font.BOLD, 18));
gridConstraints = new GridBagConstraints();
gridConstraints.gridx = 0;
gridConstraints.gridy = 0;
gridConstraints.gridwidth = 3;
movePanel.add(moveLabel, gridConstraints);

moveUpLeftButton.setIcon(new ImageIcon("UpLeft.jpg"));
moveUpLeftButton.setPreferredSize(new Dimension(30, 30));
gridConstraints = new GridBagConstraints();
gridConstraints.gridx = 0;
gridConstraints.gridy = 1;
movePanel.add(moveUpLeftButton, gridConstraints);
moveUpLeftButton.addActionListener(new ActionListener()
{
  public void actionPerformed(ActionEvent e)
  {
    moveUpLeftButtonActionPerformed(e);
  }
});
```

```
moveUpButton.setIcon(new ImageIcon("Up.jpg"));
moveUpButton.setPreferredSize(new Dimension(30, 30));
gridConstraints = new GridBagConstraints();
gridConstraints.gridx = 1;
gridConstraints.gridy = 1;
movePanel.add(moveUpButton, gridConstraints);
moveUpButton.addActionListener(new ActionListener()
{
  public void actionPerformed(ActionEvent e)
  {
    moveUpButtonActionPerformed(e);
  }
});

moveUpRightButton.setIcon(new ImageIcon("UpRight.jpg"));
moveUpRightButton.setPreferredSize(new Dimension(30, 30));
gridConstraints = new GridBagConstraints();
gridConstraints.gridx = 2;
gridConstraints.gridy = 1;
movePanel.add(moveUpRightButton, gridConstraints);
moveUpRightButton.addActionListener(new ActionListener()
{
  public void actionPerformed(ActionEvent e)
  {
    moveUpRightButtonActionPerformed(e);
  }
});

moveLeftButton.setIcon(new ImageIcon("Left.jpg"));
moveLeftButton.setPreferredSize(new Dimension(30, 30));
gridConstraints = new GridBagConstraints();
gridConstraints.gridx = 0;
gridConstraints.gridy = 2;
movePanel.add(moveLeftButton, gridConstraints);
moveLeftButton.addActionListener(new ActionListener()
{
  public void actionPerformed(ActionEvent e)
  {
    moveLeftButtonActionPerformed(e);
  }
});
```

```
    noMoveButton.setPreferredSize(new Dimension(30, 30));
    gridConstraints = new GridBagConstraints();
    gridConstraints.gridx = 1;
    gridConstraints.gridy = 2;
    movePanel.add(noMoveButton, gridConstraints);
    noMoveButton.addActionListener(new ActionListener()
    {
      public void actionPerformed(ActionEvent e)
      {
        noMoveButtonActionPerformed(e);
      }
    });

    moveRightButton.setIcon(new ImageIcon("Right.jpg"));
    moveRightButton.setPreferredSize(new Dimension(30, 30));
    gridConstraints = new GridBagConstraints();
    gridConstraints.gridx = 2;
    gridConstraints.gridy = 2;
    movePanel.add(moveRightButton, gridConstraints);
    moveRightButton.addActionListener(new ActionListener()
    {
      public void actionPerformed(ActionEvent e)
      {
        moveRightButtonActionPerformed(e);
      }
    });

    moveDownLeftButton.setIcon(new ImageIcon("DownLeft.jpg"));
    moveDownLeftButton.setPreferredSize(new Dimension(30,
30));
    gridConstraints = new GridBagConstraints();
    gridConstraints.gridx = 0;
    gridConstraints.gridy = 3;
    movePanel.add(moveDownLeftButton, gridConstraints);
    moveDownLeftButton.addActionListener(new ActionListener()
    {
      public void actionPerformed(ActionEvent e)
      {
        moveDownLeftButtonActionPerformed(e);
      }
    });
```

```
  moveDownButton.setIcon(new ImageIcon("Down.jpg"));
  moveDownButton.setPreferredSize(new Dimension(30, 30));
  gridConstraints = new GridBagConstraints();
  gridConstraints.gridx = 1;
  gridConstraints.gridy = 3;
  movePanel.add(moveDownButton, gridConstraints);
  moveDownButton.addActionListener(new ActionListener()
  {
    public void actionPerformed(ActionEvent e)
    {
      moveDownButtonActionPerformed(e);
    }
  });

  moveDownRightButton.setIcon(new
ImageIcon("DownRight.jpg"));
  moveDownRightButton.setPreferredSize(new Dimension(30,
30));
  gridConstraints = new GridBagConstraints();
  gridConstraints.gridx = 2;
  gridConstraints.gridy = 3;
  movePanel.add(moveDownRightButton, gridConstraints);
  moveDownRightButton.addActionListener(new ActionListener()
  {
    public void actionPerformed(ActionEvent e)
    {
      moveDownRightButtonActionPerformed(e);
    }
  });

  noMoveLabel.setText("Middle-No Move");
  noMoveLabel.setForeground(Color.YELLOW);
  noMoveLabel.setFont(new Font("Arial", Font.PLAIN, 12));
  gridConstraints = new GridBagConstraints();
  gridConstraints.gridx = 0;
  gridConstraints.gridy = 4;
  gridConstraints.gridwidth = 3;
  movePanel.add(noMoveLabel, gridConstraints);
```

And, add these nine empty methods:

```
private void moveUpLeftButtonActionPerformed(ActionEvent
e)
{
}

private void moveUpButtonActionPerformed(ActionEvent e)
{
}

private void moveUpRightButtonActionPerformed(ActionEvent
e)
{
}

private void moveLeftButtonActionPerformed(ActionEvent e)
{
}

private void noMoveButtonActionPerformed(ActionEvent e)
{
}

private void moveRightButtonActionPerformed(ActionEvent e)
{
}

private void moveDownLeftButtonActionPerformed(ActionEvent
e)
{
}

private void moveDownButtonActionPerformed(ActionEvent e)
{
}

private void
moveDownRightButtonActionPerformed(ActionEvent e)
{
}
```

Run the project so see:

We now see the move buttons and associated labeling. Now, let's do the **shootPanel**. It is very similar to the **movePanel**, so copy and paste skills come into play once again.

The **shootPanel** holds the buttons used to shoot prayers at lions. It also holds a couple of labels. The **GridBagLayout** is:

	gridx = 0	gridx = 1	gridx = 2
gridy = 0	**shootLabel**		
gridy = 1	**shootUpLeftButton**	**shootUpButton**	**shootUpRightButton**
gridy = 2	**shootLeftButton**		**shootRightButton**
gridy = 3	**shootDownLeftButton**	**shootDownButton**	**shootDownRightButton**

Recall all the arrow graphics are in the **\CBGJava\CBGJava Projects\Daniel** folder.

Control properties are:

shootLabel:

text	Shoot
foreground	Yellow
font	Arial, Bold, Size 18
gridx	0
gridy	0
gridwidth	3

shootUpLeftButton:

icon	UpLeft.jpg
size	30, 30
gridx	0
gridy	1

shootUpButton:

icon	Up.jpg
size	30, 30
gridx	1
gridy	1

shootUpRightButton:

icon	UpRight.jpg
size	30, 30
gridx	2
gridy	1

shootLeftButton:

icon	UpLeft.jpg
size	30, 30
gridx	0
gridy	2

shootRightButton:

icon	Right.jpg
size	30, 30
gridx	2
gridy	2

shootDownLeftButton:

icon	DownLeft.jpg
size	30, 30
gridx	0
gridy	3

shootDownButton:

icon	Down.jpg
size	30, 30
gridx	1
gridy	3

shootDownRightButton:

icon	DownRight.jpg
size	30, 30
gridx	2
gridy	3

Use these declarations for the shoot panel elements:

```
JLabel shootLabel = new JLabel();
JButton shootUpLeftButton = new JButton();
JButton shootUpButton = new JButton();
JButton shootUpRightButton = new JButton();
JButton shootLeftButton = new JButton();
JButton shootRightButton = new JButton();
JButton shootDownLeftButton = new JButton();
JButton shootDownButton = new JButton();
JButton shootDownRightButton = new JButton();
```

And, this code (again, there's lots of it) adds the controls:

```
shootLabel.setText("Shoot");
shootLabel.setForeground(Color.YELLOW);
shootLabel.setFont(new Font("Arial", Font.BOLD, 18));
gridConstraints = new GridBagConstraints();
gridConstraints.gridx = 0;
gridConstraints.gridy = 0;
gridConstraints.gridwidth = 3;
shootPanel.add(shootLabel, gridConstraints);

shootUpLeftButton.setIcon(new ImageIcon("UpLeft.jpg"));
shootUpLeftButton.setPreferredSize(new Dimension(30, 30));
gridConstraints = new GridBagConstraints();
gridConstraints.gridx = 0;
gridConstraints.gridy = 1;
shootPanel.add(shootUpLeftButton, gridConstraints);
shootUpLeftButton.addActionListener(new ActionListener()
{
  public void actionPerformed(ActionEvent e)
  {
    shootUpLeftButtonActionPerformed(e);
  }
});
```

```
shootUpButton.setIcon(new ImageIcon("Up.jpg"));
shootUpButton.setPreferredSize(new Dimension(30, 30));
gridConstraints = new GridBagConstraints();
gridConstraints.gridx = 1;
gridConstraints.gridy = 1;
shootPanel.add(shootUpButton, gridConstraints);
shootUpButton.addActionListener(new ActionListener()
{
  public void actionPerformed(ActionEvent e)
  {
    shootUpButtonActionPerformed(e);
  }
});

shootUpRightButton.setIcon(new ImageIcon("UpRight.jpg"));
shootUpRightButton.setPreferredSize(new Dimension(30,
30));
gridConstraints = new GridBagConstraints();
gridConstraints.gridx = 2;
gridConstraints.gridy = 1;
shootPanel.add(shootUpRightButton, gridConstraints);
shootUpRightButton.addActionListener(new ActionListener()
{
  public void actionPerformed(ActionEvent e)
  {
    shootUpRightButtonActionPerformed(e);
  }
});

shootLeftButton.setIcon(new ImageIcon("Left.jpg"));
shootLeftButton.setPreferredSize(new Dimension(30, 30));
gridConstraints = new GridBagConstraints();
gridConstraints.gridx = 0;
gridConstraints.gridy = 2;
shootPanel.add(shootLeftButton, gridConstraints);
shootLeftButton.addActionListener(new ActionListener()
{
  public void actionPerformed(ActionEvent e)
  {
    shootLeftButtonActionPerformed(e);
  }
});
```

```
   shootRightButton.setIcon(new ImageIcon("Right.jpg"));
   shootRightButton.setPreferredSize(new Dimension(30, 30));
   gridConstraints = new GridBagConstraints();
   gridConstraints.gridx = 2;
   gridConstraints.gridy = 2;
   shootPanel.add(shootRightButton, gridConstraints);
   shootRightButton.addActionListener(new ActionListener()
   {
     public void actionPerformed(ActionEvent e)
     {
       shootRightButtonActionPerformed(e);
     }
   });

   shootDownLeftButton.setIcon(new
ImageIcon("DownLeft.jpg"));
   shootDownLeftButton.setPreferredSize(new Dimension(30,
30));
   gridConstraints = new GridBagConstraints();
   gridConstraints.gridx = 0;
   gridConstraints.gridy = 3;
   shootPanel.add(shootDownLeftButton, gridConstraints);
   shootDownLeftButton.addActionListener(new ActionListener()
   {
     public void actionPerformed(ActionEvent e)
     {
       shootDownLeftButtonActionPerformed(e);
     }
   });

   shootDownButton.setIcon(new ImageIcon("Down.jpg"));
   shootDownButton.setPreferredSize(new Dimension(30, 30));
   gridConstraints = new GridBagConstraints();
   gridConstraints.gridx = 1;
   gridConstraints.gridy = 3;
   shootPanel.add(shootDownButton, gridConstraints);
   shootDownButton.addActionListener(new ActionListener()
   {
     public void actionPerformed(ActionEvent e)
     {
       shootDownButtonActionPerformed(e);
     }
   });
```

```
   shootDownRightButton.setIcon(new
ImageIcon("DownRight.jpg"));
   shootDownRightButton.setPreferredSize(new Dimension(30,
30));
   gridConstraints = new GridBagConstraints();
   gridConstraints.gridx = 2;
   gridConstraints.gridy = 3;
   shootPanel.add(shootDownRightButton, gridConstraints);
   shootDownRightButton.addActionListener(new
ActionListener()
   {
     public void actionPerformed(ActionEvent e)
     {
       shootDownRightButtonActionPerformed(e);
     }
   });
```

And, add these eight empty methods:

```
   private void shootUpLeftButtonActionPerformed(ActionEvent
   e)
   {
   }

   private void shootUpButtonActionPerformed(ActionEvent e)
   {
   }

   private void shootUpRightButtonActionPerformed(ActionEvent
   e)
   {
   }

   private void shootLeftButtonActionPerformed(ActionEvent e)
   {
   }

   private void shootRightButtonActionPerformed(ActionEvent
   e)
   {
   }
```

```
private void
shootDownLeftButtonActionPerformed(ActionEvent e)
{
}

private void shootDownButtonActionPerformed(ActionEvent e)
{
}

private void
shootDownRightButtonActionPerformed(ActionEvent e)
{
}
```

Run the project so see:

The shoot buttons appear. The frame design is complete.

We now begin writing code for the **Daniel and the Lions** game. We will write the code in several steps. As a first step, we will write the code that starts the program and establishes its 'initial' state. Then, we look at how to go to the state allowing Daniel to move following clicking of the **Start** button. We then write code to move Daniel (using mouse clicks or keyboard presses), move the lions toward Daniel and shoot prayers at the lions. During the code development process, recognize you may modify a particular procedure several times before arriving at the finished product.

Code Design – Initial State (Instructions)

Any time we start a program, there are certain initializations that must take place. Let's look at the initializations needed in the **Daniel and the Lions** game. When the program first begins, we want to display the game instructions (when **firstTime** is true). We also initialize the difficulty (**difficulty**) and the game status (**gameStatus**). These initializations are in **Daniel** frame constructor.

We declare three variables (**firstTime**, **difficulty** and, **gameStatus**). Do this in the class level declarations area:

```
static boolean firstTime = true;
int difficulty;
String gameStatus;
```

firstTime is declared **static** because it will be needed in the **gamePanel paintComponent** method.

Add this code at the end of the frame constructor:

```
difficulty = 1;
gameStatus = "Initial";
difficultyTextField.setText(String.valueOf(difficulty));
```

As mentioned, we initialize **difficulty** to **1** and the **gameStatus** to "**Initial**".

In this initial state, with **firstTime = true**, we want to display the game instructions. The code to do this is placed in the graphics panel **paintComponent** method. Add the shaded code:

```
public void paintComponent(Graphics g)
{
  Graphics2D g2D = (Graphics2D) g;
  super.paintComponent(g2D);
  if (Daniel.firstTime)
  {
    // draw instructions
    g2D.setFont(new Font("Arial", Font.PLAIN, 18));
    g2D.setPaint(Color.BLACK);
    g2D.drawString("DANIEL AND THE LIONS", 10, 30);
    g2D.drawString("In Daniel 6:16-28, King Darius is 
tricked into putting Daniel into the Lions Den. Daniel 
prays for God's protection", 10, 60);
    g2D.drawString("and God sends His Angel to shut the 
Lion's mouth.  God will protect you if you pray to Him 
today.", 10, 80);
    g2D.drawString("\r\n\r\nSelect Difficulty by pressing 
the left button for Easy and the right button for 
Harder.", 10, 110);
    g2D.drawString("\r\n\r\nClick on the Start Button to 
begin.", 10, 130);
    g2D.drawString("Click on the Stop Button to stop the 
program.", 10, 150);
    g2D.drawString("Use Move buttons (or keypad keys) to 
move Daniel.", 10, 170);
    g2D.drawString("Use Shoot buttons to 'shoot' prayers 
at lions.", 10, 190);
  }
  g2D.dispose();
}
```

The instructions are 'drawn' in the **gamePanel** using the **drawString** method. The positions of each line of text were found using trial and error.

Save and **Run** the program to see:

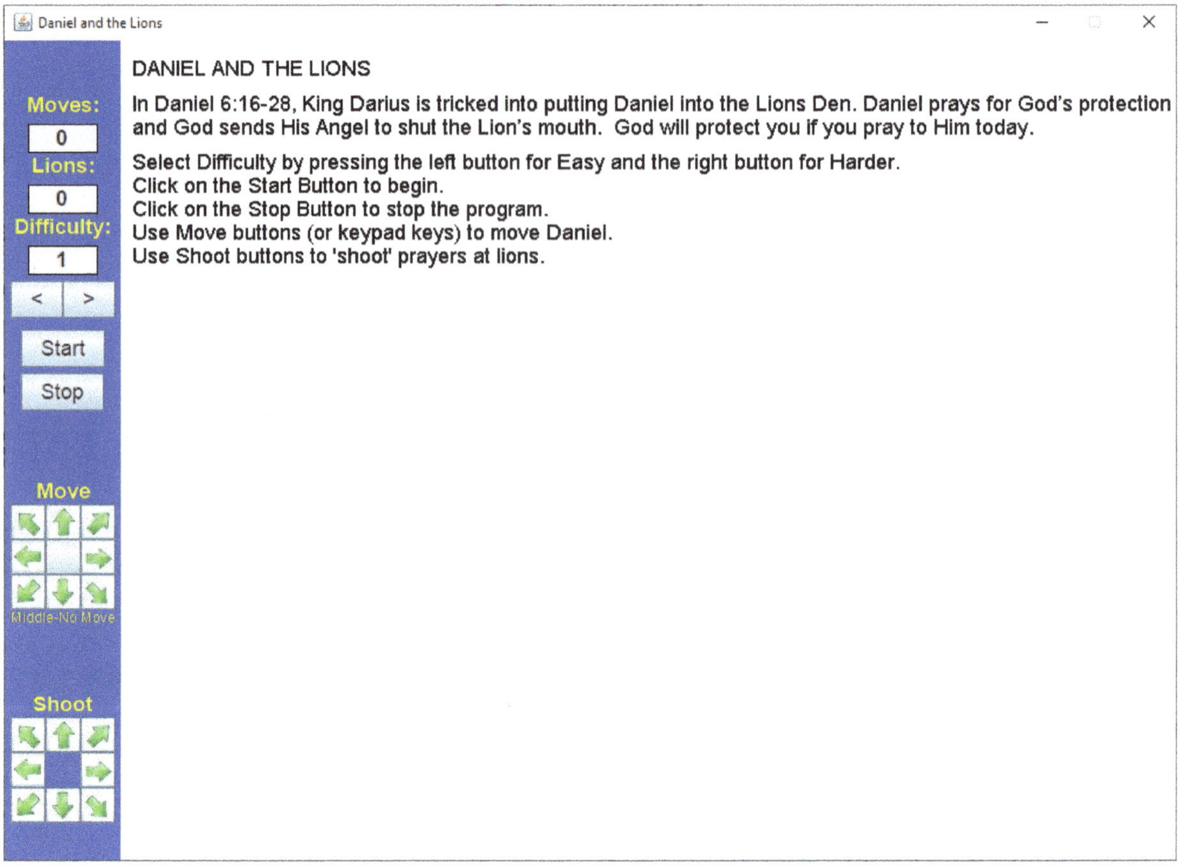

Code Design – Select Difficulty

The **difficulty** variable is used to determine how many lions are put on the game grid (the higher the difficulty, the more lions). To change the difficulty, a user clicks on either of the two arrow buttons. The code to do this goes in the **decreaseButtonActionPerformed** and **decreaseButtonActionPerformed** methods:

```
private void decreaseButtonActionPerformed(ActionEvent e)
{
  if (gameStatus.equals("Initial"))
  {
    // decrease difficulty
    difficulty--;
    if (difficulty < 1)
      difficulty = 1;

difficultyTextField.setText(String.valueOf(difficulty));
  }
}

private void increaseButtonActionPerformed(ActionEvent e)
{
  if (gameStatus.equals("Initial"))
  {
    // increase difficulty
    difficulty++;
    if (difficulty > 10)
      difficulty = 10;

difficultyTextField.setText(String.valueOf(difficulty));
  }
}
```

The code is straightforward. The difficulty can only be changed when the game is in "**Initial**" state. If the **<** button is clicked, we decrease the difficulty by one (minimum of 1). If the **>** button is clicked, we increase the difficulty (maximum of 10). The new value for the difficulty is then displayed in **difficultyTextField**.

Save and **Run** the program. Make sure the arrow buttons work – make sure the difficulty is always between 1 and 10. Here's my run where I changed the difficulty to three:

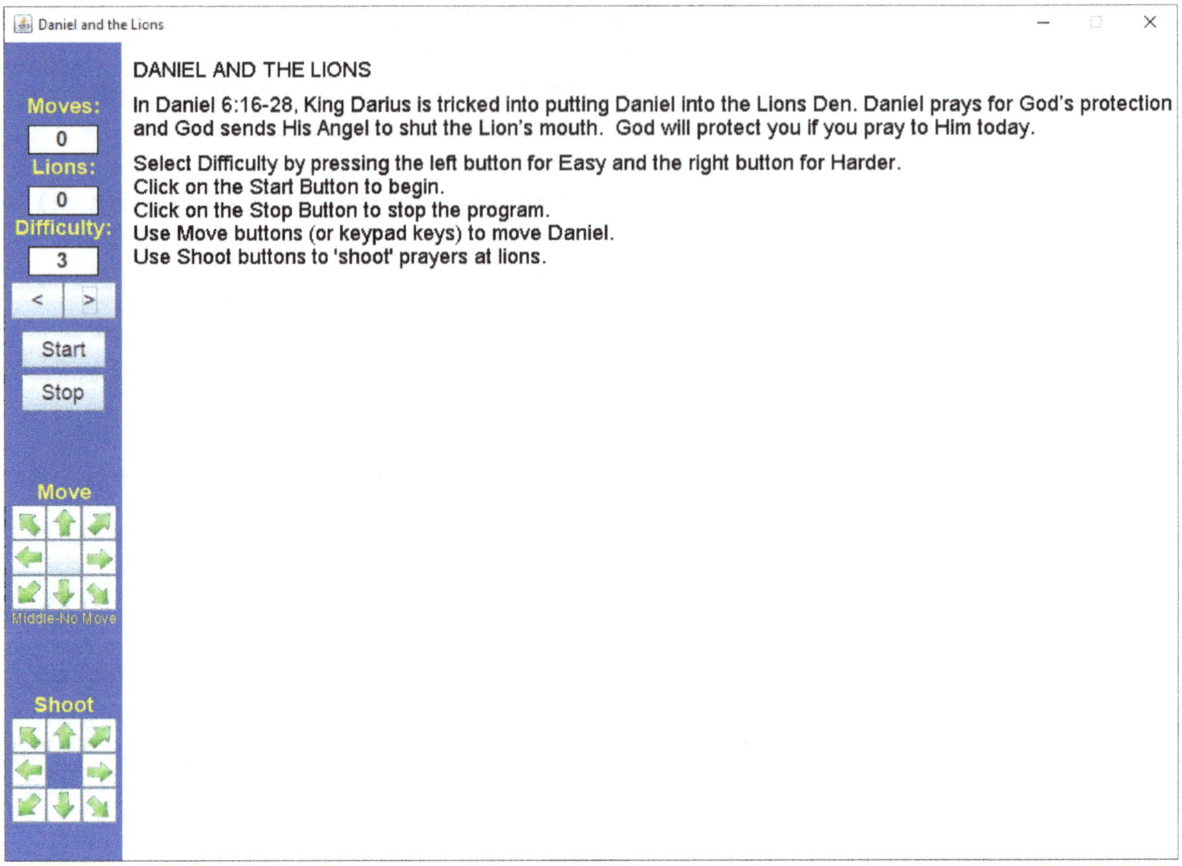

Code Design – Draw Grid

Once the difficulty is set, the next step is to click the **Start** button to allow the game to begin. Hence, we need code to move from the "**Initial**" state to what we'll call "**DanielMove**" state. When the **Start** button is clicked in "**Initial**" state, we need to take the following steps:

- Change **gameStatus** to "**DanielMove**"
- Initialize variables
- Clear game screen
- Draw game grid with rocks
- Randomly place Daniel on the grid
- Randomly place lions on the grid

There is a lot to do here, so we will take it in steps. First, we'll initialize variables and draw the grid.

Several variables are used in game control. **gameOver** is a Boolean variable that tells us if the game has ended – it is initialized at **false**. **moves** (initialized at zero) tells us how many times Daniel has moved. **numberLions** tells us how many lions are placed in the grid (initialized to **difficulty + 5**) and **lionsLeft** tells us how many lions remain in the grid. The game grid has 10 rows and 20 columns (each grid space 40 pixels wide by 50 pixels high). Add these class level declarations:

```
boolean gameOver;
int moves;
static int numberLions;
int lionsLeft;
```

numberLions is prefaced with **static** – it will be needed to draw lions in the **paintComponent** method.

Add this code to the **startButtonActionPerformed** method:

```
private void startButtonActionPerformed(ActionEvent e)
{
  //clicked start
  firstTime = false;
  gameStatus = "DanielMove";
  gameOver = false;
  moves = 0;
  numberLions = difficulty + 5;
  lionsLeft = numberLions;
  movesTextField.setText(String.valueOf(moves));
  lionsTextField.setText(String.valueOf(lionsLeft));
  gamePanel.repaint();
}
```

Once variables are established, a **repaint** of the **gamePanel** will do the drawing. We do that code now.

Add the shaded code to the **gamePanel paintComponent** method:

```
public void paintComponent(Graphics g)
{
  Graphics2D g2D = (Graphics2D) g;
  super.paintComponent(g2D);
  if (Daniel.firstTime)
  {
    // draw instructions
    g2D.setFont(new Font("Arial", Font.PLAIN, 18));
    g2D.setPaint(Color.BLACK);
    g2D.drawString("DANIEL AND THE LIONS", 10, 30);
    g2D.drawString("In Daniel 6:16-28, King Darius is
tricked into putting Daniel into the Lions Den. Daniel
prays for God's protection", 10, 60);
    g2D.drawString("and God sends His Angel to shut the
Lion's mouth.  God will protect you if you pray to Him
today.", 10, 80);
    g2D.drawString("\r\n\r\nSelect Difficulty by pressing
the left button for Easy and the right button for
Harder.", 10, 110);
    g2D.drawString("\r\n\r\nClick on the Start Button to
begin.", 10, 130);
    g2D.drawString("Click on the Stop Button to stop the
program.", 10, 150);
    g2D.drawString("Use Move buttons (or keypad keys) to
move Daniel.", 10, 170);
```

```
    g2D.drawString("Use Shoot buttons to 'shoot' prayers
at lions.", 10, 190);
  }
  else
  {
    Line2D.Double myLine;
    Rectangle2D.Double myRect;
    Ellipse2D.Double myEllipse;
    //  draw grid structure
    myRect = new Rectangle2D.Double(45, 45, 810, 510);
    g2D.setPaint(Color.BLACK);
    g2D.fill(myRect);
    myRect = new Rectangle2D.Double(50, 50, 800, 500);
    g2D.setPaint(Color.WHITE);
    g2D.fill(myRect);
    g2D.setPaint(Color.GRAY);
    for (int i = 0; i < 9; i++)
    {
      myLine = new Line2D.Double(50, 50 * i + 100, 850, 50
* i + 100);
      g2D.draw(myLine);
    }
    for (int i = 0; i < 19; i++)
    {
      myLine = new Line2D.Double(50 + 40 * i + 40, 50, 50
+ 40 * i + 40, 550);
      g2D.draw(myLine);
    }
  }
  g2D.dispose();
}
```

You should be able to identify each step in this new code. The grid structure is established as a white rectangle with a black border. Horizontal lines are drawn every 50 pixels and vertical lines are drawn every 40 pixels.

Save and **Run** the program. Choose a difficulty (I picked 3). Click **Start** and you should see:

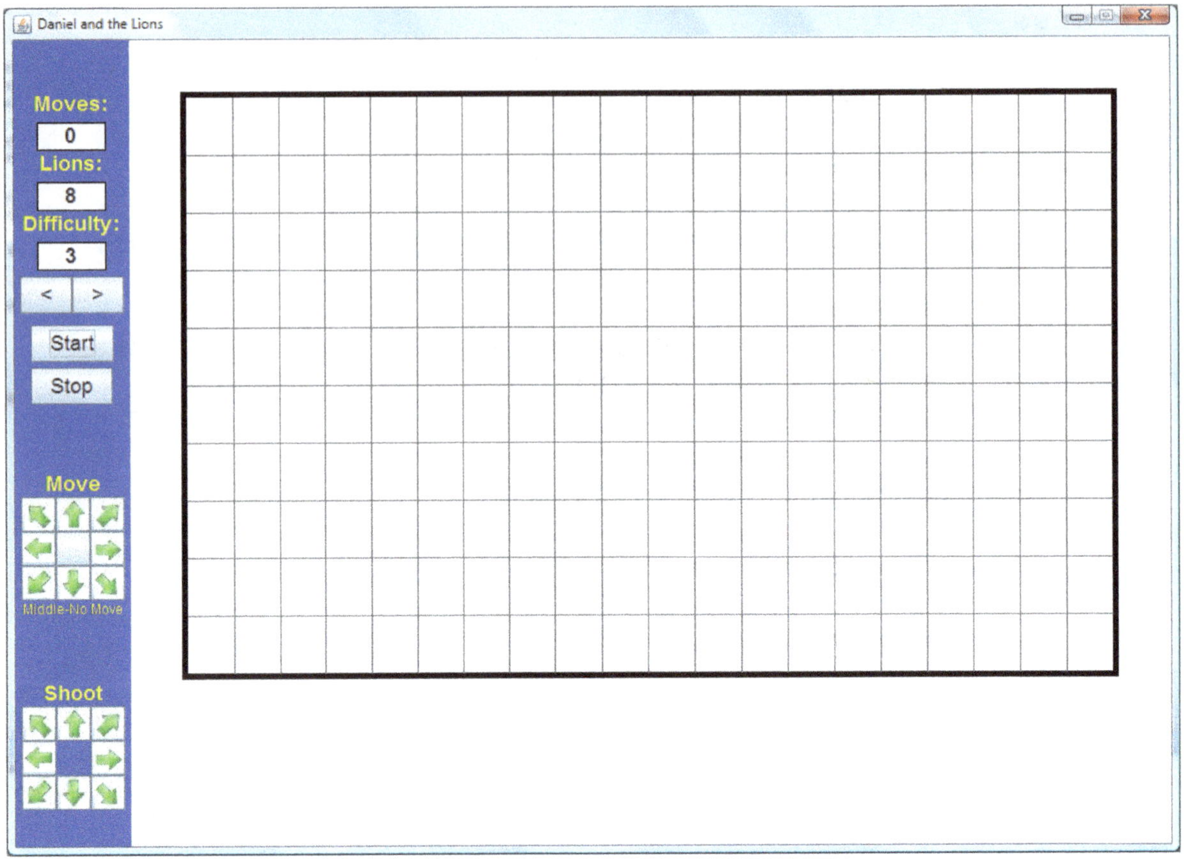

Notice the displayed values for **Moves** and **Lions**. Notice the nice grid structure.

Code Design –Position Rocks

Four rocks are placed in the grid. Daniel can hide behind these rocks if needed for protection from the lions. Elliptical shapes are used for each of the rocks.

Recall the grid has 10 rows (numbered from 0 to 9) and 20 columns (numbered from 0 to 19). We use a two-dimensional array **A** to keep track of what is in each location within the grid. The first index in the array is the **row**, the second is the **column**, so the value at:

```
A[row][column]
```

tells us what is in that location. We use this system:

```
A[row][column] = 0 Nothing is there
A[row][column] = 1 Rock is there
A[row][column] = 2 Lion is there
A[row][column] = 3 Daniel is there
```

The rocks are in fixed locations: row 3, column 4 and column 15 and row 6, column 4 and column 15.

Add this **static** declaration to the class level declarations area to define the **A** array:

```
static int[][] A = new int[10][20];
```

Add the shaded code to the **startButtonActionPerformed** method to initialize the **A** array to all zeroes, then position the four rocks on the grid:

```
private void startButtonActionPerformed(ActionEvent e)
{
  //clicked start
  firstTime = false;
  gameStatus = "DanielMove";
  gameOver = false;
  moves = 0;
  numberLions = difficulty + 5;
  lionsLeft = numberLions;
  movesTextField.setText(String.valueOf(moves));
  lionsTextField.setText(String.valueOf(lionsLeft));
  for (int i = 0; i < 9; i++)
    for (int j = 0; j < 19; j++)
      A[i][j] = 0;
  //  Place rocks
  // A array (0- nothing, 1-rock, 2-lion, 3-Daniel)
  A[3][4] = 1;
  A[3][15] = 1;
  A[6][4] = 1;
  A[6][15] = 1;
  gamePanel.repaint();
}
```

Add the shaded code to the game panel's **paintComponent** method to draw the rocks:

```
public void paintComponent(Graphics g)
{
  Graphics2D g2D = (Graphics2D) g;
  super.paintComponent(g2D);
  if (Daniel.firstTime)
  {
    // draw instructions
    g2D.setFont(new Font("Arial", Font.PLAIN, 18));
    g2D.setPaint(Color.BLACK);
    g2D.drawString("DANIEL AND THE LIONS", 10, 30);
    g2D.drawString("In Daniel 6:16-28, King Darius is
tricked into putting Daniel into the Lions Den. Daniel
prays for God's protection", 10, 60);
    g2D.drawString("and God sends His Angel to shut the
Lion's mouth.  God will protect you if you pray to Him
today.", 10, 80);
    g2D.drawString("\r\n\r\nSelect Difficulty by pressing
the left button for Easy and the right button for
Harder.", 10, 110);
    g2D.drawString("\r\n\r\nClick on the Start Button to
begin.", 10, 130);
    g2D.drawString("Click on the Stop Button to stop the
program.", 10, 150);
    g2D.drawString("Use Move buttons (or keypad keys) to
move Daniel.", 10, 170);
    g2D.drawString("Use Shoot buttons to 'shoot' prayers
at lions.", 10, 190);
  }
  else
  {
    Line2D.Double myLine;
    Rectangle2D.Double myRect;
    Ellipse2D.Double myEllipse;
    //  draw grid structure
    myRect = new Rectangle2D.Double(45, 45, 810, 510);
    g2D.setPaint(Color.BLACK);
    g2D.fill(myRect);
    myRect = new Rectangle2D.Double(50, 50, 800, 500);
    g2D.setPaint(Color.WHITE);
    g2D.fill(myRect);
    g2D.setPaint(Color.GRAY);
    for (int i = 0; i < 9; i++)
    {
```

```
        myLine = new Line2D.Double(50, 50 * i + 100, 850, 50
  * i + 100);
        g2D.draw(myLine);
      }
      for (int i = 0; i < 19; i++)
      {
        myLine = new Line2D.Double(50 + 40 * i + 40, 50, 50
  + 40 * i + 40, 550);
        g2D.draw(myLine);
      }
      // draw rocks
      g2D.setPaint(Color.DARK_GRAY);
      myEllipse = new Ellipse2D.Double(215, 205, 30, 40);
      g2D.fill(myEllipse);
      myEllipse = new Ellipse2D.Double(655, 205, 30, 40);
      g2D.fill(myEllipse);
      myEllipse = new Ellipse2D.Double(215, 355, 30, 40);
      g2D.fill(myEllipse);
      myEllipse = new Ellipse2D.Double(655, 355, 30, 40);
      g2D.fill(myEllipse);
    }
    g2D.dispose();
  }
```

The (x, y) coordinates used to create the ellipses were found by knowing where the grid lines are located (by looking at the code that draws these lines). For example, the first rock is at row 3, column 4. The top left corner at that position is (210, 200).

Save and **Run** the program. Click **Start**. The rocks will appear:

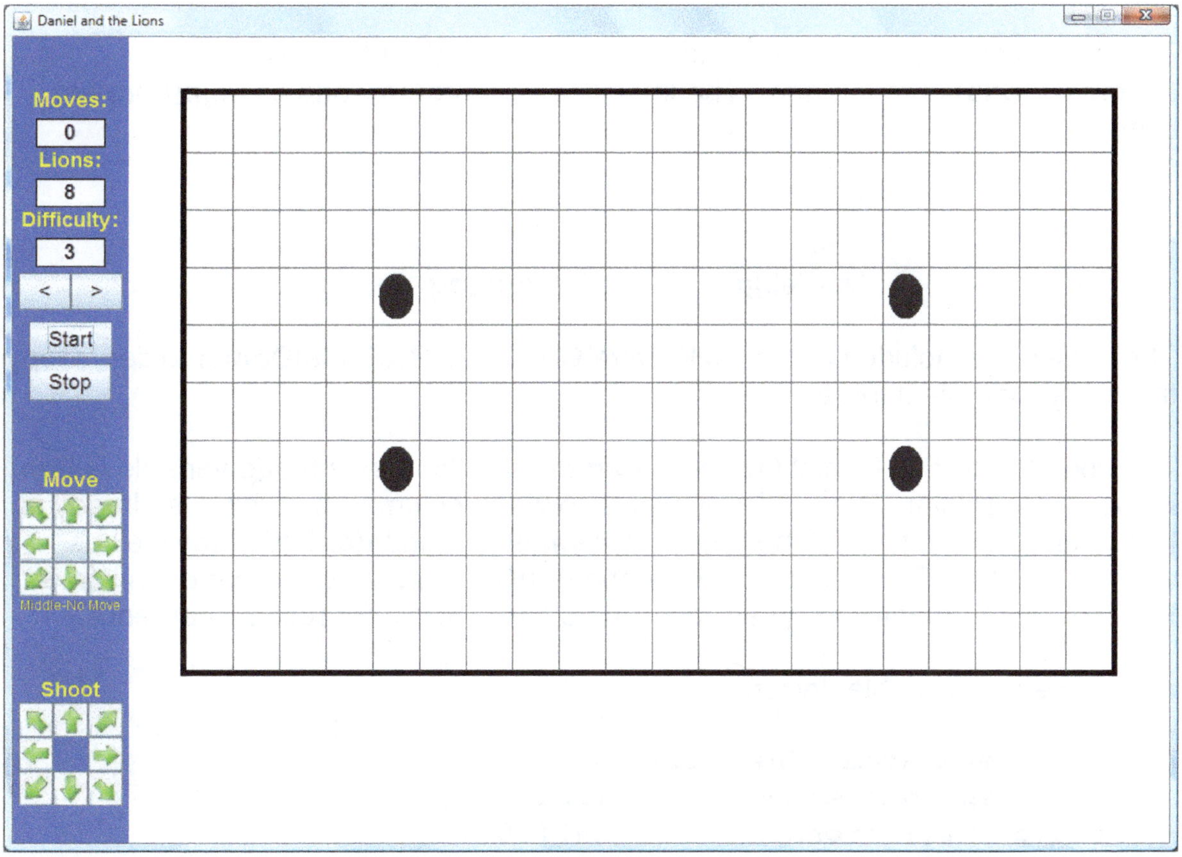

Code Design – Position Daniel and Lions

The last initialization step is to randomly place Daniel and the lions (**numberLions**) onto the grid. The image files **Daniel.jpg** and **Lion.jpg** are are used:

Daniel.jpg

Lion.jpg

These files are included in the **\CBGJava\CBGJava Projects\Daniel** folder. Copy them to your project folder.

The code to position Daniel (image is **daniel**) and the lions (image variable is **lion**) in the grid is similar. We randomly pick a row and column. If nothing is already at that position, put it there. The variables **danielRow** and **danielColumn** tell us where Daniel is. The arrays **lionRow** and **lionColumn** tell us where each lion is. Positioning coordinates (x, y) are determined like we did for rock placement.

Add these new variable declarations:

```
Random myRandom = new Random();
static int danielRow, danielColumn;
static int[] lionRow = new int[15];
static int[] lionColumn = new int[15];
static Image daniel = new
ImageIcon("Daniel.jpg").getImage();
static Image lion = new ImageIcon("Lion.jpg").getImage();
```

myRandom is needed for random number generation.

Add the shaded code to the **startButtonActionPerformed** method:

```
private void startButtonActionPerformed(ActionEvent e)
{
  //clicked start
firstTime = false;
  gameStatus = "DanielMove";
  gameOver = false;
  moves = 0;
  numberLions = difficulty + 5;
  lionsLeft = numberLions;
  movesTextField.setText(String.valueOf(moves));
  lionsTextField.setText(String.valueOf(lionsLeft));
  for (int i = 0; i < 9; i++)
  for (int j = 0; j < 19; j++)
```

```
    A[i][j] = 0;
    //  Place rocks
    // A array (0- nothing, 1-rock, 2-lion, 3-Daniel)
    A[3][4] = 1;
    A[3][15] = 1;
    A[6][4] = 1;
    A[6][15] = 1;
    // Place Daniel
    int row, column;
    do
    {
      row = myRandom.nextInt(10);
      column = myRandom.nextInt(20);
    }
    while (A[row][column] != 0);
    A[row][column] = 3;
    danielRow = row;
    danielColumn = column;
    // Place lions
    for (int i = 0; i < numberLions; i++)
    {
      do
      {
        row = myRandom.nextInt(10);
        column = myRandom.nextInt(20);
      }
      while (A[row][column] != 0);
      A[row][column] = 2;
  lionRow[i] = row;
      lionColumn[i] = column;
    }
    gamePanel.repaint();
  }
```

The code above sets up the initial values for the **A** array. It is used in the **gamePanel paintComponent** method to draw the lions and Daniel. Make the shaded changes to that method:

```
public void paintComponent(Graphics g)
{
  Graphics2D g2D = (Graphics2D) g;
  super.paintComponent(g2D);
  if (Daniel.firstTime)
  {
    // draw instructions
    g2D.setFont(new Font("Arial", Font.PLAIN, 18));
    g2D.setPaint(Color.BLACK);
    g2D.drawString("DANIEL AND THE LIONS", 10, 30);
    g2D.drawString("In Daniel 6:16-28, King Darius is
tricked into putting Daniel into the Lions Den. Daniel
prays for God's protection", 10, 60);
    g2D.drawString("and God sends His Angel to shut the
Lion's mouth.  God will protect you if you pray to Him
today.", 10, 80);
    g2D.drawString("\r\n\r\nSelect Difficulty by pressing
the left button for Easy and the right button for
Harder.", 10, 110);
    g2D.drawString("\r\n\r\nClick on the Start Button to
begin.", 10, 130);
    g2D.drawString("Click on the Stop Button to stop the
program.", 10, 150);
    g2D.drawString("Use Move buttons (or keypad keys) to
move Daniel.", 10, 170);
    g2D.drawString("Use Shoot buttons to 'shoot' prayers
at lions.", 10, 190);
  }
  else
  {
    Line2D.Double myLine;
    Rectangle2D.Double myRect;
    Ellipse2D.Double myEllipse;
    //  draw grid structure
    myRect = new Rectangle2D.Double(45, 45, 810, 510);
    g2D.setPaint(Color.BLACK);
    g2D.fill(myRect);
    myRect = new Rectangle2D.Double(50, 50, 800, 500);
    g2D.setPaint(Color.WHITE);
    g2D.fill(myRect);
    g2D.setPaint(Color.GRAY);
    for (int i = 0; i < 9; i++)
    {
```

```
        myLine = new Line2D.Double(50, 50 * i + 100, 850, 50
  * i + 100);
        g2D.draw(myLine);
      }
      for (int i = 0; i < 19; i++)
      {
  myLine = new Line2D.Double(50 + 40 * i + 40, 50, 50 + 40 *
  i + 40, 550);
        g2D.draw(myLine);
      }
      // draw rocks
      g2D.setPaint(Color.DARK_GRAY);
      myEllipse = new Ellipse2D.Double(215, 205, 30, 40);
      g2D.fill(myEllipse);
      myEllipse = new Ellipse2D.Double(655, 205, 30, 40);
      g2D.fill(myEllipse);
      myEllipse = new Ellipse2D.Double(215, 355, 30, 40);
      g2D.fill(myEllipse);
      myEllipse = new Ellipse2D.Double(655, 355, 30, 40);
      g2D.fill(myEllipse);
      // draw daniel and lions
      if (Daniel.A[Daniel.danielRow][Daniel.danielColumn] !=
  0)
        g2D.drawImage(Daniel.daniel, Daniel.danielColumn *
  40 + 55, Daniel.danielRow * 50 + 55, this);
      // Place lions
      for (int i = 0; i < Daniel.numberLions; i++)
      {
        if
  (Daniel.A[Daniel.lionRow[i]][Daniel.lionColumn[i]] == 2)
          g2D.drawImage(Daniel.lion, Daniel.lionColumn[i] *
  40 + 55, Daniel.lionRow[i] * 50 + 55, this);
      }
    }
    g2D.dispose();
  }
```

This method is now complete.

Save and **Run** the program. Set the **Difficulty** (I used 3). Click **Start**. The complete initialized game grid is now seen:

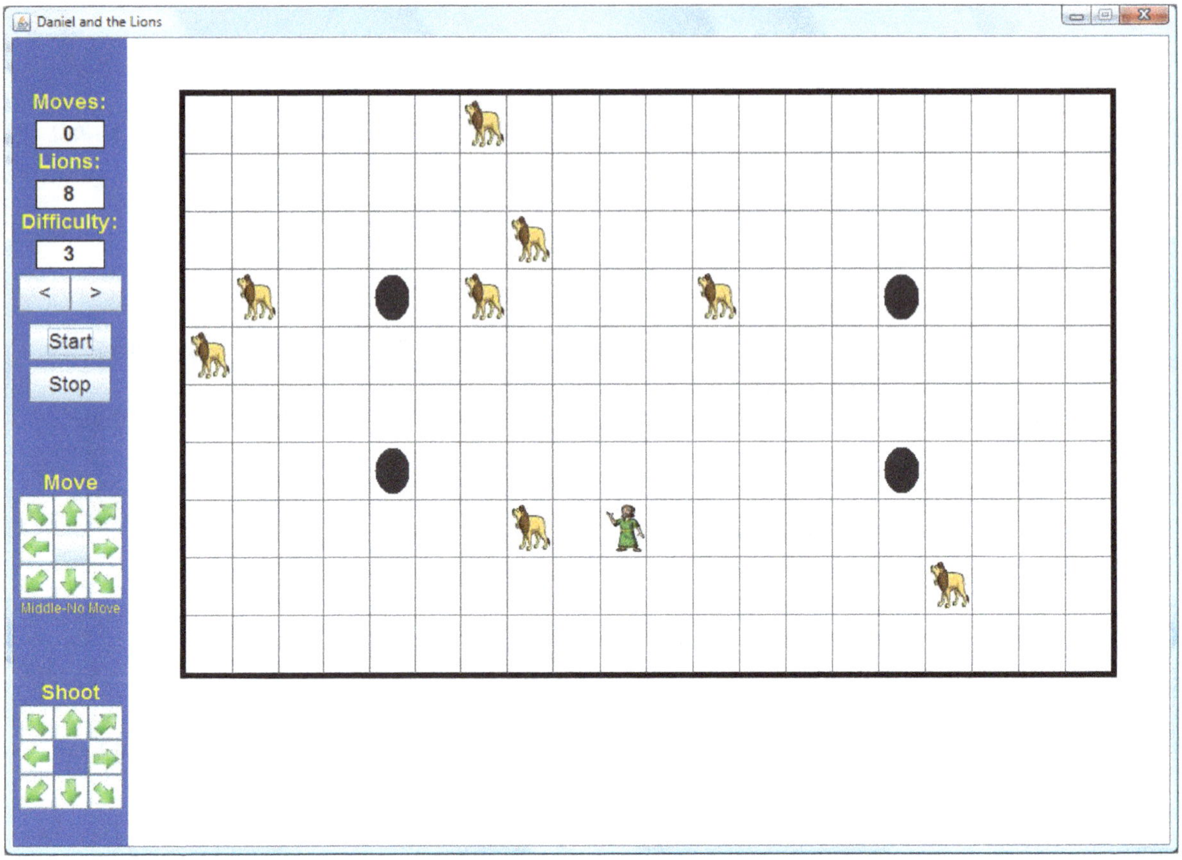

Since **Difficulty** is 3, there are 8 lions. The next step is to either move Daniel or shoot a prayer at a lion. We write code to do these steps soon. But first, let's take care of one last thing you can do while in "**Initial**" state – stop the program.

Code Design – Stop the Program

One last thing you can do while the game is in "**Initial**" state is to click on the **Stop** button. This will stop the program. The code here is simple. Add these lines to the **stopButtonActionPerformred** method:

```
private void stopButtonActionPerformed(ActionEvent e)
{
  if (gameStatus.equals("Initial"))
    // clicked stop
    System.exit(0);
}
```

As desired, if the **Stop** button is clicked, the program ends.

Save and **Run** the program. Make sure the **Stop** button works. This completes the code for moving from "**Initial**" game status to '**DanielMove**' status. Now, let's look at code to move Daniel around the grid.

Code Design – Moving Daniel

Once the game begins, you move Daniel around the grid so he can begin 'shooting' prayers at the lions. Daniel can be moved using two different methods. First, he can be moved by using the 'buttons' under the **Move** heading on the game screen:

Clicking on any of the arrow buttons will move Daniel one grid square in the corresponding direction. Clicking the middle button will leave Daniel at his current position.

The code to detect clicking on any of these buttons is placed in the corresponding button's **ActionPerformed** method. Once a move is made, we need to check to see if it is a valid move. Invalid moves include moving off the top, bottom, left or right side of the grid, moving onto a rock or moving into a lion. If an invalid move is attempted, it is not allowed, and, if a move is into a lion, the game ends! Let's do the code.

We use a method **CheckMove** (will be presented in a bit) to see if a move is valid. **CheckMove** requires two pieces of information: **deltaRow** and **deltaColumn**. **deltaRow** tells us how many rows to move Daniel – it will be either +1 (down one row), 0 (no row change), or -1 (up one row). Similarly, **deltaColumn** tells us how many columns to move Daniel - it will be either +1 (right one column), 0 (no column change), or -1 (left one column). You should be able to see that clicking any arrow button in the top row yields **deltaRow** = - 1, any button in the middle row yields **deltaRow** = 0 and any button in the bottom row yields **deltaRow** = +1. Likewise, clicking any button in the left column gives **deltaColumn** = - 1, any button in the middle column gives **deltaColumn** = 0 and any button in the right column gives **deltaColumn** = +1. Using these, we write the nine button **ActionPerformed** methods:

```
private void moveUpLeftButtonActionPerformed(ActionEvent
e)
{
  CheckMove(-1, -1);
}
```

```
private void moveUpButtonActionPerformed(ActionEvent e)
{
  CheckMove(-1, 0);
}

private void moveUpRightButtonActionPerformed(ActionEvent
e)
{
  CheckMove(-1, 1);
}

private void moveLeftButtonActionPerformed(ActionEvent e)
{
  CheckMove(0, -1);
}

private void noMoveButtonActionPerformed(ActionEvent e)
{
  CheckMove(0, 0);
}

private void moveRightButtonActionPerformed(ActionEvent e)
{
  CheckMove(0, 1);
}

private void moveDownLeftButtonActionPerformed(ActionEvent
e)
{
  CheckMove(1, -1);
}

private void moveDownButtonActionPerformed(ActionEvent e)
{
  CheckMove(1, 0);
}

private void
moveDownRightButtonActionPerformed(ActionEvent e)
{
  CheckMove(1, 1);
}
```

In each procedure, **CheckMove** is called with the appropriate values for **deltaRow** (the first number) and **deltaColumn** (the second number). Now, let's add **CheckMove**.

Add this method to your program:

```
private void CheckMove(int deltaRow, int deltaColumn)
{
  int newRow, newColumn;
  boolean moveOkay;
  moves++;
  // check if move is okay
  newRow = danielRow + deltaRow;
  newColumn = danielColumn + deltaColumn;
  moveOkay = true;
  if (newRow < 0 || newRow > 9 || newColumn < 0 ||
newColumn > 19)
    // off grid
    moveOkay = false;
  else if (A[newRow][newColumn] == 1)
    //moving to rock
    moveOkay = false;
  else if (A[newRow][newColumn] == 2)
  {
    //moving to lion
    moveOkay = false;
    gameOver = true;
    //remove Daniel
    A[danielRow][danielColumn] = 0;
  }
  if (moveOkay)
  {
    // move to new location
    A[danielRow][danielColumn] = 0;
    danielRow = newRow;
    danielColumn = newColumn;
    A[danielRow][danielColumn] = 3;
  }
  UpdateGame();
  gamePanel.repaint();
}
```

We increment **moves** and set new values for Daniel's row and column (**newRow** and **newColumn**). We then check the validity of the move. If Daniel moves off the grid, onto a rock, or into a lion, we set **moveOkay** to **false**. If Daniel moves into a lion, we set **gameOver** to **true** and remove Daniel from the grid. If we have a valid move, Daniel is moved to his new location from his old location.

Note one of the last lines in **CheckMove** is a call to another method **UpdateGame**. This method is used to change the game status after Daniel moves or after Daniel shoots a prayer (that code is added later). For now, **CheckMove** just updates the number of moves and number of lions. Add this method to your code:

```
private void UpdateGame()
{
  movesTextField.setText(String.valueOf(moves));
  lionsTextField.setText(String.valueOf(lionsLeft));
}
```

Save and **Run** the program. Choose a difficulty (I picked 3). Click **Start**. Here's what I see:

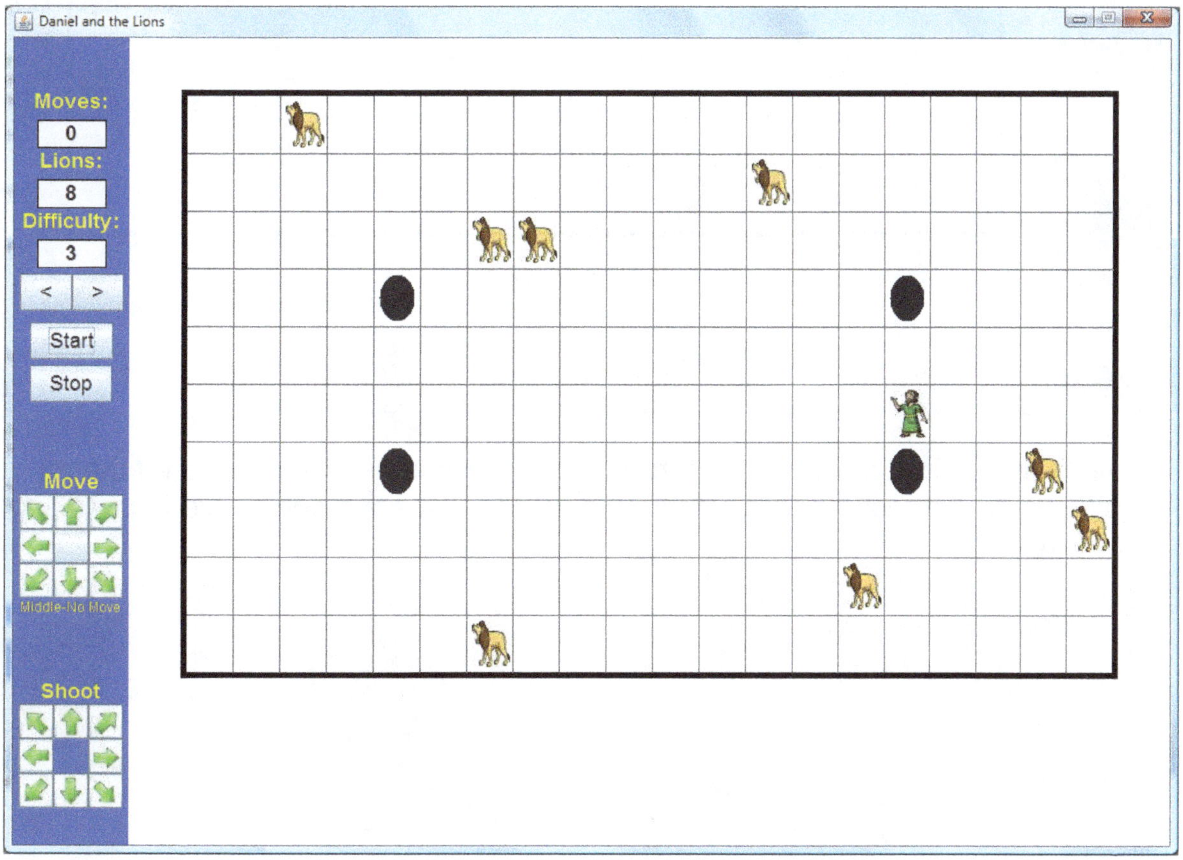

Daniel's in the middle right area (your Daniel will be at a different random location).

If I click the left move arrow, he moves one column to the right (**deltaRow** = 0, **deltaColumn** = -1):

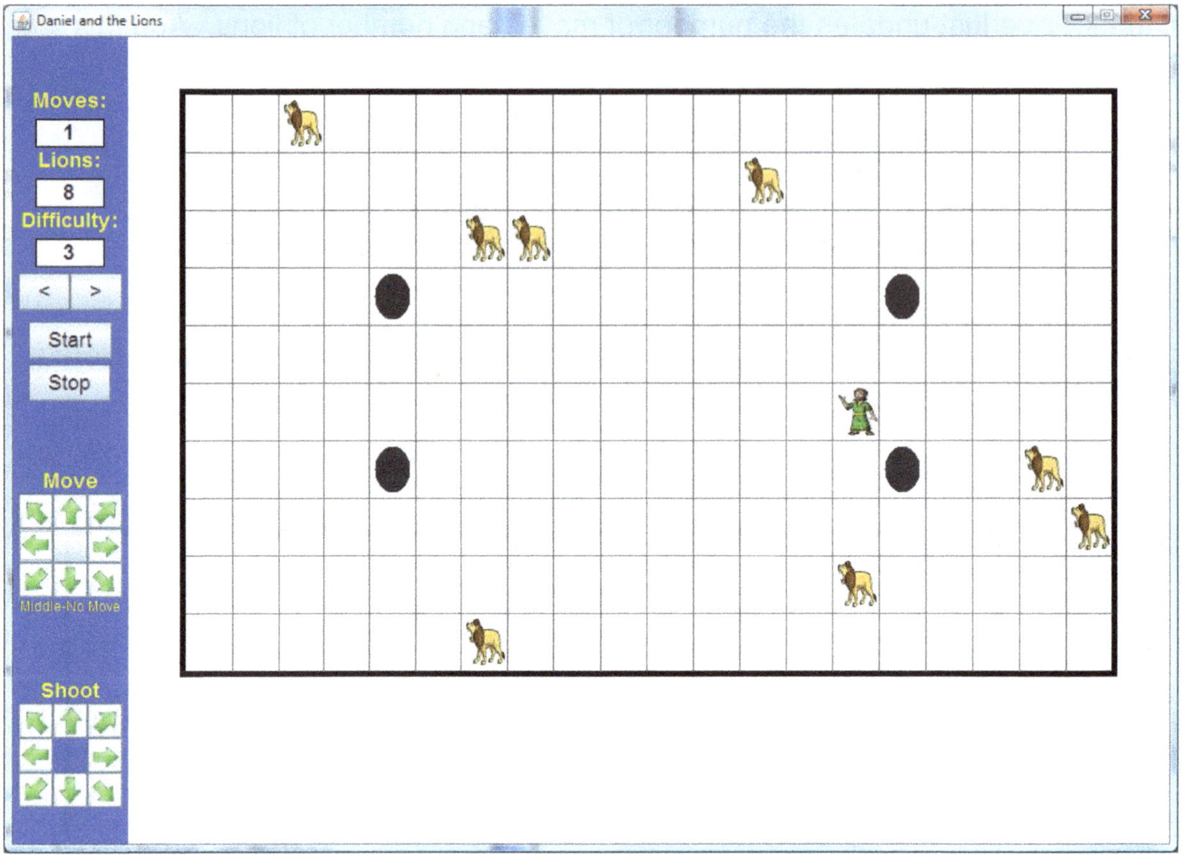

Try all the **Move** buttons to make sure they work properly. Try moving off the grid. Try moving onto a rock. Stay away from lions for now – we don't have logic to end a game yet.

When we started this section, we said there were two ways to move Daniel. Let's write code for the second method – using the numeric keypad on your keyboard. Here's a numeric keypad:

Notice the 9 number keys line up just like the **Move** buttons on the game screen. Many times, users prefer using the keyboard to the mouse. We'll add code so the 7, 8, and 9 keys work like the top row of the move buttons, the 4, 5, and 6 keys work like the middle row and the 1, 2, and 3 keys work like the bottom row.

We want to detect key presses when the game panel has focus. A few steps are needed to accomplish this. First, add this code in the frame constructor after the code that adds **gamePanel** to the frame:

```
gamePanel.addKeyListener(new KeyAdapter()
{
  public void keyPressed(KeyEvent e)
  {
    moveKeyPressed(e);
  }
});
```

With this, when a key is pressed, the event method **moveKeyPressed** is called.

To detect these key presses, we must make sure **gamePanel** always has focus during game play. To do this, we need this line in two places:

```
gamePanel.requestFocus();
```

First, place it at the end of **startButtonActionPerformed** method – this insures once a game starts, the panel has focus. Also, place it at the end of the **CheckMove** method, so after every move, the panel has focus.

Finally, the code in the **moveKeyPressed** method just replicates what we use for clicking on the corresponding arrow key. Add this method:

```
private void moveKeyPressed(KeyEvent e)
{
  int k = e.getKeyCode();
  if (k == e.VK_NUMPAD7)
    CheckMove(-1, -1);
  else if (k == e.VK_NUMPAD8)
    CheckMove(-1, -0);
  else if (k == e.VK_NUMPAD9)
      CheckMove(-1, 1);
  else if (k == e.VK_NUMPAD4)
      CheckMove(0, -1);
  else if (k == e.VK_NUMPAD5)
      CheckMove(0, 0);
  else if (k == e.VK_NUMPAD6)
      CheckMove(0, 1);
  else if (k == e.VK_NUMPAD1)
      CheckMove(1, -1);
  else if (k == e.VK_NUMPAD2)
      CheckMove(1, 0);
  else if (k == e.VK_NUMPAD3)
      CheckMove(1, 1);
}
```

Here, based on whatever key is pressed, the correct values for **deltaRow** and **deltaColumn** are set and **CheckMove** is called.

Save and **Run** the program again. Click **Start**. Make sure you can move Daniel both by clicking the move buttons and using the numeric keypad (**NumLock** must be selected to use this option). Again, be careful not to move into a lion – there is no game ending logic. We'll fix that now.

Code Design – Moving Lions

Once Daniel makes a move, all the lions also make a move – closer to Daniel! If Daniel and a lion meet, the game ends. We put this basic logic in **UpdateGame** method. Add the shaded framework:

```
private void UpdateGame()
{
  movesTextField.setText(String.valueOf(moves));
  lionsTextField.setText(String.valueOf(lionsLeft));
  if (!gameOver)
  {
    // move lions
  }
  if (gameOver)
  {
    // game is over
  }
}
```

If **gameOver** is **false**, we move the lions. If **gameOver** is **true**, we end the game. Let's add the code for both options..

For now, we'll program the game over logic. When the game ends, we change **gameStatus** to "**Initial**". If there are lions remaining (**lionsLeft > 0**), Daniel has met a lion. If no lions remain, Daniel has dispatched all the lions with prayers. This logic is reflected in the shaded code in **UpdateGame**:

```
private void UpdateGame()
{
  movesTextField.setText(String.valueOf(moves));
  lionsTextField.setText(String.valueOf(lionsLeft));
  if (!gameOver)
  {
    // move lions
  }
  if (gameOver)
  {
    // game is over
    gameStatus = "Initial";
    if (lionsLeft > 0)
    {
      JOptionPane.showConfirmDialog(null, "Daniel met a
lion but God shut the mouth of the lion at the last
minute\r\nand King Darius released Daniel from the Lion's
Den.", "Game Over", JOptionPane.DEFAULT_OPTION,
JOptionPane.PLAIN_MESSAGE);
      for (int i = 0; i < numberLions; i++)
        // clear all the lions
        A[lionRow[i]][lionColumn[i]] = 0;
    }
    else
    {
      JOptionPane.showConfirmDialog(null, "Daniel
dispatched " + numberLions + " lions in " + moves + "
moves.", "Game Over", JOptionPane.DEFAULT_OPTION,
JOptionPane.PLAIN_MESSAGE);
   A[danielRow][danielColumn] = 0;
    }
    gamePanel.repaint();
  }
}
```

Save and **Run** the program. Click **Start**. Move Daniel around until he meets a lion. You should see this message:

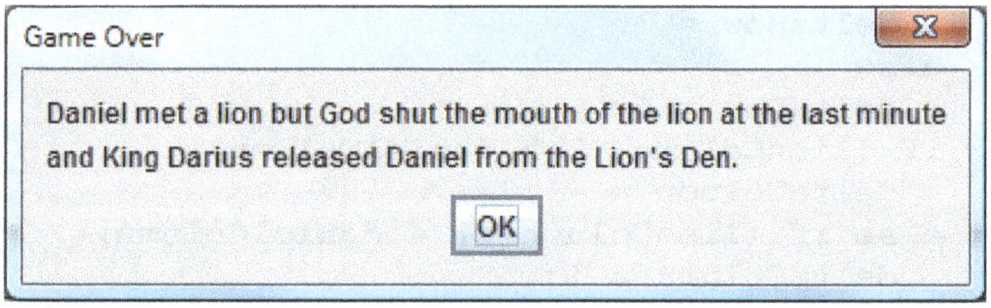

You will see a different message if Daniel dispatches all the lions. Before this can happen, though, we need code to move the lions, then code to shoot the prayers.

When the lions move, the game is switched to "**LionsMove**" status. The goal is move each lion one grid square closer to Daniel. So, for each lion remaining, the steps taken are:

- If Daniel is above lion, move lion up one grid square. If Daniel is below lion, move lion down one grid square. If Daniel and lion are in same row, do not move lion vertically.
- If Daniel is to left of lion, move lion left one grid square. If Daniel is to right of lion, move lion righ one grid square. If Daniel and lion are in same column, do not move lion horizontally.
- Lion cannot move off of grid.
- Lion cannot move into rock or another lion.
- If lion moves into Daniel, the game ends.
- Once move is complete, change **gameStatus** to "**DanielMove**"

The code that implements these steps is placed in the top part of the **UpdateGame** method. The code is shaded:

```
private void UpdateGame()
{
  int newRow, newColumn;
  int deltaRow, deltaColumn;
  boolean moveOkay;
  movesTextField.setText(String.valueOf(moves));
  lionsTextField.setText(String.valueOf(lionsLeft));
  if (!gameOver)
  {
    // move lions
    gameStatus = "LionsMove";
    for (int i = 0; i < numberLions; i++)
    {
      if (A[lionRow[i]][lionColumn[i]] == 2)
      {
```

```
        if (lionRow[i] > danielRow)
          deltaRow = -1;
        else if (lionRow[i] < danielRow)
          deltaRow = 1;
        else
          deltaRow = 0;
        if (lionColumn[i] > danielColumn)
          deltaColumn = -1;
        else if (lionColumn[i] < danielColumn)
          deltaColumn = 1;
        else
          deltaColumn = 0;
        newRow = lionRow[i] + deltaRow;
        newColumn = lionColumn[i] + deltaColumn;
        moveOkay = true;
        if (newRow < 0 || newRow > 9 || newColumn < 0 ||
newColumn > 19)
          // off grid
          moveOkay = false;
        else if (A[newRow][newColumn] == 1)
          //moving to rock
          moveOkay = false;
        else if (A[newRow][newColumn] == 2)
          //moving to another lion
          moveOkay = false;
        if (moveOkay == true)
        {
          if (A[newRow][newColumn] == 3)
          {
          System.out.println("Daniel");
            // moving to Daniel
            gameOver = true;
            // remove Daniel
            A[danielRow][danielColumn] = 0;
          }
          // move lion
          A[lionRow[i]][lionColumn[i]] = 0;
          lionRow[i] = newRow;
          lionColumn[i] = newColumn;
          A[lionRow[i]][lionColumn[i]] = 2;
        }
      }
    }
    gameStatus = "DanielMove";
    gamePanel.repaint();
  }
  if (gameOver)
```

```
    {
      // game is over
      gameStatus = "Initial";
      if (lionsLeft > 0)
      {
        JOptionPane.showConfirmDialog(null, "Daniel met a
lion but God shut the mouth of the lion at the last
minute\r\nand King Darius released Daniel from the Lion's
Den.", "Game Over", JOptionPane.DEFAULT_OPTION,
JOptionPane.PLAIN_MESSAGE);
        for (int i = 0; i < numberLions; i++)
          // clear all the lions
          A[lionRow[i]][lionColumn[i]] = 0;
      }
      else
      {
        JOptionPane.showConfirmDialog(null, "Daniel
dispatched " + numberLions + " lions in " + moves + "
moves.", "Game Over", JOptionPane.DEFAULT_OPTION,
JOptionPane.PLAIN_MESSAGE);
     A[danielRow][danielColumn] = 0;
      }
      gamePanel.repaint();
    }
  }
```

We declare some new local variables at the top. We cycle through all the lions (**numberLions**) in a **for** loop. If a lion is still on the grid, we determine values for **deltaRow** and **deltaColumn** (how much a lion moves) and the proposed new position (**newRow** and **newColumn**). If it is an acceptable move, the lion is moved by first removing it from its current location, then redrawn at its new location. Notice if the lion moves into Daniel, **gameOver** is set to **true** and Daniel is removed from the grid. This will end the game.

Save and **Run** the program. Choose a **Difficulty** (I used 3). Click **Start**. My game looks like this:

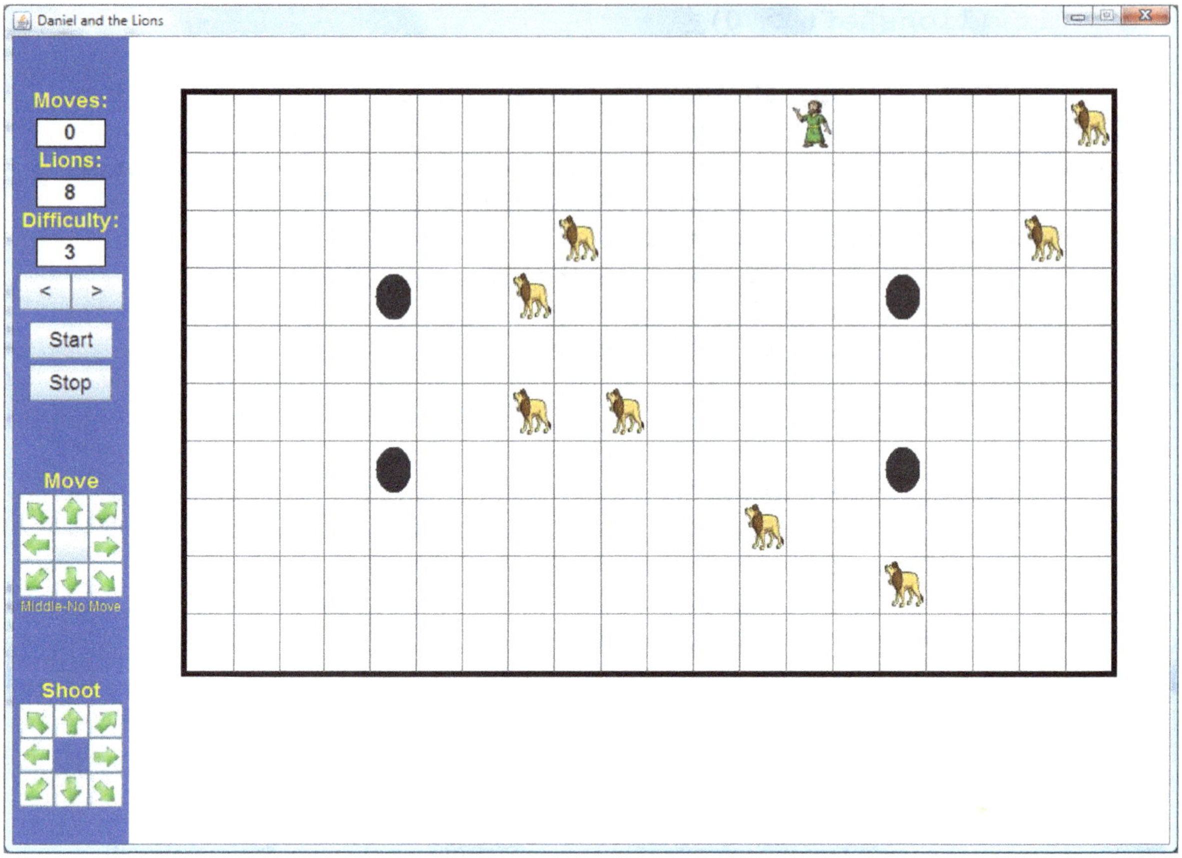

I move Daniel one square to the left.

Following my move, all the lions are closer:

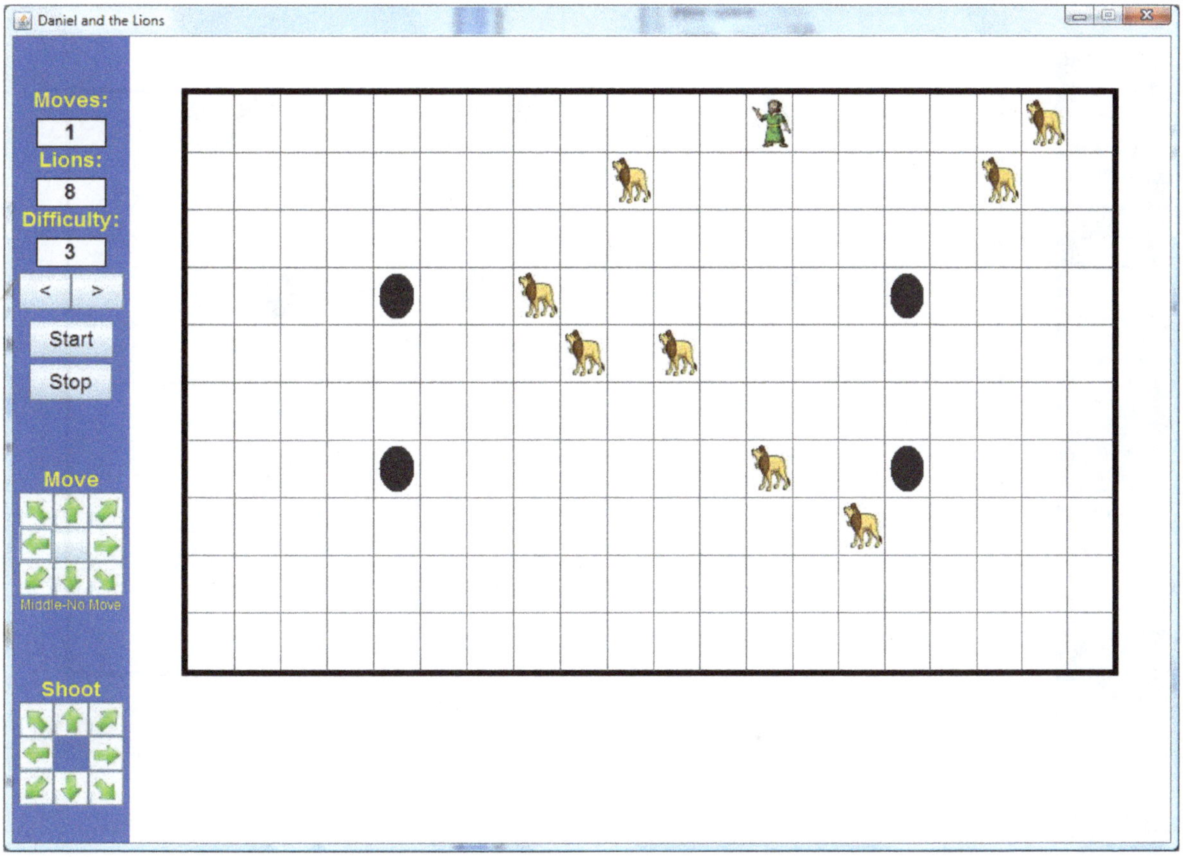

After one more move left, a lion is right next to Daniel:

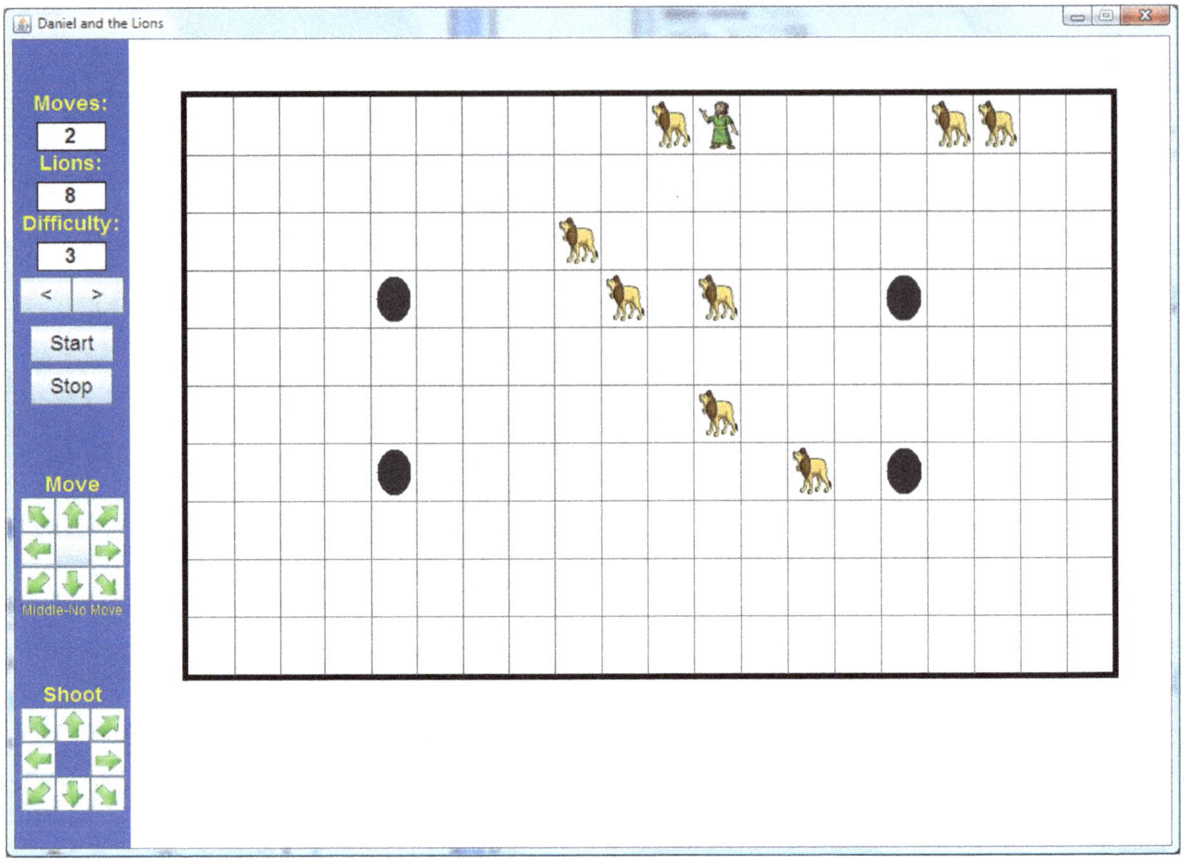

One more move and the ultimate happens:

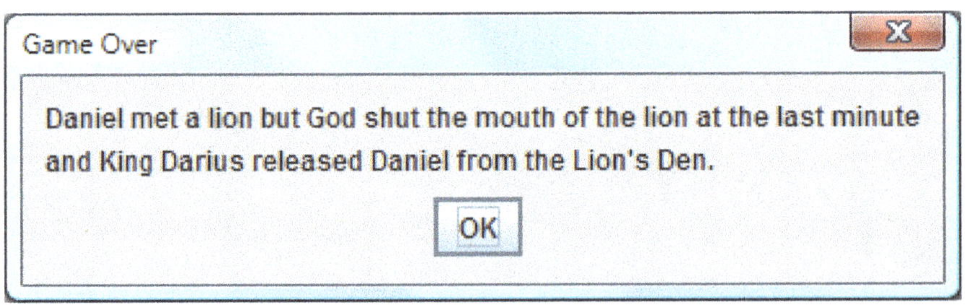

If Daniel could have shot some prayers, the lions wouldn't have gotten to him. Let's add that logic now.

Code Design – Shooting Prayers

To keep the lions away, Daniel can 'shoot' prayers at the lions to remove them from the grid. Prayers are shot by using the eight buttons under the **Shoot** heading on the game screen:

Clicking on any of the arrows will shoot a prayer in the corresponding direction. If the prayer intercepts a lion, it is removed from the grid. The logic used here is nearly identical to that used for the buttons used to move Daniel.

The code to detect clicking on any of these buttons is placed in the corresponding button's **actionPerformed** method. Once a shot is taken, we move in the corresponding direction until we hit a rock, move off the grid or hit a lion. If a lion is hit, that lion is removed. Once all lions are removed, the game ends! Let's do the code.

We use a method **ShootPrayer** (will be presented in a bit). Like the similar **CheckMove** method, **ShootPrayer** requires two pieces of information: **deltaRow** and **deltaColumn**. These tell us the direction of the prayer. **deltaRow** tells us how the vertical direction – it will be either +1 (down), 0 (no vertical motion), or -1 (up). Similarly, **deltaColumn** the horizontal direction - it will be either +1 (right), 0 (no horizontal motion), or -1 (left). You should be able to see that clicking any arrow button in the top row yields **deltaRow** = - 1, either button in the middle row yields **deltaRow** = 0 and any button in the bottom row yields **deltaRow** = +1. Likewise, clicking any button in the left column gives **deltaColumn** = - 1, either button in the middle column gives **deltaColumn** = 0 and any button in the right column gives **deltaColumn** = +1. Using this, we write the eight button **actionPerformed** methods:

```
private void shootUpLeftButtonActionPerformed(ActionEvent
e)
{
  ShootPrayer(-1, -1);
}

private void shootUpButtonActionPerformed(ActionEvent e)
{
  ShootPrayer(-1, 0);
}
```

```
private void shootUpRightButtonActionPerformed(ActionEvent
e)
{
  ShootPrayer(-1, 1);
}

private void shootLeftButtonActionPerformed(ActionEvent e)
{
  ShootPrayer(0, -1);
}

private void shootRightButtonActionPerformed(ActionEvent
e)
{
  ShootPrayer(0, 1);
}

private void
shootDownLeftButtonActionPerformed(ActionEvent e)
{
  ShootPrayer(1, -1);
}

private void shootDownButtonActionPerformed(ActionEvent e)
{
  ShootPrayer(1, 0);
}

private void
shootDownRightButtonActionPerformed(ActionEvent e)
{
  ShootPrayer(1, 1);
}
```

In each procedure, **ShootPrayer** is called with the appropriate values for **deltaRow** (the first number) and **deltaColumn** (the second number). Now, let's add **ShootPrayer**.

Add this method to your program:

```
private void ShootPrayer(int deltaRow, int deltaColumn)
{
  int prayerRow, prayerColumn;
  boolean moveOkay;
  if (deltaRow != 0 || deltaColumn != 0)
    moves++;
  prayerRow = danielRow;
```

```
    prayerColumn = danielColumn;
    do
    {
    //check if move is okay
    prayerRow += deltaRow;
    prayerColumn += deltaColumn;
    moveOkay = true;
    if (prayerRow < 0 || prayerRow > 9 || prayerColumn < 0
|| prayerColumn > 19 || (deltaRow == 0 && deltaColumn ==
0))
      // off grid or center button area clicked
      moveOkay = false;
    else if (A[prayerRow][prayerColumn] == 1)
      //moving to rock
      moveOkay = false;
    int i;
    if (moveOkay)
    {
      if (A[prayerRow][prayerColumn] == 2)
      {
        // dispatched a lion - find that lion
        for (i = 0; i < numberLions; i++)
        {
          if (prayerRow == lionRow[i] && prayerColumn ==
lionColumn[i])
            break;
        }
        moveOkay = false;
        A[prayerRow][prayerColumn] = 0;
        lionRow[i] = 0;
        lionColumn[i] = 0;
        lionsLeft -= 1;
        if (lionsLeft == 0)
          gameOver = true;
      }
    }
    }
    while (moveOkay);
    UpdateGame();
}
```

Though long, the code is fairly easy to follow. We initialize **prayerRow** and **prayerColumn** to Daniel's position (where the prayer starts). From that point on, we change **prayerRow** and **prayerColumn** (by the known **deltaRow** and **deltaColumn** values) until the prayer moves off the grid, hits a rock or hits a lion. If a lion is hit, we determine which lion and remove it from the grid. As a last step, we call **UpdateGame**. Make sure you understand how all this works.

Save and **Run** the program again. The game is nearly complete. Choose a difficulty (I use 3) and click **Start**. Here's my screen:

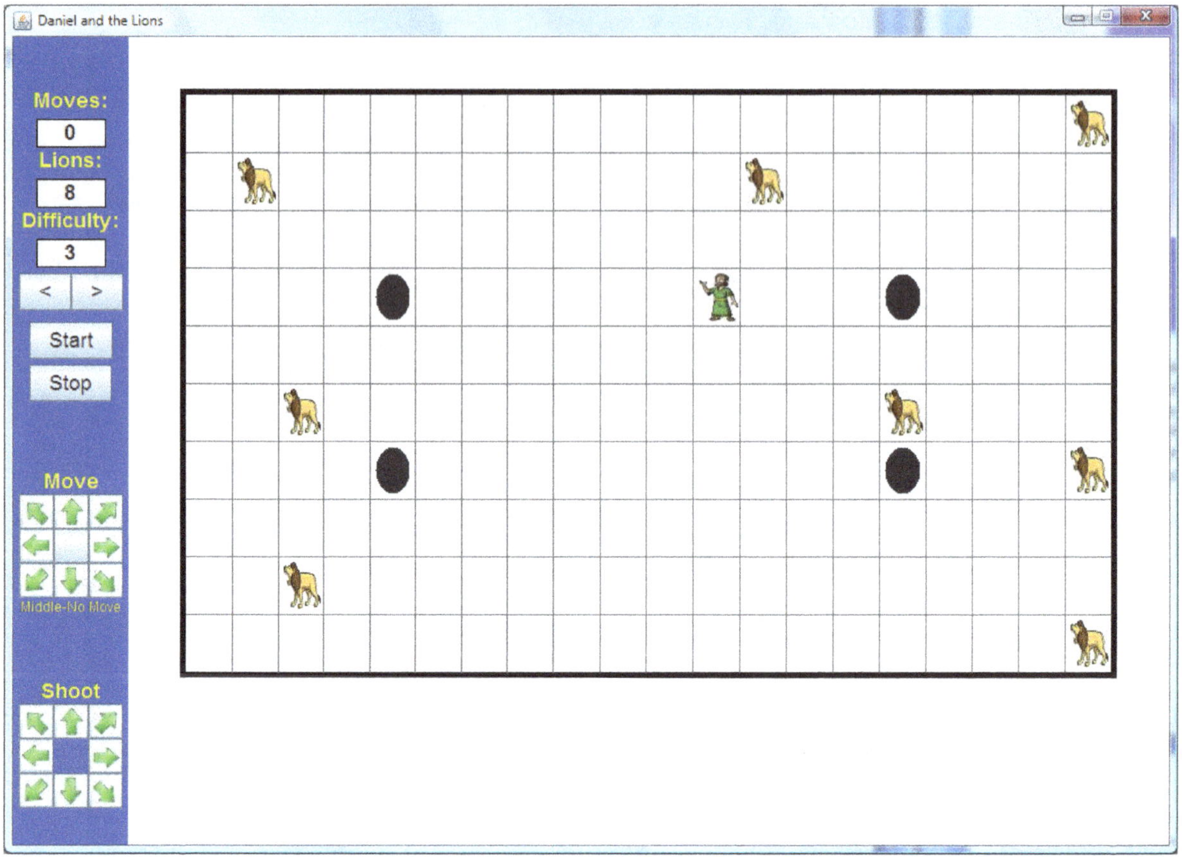

There are 8 lions to eliminate.

There are no lions in the path of a ‘prayer shot’. I move down. The lions move too:

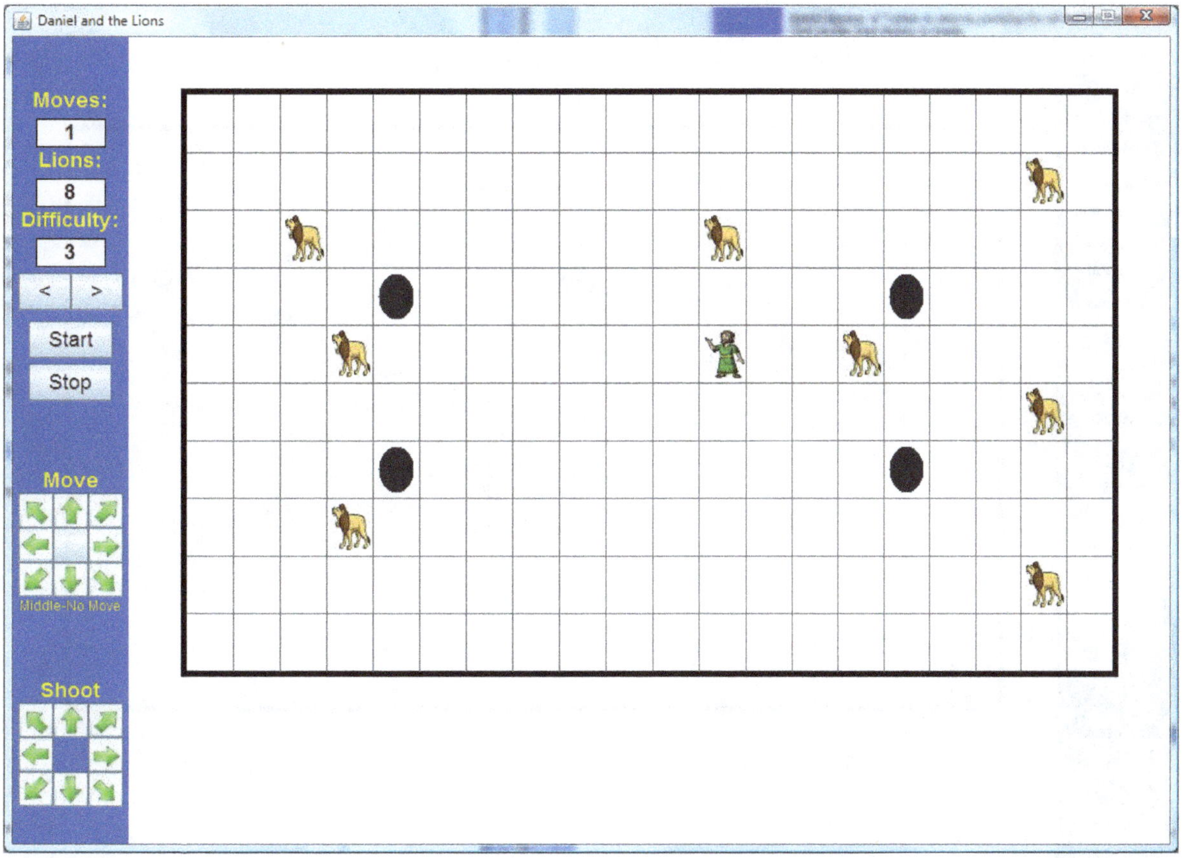

There are many in shot range. The one above Daniel is closest, so I click the up **Shoot** arrow.

Here's the result of my shot. One lion is dispatched, but the others continue to close in on Daniel:

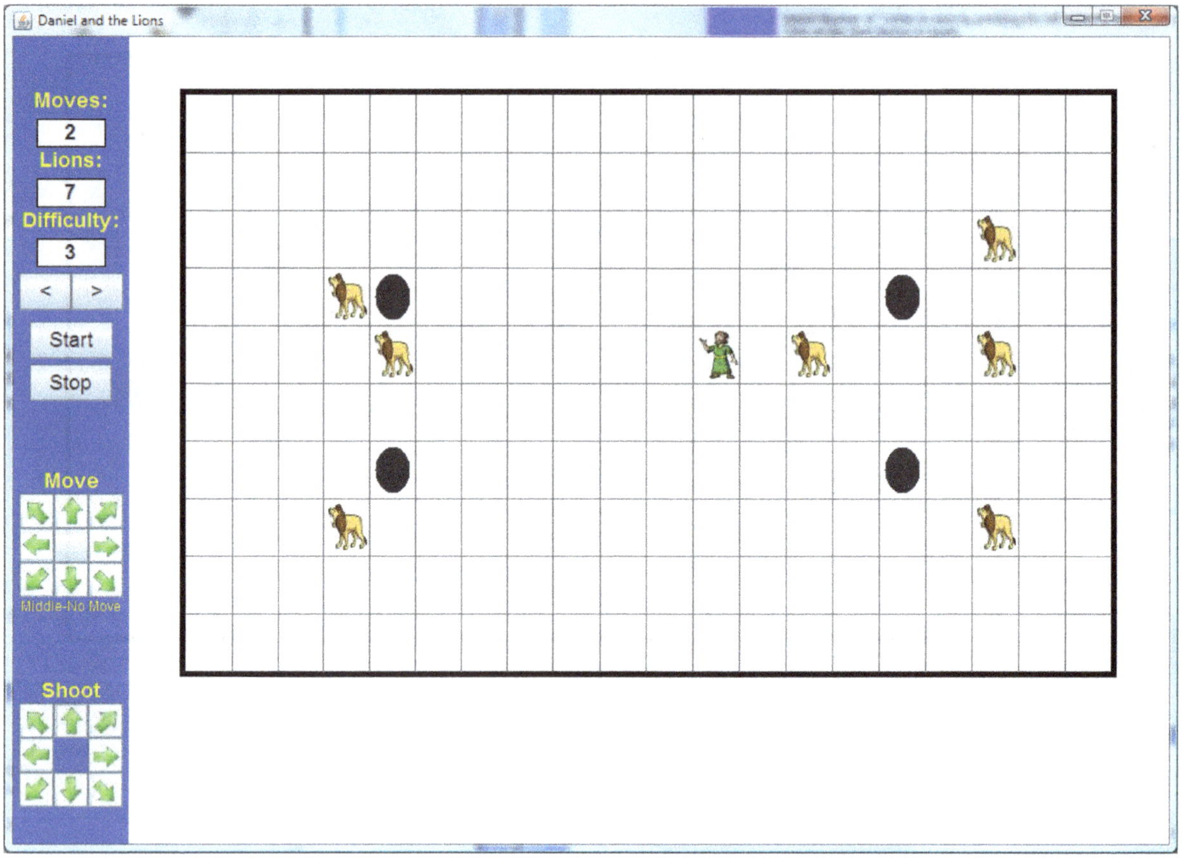

Now I need to shoot the one to the right (it's closest).

After that shot, I see:

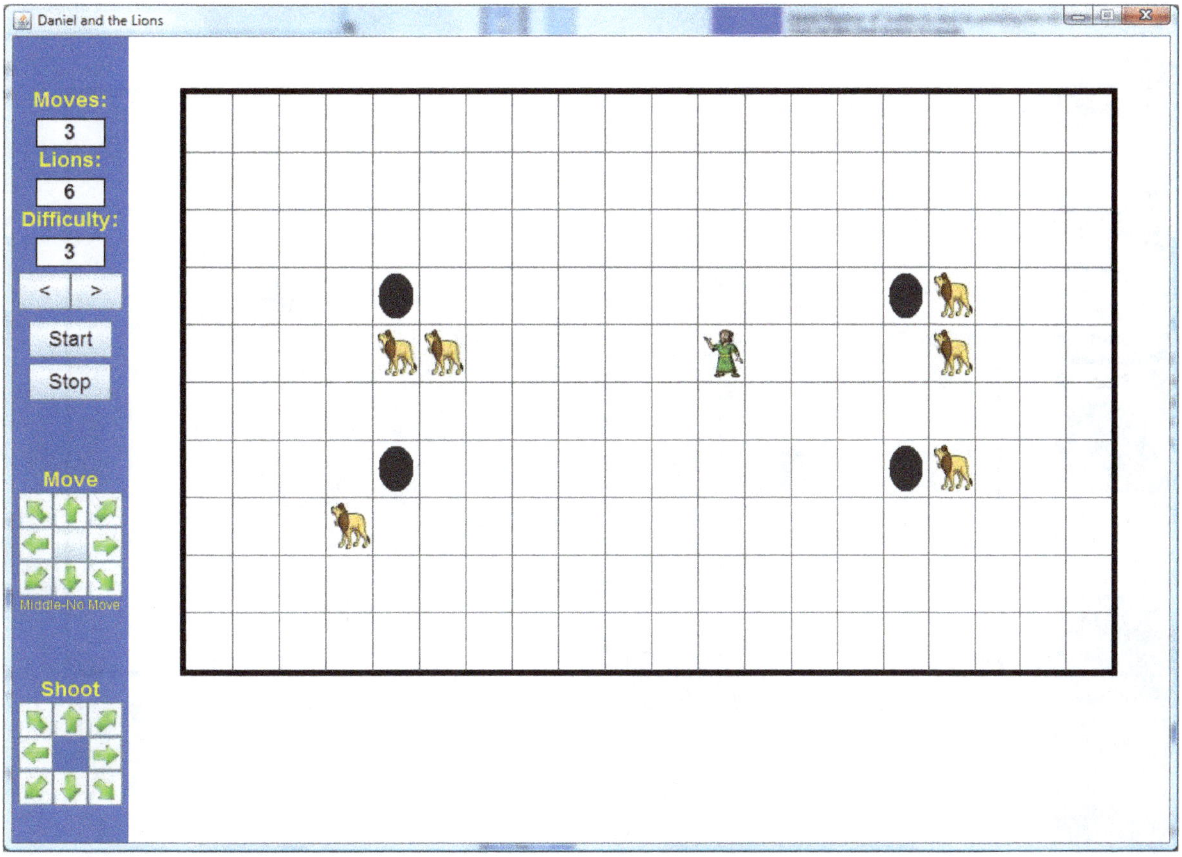

A shot to the right, then two to the left eliminates three more lions. At that point, other lions move into range.

After several shots in to the left and right, I see:

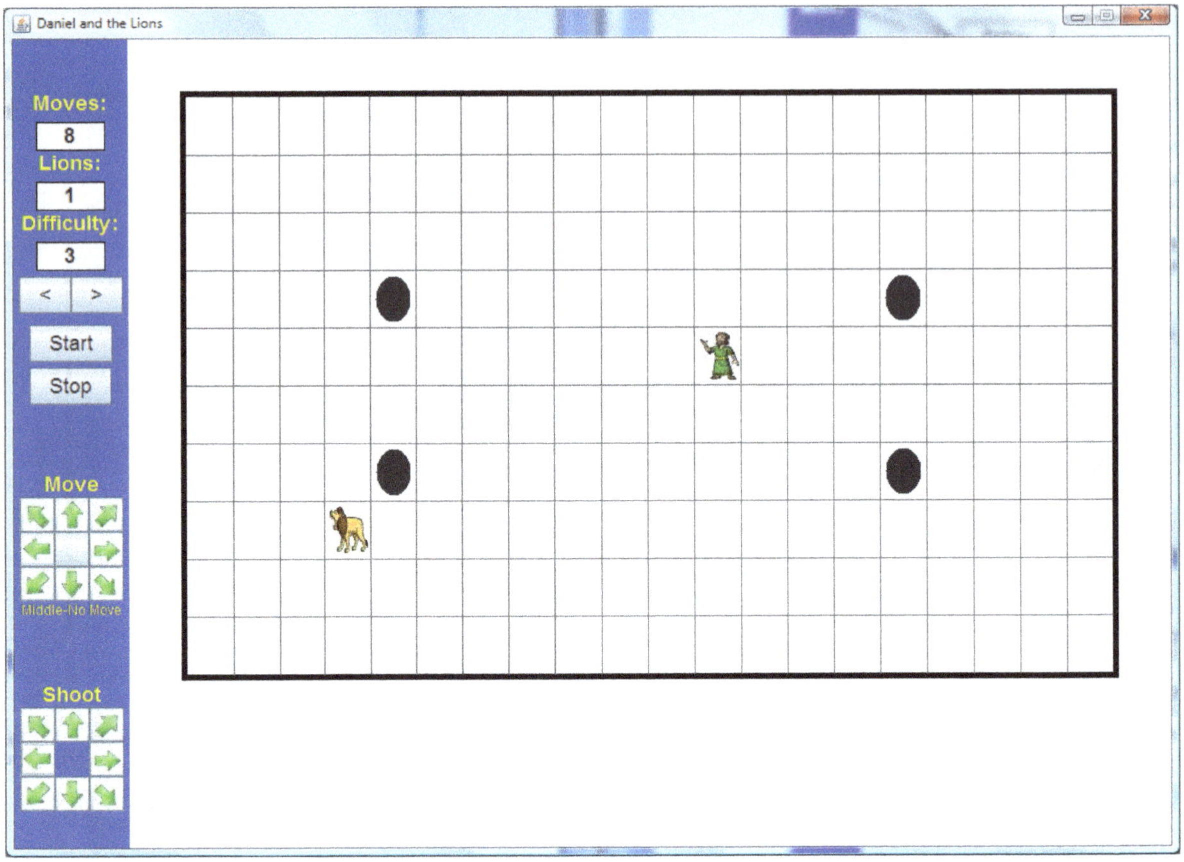

The last lion is behind a rock and can't see Daniel. And, Daniel can't shoot a prayer either. His only option is to move until the lion is in prayer shot range.

Three moves down and we have:

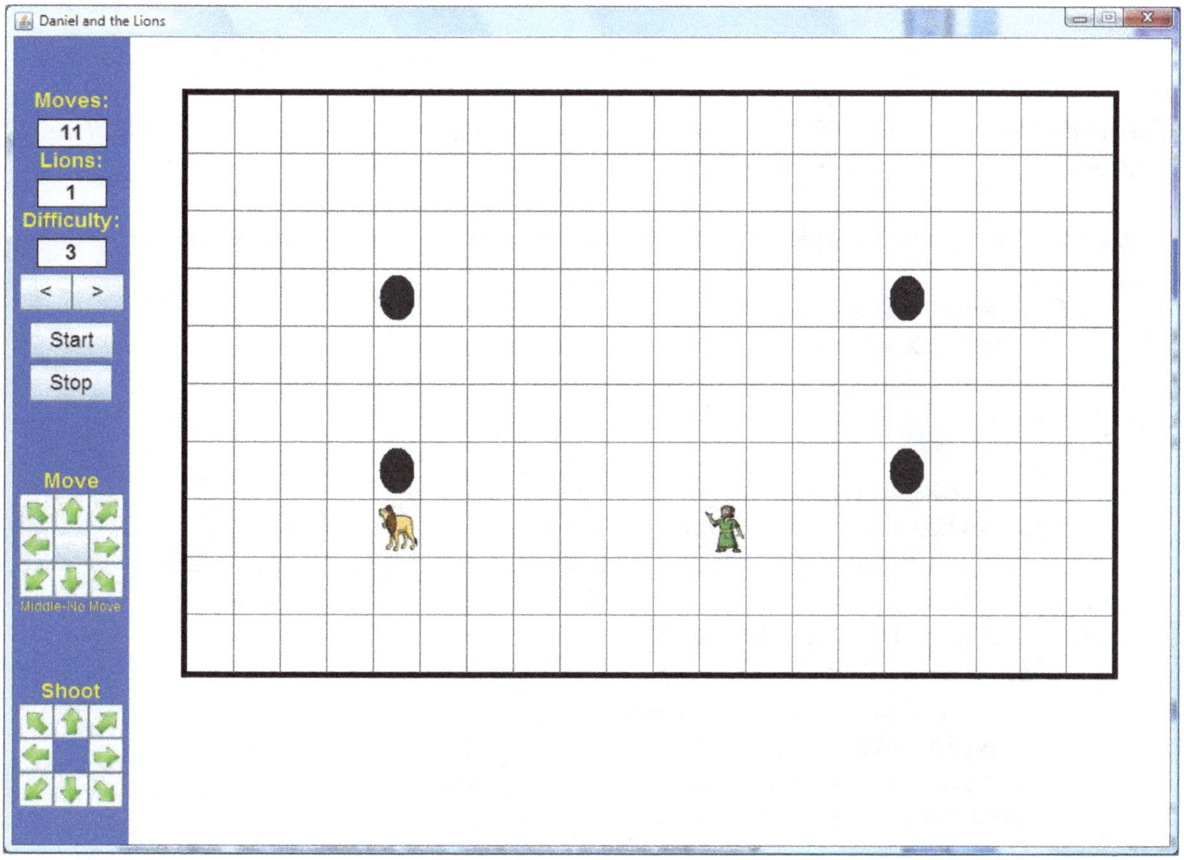

The lion can now be dispatched with a shot to the left.

I continued this game and dispatched all 8 lions in just 12 moves. At this point, I got this message:

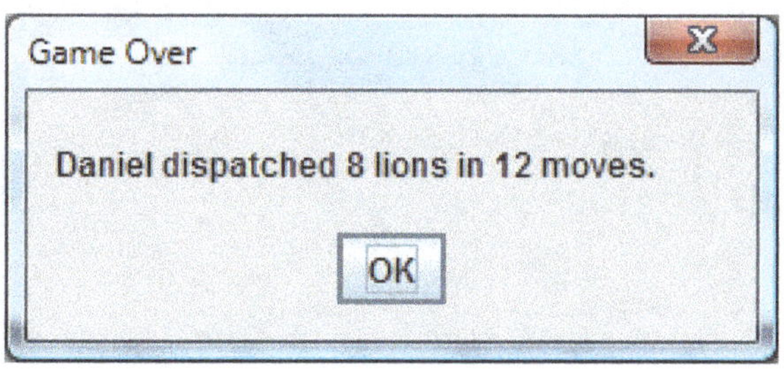

Code Design – Stop the Game

One last step and we're done. You may want to stop a game before dispatching all the lions. To do this, you can click the **Stop** button while the game is in "**DanielMove**" or "**LionsMove**" status. The code here is simple. Add the few shaded lines to the **stopButtonActionPerformed** method:

```
private void stopButtonActionPerformed(ActionEvent e)
{
  if (gameStatus.equals("Initial"))
    // clicked stop
    System.exit(0);
  else
  {
    //clicked stop while playing
    gameStatus = "Initial";
      JOptionPane.showConfirmDialog(null, "You stopped the
game.", "Game Over", JOptionPane.DEFAULT_OPTION,
JOptionPane.PLAIN_MESSAGE);
    for (int i = 0; i < numberLions; i++)
      // clear all the lions
       A[lionRow[i]][lionColumn[i]] = 0;
     A[danielRow][danielColumn] = 0;
     gamePanel.repaint();
  }
}
```

Save and **Run** the program. Click **Start**, then click **Stop**. You should see this message:

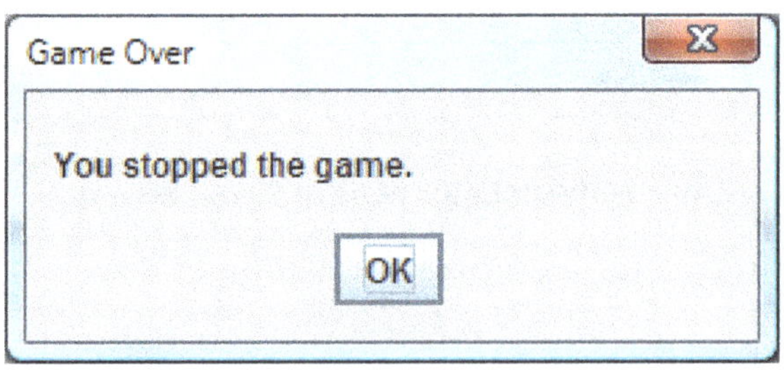

All the lions and Daniel should be removed from the screen. The game is now complete.

Daniel and the Lions Project Review

The **Daniel and the Lions** program is now complete. **Save** and **Run** the program and make sure it works as promised. Check that all options work correctly.

If there are errors in your implementation, go back over the steps of window and code design. Go over the developed code – make sure you understand how different parts of the program were coded. As mentioned in the beginning of this chapter, the finished project is saved as **Daniel** the **\CBGJava\CBGJava Projects** folder.

Daniel and the Lions Project Java Code Listing

```
/*
 * Daniel.java
 */

package daniel;
import javax.swing.*;
import java.awt.*;
import java.awt.event.*;
import java.awt.geom.*;
import java.util.Random;

public class Daniel extends JFrame
{

  JPanel controlPanel = new JPanel();
  JPanel movePanel = new JPanel();
  JPanel shootPanel = new JPanel();
  GraphicsPanel gamePanel = new GraphicsPanel();
  JLabel movesLabel = new JLabel();
  JTextField movesTextField = new JTextField();
  JLabel lionsLabel = new JLabel();
  JTextField lionsTextField = new JTextField();
  JLabel difficultyLabel = new JLabel();
  JTextField difficultyTextField = new JTextField();
  JButton decreaseButton = new JButton();
  JButton increaseButton = new JButton();
  JButton startButton = new JButton();
  JButton stopButton = new JButton();
  JLabel moveLabel = new JLabel();
  JLabel noMoveLabel = new JLabel();
  JButton moveUpLeftButton = new JButton();
  JButton moveUpButton = new JButton();
  JButton moveUpRightButton = new JButton();
  JButton moveLeftButton = new JButton();
  JButton noMoveButton = new JButton();
  JButton moveRightButton = new JButton();
  JButton moveDownLeftButton = new JButton();
  JButton moveDownButton = new JButton();
  JButton moveDownRightButton = new JButton();
  JLabel shootLabel = new JLabel();
  JButton shootUpLeftButton = new JButton();
  JButton shootUpButton = new JButton();
```

```
  JButton shootUpRightButton = new JButton();
  JButton shootLeftButton = new JButton();
  JButton shootRightButton = new JButton();
  JButton shootDownLeftButton = new JButton();
  JButton shootDownButton = new JButton();
  JButton shootDownRightButton = new JButton();

  static boolean firstTime = true;
  int difficulty;
  String gameStatus;
  boolean gameOver;
  int moves;
  static int numberLions;
  int lionsLeft;
  static int[][] A = new int[10][20];
  Random myRandom = new Random();
  static int danielRow, danielColumn;
  static int[] lionRow = new int[15];
  static int[] lionColumn = new int[15];
  static Image daniel = new
ImageIcon("Daniel.jpg").getImage();
  static Image lion = new ImageIcon("Lion.jpg").getImage();

  public static void main(String args[])
  {
    // create frame
    new Daniel().setVisible(true);
  }

  public Daniel()
  {
    // frame constructor
    setTitle("Daniel and the Lions");
    setResizable(false);
    addWindowListener(new WindowAdapter()
    {
      public void windowClosing(WindowEvent evt)
      {
        exitForm(evt);
      }
    });
    getContentPane().setLayout(new GridBagLayout());
    GridBagConstraints gridConstraints;

    // control panel
    controlPanel.setPreferredSize(new Dimension(100, 350));
    controlPanel.setBackground(Color.BLUE);
```

```
    controlPanel.setLayout(new GridBagLayout());
    gridConstraints = new GridBagConstraints();
    gridConstraints.gridx = 0;
    gridConstraints.gridy = 0;
    getContentPane().add(controlPanel, gridConstraints);

    movesLabel.setText("Moves:");
    movesLabel.setForeground(Color.YELLOW);
    movesLabel.setFont(new Font("Arial", Font.BOLD, 18));
    gridConstraints = new GridBagConstraints();
    gridConstraints.gridx = 0;
    gridConstraints.gridy = 0;
    gridConstraints.gridwidth = 2;
    gridConstraints.insets = new Insets(10, 0, 0, 0);
    controlPanel.add(movesLabel, gridConstraints);

    movesTextField.setPreferredSize(new Dimension(60, 25));

movesTextField.setBorder(BorderFactory.createLineBorder(Color
.BLACK));
    movesTextField.setText("0");
    movesTextField.setEditable(false);
    movesTextField.setBackground(Color.WHITE);

movesTextField.setHorizontalAlignment(SwingConstants.CENTER);
    movesTextField.setFont(new Font("Arial", Font.BOLD, 18));
    gridConstraints = new GridBagConstraints();
    gridConstraints.gridx = 0;
    gridConstraints.gridy = 1;
    gridConstraints.gridwidth = 2;
    gridConstraints.insets = new Insets(5, 0, 0, 0);
    controlPanel.add(movesTextField, gridConstraints);

    lionsLabel.setText("Lions:");
    lionsLabel.setForeground(Color.YELLOW);
    lionsLabel.setFont(new Font("Arial", Font.BOLD, 18));
    gridConstraints = new GridBagConstraints();
    gridConstraints.gridx = 0;
    gridConstraints.gridy = 2;
    gridConstraints.gridwidth = 2;
    controlPanel.add(lionsLabel, gridConstraints);

    lionsTextField.setPreferredSize(new Dimension(60, 25));

lionsTextField.setBorder(BorderFactory.createLineBorder(Color
.BLACK));
    lionsTextField.setText("0");
```

```
    lionsTextField.setEditable(false);
    lionsTextField.setBackground(Color.WHITE);

lionsTextField.setHorizontalAlignment(SwingConstants.CENTER);
    lionsTextField.setFont(new Font("Arial", Font.BOLD, 18));
    gridConstraints = new GridBagConstraints();
    gridConstraints.gridx = 0;
    gridConstraints.gridy = 3;
    gridConstraints.gridwidth = 2;
    gridConstraints.insets = new Insets(5, 0, 0, 0);
    controlPanel.add(lionsTextField, gridConstraints);

    difficultyLabel.setText("Difficulty:");
    difficultyLabel.setForeground(Color.YELLOW);
    difficultyLabel.setFont(new Font("Arial", Font.BOLD,
18));
    gridConstraints = new GridBagConstraints();
    gridConstraints.gridx = 0;
    gridConstraints.gridy = 4;
    gridConstraints.gridwidth = 2;
    controlPanel.add(difficultyLabel, gridConstraints);

    difficultyTextField.setPreferredSize(new Dimension(60,
25));

difficultyTextField.setBorder(BorderFactory.createLineBorder(
Color.BLACK));
    difficultyTextField.setText("1");
    difficultyTextField.setEditable(false);
    difficultyTextField.setBackground(Color.WHITE);

difficultyTextField.setHorizontalAlignment(SwingConstants.CEN
TER);
    difficultyTextField.setFont(new Font("Arial", Font.BOLD,
18));
    gridConstraints = new GridBagConstraints();
    gridConstraints.gridx = 0;
    gridConstraints.gridy = 5;
    gridConstraints.gridwidth = 2;
    gridConstraints.insets = new Insets(5, 0, 0, 0);
    controlPanel.add(difficultyTextField, gridConstraints);

    decreaseButton.setText("<");
    decreaseButton.setFont(new Font("Arial", Font.PLAIN,
18));
    gridConstraints = new GridBagConstraints();
    gridConstraints.gridx = 0;
```

```
    gridConstraints.gridy = 6;
    gridConstraints.insets = new Insets(5, 0, 0, 0);
    controlPanel.add(decreaseButton, gridConstraints);
    decreaseButton.addActionListener(new ActionListener()
    {
      public void actionPerformed(ActionEvent e)
      {
        decreaseButtonActionPerformed(e);
      }
    });

    increaseButton.setText(">");
    increaseButton.setFont(new Font("Arial", Font.PLAIN,
18));
    gridConstraints = new GridBagConstraints();
    gridConstraints.gridx = 1;
    gridConstraints.gridy = 6;
    gridConstraints.insets = new Insets(5, 0, 0, 0);
    controlPanel.add(increaseButton, gridConstraints);
    increaseButton.addActionListener(new ActionListener()
    {
      public void actionPerformed(ActionEvent e)
      {
        increaseButtonActionPerformed(e);
      }
    });

    startButton.setText("Start");
    startButton.setFont(new Font("Arial", Font.PLAIN, 18));
    gridConstraints = new GridBagConstraints();
    gridConstraints.gridx = 0;
    gridConstraints.gridy = 7;
    gridConstraints.gridwidth = 2;
    gridConstraints.insets = new Insets(10, 0, 0, 0);
    controlPanel.add(startButton, gridConstraints);
    startButton.addActionListener(new ActionListener()
    {
      public void actionPerformed(ActionEvent e)
      {
        startButtonActionPerformed(e);
      }
    });

    stopButton.setText("Stop");
    stopButton.setFont(new Font("Arial", Font.PLAIN, 18));
    gridConstraints = new GridBagConstraints();
    gridConstraints.gridx = 0;
```

```
gridConstraints.gridy = 8;
gridConstraints.gridwidth = 2;
gridConstraints.insets = new Insets(5, 0, 0, 0);
controlPanel.add(stopButton, gridConstraints);
stopButton.addActionListener(new ActionListener()
{
  public void actionPerformed(ActionEvent e)
  {
    stopButtonActionPerformed(e);
  }
});

// move panel
movePanel.setPreferredSize(new Dimension(100, 175));
movePanel.setBackground(Color.BLUE);
movePanel.setLayout(new GridBagLayout());
gridConstraints = new GridBagConstraints();
gridConstraints.gridx = 0;
gridConstraints.gridy = 1;
getContentPane().add(movePanel, gridConstraints);

moveLabel.setText("Move");
moveLabel.setForeground(Color.YELLOW);
moveLabel.setFont(new Font("Arial", Font.BOLD, 18));
gridConstraints = new GridBagConstraints();
gridConstraints.gridx = 0;
gridConstraints.gridy = 0;
gridConstraints.gridwidth = 3;
movePanel.add(moveLabel, gridConstraints);

moveUpLeftButton.setIcon(new ImageIcon("UpLeft.jpg"));
moveUpLeftButton.setPreferredSize(new Dimension(30, 30));
gridConstraints = new GridBagConstraints();
gridConstraints.gridx = 0;
gridConstraints.gridy = 1;
movePanel.add(moveUpLeftButton, gridConstraints);
moveUpLeftButton.addActionListener(new ActionListener()
{
  public void actionPerformed(ActionEvent e)
  {
    moveUpLeftButtonActionPerformed(e);
  }
});

moveUpButton.setIcon(new ImageIcon("Up.jpg"));
moveUpButton.setPreferredSize(new Dimension(30, 30));
gridConstraints = new GridBagConstraints();
```

```
    gridConstraints.gridx = 1;
    gridConstraints.gridy = 1;
    movePanel.add(moveUpButton, gridConstraints);
    moveUpButton.addActionListener(new ActionListener()
    {
      public void actionPerformed(ActionEvent e)
      {
        moveUpButtonActionPerformed(e);
      }
    });

    moveUpRightButton.setIcon(new ImageIcon("UpRight.jpg"));
    moveUpRightButton.setPreferredSize(new Dimension(30,
30));
    gridConstraints = new GridBagConstraints();
    gridConstraints.gridx = 2;
    gridConstraints.gridy = 1;
    movePanel.add(moveUpRightButton, gridConstraints);
    moveUpRightButton.addActionListener(new ActionListener()
    {
      public void actionPerformed(ActionEvent e)
      {
        moveUpRightButtonActionPerformed(e);
      }
    });

    moveLeftButton.setIcon(new ImageIcon("Left.jpg"));
    moveLeftButton.setPreferredSize(new Dimension(30, 30));
    gridConstraints = new GridBagConstraints();
    gridConstraints.gridx = 0;
    gridConstraints.gridy = 2;
    movePanel.add(moveLeftButton, gridConstraints);
    moveLeftButton.addActionListener(new ActionListener()
    {
      public void actionPerformed(ActionEvent e)
      {
        moveLeftButtonActionPerformed(e);
      }
    });

    noMoveButton.setPreferredSize(new Dimension(30, 30));
    gridConstraints = new GridBagConstraints();
    gridConstraints.gridx = 1;
    gridConstraints.gridy = 2;
    movePanel.add(noMoveButton, gridConstraints);
    noMoveButton.addActionListener(new ActionListener()
    {
```

```
      public void actionPerformed(ActionEvent e)
      {
        noMoveButtonActionPerformed(e);
      }
    });

    moveRightButton.setIcon(new ImageIcon("Right.jpg"));
    moveRightButton.setPreferredSize(new Dimension(30, 30));
    gridConstraints = new GridBagConstraints();
    gridConstraints.gridx = 2;
    gridConstraints.gridy = 2;
    movePanel.add(moveRightButton, gridConstraints);
    moveRightButton.addActionListener(new ActionListener()
    {
      public void actionPerformed(ActionEvent e)
      {
        moveRightButtonActionPerformed(e);
      }
    });

    moveDownLeftButton.setIcon(new
ImageIcon("DownLeft.jpg"));
    moveDownLeftButton.setPreferredSize(new Dimension(30,
30));
    gridConstraints = new GridBagConstraints();
    gridConstraints.gridx = 0;
    gridConstraints.gridy = 3;
    movePanel.add(moveDownLeftButton, gridConstraints);
    moveDownLeftButton.addActionListener(new ActionListener()
    {
      public void actionPerformed(ActionEvent e)
      {
        moveDownLeftButtonActionPerformed(e);
      }
    });

    moveDownButton.setIcon(new ImageIcon("Down.jpg"));
    moveDownButton.setPreferredSize(new Dimension(30, 30));
    gridConstraints = new GridBagConstraints();
    gridConstraints.gridx = 1;
    gridConstraints.gridy = 3;
    movePanel.add(moveDownButton, gridConstraints);
    moveDownButton.addActionListener(new ActionListener()
    {
      public void actionPerformed(ActionEvent e)
      {
        moveDownButtonActionPerformed(e);
```

```
      }
    });

    moveDownRightButton.setIcon(new
ImageIcon("DownRight.jpg"));
    moveDownRightButton.setPreferredSize(new Dimension(30,
30));
    gridConstraints = new GridBagConstraints();
    gridConstraints.gridx = 2;
    gridConstraints.gridy = 3;
    movePanel.add(moveDownRightButton, gridConstraints);
    moveDownRightButton.addActionListener(new
ActionListener()
    {
      public void actionPerformed(ActionEvent e)
      {
        moveDownRightButtonActionPerformed(e);
      }
    });

    noMoveLabel.setText("Middle-No Move");
    noMoveLabel.setForeground(Color.YELLOW);
    noMoveLabel.setFont(new Font("Arial", Font.PLAIN, 12));
    gridConstraints = new GridBagConstraints();
    gridConstraints.gridx = 0;
    gridConstraints.gridy = 4;
    gridConstraints.gridwidth = 3;
    movePanel.add(noMoveLabel, gridConstraints);

    // shoot panel
    shootPanel.setPreferredSize(new Dimension(100, 175));
    shootPanel.setBackground(Color.BLUE);
    shootPanel.setLayout(new GridBagLayout());
    gridConstraints = new GridBagConstraints();
    gridConstraints.gridx = 0;
    gridConstraints.gridy = 2;
    getContentPane().add(shootPanel, gridConstraints);

    shootLabel.setText("Shoot");
    shootLabel.setForeground(Color.YELLOW);
    shootLabel.setFont(new Font("Arial", Font.BOLD, 18));
    gridConstraints = new GridBagConstraints();
    gridConstraints.gridx = 0;
    gridConstraints.gridy = 0;
    gridConstraints.gridwidth = 3;
    shootPanel.add(shootLabel, gridConstraints);
```

```
    shootUpLeftButton.setIcon(new ImageIcon("UpLeft.jpg"));
    shootUpLeftButton.setPreferredSize(new Dimension(30,
30));
    gridConstraints = new GridBagConstraints();
    gridConstraints.gridx = 0;
    gridConstraints.gridy = 1;
    shootPanel.add(shootUpLeftButton, gridConstraints);
    shootUpLeftButton.addActionListener(new ActionListener()
    {
      public void actionPerformed(ActionEvent e)
      {
        shootUpLeftButtonActionPerformed(e);
      }
    });

    shootUpButton.setIcon(new ImageIcon("Up.jpg"));
    shootUpButton.setPreferredSize(new Dimension(30, 30));
    gridConstraints = new GridBagConstraints();
    gridConstraints.gridx = 1;
    gridConstraints.gridy = 1;
    shootPanel.add(shootUpButton, gridConstraints);
    shootUpButton.addActionListener(new ActionListener()
    {
      public void actionPerformed(ActionEvent e)
      {
        shootUpButtonActionPerformed(e);
      }
    });

    shootUpRightButton.setIcon(new ImageIcon("UpRight.jpg"));
    shootUpRightButton.setPreferredSize(new Dimension(30,
30));
    gridConstraints = new GridBagConstraints();
    gridConstraints.gridx = 2;
    gridConstraints.gridy = 1;
    shootPanel.add(shootUpRightButton, gridConstraints);
    shootUpRightButton.addActionListener(new ActionListener()
    {
      public void actionPerformed(ActionEvent e)
      {
        shootUpRightButtonActionPerformed(e);
      }
    });

    shootLeftButton.setIcon(new ImageIcon("Left.jpg"));
    shootLeftButton.setPreferredSize(new Dimension(30, 30));
    gridConstraints = new GridBagConstraints();
```

```
    gridConstraints.gridx = 0;
    gridConstraints.gridy = 2;
    shootPanel.add(shootLeftButton, gridConstraints);
    shootLeftButton.addActionListener(new ActionListener()
    {
      public void actionPerformed(ActionEvent e)
      {
        shootLeftButtonActionPerformed(e);
      }
    });

    shootRightButton.setIcon(new ImageIcon("Right.jpg"));
    shootRightButton.setPreferredSize(new Dimension(30, 30));
    gridConstraints = new GridBagConstraints();
    gridConstraints.gridx = 2;
    gridConstraints.gridy = 2;
    shootPanel.add(shootRightButton, gridConstraints);
    shootRightButton.addActionListener(new ActionListener()
    {
      public void actionPerformed(ActionEvent e)
      {
        shootRightButtonActionPerformed(e);
      }
    });

    shootDownLeftButton.setIcon(new
ImageIcon("DownLeft.jpg"));
    shootDownLeftButton.setPreferredSize(new Dimension(30,
30));
    gridConstraints = new GridBagConstraints();
    gridConstraints.gridx = 0;
    gridConstraints.gridy = 3;
    shootPanel.add(shootDownLeftButton, gridConstraints);
    shootDownLeftButton.addActionListener(new
ActionListener()
    {
      public void actionPerformed(ActionEvent e)
      {
        shootDownLeftButtonActionPerformed(e);
      }
    });

    shootDownButton.setIcon(new ImageIcon("Down.jpg"));
    shootDownButton.setPreferredSize(new Dimension(30, 30));
    gridConstraints = new GridBagConstraints();
    gridConstraints.gridx = 1;
    gridConstraints.gridy = 3;
```

```
    shootPanel.add(shootDownButton, gridConstraints);
    shootDownButton.addActionListener(new ActionListener()
    {
      public void actionPerformed(ActionEvent e)
      {
        shootDownButtonActionPerformed(e);
      }
    });

    shootDownRightButton.setIcon(new
ImageIcon("DownRight.jpg"));
    shootDownRightButton.setPreferredSize(new Dimension(30,
30));
    gridConstraints = new GridBagConstraints();
    gridConstraints.gridx = 2;
    gridConstraints.gridy = 3;
    shootPanel.add(shootDownRightButton, gridConstraints);
    shootDownRightButton.addActionListener(new
ActionListener()
    {
      public void actionPerformed(ActionEvent e)
      {
        shootDownRightButtonActionPerformed(e);
      }
    });

    // game panel
    gamePanel.setPreferredSize(new Dimension(900, 700));
    gamePanel.setBackground(Color.WHITE);
    gridConstraints = new GridBagConstraints();
    gridConstraints.gridx = 1;
    gridConstraints.gridy = 0;
    gridConstraints.gridheight = 3;
    getContentPane().add(gamePanel, gridConstraints);
    gamePanel.addKeyListener(new KeyAdapter()
    {
      public void keyPressed(KeyEvent e)
      {
        moveKeyPressed(e);
      }
    });

    pack();
    Dimension screenSize =
Toolkit.getDefaultToolkit().getScreenSize();
```

```
    setBounds((int) (0.5 * (screenSize.width - getWidth())),
(int) (0.5 * (screenSize.height - getHeight())), getWidth(),
getHeight());

    difficulty = 1;
    gameStatus = "Initial";
    difficultyTextField.setText(String.valueOf(difficulty));

   }

  private void decreaseButtonActionPerformed(ActionEvent e)
  {
    if (gameStatus.equals("Initial"))
    {
      // decrease difficulty
      difficulty--;
      if (difficulty < 1)
        difficulty = 1;

difficultyTextField.setText(String.valueOf(difficulty));
    }
  }

  private void increaseButtonActionPerformed(ActionEvent e)
  {
    if (gameStatus.equals("Initial"))
    {
      // increase difficulty
      difficulty++;
      if (difficulty > 10)
        difficulty = 10;

difficultyTextField.setText(String.valueOf(difficulty));
    }
  }

  private void startButtonActionPerformed(ActionEvent e)
  {
    //clicked start
    firstTime = false;
    gameStatus = "DanielMove";
    gameOver = false;
    moves = 0;
    numberLions = difficulty + 5;
    lionsLeft = numberLions;
    movesTextField.setText(String.valueOf(moves));
    lionsTextField.setText(String.valueOf(lionsLeft));
```

```
    for (int i = 0; i < 9; i++)
      for (int j = 0; j < 19; j++)
        A[i][j] = 0;
    //  Place rocks
    // A array (0- nothing, 1-rock, 2-lion, 3-Daniel)
    A[3][4] = 1;
    A[3][15] = 1;
    A[6][4] = 1;
    A[6][15] = 1;
    // Place Daniel
    int row, column;
    do
    {
      row = myRandom.nextInt(10);
      column = myRandom.nextInt(20);
    }
    while (A[row][column] != 0);
    A[row][column] = 3;
    danielRow = row;
    danielColumn = column;
    // Place lions
    for (int i = 0; i < numberLions; i++)
    {
      do
      {
        row = myRandom.nextInt(10);
        column = myRandom.nextInt(20);
      }
      while (A[row][column] != 0);
      A[row][column] = 2;
      lionRow[i] = row;
      lionColumn[i] = column;
    }
    gamePanel.repaint();
    gamePanel.requestFocus();
  }

  private void stopButtonActionPerformed(ActionEvent e)
  {
    if (gameStatus.equals("Initial"))
      // clicked stop
      System.exit(0);
    else
    {
      //clicked stop while playing
      gameStatus = "Initial";
```

```
      JOptionPane.showConfirmDialog(null, "You stopped the
game.", "Game Over", JOptionPane.DEFAULT_OPTION,
JOptionPane.PLAIN_MESSAGE);
      for (int i = 0; i < numberLions; i++)
        // clear all the lions
         A[lionRow[i]][lionColumn[i]] = 0;
       A[danielRow][danielColumn] = 0;
       gamePanel.repaint();
    }
  }

  private void moveUpLeftButtonActionPerformed(ActionEvent e)
  {
    CheckMove(-1, -1);
  }

  private void moveUpButtonActionPerformed(ActionEvent e)
  {
    CheckMove(-1, 0);
  }

  private void moveUpRightButtonActionPerformed(ActionEvent
e)
  {
    CheckMove(-1, 1);
  }

  private void moveLeftButtonActionPerformed(ActionEvent e)
  {
    CheckMove(0, -1);
  }

  private void noMoveButtonActionPerformed(ActionEvent e)
  {
    CheckMove(0, 0);
  }

  private void moveRightButtonActionPerformed(ActionEvent e)
  {
    CheckMove(0, 1);
  }

  private void moveDownLeftButtonActionPerformed(ActionEvent
e)
  {
    CheckMove(1, -1);
  }
```

```
  private void moveDownButtonActionPerformed(ActionEvent e)
  {
    CheckMove(1, 0);
  }

  private void moveDownRightButtonActionPerformed(ActionEvent
e)
  {
    CheckMove(1, 1);
  }

  private void CheckMove(int deltaRow, int deltaColumn)
  {
    int newRow, newColumn;
    boolean moveOkay;
    moves++;
    // check if move is okay
    newRow = danielRow + deltaRow;
    newColumn = danielColumn + deltaColumn;
    moveOkay = true;
    if (newRow < 0 || newRow > 9 || newColumn < 0 ||
newColumn > 19)
      // off grid
      moveOkay = false;
    else if (A[newRow][newColumn] == 1)
      //moving to rock
      moveOkay = false;
    else if (A[newRow][newColumn] == 2)
    {
      //moving to lion
      moveOkay = false;
      gameOver = true;
      //remove Daniel
      A[danielRow][danielColumn] = 0;
    }
    if (moveOkay)
    {
      // move to new location
      A[danielRow][danielColumn] = 0;
      danielRow = newRow;
      danielColumn = newColumn;
      A[danielRow][danielColumn] = 3;
    }
    UpdateGame();
    gamePanel.repaint();
    gamePanel.requestFocus();
```

```
  }

  private void UpdateGame()
  {
    int newRow, newColumn;
    int deltaRow, deltaColumn;
    boolean moveOkay;
    movesTextField.setText(String.valueOf(moves));
    lionsTextField.setText(String.valueOf(lionsLeft));
    if (!gameOver)
    {
      // move lions
      gameStatus = "LionsMove";
      for (int i = 0; i < numberLions; i++)
      {
        if (A[lionRow[i]][lionColumn[i]] == 2)
        {
          if (lionRow[i] > danielRow)
            deltaRow = -1;
          else if (lionRow[i] < danielRow)
            deltaRow = 1;
          else
            deltaRow = 0;
          if (lionColumn[i] > danielColumn)
            deltaColumn = -1;
          else if (lionColumn[i] < danielColumn)
            deltaColumn = 1;
          else
            deltaColumn = 0;
          newRow = lionRow[i] + deltaRow;
          newColumn = lionColumn[i] + deltaColumn;
          moveOkay = true;
          if (newRow < 0 || newRow > 9 || newColumn < 0 ||
newColumn > 19)
            // off grid
            moveOkay = false;
          else if (A[newRow][newColumn] == 1)
            //moving to rock
            moveOkay = false;
          else if (A[newRow][newColumn] == 2)
            //moving to another lion
            moveOkay = false;
          if (moveOkay == true)
          {
            if (A[newRow][newColumn] == 3)
            {
              System.out.println("Daniel");
```

```
          // moving to Daniel
          gameOver = true;
          // remove Daniel
          A[danielRow][danielColumn] = 0;
        }
        // move lion
        A[lionRow[i]][lionColumn[i]] = 0;
        lionRow[i] = newRow;
        lionColumn[i] = newColumn;
        A[lionRow[i]][lionColumn[i]] = 2;
      }
    }
  }
  gameStatus = "DanielMove";
  gamePanel.repaint();
}
if (gameOver)
{
  // game is over
  gameStatus = "Initial";
  if (lionsLeft > 0)
  {
    JOptionPane.showConfirmDialog(null, "Daniel met a
lion but God shut the mouth of the lion at the last
minute\r\nand King Darius released Daniel from the Lion's
Den.", "Game Over", JOptionPane.DEFAULT_OPTION,
JOptionPane.PLAIN_MESSAGE);
    for (int i = 0; i < numberLions; i++)
      // clear all the lions
      A[lionRow[i]][lionColumn[i]] = 0;
  }
  else
  {
    JOptionPane.showConfirmDialog(null, "Daniel
dispatched " + numberLions + " lions in " + moves + "
moves.", "Game Over", JOptionPane.DEFAULT_OPTION,
JOptionPane.PLAIN_MESSAGE);
     A[danielRow][danielColumn] = 0;
  }
  gamePanel.repaint();
}
}

private void shootUpLeftButtonActionPerformed(ActionEvent
e)
{
  ShootPrayer(-1, -1);
```

```
  }

  private void shootUpButtonActionPerformed(ActionEvent e)
  {
    ShootPrayer(-1, 0);
  }

  private void shootUpRightButtonActionPerformed(ActionEvent
e)
  {
    ShootPrayer(-1, 1);
  }

  private void shootLeftButtonActionPerformed(ActionEvent e)
  {
    ShootPrayer(0, -1);
  }

  private void shootRightButtonActionPerformed(ActionEvent e)
  {
    ShootPrayer(0, 1);
  }

  private void shootDownLeftButtonActionPerformed(ActionEvent
e)
  {
    ShootPrayer(1, -1);
  }

  private void shootDownButtonActionPerformed(ActionEvent e)
  {
    ShootPrayer(1, 0);
  }

  private void
shootDownRightButtonActionPerformed(ActionEvent e)
  {
    ShootPrayer(1, 1);
  }

  private void ShootPrayer(int deltaRow, int deltaColumn)
  {
    int prayerRow, prayerColumn;
    boolean moveOkay;
    if (deltaRow != 0 || deltaColumn != 0)
      moves++;
    prayerRow = danielRow;
```

```
    prayerColumn = danielColumn;
    do
    {
      //check if move is okay
      prayerRow += deltaRow;
      prayerColumn += deltaColumn;
      moveOkay = true;
      if (prayerRow < 0 || prayerRow > 9 || prayerColumn < 0
|| prayerColumn > 19 || (deltaRow == 0 && deltaColumn == 0))
        // off grid or center button area clicked
        moveOkay = false;
      else if (A[prayerRow][prayerColumn] == 1)
        //moving to rock
        moveOkay = false;
      int i;
      if (moveOkay)
      {
        if (A[prayerRow][prayerColumn] == 2)
        {
          // dispatched a lion - find that lion
          for (i = 0; i < numberLions; i++)
          {
            if (prayerRow == lionRow[i] && prayerColumn ==
lionColumn[i])
              break;
          }
          moveOkay = false;
          A[prayerRow][prayerColumn] = 0;
          lionRow[i] = 0;
          lionColumn[i] = 0;
          lionsLeft -= 1;
          if (lionsLeft == 0)
            gameOver = true;
        }
      }
    }
    while (moveOkay);
    UpdateGame();
  }

  private void moveKeyPressed(KeyEvent e)
  {
    int k = e.getKeyCode();
    if (k == e.VK_NUMPAD7)
      CheckMove(-1, -1);
    else if (k == e.VK_NUMPAD8)
      CheckMove(-1, -0);
```

```
    else if (k == e.VK_NUMPAD9)
      CheckMove(-1, 1);
    else if (k == e.VK_NUMPAD4)
      CheckMove(0, -1);
    else if (k == e.VK_NUMPAD5)
      CheckMove(0, 0);
    else if (k == e.VK_NUMPAD6)
      CheckMove(0, 1);
    else if (k == e.VK_NUMPAD1)
      CheckMove(1, -1);
    else if (k == e.VK_NUMPAD2)
      CheckMove(1, 0);
    else if (k == e.VK_NUMPAD3)
      CheckMove(1, 1);
  }

  private void exitForm(WindowEvent evt)
  {
    System.exit(0);
  }
}

class GraphicsPanel extends JPanel
{
  public GraphicsPanel()
  {
  }
  public void paintComponent(Graphics g)
  {
    Graphics2D g2D = (Graphics2D) g;
    super.paintComponent(g2D);
    if (Daniel.firstTime)
    {
      // draw instructions
      g2D.setFont(new Font("Arial", Font.PLAIN, 18));
      g2D.setPaint(Color.BLACK);
      g2D.drawString("DANIEL AND THE LIONS", 10, 30);
      g2D.drawString("In Daniel 6:16-28, King Darius is
tricked into putting Daniel into the Lions Den. Daniel prays
for God's protection", 10, 60);
      g2D.drawString("and God sends His Angel to shut the
Lion's mouth.  God will protect you if you pray to Him
today.", 10, 80);
      g2D.drawString("\r\n\r\nSelect Difficulty by pressing
the left button for Easy and the right button for Harder.",
10, 110);
```

```
      g2D.drawString("\r\n\r\nClick on the Start Button to
begin.", 10, 130);
      g2D.drawString("Click on the Stop Button to stop the
program.", 10, 150);
      g2D.drawString("Use Move buttons (or keypad keys) to
move Daniel.", 10, 170);
      g2D.drawString("Use Shoot buttons to 'shoot' prayers at
lions.", 10, 190);
    }
    else
    {
      Line2D.Double myLine;
      Rectangle2D.Double myRect;
      Ellipse2D.Double myEllipse;
       //  draw grid structure
       myRect = new Rectangle2D.Double(45, 45, 810, 510);
       g2D.setPaint(Color.BLACK);
      g2D.fill(myRect);
       myRect = new Rectangle2D.Double(50, 50, 800, 500);
      g2D.setPaint(Color.WHITE);
      g2D.fill(myRect);
      g2D.setPaint(Color.GRAY);
      for (int i = 0; i < 9; i++)
      {
        myLine = new Line2D.Double(50, 50 * i + 100, 850, 50
* i + 100);
        g2D.draw(myLine);
      }
      for (int i = 0; i < 19; i++)
      {
        myLine = new Line2D.Double(50 + 40 * i + 40, 50, 50 +
40 * i + 40, 550);
        g2D.draw(myLine);
      }
      // draw rocks
      g2D.setPaint(Color.DARK_GRAY);
      myEllipse = new Ellipse2D.Double(215, 205, 30, 40);
      g2D.fill(myEllipse);
      myEllipse = new Ellipse2D.Double(655, 205, 30, 40);
      g2D.fill(myEllipse);
      myEllipse = new Ellipse2D.Double(215, 355, 30, 40);
      g2D.fill(myEllipse);
      myEllipse = new Ellipse2D.Double(655, 355, 30, 40);
      g2D.fill(myEllipse);
      // draw daniel and lions
      if (Daniel.A[Daniel.danielRow][Daniel.danielColumn] !=
0)
```

```
        g2D.drawImage(Daniel.daniel, Daniel.danielColumn * 40
+ 55, Daniel.danielRow * 50 + 55, this);
      // Place lions
      for (int i = 0; i < Daniel.numberLions; i++)
      {
        if (Daniel.A[Daniel.lionRow[i]][Daniel.lionColumn[i]]
== 2)
          g2D.drawImage(Daniel.lion, Daniel.lionColumn[i] *
40 + 55, Daniel.lionRow[i] * 50 + 55, this);
      }
    }
    g2D.dispose();
  }
}
```

Appendix - Installing Java and NetBeans

Downloading and Installing Java

To write and run programs using Java, you need the **Java Development Kit** (JDK) and the **NetBeans Integrated Development Environment** (IDE). These are free products that you can download from the Internet. This simply means we will copy a file onto our computer to allow installation of Java. Each product requires a separate download and installation process.

Java Development Kit

1. Start up your web browser (Internet Explorer, Chrome, Firefox, Safari or other browser) and go to Java web site:

https://www.oracle.com/technetwork/java/javase/downloads/jdk11-downloads-5066655.html

This web site has lots of useful Java information. As you become more proficient in your programming skills, you will go to this site often for answers to programming questions, interaction with other Java programmers, and lots of sample programs.

2. Once on the page with the JDK download links, accept the Licensing Agreement and choose the link corresponding to your computer's operating system.

For Microsoft Windows: select the Windows exe file

Java SE Development Kit 11.0.3

You must accept the Oracle Technology Network License Agreement for Oracle Java SE to download this software.

Thank you for accepting the Oracle Technology Network License Agreement for Oracle Java SE; you may now download this software.

Product / File Description	File Size	Download
Linux	147.31 MB	jdk-11.0.3_linux-x64_bin.deb
Linux	154.04 MB	jdk-11.0.3_linux-x64_bin.rpm
Linux	171.37 MB	jdk-11.0.3_linux-x64_bin.tar.gz
macOS	166.2 MB	jdk-11.0.3_osx-x64_bin.dmg
macOS	166.52 MB	jdk-11.0.3_osx-x64_bin.tar.gz
Solaris SPARC	186.85 MB	jdk-11.0.3_solaris-sparcv9_bin.tar.gz
Windows	150.98 MB	jdk-11.0.3_windows-x64_bin.exe
Windows	171 MB	jdk-11.0.3_windows-x64_bin.zip

Instructions for installing Java on other platforms such as Linux or Solaris can also be found on the website. My screenshots in these notes will be Microsoft Windows.

<u>For Mac OS:</u> click on the macOS dmg file

Java SE Development Kit 11.0.3

You must accept the Oracle Technology Network License Agreement for Oracle Java SE to download this software.

Thank you for accepting the Oracle Technology Network License Agreement for Oracle Java SE; you may now download this software.

Product / File Description	File Size	Download
Linux	147.31 MB	jdk-11.0.3_linux-x64_bin.deb
Linux	154.04 MB	jdk-11.0.3_linux-x64_bin.rpm
Linux	171.37 MB	jdk-11.0.3_linux-x64_bin.tar.gz
macOS	166.2 MB	jdk-11.0.3_osx-x64_bin.dmg
macOS	166.52 MB	jdk-11.0.3_osx-x64_bin.tar.gz
Solaris SPARC	186.85 MB	jdk-11.0.3_solaris-sparcv9_bin.tar.gz
Windows	150.98 MB	jdk-11.0.3_windows-x64_bin.exe
Windows	171 MB	jdk-11.0.3_windows-x64_bin.zip

<u>For Linux OS:</u> click on the Linux deb file

Java SE Development Kit 11.0.3

You must accept the Oracle Technology Network License Agreement for Oracle Java SE to download this software.

Thank you for accepting the Oracle Technology Network License Agreement for Oracle Java SE; you may now download this software.

Product / File Description	File Size	Download
Linux	147.31 MB	jdk-11.0.3_linux-x64_bin.deb
Linux	154.04 MB	jdk-11.0.3_linux-x64_bin.rpm
Linux	171.37 MB	jdk-11.0.3_linux-x64_bin.tar.gz
macOS	166.2 MB	jdk-11.0.3_osx-x64_bin.dmg
macOS	166.52 MB	jdk-11.0.3_osx-x64_bin.tar.gz
Solaris SPARC	186.85 MB	jdk-11.0.3_solaris-sparcv9_bin.tar.gz
Windows	150.98 MB	jdk-11.0.3_windows-x64_bin.exe
Windows	171 MB	jdk-11.0.3_windows-x64_bin.zip

Once you select a file, you may be asked to create an Oracle Account - follow the requested steps.

3. You will be asked what you want to do with the selected download file. Click **Run**. The installation begins.

4. The Java installer will unpack some files and an introductory window will appear:

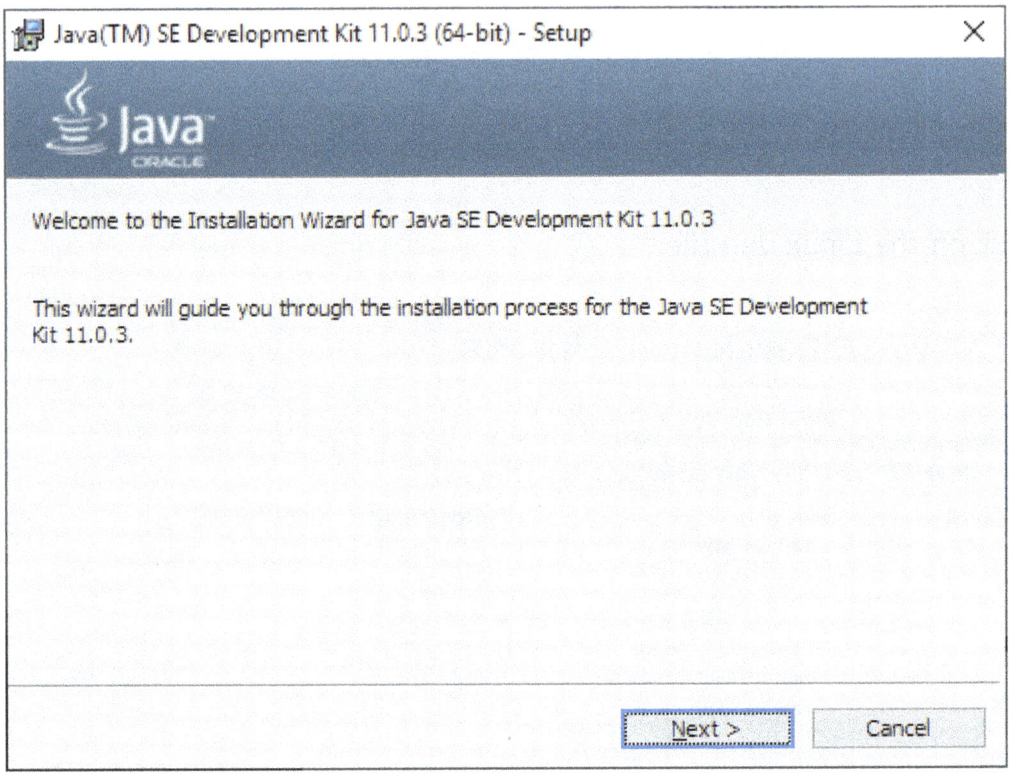

Click **Next** to start the installation. Several windows will appear in sequence. Accept the default choices by clicking **Next** at each window.

When complete (it will take a while), you will see this window:

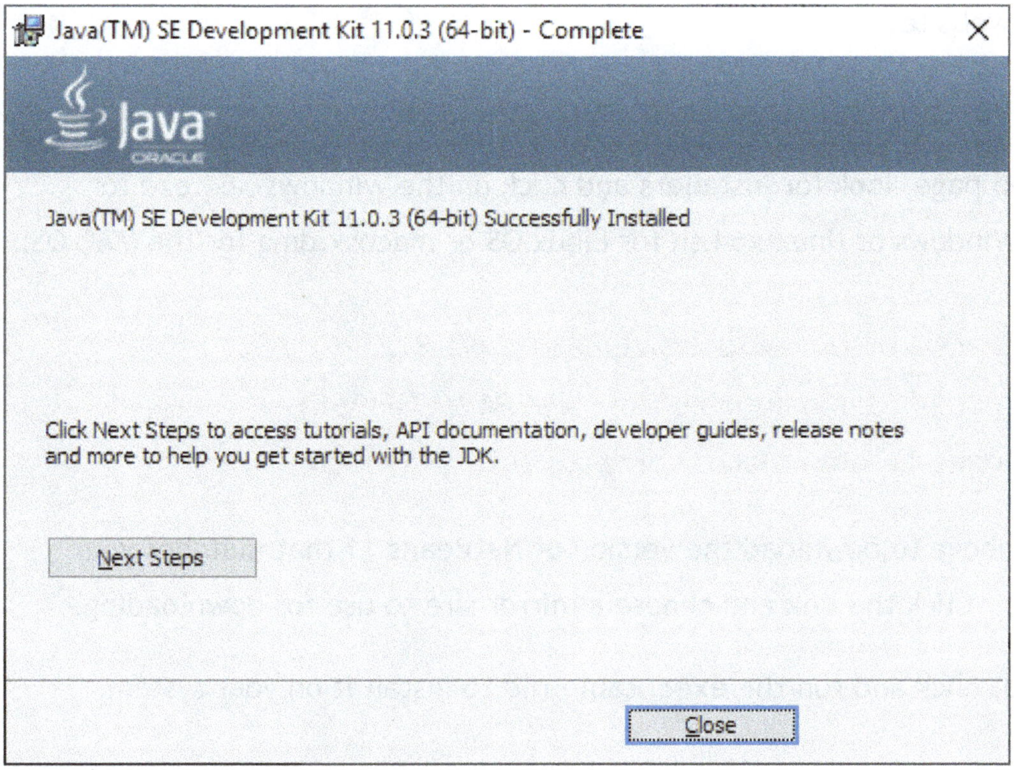

Click **Close** and the installation will complete. Next, let's install NetBeans.

NetBeans Integrated Development Environment

1. Go to this website:

2. https://netbeans.apache.org/download/nb111/nb111.html

3. On this web page, look for Installers and click on the windows-x64.exe for Microsoft Windows or linux-x64.sh for Linux OS or macosx.dmg for the MAC OS:

- Apache-NetBeans-11.1-bin-windows-x64.exe (SHA-512, PGP ASC)
- Apache-NetBeans-11.1-bin-linux-x64.sh (SHA-512, PGP ASC)
- Apache-NetBeans-11.1-bin-macosx.dmg (SHA-512, PGP ASC)

Click on the link above to download the version of NetBeans 11 that matches your Operating System. Click the link and choose a mirror site to use for downloading.

Once downloaded, click and run the **executable** file to install it on your system.

Running NetBeans

You now have Java and the **NetBeans** IDE installed on your computer. All of our programming work will be done using NetBeans. Let's make sure **NetBeans** installed correctly. To start using NetBeans under Microsoft Windows,

- Double-click the **NetBeans** shortcut on your computer's desktop

You can rename this shortcut if you choose. To start using NetBeans under the MAC OS,

- Click on the **Finder** and go to the **Applications Folder**.

The NetBeans program should start (several windows and menus will appear).

We will learn more about NetBeans in the notes. For now, we want to make some formatting changes. In Java programming, indentations in the code we write are used to delineate common blocks. The NetBeans IDE uses four spaces for indentations as a default. This author (and these notes) uses two spaces. To make this change, choose the **Tools** menu item and click **Options**. In the window that appears, choose the **Editor** option and the **Formatting** tab:

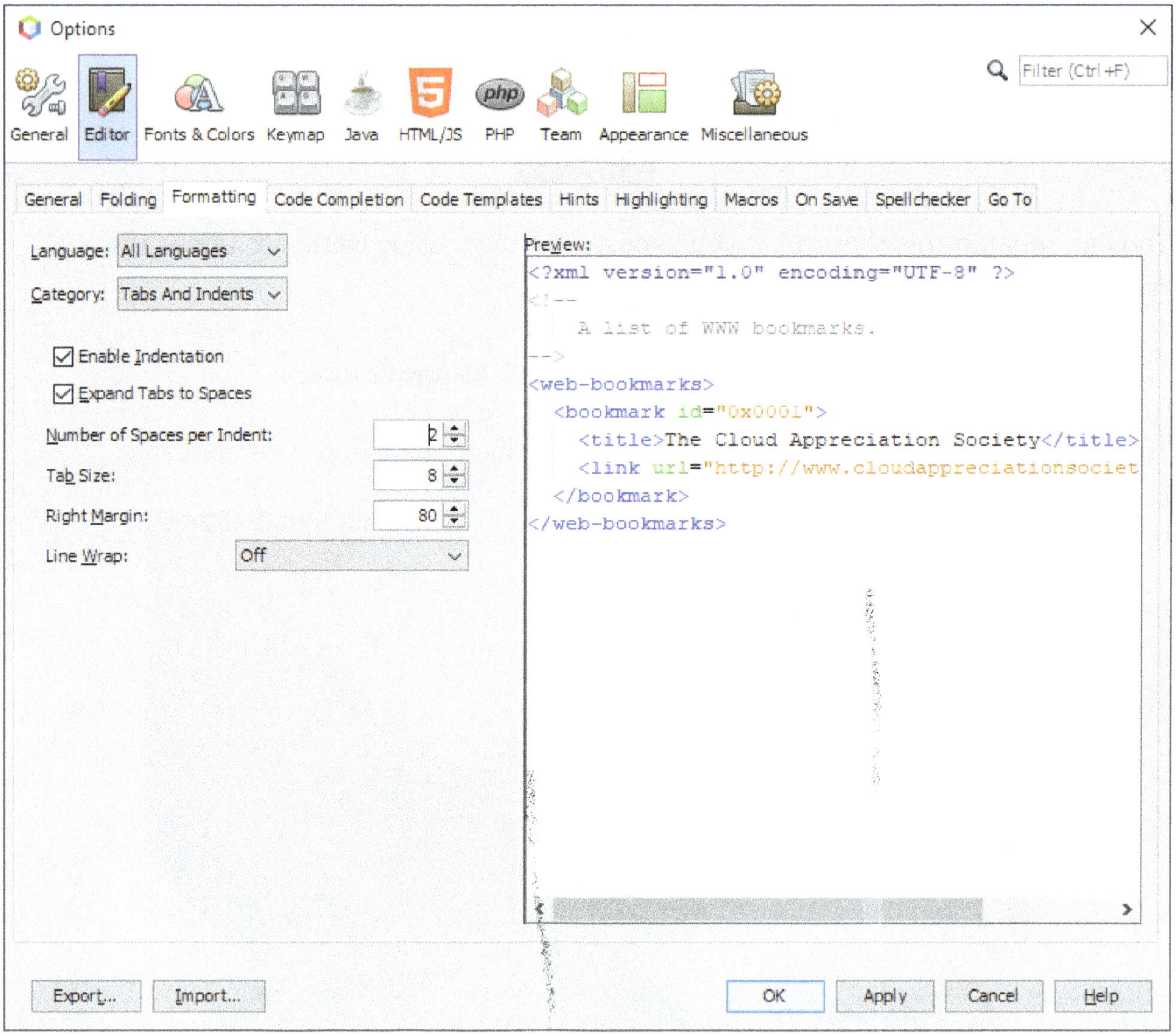

As shown, choose the **Tabs and Indents Category** and set the **Number of Spaces per Indent** to **2**.

Before leaving this window, we make another change. Braces (curly brackets) are used to start and stop blocks of code. We choose to have these brackets always be on a separate line - it makes checking code much easier.

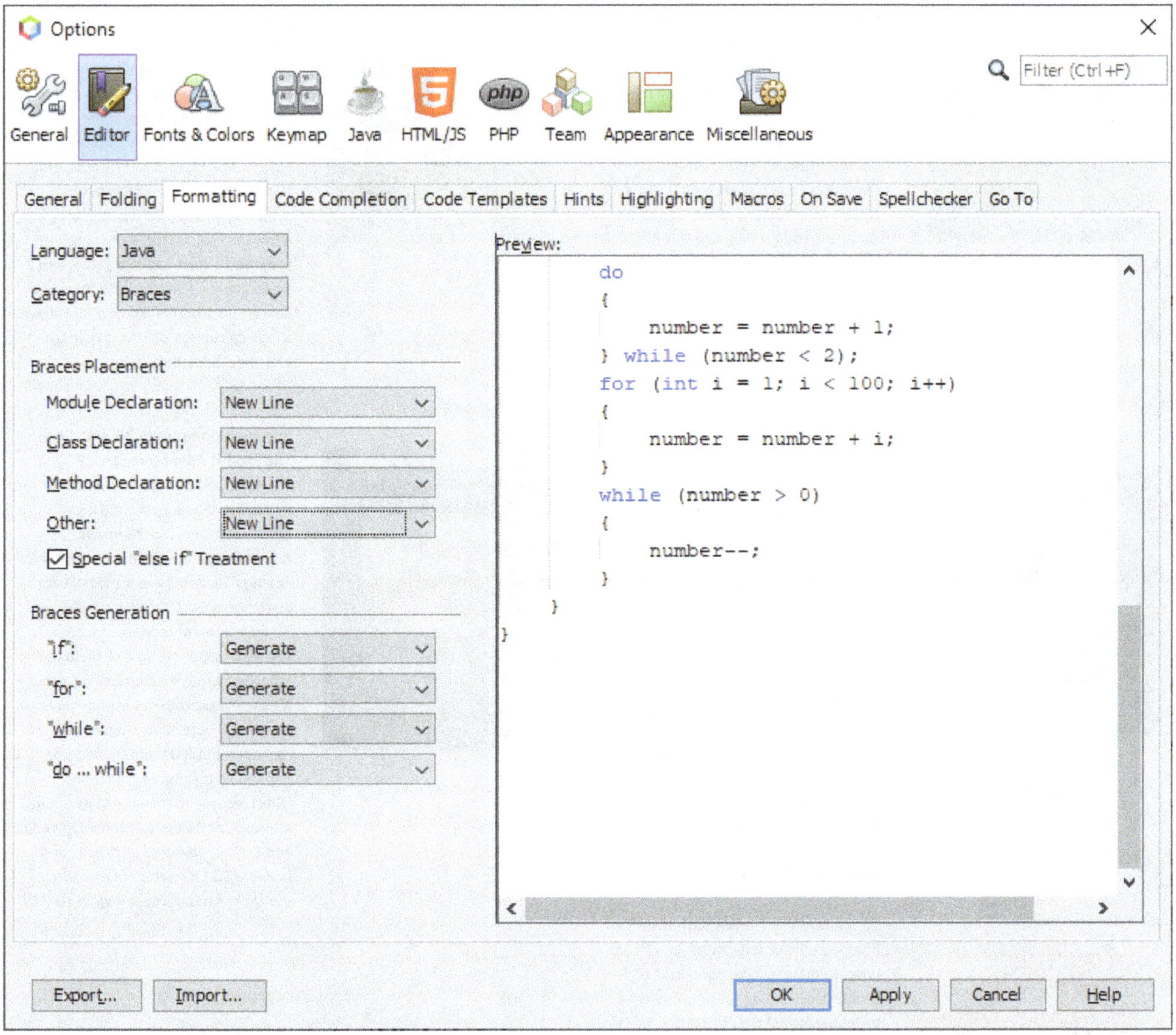

As shown, choose the **Braces Category** and under **Braces Placement**, set all choices to **New Line**. Click **Apply**, then **OK**. Stop **NetBeans** - you're ready to go!

Other Self-Study and/or Instructor-Led Programming Tutorials By BibleByte Books

Computer Bible Games for Microsoft Small Basic is a self-paced "beginner" programming tutorial for Middle-School students. This tutorial consists of 13 chapters explaining (in simple, easy-to-follow terms) how to build Computer Bible Games in Small Basic. It also includes the Small Basic source code for the several of the original Computer Bible Games. The Computer Bible Games built include Noah's Ark, Daniel and the Lions, Elijah and the Ravens, The Good Shepherd, The Prodigal Son, The Lost Coin, and Bible Scramble. Other learning projects include a card game, an allowance calculator, a drawing program, a state capitals game, and a video game.

Computer Bible Games with Visual Basic® is a self-paced semester long self-study "beginner" programming tutorial consisting of 13 chapters explaining (in simple, easy-to-follow terms) how to build a Visual Basic Express Windows application and Computer Bible Games. The Computer Bible Games built include Noah's Ark, Elijah & the Ravens, and Daniel & the Lions. Other learning projects include a card game, an allowance calculator, a drawing program, a state capitals game, and a video game. We also include several college prep bonus projects including a loan calculator, portfolio manager, and checkbook balancer.

Computer Bible Games with Visual C#® is a semester long self-paced "beginning "programming tutorial consisting of 13 chapters explaining (in simple, easy-to-follow terms) how to build a C# Express Windows applications and several Computer Bible Games. The Computer Bible Games built include Noah's Ark, Elijah & the Ravens, Daniel & the Lions and a Unity 3D Cartoon Moses Rod Adventure game. Other learning projects include a card game, an allowance calculator, a drawing program, a state capitals game, and the Pong video game. We also include several bonus projects including a loan calculator, portfolio manager, and checkbook balancer.

Introduction to Unity 3D with C# – The Exodus Adventure is a 2nd semester self-paced tutorial that teaches you how to build a high quality Third Person 3D Puzzle Adventure game based on the Book of Exodus. Students are provided with high quality 3D Character models and 3D Environment models to work with. We teach students how to build the following game mechanics: 3rd person Mecanim controller to Interact with actors and objects; Dialogue; Item Management; Full screen map and mini-map showing key locations; Quest Journal to manage quests; Cut-scenes; Cinematics for Game Opening and Ending, Game soundtrack, and building 3D Character Models using the Unity Multipurpose Avatar (UMA).

Computer Bible Games with Java™ is a semester long self-paced programming tutorial consisting of 7 chapters explaining (in simple, easy-to-follow terms) how to build a Java® Computer Bible Games. This Tutorial requires a complete understanding of the Java Swing Control Library before attempting so it is an Advanced Java Tutorial. We recommend that you compete the *Learn Java GUI Applications* tutorial by Kidware Software before attempting this advanced tutorial. The Computer Bible Games built include Noah's Ark, Elijah & the Ravens, and Daniel & the Lions, Bible Safecracker, Bible Match, and Bible Trivia Tic-Tac-Toe.

www.ingramcontent.com/pod-product-compliance
Lightning Source LLC
Chambersburg PA
CBHW081132090925
32270CB00108B/6070
* 9 7 8 1 9 5 1 0 7 7 0 4 4 *